A

COMPLETE DICTIONARY

OF

MUSIC

Owing to the antiquity and rarity of this book, certain pages are regrettably absent, and readability is compromised due to the blurring of the original text. If you possess any insights regarding the availability of these missing sections, kindly inform us. Your assistance is crucial in ensuring the completion of this significant work for the benefit of future generations.

A

COMPLETE DICTIONARY

OF

MUSIC

CONSISTING OF

A COPIOUS EXPLANATION OF ALL WORDS NECESSARY TO A TRUE KNOWLEDGE AND UNDERSTANDING OF

MUSIC

J. J. ROUSSEAU, TRANSLATOR: WILLIAM WARING

Published by

FacsiMile Publisher
12 Pragati Market
Ashok Vihar, Ph-2
Delhi - 110052, India
Phone: 011-47034999
Email: www.facsimilepublishers.com
info@facsimilepublishers.com

Distribution Network
gyanbooks.com
India, USA, Canada, UK, Australia

© Publisher
All rights reserved. No part of this work may be reproduced, stored, adapted, or transmitted in any form or by any means, electronic, mechanical, photocopying, micro-filming, recording or otherwise, or translated in any language, without the prior written permission of the copyright owner and the publisher.

ISBN: 978-93-5308-715-9 (HB)
First Published, 1779

2nd Impression 2025

Printed at: Gyan Press, Delhi.

The book is sold subject to the condition that it shall not, by way of trade or otherwise, be lent, resold, hired out, or otherwise circulated without the prior publisher's written consent.

A COMPLETE DICTIONARY OF MUSIC
Arthur J. J. Rousseau, Translator: William Waring

A COMPLETE DICTIONARY OF MUSIC

A COMPLETE DICTIONARY OF MUSIC.

CONSISTING OF

A copious Explanation of all Words neceſſary to a true Knowledge and Underſtanding of

MUSIC.

Tranflated from the Original French of

J. J. ROUSSEAU.

By WILLIAM WARING.

SECOND EDITION.

LONDON,
PRINTED FOR J. MURRAY, N°. 32, FLEET-STREET; AND
LUKE WHITE, DUBLIN.
MDCCLXXIX.

MUSICAL DICTIONARY.

A

A BATTUTA. Vide TIME.

A MI LA, or, A LA MI RE, or ſimply A, the ſixth note of the natural and diatonic Gamut, which is alſo indifferently called LA.

A TEMPO, This expreſſion is of a ſimilar ſignification to a Battuta, and is uſed when following a Recitative, to denote the place where one ſhould begin to ſing in time.

ACADEMY OF MUSIC, or MUSICAL ACADEMY, By this name, formerly in France, and ſtill in Italy, were called an aſſembly of Muſicians, or of Dilettantes, that is to ſay, thoſe who frequented Concerts for pleaſure only, to which the French have ſince given the name of Concertos. Vide CONCERTO.

ROYAL MUSICAL ACADEMY, Is a title which is ſtill borne by the Opera of Paris. I will not here make any mention of this celebrated eſtabliſhment, unleſs, that amongſt all the Academies of that kingdom, or of the world in general, *that* may, aſſuredly, lay the greateſt claim to fame. Vide OPERA.

ACCENT, By this name is called, according to the moſt general acceptation, every modulation of the voice, while ſpeaking, during its continuance, or in the ſound of the ſyllables, and words, of which the diſcourſe is compoſed, which denotes an exact uniſon between the two variations of the Accents, and the two diviſions of Melody.

AC, That is to ſay, the Rhyme, and the Muſical Harmony. Accentus, ſays the Grammarian Sergius in Donatus, is, as it were, ad Cantus. There are as many different Accents, as there are methods of modulating the voice thereunto, and there are as many various kinds of Accents as there are general cauſes for ſuch modulations. In common diſcourſe, there are diſtinguiſhed three of theſe kinds, to wit, the Grammatical Accent which confines the rule of Accents, properly ſo called, by which the ſound of the ſyllables is grave or acute, and that of the quantity, by which each ſyllable is ſhort or long: Secondly, The Logic or Rational Accent, which, by many, is confuſedly intermixed with the foregoing: This ſecond kind of Accent, denoting the relation, the lesser or greater connection, that Propositions or Ideas have between themselves, is marked chiefly by Punctuation. Lastly, The Pathetic, or Accent of Oratory, which, by different variations of the voice, by a tone more or less elevated, by a method of discourse quicker, or more slow, expresses those sentiments which agitate the speaker, and communicates them to the audience. A study of these various Accents, and of their uses in language, should be the main business of a musician; and Dennis of Halicarnassus, looks, with justice, on Accent in general, as the foundation of every branch in music: For which reason, we also ought to admit as an incontestible maxim, that a greater or less degree of Accent, is the real cause which renders language more or less musical; for what relation could music bear to discourse, were not the modulations of the singer an imitation of the verbal Accents. From whence it follows, that the less quantity a language has of such like Accents, more the harmony thereof must be monolonized, languishing, and disgustful, unless it seeks, in the height and force of sounds, those charms which cannot be found in their variety.

In regard to the Pathetic and Oratorical Accent, which is the most principal object of the imitative music of the theatre, no one can oppose the maxim which I have just lain down, that every man being subject to the same passions, ought to have a similar expression of them; for the universal Accent of nature, which draws from every man inarticulate sounds, is one thing, and the Accent of language, which produces an harmony peculiar to a nation, is another. The difference of a greater or less imagination or sensibility which may be distinguished between one people and another, ought of itself to introduce an infinite variety in the accented idioms of a tongue, if I have liberty to express myself thus. The German, for example, raises equally and roughly his voice, when in a rage, he cries ever in the same tone; the Italian, whom a thousand different motions agitate quick and successively from the same cause, varies his voice in a thousand different strains. The same foundation of passion directs *his* soul; but what a variety of expression in his Accents and his language! Moreover, 'tis to this variety alone, when the musician knows the imitation of it, that he owes the energy and beauty of his Cantata. Unluckily all these different Accents, which are perfectly concordant in the mouth of an orator, are not so easy to collect under the pen of a musician, already so restrained by the particular rules of his art. There is no doubt to be made, but that the most perfect, or at least the most expressive music, is *that* wherein all the Accents are observed with the greatest nicety; but what renders this assemblage so difficult, is, that too many rules in this art are subject to a mutual

tual contrariety, and are so much the more contrary, as the language is less musical, for none is perfectly so, otherwise those who use it would sing, instead of speaking.

This great difficulty in following, upon trust, the rules of all the Accents, obliges then often the composer to give the preference to one or the other, according to the different kinds of music of which he is beating. For example, the airs of dancing require particularly an Accent of rhyme and cadence, the nature of which is in every nation determined by the language. The Grammatical Accent ought to be the first consulted in the Recitative, to render the pronunciation of the words more articulate, which is used to be lost through the volubility of the discourse, in the harmonic sound; but that Accent which expresses the passion, claims the precedence in its turn in dramatic airs; and both are subordinate, particularly in symphony, to a third kind of Accent, which might be stiled musical, and is in some respects determined by the nature of that melody which the musician wishes to appropriate to the words.

In fine, the first and chief design of every kind of music, is to please the ear, wherefore every air should have an agreeable note: herein lies the first law, which is never suffered to be violated.—It is necessary then, first to consult the harmony and the musical Accent in the composition of any air whatsoever; then, should our design be a dramatic and imitative Cantata, we must seek the Pathetic Accent, which gives to each sentiment its proper expression, and the rational Accent, by the assistance of which, the musician enters with justice into the ideas of the poet; for to inflame others with that warmth, wherewith ourselves are animated in speaking to them, we must make *them* comprehend what is the subject of our discourse. The Grammatical Accent is necessary for the same reason; and this rule, though placed here the last in order, is not less indispensable than the two former, since the sense of propositions and phrases depends entirely on that of words. But the musician who understands his language, has seldom occasion to be attentive to this Accent; he cannot sing his air without perceiving if he speaks ill or well; and it is sufficient that he knows, that it is always necessary to speak well. Happy is it always, when a flowing and flexible melody never ceases to unite itself to the natural exigencies of language. The French musicians in particular, have assistances, which in this case render their errors unpardonable; and above all, the Treatise on the French Rosody, by Mons. L'Abbi d'Olivet, which every one should consult. Those, who will be in a condition to raise themselves to a higher sphere, should study the Grammar of Port Royal, and the ingenious notes of the philosopher who has commented on it: then, by building the experiments on the rules, and the rules on their principles,

principles, they will be always certain of what they should do in the management of the Grammatical Accent in every shape.

In regard to the two other kinds of Accents, they can be reduced into a lesser number of rules, and the practice of them requires less study, and more genius. There cannot be found any kind of Sang-froid in the language of the passions; and it is a well known truth, that to inspire another with feeling, we must feel ourselves. Nothing then can, in the search of the Pathetic Accent, supply the place of that natural fire, which awakens at pleasure every sentiment; and there is no other art in this case necessary, but to light up in one's own soul, that flame, which we wish to convey into the hearts of others. (Vide FIRE.) Is the rational Accent the object of our concerns? Art has but little to do in the acquiring of it, for this reason, that the deaf cannot be taught to hear. It must be confessed also, that this Accent is, in a less degree than the others, the result of music, because music is much more the language of the senses than of the mind. Give then a number of images, or sentiments, and few simple ideas, to be discussed by the musician, for it is the passions alone that sing, the understanding consists but in the speech.

ACCENT, A kind of mark in the French singing, which was formerly affixed to the music, but which at present the masters of the Gout du Chant, or Parte in singing, mark with pencil only, until the scholars understand themselves the method of placing it. This Accent is only used on a long syllable, and serves as a conveyance from one note thus marked to another note without this mark, placed upon the same degree. It consists in an elevation of the throat, which raises the sound a degree, to give, in that instant, the following note the same sound which it has left. Many have given the name of Plainte to this Accent. Vide the Sign and Effect of the ACCENT.

ACCENTS, The poets often use this word in the plural to signify the song itself, and ordinarily adjoin to it an epithet, as sweet, tender, mournful Accents. In this case, this word receives exactly the sense of its root, from whence arises the derivation; for it is formed from Canere, Cantus, whence is derived Accentus, as well as Concentus.

ACCIDENT, ACCIDENTAL, We call accident, or accidental signs, the B mollare's, the Diesis's, or B Quadrato's, which are met with by accident in the course of an air, and which, consequently not being at the key, have no relation to the mode or principal system. (Vide Diesis, B mollare, Mode, Cleff or Key.) We call also accidental or ledger lines, those which are added above or below the usual horizontal five, to fix the notes which are beyond their limits. Vide LINE.

ACCOMPANIST, He, who in a Concert, accompanies the band with the organ, the harpsichord, or any other accompanying instrument. Vide ACCOMPANYING.

It is absolutely necessary, that a good accompanist be a skilful musician; that he be acquainted with the foundation of harmony; that he know perfectly his system of music; that he have a sensible ear, pliant fingers, and a well founded taste.

'Tis the business of the accompanist to fix the key for the voices, and to give the change of motion to the orchestra. The first of these offices requires him to have always under the finger the note of music, to restrike it when necessary, and to raise or set right the voice when it weakens, or is bewildered. The second requires him to strike the bass; and his accompanying with a firm stroke, equal lain out, and well regulated on each side, for the purpose of rendering the musicians sensible of the time, particularly in the beginning of airs.

In the three following articles may be found those details which are wanting in the present.

ACCOMPANYING, Is the execution of a complete and regular harmony on an instrument proper for rendering it so, viz. the organ, the harpsichord, the theorbo, the guittar, &c. &c. We will take here, as an example, the harpsichord, as it is the only instrument continued in use for accompanying.

There is given, as a direction, one of the parts of music, which is ordinarily the bass. That bass must be touched with the left-hand, and with the right the harmony expressed by the tone of the bass, by the melody of the other parts, which are playing at the same time, by the partition which is placed before the eyes, or by the cyphers which are found added to the bass. The Italians hold the cyphers in contempt, the partition itself is of little service to them; the quickness and nicety of the ear supplies their place, and they accompany extremely well without

without all this preparation: but it is to their natural disposition alone that they are indebted for this facility; and another people, not born to music like themselves, find in the execution of the accompanying, several difficulties almost insurmountable. Eight or ten years are necessary for succeeding therein in any tolerable degree. What then can be the causes that retard, in this manner, the advancement of young practitioners, and embarrass, for so long a time, the masters, unless the difficulty of the art alone is the occasion of it? There are two principal reasons: the one lies in the method of marking the cyphers on the bass; the other, in the manner of the accompaniment. Let us first treat of the former.

The signs which are made use of for the purpose of forming the cyphers on the bass, are far too numerous. Since there are so few fundamental concords, why are so many cyphers necessary to express them? These same signs are equivocal, obscure, insufficient: for example, they very seldom determine the nature of the intervals which they express, or what is worse, they denote those of another nature. We fix a bar to the one to mark the Diesis's, and to others, to mark the B mollare's. The major and superfluous intervals, and even the deminished, are often expressed in the same manner. When the cyphers are double, they are too confused, when single, they very seldom express more than the idea of one interval alone; so that we have always a great number to understand and to determine. But how can we remedy these inconveniences? Must it be necessary to increase the number of signs to express each part? But the complaint is, that there are already too many. Should we reduce them? In that case, we shall leave more things for the accompanist to guess at, who is already too much embarrassed; and provided we go so far as to make use of cyphers, they should be of such a nature as to express every thing. What then is to be done? Should we invent new signs, render the method of placing the finger more perfect, and from those signs, and that position of the finger, compose two united methods which combine in assisting the accompanist? That is what Monf. Rameau has attempted with great sagacity, in his Dissertation on the different Methods of Accompanying. We will point out, under the words cypher and to finger, the means which he proposes. Let us pass on to the methods.

As the ancient music was not composed on the same plan as ours, neither for the song, nor its harmony, and as there was no other bass but the fundamental, the whole accompaniment consisted only in a series of perfect accords; in the which, the accompanist substituted, from time to time, some sixth to the fifth, according as the ear required: they knew no farther. At present, fent, fince they have changed the modulations, overturned each feparate party, furcharged, perhaps, fpoiled, the harmony by a quantity of difcords, we are obliged to purfue a different rule. Campion gave the preference, it is faid, to the rule of the octave, (Vide Rule of the OCTAVE) and, according to this method, many mafters ftill teach at prefent the accompaniment. The concords are determined by the rule of the octave, according to the rank which is held by the notes of the bafs, and to the courfe which they follow in a given tone. Therefore the tone being known, the note of the bafs continues known alfo. The rank of this note in the tone, the rank of the note that immediately precedes it, and the rank of the note that follows it, if accompanied by the rule of the octave, cannot lead us into any great error, provided that the compofer has followed the moft fimple and moft natural harmony; but that is what we ought rarely to expect in the prefent mufic, as hardly in Italy itfelf does the harmony appear to increafe its fimplicity, in proportion as it leffens it elfewhere. More than this, what method muft we follow to have thefe things continually prefent? And whilft the accompanift is inftructing himfelf, what becomes of the fingers? Hardly have we formed an idea of one Accord, but there prefents itfelf another, and the inftant of our reflection is precifely that of execution.

There is but one determined method in mufic, one reflected experience, i. e. the facility of reading a line of mufic in the caft of the eye, which can be of fervice at this time. And ftill the moft fkilful are often deceived with this affiftance. What a number of faults efcape them during the execution, even let the accompanift be ever fo well experienced! Can we expect, even for the accompanift that the ear be formed, that the mufician be able to read with eafe and rapidity every kind of mufic, that he can, at the inftant the book is opened, unravel a partition? And ftill, were this poffible, we fhould want a motion of the fingers founded on different principles of accompaniment than thofe made ufe of until Monf. Rameau.

Zealous mafters have very clearly feen the infufficiency of their rules. To fupply the defect, they have had recourfe to the enumeration and defcription of confonances, every diffonance of which is extended, accompanied, and prevented, in all its different cafes. A prodigious detail! which the quantity of diffonances and of their combinations fufficiently evince, and with which the memory remains loaded.

Many advife the compofition to be ftudied before we pafs to the accompaniment, as if the accompaniment was not compofition itfelf, except in regard to the invention, that more is neceffary to the compofer. It is as if it was propofed to begin to learn to read by making one's felf an orator. On the contrary, how many insist on beginning by the accompaniment to learn composition! and this plan is certainly more reasonable and more natural.

The course of the bass, the rule of the octave, the method of extending and preventing the dissonances, composition itself in general, all this concurs to no other purpose, than to shew the succession of one accord to another; so that in every accord there are fresh objects, new subjects for reflection! What a continual labour! When will the mind be sufficiently instructed, and when the ear sufficiently exercised, so that the fingers be no longer stopt?

These are the difficulties which Monf. Rameau has proposed to remedy by his new cyphers, and by his new rules for accompaniment. I will endeavour to point out, in few words, the principles upon which his methods are founded.

In harmony there are but consonances and dissonances. Consequently there are only consonant accords and dissonant.

Each one of these accords is fundamentally divided by tierces or thirds (this is Monf. Rameau's system). The concinnous accord is composed of three notes, viz. ut, mi, sol, and the dissonant of four, viz. sol, si, re, fa, laying aside the supposition and suspension, which, in the place of those notes, whose removal is required, introduce others, as it were, by licence; but the accompaniment bears never more than four. (Vide SUPPOSITION and SUSPENSION.)

Where concinnous accords succeed each other, where dissonant accords are followed by others dissonant also, and where the concinnous and the dissonant are intermixt.

Whereas the perfect concinnous accord agrees only to the tonic, the succession of concinnous accords furnishes so many tonics, and consequently an equal number of changes of the tone.

The dissonant accords succeed each other commonly in the same tone, if the sounds therein are not greatly varied. Dissonance unites together the harmonic sense, one accord thereof excites the desire of another.

If the tone be changed in this succession, this change is always denoted by a diesis, or a B mollare. In regard to the third succession, that is to say, the intermixture of consonant and dissonant accords, Monf. Rameau reduces it to two cases only, and he gives it as his opinion in general, that a consonant accord cannot be immediately preceded by any other dissonant accord, than that of the seventh of the dominant tonic, or that of the sixte quinte of the sous dominant, except in the broken cadence and the suspensions; and farther he advances, that there are no exceptions in regard to the foundation. It appears evident to me, that a perfect accord may yet be preceded by the accord

accord of the diminished seventh, and even by that of the superfluous sixth, two original accords, the latter of which suffers no alteration.

Herein then we see three different textures of harmonic phrases. First, the tonics, which succeed each other, and form an equal number of new modulations. Secondly, the dissonances, which succeed each other ordinarily in the same tone. Thirdly, and lastly, the consonances and dissonances, which are intermixt, and where the consonance is, according to Mons. Rameau, preceded by the seventh of the dominant, or by the sixte quinte of the sous dominant. What then remains to be done for the facility of the accompaniment, except to point out, to the accompanist, which it is of those textures that is predominant in whatever he accompanies. Moreover, this is what Mons. Rameau would have executed by characters of his invention.

One sign alone can easily denote the tone, the tonic, and its accord. From thence is derived the knowledge of the diesis's and B mollare's, which must enter into the composition of accords from one tonic to another.

The fundamental succession by thirds, or by fifths, as well in rising as in descending, gives the first texture of harmonic phrase, entirely composed of consonant accords

The fundamental succession by fifths, or by thirds, in descending, gives the second texture, composed of dissonant accords, that is to say, of accords of the seventh, and this succession gives a descending harmony.

The ascendant harmony is furnished by a succession of fifths in rising, or of fourths in descending, accompanied by a dissonance appropriated to this succession, which is la sixte ajoutee, or the sixth added, and this is the third texture of harmonic phrases. This last had not till this time been discovered by any one, not even by Mons. Rameau, though he discovered the principle of it, in that cadence, which he called irregular. Therefore, by the ordinary rules, the harmony which arises from a succession of dissonances, always descends, although, according to the true principles, and according to reason, it ought to have, in its rise, a progression equally as regular, as in its descent.

The fundamental cadences give the fourth texture of harmonic cadences, where the consonances and dissonances are interunited.

All these textures may be denoted by characters, simple, few in number, evident, which can at the same time point out, when it is necessary, the dissonance in general, for the nature of it is always determined by the texture itself. We must begin by exercising ourselves on these textures taken separately, then we must make them succeed each other on every tone, and on every mode successively.

With these precautions, Monf. Rameau pretends that we may learn more of accompaniment in six months, than could be learned before in six years, and he has experience on his side (Vide CYPHERS). In regard to the method of accompanying with intelligence, as it depends more from the use and taste, than from any rules which can be given, I shall content myself to make here some few general observations, of which no accompanist ought to be ignorant.

First, Although in the principles of Monf. Rameau, it is necessary to strike every sound of each accord, we must be very careful always to observe this rule literally. There are accords which would be insupportable with all this confusion. In the greatest part of dissonant accords, particularly in the accords by supposition, we must abstract some sound for the purpose of diminishing its duration. This sound is sometimes the seventh, sometimes the fifth: now and then, both the one and the other are cut off. We cut off also very often the fifth, or the octave of the bass in the dissonant accords, to avoid the octaves or fifths that follow, which may create an ill effect, particularly at the extremity of the piece. For the same reason, when the sensible note is in the bass, it is never placed in the accompaniment, and to supply its place, we double the third or the sixth, on the right hand. We ought also to avoid the intervals of the sixth, and to keep the two fingers joined, for that renders the dissonance very rough, which we ought to preserve for some occasions, where the expression requires it. In general, we ought to reflect, in accompanying, that when Monf. Rameau wishes every accord to be filled up, he has a greater attention to the mechanism of the fingers, and to his particular system of accompaniment, than to the purity of the harmony. Instead of that confused sound which is made by a like accompaniment, we should seek to render it agreeable and sonorous, and make it nourish and strengthen the bass, instead of concealing and stifling it.

If it should be asked how this abstraction of sounds can agree to the difinition of the accompaniment by a complete harmony, I answer, that these abstractions are in reality but hypothetic, and only within the system of Monf. Rameau; that, according to nature, these accords, thus mutilated in appearance, are not less complete than the others; since the sounds which are supposed therein being cut off here, would render them disagreeable, and often insupportable; that in effect the dissonant accords are not at all fulfilled in the system of Monf. Partins, as in that of Monf. Rameau; that consequently the defective accords in the one are completed in the other; that in fine, a nice taste in the execution requiring that we abstract often from the general rule, and the accompaniment not being always the most agreeable, the definition

definition ought to fix the rule, and custom teach when we ought to differ from it.

Secondly, We ought always to proportionate the sound of the accompaniment to the character of the music, and to that of the instruments or voices which we are to accompany. Wherefore in a choir, we strike with the right hand the full accords, with the left we redouble the octave or the fifth, sometimes the whole accords.

We ought to follow the same plan in the Italian recitative, for the sounds of the bass not being maintained therein, should not make themselves understood, unless with their whole harmony, and for the purpose of recalling forcibly, and for a long duration of the idea of the modulation. On the contrary, in a slow and sweet air, when there is but a weak voice, or a single instrument for the accompaniment, we cut off the sounds, we slacken slowly, we touch the small key. In a word, attention should be always paid, lest the accompaniment, which is formed but to sustain and embellish the song, spoil, and entirely conceal it.

Thirdly, When we strike the same strings to prolong the sound in a long note, or in a session, let it be rather at the beginning of the measure, or the strong time, than at another moment. We ought not to repeat the stroke till we have well examined the measure. In the Italian recitative, how long a duration soever a note of the bass may contain, we should never strike it but once, and that forcibly with its whole accord. We restrike the accord only when it changes on the same note; but when an accompaniment of violin is attendant on the recitative, then we should sustain the bass and slacken its accord.

Fourthly, When we accompany vocal music, we ought, by the accompaniment, to sustain the voice, to guide it, give it its tone in all its takings in, and correct it whenever it is out of tune. The accompanist always having the cantata before his eyes, and the harmony present in his memory, is especially charged to be careful that the voice lose not itself in an error. (Vide Accompanist.)

Fifthly, We ought not to accompany in the same manner the Italian and French music. In the latter, we should sustain the sounds, sweeten them continually with grace in a gradual rise, always fill up the harmony as much as possible, play the bass with propriety, in a word, fall in with every thing that the nature of it requires. On the contrary, in accompanying the Italian music, we must simply strike, and withdraw the notes of the bass, make neither trills nor graces, but preserve in it that equal and simple course which appertains to it. The accompaniment ought to be full, bold, and without slackening, except the case, of which I have treated numero 3, and some takings in in, or points d'orgue. We may therein, without ſcruple, diminiſh the ſounds, but in that caſe, we muſt carefully chooſe thoſe which are underſtood, for this purpoſe, that they may be founded in harmony, and be applicably adapted to the voice. The Italians hold it as their opinion, that nothing is heard in the accompaniment, or in the baſs, which can abſtract the ear for one moment from the air; and their accompaniments are always directed on this principle, that the pleaſure and attention evaporate in a diviſion of each.

Sixthly, Though the accompaniment of the organ be the ſame with that of the harpſichord, the taſte of it is very different: as the ſounds of the organ are ſuſtained, the courſe of it ought to be more bounded and leſs changeable. We ſhould raiſe the hand entire as little as poſſible, ſlide the fingers from one ſtop to another without removing thoſe, which, in the place where they are fixt, may be neceſſary to the accord wherein we are intereſted. There is nothing ſo diſagreeable as to hear grate on the organ, that kind of dry ſlackening accompaniment, which we are obliged to practice on the harpſichord. In general the organ, *that* inſtrument, ſo ſonorous and majeſtic, has no aſſociation with any other, and makes but an ill effect in the accompaniment, if it is not, at the moſt, to ſtrengthen the ripeano's and the choirs.

Monſ. Rameau, in his Errors in Muſic, has lately eſtabliſhed, or at leaſt advanced, a new principle, for the omiſſion of which, in my Encycopledie, he cenſures me highly, i. e. that the accompaniment is a repreſentation of the ſonorous body. As I examine this principle in another writing, I ſhall diſpenſe mentioning it in this article, which is already too long. My diſputes with Monſ. Rameau are the moſt uſeleſs circumſtances in the world towards the advancement of art, and conſequently towards the plan of this Dictionary.

ACCOMPANIMENT, Is moreover every part of the baſs, or any other inſtrument, which is compoſed under an air, to render a harmony therein. On this method a ſolo of the violin is accompanied by the violincello, or harpſichord, and an accompaniment of the flute, is very well adapted to the voice. The harmony of the accompaniment is an addition to the agreements of the air, by rendering its ſounds more ſure, their effect more ſweet, the modulation more ſenſible, and by conveying to the ear a teſtimony of juſtneſs which gives pleaſure. In the ſame manner, in regard to the voice, there is a ſolid reaſon for its being always accompanied with ſome inſtrument, whether it be in part, or in uniſon, for though numbers that in ſinging the voice modifies itſelf naturally according to the laws of modification, (Vide MODIFICATION) however, experience teaches us, that the moſt juſt and beſt exerciſed voices have a great trouble in in maintaining themselves any long time in the justness of the tone, when there is nothing to sustain them therein. By strength of singing we rise and fall insensibly, and it is very uncommon that we find ourselves exactly at the conclusion in the same tone from whence we set off. 'Tis for the purpose of preventing these variations, that the harmony of an instrument is employed. It maintains the voice in the same diapason, and when it loses itself, we recall it in an instant. The bass is, of all the parts, the most necessary for the accompaniment, being that which best sustains the voice, and gives a greater pleasure to the ear, because there are none whose vibrations are so strong, so determinant, or which leave a less equivocation in the judgment of fundamental harmony.

To ACCOMPANY, Is in general to play the parts of accompaniment, in the execution of a piece of music; or more particularly on a suitable instrument, to strike with each note of the bass the accords which it ought to bear, and which are called the accompaniment. I have sufficiently explained, in the precedent articles, in what consists this accompaniment; I will only add, that this word also points out to the accompanist in a concert, that he is employed only in an accessary part; that he ought but to be diligent in giving a greater weight to the parts of others; that the moment he has the least pretensions for himself, he spoils the execution, and tires out, at the same time, the musicians, and the audience. The more he thinks to make himself admired, the more ridiculous he appears; and as soon as, by the strength of his notes, or misplaced flourishes, he fixes on himself that attention due to the principal parts, whatever talents or execution he may display, he displays at the same time, his vanity and ill judgment. To accompany with merit and with applause, our only attention should be to sustain and give weight to the essential parts; and he executes very ingeniously his own, who causes its effect to be preserved, without permitting the part to be remarked.

ACOUSTIC, The doctrine or theory of sounds. (Vide SOUND) This word is from the invention of Monf. Sauveur, and is derived from the Greek ακουω, I hear. The acoustic is properly the theoretic part of music; 'tis that which gives, or ought to give, the causes for that pleasure which we receive from harmony and singing, which determines the references of the harmonic intervals, and which discovers the bearings and niceties of the vibrations in the chords. (Vide CHORD) Harmony acoustic is also sometimes used adjectively, we say the acoustic organ, an acoustic phœnomenon, &c. &c.

ACT, That part of an opera which is separated from any other in representation by a space called interlude, or entr' acte. (Vide INTERLUDE) The unity of time and place should be be obſerved with as much caution in the act of an opera, as in an entire tragedy of an ordinary kind, and even more ſo, in certain points; for the poet ought not to give to an act of the opera, a ſuppoſed duration longer than that which it really has, becauſe we cannot ſuppoſe that what is tranſacted before our eyes takes up a greater duration than that which we ſee it demand in effect; but it depends on the muſician to haſten or retard the action to a certain point, to encreaſe the natural reſemblance or his intereſt, a liberty which obliges him to ſtudy well the gradation of theatrical paſſions, the time that is neceſſary for the extenſion of them, *that* wherein the progreſs is at its higheſt pitch, and *that* where it is incumbent on him to ſtop, to prevent the inattention, the langour, and drowſineſs of the ſpectator. Neither is it permitted to change the ſcenery, and tranſport the theatre from one ſpot to another in the middle of an act, even in the *marvellous*, becauſe ſuch a tranſition is an oppoſition to reaſon and nature, and deſtroys the illuſion, which it is the firſt foundation of the theatre to favour in every reſpect. When then the performance is interrupted by ſuch changes, the muſician can neither tell how he ſhould be prepared for them, nor what he ought to do in his orcheſtra during their continuance, unleſs it be to repreſent the ſame chaos that then reigns within the ſcene.

Sometimes the firſt act of an opera has little reference to the principal action, and ſerves but as an introduction. In that caſe, it is called prologue (Vide PROLOGUE). As the prologue makes no part of the piece, it is never reckoned within the number of acts which it contains, which is commonly five in the French opera, but always three in the Italian. (Vide OPERA.)

ACT OF CADENCE, Is a movement in one of the parts, and chiefly in the baſs, which obliges all the other parts to concur in forming a cadence, or in expreſſly avoiding it. (Vide CADENCE.)

ACTOR, A ſinger who plays a part in the repreſentation of an opera. Beſides all thoſe qualities which he ſhould poſſeſs in common with the dramatic player, he ſhould have many particular ones to ſucceed in his art; for this reaſon, it is not ſufficient that he has a fine voice for ſpeaking, unleſs he has an equally good one for ſinging, for there is not ſuch an union between the ſpeaking and the ſinging voice, that the beauty of the one comprehends that of the other. Though we may forgive an actor the default of ſome one quality, which he flattered himſelf to be able to acquire, we cannot forgive him the audacity of deſtining himſelf for the ſtage, when deſtitute of the natural qualities which are therein neceſſary; as for example, the voice in a ſinger. But by this word voice, I underſtand more the extent, juſtneſs, and flexibility, than the ſtrength of the brain. It is wish that the Theatre, whose plan is to touch the heart by singing, should be forbid to those rough roaring voices which but stun the ear; and that, how little voice soever an actor may possess, if it be just, striking, easy, and sufficiently dilated, he has every thing necessary; for he will very easily make himself understood, if he can gain the attention of his hearers. With a suitable voice, the actor should be attentive to improve it by art; and though his voice may not require it, he will himself want it to catch, and render with nicety, the musical parts of his speeches. Nothing is more insupportable and disgusting, than to see a hero, in the most lively transports of his passion, constrained and retarded in his part, straining and imitating a school-boy, who blunders in his task, shewing, instead of the opposition between Love and Virtue, *that* of a bad singer between the Measure and the Orchestra; and more dubious on the tone of his voice, than on the side which he ought to take. There is neither warmth nor grace without ease, and that actor who labours in his part, will afford neither the one or the other.

It is not sufficient that the actor in an opera be an excellent singer, unless he is an ingenious mimic; for he ought not only to cause what he speaks to be felt, but also what he leaves to be spoken by the symphony. The orchestra does not deliver a sentiment, but what should arise from *his* soul; his steps, his eyes, his gesture, all should incessantly agree with the music, and even without his appearing to notice it. He ought always to interest, even when he is silent; and tho' busied in a difficult part, if he forgets one instant the personage, to pay attention to the singer, he is but a musician on the stage, he is no longer actor. Many a one has excelled in every other particular, who has got himself hissed for neglecting *this*. There is no actor to whom, in this respect, we may not give the celebrated Chassé as a model. This excellent mimic, always placing his art above him, and constraining himself to excell in it, by that means placed himself very much above his companions. Inimitable actor and excellent man! He will leave the admiration and regret of his talents to the lovers of his theatre, and an honourable memory of himself to every honest man.

ACUTE, Is so said of a sound piercing, or elevated through reference to some other sound. (Vide Sound.)

In this sense, the word Acute, is opposed to the word flat. The more the vibrations of the corpo sonoro are numerous, the more the sound is acute. The sounds considered under the references of acutes and flats, are the subject of harmony. (Vide Harmony. Concord.)

ADAGIO, This word, written at the beginning of an air, denotes the second, from slow to quick, of the five principal degrees of

movement,

movement, distinguished in the Italian music. (Vide MOVEMENT.) Adagio is an Italian adverb, which signifies a l'Aise, or gradually; and it is also by this Method, that we should strike the measure of those airs to which it is applied. The word Adagio is sometimes used substantively, and is applied metaphorically to those pieces of music whose movement it determines. Other words of a like nature are similarly used. So we say, an Adagio of Partini, an Andante of Martino, and an Allegro of Locarelli, &c.

ADQUISITA, This was in the Greek music that chord or sound which they called Proslambanomenos. (Vide this Word.)

A sixte ajoutée, or a sixth ad quisita, is a sixth added to a perfect accord, and whose name, an accord thus augmented, ordinarily takes. (Vide CONCORD and SIXTH.)

AFFETUOSO, An adjective taken as an adverb.

This word, written at the beginning of an air, denotes a movement, something between the Andante and the Andagio, and in the character of the air itself, an expression affecting and sweet.

AGOGE, One of the sub-divisions of the ancient Melopœia, which gives the rules for the course of an air by degrees alternatively, conjoint or disjoint, whether in arising or descending, (Vide MELOPOEIA.) Martianus Capella gives, after Aristides Quintilian, to the word Agogé another sense, which I shall treat of under the word Tirata.

AIR, A piece of music which is adapted to the words of a song, or of a piece of poetry proper for singing; and in an extensive sense, the song itself is called Air. In the opera, the name of Air is given to all the measured chants, to distinguish them from the recitative; and in general, every complete piece of vocal and instrumental music which forms a Tune, is called Air, whether this composition makes of itself an entire piece, or that it can be detached from *that* whole, of which it is a part, and executed separately.

If the subject or air be divided into two parts, it is called Duo, or Duet; if into three, Trio.

Saumaise imagines, that this word comes from the Latin æra; Baretti is of his opinion: tho' Menage opposes them in his Etymologies of the French language.

The Romans had *their* signs for the rhyme, in the same manner as the Greeks had theirs, and these signs, drawn also from their Characters, were not only called numerus, but æra; that is to say, number, or the marks of the number, numeri nota, says Nominus Marcellus. 'Tis in this sense that the word æra is found used in this verse of Lucilius,

Hæc est ratio: Perversa æra! Summa subducta improbé!

And Sextus Rufus uses it in the same manner.

Moreover,

Moreover, though this word was originally taken only for the number or measure of the chant, in the end it was made use of in the same manner as in the word numerus; and æra was used to denote the song itself; from whence is derived, according to the two authors I have cited, the French word Air, and the Italian Aria taken in the same sense.

The Greeks had a number of different airs, which they called Nomes: the nomes had each their character and their use, and many were appropriated to some particular instrument, almost the same thing as what we now call pieces or sonatas.

Modern music has divers kinds of airs, each of which has reference to some sort of dance, whose name these airs generally bear. (Vide MINUET, &c. &c.) The airs of our operas are (if I may use the expression) the canvas or foundation, on which the paintings of imitative music are coloured. The melody is the design, the harmony the colouring,—all the picturesque objects of nature's beauty, all the reflected sentiments of the human heart, are the models which are imitated by the artist. Attention, interest, the charms of the ear, and the emotion of the heart, are the result of these imitations. (Vide IMITATION) An ingenious and agreeable air, an air composed with taste and discovered genius, is the chef d'auvre of music. 'Tis *there*, that a fine voice dilates itself, that a noble symphony shines with lustre; 'tis *there*, that the passion insensibly strikes the soul by the sense. After a fine air we are satisfied, the ear desires nothing more. It rests in our imagination, we convey it away with us, we repeat it at our pleasure. Without being able to render a single note, we preserve it in our minds as we heard it in the performance; we view the scene, the actor, the theatre; we hear the accompaniment and the applause. A true lover of music never loses the fine airs which he has heard during life, but makes the opera re-commence whenever he chooses. The words of airs do not always follow in a regular suit, neither are they spoken as those of the recitative, tho' they are generally short, they divide, they are repeated, and are extended to such a length as it pleases the composer; they do not form a part of the narration, but paint, either a picture, which must be seen from different points of sight, or a sentiment, in the which the heart is interested, and from which it cannot (to use the expression) detach itself; and the different variations of the air, are but so many methods of viewing the same image. 'Tis for this reason that the subject should be one and the same; 'tis by these well understood repetitions, by these redoubled strokes, that an expression, that at first might escape your notice, in fine agitates you, and transports you from yourself; and it is still through the same principle that the shakes, which in pathetic airs seem so misplaced,

placed, are not so always: the heart, impressed with a very lively sentiment, often expresses it more feelingly by inarticulate sounds than by words.

The form of airs is of two kinds: the lesser airs are often composed of two divisions, each of which, is sung twice; but the greater airs of the opera are more frequently in Rondeau's. (Vide RONDEAU.)

AL SEGNO, or DA CAPO, These words written at the end of an air, denote, that the first part must be re-commenced, not entirely at the beginning, but at that place where the return is marked.

ALLA BREVE, An Italian term, which denotes a kind of measure of two times very quick, and which however is marked with a ronde or semibreve per tempo. It is no longer made use of in Italy, and only in church-music. It answers almost to what they call in France the Gros-fa.

ALLA ZOPPA, An Italian term, which makes a constrained movement, syncopating between two times, without syncopating between two measures, which gives to the notes an irregular, and, as it were, a lame direction. 'Tis a notice also, that this same course continues to the end of the air.

ALLEGRO, adjective taken adverbly.

This Italian word written at the beginning of an air, denotes, from quick to slow, the second of the five principal degrees of movement, distinguished in the Italian music. Allegro signifies lively, and it is also the indication of a lively movement, the most so of any after presto. But we must not think, on that account, that this movement is proper for gay subjects only; it is often applicable to transports of passion, distraction, or despair, which partake of nothing less than of gaiety. The diminutive Allegretto denotes a more moderated gaiety, and a little less vivacity in the measure. (Vide MOVEMENT)

ALLEMANDE, A kind of air or piece of music, the measure of which is a quatre temps, and is struck with a flat. It appears by its name, that this kind of air first came from Germany, tho' they know not the least of it in that country. The Allemande in a sonata is quite absolete, and the musicians very rarely make use of it at present; those also who still employ it, give it a far more lively movement.

ALLEMANDE, Is also the air of a dance very common in Switzerland and Germany. This air, as well as the dance, has much gaiety, it is played a deux temps.

ALTUS. (Vide HAUTE CONTRE)

AMBITUS, Is a name which was formerly given to the extent of every tone or mode from flat to sharp; for tho' the extent of a mode was in some respects fixed to two octaves, there were irregular modes, the Ambitus of which exceeded this extent, and others imperfect, where it did not reach it.

In the plain chant, this word is again ufed, but the Ambitus of perfect modes is only of one octave therein; thofe that exceed it, are called fuperfluous modes; thofe that do not reach it, diminifhed modes. (Vide MODES)

AMOROSO. (Vide TENDERLY)

ANACAMPTOS, A term of the Greek Mufic, which fignifies a collection of retrograde notes, or of notes proceeding from the fharp to the flat. 'Tis the contrary to Euthia. One of the parts of the ancient melopœia had alfo the name of Anacamptofa. (Vide MELOPOEIA)

ANDANTE, This word written at the beginning of an air, denotes, from flow to quick, the third of the five principal degrees of movement, diftinguifhed in the Italian mufic. Andante is the participle of the Italian verb, Andare, to go. It denotes a movement marked, without being gay, and anfwers very nearly to that which is defcribed by the word Gracieufement. (Vide MOVEMENT)

The diminutive Andantino denotes a little lefs gaiety in the meafure, which muft be particularly obferved, as the word Larghetto fignifies exactly the contrary. (Vide LARGO)

ANTIPHONA, Is a kind of chant made ufe of in the catholic church.

The Antiphonæ were fo named, becaufe in their origin they were fung with two chorufſes, which anfwered each other alternately; and the pfalms and hymns fung in the church were comprehended under this name. Ignatius, difciple of the apoftles, was, according to Socrates, the inventor of this method of finging amongft the Greeks; and Ambrofius introduced it into the latin church: Theodore attributes the Invention to Diodorus and Flavian.

At prefent, the fignification of this term is confined to certain fhort paffages drawn from fcripture, which are applicable to the feaft which is celebrating, and which preceding the pfalms and cantics, direct their intonation: the name of Antiphona is alfo preferved in fome hymns fung in honour of the Virgin, fuch as Regina Cœli, Salve Regina.

ANTIPHONY, A name which the Greeks gave to that kind of fymphony, which was performed by divers voices, or by different inftruments to the octave or double octave, in oppofition to that which was executed in fingle unifon, and which they called Homophony. (Vide SYMPHONY)

This word is derived from Ἀντὶ contra and Φωνὴ vox, as if one were to fay an oppofition of the voice.

ANTIPHONARY, A book which contains in notes the Antiphony and other chants, which are ufed in the catholic church.

APOTHETUS, A kind of name applicable to the flutes in the ancient mufic of the Greeks.

APOTOME,

APOTOME, That which remains of a tone major, after that a limma has been abstracted, which is an interval, less by a comma, than the semitone major, consequently the Apotome is greater by a comma than the middle semitone. (Vide COMMA, SEMITONE.) The Greeks, who knew perfectly well that the tone major cannot, by reasonable divisions, be divided into two equal parts, divided it unequally by many methods. (Vide INTERVAL.)

From one of these divisions, invented by Pythagoras, or rather by Philolaus, his scholar, resulted the diesis or limma on one side, and the Apotome on the other, the standard of which is from 2048 to 2187. The derivation of this Apotome is found at the Septieme Quinte, ut Diesis, beginning by ut Natural, for the quantity by which this ut Diesis surpasses the ut Natural drawn nearest, is precisely the reference which I have just observed.

The ancients gave also the same name to other intervals. They called Apotome major a little Interval, which Mons. Rameau calls the inharmonic Quart de ton, the which is formed of two sounds in the standard of 125 to 128.

And they called minor Apotome, the interval of two sounds, whose distinction was from 2025 to 2048, an interval still less sensible to the ear than the preceding.

Jean de Muris and his contemporaries give the name of Apotome chiefly to the minor semitone, and that of diesis to the semitone major.

APYCNI, plural, The ancients called by this name in their scale, three of eight solid sounds of their system or diagramma, the which touched not on any side the compact intervals, that is, to the proslambanomenos, the note synnemenon, and the note hyperboleon.

They called also Apycnos, or not crouded, the diatonic genus, because in the tetrachords of that genus the sum of the two first intervals was greater than the third. (Vide CROUDED, GENUS, SOUND, TETRACHORD)

ARBITRIO. (Vide CADENZA)

ARCO, A Bow, These Italian Words Con l'Arco, denote, that after having slipped off the chords, we must replace the bow to the part where they are written.

ARIETTA, This diminutive, derived from the Italian, signifies properly a little air; but the sense of this word is altered in France, and the name of Arietta's is given to greater pieces of music, of a movement generally rather gay, which are sung with accompaniments and symphony, and which are commonly in rondeau. (Vide AIR, RONDEAU)

ARIOSO, This Italian word at the beginning of an air, denotes a kind of singing well sustained, open, and appropriated to the greater airs.

ARISTOXENIANS

ARISTOXENIANS, A ſect that had for their chief Ariſtoxenes, of Tarentum, Scholar of Ariſtotle, and which was repugnant to the Pythagoreans, in regard to the meaſure of intervals, and on the method of determining the references of the ſounds; ſo that the Ariſtoxenians made application ſolely to the judgment of the ear, and the Pythagoreans to the preciſion of calculations. (Vide PYTHAGOREANS)

ARPEGGIO, The method of cauſing the different ſounds of an accord to be heard ſucceſſively and rapidly, inſtead of ſtriking them all at a time. There are inſtruments on which there cannot be formed a full accord but thro' the Arpeggio. Such are the violin, the violincello, the viol, and all thoſe which are played with the bow; for the convexity of the bridge hinders the bow from fixing itſelf at once on all the ſtrings. For the formation then of accords on theſe inſtruments, we are obliged to uſe the Arpeggio, and as we cannot draw more ſounds than there are ſtrings, the Arpeggio of the violincello, or of the violin, cannot be compoſed of more than four ſounds. In the Arpeggio each of the fingers muſt be arranged on its chord, and the Arpeggio muſt be drawn from a ſingle and forcible ſtroke of the bow or fiddle-ſtick, which muſt begin ſtrongly on the largeſt ſtring, and conclude by turning and ſoftening on the leſſer gradually. If the fingers were only arranged ſucceſſively on the ſtrings, or that many ſtrokes of the fiddle-ſtick were given, it would no longer be Arpeggio, but only a very quick paſſage on ſeveral notes in continuance.

What is done on the violin thro' neceſſity, is practiſed by taſte on the harpſichord. As we can only draw from that inſtrument ſounds of a ſhort continuance, we are obliged to re-ſtrike them in notes of a long duration. To make an accord of a longer duration, we ſtrike by the Arpeggio, beginning with the lower ſounds, and remarking, that the fingers which have firſt ſtruck quit not their ſtroke until all the Arpeggio be finiſhed, for the purpoſe of hearing at once every ſound of the accord. (Vide ACCOMPANIMENT)

Arpeggio is an Italian word, which is Frenchified into that of Arpege. It is derived from the word Arpa, becauſe 'tis from the playing of the harp that we have taken the idea of the Arpeggio.

ARSIS and THESIS, Terms of muſic and proſody.—Theſe two words are Greek. Arſis comes from the verb ἄιρω tollo, I raiſe, and denotes the elevation of the voice or of the hand: the falling which follows this elevation, is what is called θέσις depoſitio. Remiſſio.

In regard then to the meaſure, per arſin, ſignifies in raiſing, or continuing the higheſt time; per theſin, in lowering, or continuing

tinuing the lowest time: in which case we ought to take notice, that our method of marking the measure is very different from that of the ancients, for we strike the highest time and elevate the lowest. To remove every equivocal term, we may say, that Arsis signifies the bold and strong time; and Thesis, the fainter and weak. (Vide MEASURE, TIME, to BEAT TIME.)

In regard to the voice, we say that a chant, a counterpoint, a fugue, are per thesin, when the notes rise from flat to sharp; per arsin when they descend from sharp to flat. Fugue per arsin and thesin, is what is now called counter fugue, in the which the answer is made in a contrary sense, that is to say, in descending if the guida has risen, and in rising if the guida has descended. (Vide FUGUE.)

ASSAI, An augmentative adverb, which is often found joined to the word which denotes the movement of an air: wherefore presto assai, largo assai, signify very quick, very slow. The Abbé Brassard has made out of this word one of his ordinary double senses, by substituting, instead of its true and only meaning, that of an ingenious mediocrity of slowness and quickness. He believed, that Assai signified assez, i. e. enough: for which reason we ought to admire the singular fancy that this author had of preferring in his vocabulary, to his mother-tongue, a foreign language which he understood nothing of.

AUBADE, A nightly concert in the open air, under the windows of a house. (Vide SERENADE.)

AUTHENTIC, When the octave is found harmonically divided, as in this proportion, 6, 4, 3, that is to say, when the fifth is in the flat, and the fourth in sharp, the mode or tone is called Authentic, except in regard to the tone plagal, where the octave is arithmetically divided, as in this proportion, 4, 3, 2, which fixes the fourth in flat, and the fifth in sharp.

To this explanation, adopted by all the authors, but which is to no purpose, I will add the following: the reader may take his choice. When the finale of a chant is also its tonic, and the chant does not descend so far as to the Dominant au dessous, the tone is called authentic; but if the chant descends or concludes at the dominant, the tone is plagal. I here take the words tonic and dominant in their musical acceptation. These differences of authentic and plagal are observed but in the plain chant, whether the finale be placed at the bottom of the diapason, which makes the tone authentic, or whether we place it in the middle, which makes it plagal, provided that on the whole, the modulation be regular. Modern music admits all the chants as equally authentic, in whatever place of the diapason the finale may chance to fall. (Vide MODE.) There are

are in the eight tones of the Roman church four *authentic*, to wit, the first, the third, the fifth, and the seventh. (Vide Tones of the Church) Formerly, the name of *authentic fugue* was given to that whose subject proceeded in a gradual rise, but that Denomination is no longer in use.

B.

B FA SI, or B FA B MI, or simply B, The name of the seventh sound of the gamut of Aretin, for the which the Italians and other Europeans repeat the B, saying B MI, when it is natural; B FA, when it is a B Flat; but the French call it SI. (Vide Si.)

B FLAT, Character of music, to which is given nearly the figure of a ♭, and which lessens the note to which it is join'd by a semitone minor. (Vide Semitone.)

Guy d'Arezzo, having formerly given names to six of the sounds of the octave, from the which he composed his celebrated Hexacord, left the seventh without any other name than that of the letter B, which is proper to it, as the C to ut, and the D to re, &c. Moreover this B was sung in two methods, that is to say, in a tone below la, according to the natural order of the gamut, or only in a semitone of the same la, when they wished to unite the tetrachords, for at that time they knew nothing of our modes or modern tones. In the first case, the si sounding very roughly, on account of the three consecutive tones, it was judged that it caused to the ear an effect similar to that which angulated and hard bodies cause to the hand, for which reason it was called B hard, or B sharp, in Italian B quadro. In the second case, on the contrary, it was found that the si was extremely soft, therefore they called it B flat. By the same analogy it might have also been called B round, and effectually the Italians called it often B rondo.

There are two methods of making use of the B flat, the one accidental, when in the course of an air it is placed on the left of a note. This note is almost always the sensible note in the major tones, and sometimes the sixth in the minor tones, when the cleff is not correctly numbered. The accidental B flat changes only the note which it touches, and those which immediately answer to it, or at the most, those, which, in the same bar or measure, are found on the same degree, without any contrary sign.

The other method is to employ the B flat in the cleff, and in that case it modifies it, it acts in the whole course of the air, and upon all the notes placed upon the same degree, unless this B flat be accidentally destroyed by some diesis or B sharp, or that the cleff undergoes some change.

The position of the B flat on the cleff is by no means arbitrary; herein lies the reason: it is intended to change the place of the semitones of the scale; moreover, those two semitones ought always to preserve between them prescribed intervals, i. e. that of a fourth on one side, and of a fifth on the other. Wherefore the note mi, inferior to its semitone, makes in the flat the fifth of si, which is its homologue in the other semitone; and in the sharp, the fourth of the same si, and the note si, reciprocally make in the flat the fourth of mi, and in the sharp, the fifth of the same mi. If then, as in example, leaving out the natural si, a B flat was given to mi, the semitone would change its place, and be found a degree lower, between the re and the mi B flat. Moreover, in this position, we see that the two semitones would no longer preserve the prescribed distance between each other; for the re, which would be the inferior note of the one, would make in the flat the sixth of si, its homologue in the other, and in the sharp, the third of the same si; and this si would make in the flat the third of re, and in the sharp, the sixth of the same re. Wherefore the two semitones would be placed too near on the one side, and too great a distance on the other.

The order of B's flat ought not then to begin by mi, nor by any other note of the octave but si, the only one which has not the same inconvenience; for as much as the semitone changes its place therein, and ceasing to be between the si and the ut, descends between the si B flat, and the la, still the prescribed order is not demolished. The la, in this new arrangement, being found on one side at the fourth, and on the other at the fifth of mi. its homologue, and *that* reciprocally.

The same reason which fixes the first B flat on the si, fixes the second on the mi, and so in continuance, in ascending a fourth, or descending a fifth as far as sol, at which is commonly made a stop, because the B flat of ut, which will be found hereafter, differs not from the si in practice. That causes then a collection of five B flat's in this order.

1.	2.	3.	4.	5.
Si.	Mi.	La.	Re.	Sol.

By the same reason also, we cannot use the latter B's flat in the cleff, without using also those which precede them; wherefore the B flat of mi, is never placed but with that of si, and that of la, but with the two preceding, and each of the following, but with all those which precede it.

In the article cleff may be found a *Formula*, to know immediately if a tone or a mode given, ought to bear B's flat within the cleff, and how many.

B SHARP, A character of music which is written thus, ♮; and which, being placed on the left of the note, denotes that *that* note, having been precedently elevated by a diesis, or lowered by a B flat, ought to be replaced in its natural and diatonic elevation.

The B sharp was invented by Guy d'Arezzo. This author, who gave names to the six first notes of the octave, left none but the letter B to express the natural si: For every note had, at that time, its correspondent letter; and as the diatonic chant of this si is rough, when we ascend to it from the fa, he called it simply B dur, or hard, B quarré, by an allusion which I have mentioned in the preceding article.

The B sharp served in the end to destroy the effect of the anterior B flat, on the note which followed the B sharp, that is, that the B flat being generally placed on the si, the B sharp which followed directly after, by destroying this B flat, produced only its natural effect, which was to represent the note si without alteration. In the end, it was used for extension, and in default of another sign, to destroy also the effect of the diesis; and 'tis in this manner that it is employed till this time. The B sharp effaces equally the B flat, or the diesis, which have preceded it.

There is, however, a distinction to be made. If the diesis or the B flat were accidental, they are destroyed without return by the B sharp, in all the notes which follow it mediately or immediately on the same degree, until there presents itself a new B flat or a new diesis. But if the B flat or the diesis are on the cleff, the B sharp effaces them only for the note which it immediately precedes, or at the most, for all those which follow in the same measure and on the same degree; and in every note changed at the cleff, whose alteration we wish to destroy, so many new B sharp's are necessary. All this is very poorly understood, but such is the custom.

Some have given another sense to B sharp, and granting it only the right of effacing the accidental diesis's or B flat's, deny it that of changing any thing in the state of the cleff; so that, in this sense, on a fa diesis'd, or a si marked with B flat on the cleff, the B sharp would serve but to destroy an accidental diesis on this si, or a B flat on this fa, and would always signify the fa diesis, or the si B flat, just as it is on the cleff.

Others also made use of the B sharp to efface the B flat, and even that of the cleff, but never to efface the diesis. 'Tis the B flat only which they employ in this last case.

The first custom has entirely prevailed; the latter become more uncommon, and are abolished day by day; but it is necessary to give attention to it in the reading of ancient music, without which we should often be deceived.

BALLET, A theatrical action which is represented by the dance directed by the music: This word is derived from the old French Baller, to dance, to sing, to amuse one's self. The music of a ballet ought to have still more cadence and accent than that of the vocal, because it is changed to express a greater number of things; and 'tis in it alone to inspire the dancer with the warmth and expression that the singer may receive from the words; and what is still more, it must supply, in the language of the soul and of the passions, every thing that the dance cannot express to the eyes of the spectators.

Ballet is also the name that is given in France to a confused kind of opera, wherein the dance is not in the least better regulated than in the rest, and causes no better effect. In the greatest part of these operas, the acts form so many different subjects, united together only by some general systems, foreign to the action, and which the spectator could never perceive, had not the author given him a hint in the prologue. These ballets contain other ballets, which are generally called Fêtes. They are a collection of dances which succeed each other without plot, without an union in themselves, or with the principal action, and where the best dancers inform you of nothing but that they dance well. This conduct, so little theatrical, suffices for a ball, where every actor satisfies his desire, provided that he amuses himself, and where the interest which the spectator takes in the personages, dispenses with an attention to things; but such a deficiency in subjects and union, should never be suffered on the stage, not even in the representation of a ball, where the whole ought to be united together by some secret action, which awakens the attention, and interests the spectator. This plan in composition is not without example, even in the French opera; and there may be seen a very agreeable proof of it in the Fêtes Venetiennes.

In general every dance that describes itself alone, and every ballet, which is only a ball, should be banished entirely from the lyric theatre. In short, the action of the scene is always the representation of another action, and what we see therein, is but the image of what strikes our ideas; so that it ought not to be this, or that dancer, who presents himself before you, but the character itself which he represents. Therefore, altho' a private dance represents nothing more than itself, *that* of the theatre should necessarily be the imitation of something else, as well as the actor, who, in his character, represents a person in discourse, and

and the ſcenes which exhibit a different place from that wherein they ſtand.

The worſt kind of ballets, is that which treats of allegorical ſubjects, and wherein, in conſequence, there is but imitation on imitation. The whole art of theſe ſorts of dramas conſiſts, in repreſenting under ſenſible images, a reference purely intellectual, and in making the ſpectator reflect on things quite different from thoſe he ſees, as if, inſtead of drawing his attention to the ſcence, it were a merit to divert it from its objects. Theſe kinds of ballets, beſides, demand ſo great an ingenuity in the dialogue, that the muſician rambles, as it were, in an unknown country, between the points, the alluſions, and epigrams, whilſt the ſpectator does not forget himſelf for an inſtant. According to ſuch a proceeding, there will never be any thing but the ſentiment which can introduce this on the ſtage, and identify it with the actors; every thing that is only intellectual bears it away to the piece, and reſtores it to itſelf. As a proof, we ſee that thoſe perſons, who wiſh to place the moſt wit in the theatre, are the very men that leaſt regard the illuſion. What then can the muſician do in thoſe dramas which pay no reſpect or value to his art? If muſic expreſſes but ſentiments or images, how can it render ideas purely metaphyſic, ſuch as allegories, where the mind is inceſſantly employed with the reference which the objects which are preſented to it, bear to thoſe which it muſt recollect in itſelf?

Would the compoſers but reflect on the true principles of their art, they would uſe greater caution in the dramas which they receive, as well as more truth in the expreſſion of their ſubjects; and when the words of an opera will but give ſome ideas, the muſic will ſoon be taught to ſpeak.

BARCAROLLES, A kind of ſongs in the Venetian language which are ſung by the Gondoliers in Venice. Though the airs of theſe Barcarolles are chiefly formed for the people, and often compoſed by the Gondoliers themſelves; they have ſo great a melody, and ſo pleaſing an accent, that there is no muſician in Italy but piques himſelf on knowing and ſinging them. The liberty that the Gondoliers have of viſiting all the theatres gratis, gives them an opportunity of forming the ear and taſte without any Expence, ſo that they compoſe and ſing their airs, as perſons, who, though converſant in the niceties of muſic, will not vary the ſimple and natural diſpoſition of their Barcarolles. The words of theſe ſongs are generally more than natural, like the converſation of thoſe who ſing them; but thoſe who are delighted with the faithful picture of a people's manners, and who, beſides, love the Venetian dialect, are eaſily led into a fondneſs for them, ſeduced by the beauty of the airs, ſo that many curioſos have very large collections of their pieces.

We

We cannot in conſcience omit remarking, to the glory of Taſſo, that the greateſt part of the Gondoliers can recite by heart, the chief part of his Jeruſalem Delivered; that many know it entirely, and ſpend the nights in their boats, ſinging it alternatively from one veſſel to another, that it is aſſuredly a moſt inimitable Barcarolle. Homer alone had the honour before himſelf of being thus celebrated, and no other epic poem has ſince met with any ſimilar renown.

BARDS, A kind of men, very ſingular, and to this time much reſpected among the Gauls, which were at the ſame time prophets, poets, and muſicians. Bochard derives the word from Parat, to ſing; and Camden agrees with Feſtus, that Bard ſignifies a ſinger, in the Celtic language, BARD.

BARIPYCNI, The ancients called by this term, five of the eight ſounds, or ſtable chords of their ſyſtem, or diagram, that is to ſay, the Hypaté-Hypaton, the Hypaté-Meſon, the Meſe, the parameſe, and the Neté, Diazeugmenon. (Vide PYCNI. TETRACHORD.)

BARITONO, A kind of note between tenor and baſs. (Vide CONCORDANT.)

BAROQUE, A Baroque, or rough muſic, is that, whoſe harmony is confuſed, filled with modulations and diſſonances, its notes hard and unnatural, the intonation difficult, and the movement conſtrained.

It appears evidently that this term muſt be derived from the Baroco of the logicians.

BARRE, C Barré, A kind of meaſure. (Vide C.)

BARS, Lines drawn perpendicularly at the end of each meaſure, on the five lines of the ſcale, to ſeparate the meaſure which finiſhes from that which begins. For which reaſon, thoſe notes contained between two bars, always form a complete meaſure, equal in quantity and duration to each of the other meaſures compriſed between two other bars, provided the movement does not change; but as there are many ſorts of meaſures which greatly differ in their duration, the ſame differences are perceived in the quantities contained between two bars of each of theſe kinds of meaſures. So in the great triple which is marked by this ſign $\frac{2}{3}$ and which is ſtruck deliberately, the ſum of the notes compriſed between two bars ought to make a circular note and a half, and in the ſmall triple $\frac{3}{8}$ which is ſtruck quick, the two Bars incloſe only three crotchets, or their quantity; ſo that eight times the quantity contained between the two bars of of this last measure, composes only once the quantity contained between two bars of the other.

The chief service of bars is to distinguish the measures, and to express their time, which is always fixed on that note which immediately follows the bar. They are also used in partitions to denote the correspondent measures within each division. (Vide PARTITION.)

Some hundred years ago, a plan was laid down for drawing bars from measure to measure: The music before-hand was simple. There was nothing seen therein but rounds, minums, and black notes, few crotchets, and hardly ever double crotchets. As the divisions were more equal, the measure was more easy to be followed. However, I have seen some of our best musicians embarrassed to execute the ancient music of Orlando and Claudin. They were lost in the measures, thro' an omission of those bars, to which they had been accustomed, and followed, with difficulty, such parts as had been formerly sung with rapidity by the musicians of Henry III. and Charles IX.

BASS, That of the four parts of music which is below the rest, the lowest of all, whence is derived its appellation of bass. (Vide PARTITION.)

The bass is the most necessary of all the parts, 'tis on that the whole of harmony is established; and 'tis a general maxim among musicians, that when the bass is good, the harmony is rarely contrary.

There are a great number of different kinds of the bass, viz. The *Fundamental Bass*, which we shall treat of in the following article.

The *Continued, or Thorough Bass*, so called because it lasts throughout the whole piece: its chief use, omitting that of directing the harmony, is to sustain the voice, and preserve the tone. It is believed, that it was one Lodovico Viana, one of whose treatises is extant, who, about the beginning of the last century, first brought it into use.

The *Figured Bass*, which in lieu of a single note, divides its quantity in several other notes under the same concord. (Vide FIGURED HARMONY.)

The *Constrained Bass*, whose air or subject, bounded to a small number of measures, as four or eight, begins afresh incessantly, whilst the superior parts pursue their air and harmony, and vary them by different methods. This bass belongs originally to the couplets of the chacon, a kind of tune, but at present it is no longer used. The constrained bass descending diatonically, or chromatically, and with slowness from the tonic, or from the dominant, is admirable for pathetic pieces. Those frequent and periodical returns touch insensibly the soul, and inspire it with a disposition of languor and melancholy. Examples may be seen in in ſeveral ſcenes of the French opera. But tho' theſe kinds of the baſs have a good effect to the ear, it is ſeldom the ſame in regard to the airs that they are adapted to, which generally conſtitute only a ſimple accompaniment. Beſide the rough and ill conducted modulations, which can be ſcarcely avoided, theſe airs varied in a thouſand methods, and ſtill monotonic, produce a confuſion by no means harmonious; and as they have but little muſic in themſelves, the parts above are greatly detained thro' the conſtraint of the baſs.

The *Singing Baſs*, is that kind of voice which ſings the part of the baſs. There are the baſs recitative, and the baſs in chorus; concordants, or baſs tenor, which have their place between the tenor and the baſs; baſs's diſtinguiſhed properly by that name alone, to which cuſtom has given the name of baſs tenor; and laſtly, counter baſs, the moſt ſo of all the notes which ſing the baſs below the baſs itſelf, and which we muſt not confound with a kind of inſtrument that bears a ſimilar name.

FUNDAMENTAL BASS, Is that which is formed only from the fundamental ſounds of harmony, ſo that below every concord it gives the true fundamental ſound of that concord, i. e. the ſound from whence it is derived by the laws of harmony. Wherein we ſee that the fundamental baſs can have no other texture than that of a regular and fundamental ſucceſſion; without which, the order of the ſuperior parts would be diſcordant. To underſtand this well, it muſt be premiſed, that according to the ſyſtem of Monſ. Rameau, which I have conformed to in this work, every concord, tho' formed of ſeveral ſounds, has but one fundamental to it, that is to ſay, that which has produced this concord, and which ſerves as a baſs to it, in direct and natural order. Moreover, the baſs which reigns under all the other parts, does not always expreſs the fundamental ſounds of the concords; for amongſt all the ſounds that form a concord, the compoſer may appropriate to the baſs whichever he thinks preferable, with a view to the order of this baſs, to the beauty of his air, and above all, to the expreſſion, as I ſhall explain it in the future pages. In this caſe, the true fundamental ſound, inſtead of being in its natural place, which is the baſs, is tranſported into the other parts, or perhaps is not expreſſed at all; and *ſuch* a concord is ſtiled a ſubverted concord. In its foundation, a ſubverted concord differs not from the direct accord which has produced it, for they are ſtill the ſame ſounds, but theſe ſounds forming a different combination, all thoſe combinations have been long taken for ſo many different fundamental concords, and they have received different names, which may be ſeen under the word Concord; and which have continued to diſtinguiſh them, as if the difference of names could produce any variation in their nature.

Monſ.

Monſ. Rameau has ſhewn in his Treatiſe of Harmony, and M. d'Alembert, in his Elements of Muſic, has given a ſtill clearer evidence, that many of theſe pretended concords were only the ſubverſions of a ſingle one. So, the concord of the ſixth is only a perfect concord, whoſe third is tranſported to the baſs; in conveying to it the fifth, we ſhall have the concord of the ſixth fourth. Herein then we ſee three combinations of a concord which has but three ſounds; thoſe which have four are capable of four combinations, as every ſound may be conveyed to the baſs. But by introducing, under this, another baſs, which under all the combinations of the ſame concord, prevents us always a fundamental ſound; it is evident, that the number of conſonant concords is reduced to a third, and the number of diſſonant to a fourth. Add to that, all the concords by ſuppoſition which are ſtill reduced to the ſame fundamentals, and you will find the harmony ſimplified to a degree that one could not have expected, conſidering the confuſed ſtate in which its rules were founded before the time of M. Rameau. It is certainly, as that author obſerves, an aſtoniſhing thing that it has been poſſible the practice of that art to be carried to the height to which it has arrived without knowing its foundation, and that we have found exactly every rule, without being able to diſcover the principles from whence it is derived.

After having ſhewn what is the fundamental baſs under the accords, let us now ſpeak of its direction, and of the method by which it unites the concords together. The precepts of art on this head, may be reduced to the ſix following rules.

I. The fundamental baſs ſhould never ſound any other notes than thoſe of the Gamut of that tone, in which we are employed, or of that thro' which we intend to paſs. This is the firſt and moſt indiſpenſible of all its rules.

II. In the ſecond place, its courſe ſhould be ſo ſubmitted to the laws of modulation, that it ſhould never ſuffer the idea of a note to be loſt, but in taking up that of another, that is to ſay, the fundamental baſs ſhould never wander, or ſuffer the tone which is before us, to be forgot an inſtant.

III. In the third place, it is ſubjected to the union of concords, and to the preparation of diſſonances, a preparation which, as I will ſhew, is only one of the caſes of union, and which, conſequently, is never neceſſary when the union can exiſt without it. (Vide UNION, to PREPARE.)

IV. By the fourth rule it ought, after every diſſonance, to follow the progreſs, which is preſcribed to it thro' the neceſſity of preſerving it.

V. By the fifth, which is only a ſummary of the precedent, the fundamental baſs ought only to move in conſonant intervals; as it is only in a caſe of broken cadence, or after a concord of the diminiſhed ſeventh, that it aſcends diatonically. Every other movement of the fundamental baſs is erroneous.

VI. Finally, by the ſixth, the fundamental baſs or harmony, ſhould undergo no ſyncope, but ſhould denote the measure and time by a well cadenced change of concords; for the purpoſe that the diſſonances, which ought to be prepared, ſhould be ſo on a weak time, but particularly that all the ſtops ſhould be found on a ſtrong time. This ſixth rule meets with a great number of exceptions, but the compoſer ſhould ſtill be attentive to it if he wiſhes to form a piece, wherein the movement may be well pointed, and whoſe meaſure may fall with grace.

Wherever theſe rules are obſerved, the harmony will be regular, and without error, which will not however prevent the muſic from being diſpleaſing. (Vide COMPOSITION.)

One word of diſcuſſion on the fifth rule will not be by any means uſeleſs. Let the fundamental baſs be ſhifted as we pleaſe, if it be well formed, we ſhall find therein but theſe two things, either perfect concords or conſonant movements, without which theſe concords could have no union, or diſſonant accords in the acts of cadence; in every other caſe, the diſſonance can neither be well placed, or well preſerved.

Thence it follows, that the fundamental baſs can have no regular courſe, but by one of theſe three methods. 1ſt. To aſcend or deſcend from a third or ſixth. 2dly. From a fourth or fifth. 3dly. To aſcend diatonically to the method of the diſſonance, which forms the union, or by courlery, on a perfect concord. In regard to the diatonic deſcent, it is a plan entirely aboliſhed in the fundamental baſs, or at the moſt tolerated in caſe of two conſecutive perfect concords, ſeparated by a ſtop expreſt or underſtood therein. This rule has no other exception; and 'tis thro' not having diſcovered the true foundation of certain paſſages, that M. Rameau has made the fundamental baſs deſcend diatonically on the concords of the ſeventh, which cannot be ſuffered in a complete harmony. (Vide CADENCE, DISSONANCE.)

The fundamental baſs, which is added only as a proof of harmony, is cut off in the execution, and often it would form a very ill effect; for it is according to M. Rameau, for the judgment and not the ear:—It would at leaſt produce a very diſguſting monotony by the frequent returns of the ſame concord, which is diſguiſed and varied more agreeably in a combination, by different methods on the thorough baſs, without reckoning that the different revolutions of harmony furniſh a thouſand methods of adding freſh beauties to the air, and a new energy to the expreſſion. (Vide CONCORD.)

If the fundamental baſs does not ſerve for the compoſition of good muſic, if even it ought to be retrenched in the execution,

I ſhall be aſked in what particular it is of ſervice? I anſwer, that in the firſt place it ſerves as a rule for ſcholars to learn the methods of forming a regular harmony, and giving to every part the diatonic and elementary courſe which is preſcribed to them by this fundamental baſs. It ſerves, ſecondly, as I have already ſaid, to diſcover if an harmony already compoſed be good and regular; for every harmony which cannot be ſubmitted to a fundamental baſs, is regularly incorrect. It is of uſe laſtly, to find a thorough baſs under a given air; although, in fact, he who is not able to compoſe directly a thorough baſs, will not be ſuperior in the compoſition of a fundamental; and much leſs will he know the art of transforming this fundamental baſs into a good thorough baſs. Herein then lie the principal rules that M. Rameau lays down for the diſcovering the fundamental baſs in a given air.

I. To be certain of the tone or mode by which the air is begun, and of all thoſe thro' which we paſs. There are alſo rules for this diſcovery of the tone, but ſo long, ſo vague, and incomplete, that the ear is formed a long time before the rules are learned; and the fool, who would endeavour to make uſe of them, will only gain the habit of proceding note by note, without ever knowing where he is.

II. To try ſucceſſively on each note the principal chords of the tone, beginning by the moſt analogous, and continuing to the moſt diſtant, if we lie under that neceſſity.

III. To be attentive if the choſen chord can time with the inferior parts in what precedes, and what follows, by a good fundamental ſucceſſion; and when that cannot be done, to return to our former plan.

IV. Never to vary the note of the fundamental baſs till we have exhauſted all the conſequent notes of the parts below, which can enter into its accord, or till ſome ſyncopating note in the air, may receive two or more notes of the baſs, to prepare the preſerved diſſonances in a regular continuance.

V. To ſtudy well the inter-union of phraſes, the poſſible ſucceſſion of cadences, whether full, whether avoided, and particularly the ſtops which come generally every four or two meaſures, for the purpoſe of making them always fall on perfect or on irregular cadences.

VI. Laſtly, to obſerve all the foregoing rules for the compoſition of the fundamental baſs. Here then, are the chief obſervations to be made for finding one under a given air, for there are often ſeveral to be found; but whatever may be ſaid, if the air has accent and character, there is one fundamental baſs only which we can adapt to it.

After having given a clear ſummary of the method of compoſing a fundamental baſs, there would remain alſo to ſhew the method of transforming it into a thorough bass; and that would be easy, if it were necessary to look only at the diatonic course, and the pleasing notes of this bass; but let us not think, that the bass, which is the guide and support of harmony, the soul, and, to use the expression, the interpreter of the air, is confined to rules so simple. There are others which arise from a more sure and radical principle, a principle ingenious, tho' concealed, which has been felt by all the artists of genius, without having been ever unravelled by any one. I think I have hit on the bud of it in my Letter on the French Music: I have have spoken sufficiently for those who comprehend me:—I shall never explain it clearly to those who do not. (Vide through the whole, UNITY of MELODY.)

I make no mention here of the ingenious System of Monf. Serre, of Geneva, or of his double fundamental bass, because the principles, which he had examined with a sagacity worthy of praise, have been since exposed to view, by Monf. Tartins, in a work, which I will treat of before the conclusion of the present. (Vide SYSTEM.)

BEATING, A particularity or grace in the French airs, which consists in elevating and striking a quaver, on a note instantaneously begun. There is this difference between the cadence and the beating, that the cadence begins by the note superior to that whereon it is marked, after which we strike alteratively the superior note, and the true one, whereas the beating begins by the sound itself of the note that bears it, after which we strike alternatively *that* note, and that which is above it, *E, G:* these tones of the throat, mi, re, mi, re, mi, re, ut, ut, are a cadence; and the following re, mi, re, mi, re, mi, re, ut, re, mi, are a beating.

BEATINGS, in the plural, Whenever two strong and well sustained notes, like those of the organ, are harsh and dissonant together, on the approach of a consonant interval, they form, by more or less frequent shakes, an irregularity of sound which impresses on the ear, an effect nearly similar to the beating of the pulse on the hand, for which reason, Monf. Sauveur has given them also the term of beatings: these strokes become so much the more frequent, as the interval draws nearer to justness, and whenever they reach it, they are confounded with the vibrations of the sound.

Monf. Serre pretends, in his Essay on the principles of Harmony, that these beatings, produced through the concurrence of two sounds, are only an acoustic appearance, occasioned by the vibrations of their two sounds. These beatings, according to him, have equally a place when the interval is consonant, but the rapidity, in which they are then counfounded, not suffering them to be distinguished by the ear, there ought to follow, not an an abſolute ceſſation of the ſtrokes, but an appearance of a flat and thorough ſound, a kind of leſs perceptible humming, ſuch an one preciſely as reſults in the proofs cited by Monſ. Serre, and ſince expanded by Monſ. Tartins, from the concurrence of two ſharp and conſonant ſounds, (under the word ſyſtem may be ſeen, that the diſſonances alſo produce them). "What is "very certain," continues Monſ. Serre, "is, that their beat- "ings, their co-incident vibrations, which are followed with "more or leſs rapidity, are exactly ſimilar in meaſure to the "vibrations, which the fundamental ſound would really pro- "duce, if, thro' means of a third corpo ſonoro, it was actually "made to reſound."

This very ſpecious explanation is not perhaps without its difficulties; for the connection of two ſounds is never more compoſed than when it approaches to the ſimplicity which produces from it a conſonance; and the vibrations ought never to coincide more rarely than when they reach almoſt to an iſochroniſm; from whence it muſt follow, in my opinion, that the Beatings ought to ſlacken, in proportion as they become more quick, then in an inſtant reunite, in the moment that the concord is juſt.

The obſervation of the beatings is an excellent rule to be conſulted on the beſt ſyſtem of modification. (Vide MODIFICATION) For it is evident, that amongſt all poſſible modifications, *that* which leaves the feweſt beatings in the organ, is moſt pleaſing to nature and the ear. Moreover, it is a conſtant and well-known circumſtance among organiſts, that the changes of thirds major, produce beatings more forcible and more diſagreeable than thoſe of the Fifths. In this caſe nature herſelf has choſen.

BATTERY, The method of ſtriking and repeating ſucceſſively on different ſtrings of an inſtrument, the various ſounds which compoſe a concord, and of paſſing in this manner from concord to concord by the ſame variation of notes. This battery is but a continued arpeggio, but the whole of its notes are detatched inſtead of being conjoined as in the arpeggio.

BEATER OF TIME, One whoſe office is in beating time in a concert. (Vide the following Article.)

TO BEAT TIME, Is to ſpecify the variety of time, by motions of the hand or foot, which denote its duration, and by which all ſimilar meaſures are rendered exactly equal in their chronical powers or time in the execution. There are meaſures which are ſtruck by one time only, others by two, three, or four, which is the greateſt number of times ſpecified, that can be contained within a meaſure. A four tim'd meaſure alſo can always be divided into two meaſures of two times each. In all their different meaſures, the beaten time is always on the note which

which immediately follows the bar: the raised time is always that which precedes, unless it happens that the measure contains but one time, and even in that case we must always suppose a weaker time, since we cannot beat without having raised.

The degrees of slowness or of quickness which are given to measure, depend on many circumstances. 1st, From the powers of the notes which compose the measure, we may very plainly see, that a measure which contains a circle, viz. O, should be struck more forcibly, and have a longer duration than that which contains a crotchet, viz. ♩ 2dly, From the movement expressed by the French or Italian word, which is often placed at the beginning, *Gai*, *Vite*, *Lent*, *&c.* All these words denote an equal number of modulations in the movement of a similar kind of measure. 3dly and lastly, From the character of the air itself, which, if well executed, will necessarily strike us with its true movement.

The French musicians beat time differently from the Italians. The one, in a four timed measure, strikes the two first successively, and raises the others. They strike also the two first in a three tim'd measure, and raise the third. The French strike the first time only, and specify the others by different motions of the hand on the right and left. However, the French music would be in want of a well-marked measure, much more than the Italian, for it does not convey its cadence within itself; its movements have no natural precision: the measure is extended or diminished at the option of the singer. How greatly are our ears disgusted at the French opera with the disagreeable and continual noise, which is made by the strokes of him who beats the time, and who has been ingeniously compared to a wood-cutter felling a tree! But 'tis an inevitable evil. Without that noise the measure could not be felt. The music itself does not express it. On which account foreigners can perceive no movements in the French airs. If we pay attention to this, we shall find, that herein lies one of the specific differences between the French and Italian music. In Italy, the measure is the whole spirit of the music; 'tis a well expressed measure which gives it that accent which renders it so delightful. 'Tis the measure also which directs the musician in the execution. In France, on the contrary, 'tis the musician who directs the measure: He enervates and disfigures it without hesitation or scruple. But what am I saying? The excellence of taste itself consists in not suffering it to be perceived; a precaution of which (into the bargain) it stands in no great need. The opera of Paris is the only European theatre where the measure is struck without being followed. In every other part they follow it without beating.

There

There reigns herein a general error, which a little reflection will eaſily aboliſh. It is imagined, that a hearer beats the time of an air which he hears, only becauſe he feels it forcibly; and 'tis, on the contrary, becauſe it is not ſufficiently ſenſible, or that he does not well enter into its ſpirit, that he endeavours, by the addition of motions of the hand or foot to make amends for what is wanting in this particular to the ear. As little as a piece of muſic regards its cadence, we may ſee the generality of the French, in attending to it, make a thouſand contorſions, and an inconceivable jargon to aſſiſt the meaſure in its courſe, and the ear, in feeling it. Subſtitute Italians or Germans in their place, you will not perceive the leaſt noiſe, or ſee the moſt minute geſture that has any connection with the meaſure. Is it, poſſibly, that the Germans and Italians were leſs ſenſible of the meaſure than the French? There are ſeveral of my readers who would not in the leaſt ſcruple in ſaying ſo; but would they alſo advance, that the moſt ingenious muſicians are thoſe who enter leaſt into the ſpirit of the muſic. It is inconteſtable that they are thoſe who *beat* the leaſt, and when, by dint of exerciſe, they have gained the habit of always feeling it, they do not *beat* at all: this is a proof of experience that may be ſeen daily throughout the world. It may be ſaid alſo, that the ſame perſons, whom I accuſe of beating time only thro' an inſufficient feeling, do not beat in the airs where it is not to be felt; and I anſwer, that in that caſe 'tis becauſe they do not feel it at all. The ear muſt be ſtruck at leaſt with ſome kind of connection with the meaſure, that inſtinct may endeavour to ſtrengthen it.

The ancients, ſays Monſ. Burette, beat time in many different methods. The moſt general conſiſted in the motion of the foot, which was raiſed from the ground, and ſtruck it alternatively, according to the meaſure of the two equal or unequal times. (Vide RHYME.) This was commonly the office of the muſic-maſter, who was called Κορυφαιος, becauſe he was ſituated in the midſt of the choir of muſicians, and in an elevated ſituation, that he might be more eaſily ſeen and heard by all the company. Theſe time beaters were called in Greek ποδόκτυποι and ποδοψόφοι, on account of the noiſe of their feet συντονάριοι, on account of the uniformity of their geſtures, and, if I may be allowed the expreſſion, of the monotony of the rhyme, which they always beat à deux tems. They were called in Latin pedarli, podarii, pedicularii. They beat time not only with the foot, but alſo with the right hand, and conjoined all the fingers to ſtrike within the hollow of the left, and he who expreſſed the harmony in this manner, was called Manuductor. Beſide this, beating of hands and noiſe of ſlippers, the ancients had ſtill, for ſtriking the time, that of cockell-ſhells, oyſter-ſhells, and the ſmall bones of animals, which they ſtruck againſt one another, as we at preſent perform with caſtanets and other ſimilar inſtruments. All this ſo diſagreeable and ſuperfluous noiſe among us, on account of the equality of the meaſure, was not the ſame in thoſe times, where the frequent changes of feet and rhyme required a concord much more difficult, and gave to the noiſe itſelf a variety much more harmonious, and more ſtriking. We may moreover ſay, that the cuſtom of beating in this manner was introduced only in caſe the harmony ſhould become languiſhing, and ſhould loſe its accent and energy, The higher we riſe, the fewer examples we find of theſe beaters of time, and in muſic of the remoteſt antiquity, we cannot diſcover any.

TO BAWL, Is to exert the voice in ſinging in ſuch a manner, as that the ſounds can be no longer diviſible, and have a greater reſemblance to cries than ſinging. The French muſic muſt be bawled: 'tis in that that its moſt forcible expreſſion conſiſts.

BI, A ſyllable which ſeveral foreign muſicians uſed formerly for the pronunciation of the ſound of the gamut, which is called by the French ſi. (Vide Si.)

BISCHROMA, An Italian word which expreſſes triple crotchets. Whenever this word is written under a collection of notes, equal, and of a greater power than the triple crotchets, it denotes, that the powers of thoſe notes ſhould be divided into triple crotchets, according to the real diviſion which is generally found in the firſt time. 'Tis an invention of authors adopted by imitators, particularly in the partitions, to ſpare pains and paper. (Vide Crotchet.)

BOREE, A kind of air, appropriated to the dance which goes under the ſame name as that which is generally ſuppoſed to take its origin from Auvergne, and which is ſtill in uſe in that province. The boree has two lively times, and begins with a crotchet before it is ſtruck. It ſhould have, as the generality of dances, two parts and four meaſures, or a multiple of four to each. In theſe kinds of airs we frequently join the latter half of the firſt time to the former of the ſecond by a ſyncopated minum.

BOUTADE, An ancient kind of leſſer ballet, which was executed, or appeared to be, impromptu, The muſicians have ſometimes given this name to pieces or ideas which they executed in the ſame manner on their inſtruments, and which are otherwiſe ſtiled caprices or fantaſies, (Vide thoſe words.)

TO BRAWL, Is to outdo the natural extent of the voice, and ſing with all our poſſible violence, as the church-wardens in the villages of Lutrin, and ſeveral muſicians elſewhere.

BRAWL,

BRAWL, A kind of dance very lively, which is performed in a circle, with a short tune in rondeau, that is to say, with the same conclusion at the end of every couplet.

BREF, An adverb which we often find in ancient music, written above the note which concludes a phrase or an air, to denote that this finale should be lessened by a quick and short sound, instead of preserving its entire force. (Vide To Clip.) This word is however useless, as we have a sign which may express it.

BREVE, A note which passes with double the quickness of the preceding; for which reason the crotchet is short after a pricked minum, and the quaver after a pricked crotchet. We could not call a note that is equal to the half of the preceding a breve, wherefore a crotchet is not breve after a simple minum, nor a quaver after a crotchet, unless we make use of a syncope.

In church music it is quite different. To answer exactly to the quantity of syllables, the breve is equal to the half of a long syllable. Moreover, a long note has often a tail to distinguish it from a short, which never has any, which circumstance is a direct opposition to music, where the round which has no tail, is the double of the minum which has one. (Vide Measure, Powers of the Notes.)

BREVE, Is also a name which our ancient musicians gave, and the Italian still give to that old kind of note that we express by the term quarrée. There were two sorts of Breve's, for instance, the true and perfect, which is divided into three equal parts, and is equal to three rounds, or semi-breves in triple measure; and the changed or imperfect breve, which we divide into two equal parts, and which is equal to two semi-breves only in a double measure. This last kind of breve, is that which is marked by the sign of C barré, and the Italians call still by the name of alla breve, the measure of two quick times, which they make use of in pieces of music, da Capella. (Vide Alla Breve.)

BUZZING, A thorough bass which is always continuing in the same sound, as are those generally from the instruments which we call Bag-pipes.

BUCOLIASM, An ancient rustic song. (Vide Song.)

C.

C. This letter, in our ancient music, was the sign of the minor imperfect extent, from whence the same letter has continued among us, as that of a four timed measure, which includes exactly an equal power of notes. (Vide MODE.)

C BARRE, The sign of a quick four timed measure, or a set two timed. It is marked by a perpendicular line which passes from the top to the bottom of the C within the stave, thus ₵.

C SOL UT, C SOL FA UT, or simply C, A character or term of music, which indicates the first Note of the gamut, which we call ut. (Vide GAMUT.) It is also the ancient sign of one of the three keys of music. (Vide CLEFF.)

CACOPHONY, A discordant unison of several ill chosen, or disagreeing sounds.—This word is derived from κακος, ill, and φωνη, a sound. For which reason it is called cacaphony by the generality of musicians in an improper pronunciation.

CADENCE, The termination of an harmonic phrase, either on a stop, or a perfect concord, or, to speak in a more extensive sense, it is every passage from a dissonant accord to any other whatsoever, for we can never remove from a dissonant accord but by an act of cadence. Moreover, as every harmonic phrase is by necessity conjoined by dissonances expressed or understood, it follows, that harmony in general is properly a collection of cadences only.

That which we call act of cadence, takes it origin always from two fundamental sounds, one of which denotes the cadence, and the other its termination.

As there can be no dissonance without a cadence, neither can there be any cadence without its dissonance expressed or understood; for to give expression to a stop, something anterior must suspend it, and this something can be nothing, unless a dissonance, or the implicit sentiment of that dissonance: were it otherwise, the two concords, being equally perfect, we might make a pause on the first; the second would not discover itself, and therefore must become unnecessary. The concord formed on the first sound of a cadence, should, consequently, be always dissonant, that is to say, should sustain or suppose a dissonance.

In regard to the second, it may be consonant or dissonant, just as we chuse, either to preserve or to elude the stops. If it be consonant, the cadence is full; if dissonant, the cadence is avoided or imitated.

We generally reckon four kinds of cadences, that is to say, perfect cadence, imperfect or irregular cadence, cadence interrupted, and broken cadence. These are the denominations which

Monſ. Rameau has given to them, and the reaſons whereof ſhall be ſeen hereafter.

I. Whenſoever after a concord of the ſeventh, the fundamental baſs deſcends from the fifth on a perfect concord, 'tis a full perfect cadence, which proceeds always from a dominant tonic to a tonic; but if the perfect cadence be avoided by a diſſonance added to the ſecond note, we may begin a ſecond cadence, in avoiding the firſt on that ſecond note, avoid this ſecond cadence, and begin a third on the third note; then go on in the ſame plan as far as we pleaſe, by aſcending from the fourth, or deſcending from the fifth on all the chords of the tune, and this forms a ſucceſſion of avoided perfect cadences. In this ſucceſſion, which is without a doubt, the moſt harmonious, two parts, viz. thoſe which form the ſeventh and the fifth deſcend on the third and eighth of the following concord, whereas the two other parts, viz. thoſe which form the third and eighth, remain to compoſe in their turn, the ſeventh and the fifth, and deſcend immediately in an alternate direction with the two others. In this manner ſuch a ſucceſſion promotes a deſcendant harmony. It ſhould never ſtop but on a dominant tonic, to fall immediately on the tonic by a full cadence.

Perfect Cadences avoided.

II. If the fundamental baſs, inſtead of deſcending from the fifth after a concord of the ſeventh, deſcends only on the third, the cadence is called interrupted. This can never be full, but it muſt neceſſarily fall out, that the ſecond note of this cadence ſuſtains another diſſonant accord. We may in the ſame manner continue to deſcend from the third, or aſcend from the ſixth, by concords of the ſeventh, which makes a ſecond ſucceſſion of avoided cadences, but much leſs perfect than the preceding, for the ſeventh, which unites with the third in the perfect cadence, unites

unites here with the eighth, whence proceeds a lesser harmony, and which makes also two eighths to be understood, so that to avoid them, we must either remove the dissonance or destroy the harmony.

Whereas the interrupted cadence can never be full, it follows thence that a phrase can never be concluded by it, but we must have recourse to the perfect cadence to make the concord dominant be understood.

Interrupted Cadences avoided.

The interrupted cadence forms also, by its succession, a descendant harmony, but there is one found only which descends. The three others remain in order to descend, each in its turn, in a similar direction.

There are some who erroneously mistake an overthrow of the perfect cadence for an interrupted cadence, wherein the bass, after a concord of the seventh, descends from the third, sustaining a concord of the sixth, but every one must see that such a course, not being fundamental, can by no means constitute a cadence proper to it.

III. Broken cadence is that wherein the fundamental bass, instead of ascending from the fourth after a concord of the seventh, as in the perfect cadence, ascends only a degree. This cadence is ofteneſt avoided by a seventh on the second note. It is certain that it cannot be rendered full but by licence, for in such a case there is necessarily a want of unison.

Broken

Broken Cadence
Full with a Tie A.
Avoided with a Tie B.

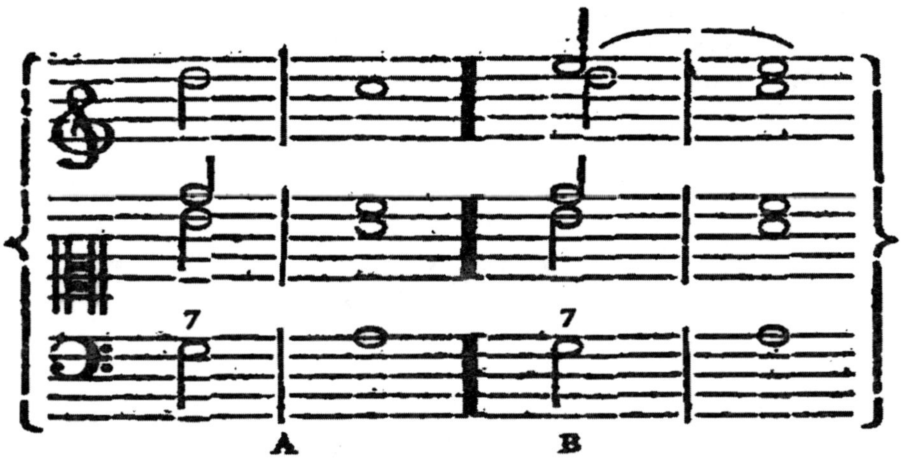

A ſucceſſion of broken cadences avoided is ſtill deſcendant. Three ſounds therein deſcend, the eighth remains alone to prepare the diſſonance; but ſuch a ſucceſſion is rough, badly modulated, and is ſeldom put in practice.

IV. When the Baſs deſcends by an interval of the fifth, from the dominant on the tonic, it is, as I have ſaid, an act of perfect cadence. If, on the contrary, the baſs aſcends by a fifth from the tonic to the dominant, 'tis an act of irregular and imperfect cadence. To diſcover it, we add to the concord of the tonic a ſixth major, whence this concord takes the name of ſixth added. (Vide Concord.) This ſixth, which forms a diſſonance on the fifth, is alſo healed as a diſſonance on the fundamental baſs, and, as ſuch, obliged to extend itſelf by aſcending diatonically on the third of the following concord.

The imperfect cadence forms almoſt an abſolute oppoſition to the perfect cadence. In the firſt concord of each we divide the fourth, which is placed between the Fifth and the eighth, by a diſſonance, which forms therein a new third, and this diſſonance ought to be reduced on the following concord; therein lies what theſe two cadences have in common with each other, but hereafter the contrariety which they maintain.

In the perfect cadence, the ſound which is added fixes itſelf at the top of the interval of the fourth, near to the eighth, forming a third before the fifth, and produces a diſſonance minor, which is avoided by deſcending; whereas the fundamental baſs aſcends from the fourth, or deſcends from the fifth of the dominant to the tonic, to maintain a perfect pauſe. In the imperfect cadence, the ſound which is added is fixed at the bottom of the interval of the fourth, near to the fifth, and forming a third with the eighth, it produces a major diſſonance, which is avoided by aſcending; whereas the fundamental baſs deſcends from the fourth, or aſcends from the fifth of the tonic to the dominant, to eſtabliſh an imperfect pauſe.—Monſ. Rameau, who firſt made mention of this cadence, and who admits many exceptions from it, forbids us in his Treatiſe on Harmony, page 117, to admit that wherein the added ſound is in the flat, ſuſtaining a concord of the ſeventh, and that, with a very weak argument, which I have made mention of under the word concord. He has taken this concord of the ſeventh as fundamental, ſo that we muſt preſerve a ſeventh by another ſeventh, a diſſonance by an equal diſſonance, by a ſimilar movement on the fundamental baſs. If ſuch a method of treating the diſſonances could be ſuffered, we had as well ſhut our ears, and throw our rules into the flames. But the harmony, under which this author has placed ſo ſtrange a fundamental baſs, is clearly overthrown by an imperfect cadence, avoided by a ſeventh added upon the ſecond note.

Reverſion of the Sixth added.

B. F. from M. Rameau. *The true B. F.*

And this is ſo true, that the thorough baſs, which ſtrikes the diſſonance, is neceſſarily obliged to aſcend diatonically to preſerve it, without which the paſſage could be of no avail. I confeſs, that in the ſame work, page 272, Monſ. Rameau gives a ſimilar example with the fundamental baſs; and ſince he diſapproves in formal terms, the overthrow which reſults from this baſs, ſuch a paſſage ſerves only to diſcover, in his book, one contradiction more. And as much as this ſame author, in a future work (Gener. Harmon, page 186) ſeems to recollect the true origin of this paſſage; he ſpeaks of it ſo obſcurely, and ſays again ſo poſitively, that one ſeventh is preſerved by another, that we may ſee clearly, that he only takes therein a comparative view, and that at the bottom his ſentiments remain the ſame, ſo that we have the privilege of retorting againſt him the reproach

reproach which he confers on Maſſon, not to have known how to ſee the imperfect cadence in one of his perverſions.

This ſame imperfect cadence extends itſelf alſo from the ſub-dominant to the tonic. We may alſo avoid it, and give it, by this method, a ſucceſſion of ſeveral notes, whoſe concords will compoſe an aſcendant harmony, in the which the ſixth and eighth aſcend on the third and fifth of the concord, whereas the the third and fifth remain to form the eighth and prepare the ſixth.

No author that I know of, before Monſ. Rameau, has ſpoken of this harmonic riſe, himſelf has only given us a view of it; and it is certain, that we could neither practiſe a long continuance of ſimilar cadences, on account of the major ſixths which would remove the modulation, nor even fill the whole of its harmony without a precaution.

After having laid open the rules and conſtitution of the different cadences, let us take a view of the reaſons which Monſ. D'Alembert gives, from Monſ. Rameau, of their denominations.

The perfect cadence conſiſts in a courſe of the fifth, by deſcending; and, on the contrary, the imperfect conſiſts in a courſe of the fifth in aſcending. Herein lies the reaſon: When I ſay ut ſol, ſol is already encloſed within ut, ſince every ſound, as ut, carries its twelfth with it, the fifth of which, viz. ſol, is the eighth; ſo when we go from ut to ſol, 'tis the generating ſound which paſſes to its product, in ſuch a manner though, that the ear always wiſhes to return to this firſt generator; on the contrary, when we ſay ſol ut, 'tis the product which returns to its generator, the ear is ſatisfied, and wiſhes nothing more. Moreover in this courſe, ſol ut, the ſol makes itſelf again underſtood in ut; by this means the ear hears at once the generator and its product, whereas, in the courſe ut ſol, the ear, which in the firſt ſound had heard ut and ſol, hears nothing more in the ſecond than ſol without ut. Wherefore the ſtop or cadence from ſol to ut, has a greater perfection than the cadence or ſtop, from ut to ſol.

It ſeems, continues Monſ. D'Alembert, that in the principles of Monſ. Rameau, we may furthermore explain the effect of the broken cadence, and the interrupted.* Let us ſuppoſe, for this purpoſe, that after a concord of the ſeventh, ſol, ſi, re, fa, we aſcend diatonically, by a broken cadence to the concord la, ut, mi, ſol: It is viſible that this concord is deſtroyed by the concord of the ſub-dominant, ut, mi, ſol, la; wherefore, the courſe of broken cadence is equivocal to this ſucceſſion, ſol, ſi, re, fa, ut, mi, ſol, la, which is nothing different from a perfect cadence, in the which ut inſtead of being uſed as tonic is rendered ſub-dominant.

dominant. Every tonic, ſays Monſ. D'Alembert, can always be rendered ſub-dominant by changing its mode. I will add, that it can even bear the concord of a ſixth added, without undergoing any change.

In regard to the interrupted cadence, which conſiſts in deſcending from one dominant on another by the interval of the third in this method, ſol, ſi, re, fa,—mi, ſol, ſi, re, it ſeems, that we may ſtill explain it. In effect, the ſecond concord, mi, ſol, ſi, re, is overthrown by the concord of the ſub-dominant, ſol, ſi, re, mi; for which reaſon the interrupted cadence is equivocal to this ſucceſſion, ſol, ſi, re, fa,—ſol, ſi, re, mi, where the note ſol, after having been uſed as dominant, is rendered ſub-dominant by changing the mode, which is permitted, and left to the option of the compoſer.

Theſe explanations are ingenious, and ſhew what uſe we may make of the double employ in thoſe paſſages, which ſeem to have the leaſt connection with it. However, the intention of Monſ. D'Alembert, is not ſurely that we ſhould make uſe of them in reality in theſe paſſages for practice, but only for the comprehenſion of the changes. For inſtance, the double employ of the interrupted cadence would prevent the diſſonance fa, by the diſſonance mi, which is contrary to rules, to the utility of rules, and particularly to the judgment of the ear; for in the ſenſation of the ſecond concord, ſol, ſi, re, mi, at the continuance of the firſt ſol, ſi, re, fa, the ear is more attached towards the removal of the re, than to admit the mi as diſſonant. Beginners, in general, ſhould be acquainted, that the double employ may be admitted on a concord of the ſeventh, in the continuance of a conſonant accord; but that as ſoon as the concord of the ſeventh follows one ſimilar to itſelf, the double employ can have no admiſſion. It is neceſſary that they know alſo that the tone ought not to be changed by any other diſſonant accord than the ſenſible; whence it follows, that in the broken cadence we cannot ſuppoſe any variation of tone.

There is another kind of cadence which the muſicians do not look upon as ſuch, and which, according to its definition, is, however, a true one: 'Tis the paſſage of the concord of the ſeventh diminiſhed on the ſenſible note, to the concord of the tonic. In this paſſage, there is found no harmonic union, and it is the ſecond example of this default, in what is called cadence. One might regard the harmonious tranſitions as methods of avoiding this ſame cadence, in the ſame manner as we avoid the perfect cadence of a dominant to its tonic, by a chromatic tranſition, but I confine myſelf here to the explanation of eſtabliſhed denominations only.

CADENCE, Is, in terms of singing, that motion of the throat which the Italians call trillo, and which we call warbling, which is generally on the last note but one of a musical phrase, from whence it has, doubtless, taken the name of Cadence. We say, "That actress has a fine cadence." "Such a singer strikes the cadence ill."

There are two kinds of cadences. The one is the full cadence, which consists in not beginning the warbling of the voice, until we have rested on the higher note: The other is called broken cadence, and in that we begin the trill of the voice without any preparation.

The CADENCE, Is a quality of good music, which gives to those who execute it, or who listen to it, a lively feeling of the measure, so that they remark it, and perceive it fall justly, without reflecting on it, as it were thro' instinct. This quality is particularly requisite in the airs for dancing. "This minuet has an agreeable Cadence." "That chacon wants a cadence." The cadence being, in that sense a quality, is generally preceded by the definite article *the*, whereas the harmonic cadence bears, as individual, the numerical article, viz. A perfect *cadence.*—*Three cadences* avoided.

Cadence signifies also the conformity of the dancer's steps, with the measure, expressed by the instrument. He goes out of *cadence*, or tune.---He keeps well the *cadence* or time. For this reason, the music master denotes the movement of the minuet, by beating time, at the beginning of each measure; whereas the dancing master beats time only every two measures, because so much is requisite to form the four steps of the minuet.

CADENCED, A well cadenced music is that wherein the cadence is most sensible, wherein the rhime and harmony most perfectly concur in giving life, as it were, to the movement; for the choice of concords is by no means indifferent to denote the time and measure; and we ought not to practise indifferently the same harmony on the stroke and its rise. Neither is it sufficient to divide the measures into equal powers, to make their equal returns be felt, since the rhime does not depend less from the accent which is given to the melody, than from the powers which are given to the notes, for we may have times very equal, and yet very ill cadenced: 'Tis not sufficient that there *be* an equality, but it must be of such a nature as to be felt.

CADENZA, An Italian word, by which we denote a point d'orgue, or sign of a pause, not written, and which the author leaves to the will of him who performs the principle part, for the purpose of his making, relatively to the character of the air, the passage most suitable to his voice, his instrument, or his taste.

Thi- ſign of a pauſe is called Cadenza, becauſe it is generally made on the firſt note of a final cadence; and it is alſo called arbitrio, on account of the liberty which we learn therein to the performer to ſuit his own ideas, and follow his particular taſte. The French muſic, particularly the vocal, which is extremely ſtrict, leaves no ſimilar liberty to the ſinger, which, were it ſo, he would with difficulty know how to uſe.

The CANARIES, A kind of gigue, the air of which is even of a more lively movement than that of the ordinary gigue, for which reaſon, it is ſometimes marked by $\frac{3}{16}$: This dance is at preſent no longer in uſe. (Vide GIGUE.)

CANEVAS, It is by this name that, in the opera of Paris, thoſe words are called, which the muſician adjuſts to the notes of an air, as a parody. From theſe words, which have no ſignification, the poet adjuſts others, which expreſs little more, wherein in general we find no more ingenuity than ſenſe, where the French proſody is infamouſly murdered, and which are therefore with great reaſon ſtiled

CANON; This was, in the ancient muſic, a rule or method to determine the reference and connection of intervals. They gave alſo the name of Canon to the inſtrument, by which they diſcovered theſe connections, and Ptolemy has given this ſame name to the book which we have of his on the reference of all the harmonic intervals. They called in general the diviſion of the monochord by all theſe intervals, ſextis canonis, and the monochord, thus divided, or the Table which repreſented it, Canon univerſalis. (Vide MONOCHORD.)

CANON, In modern muſic, is a kind of fugue, which is called perpetual, becauſe the parts ſucceeding each other, continually repeat the ſelf-ſame air.

Formerly, ſays Zarlin, there were placed at the head of the perpetual fugues, which he calls *Fughe in conſequenza*, certain notes which directed the method of ſinging thoſe kinds of fugues, and theſe directions, being properly the rules of theſe fugues, were called Canoni-Rules---Canons --From thence, taking the title for the thing, that kind of fugue, by Metonymy, has been ſtiled canon.

The canons, eaſieſt to be made, and moſt general, fix them at the uniſon, or at the 8th; that is to ſay, that every part repeats, on the ſame tone, the air of that which precedes it. For the compoſition of this kind of canon, we have only to chuſe an air to our liking; add thereto a partition, as many parts as we pleaſe with equal notes, then, from all theſe parts ſung in ſucceſſion, to form a ſingle air; uſing our endeavours that this ſucceſſion may produce a ſomething completely agreeable, whether it be in the harmony, or in the canto.

To

To execute a single canon, he, who is to sing the first, begins alone, singing the air throughout, and then again beginning it without interrupting the measure. As soon as he has finished the first couplet, which ought to serve as a continual subject, and on which the whole of the canon has been composed, the second enters, and begins this same first couplet, whilst he who entered first continues the second: The others pursue the same plan successively, as soon as he who precedes them is at the end of the first couplet; in re-beginning after this method, continually, there can be found no general conclusion, and they extend the canon to whatsoever length they please.

We may also take a perpetual fugue in the fifth or fourth, that is to say, that every part shall repeat the air of the foregoing, a fifth or a fourth higher or lower. But in that case the canon must be supposed quite entire, *di prima intenzione*, as the Italians say, and B sharp's or diesis's must be added to the notes, whose natural degrees could not exactly render, in the fifth or fourth, the air of the preceding part. We ought not here to pay the least regard to any modulation, but only to the identity of the air, which renders the composition of the canon more difficult; for every time that a part receives its fugue, it enters into a different tone: it has variations in almost every note, and what is worse, no one part is found at the same time in the same tone as another; which occasions that these kinds of canons, besides being difficult to follow, never form an agreeable effect, however good its harmony may be, and however well they may be sung.

There is a third kind of canons very scarce, as much on account of their exceeding difficulty, as because being generally bereft of arguments, they have no other merit than having cost a great deal of trouble to compose them. This is what might be called double canon varied, as much through the inversion which is placed therein in the singing of the parts, as thro' *that* which we find amongst the parts themselves in singing them. There is such an artifice in this kind of canons, that whether we sing the parts in their natural order, or change the paper to sing them in a retrogade direction by beginning at the end, and placing the bass above, we always find a good harmony, and a regular canon.

Double Canon perverted.

Another Double Canon perverted.

The above examples of thoſe kinds of canons are taken from Botempi, who alſo gives rules for the compoſition of them. But we ſhall find the true principle of theſe rules under the word Syſtem, in the expoſition of that of Monſ. Tartins.

To compose a canon where harmony may be a little varied, the parts must not follow each other too suddenly, and one must not enter till sometime after the other. When they follow one another with such velocity, as, at a pause, or demi-pause, there is no time for making several concords pass, and the canon cannot fail of being monotonous. But it is a method of making without much trouble, a canon at whatever part we please, for a canon of four measures only will be instantly of eight, if they follow each other at the demi-pause; and in every measure which is added, two other parts will be also gained. The emperor Charles VI. who was a great musician, and an excellent composer, took great pleasure in making and singing canons. Italy is still full of very fine canons, which had been made for that prince, by the best masters of the country.

CANTABILE, An Italian adjective, which signifies, convenient for singing. It is proper to every air, whose intervals, in whatsoever measure they may be, are not too large, nor the notes too precipitate, so that they can be easily sung without forcing or injuring the voice. The word cantabile is by degrees also past into the French language.

CANTATA, A kind of little lyric poem, which is sung with accompaniments, and which, though composed for a private room, ought to receive from the musician the fire and graces of imitative and theatrical music. Cantatas are generally composed of three recitatives, and as many airs. Those which are a recital, and the airs, their maxims are always cold and disagreeable: The musician ought to abolish them. The best are those wherein the principal person speaks himself in a situation lively and affecting; for our cantatas are in general composed for one voice. There are, however, some for two voices, in form of a dialogue, and those are somewhat agreeable when the composer knows the art of introducing something in them of an interesting nature. But as a few preambles are always necessary to make a kind of exposition, and give the hearer some ideas, 'tis not without reason that cantatas have changed their form, and that even in concerts they have substituted opera scenes in their place. The mode of cantatas takes its origin from Italy, as we may see by their name in Italian, and 'tis Italy also which first placed bounds to them. The cantatas made there at present, are absolutely dramatic pieces to many actors, which differ from operas only in what the one represents on the stage, and the other executes in concert, so that the cantata is, on a profane subject, what the oratorio is on one that is sacred.

CANTATILLE, Is a diminutive of cantata, and in reality only a very short cantata, whose subject is united by some verses in recitative, in two or three airs in rondeau for the most

part,

part, with ſome accompaniments of ſymphony. The nature of the cantatilla is ſtill more trifling than that of the cantata, in whoſe place it has been ſubſtituted amongſt us. But as we can neither diſcover paſſions or painting therein, and as it is ſuſceptible of gentility only, 'tis a reſource for the inferior verſe ſcribblers, and for muſicians without genius.

CANTIC, A hymn ſung in honour of the divinity. The firſt and moſt ancient cantics were compoſed on account of ſome memorable event, and may well be reckoned as the moſt ancient hiſtorical monuments.

Theſe cantics were ſung by choirs of muſicians, and often accompanied with dances, as it appears by writings. The moſt diſtinguiſhed piece that we meet with of this nature, is the cantic of cantics; a work attributed to Solomon, and which ſome authors pretend to be his epithalamium only, on his marriage with the daughter of the king of Ægypt. But the Theologicians diſcover under this emblem, the union of Jeſus Chriſt and the Church. The Sieur de Cahuſac ſaw, in this cantic of cantics, nothing more than a well compoſed opera, the ſcenes, the dialogue, the duo, the choirs, were intirely perfect; nothing was wanting, and he made no doubt but that the opera had been repreſented.

I do not know any of the pieces of muſic in the Roman church, which have yet retained the name of cantic, unleſs it be the cantic of Simeon, that of Zachara, and the Magnificat, ſtiled the cantic of the Virgin. But amongſt us every thing ſung in our temples is called cantic, except the pſalms, which retain their proper name.

The Greeks gave the name of cantics alſo to ſeveral paſſionate ſoliloquies of their tragedies, which we ſung in the hypo-dorian or hyphrygian ſtile, as Ariſtotle teaches us in his nineteenth problem.

CANTO, This Italian word, written in a partition, on the ſcale fixed for the firſt violin, ſhews that it ſhould play in uniſon on the ſinging part.

CAPRICIO, A kind of irregular piece of muſic, in the which the author, without confining himſelf to any ſubject, gives ſcope to his genius, and indulges the whole fire of compoſition. The capricio of Rebel was eſteemed in its day. At preſent the capricios of Locatelli are become the exerciſe of our violins.

CARRILLON, A kind of air made to be performed by a number of bells, tuned in a different harmony. As the carrillon is rather made for the bells than the bells for the carrillon, there are no more ſounds permitted therein than there are bells. We muſt moreover obſerve, that all their ſounds, having ſome duration, each one of thoſe which are ſtruck ſhould form a harmony

mony with that which precedes it, and that which follows; a ſubjection which, in a lively movement, ought to extend itſelf through a whole meaſure, and even farther, ſo that the ſounds which continue together may make no diſſonance to the ear. There are ſeveral other obſervations to be made for the compoſition of a good carrillon, which renders this work more laborious than ſatisfactory, for the muſic of bells is ſilly at the beſt, tho' all their ſounds be exactly true, which never happens.

A Conſonant Carrillon of Nine Bells.

We may here ſee the example of a conſonant carillon, compoſed to be executed on a pendulum of nine bells, formed by Monſ. Romilly, a celebrated clock-maker. It is generally imagined, that the exceeding difficulties to which the harmonic ſucceſſion of ſounds, and the ſmall number of bells are ſubject, will not permit any thing vocal in an air of this nature.

CARTELS, Large ſheets of aſſes-ſkin prepared for the purpoſe, on which are drawn the lines of the ſcale, for the benefit of marking thereon every thing neceſſary for compoſition, and rubbing it out at pleaſure with a ſpunge: The other ſide, which has no ſcale, may ſerve for ſcribbling, and is rubbed out in the ſame manner, provided that the ink is not left to dry. With a cartel, a diligent compoſer may be ſupplied for ever, and ſpare many quires of ruled paper; but there is this inconvenience, that the pen paſſing continually on the engraved lines, eaſily wears out and ſoftens. All the cartels take their riſe from Rome or Naples.

CASTRATO, A musician, who in his infancy had been deprived of the organs of generation, for the sake of preserving a shrill voice, who sings that part called sophrano. However small the connection may appear between two such different organs, it is a certain fact that the mutilation of the one prevents and hinders in the other that change which is perceptible in mankind, near the advance of manhood, and which, on a sudden, lowers their voice an eighth. There exist in Italy, some inhuman fathers, who sacrificing nature to fortune, give up their children to this operation, for the amusement of voluptuous and cruel persons, who have the barbarity to require the exertion of voice which the unhappy wretches possess. Let us leave to the modest ladies of great cities, the stifled laughs, the disdainful air, and the jocular sneers, whose external object they are; but let us explain, if we are able, the voice of modesty and of humanity, which vociferates loudly against this horrid custom; and let those princes, who encourage it by their endeavours, blush for once, at the thought of injuring, in so many respects, the preservation of the human race!

In the next place, the advantage of voice in these castrati is amply recompensed by many other losses.---These men, who sing so well, but without fire or passion, become on the stage the most miserable actors in the world: They love their voice at an early period, and gain, in return, an affectation very disgusting. They speak and pronounce worse than *men themselves*, and there are also several letters, such as the *r*, which they cannot pronounce at all.

Though the word castrato cannot offend the most delicate ear, 'tis not the same thing in regard to its French synonymy. An evident proof, that what renders words indecent or immouest, depends less from the ideas attached to them, than from the practice of genteel company, in regard to their toleration or abolition of them.

CATABAUCALESIO, A nurse's humdrum ditty amongst the ancients.

CATACOUSTIC, A science whose chief objects consist in reflected sounds, or that part of the acoustic which considers the propriety of the eccho. For which reason the catacoustic is to the acoustic what the catoptric is to the optic.

CAVATINA, A kind of air, in general rather short, which neither has a return nor second part, and which is often found in confined recitatives. This sudden change from recitative to a measured harmony, and the unexpected return of the measured harmony to the recitative, produce an admirable effect in sublime expressions, as are always those of the confined recitative.

The

The word cavatina is Italian, and tho' I wiſh not in this dictionary all the technical Italian words, particularly when theſe words are ſynonymous to another language, yet I think myſelf obliged to explain *thoſe* of ſuch words which are employed in the marked muſic; becauſe, that in executing this muſic, it is neceſſary to underſtand the terms which are therein, and which the author has not placed without a reaſon.

CENTONIZARE, A term in church-muſic. 'Tis to compoſe an air with backward lines, properly arranged for the melody in queſtion. This method of compoſition is not the invention of the modern ſymphoniſts, ſince, according to Monſ. L'Abbé de Bœuf, Saint Gregory himſelf was converſant in the art.

CHACON, A kind of muſical piece formed for the dance, the meaſure of which is well marked, and the movement moderate. Formerly there were chacons of two and three times, but at preſent they compoſe them only of three. They are in general airs, which are called couplets, compoſed and varied in different manners on a conſtrained baſs, from four to four meaſures, beginning almoſt always by the ſecond time to prevent an interruption. We have by degrees aboliſhed this conſtraint of the baſs, and pay little or no attention to it.

The beauty of the chacon conſiſts in finding notes which expreſs the movement well, and, as it is often very long, in varying the couplets in ſuch a manner that they may make a mutual contraſt, and continually enliven the attention of the hearer. For this purpoſe we paſs and repaſs at pleaſure from the major to the minor, without quitting, however greatly, the principal tone; and from the grave to the gay, or from the tender to the lively, without ever exceeding or leſſening the meaſure.

The chacon was firſt introduced in Italy, and formerly in great eſteem there, as well as in Spain. But at preſent it is no longer known, except in the French operas.

AMBROSIAN CHANT, A kind of church-muſic, the invention of which is attributed to St. Ambroſe, archbiſhop of Milan. (Vide CHURCH-MUSIC.)

GREGORIAN CHANT, A kind of church-muſic, the invention of which has been attributed to Pope St. Gregory, and which has been ſubſtituted or preferred in moſt churches to the ambroſian chant. (Vide CHURCH-MUSIC.)

CHANT en ISON, By this name is called an air, or pſalmody, which varies only in two ſounds, and conſequently forms one interval only. Some religious orders have no other chant in their churches than the Chant en Iſon.

CHANT SUR LE LIVRE, A kind of plain chant, or counterpoint in four parts, which the musicians compose and sing extempore on one only, i. e. the book of choruſſes at the Lutrin, ſo that, except the pricked part, which is generally put on the tenor, the musicians being attentive to the three other parts, have that only for their guide; and each composes his ſeparate part whilſt ſinging.

The Chant ſur le Livre requires great knowledge, practice, and a fine ear in thoſe who execute it, ſo much the more, as it is not always eaſy to render the tones of the church-music ſimilar to thoſe of ours. However, there are ſome church-muſicians, ſo well verſed in this kind of ſinging, that they can begin and even go through the fugues whenever the ſubject can permit, without confounding or cruſhing the parts, or making any errors in the harmony.

CHANTEREL, That of the ſtrings of the violin, and ſimilar inſtruments, whoſe ſound is ſharpeſt. We ſay of a ſymphony, that it does not quit the chanterel, when it actuates only between the ſounds of that ſtring, and thoſe which are neareſt to it, as are almoſt all the violin parts of Lully's operas, and of the ſymphonies of his time.

CHAPEAU, or TIE, A demi circular ſtroke, with which two or more notes are covered, and which is more commonly called Liaiſon.

CHARACTERS of MUSIC, Are the different ſigns which are uſed to repreſent all the ſounds of melody, and all the powers of the times and meaſure, ſo that by the aſſiſtance of thoſe characters one may read and execute muſic exactly as it has been compoſed, and this method of writing is called pricking. (Vide NOTES.)

There are no nations but the European, who underſtand the art of writing their muſic. Tho' in the other parts of the world every people has its own; it does not appear that any of them have extended their reſearches ſo far as the formation of characters to denote it. At leaſt, it is certain that neither the Arabians or Chineſe, the two foreign people who have moſt cultivated the arts, have any ſuch ſimilar characters. It muſt be confeſſed, that the Perſians give the names of their citus, or parts of the human body to the forty-eight ſounds of their muſic. They ſay, for inſtance, to give the tone of any air, "Go from ſuch to ſuch a city," or "Go from the finger to the elbow;" but they have no ſign proper for expreſſing theſe ſame ſounds on paper; and in regard to the Chineſe, we find in P. du Halde, that they were extremely ſurpriſed to ſee the Jeſuits mark and read on the ſame note, all the Chineſe airs, with which they made them acquainted.

The

The ancient Greeks in their music, as in their arithmetic, made use of the letters of their alphabet, but instead of giving them in music a numerous power, which might mark the intervals, they were contented with using them as signs, combining them in different ways, clipping them, coupling, rendering them silent, and changing them differently, according to their kinds and modes, as we may see in the miscellany of Alypius.----The Latins imitated them in making use of the letters of the alphabet, by their example, and there still remains amongst us the letter joined to the name of every note of our diatonic and natural scale,

Guy Aretin invented the lines, and particular signs, which have remained to us under the name of notes, and which are at present the musical and universal language of all Europe. As these last signs, though unanimously admitted, and perfectionated since the time of Aretin, have yet some great faults; many have endeavoured to substitute other notes in their places: Of this number have been Parran, Souhaitti, Sauveur, Dumas, and myself. But as, at bottom, all these systems, in correcting old faults to which we were accustomed, only substituted others, which custom is *yet* to make familiar to us; I think that the public acted very wisely in leaving things as they were, and sending us and our systems back into the country of vain speculations,

CHORISTER, Those who sing in the choir of Catholic churches are called choristers. We do not say singer in a church, or chorister in a concert.

Among the reformed, they call chorister, him who gives the tone and sustains the air of the psalms in their temple: He is seated below the minister's choir forwards; his office requires a very strong voice, capable of exceeding that of the congregation, and of making himself heard to the very extremity of the temple. Though there be neither prosody nor measure in the French method of singing psalms, and tho' the tune is so slow that every one may easily follow it, yet, it seems to me that it must be necessary for the chorister to mark a kind of measure. The reason of it is, that the chorister being very distant from several parts of the church, and the sound passing slowly thro' the greater intervals, his voice can hardly be heard at the extremities till it has taken another tone, and began a different note, which becomes so much the more sensible in certain places, as the sound passing still more slowly from one extremity to the other, than from the middle, where the chorister is, the mass of air which fills the temple becomes at once divided into several very discordant sounds, which incessantly press one on the other, and

and disgust greatly a nice ear; a fault that the organ itself only increases, because instead of being in the middle of the edifice, as the chorister, it gives the tone only from one end.

The remedy of such an inconvenience appears to me exceedingly simple; for as the visual rays are instantly communicated from the object to the eye, or at least, with a velocity much greater than that with which the sound is transmitted from a sonorous body to the ear, it is sufficient to substitute one for the other, to have in the whole compass of the temple, a tune well sustained, and of a perfect concord. For this purpose, we have nothing to do but to place the chorister, or some one who discharges that part of his office, so that he may be in view of the whole congregation, and let him make use of a time-stick, the motion of which may be easily perceived at a distance, for instance, a roll of paper; for then, with the precaution of giving a sufficient duration to the first note, that the intonation of it may be extended on all sides before it's followed; all the rest of the tune will proceed perfectly well together, and the discord which I mentioned, must infallibly disappear. We might even, instead of a man, make use of a chronometre, the motion of which would be still more equal in so slow a measure.

From thence would result two other advantages also; one, that almost without changing the air of the psalms, it would be easy to introduce therein a little prosody, and at least to observe the most sensible long and short; the other, that whatever languor and monotony there might be in the tune, might, according to the first intention of the author, be extirpated by the bass and other parts, whose harmony is certainly the most majestic and sonorous that can be heard.

CHORUS, A piece of music, complete in four or more parts, sung at the same time by all the voices, and played by the whole band. In chorusses we seek for an agreeable and harmonious melody, which may charm and satisfy the ear. A pleasing chorus is the master-piece of a beginner, and 'tis by a work this kind that he shews himself sufficiently instructed in all rules of harmony. The French, in France, pass for the most excellent in that particular branch, of any European nation. The chorus, in the French music, is sometimes called grand-chœur, in opposition to the petit-chœur, which is composed of three parts only, that is to say, two trebles and the tenor, which serves as their bass. This petit-chœur is now and then played separately, the sweetness of which makes an agreeable contrast to the loud harmony of the greater.

They give the name of petit-chœur also, in the opera of Paris, to a certain number of the best instruments in every kind, which as a particular orchestra are placed next to the harpsichord, and

him

him who beats the time. This petit-chœur is deſtined for the accompaniments, which requires a greater delicacy and preciſion.

There are ſome pieces of muſic of two or more choruſſes, which anſwer each other, and ſometimes are all ſung together. We may find an example of this in the opera of Jephtha. But this plurality of choruſſes, which is very often practiſed in Italy, is ſeldom uſed in France. They find that it does not produce a very pleaſing effect, that its compoſition is not very eaſy, and that too great a number of muſicians are wanted for the execution of it.

CHORION, A piece of Greek muſic, which was ſung in honour of the mother of the gods, and which is ſaid to have been invented by Olympus of Phrygia.

CHRESES or CHRESIS, One of the parts of the ancient melopea, which teaches the compoſer to place ſuch an arrangement in the diatonic direction of ſounds, as to form from them a good modulation and an agreeable melody. This part is applicable to different ſucceſſions of ſounds, called, by the ancients, agoge, euthia, anacamptos.

CHROMATIC, A kind of muſic which proceeds in ſeveral conſecutive ſemi-tones. This word is derived from the Greek χρῶμα, which ſignifies colour, either becauſe the Greeks marked theſe notes with red characters, or differently coloured; or, according to authors, becauſe the chromatic kind is a medium between the two others, as colour is between black and white; or according to others, becauſe this kind varies and embelliſhes the diatonic by its ſemi-tones, which, in muſic, produces the ſame effect as the colours in painting.

Boetius attributes the invention of this chromatic muſic to Timotheus of Milet; but Athenæus to Epigonus.

Ariſtoxenes divides this kind into three ſorts, which he calls molle, hemiolion, and tonicum; the connections of which we may here find, the tetrachord being ſuppoſed to be divided in 60 equal parts.

According to Ariſtoxenes.

Diatonic.

The tender or ſoft	12 + 18 + 30 = 60
Syntonic or hard	12 + 24 + 24 = 60

Chromatic.

		Harmonic.
Molle	8 + 8 + 44 = 60	6 + 6 + 48 = 60
Hemiolon	9 + 9 + 42 = 60	
Tonic	12 + 12 + 35 = 60	

Ptolomæus divides this ſame kind into two ſorts only, molle, or anticum, which proceeds by leſſer intervals ; and intenſum, the intervals of which are greater.

According to Ptolomæus.

Diatonic.

$$\text{Diatonic } \frac{256}{243} + \frac{9}{8} + \frac{9}{8} = \frac{4}{3}$$

Chromatic.

$$\text{Molle } \frac{28}{27} + \frac{15}{14} + \frac{6}{5} = \frac{4}{3}$$

$$\text{Intenſe or Syntonic } \frac{22}{21} + \frac{12}{11} + \frac{7}{6} = \frac{4}{3}$$

Harmonic.

$$\frac{45}{45} + \frac{24}{23} + \frac{5}{4} = \frac{4}{3}$$

At preſent the chromatic kind conſiſts in giving ſuch a courſe to the fundamental baſs, that the parts of the harmony, or at leaſt ſome one of them, may proceed by ſemi-tones, as much in aſcending as deſcending, which is moſt frequently found in the minor mode, on account of the alterations to which the 6th and 7th notes are ſubject, by the very nature of the mode.

The ſucceſſive ſemi-tones practiſed in the chromatic, are not all of the ſame kind, but almoſt alternately minors and majors ; that is to ſay, chromatics and diatonics : for the interval of a minor tone contains a ſemitone minor or chromatic, and a ſemitone major or diatonic, a meaſure which its government makes common to all the tones ; ſo that we cannot proceed by two conjoint and ſucceſſive ſemi-tones minor, without entering on the harmonic ; but two major ſemi-tones follow each other twice in the chromatic order of the gamut.

The elementary route of the fundamental baſs, to produce an aſcendant chromatic, is to deſcend from the third, and aſcend to the fourth alternately, all the concords ſuſtaining the major third. If the fundamental baſs proceeds from dominant to dominant, by perfect cadences avoided, it produces a deſcendant chromatic. To produce at the ſame time the one and the other, we intermix the perfect cadence, and the interruption by avoiding them.

As in every note the tone is changed in the chromatic, we muſt ſet bounds and regulate theſe ſucceſſions for fear of loſing ourſelves ; and for this purpoſe, it muſt be remembered, that the ſpace which is moſt ſuitable for the chromatic movements, is between the dominant and tonic in aſcending, and between the tonic and dominant in descending. In the major mode we may also descend chromatically from the dominant on the second note. This passage is very common in Italy, and, tho' beautiful, is rather too much so in France.

This chromatic is admirable for expressing sorrow and affliction, its forcible sounds in rising strike the soul. It is not less energic in descending: We seem then even to hear the identical groans. When accompanied by its harmony, this kind becomes proper for every thing; but its fulness, by stifling the air, takes away a part of its expression, and 'tis then the office of the movement to restore to it *that* which it is deprived of by the plenitude of its harmony. Moreover, the greater energy this kind possesses, the less should it be augmented: Like those delicate dishes whose abundances soon disgust, so it charms when prudently conducted, so it becomes satiated when overdone.

CHRONOMETRE, The general name of instruments which serve to measure the time. This word is composed of χρόνος, time, and μέτρον, measure.

In this sense we call watches or clocks by the name of chronometres. There are however some instruments which are particularly called chronometres, and one in chief which Mons. Sauveur describes in his principles of the acoustic. This was a particular pendulum, which he intended to determine exactly the movements of music. L'Affilard, in his principles dedicated to a convent of nuns, placed at the head of all his airs, cyphers, which expressed the number of the vibrations of this pendulum, during the continuation of each measure.

About thirty years ago there appeared a plan of a similar instrument under the name of Metrometre, which beat time alone, but it neither succeeded in one or the other. Many pretend, however, that it were much to be wished, that such an instrument might be had, to fix with precision the time of each measure in a piece of music: by this means we might easily preserve the true movement of the airs, without which they lose their value, and which one cannot know after the death of the authors, but, by a kind of tradition, very subject to change or obscurity. It is already a complaint, that we have forgot the movements of a great number of airs, and it is to be believed, that all have undergone a change. If they had had the precaution which I have mentioned, and in which I see nothing inconvenient, we should at present have had the pleasure of hearing those same airs, such as the author intended them to be executed.

To this the connoisseurs in music do not remain without an answer: They will object, says Mons. Diderot, in his Memoirs on different Subjects of the Mathematics, against all chronome-

 tres

tres in general, that there is not, perhaps, in an air two measures which are exactly of the same duration: two things contributing thro' necessity, to slacken the one and hasten the other, taste and harmony in pieces of many parts, taste and a presentiment of the harmony in the solo. A musician who understands his art, has not played four measures of an air but he enters into the character of it, and is intirely wrapt up in it: The pleasure of the harmony only suspends him. He wishes the concords to be struck *here* and *there*, that they should be omitted, that is to say, that he should sing or play more or less slowly, from one measure to another, and even from a time or quarter time, to him who follows.

In fact, this objection, which is of great weight in the French music, is of no kind of consequence in the Italian, it being most strictly confined to the most exact measure: Nothing even can more plainly shew the opposition of these two musics; since, what is a beauty in the one, would be a capital fault in the other. If the Italian music draws its energy from that slavery to the rigour of the measure, the French seeks her's by modulating this same measure at her pleasure; by augmenting or diminishing it, according to what the nature of the air requires, or the degree of flexibility in the voice of the singer.

But should we admit the utility of a chronometre, we must always, says Monf. Diderot, begin by rejecting all those which we have proposed to follow, because we form, from the musician and the chronometre, two separate machines, the one of which can never be aptly subject to the other: This hardly can require a proof. It is impossible that the musician can have, throughout the whole of his piece, his eye on the movement, and his ear attentive to the sound of the pendulum; and if he is lost but one moment, lost is the rein also which they have pretended to have given him.

I will add, that whatever instrument may be found to regulate the duration of the measure, it must be impossible, tho' the execution should be of never so great facility, that it can ever have a place in practice. The musicians confident, and, like many others, forming the rules of a good taste from their own, would never adopt it. They would leave the chronometre, and would apply to themselves only the true character and true movement of the airs. For which reason, the only good chronometre we can have, is an ingenious musician, who has taste, who has well read the music he is to execute, and who is skilled in beating its time. Amongst the variety of machines, this certainly is the safest to confide in.

CHURCH MUSIC, or PLAIN CHANT, Was a name given in the Roman church to the ecclesiastic airs. This chant, just

just as it remains to this time, is an antiquity very much disfigured, but very precious, of the Greek music, which after having passed thro' the hands of barbarians, has not, however, been able to lose all its primitive beauties. There remains yet enough of it to render it much preferable, even in its present condition, and for the use to which it is intended to those effeminate and theatrical pieces, which in some churches are substituted in its place, without gravity, without taste, without agreement, and without respect for the place which they dare thus to profane.

The time when the christians began to have churches, and to sing psalms and hymns therein, was that wherein music had already lost all its ancient energy, by a progress, the causes of which I have mentioned elsewhere. The christians entering upon music in the condition which they found it in, took from it even the greatest strength that had remained to it, that is to say, that of the rhyme and metre; when, instead of the verses, to which it had been always applied, they changed it into the prose of their sacred writings, or some strange kind of barbarous poetry, worse for music than the prose itself. In that case, one of the two consecutive parts vanishes, and the air extending itself uniformly, and without any kind of measure, from notes to notes almost equal, loses, with its rhymic and cadenced form, all the energy which it received from it. There were but a few hymns, in the which the prosody and quantity of feet being preserved, we still felt, in a lesser degree, the cadence of the verse, but it was no longer the general characters of the plain-chant, most generally degenerated in a psalmody, always monotonous, and sometimes silly, in a language such as the latin, much less harmonious and accented than the Greek.

In spite of all these so great and so essential losses, the plain-chant preserved elsewhere by the priests in its primitive character, as well as all the exterior and ceremonious parts of their church, still presents some precious fragments of the ancient melody, and its different modes to connoisseurs, as much as it can make itself felt without measure, and without rhyme, and in the only diatonic kind, which we can attribute in its purity to the plain-chant. The different modes therein preserve their two principal distinctions; the one thro' the difference of the fundamentals or the tonics, and the other by the different position of the two semi-tones, according to the degree of the diatonic natural system, wherein the fundamental is found, and according to what the modo authentico, or plagal, represents the two tetrachords, conjoint or disjoint. (Vide SYSTEMS, TETRACHORDS, TONES of the CHURCH.

These modes, such as they have been transmitted to us in the ancient ecclesiastic chant, preserve therein a beauty of character, and

and a variety of affections, very sensible to an impartial connoisseur, and which have preserved some judgment of the ear for the melodious systems, established on principles different from ours: but we may well say, that there is nothing more ridiculous and more flat, than these plain-chants suited to our modern music, embellished with the ornaments of our melody, and modulated on the chords of our modes; as if our harmonic system could at any time be united to that of the ancient modes, which is established on principles exactly opposite. We ought to thank the bishops, prevosts, and choristers, who have opposed this barbarous mixture, and use our utmost endeavours for the progress and perfection of an art, which is very far from the point at which it has been placed, that these valuable remains of antiquity may be faithfully transmitted to those who have sufficient talents and authority to enrich the modern system by the addition of them. How far soever our music may have been extended into that of the church, I am persuaded that it would be preferable to convey the church music into ours; but for that, much taste is necessary, still *more* knowledge, and above all, an exemption from every kind of prejudice.

The church music is pricked on four lines only, and there are but two cleffs used in it, i. e. that of ut, and the cleff of fa; one transposition only, that is to say, a B flat, and but two representations of notes, which are the long or sharp, to which is sometimes added, a tail, and the short which is formed as a lozenge.

Ambrosius, archbishop of Milan, is said to have been the inventor of the plain-chant; that is to say, that he was the first who gave a form and rules to the ecclesiastic chant, to suit it better to its object, and to defend it from the barbarity and obscurity into which music was fallen in his time. Pope Gregory perfected it, and gave it the form which it preserves at present in Rome, and the other churches, in which the Roman melody is practised. The French church allows the Gregorian chant but in part, with much ill-will and almost thro' necessity. The following extract from a work about that time, printed at Francfort in 1594, contains the account of an ancient quarrel on account of the plain chant, which was renewed in our days on music, but which had not, God and king Charlemagne be praised, the same issue.

"The pious king Charles being returned to celebrate the "festival of Easter with our apostolic lord at Rome, there "arose, during the feast, a quarrel between the French and "Italian choristers. The French pretended to sing better and "more agreeably than the Italians. The latter declaring them-"selves superior in the ecclesiastic music, which they had learned

from

" from Pope St. Gregory, accused the French of corrupting and " disfiguring the true melody. This dispute being laid before " his majesty, the French, who relied greatly on his partiality, " insulted the Italian singers. *They*, proud of their superior " knowledge, and comparing the learning of St. Gregory to " the rusticity of the others, treated them as clowns, fools, and " silly pretenders. As this altercation still continued, the pi- " ous monarch said to his choristers, Tell us, which is the purest " and most excellent water, that drawn from the fountain head, " or that of the streams which flow at an extensive distance " from it. All consented in pronouncing that of the fountain " head the most pure, and that of the rivulets so much inferior " as the distance whence it flowed. Have recourse then, re- " plied Charles, to the fountain of St. Gregory, whose music " you have undoubtedly corrupted. The king then desired of Pope " Adrian some choristers to correct the French chant, and his " holiness gave him Theodorus and Benoit, two very ingenious " singers, and instructed by St. Gregory himself; he gave him " also some Antiphonaries of St. Gregory, which he had himself " set down in Italian Notes. Of these two choristers, the king, " on his return into France, sent one to Metz, and the other " to Soissons, giving all the music-masters in the cities of France " orders to give them their Antiphonaries to correct, and learn " from them to sing. Thus were the French Antiphonaries " corrected, which every one had changed by additions and re- " trenchments after his fancy; and all the choristers of France " learned the Roman chant, tho' they have now given it the " name of French: but in regard to the trembling, broken, and " clipp'd notes in this kind of music, the French could never " render them, making rather an uncouth noise than a trill, on " account of the natural and barbarous roughness of their " throats. As for the remainder, the principal school was al- " ways kept at Metz; and as much as the Roman chant sur- " passes that of Metz, so much that of Metz excells the other " schools of France. The Roman choristers taught the French " also the accompaniment of instruments; and the king, having " at the same time taken with him into France grammarians " and arithmeticians, ordered that the study of letters should " be established throughout; for before this said king Charles, " the knowledge of the liberal arts was intirely unknown in " France."

CIRCUMVOLUTION, A term in church-music. 'Tis a kind of perielesis, which is made by inserting between the penultimate and the last note of the intonation of a piece of music, three other notes, viz. one above and two below the last note, which three are united with it, and form the compass of a third

third before meeting with it, as if you were to have these three notes, mi, fa, mi, to terminate the intonation, you would intermix these other three, fa, re, re, and in that case your intonation must be finished in this manner, mi, fa, fa, re, re, mi, &c.

CITHARISTIC, A kind of music and of poetry appropriated to the accompaniment of the harp. This kind, of which Amphion, son of Jupiter and Antiope, was the inventor, has since taken the name of lyric.

CLEFF, A character of music, which is placed at the beginning of a stave to determine the degree of elevation of that stave in the general key, and to express the names of all the notes which it contains within the line of that cleff.

Formerly the name of cleff was given to the letter, by which the signs of the gamut were denoted. Thus the letter A was the cleff of the note la; C the cleff of ut; E the cleff of mi, &c. In proportion as the system was extended, they found the difficulty and the inutility of this quantity of cleffs. Gui d'Arrezzo, who had invented them, marked a letter of cleff at the beginning of each line of the scale, for he had not yet placed the notes within the spaces. In some little time, they marked only one of the seven cleffs at the beginning of one line only, that being sufficient to fix the position of all the rest, according to their natural order. At last, from these seven lines or cleffs, four were chosen, which they called claves signatæ, because they were satisfied with marking one on one of these lines to give the idea of all the others; in time, one of the four was removed; that is, the gamma which they made use of to denote the sol below, viz. the hypoproslambanomenos added to the system of the Greeks.

Kitcher effectually pretends that if we were acquainted with the ancient writings, and were to examine the figure of our cleffs, we should find, that each one has a connection with the letter a little varied of the note which it represents. For instance, the cleff of sol was originally a G; the cleff of ut a C; and that of fa an F.

We find then in the fifth, three cleffs, one after the other. The cleff of F, ut, fa, or of fa, which is the lowest; the cleff of ut, or of C, sol, ut, which is a fifth above the first; and the cleff of sol, or of G, re, sol, which is a fifth above that of ut, in the order marked as follows.

The Keys.

Cleff of ſol, or of G, re, ſol.
Cleff of ut, or of C, ſol, ut.
Cleff of fa, or of F, ut, fa.

In regard to which we ſhould remark, that by a remain of antient cuſtom, the cleff is always plac'd on one line, and never in the ſpace. We ſhould know alſo that the cleff of fa is made in three different manners; the one in printed muſic, another in the written or engraved, and the laſt in church-muſic.

The three different repreſentations of the Cleff Fa.

Printed Muſic.

Written Muſic.

Church-Muſic.

By adding four lines above the cleff of ſol, and three below the cleff of fa, which gives, on each ſide, the greateſt extent of ſtable lines, we may ſee, that the whole ſyſtem of notes which can be placed on the relative degrees of theſe cleffs, amounts to 24; that is to ſay, 3 eighths and a fourth from the fa, which is placed below the firſt line to the ſi, which is found above the laſt, and all this together forms, what is called, the general key; by which we may judge, that this extent has for ſome time made that of the ſyſtem. At preſent, whilſt new degrees are inceſſantly forming, as well in ſharp as flat, thoſe degrees are marked on lines added on the top or bottom, juſt as required.

Inſtead of joining together all the lines as I have done, to expreſs the connection of the cleffs, they are ſeparated into fives, because the extent of the voice in general is bounded nearly by the degrees contained within that ſpace. This collection of five lines is called ſtave, and a cleff is there placed to determine the name of the notes, the place of the ſemitones, and to ſhew what part the ſtave requires within the key.

By whatſoever method we take five conſecutive lines, within the gamut we always find a cleff compriſed therein, and ſometimes two, in which caſe we cut off one as uſeleſs. Cuſtom has even preſcribed which of the two ſhould be effaced, and which ſhould ſtand, which has alſo fixed the number of poſitions aſſigned to each cleff.

If I make a ſtave of the five firſt lines of the gamut, beginning at the bottom, I find the cleff of fa on the fourth line. Here then is the poſition of a cleff, and that poſition evidently belongs to the flatteſt notes. In like manner is it the poſition of the baſs cleff.

If I wiſh to have a third at the top, I muſt add a line above, but in that caſe I muſt eraſe one below, otherwiſe the ſtave would conſiſt of more than five lines. The cleff of fa is then removed from the fourth to the third line, and the cleff of ut alſo on the fifth; but as two cleffs are uſeleſs, that of ut is here rejected. We ſee that the ſtave of this cleff is elevated a third more than the preceding.

By loſing alſo a line below to gain one above, we have a third ſtave, wherein the cleff of fa muſt be placed on the ſecond line, and that of ut on the fourth: here we loſe the cleff of fa, and take that of ut. We have gained alſo a third in ſharp, and loſt it in flat.

By continuing thus from line to line, we paſs ſucceſſively through four different poſitions of the cleff of ut. Coming to that of ſol, we find it placed on the ſecond line, and again on the firſt: This poſition extends itſelf to the five higheſt lines, and gives the ſharpeſt diapaſon, that can be eſtabliſhed by the cleffs.

We may ſee this ſucceſſion of cleffs from flat to ſharp, which makes in all eight ſtaves, cleffs, or different poſitions of cleffs.

Whatever may be the character of a voice or inſtrument, provided that its extent does not exceed in ſharp or flat, that of the general gamut, we may in this number find a ſtave and cleffs ſuitable to it; and there are in reality ſome determined for all the parts of muſic. (Vide PARTS) If the extent of a part is very great, ſo that the number of lines, which muſt be added above or below, becomes inconvenient, in that caſe, the cleff is changed within the courſe of the air. We evidently ſee by the figure, what cleff we muſt take to elevate or lower the ſtave,

whatever

whatever may be the key with which it is actually numbered.

We also see, that to connect one cleff with another, we must connect them both on the general scale; by the method of which, we see what each note of one of the cleffs is in proportion to the other. 'Tis by this reiterated exercise, that we learn the art of easily reading the partitions. From this mechanism it follows, that we may place whatever note of the gamut we please on any line or space of the stave; since we have the choice of eight different positions, the number of the notes of the octave. In this manner, we might prick an entire air on the same line, by changing the cleff in every degree. The figure seven, shews, through the course of cleffs, the course of the notes re, fa, la, ut, mi, sol, si, re, ascending from third to third, and all placed on the same line.

The following figure 8 represents in the course of those same cleffs, the note ut, which seems to descend by thirds on all the lines of the stave, and below; and which, however, by means of the change in the cleff, preserves always its unison. 'Tis on similar examples that we ought to practice, to know at first sight the play of all these cleffs.

Here are two of their positions; that is to say, the cleff of sol on the first line, and the cleff of fa on the third, the use of which seems daily to abolish. The first may appear less necessary, since it forms one position only quite similar to that of fa on the fourth line, which, however, it is different from by two eighths. As for the cleffs of fa, it is evident, that by removing it entirely from the third line, we shall no longer have an equivalent position; and the composition of the gamut, which is at present complete, must by that means become defective.

TRANSPOSED CLEFF, By this name we call every cleff, numbered with diesis's, or B's flat. These signs serve there to change the place of the two semi-tones of the octave, as I have explained under B flat, and to establish the natural order of the gamut, on whatever degree of the scale we may desire.

The necessity of these alterations arises from the similitude of modes in all the tones; for as there is but one form for the major mode, all the degrees of this mode must be placed in the same method on their tonic, which cannot be done but by the assistance of diesis's, or of B mollare's. The minor mode is conducted in the same manner; but as the same combination which gives the form for a major tone, gives it also for a minor on another tonic, (Vide MODE) it follows thence, that for the twenty-four modes, twelve combinations are sufficient; moreover, if with the natural gamut, we count six modifications by diesis, and five by B's flat, or six by B's flat, and five by diesis's, diesis's, we shall find these twelve combinations, by which are bounded, all possible varieties of tones and modes in the established system. I explain, under the words diesis's, or B's flat, the order, according to which they ought to be placed in the cleff. But for transposing on a sudden the cleff, suitable to any tone or mode soever, here is a general form discovered by Mons. Boisgelou, president of the Grand Council, and which he has obligingly communicated to me.

Taking the natural ut, as a term of comparison, we will call minor intervals the fourth ut fa, and all the intervals of the same ut, to any note with B flat; every other interval is major. Take notice that we ought not to take by diesis, the superior note of a major interval, because in that case we should form a superfluous interval; but we must attempt the same thing by B flat, which will give a minor interval. Wherefore we shall not compose in the diesis la, because the sixth ut la, being naturally major, would become superfluous by this diesis; but we must take the note si B flat, which gives the same force by a minor interval, which returns into the rule.

Table of INTERVALS.

For the Formula of Cleffs *transposed.*

Space of the Interval.		Minor	Major	Minor	Major	Minor	Major	Major	Minor	Major	Minor	Major	
The Notes which give it.	Ut,	re♭,	re,	mi♭,	mi,	fa,	fa✱,	sol,	la♭,	la,	si♭,	si,	ut.
Name of the Interval.	Term of Comparison.	Second.	Second.	Thi.d.	Third.	Fourth.	Fourth.	Fifth.	Sixth.	Sixth.	Seventh.	Seventh.	

We here find a table of the twelve sounds of the octave, divided by major and minor intervals, on the which we may transpose the cleff in the following manner, according to the tone or mode in which we chuse to compose.

Having taken one of those twelve notes for tonic or fundamental, we must immediately see if the interval which it makes with ut is major or minor; if 'tis major, diesis's are necessary; if minor, we must use B's flat. If that note be ut itself, the interval is null, and we want neither diesis's or B's flat. To determine now how many diesis's or B's flat are wanting, let *a* be the number which expresses the interval of ut in the note in question. The form by diesis's will be $\frac{a - 1 + 2}{7}$ and the remainder will give

give the number of diesis's, which we ought to place at the cleff. The formula by B's flat will be $\frac{x-1+5}{7}$, and the rest will be the number of B's flat which we must place to the cleff.

I will, for instance, compose in la a major mode. I immediately see that diesis's are wanting, because la makes a major interval with ut. The interval is a sixth, whose number is 6, I remove 1, I multiply the remaining 5 by 2, and from the product 10 rejecting 7 as often as possible, I have the remainder 3, which marks the number of diesis', with which I must number the cleff for the major tone of la.

If I wish to take fa, a major mode, I see by the table that the interval is minor, and that in consequence B's flat are necessary. I take away then 1, from 4 the number of the interval, I multiply the remaining 3 by 5, and from the product 15, throwing away 7 as often as possible, I have 1 remaining, that is a B flat, which I must place to the cleff.

We see by this means that the number of diesis's or B's flat can never exceed six, since they must be the remainder of a division by seven.

For the minor tones we must still use the same forms as that of the major, not on the tonic, but on the note, which is a minor 3d above this same tonic, on its mediant.

So, to compose in si a minor mode, I will transpose the cleff as for the major tone of re. For fa, a minor diesis, I will transpose it as for la major.

Musicians determine the transposition only by force of custom, but the rule which I give is demonstrated, general, and without exception.

COMARCHIOS, A kind of appellation for the flute in the ancient music of the Greeks.

COMMA, A small interval, which in some cases is found between two sounds, produced under the same denomination, by different progressions.

We distinguish three kinds of commas. First, the minor, the computation of which is from 2025 to 2048, which is the quantity by which the si diesis fourth 5th of the sol diesis, taken as a major third of mi, is surpassed by the natural ut which corresponds to it. This comma is the difference of the major and middle semitone.

Secondly, The major comma is that which is placed between the mi produced by triple progression, as a fourth fifth, beginning by ut and the same mi, or its respondent, considered as a major third of that same ut. Its numerical powers are from 80

 to

to 81. This is the ordinary comma, and it is the difference between the major and minor tone.

Thirdly, The comma maxima, which is called the comma of Pythagoras, has its computation from 524288 to 531441, and it is the excess of the si diesis produced by triple progression, as the twelfth fifth of the ut on the same ut elevated by its eighth to the correspondent degree.

The musicians understand by comma the eighth or ninth part of the tone, the half of what they call a quarter of a tone. But we may rest assured that they know not what they say, in expressing themselves thus, since, for ears like ours, so small an interval is useless, unless in calculation. (Vide INTERVAL.)

COMPAIR, The compair tones in church-music, are the authentic and the plagal which answers to it. So, the first tone is compair with the second, the third with the fourth, and so on. Every equal tone is compair with the unequal that precedes it.

COMPLEMENT Of an interval, is the quantity which is wanting to it to arrive at the octave, so the second and seventh, the third and sixth, the fourth and fifth, are complements one of the other. When we treat of one interval only, complement is the same thing with the general variation of notes. In regard to their kinds, the major is complement of the minor, the superfluous of the diminished, and so reciprocally. (Vide INTERVAL.)

COMPOS'D, This word has three meanings in music; two in regard to the intervals, and one to the measure.

I. Every interval which passes the extent of the Octave, is a compos'd interval, because by removing the octave, we simplify the interval without changing it. For instance, the ninth, the tenth, and the twelfth, are compos'd intervals; the first, of the second and eighth; the second, of the third and eighth; the third, of the fifth and eighth, &c.

II. Every interval which can be musically divided into two intervals, may be considered as compos'd. By this means, the fifth is compos'd of two thirds; the third of two seconds; the major second of two semitones; but the semitone is by no means composed because it can neither be divided on the gamut or by notes. 'Tis the sense of the discourse which out of the two foregoing acceptations must determine that according to which an interval is composed.

III. We call composed measures, all those which are expressed by two cyphers. (VIDE MEASURE.)

TO COMPOSE, To invent new music, according to the rules of the art.

COMPOSER, He who composes music, or forms the rules of composition. Under the word composition, may be seen the detail of of knowledge, necessary for the art of composing. This is not yet sufficient without a genius to put it into execution. Whatever efforts we may make, whatever acquisitions we may have, we must still be born to the art, otherwise our works can never mount above the insipid. It is with the composer as with the poet. Nature herself must have form'd him so. What I would express by genius is by no means that strange capricious taste, which spreads on all sides uncouth and idle difficulties, which knows not how to ornament its harmony but by dint of dissonances, contracts and confusion, 'Tis an inward flame which burns, torments the composer, spite of himself, which continually inspires him with airs new, and always agreeable, with expressions lively, majestic, and which touch the heart, with a harmony pure, affecting, and forcible, which adorns the air without obscurity. 'Tis this divine guide which led Correlli, Vinci, Perez, Rinoldo, Jomelli, Durante, more ingenious than all the rest, into the sanctuary of harmony; Leo, Pergolese, Hasse, Terradeglias, and Galuppi, into that of taste and expression.

COMPOSITION, Is the art of inventing and writing airs, of accompanying them with a suitable harmony; in a word, to make a complete piece of music with all its parts.

The knowledge of harmony and its rules, is the foundation of composition. Without doubt, we ought to be skill'd in filling concords, preparing and avoiding dissonances, finding fundamental basses, and possessing every other trifling elementary knowledge; for, with the rules of harmony only, we are no more advanced in the knowledge of composition, than an orator with those of the Grammar. I will not say, that it is also necessary to understand well the stave, and character of the voice and instruments; the airs which are easy or difficult of execution; what forms, and what does *not* form any effect; to feel the character of the different measures, and that of the different modulations; to apply the one or the other always à propos; to know all the particular rules established by agreement, taste, caprice or pedantry, as the fugues, imitations, constrain'd subjects, &c. All these things are nothing more than preparatives to composition; but we must discover in ourselves the beautiful airs of the greater harmony, the painting, the expression; in a word, we must be capable of collecting and forming the plan of a whole work, following its correspondences of every kind, and making ourselves acquainted with the mind of the poet, instead of amusing ourselves with running after the words. 'Tis with reason that our musicians have given the name of words to the poems which they set to music. We clearly see, by their method of rendering them, that they are but words to them. It seems, particularly these last years, that the rules of concord have abolished, or at least rendered neglected every other; and that harmony has gained its facility only at the expence of the art in general. All our artists understand the art of filling up their music, but very few its composition.

Though the fundamental rules of counter-point be always the same, they yet have more or less rigour, according to the number of divisions; for in proportion to the increase of parts, the composition becomes more difficult, and the rules are less severe. The composition in two parts is called duo, when the two parts tune equally, that is, when the subject is equally divided between them. If the subject is in one part alone, and the other only acts in accompaniment, the first is then called recital, or solo; and the other, accompaniment, or thorough Bass, if it be a bass. It is the same thing with the trio or composition in three parts, with the quatuor, the quinque, &c. (Vide those words.)

The name of composition is also given to the pieces of music themselves, made in the rules of composition; for which reason, the duo, trio, quatuor, which I have just mentioned, are called compositions.

We compose either for the voices only, or for instruments, or for the instruments and the voice. Church-music and songs are the only compositions which are for the voice alone, and to those also some instruments are very often joined for the sustaining of them. Instrumental compositions are for the choir of the orchestra; and in that case they are called symphonies and concerts, or for some particular kind of instrument, and they are then called pieces, sonatas. (Vide those Words.)

In regard to the compositions intended for the voice and for the instruments, they are generally divided into two principal sorts, viz. Latin or church-music, and French music. The music destined for the church, whether psalms, hymns, or antiennes, generally bear the name of molets. (Vide MOLET.) The French music is also divided into theatrical music, such as our operas, and in that of a private room, as our cantatas or cantatillas. (Vide CANTATA, OPERA.)

The latin composition is imagined in general to require the most knowledge and rules, and the French the most genius and taste.

In a composition the author has for his subject, the sound physically considered, and for his object the pleasure only of the ear, or now and then he rises to imitative music, and seeks to touch his hearers by moral effects. In the first case, it is sufficient for him to seek pleasing sounds and agreeable concords; but in the second he should consider music by its connection with the accents, eents of the human voice, and by the possible conformities between sounds harmonically combined and imitable objects. Under the article opera, may be found some thoughts on the methods of elevating and ennobling this art, by making of music a language more eloquent than the discourse itself.

CONCERT, An assembly of musicians who perform pieces of vocal and instrumental music. This word concert is seldom used for an assembly of less than seven or eight musicians, or a piece of music of many parts. In regard to the ancients, as they were ignorant of the counter-point, their concerts were executed only in unison or in the octave. and they seldom had any other but in their theatres and temples.

SPIRITUAL CONCERT, A concert which supplies the place of the public spectacle at Paris, during the time that the other amusements are shut up. It is established at the Château des Thuilleries, the band is very numerous, and the hall beautifully decorated. They perform their molets and symphonies, and amuse themselves now and then with sporting in Italian airs.

CONCERTANT, Concertant parts are those, according to the Abbé Bropard, which have something of recital in a piece or concert, and this word serves to distinguish them from those parts which contain singing only. If this has ever been its sense, it is now obsolete. We say at present reciting parts, but we use *that* of concertant in speaking of a number of musicians who perform in a concert, and we then say, "We were five and twenty concertants." "An assembly of eight or ten concertants."

CONCERTO, An Italian word Frenchified, which signifies in general, a symphony made to be performed by the whole orchestra; but we call more particularly by the name of concerto, a piece made for some separate instrument, which plays alone at set times with a simple accompaniment, after a beginning by the whole orchestra, and the piece continues always thus alternatively between the same instrument reciting, and the orchestra in chorus. In regard to the concertos, where all is played in Rippiéno, and where no instrument recites, the French call it sometimes trio, and the Italians sinfonie,

CONCINNOUS, I will not make any digressions on the explanation of this word, taken as the suitable connection of all the parts of a work between themselves, and with the whole, because it is a sense that is seldom given to it in music. 'Tis to the execution generally that this term is applied, when the concertants are perfectly in concord, whether for the intonation or the measure, when they all appear to be animated with the same soul, and when the execution affords faithfully to the ear, all that the eye beholds on the partitions.

The

The concinnous does not only depend on the ingenuity with which each one reads his part, but on the underſtanding with which he feels its particular character, and its union with the whole; whether for compoſing with exactneſs, for following the preciſion of the movements, or for catching the moment and variety of the *bold*, and *ſweet*; or laſtly, for adding to the mark'd ornaments, thoſe which are ſo neceſſarily ſuppoſed by the author, that no one can be permitted to omit them. 'Tis in vain for a muſician to be ingenious; there can be nothing concinnous but from the knowledge of the muſic which he executes, and from the mutual underſtanding that he maintains with others; for it would be impoſſible to place a good *concinnous* in a concert of deaf men, or in a piece of muſic whoſe ſtile is perfectly oppoſite to thoſe who execute it. Muſic-maſters, conductors and managers of the orcheſtra, ought particularly to guide, reſtrain, or forward their muſicians, in fixing throughout a good concinnity, and this is what always forms a good firſt violin, by a particular force in the execution, which impreſſes ſtrongly its character on every ear. The reciting voice is ſubject to the baſs and meaſure; the firſt violin ſhould always attend to and follow the voice. The ſymphony ought to be attentive to the violin; and laſtly, the harpſichord, which we ſuppoſe to be held by the compoſer, ſhould be the true and firſt direction of the whole.

In general, the more character the ſtile, periods, phraſes, and harmony poſſeſs, the more eaſy is the concinnous to catch, becauſe the ſame idea impreſſed with life on every mind, preſides over the whole of the execution. On the contrary, when the muſic is ſilent, and we feel nothing more than a continuance of notes without an uniſon, there is no general object to which each one connects his part, and the execution proceeds always in a diſagreeable ſtrain. For this reaſon it is, that the French muſic is never concinnous.

TO CONFINE THE HARMONY, Is to collect each part within the ſmalleſt intervals that can be poſſible. For inſtance, to confine this concord, ut, ſol, mi, which comprehends a tenth, we muſt vary it thus, ut, mi, ſol, and in that caſe it contains no more than a fifth. (Vide CONCORD, VARIATION.)

CONCORD, An union of two or more ſounds uttered at once, and forming together a general harmonic.

The natural harmony produced by the reſounding of a ſonorous body, is compoſed of three different ſounds, without reckoning their octaves, the which form together the moſt agreeable and moſt perfect concord that can be heard; from whence, on account of its excellence, it is called a perfect concord. Thus, to render the harmony complete, every concord muſt be at leaſt compoſed of three ſounds. The muſicians alſo find in the trio, an an harmonic perfection, either becauſe the concords are therein entirely employed, or becauſe in the occaſions, where they do not employ them entirely, they have the art of giving a change to the ear, and produce a contrary ſenſation, by preſenting to it the principal ſounds of the concords, in ſuch a manner as to obliterate entirely the others. (Vide TRIO.) The octave, however, of the principal ſound, producing freſh connections, and new conſonances by the complements of intervals, (Vide COMPLEMENT) we generally add that octave to form the concinnity of all the conſonnances within the ſame concord. (Vide CONSONNANCE.) Moreover, the addition of the diſſonance (Vide DISSONANCE) producing a fourth ſound added to the perfect concord, it is abſolutely neceſſary, if we wiſh to fill the concord, to have a fourth part to expreſs this diſſonance. Wherefore the ſyſtem of concords can never be complete and united but by the means of four parts. We divide the concords into perfect and imperfect. The perfect concord is that which we have juſt mentioned, which is compoſed of the fundamental or flat ſound, of its third, fifth and eighth: It is ſub-divided into major or minor, according to the nature of its third. (Vide MAJOR and MINOR.)

Some authors give the name of perfect alſo to all the concords, even diſſonant, whoſe fundamental ſound is in flat. The imperfect concords are thoſe which retain a ſixth inſtead of a fifth; and in general all thoſe where the flat ſound is not the fundamental. Theſe denominations, which were given before the fundamental baſs was known, are by no means applicable. Thoſe of direct or varied concords would be much more ſuitable in the ſame ſenſe. The concords are again divided into conſonant and diſſonant. The conſonant concords are the perfect concord and its derivatives; every other concord is diſſonant. (See the under-written table of each, according to M. Rameau's ſyſtem.)

T A B L E

Of all the Concords *admitted into Harmony.*

Fundamental Concords.

Perfect Concord and its Derivatives.

The fundamental Sound in flat. | Its Third in flat. | Its Fifth in flat.

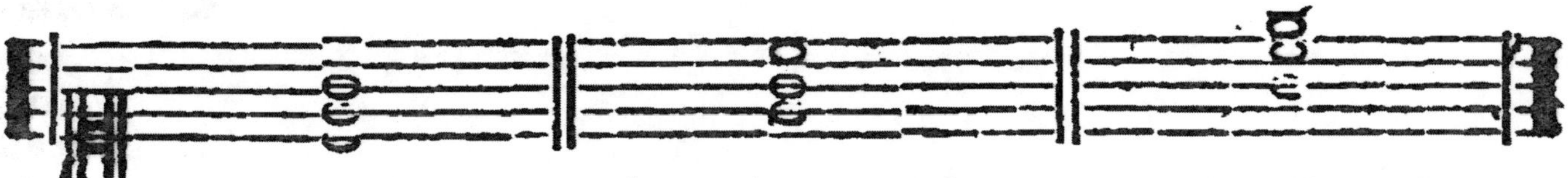

Perfect Concord. | Concord of Sixth. | Concord of Sixth-fourth.

This concord constitutes the tone, and is formed only on the tonic: Its third may be either major or minor; and it is that which constitutes the mode.

Sensible or Dominant Concord, *and its* Derivatives.

The fundamental Sound in flat. | Its Third in flat. | Its Fifth in flat. | Its Seventh in flat.

Sensible Concord. | False Fifth. | Small Sixth-major. | Triton.

No one of the sounds of this concord can be varied.

Concord of the Seventh *and its* Derivatives.

The fundamental Sound in flat. | Its Third in flat. | Its Fifth in flat. | Its Seventh in flat.

Concord of the 7th. | Of great 6th. | Of small 6th Minor. | Of the 2d.

The third, fifth, and seventh may be varied in this concord.

Concord *of the diminished* Seventh, *and its* Derivatives.

The Fundamental Sound in Flat. | Its Third in flat. | Its Fifth in flat. | Its Seventh in flat.

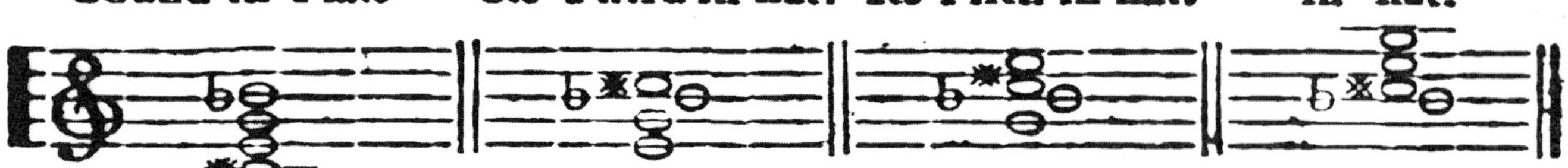

Concord of 7th diminished. | Of 6th Major and false Fifth. | Of Minor 3d and Triton. | Of the superfluous 2d.

No one of the Sounds of this concord can be varied.

Concord

Concord *of the* Sixth *added, and its* Derivatives.

The fundamental Sound in flat.	Its Third in flat.	Its Fifth in flat.	Its Sixth in flat.

Concord of the 6th added.	Of ſmaller 6th added.	Of the 2d added.	Of the 7th added.

I join the word *added* throughout this work, to diſtinguiſh this concord and its variations from the ſimilar productions of the concord of the ſeventh. This laſt variation of the ſeventh added, is not admitted by Monſ. Rameau, becauſe this variation forms a concord of the ſeventh, and the concord of the ſeventh is fundamental. This reaſon ſeems to have little weight. We ought not then, on this plan, to admit the greater ſixth, as a variation, ſince, in the particular principles of Monſ. Rameau, this ſame concord is often fundamental. But the practice of the greateſt muſicians, and even his own, contradicts the execution which he wiſhes to eſtabliſh.

Concords *of the ſuperfluous* Sixth.

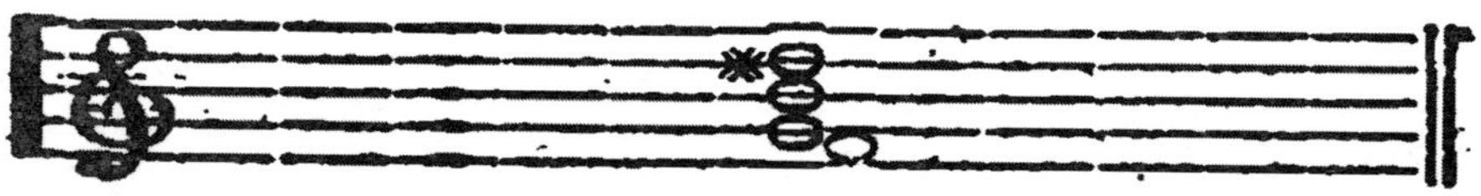

This concord has no variation; and no one of its ſounds can undergo a change. 'Tis properly no more than a concord of ſmall major ſixth dieſis'd by accident, and in which we ſubſtitute ſometimes the fifth for the fourth.

Concords *by* Suppoſition.

(Vide Supposition.)

Concord *of the* Ninth, *and its* Derivatives.

The ſuppoſed Sound in flat.	The fundamental Sound in flat.	Its Third in flat.	Its Seventh in flat.

Concord of the 9th.	Of the 7th and 6th.	Of the ſixth-fourth and 5th.	Of 7th and 2d.

N

This

This is a concord of the Seventh, in the which we add a fifth ſound to the third beneath the fundamental.

We generally remove the ſeventh, i. e. the fifth of the fundamental ſound, which here is that note marked in black: in this caſe, the concord of the ninth may vary in removing again from the accompaniment, the eighth of the note which we carry to the baſs,

Concord *of the ſuperfluous* Fifth.

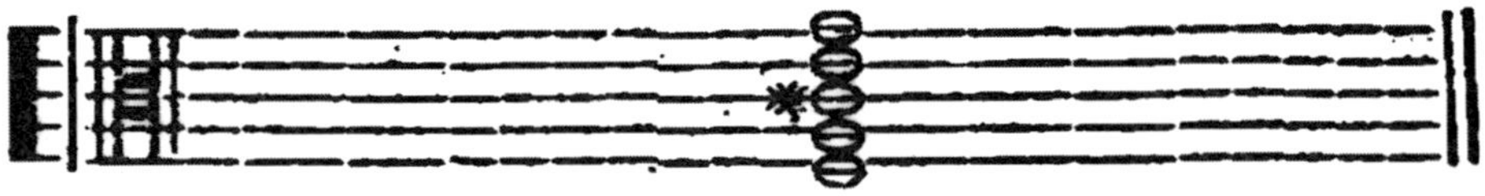

This is the ſenſible concord of a minor tone, below which we make the mediant underſtood; for which reaſon, 'tis a true concord of the ninth. But it does not vary on account of the diminiſhed fourth, which the ſuppoſed ſound carried into ſharp, would produce with the ſenſible note, which fourth is an interval expelled from harmony.

Concord *of the* Eleventh *or* Fourth.

The ſuppoſed Sound in flat.	Idem, by removing two Sounds	The fundamental Sound in flat.	Its Seventh in flat.

Concord of the 9th and 4th.	Concord of the 4th.	Of 7th and 4th.	Of 2d and 5th.

This is a concord of the ſeventh, below which we add a fifth ſound to the fifth of the fundamental. We never ſtrike this concord full, on account of its duration. Its ninth and ſeventh are generally removed; and to vary it, this removal is indiſpenſably neceſſary.

Concord *of ſuperfluous* Seventh.

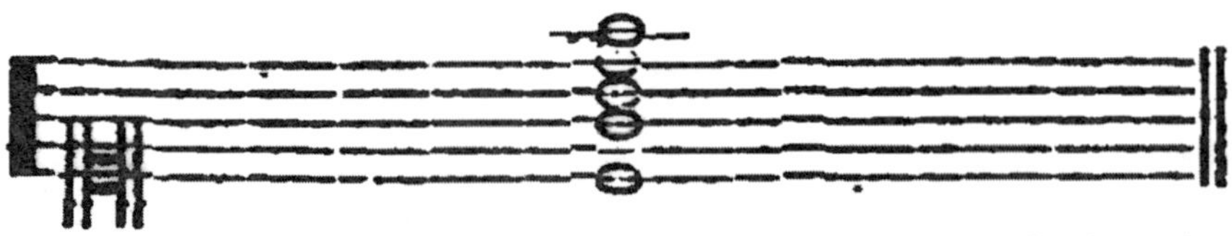

This is the dominant concord, under which the baſs forms the tonic.

Concord

Concord *of ſuperfluous* Seventh *and* Minor Sixth.

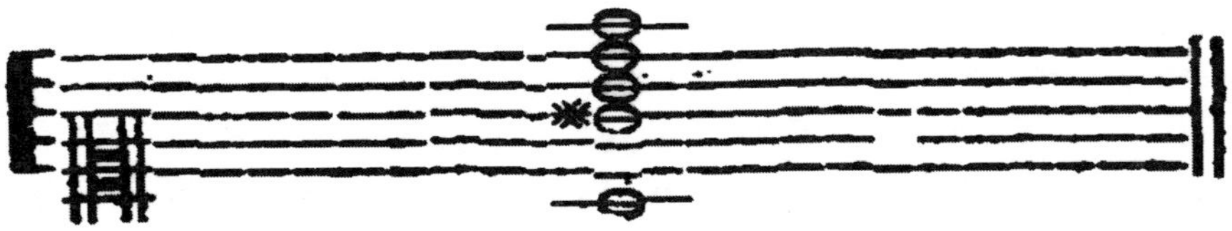

This is the concord of the diminiſhed ſeventh on the ſenſible note, under which the baſs forms the tonic.

Theſe two laſt concords have no variation, becauſe the ſenſible note and the tonic muſt then be heard together in the ſuperior parts, which can never ſucceed.

Though all the concords in this table be full and complete, as was neceſſary to ſhew all their elements, yet it is not laid down that we muſt uſe them thus: we cannot always, and we ought not often. In regard to the ſounds which ought to be preferred according to the place and cuſtom of concords; it is in this exquiſite and neceſſary choice, that the grand art of the compoſer conſiſts. (Vide Composition, Melody, Effect, Expression, &c.)

End of the Table of Concords.

We will ſhew, under the words *Harmony, Fundamental Baſs, Compoſition, &c.* the method of employing all theſe concords, to form by them a regular harmony. I will only here add the following obſervations.

I. 'Tis a very great miſtake to imagine that the choice of variations in the ſame concord can be indifferent, either for the harmony or the expreſſion. There is not one of theſe variations but has its proper characters. Every body muſt perceive the contrariety which is found between the ſweetneſs of the falſe fifth, and the ſharpneſs of the triton, and ſtill one of theſe intervals is varied from the other. It is the ſame thing with the diminiſhed ſeventh and ſuperfluous ſecond, with the general ſecond and the ſeventh. Who does not know the ſonorous difference between the fifth and the fourth? The concord of greater ſixth and that of ſmall minor ſixth, are two repreſentations of the ſame fundamental concord: But how much is the one more harmonious than the other! The concord of ſmall major ſixth, on the contrary, is much more brilliant than that of the falſe fifth. And to ſpeak only of the moſt ſimple of all the concords, reflect on the dignity of the perfect concord, the ſweetneſs of the

the concord of ſixth; and the flatneſs of that of ſixth-fourth; all theſe are however compoſed of the ſame ſounds.

The ſuperfluous intervals, in general the dieſis's above, are proper on account of their duration, to expreſs rage, anger, and the ſharper paſſions. On the contrary, the B mollare's in ſharp, and the diminiſhed intervals, form a plaintive harmony, which touches the ſoul. There are a multitude of ſimilar obſervations, which, when a muſician knows how to manage them, render him maſter of the affections of thoſe, who liſten to him.

II. The choice of ſimple intervals is not leſs important than that of concords, in regard to the place where they ſhould be employed.. For inſtance, 'tis below where the fifths and octaves muſt in preference be placed above the thirds and ſixths. Tranſpoſe this order, and you will demoliſh the harmony, tho' you leave the ſame concords.

III. Laſtly, we may render the concords ſtill more harmonious by uniting them by ſmaller intervals, much more ſuitable to the capacity of the ear than the larger. This is what we call to confine the harmony, and which ſo few muſicians are ſkilled in practiſing. The boundaries of the diapaſon of the voice are another reaſon for confining the choirs. We may be aſſured, that a choir is ill compoſed when the concords are ſcattered, when the parts have a ſqueaking note, loſe their diapaſon, and are ſo removed one from the other, as to ſeem to have no kind of connection between themſelves.

We call alſo by the name of concord, the condition of an inſtrument whoſe fixed ſounds are connected together in the exact juſtneſs which they ought to preſerve. In this ſenſe, we ſay, that an inſtrument is, or is not in concord or tune; that it keeps or does not keep its concord. The ſame expreſſion is uſed in regard to two voices which ſing together, for two ſounds, which are heard at a time, whether in uniſon or counterpart.

DISSONANT CONCORD, FALSE CONCORD, CONCORD UNTRUE, Are things ſo different, that they muſt not be confounded. The diſſonant concord is that which contains ſome diſſonance. An untrue concord, that whoſe ſounds are ill adapted, and do not preſerve together the juſtneſs of the intervals. Falſe concord, that which diſguſts the ear becauſe it is ill compoſed, and the ſounds, tho' juſt, do not form therein an entire harmonic.

CONCORDANT, or, BARYTON, is that part of muſic which is fixed in the middle, between the tenor and baſs. The

name

name of concordant is no longer in uſe, but in church-muſic, no more than the part which it denotes. Every where elſe, this part is call'd common pitch of baſs, and is counfounded with the baſs. The concordant is properly the part which in Italy is called tenor. (Vide PARTS.)

CONCOURSE, An aſſembly of muſicians and authoriſed connoiſſeurs, in the which a vacant place of muſic-maſter or organiſt is gained, by the majority of votes, by him who has compoſed the beſt molet, or who has diſtinguiſhed himſelf by the beſt execution

The concourſe was in uſe formerly in a great number of cathedrals; but in theſe partial times, when the ſpirit of intrigue engroſſes the generality of places, it is clear that this muſt gradually be aboliſhed, and that in its place they have ſubſtituted methods more eaſy, by giving to favour or intereſt, the rewards due to ingenuity and merit.

CONJOINT, A conjoint tetrachord is, in ancient muſic, that whoſe flatteſt chord is in uniſon with the ſharpeſt chord of the tetrachord, which is immediately below it; or whoſe ſharpeſt chord is in uniſon with the flatteſt of the tetrachord immediately above it. So, in the ſyſtem of the Greeks, all the five tetrachords are conjoint on ſome ſide that is firſt. The tetrachord meſon is conjoint to the tetrachord hypaton. 2dly. The tetrachord ſynnéménon is conjoint to the tetrachord meſon. 3dly, The tetrachord hyperboleon is conjoint to the tetrachord diazeugmenon; and as the tetrachord, to which another was conjoint, was reciprocally conjoint to that, this would have made ſix tetrachords in all, had not the tetrachord meſon, being conoint by its two extremities, been taken twice for once.

Amongſt us, conjoint is ſaid of an interval or degree. We call conjoint degrees, thoſe which are ſo diſpoſed between themſelves, that the ſharpeſt ſound of the inferior degree becomes in uniſon with the flatteſt ſound of the ſuperior. Moreover, neither of theſe degrees conjoined muſt be divided into other ſmaller degrees, but they themſelves muſt be as ſmall as poſſible, viz. thoſe of a ſecond. Wherefore, theſe two intervals ut re and re mi are conjoint, but ut re and ſol fa are not ſo, for want of the firſt condition, ut mi and mi ſol are not alſo, for want of the ſecond.

An extent by conjoint degrees ſignifies the ſame thing as a diatonic extent. (Vide DIATONIC DEGREE.)

CONNECTED, A term in church-muſic. (Vide MIXT.)

CONSONANCE, Is, according to the Etymology of the Word, the effect of two or more ſounds heard at a time; but the ſignification of this word is generally reſtrain'd to intervals formed by two ſounds, the concord of which is pleaſing to the

O ear,

ear, and 'tis in this sense, that I shall speak of it under this head.

From this infinity of Intervals which can divide the sounds, there is but a small number, which form a consonance; all the rest disgust the ear, and are therefore called dissonances. 'Tis not fixt absolutely that many of these may not be employed in harmony, but they are fixt only with those precautions, of which the consonances, always agreeable in themselves, are not equally in want. The Greeks admitted five consonances only, i. e. The octave, the 5th, the 12th, which is the replication of the 5th, the 4th, and the 11th, which is its replication. We add to these, the 3ds and 6ths major and minor, the double and triple octaves, and, in short, the different replications of all these without exception, according to the whole extent of the system.

We distinguish the consonances, as perfect or just, whose interval has no variation, and as imperfect, those which may be major or minor. The perfect consonances are the 8th, 5th, and 4th; the imperfect, the 3ds and 6ths.

The principal character of consonances is drawn from their production in a similar sound, or, if we will, from the rustling of the chords. Of two chords, in full concord, forming together an interval of octave, or of 12th, which is the octave of the 5th, or of 17th major, which is the double octave of the major 3d; if we make the flattest sound, the other shakes and resounds. In regard to the major and minor 6th, the minor 3d, the simple major 5th and 3d which are all combinations of the precedent consonances, they are found, not directly, but between the different chords that shake in the same sound.

If I touch the chord ut, the chords ascending to its octave ut, to the 5th sol of that octave, to the third mi of the double octave, even to the octaves of all these, will all shake, and resound at a time; and if the first chord should be alone, we should still distinguish all these sounds in its resounding. Here then are the octave, the major third, and the fifth direct. The other consonances are found also by combinations, viz. the minor third from mi to sol; the minor sixth from the same mi to the ut above; the fourth from sol to the same ut; and the major sixth from the same sol to the mi which is above it. Such is the generation of all the consonances. It would be necessary to give an account also of the phœnomena.

First, The shaking of the chords is explained by the action of the air, and the concourse of vibrations. (Vide UNISON) Secondly, The sound of a chord must be always accompanied by its harmonics, (Vide that word.) This appears a propriety of the sound, which depends on its nature, which is inseparable from it, and which can be explained only by hypothesis's, which are not without their difficulties. The most ingenious that has yet been hit on, on this matter, is, without doubt, that of Monf. de Mairan, from which M. Rameau fays, he has greatly profitted.

Thirdly, In regard to the pleafure which confonances afford the ear by the exclufion of every other interval, we fee from thence clearly their fource in their generation. All confonances arife from a perfect concord, produced by one only found, and the perfect concord reciprocally is formed by an affemblage of confonances. It is therefore natural, that the harmony of this concord fhould be communicated to its parts, that each of them fhould partake therein, and that every other interval which does not form a part of this concord fhould not partake in it. Nature, moreover, which has endowed the objects of every fenfe, with qualities proper for flattering it, has chofen, that one found, whatever it be, fhould be accompanied with their agreeable founds, as fhe has willed, that one ray of light fhould be always formed of the fineft colours. But if we remove this queftion, and enquire whence arifes the pleafure which a perfect concord caufes to the ear, whilft it is difgufted with the concourfe of every other found, what can we anfwer to that, unlefs to demand in our turn, why green delights the eye more than grey? and why the odour of the rofe is pleafing, whilft the poppy's fmell difgufts?

I don't deny, but that the phyficians have explained all this, and what is there they do not explain? But how much do thefe explanations depend on conjecture, and how little folidity do we find in them when they are nearly examined? The reader will judge of this by the expofition of the chief of them, which I fhall endeavour at in as few words as poffible.

They fay, that when the fenfation of the found is produced by the vibrations of the fonorous body, propagated as far as the tympanum by thofe which the air receives from this fame body, when two founds are heard together, the ear is affected at the fame time with their different vibrations. If thefe vibrations are ifochronic, that is to fay, if they agree in beginning, and finifhing at the fame time, this concurrence forms the unifon, and the ear, which catches the concord of thefe equal and juftly concordant returns, is agreeably affected by them. If the vibrations of one of the two founds are double in duration to thofe of the other, during each flatteft vibration, the fharp will make precifely two, and at the third they will fet off together. Wherefore every two times each unequal vibration of the fharp concurs with every vibration of the flat, and this frequent concordance, which conftitutes the octave, lefs fweet in their opinion than the unifon, will be more fo than any other confonance.

nance. The 5th comes after, one of whose sounds forms two vibrations, whilst the other forms three, so that they agree only in every 3d vibration of the sharp; next comes the double octave, one of whose sounds forms four vibrations, whilst the other forms but one, agreeing only in every fourth vibration of the sharp: as to the fourth, the vibrations answer each other every fourth in sharp, and every third in flat; those of the major third are as 4 and 5; of the major sixth as 3 and 5; of the minor third as 5 and 6; and of the minor sixth as 5 and 8. Above those numbers there are only their multiples, which produce consonances, that is to say, the octaves of the former: all the remaining parts are dissonant.

Others finding the octave more agreeable than the unison, and the fifth more agreeable than the octave, give it as a reason, that the equal returns of the vibrations in the unison, and their too frequent concurrence in the octave, confound, identify the sounds, and prevent the ear from perceiving their diversity. That it may feel the sounds with pleasure, they say that it is necessary for the vibrations to accord by intervals, but not for them to confound each other too often; otherwise, instead of two sounds, we should think to hear one only, and the ear would lose the pleasure of the comparison. 'Tis in this manner, that from the same principle we deduce, according to our liking, the pro and con, just as we imagine that experience requires.

But in the first place, all this explanation is, as we may see, founded on the pleasure only that we pretend the soul receives thro' the organ of hearing, from the concurrence of vibrations, which, at bottom, is nothing more than a mere supposition. Moreover, we must again suppose, to authorise this system, that the first vibration of each of the two sonorous bodies begins exactly with that of the other; for, however little one may precede, they no longer concur in a determined connection, perhaps even they can in no case concur, and, consequently, the sensible interval must be subjected to change; the consonance could no longer exist, or, at least, would be entirely different. Lastly, we must suppose, that the different vibrations of the two sounds of a consonance strike the organ without confusion, and transmit to the brain, the sensation of the concord, without a mutual injury: a thing difficult to conceive, and of which I shall have occasion to speak elsewhere.

But, without disputing on so many suppositions, let us see what ought to follow from this system. The vibrations or sounds of the last consonance, which is the minor third, are as 5 and 6, and its concord is very agreeable. What then should naturally result from two other sounds, whose vibrations were between themselves as 6 and 7? A consonance, a little less harmonious, I confess,

confess, but still very agreeable, on account of the small difference of their calculations, for they differ a 36th only. But let me be told how it can happen that two sounds, the one of which forms five vibrations, whilst the other makes six, can produce an agreeable consonance; and that two sounds, one of which makes six vibrations, whilst the other forms seven, produce a disagreeable dissonance. How can it be, that in one of these connections the vibrations agree from six to six, and my ear is delighted; whilst in the other they agree from seven to seven, and my ear is disgusted? I will again enquire how it happens, that after this first dissonance, the duration of the others does not increase in proportion to the composition of their connection? Why, for instance, is not the dissonance which results from the connection of 89 to 90, much more disgusting than than of 12 to 13? If the more or less frequent return of the concurrence of vibrations was the cause of the degree of pleasure or pain which the concords afford me, the effect must be proportionate to this cause, and I cannot find the least proportion in them.—This pleasure and pain then cannot be derived from thence.

It still remains to pay attention to the alterations of which a consonance is susceptible, tho' these alterations misplace entirely the periodical concurrence of vibrations; and the concurrence itself becomes more scarce in proportion as the alteration is less. It remains to consider that the concord of the organ or harpsichord can offer to the ear nothing more than a cacophony, so much the more disgusting, as these instruments are more in tune, since, except the octave, there is found no other consonance in its exact connection.

Can one say, that an approaching connection is supposed to be entirely exact, that it is received as such by the ear, and that it supplies by instinct whatever is wanting to the justness of the concord? In that case, I enquire the cause of this inequality of judgment and perception, thro' which it admits connections more or less approaching, and banishes others according to the different nature of consonances? In the unison, for instance, the ear can supply nothing: It is either just or false; there is no medium. In the same manner in the octave also, unless the interval be exact, the ear is disgusted; it admits no approximation. For what reason does it admit more in the fifth, and less in the major third? An explanation vague, opposite to the principle which should be established, and without proof, can give no reason for these differences.

The philosopher, who has given us some principles of the acoustic, laying aside all these concurrences of vibrations, and renewing on this point the system of Descartes, gives a reason for the pleasure which consonances cause to the ear by the simplicity of of connections which are between the sounds that form them. According to this author, and Descartes also, the pleasure diminishes in proportion as these connections become more composed, and when the mind partakes in them no more, they are veritable dissonances; wherefore it is an operation of the mind which they take as the principle of an harmonic sentiment. Moreover, though this hypothesis may agree with the result of the first harmonic divisions, and tho' it may extend itself even to other phœenomena that are discovered in the fine arts, as it is subject to the same objections as the preceding, it is not possible for reason to render a satisfactory account of it.

That of all, which appears the most satisfactory, has for its author Monf. Estéve, of the Royal Society of Montpélier.— Here are his reasonings thereon:

The sentiment of sound is inseparable from that of its harmonics; and since every sound bears its harmonics, or rather its accompaniment with it; this same accompaniment is in the order of our organs. There is in the most simple sound, a gradation of sounds, which are sharper and weaker, which sweeten, by their variety, the principal sound, and render it lost in the great velocity of the higher sounds. Here then we see the explanation of a sound; the accompaniment is essential to it, and forms its sweetness and its melody. Werefore, every time that this sweetening, this accompaniment, these harmonics are enforced, and better disclosed, the sounds will be more melodious, the varieties better sustained. This is a perfection, and the soul ought to be sensible of it.

These consonances, moreover, have this propriety, that the harmonics of each of the two sounds, concurring with the harmonics of the other, their harmonics are mutually sustained, become more sensible, have a longer duration, and by this means, make the concord of sounds which produce them much more agreeable.

To make the application of this principle more evident, Monf. Estéve has formed two tables, the one of consonances, and the other of dissonances, which are in the order of the gamut; and these tables are so disposed, that we may perceive in each the concurrence or opposition of the harmonics of the two sounds which form each interval.

By the table of the consonances, we see that the concord of octave preserves almost all its harmonics, and this is the reason of the identity which we suppose, in the practice of harmony, to be between the two sounds of the octave: we see that the concord of the fifth preserves three harmonics only; that the fourth has only two; and lastly, that the imperfect consonances preserves but one, except the major sixth, which bears two.

By

By the table of dissonances, we see that they preserve no kind of harmonic, except the minor seventh alone, which preserves its harmonic fourth, that is, the major third of the third octave of sharp sounds.

From these observations, the author concludes, that the more concurrent harmonics there are between two sounds, more will the concord be agreeable, and in this consist the perfect consonances.

The more harmonics there are destroyed, the less will the soul be satisfied with its concords: Such are imperfect consonances. Lastly, if it should ever happen that no harmonic is preserved, the sounds will be deprived of their sweetness and melody, they will be disagreeable, and rendered, as it were, thin; the soul will be disgusted with them, and instead of the harmonious sweetness, which it discovered in the consonances, finding nothing but a continued roughness, it must feel a sensation of inquietude very disagreeable, which is the effect of dissonances.

This is, without contradiction, the happiest, most simple and most natural of every hypothesis, but it still leaves something to be wished for the satisfaction of the mind, since the causes which are assigned are not always in proportion to the difference of the effects; as, for instance, it confounds in the same cathegory, the minor third and the minor seventh, as equally reduced to one harmonic only, tho' the one is consonant and the other dissonant, and the effect, to the ear, is as different as possible.

In regard to the principle imagined by Monf. Sauveur, which he made to consist in the strokes, as it can by no means be sustained, and has been adopted by no one, I will not employ it here, as it will suffice to direct the reader to what I have spoken of it under the word Beatings.

CONSONANT, A consonant interval is that which gives a consonance, or produces the effect of one, which happens, in certain cases, to dissonances, thro' the force of the modulation. A consonant concord is that which is composed of consonances only.

CONSTRAIN'D, This word is applied either to the harmony, the air, or the power of the notes, when, through the nature of the design, we are tied down to a law of uniformity in some one of the three parts. (Vide Bass Constrain'd.)

TO CONTINUE, To continue on a syllable, is to prolong it farther than prosody requires, as we do in trills; and to continue on a note, is to make a line therein, or to prolong it until the sensation of the measure be forgotten.

CONTRA,

CONTRA, A name given formerly to that part which was more generally called Altus, and which, at present, we name Haute Contre.

CONTRAST, An opposition of characters. There is a contrast in a piece of music when the movement passes from slow to quick, or from quick to slow; when the diapason of the melody passes from flat to sharp, or from sharp to flat; when the air passes from sweet to bold, or from bold to sweet; when the accompaniment passes from simple to figured, or from figured to simple. Lastly, when the harmony has clear and full alternatives; and the most perfect contrast is that which reunites all these oppositions at the same time.

It is very common for composers, who are barren in invention, to make a wrong use of the contrast, and to seek in that, for the sake of preserving the attention, those resources with which their genius is incapable of finishing them. But the contrast, employed à propos, and managed with propriety, produces an effect particularly admirable.

CONTRA TENOR, A name given in the beginning of counter point, to that part, which has since been stiled, tenor only.

CONTRARY SENSE, A fault, into which the musician falls, when he renders a different thought from that which he ought.—Music, says Mons. D'Alembert, being nothing more than a translation of the words which are set to an air, it is visible, that we can fall into a contrary sense, neither can it be avoided more easily than in a literal translation. Contrary sense, in expression, is when the music is sad instead of being gay, gay instead of being sad, light instead of being heavy, heavy instead of being light, &c. Contrary sense, in prosody, is when we render long syllables short; or short, long; when we do not observe the accent of the language, &c. Contrary sense, in declamation, is when we express, by the same modulations, opposite and different sentiments; when we are more attentive to the words than the sentiments; when we lay a stress on such details as we ought to slide over; and when our repetitions are brought in contrary to nature. Contrary sense, in punctuation, is when a musical phrase is terminated by a perfect cadence in those places where the sense is suspended, or forms an imperfect stop where the sense is concluded. I speak here of contrary senses in the rigour of the word; but a want of expression is, perhaps, more disgusting than all these. I even had rather the music should speak contrary to what it absolutely ought, than that it should produce a confusion of nothing at all.

CONTRE CHANT, A name given by Gerſon, and others, to that which was then more generally called Deſcant, or Counter-point. (Vide thoſe words.)

COPIER, He whoſe profeſſion it is to copy muſic.

How great a progreſs ſoever the art of typography may have made, we have never been able to apply it to muſic with ſo great ſucceſs as to writing: whether it be becauſe the taſte of the mind being more ſtable than that of the ear, we are not ſo ſoon tired with the ſame books as with the ſame ſongs, or by the particular difficulties which the combination of the notes and lines add to the impreſſion of muſic; for if we draw firſt the lines, and then the notes, it is impoſſible to give their relative poſitions that juſtneſs which is neceſſary; and if the character of each note engroſſes a portion of the ſcale, as in our printed muſic, the lines are ſo miſerably adjuſted together, ſo great a quantity of characters are required, and the whole produces ſo diſagreeable an effect to the ear, that this method has been aboliſhed with reaſon, and the engraving has been ſubſtituted in its place. But beſides the other inconveniencies that engraving is ſubject to, it has particularly that of augmenting too much or too little the examples or parts; of placing in partition what ſome would chuſe in ſeparate parts; and in ſeparate parts what others would chuſe to be in partition; and laſtly, of offering to the curious nothing but ancient muſic, which has paſſed thro' the hands of half the world. It is certain, that in Italy, the country which produces the greateſt variety of muſic, they have aboliſhed ſome time the printed note, without the engraving having been able to eſtabliſh itſelf; from whence I conclude, that in the opinion of the ingenious, that of the ſimple copy is the moſt preferable.

It is of greater importance, that muſic ſhould be correctly and neatly copied than ſimple writing, becauſe he who reads and reflects in his cloſet, may eaſily correct the errors of his book, whilſt nothing prevents him from ſuſpending and re-beginning his diſcourſe; but in a concert, where each one ſees but his part, and where the velocity and continuance of the execution leave no time for rectifying any error, they are all irreparable; a moſt ſublime piece is often murdered, the execution is interrupted, and even ſtopped; every thing goes contrary, the effect and uniſon fails throughout, the hearer is diſguſted, and the author diſcountenanced thro' the error only of the copier.

Moreover, the underſtanding of a difficult piece of muſic depends greatly on the manner of its being copied, for beſides the neatneſs in the notes, there are different methods to repreſent more clearly to the reader, the ideas that we would paint to him, and which he ſhould underſtand. We often find the copy of one man more legible than that of another, tho' the latter may prick his notes more agreeably; the cause of which is, that the one wishes to please the eye, whilst the other is attentive to more serviceable endeavours!

The most ingenious copier is he whose music is executed with the most ease, without the musicians perceiving ever the reason why.—All this has persuaded me that I should not compile an useless article, if I demonstrated in brief an account of the duties and cares of a good copier. Every thing that tends to facilitate the execution, is by no means indifferent in the perfection of an art, of which it is always the most material beauty. I feel how much I shall injure myself if my works are compared with my rules; but I am not ignorant that he who seeks the public utility, should never have a remembrance of his own. As a man of letters, I have spoken of my condition all the evil I think of it: I have composed French music, and love only the Italian; I have shewn all the disadvantages of society, at the time when it gave me a sincere pleasure; as a bad copier, I here demonstrate the laws by which the ingenious are directed. O truth! my interest never prevailed in opposition to thee, and may it never in any respect erase the adoration which I owe to thee!

I must primarily suppose, that the copier is possessed of all the knowledge necessary to his profession. I even suppose him endued with the talents necessary for a superiority in its performance. What are these talents, and what is this knowledge? Without absolutely delineating them, I can, under this head, give a sufficient idea of them. All that I am privileged to say here, is, that the composer who thinks himself ingenious, may be very far from being sufficiently so to copy correctly the composition of another.

As written music, particularly in partition, is made to be read by concertants at a distance, the chief thing to be observed by the copier, is to make use of the convenient materials for rendering his notes most neat and legible. For this reason, he should chuse strong fair paper, rather thin, and which does not sink; that which does not require washing is generally preferred, because the washing with allum takes off something of its whiteness. The ink ought to be very black, without either gloss or gum; the ruling neat, equal, and well fixed, but not so black as the notes; on the contrary, the lines should be rather pale, so that the crotchets, double crotchets, pauses, and other smaller signs may not be confounded with them, and that the note may be expressed the fuller. The paleness of the lines, far from preventing the music to be read at a fixed distance, on the contrary, assists it by its neatness, and tho' the line should now and then escape the sight for a moment, the position of the notes very often

often of itſelf denotes it. The ruling of the paper is but an uſeleſs labour. If the copier would gain himſelf credit, let him rule his paper himſelf

There are two formations for ruled paper, one for the French muſic, the length of which is from the bottom to the top; the other, for the Italian, the length of which is according to the direction of the lines. We may make uſe of the ſame paper for the two, by clipping and ruling it contrary ways; but when we buy it ruled we muſt change the names at the paper-ſellers, and aſk for Italian paper when we want the French, and French when we want Italian; this qui pro quo is of little importance when we are acquainted before-hand.

To copy a partition, we muſt reckon up the parts which the ſcale comprehends, and chooſe paper which has by the page the ſame number of ſtaves, or a multiple of that number; finally, we ſhould loſe no ſtave, or, at leaſt, as little as poſſible when the multiple is not exact. The Italian paper has generally ten ſtaves, which divides every page into two columns, each of five ſtaves for the ordinary airs, that is to ſay, two ſtaves, for the two trebles of the violin, one for the fifth, one for the air, and one for the Baſs. When we have duo's, or pieces of muſic for flutes, hautboys, horns, or trumpets, in that caſe, to that number of ſtaves we can put no more than one column in the page, unleſs we can find a method for ſuppreſſing ſome uſeleſs ſtave, as that of the fifth, when it is continually in motion on the baſs.

Herein, however, are ſome obſervations, which we ſhould make to diſtribute the partitions with exactneſs. Firſt, whatever number of parts of ſymphony we may have, it is always neceſſary that the parts of the violin, as being principal, ſhould be placed at the top of the column, where the eyes may be moſt eaſily conveyed. Thoſe who place them at the bottom of all the reſt, and immediately on the fifth, for the convenience of the accompaniment, are in an error, without obſerving that it is ridiculous to ſee in a partition, the parts of the violin below, for inſtance, thoſe of the horn which are of a much deeper baſs. Secondly, in the whole length of every piece, we ought never to change any thing in the number of the parts, ſo that every part may have its properties in the ſame place.

It would be better to leave the ſtaves vacant, or, if there is a neceſſity, place two parts in ſome of them, than to extend or diminiſh the column unequally. This rule is for the Italian muſic only, for the uſe of engraving has made the French muſic more attentive to the œconomy of the ſpace, than to the commodity of the execution. Thirdly, it is only at the greateſt extremity that we ſhould place two parts on the ſame ſtave, and this is what we ought particularly to avoid in the parts of the violin;

violin; for, beſides that there is much confuſion to be feared, there would be an equivocation with the double chord; we muſt always alſo be careful, that the parts do not interfere croſs ways, which we could not expreſs on the ſame ſtave. in a method clear and legible. Fourthly, the keys being correctly written, and once numbered, ſhould never be repeated any more than the ſign of the meaſure, unleſs in the French muſic, when, the columns being unequal, each one could not recollect his parts; but in the ſeparated parts, we muſt repeat the cliff at the beginning of each ſtave, were it only to denote the beginning of the lines, on a failure of the column.

The number of ſtaves being thus fixed, we muſt make a diviſion of the meaſures, and theſe meaſures ought to be all equal in ſpace as well as duration, to meaſure in ſome reſpect the time by the compaſs, and to guide the voice by the eyes. This ſpace ought to be ſufficiently extended in each meaſure, to receive all the notes which can enter therein, according to its greateſt ſub-diviſion. It cannot be imagined how great a clearneſs this caſe throws on a partition, and in what an embarraſſment a neglect of it throws them. If we confine a meaſure on a crotchet, how can we place the ſixteen double crotchets, which, perhaps, another part contains in the ſame meaſure. If we confine ourſelves to the vocal part, how can we fix the ſpace of the returns? In a word, if we are attentive only to the diviſions of one of theſe parts, how can we make the diviſions of the other parts, often contrary to coincide with them.

It is not ſufficient to divide the air into equal meaſures, we muſt alſo divide the meaſures into equal times. If in each part we proportionate thus the ſpace to the duration, all the parts, and all the ſimultaneous notes of each part will correſpond with a juſtneſs which will give pleaſure to the eye, and will greatly facilitate the reading of a partition. If, for inſtance, we divide a meaſure into four times, into four ſpaces very equal together, and in each part, if we extend the crotchets, draw the quavers nearer, and confine the ſemi-quavers in proportion, and each in its ſpace, without wanting to look at one part, in copying another, all the correſponding notes will be more exactly perpendicular than if they had been confronted by writing them, whether between the different meaſures of the ſame part, or between the different parts of the ſame meaſure.

To the exactneſs of the connections, we muſt join as much as poſſible, a neatneſs in our ſigns. For inſtance, we ſhall never prick uſeleſs notes; but as ſoon as we perceive that two notes re-unite, and are in uniſon, we ought to ſeparate the one from the other, when they are near each other, and on the ſame cliff. In regard to the fifth, as ſoon as its courſe is on the octave of the

the bafs, we muft act alfo in the fame manner. An equal attention of not multiplying our figns without a caufe, fhould prevent us from making piano's as a fymphony at the beginning of an air, and the forte's when it concludes. Every where elfe we muft write them exactly under the firft violin and the bafs; and this is fufficient in a partition where all the parts can, and ought to make thofe their grand object.

Laftly, It is the duty of a copier, when he writes a partition, to correct all the falfe notes which he may find in the original. I don't mean, by falfe notes, the faults of the work, but thofe of the copy which ferves as its original. The perfection of his confifts in rendering faithfully the ideas of the author; good or ill, that is not his bufinefs, fince he is neither author or corrector but copier only. It is very true, that if the author has, by miftake, placed one note for another, he ought to correct it. but if this fame author has, through ignorance, made an error in the compofition, he fhould leave it. Let him compofe better himfelf if he will or can, and well; but whenfoever he copies, he fhould have an eye to his original. We fee by this means, that it is not fufficient for a copier to be a good harmonift, and to underftand well the compofition, but he fhould, into the bargain, be well fkilled in the different ftyles, and be converfant in an author by his method, to know what he has, and what he has not compofed. There is, moreover, a kind of criticifm neceffary to reftore a paffage by the comparifon of another, to replace a forte or a dolce where it has been omitted, which is not uncommon in the partitions; even to difunite alfo phrafes improperly joined, and to reftore meafures before ejected. Knowledge and tafte are certainly neceffary to re-eftablifh a text in its full purity. It may be faid, few copifts can perform it; I anfwer, that it is incumbent on all.

Before I finifh what appertains to the partitions, I muft fpeak of the method of collecting the feparated parts; a laborious tafk from many copiers, but fimple and eafy when we undertake it by method.—For this purpofe, we muft firft reckon carefully the meafures in each part, to fatisfy ourfelves that they are correct. Then we place all the parts one on the other, beginning by the bafs, and covering it fucceffively with the other parts in the fame order as they ought to have in the partition. We compofe the columns of as many ftaves as there are parts, divide them into equal meafures, then placing all thefe parts thus ranged before us, on the left hand, we firft copy the firft line of the firft part, which I imagine to be the firft violin, make a flight mark with the pencil at the place where we ftop, and then continue it, being turned back to the right. We copy in the fame manner the firft line of the fecond violin, returning to the firft where-ever their courſe is in uniſon; then making a mark as before, we change the preceding part to the right, and proceed in the ſame manner with all the parts one after the other. When we are at the baſs, we run over with the eye the whole column, to diſcover if the harmony is good, if the whole is in concord, and if there are no errors: The firſt line being made, we take together all the parts which were changed one on the other on the right hand, and we once again change them on the left; they are then found in the ſame order, and in the ſame ſituation, as when they began: we then begin the ſecond column at the pencil mark; we make another mark at the end of the ſecond line, and we continue as before till the whole is completed.

I ſhall have little to ſay on the method of drawing a partition into ſeparate parts, for this is the moſt ſimple operation of the art, and it will be ſufficient to make thereon the following obſervations. Firſt, we muſt ſo compare the length of the pieces to what a page may contain, as never to be obliged to turn on the ſame piece in inſtrumental parts, unleſs there are a great number of meaſures to reckon, which will afford time. This rule obliges us to begin at the page verſo all the pieces, which takes up more than a page, and there are none which fill more than two. Secondly, the dolce's and the forte's ſhould be marked with the greateſt exactneſs on all the parts, even thoſe where the air begins and finiſhes, which are not ordinarily on the partition. Thirdly, we ought never to divide a meaſure frome one line to another, but endeavour that there ſhould be always a bar at the end of each ſtave. Fourthly, all the additional lines which exceed, either above or below, the five of the ſtave, ſhould by no means be continued, but ſeparated at each note, for fear that the muſician, confounding them with thoſe of the ſtave, ſhould be deceived in his note, and know no longer where he is. This rule is not leſs neceſſary in the partitions, and is followed, however, by no French copier. Fifthly, the parts of the hautboy which are drawn on the parts of the violin for a full band, ſhould never be exactly copied as they are in the original, but, beſides the extent which that inſtrument has leſs than the violin, beſides the dolce's which it cannot equally perform, beſides the velocity which is wanting, or which ſuits it ill in certain quick paſſages, the force of the hautboy ſhould be managed to mark the principal notes better, and give a greater accent to the muſic. If I had to judge of the taſte of a ſymphoniſt without hearing him, I would give him a leſſon on the part of the violin and hautboy; every copier ſhould be ſkilled in thoſe. Sixthly, the parts of horns and trumpets are ſometimes pricked on a different tone from the reſt of the air; we muſt tranſpoſe them in the tone, or at leaſt, if we copy them juſt as they are, we muſt write

write above the titles of the true tonic, Corni in D sol, re; Corni in E la, fa, &c. &c. Seventhly, we must never vary the part of fifth, or of the viol from the cleff of the bass, and its own, and thereon we have another attention to bestow, which is to transpose to the cleff of the viol all the places wherein its course is with the bass: we must never let the viol rise above the parts of the violin, so that, when the bass ascends too high, we must not take down the octave, but the unison, so that the viol may never leave that medium which is suitable to it. Eighthly, the vocal part should never be copied but in partition with the bass, so that the singer may accompany himself, and not have the trouble either to hold his part in the hand, or to reckon his pauses. In the duets and trios, each part of the air ought to contain, besides the bass, its counter part, and when we copy a limited recitative, we should for each instrumental part add to its own the part of the air, to guide it on a default in the measure. Ninthly and lastly, in the vocal parts we must be careful to unite or disunite the chords, so that the singer may clearly see those which belong to every syllable. The partitions which come out of the composer's hands, are very equivocal in this point, and the singer cannot tell, the chief part of the time, how to render the notes suitable to the words. The copier, skill'd in prosody, and who knows exactly the accent of the words and that of the air, determines the division of the notes, and prevents the doubts of the singer. The words should be written exactly under the notes, and very correct in regard to the accent and orthography; but they should have neither stops or commas, as the frequent repetitions being so irregular, render a grammatical punctuation impossible; 'tis for the music to punctuate the words; the copier has no concern therein; for this would be an addition of those signs which the composer is bound to render useless.

I will conclude for fear of carrying this article to too great a length, I have already said too much for a good copist, who is ingenious, and has a taste for his occupation: I can never say enough for others. I will only add a word in finishing: There are several intermediaries between what the composer plans, and what the audience hear. 'Tis the duty of the copier to connect these two terms as near as possible, to mark with precision every thing which should be done, that the music when executed may render to the composer's ear, exactly what was plann'd within his head at the time of the composition.

CORD or CHORD SONOROUS, Is every extended Chord from whence a sound can be drawn. For fear of going out of my depth on this article, I will transcribe, in part, that of Monf. D'Alembert,

D'Alembert, and add nothing more of my own than what has an immediate connection with ſound and muſic.

" If an extended chord is ſtruck in ſome one of its points by " any power, it will dilate itſelf to a certain diſtance from the " ſituation in which it before reſted, it will then return and " make vibrations by virtue of the elaſticity which its extenſion " gives it. If, moreover, the compoſition of this chord is na- " turally elaſtic, or ſufficiently homogenous for the ſame mo- " tion to be communicated to all its parts, it will make a ſound " in ſhaking, and a reſounding will always accompany its vi- " brations. The geometricians have diſcovered the laws of " theſe vibrations, and muſicians, thoſe of the ſounds which re- " ſult from them.

" It has been long known by experience, and reaſonings fool- " iſh enough, that every thing elſe being equal, the more a " chord was extended, the quicker were its vibrations; that on " an equal extenſion, the chords cauſed their vibrations more or " leſs quick, in proportion as they were leſs or longer, that is " to ſay, that the proportion of the lengths was always inverſe " to that of the number of vibrations. Mr. Taylor, a cele- " brated Engliſh geometrician, is the firſt who has demonſtrated " the law of the vibrations of the chords with any exactneſs, " in his ingenious work, entitled Methodus Incrementorum " Directa & Inverſa, 1715; and theſe ſame laws have been ſince " demonſtrated by Monſ. Jean Bernouilli, in the ſecond volume " of his Memoirs of the Imperial Academy of Peterſburg." From the formula which reſults from theſe laws, and which may be found in the Encyclopoedia, under the article chord, I draw the three following corollaries, which ſerve as principles to the theory of muſic.

I. If two chords of the ſame compoſition are equal in length and thickneſs, the number of their vibrations in equal times will be as the roots of the numbers, which expreſs the connection of the extenſion of the chords.

II. If the extenſions and lengths are equal, the numbers of the vibrations in equal times will be in inverſe proportion to the thickneſs or diameter of the chords.

III. If the extenſions and the thickneſſes are equal, the number of vibrations in equal times will be in inverſe proportion to the lengths. For the underſtanding theſe theorems, I ſhould have firſt lain down as a rule, that the extenſion of the chords is not repreſented by the extending weights, but by the roots of thoſe weights; wherefore the vibrations being as the fourth of the roots of the extenſions, the extending weights are between themſelves as the cubes of thoſe vibrations, &c. &c.

From

From the laws of the vibrations of the chords are deduced those of the sounds, which result from those same vibrations in the sonorous chord. The more vibrations a chord performs within a given time, the more sharp are its sounds; the less vibrations it forms, the flatter: so that the sounds following between themselves, the connections of the vibrations, their intervals are expressed by the same connections, which submits the whole of the music to a calculation.

We see by the preceding theorems, that there are three methods of changing the sound of a chord, i. e. by changing the diameter; that is, the thickness of the chord, or its length, or its extension. What these alterations produce successively on the same chord, may be produced at once on different chords, by giving them different degrees of thickness, length or extension. This method combined is what is used in general in the concord and playing of the harpsichord, the violin, the bass, guittar, and other similar instruments composed of chords of different thicknesses and differently extended, which consequently must have different sounds.

Moreover, in the one, as the harpsichord, these chords have different lengths fixed, by the which the sounds are varied again, and in the others as the violin, the chords, tho' equal in fixed length, are shortened or lengthened by the finger of the player, at will; and this finger being advanced or drawn back on the handle, perform then the office of moveable bridges, which give to the chord shaken by the fiddle stick, as many different sounds as lengths. In regard to the connection of the sounds and their intervals, in relation to the length of the chords and their vibrations, see SOUND, INTERVAL, CONSONANCE.

The sonorous chord, besides the principal sound which results from the whole of its length, emits other necessary sounds less sensible, and these sounds seem to prove that this chord does not only vibrate in its whole length, but makes each of its aliquots also vibrate in particular, according to the law of their dimensions. To which I should add, that this propriety which serves, or ought to serve as a foundation for all harmony, and which many attribute not to the sonorous chord, but to the air which this sound emits, is not particular to chords only, but may be found in all sonorous bodies. (Vide CORPO SONORO.)

Another not less surprising propriety of the sonorous chord, and which attends on the preceding, is that if the bridge that divides it leans but lightly, and leaves a little communication between the vibration of one part and the other, then, instead of the total sound of one or both parts, we hear only the sound of the greater aliquot common to both parts. (Vide HARMONIC SOUNDS.)

The

The word chord is taken figuratively in composition for the fundamental sounds of the mode; and we often call *Chords of Harmony* those notes of the bass, which, by favour of certain dissonances, prolong the phrase, vary and incorporate the modulation.

CORPO SONORO, By this name is called every body which renders, or may immediately render, a sound. It does not follow from this definition, that every instrument of music is a corpo sonoro; this name should be given only to that part of the instrument which sounds from itself, and without which there would be no sound. Thus in a violincello, or in a violin, every chord is a corpo sonoro; but the case of the instrument, which only resounds or reflects, the sound is by no means a a corpo sonoro, neither does it form a part. We should have this article before us, whenever there is occasion to speak of a corpo sonoro in this work.

CORPO VOCE, The voice has different degrees of force as well as of extent. The number of these degrees which each contain, bears the name of corpo voce, when we speak of the force, and *volume*, when of extent. Vide VOLUME. So, from two sounds similar, and producing the same sound, that which fills the ear strongest, and is heard at the greatest distance, is said to have a greater corpo or body. In Italy, the chief qualities that are sought for in voices, are justness and flexibility, but in France, the corpo voce is the grand aim.

CORYPHÆA, He who conducted the band in the Grecian entertainments, and beat the time in their music. (Vide TO BEAT TIME.)

COUNTER FUGUE, A kind of fugue whose direction is opposite to that of another fugue, which has been before established in the same piece. So when the fugue is heard by ascending from the tonic to the dominant, or from the dominant to the tonic, the counter fugue should be heard by descending from the dominant to the tonic, or from the tonic to the dominant, and vice versa. In other particulars, these rules are entirely similar to those of the fugue. (Vide FUGUE.)

COUNTER HARMONIC, The name of a kind of proportion. (Vide PROPORTION.)

COUNTER PART, This term is used in music, only to signify one of the two parts of a duet considered relatively with the other.

COUNTER POINT, This is nearly the same thing with composition, unless that composition may be said of airs, and of a single part; and counter-point is said of harmony only, and of a composition of two or more different parts.

This

This term of counter-point is derived from what in ancient times the notes or signs of sounds were with simple points, and in composing these with many parts, these points were placed over each other, or opposite.

At present, the name of counter-point is especially applied to the parts added on a given subject, taken ordinarily from the music of the church. The subject may be in tenor, or some other superior part; and in that case we say, that the counter-point is below the subject; but it is generally in the bass, which places the subject below the counter-point. When the counter-point is syllabic, or note upon note, it is called simple counter-point; figured counter-point, when there are found different figures or powers of the notes, and when there are formed designs, fugues, or imitations. We easily see that this cannot be done but by assistance of the measure, and that this church melody then becomes a true music. A composition formed and instantly executed, without preparation, on a given subject, is called an air at sight, because then each one composes extempore his part, and his air on the book of the choir.

COUNTER TEMS, A measure in counter-time is that in which we pause on a weak time, and slide over in a strong, and in which the air seems to be in contrary sense with the measure.

COUNTER TENOR, That of the four parts of music, which belongs to the shrillest and clearest voices of men, in opposition to the counter bass, which is for the deepest and most flat. (Vide PARTS.)

In the Italian music, this part which they call contr 'alto, and which answers to the counter-tenor, is almost always sung by the upper bass, whether of women or of castratos. In effect, the counter-tenor is by no means natural for a man's voice, it must be forced to be raised to that diapason, and whatever we do, it has always a sharpness, and seldom any justness.

COUNTRY DANCE, The air of a kind of dance which bears the same name, which is performed by 4, 6, or 8 persons, and which is generally danced at a ball after the minuets, as being the most lively and entertaining of any thing of the kind. The tunes of the country dances are commonly of two times; they should be full cadenced, pleasing and gay, and still have a great deal of simplicity; for as they are often re-performed, they would be disgusting if of a heavy composition. The most simple things in every kind are always those of which we are least tired.

COUPLET, A name given in country ballads and other songs to that part of the poetry which in odes is called strophe. As all couplets are composed in the same measure of verse, they

are

are alſo ſung to the ſame air, which is often the cauſe of murdering the accent and proſody, becauſe two French verſes are not leſs in the ſame meaſure, though the long and ſhort may not be in the ſame places.

COUPLETS, Is alſo ſaid of the doubles and variations which are made in the ſame air, by taking it up ſeveral times with freſh changes, but always without disfiguring the foundation of the air, as in the Spaniſh airs and antient chacons. Every time that an air is taken up with a different variation, a freſh couplet muſt be made. (Vide VARIATIONS.)

COURANT, An air appropriated to a kind of dance which has the ſame name, on account of the goings in and out with which it is filled more than any other. This air is generally of a three flat timed meaſure, and is marked in a triple of minums with two renewals. It is no longer uſed, any more than the dance which bears its name.

COURONNE, A kind of C contrary ways, with a dot in the middle, which is formed thus 𝄐.

When the couronne, which is alſo called the ſign of a pauſe, is at once on all the parts of the correſponding note, it is the ſign of a general ſtop; the meaſure ſhould be ſuſpended there, and we may even ſometimes finiſh by this note. In general, the principal part therein makes at will ſome paſſage which the Italians call cadenza, whilſt all the reſt prolong and ſuſtain the ſound which is ſet down for them, or even make an entire pauſe. But if the couronne is on the final note of a ſingle part, then it is called point d'orgue, and denotes, that the ſound of that note muſt be continued until the other parts reach their natural concluſion. It is uſed alſo in canons, to ſpecify the place where all the parts may finiſh when they draw near a concluſion. (Vide PAUSE, CANON, &c. &c.)

CROME, This Italian plural ſignifies demi-crotchets. When this word is found written under crotchets or minums, it ſignifies the ſame as the parentheſis would, and denotes, that each note muſt be divided into demi-crotchets, according to its powers.

CROQUE NOTE, A name given in deriſion to thoſe ſilly muſicians, who, verſed in the combination of notes, and capable of performing the moſt difficult compoſitions at ſight, execute in general without ſentiment, without expreſſion, and without taſte. A croque ſol rendering rather the ſounds than the phraſes, reads the moſt energetic muſic, without the leaſt comprehenſion, as a ſchool maſter would read a maſter piece of eloquence, written in his own language, in a language of which he had no ideas.

CROTCHET, a note of muſic which is formed thus , or thus , and which is equal to two demi-crotchets, or the half of a minum. In our ancient muſic they made uſe of ſeveral ſorts of crotchets: crotchet with a tail, ſquare crotchets, and crotchets in a lozenge. Theſe two laſt ſorts continue in church muſic, but in ours we only uſe the crotchet with a tail. (Vide POWER of the NOTES.)

CROCHET DEMI, A note in muſic which is equal in duration to the fourth of a minum only, or the half of a crotehct. Eight demi-crotchets are conſequently neceſſary for a ſemi-breve, or a four timed meaſure.

We may here ſee the form of the demi-crotchet, whether alone, or ſung alone on a ſyllable; whether united with others when we paſs over many at the ſame time in playing, or on the ſame ſyllable in ſinging. They are generally united by fours in a four or a two timed meaſure; by threes in the ſix or eight timed meaſures, according to the diviſion of the time; and by ſixes in a third timed meaſure, according to the diviſion of the meaſures.—CORRESPONDENT.

EQUAL POWERS.

CROWDED, A crowded genus, πυκνός, is according to the definition of Aristoxenes, that wherein in every tetrachord, the sum of the two first intervals is less than the third. For this reason, the harmonic kind is crowded, because the two first intervals, which are each of a quarter tone, form no more than a semi-tone together, a sum much less than the third interval, which is a major third. The chromatic is also of the crowded kind, for these two first intervals form but one tone, less even than the minor third which follows. But the diatonic is by no means crowded, since its two first intervals form a tone and an half, a sum greater than the tone which follows. (Vide GENUS, TETRACHORD.)

From this term πυκνός, as radical, are composed the words Apycni, Barypicni, Mesopycni, Oxypycni, each of which articles will be found in its place. This determination is no longer in use in the modern music.

TO CYPHER, Is writing on the notes of the bass, cyphers or other characters, denoting the concords that these notes should bear, to serve as a guide to the accompanist. (Vide CYPHERS, CONCORD.)

CYPHERS, Characters which are placed above or below the notes of the bass to denote the concords which they ought to bear. Though amongst these characters there are many which are not cyphers, this name has been generally given to them because that is the sort of signs which is most commonly presented to our view.

As every concord is composed of many sounds, if it had been necessary to express each of these sounds by a cypher, the cyphers would have been so multiplied and confused, that the accompanist could never have found time to read them at the instant of the execution. Application has therefore been made as much as possible to characterize each concord by a cypher, so that this cypher may suffice to specify, in relation to the bass, the nature of the concord, and consequently all the sounds which are to compose it. There is even a concord which is cyphered without a cypher; for, according to the precision of the cyphers, every note which is not cyphered, either bears no concord, or the perfect chord.

The cypher which denotes each concord, is generally that which answers to the name of the concord; wherefore the concord of the second is cyphered by 2, the seventh by 7, and the sixth by 6, &c. &c. There are concords which bear a double name, and which are also expressed by a double cypher, such are the concords of sixth fourth, sixth fifth, of seventh and sixth, &c. Sometimes even three are placed, which occasions that inconvenience which we would wish to avoid, but as the composition of cyphers is derived from time and chance, rather than from reflecting study, it is not strange that it is not free from fault and contradictions.

I have composed a table of all the cyphers practised in the accompaniment, in which it must be observed, that there are many concords which are differently cyphered in different countries, or in the same country by different authors, and even sometimes by the same. I have given the various methods, so that every one may chuse what appears cleareſt to himself; for cyphering and occompanying, connect each cypher to the suitable concord, according to the method of the author's cyphering.

GENERAL TABLE

OF ALL THE

CYPHERS of the ACCOMPANIMENT.

N. B. An Asterisk as added to those which are most used at present in France.

Cyphers.	Names of Concords.
* . .	Perfect Concord.
8 . .	Idem.
5 . .	Idem.
3 . .	Idem.
5 3 } .	Idem.
3 ♭ .	Perfect Concord. Third Minor.
♭ 3 .	Idem.
* ♭ .	Idem.
5 ♭ } .	Idem.
3 ✕ .	Perfect Concord Major Third.
✕ 3 .	Idem.
* ✕ .	Idem.
5 ✕ } .	Idem.
3 ♮ .	Perfect Concord Natural Third.
♮ 3 .	Idem.
* ♮ .	Idem.
5 ♮ } .	Idem.
6 3 } . .	Concord of Sixth.
* 6 . .	Idem. The different Sixths in this Concord are marked accidentally with the Cypher, as the Thirds in the perfect Concord.
* 6 4 } .	Concord of Sixth Fourth
6 . .	Idem.
7 5 3 } .	Concord of Seventh.

Cyphers.	Names of Concords.
7 5	Idem.
7 3	Idem.
* 7	Idem.
* 7 ♯	Seventh with Major Third.
* 7 ♭	With minor Third.
* 7 ♮	With natural Third.
7♭	Concord of Minor Seventh.
*♭ 7	Idem.
7♯	Concord of Major Seventh.
*♯ 7	Idem.
7 ♮	Of natural Seventh.
*♮ 7	Idem.
* 7 5	Seventh with false Fifth.
7 5♭	Idem.
* 7̸	Diminished Seventh.
7 ♭	Idem.
♭ 7	Idem.
7♭ 5	Idem.
7♭ 5♭	Idem.
♭7 5	Idem.
♭7 ♭5	Idem.
7♭ 5♭ 3	Idem.
	&c.
*♯7	Superfluous Seventh.
7♯	Idem.
7	Idem.
7 2	Idem.

Cyphers.	Names of Concord.
7♯ 4 2	Idem.
♯7 5 4 2	Idem.
	&c.
7♯ 6♭	Superfluous Seventh, with minor Sixth.
*x7 ♭6	Idem.
x7 6♭ 2	Idem.
x 7 6 4	Idem.
	&c.
*7 2	Seventh and Second.
*6 5	Greater Sixth.
6	Idem.
*5	False Fifth.
5♭	Idem.
♭5	Idem.
6 ♭5	Idem.
6 5	Idem.
6̸ 5̸	False Fifth and major Sixth.
*x6 5̸	Idem.
x6 ♭5	Idem.
6♯ 5♭	Idem.
4 3	Smaller Sixth.
6 4 3	Idem.
*6̸	Idem.

Cyphers.	Names of Concords.
6	Idem.
x6̸	Idem major.
x6 4 3	Idem.
	&c.
*x6̸	Smaller superfluous Sixth.
x6 4 3	Idem.
x6	Idem.
x6 5 3	Idem with the Fifth.
x6 5	Idem.
6 4 3	Smaller Sixth, with superfluous Fourth.
6 x4 3	Idem.
6̸ *x4	Idem.
x4 3	Idem.
*2	Concord of the Second.
4 2	Idem.
6 2	Idem.
*5 2	Second and Fifth.
6 4	Triton.
6 4x	Idem.
6 x4	Idem.
6 4̸	Idem.

Cyphers.	Names of Concords.
6 4 2	Idem.
4 2	Idem.
4x 2	Idem.
x4 2	Idem.
4x	Idem.
*x4	Idem.
4̸	Idem.
4x 3♭	Triton with minor Third.
*4̸ ♭	Idem.
6 4 3♭	Idem.
*x4	Idem.
*x2	Superfluous Second.
x4 x2	Idem.
4̸ 7̸	Idem.
6 4 7̸	Idem.
	&c.
*9	Concord of the Ninth.
9 5	Idem.
9 3	Idem.
*9 7	Ninth with Seventh.
9 7 5	Idem.
*4	Fourth or Eleventh.
5 4	Idem.

Cyphers.	Names of Concords.	Cyphers.	Names of Concords.
*4 9	. Fourth and Ninth.	*x5 ♮4	. Superfluous Fifth and Fourth.
*4 7	. Seventh and Fourth.	5x 4♮	. Idem.
*x5	. Superfluous Fifth.	*7 6	. Seventh and Sixth.
5x	. Idem.	*9 6	. Ninth and Sixth.
x5 9	. Idem.		
x5 9 7	. Idem.		

End of the Table of Cyphers.

Some authors had introduced a custom of covering with a ſtroke, all the notes of the baſs which paſſed under the ſame concord: In this manner, the pleaſing cantatas of Monſ. Clerambault are cyphered, but this invention was of too much utility to continue; it ſhewed alſo, too clearly to the eye, all the ſyncopes of harmony. At preſent, when the ſame concord is ſuſtained on four different notes of the baſs, there are four different cyphers which they are obliged to bear, ſo that the accompaniſt, led into an error, is haſtening even to ſeek the concord which he has under his hand. But it is the faſhion in France to load the baſs with a confuſion of uſeleſs cyphers; every thing is cyphered, even to the moſt evident concords: and he who places the greateſt number of cyphers is reckoned the moſt ingenious. A baſs thus confuſed with trivial cyphers retards the accompaniſt, and often makes him neglect the neceſſary cyphers.

The author, I think, muſt ſuppoſe, that the accompaniſt knows the elements of accompaniment, that he knows how to place a ſixth on a mediant, a falſe fifth on a ſenſible note, a ſeventh on a dominant, &c. he ſhould not therefore cypher theſe evident concords, unleſs that it be neceſſary to announce a change of the tone. The cyphers are made only to determine the choice of the harmony in dubious caſes, or the choice of ſounds in the concords which ought not to be filled: otherwiſe it is very well to have cyphered baſſes for ſcholars only. Cyphers muſt ſhew them the application of the rules; as for the maſters, it is ſufficient to ſpecify the exceptions.

 Monſ.

Monſ. Rameau, in his Diſſertation on the different Methods of Accompaniment, has diſcovered a number of faults in the eſtabliſhed cyphers.—He has ſhewn, that they are too numerous, and, moreover, inſufficient, obſcure, and equivocal; that they multiply concords uſeleſſly, and that they diſcover no kind of union.

All theſe errors come from having been deſirous of connecting the cyphers to the arbitrary notes of the thorough baſs, inſtead of connecting them immediately to the fundamental harmony. The thorough baſs forms, without a doubt, a part of the harmony, but not the foundation: this harmony is independent of the notes of that baſs, and has its determined progreſs, to which the baſs itſelf ought to ſubject its direction. By making the concords and cyphers, which vary them from the notes of the baſs and their different directions, dependent, we ſhew only the combinations of the harmony inſtead of their baſs; we infinitely multiply the ſame number of fundamental concords, and oblige, in ſome reſpects, the accompaniſt to loſe ſight of the true harmonic ſucceſſion every inſtant.

After having made ſome excellent obſervations on the mechaniſm of the fingers in practiſing the accompaniment, M. Rameau propoſes ſubſtituting more ſimple cyphers in the place of ours, which render this accompaniment independent of the thorough baſs; ſo that, without any attention to this baſs, and even without ſeeing it, we could accompany on the cyphers alone with more preciſion than by the method eſtabliſhed with the concurrence of the baſs and cyphers.

All the cyphers invented by Monſ. Rameau denote two things. 1ſt. The fundamental harmony in perfect concords, which have no other neceſſary ſucceſſion, but which always conſtitute the tone. 2dly. The harmonic ſucceſſion determined by the regular direction of the fingers in the diſſonances.

All this is done by means of ſeven cyphers only. I. One letter of the gamut denotes the tone, the tonic, and its concord. If we paſs from a perfect concord to another, the tone is changed, a new letter is then made uſe of. II. To paſs from the tonic to a different concord, Monſ. Rameau admits but ſix methods, to each of which he aſſigns a particular character, that is to ſay,

1. An X for the ſenſible concord; for the diminiſhed ſeventh it is ſufficient to add a B flat under that X.

2. A 2 for the concord of the ſecond in the tonic.

3. A 7 for the concord of the ſeventh.

4. This abbreviation aj for the ſixth added.

5. Theſe two cyphers $\frac{4}{3}$ relative to this tonic for the concord

which

which he calls of third-fourth, and which answers to the concord of the ninth on the second note.

6. Lastly, this cypher 4 for the concord of fourth and fifth on the dominant.

III. A dissonant accord is followed by a perfect concord, or another dissonant accord: In the first case, the concord is specified by a letter; the second is applied to the mechanism of the fingers. 'Tis one, two, or three fingers which ought to descend diatonically.

This is shewn by as many points, one on the other, as the number of fingers which should descend. The diesis's or B's flat which should be made are known by the tone, or substituted in the cyphers correspondent to the points; or indeed, in the chromatic or harmonic they are specified by a small line inclining in its descent or ascent, after the sign of a known note, to denote that it should descend or rise a semitone. By this means the whole is foreseen, and this small number of signs is sufficient to express the finest harmony possible.

It is easily seen, that we must here suppose every dissonance to be prevented in descending; for if there were any which could be prevented in ascending, if there were ascendant directions of the fingers in dissonant accords, the points of M. Rameau could not answer their purpose.

How simple soever this method may be, how favourable soever for practice, it has had no success. It might perhaps be thought, that Mons. Rameau's cyphers, corrected one error only to substitute another; for if he simplifies the signs, and diminishes the number of concords, he not only does not express the true fundamental harmony, but, moreover, he makes those signs so much dependent on each other, that if we should chance to err or lose ourselves a moment, to take perhaps one finger for another, we are irrecoverably lost; the points are no longer significant, and there is more room for entering upon a fresh perfect concord. But with so many preferable reasons, should there not be other objections to cause M. Rameau's method to be rejected? It was new; it was proposed by a man whose abilities were superior to those of all his rivals: This was the cause of its condemnation.

D.

D. This letter in French music signifies the same thing as P in the Italian; that is to say, Sweet. The Italians use it also sometimes for the term dolce, and this word dolce is not only an opposition to forte, but to rude also.

D. C. Vide Da Capo.

D LA RE, D SOL RE, or simply D, The second note of the natural or diatonic gamut, which is indifferently called Re. (Vide Gamut.)

DA CAPO, These two Italian words are frequently found written at the end of airs in rondeau, sometimes at full length, and often abridged by these two letters D. C. They specify that when the second part of the air is finished, we must take up the beginning as far as the final point. Now and then we must not return to the beginning entirely, but to a specified place. In that case, instead of the words Da Capo, we find these written, Al Segno.

DACTYLIC, A name given in ancient music to that kind of rhyme whose measure was divided into two equal times. (Vide Rhyme.)

A kind of ode, wherein this rhyme was frequently used, was also stiled dactylic, such as the Harmathian and Orthian odes.

Julius Pollius seems to make a doubt whether the dactylic was a kind of instrument or an air, a doubt, which is however, confirmed by what Aristides Quintilian says of it in his second book; and which cannot be resolved but by supposing that the word dactylic signified, at the same time, an instrument and an air, as several words with us.

DECAMERIDES, The name of one of the elements in Mons. Sauveur's System, which may be seen in the Memoirs of the Academy of Sciences, A. D. 1701.

To form a general system, which might afford the best temperament, and be adjusted to every system, this author, after having divided the octave into 43 parts, which he calls merides, and sub-divided each mende into 7 parts called Eptamerides, divides again each eptameride into two other parts, to which he gives the name of decamerides. The octave is by this means divided into 3010 parts, by the which we may express, without any perceptible error, the connections of all the intervals in music.—This word is formed from δέκα, ten, and μέρις a part.

DASH, A term in church-music, denoting the psalm, or psalmody of a psalm, or some staves of the psalm, drawn and lengthened on a mournful air, substituted on some occasions in lieu

lieu of the joyous airs of the Hallelujah, &c. &c. An air with dashes should be composed in the second or eighth tone. The rest are not suitable to it.

DASH TRACTUS, Is also the name of an ancient figure of a note, called also Plica.

DECLAMATION, In music, is the art of rendering a grammatical and oratorical accent, by the inflexions and number of the melody. (Vide ACCENT, RECITATIVE.)

DEDUTTIONE, A collection of notes ascending diatonically, or by conjoint degrees. This term is in use only in church music.

DEGREE, The difference of position or elevation which is found between two notes placed in the same direction. On the same line, or in the same space, they are in the same degree, and they would be so still, though one of the two be raised or lowered a semi-tone by a diesis or B flat. On the contrary, they might be in unison, though placed on different degrees; as the ut B flat, and the si natural; the fa diesis, and the sol B flat, &c.

If two notes follow each other diatonically, so that one being on a line, the other is in the adjoining space, the interval is of one degree; of two, if they are in a third; of three, if in a fourth; of seven, if in the octave, &c.

Thus, by taking away one of the number expressed by the name of the interval, we always have the number of the diatonic degrees, which separate the two notes.

These diatonic degrees, or degrees simply, are also called conjoint degrees, in opposition to disjoint degrees, which are composed of many degrees conjoined. For instance, the interval of the second is a conjoin'd degree; but that of the third is disjoint, composed of two conjoint degrees; and in the same manner with the rest. (Vide CONJOINT, DISJOINT, INTERVAL.)

DEMI JEU, A DEMI JEU, or simply A DEMI, A term of instrumental music, which answers to the Italian sotto voce, or mezza voce, or mezzo forte, and which expresses a method of playing which holds a medium between the forte and dolce.

DEMI MEASURE, A space of time which equals the duration of a measure. There are properly demi-measures in those measures only whose times are in equal number; for in a three-timed measure, the first demi-measure begins with a tempo forte, and the second in contrary time, which renders them unequal.

DEMI MINIME REST, A character of music denoting a silence, the duration of which is equal to that of a demi-crotchet, or the half of a minime.

DEMI

DEMI PAUSE, A character of music, which expresses a silence, whose duration should be equal to that of a four timed demi-measure, or of a minum. As there are measures of different powers, and as that of the demi-pause has no variation, it is equal to the half of a measure, only when the entire measure is equal to a semi-breve, the difference of the entire pause excepted, which is always exactly equal to a measure, great or small. (Vide PAUSE.)

DEMI TIME, A power which is of exact duration with the half of a time. What I have said in regard to time, must be applied to the demi-time, when I spoke of the demi-measure in regard to measure.

DEMI TONE, An interval of music, nearly equal to the half of a tone, and which is more commonly stiled semi-tone. (Vide SEMI-TONE.)

TO DESCEND, Is to lower the voice *vocem remettere*, that is, to make the sounds succeed from sharp to flat, or from high to low. This is presented to the eye by our method of pricking the notes.

DESIGN, Is the invention and conduct of a subject, the disposition of each part, and the general direction of the whole.

It is not sufficient to compose beautiful airs and a pleasing harmony. All this must be conjoined by a principal subject, to which all the parts of the work must be connected, and by which it may become one. Thus unity should reign in every air, in the movement, the character, the harmony, and modulation. The whole must have reference to one general idea, which unites it. The difficulty is to unite these precepts with an elegant variety, without which, the whole becomes fatiguing. Doubtless, the musician, as well as the poet and painter, dares every thing in favour of this charming variety, provided, that under pretext of contrasting, we have not, for a well conducted work, some broken, murdered music given us, composed of shattered pieces, the connection of which make a complete opposition ——

Non ut placidis coeant immitia, non ut
Serpentes avibus geminentur, tigribus agni.——

'Tis therefore in a well extended distribution, in a just proportion between all the parts, that the perfection of the design consists; and 'tis particularly in this point, that the immortal Pergolesis has discovered his judgment, taste, and left all his rivals at such a distance behind him.—His Stabat Mater, his Orpheus, his Serva Padrona, in three different kinds, are three complete Chef d'Oeuvres, equally excellent in their design.

This idea of the general design of a work is also separately applied to each part, which composes it. So we design an air,

a

a duo, trio, &c. &c. For this purpoſe, after having fixed on a ſubject, we lay it out, according to the rules of a good modulation, into every part wherein it ſhould be extended, with ſo exact a proportion, as not to be effaced from the mind of the audience, and ſtill never to preſent itſelf to their ear, but with all the graceful beauties of novelty. 'Tis a fault in the deſign to ſuffer the ſubject to be forgotten, and a much greater to continue it till it becomes diſguſting.

TO DESIGN, To form the deſign of a piece or an air in muſic. (Vide DESIGN.) "Such a compoſer deſigns his works ill." "This choir is ſhockingly deſigned."

DESCANT, An ancient term, by which was ſpecified what has been ſince called counter point. (Vide COUNTER POINT.)

DESK, A ſtructure in the choir, on which were placed the muſic books in the catholic churches.

DETACHED, uſed ſubſtantively, A kind of execution, by which, inſtead of ſuſtaining the notes in the duration of their whole powers, we ſeparate them by ſilences taken on the ſame powers. The *Detatched*, entirely dry and ſhort, is marked on the notes by lengthened points.

DIACOMMATIC, A name given by Monſ. Serre to a kind of fourth genus, which conſiſts in certain harmonic tranſitions, by which the ſame note continuing apparently on the ſame degree, aſcends or falls a comma in paſſing from one concord to another, with which we ſeem to form an union.

For inſtance, on this paſſage of the baſs $\overset{32}{\text{fa}}$ $\overset{27}{\text{re}}$ in the major mode of ut, the $\overset{80}{\text{la}}$, major third of the firſt note, remains to become the fifth of re; moreover the true fifth of $\overset{27}{\text{re}}$ or of $\overset{54}{\text{re}}$ is not $\overset{80}{\text{la}}$ but $\overset{81}{\text{la}}$: wherefore the muſician who tunes the la ſhould naturally give it the two conſecutive intonations $\overset{80}{\text{la}}$ $\overset{81}{\text{la}}$, which differ by a comma.

In the ſame manner, in an air called la Folie d'Eſpagne, in the third time of the third meaſure, one muſt imagine that the tonic $\overset{80}{\text{re}}$ aſcends a comma to form the ſecond $\overset{81}{\text{re}}$ of the major mode of ut, which is explained in the following meaſure, and is found ſuddenly conducted by this muſical paralogiſm, and double uſe of the re.

We muſt obſerve, that to paſs briſkly from the minor mode of la to that of ut major, the concord of diminiſhed ſeventh is changed ſol dieſis, ſi, re, fa, into the concord of the ſimple ſeventh, ſol, ſi, re, fa. The chromatic movement of the ſol dieſis in oppoſition to the natural ſol, is much the moſt ſenſible, but that is not the only one. The re ascends also by a diacommatic movement from $\overset{80}{\text{re}}$ to $\overset{81}{\text{re}}$, tho' the notes supposes it permanent on the same degree.

We may find a great number of examples of this diacommatic genus, particularly when the modulation passes suddenly from the major to the minor, or the minor to the major: It is chiefly in the adages, adds Monf. Serre, that excellent masters, tho' principally guided by sentiment, make use of this kind of transition, so necessary to give the modulation an appearance of indecision, whose effects the ear and sentiment often approve, as they are by no means equivocal.

DIACOUSTIC, Is a search for the proprieties of a sound, broken by passing across different middles, i. e. from a condense to a more rarified, and so vice versa. As visual rays direct more easily than sounds by lines on certain points, so the experience of the diacoustic is infinitely more difficult than that of the dioptric.

This word is formed from the Greek διὰ through, & ἀκούω, to hear. (Vide Sound.)

DIAGRAM, This was, in the ancient music, the table or model which presented to the eye a general extent of all the sounds of a system, and what we call at present Scale, Gamut, Keys. (Vide those words.)

DIALOGUE, A composition for two voices or instruments, which answer to each other, and often reunite. The greatest part of scenes in an opera, are in this sense dialogues, and the Italian duo's are so always; but this word is more particularly applied to the organ. 'Tis on this instrument that an organist plays dialogues, by answering in different tunes, or on different keys.

DIAPASON, A term in ancient music, by which the Greeks expressed the interval or consonance of the octave. (Vide Octave.)

The musical instrument-makers call, at present, diapasons, certain tables, wherein are marked the measures of these instruments, and of all their parts.

We call also diapason, a suitable extent for a voice or an instrument. Wherefore when a voice is raised to a great height, we say, that it goes out of the diapason; and we say the same of an instrument, whose chords are too loose or too tight, which render but a little sound, or a sound very disagreeable, because its tone is either too high or too low.

This word is formed from διὰ through, and πᾶσων, all, because the octave comprehends all the notes of the perfect system.

DIAPENTE, A name given by the Greeks to the interval which

which we now call Fifth, and which is the ſecond of the conſonances. (Vide CONSONANCE, INTERVAL, FIFTH.)

This word is formed from διὰ, by and πέντε, five, becauſe by going through this interval diatonically, we find five different ſounds pronounced.

DIAPENTISSARE, A barbarous word uſed by Muris, and other ancient muſicians.

It was a method of proceeding in the deſcant or counter-point, by fifths rather than fourths. Muris diſſerts extenſively on the proper art, and convenient rules for this branch.

DIAPHONY, A name given by the Greeks to every interval or diſſonance, becauſe the two ſounds contradicting each other mutually, are divided, and make their difference appear very diſagreeably.

Guy Aretin gives alſo the name of diaphony to what has been ſince called deſcant, on account of the two parts which are therein diſtinguiſhed.

DIAPTOSE, An inter-cadence or leſſer fall. 'Tis in church-muſic a kind of Perielesis, or paſſage, which is formed on the laſt note of an air, generally after a greater interval in aſcending. In that caſe, to certify the juſtneſs of this finale, it is twice marked, by ſeparating that repetition by a third note, which is lowered by a degree, after the method of a ſenſible note, as ut ſi ut, or mi re mi.

DIASCHISMA, Is, in ancient muſic, an interval forming the half of a minor ſemi-tone. The reference is from 24 to $\sqrt[2]{600}$, and conſequently irrational.

DIASTEME, This word, in ancient muſic, ſignifies properly interval, and is the name given by the Greeks to the ſimple interval, in oppoſition to the compounded interval, which is called ſyſtem. (Vide INTERVAL, SYSTEM.)

DIATESSARON, A name given by the Greeks to the interval which we call Fourth, and which is the Third of the conſonances. (Vide CONSONANCE, INTERVAL, FOURTH.)

DIATESSERONARE, Was, amongſt our ancient muſicians, a method of proceeding in the deſcant or counterpoint, rather by fourths than fifths.

The word is compounded of διὰ, by, and τέσσαρες, four, becauſe in going diatonically over the interval, we pronounce four different ſounds.

DIATONIC, The diatonic genus is that of the three which proceeds by major tones and ſemi-tones, according to the natural diviſion of the gamut; that is, that whoſe leaſt interval is of a conjoint degree, which does not prevent the parts from proceeding by greater intervals, provided they are all taken on diatonic degrees.

This word is derived from the Greek διὰ, by, and τόνος, the tone; that is, passing from one tone to another.

The diatonic genus of the Greeks resulted from one of the three principal rules which were established for the concordance of the tetrachords.—This genus was divided into many different kinds, according to the different connections, into which the interval could be divided which determined them, as this interval could not be confined below a certain point without changing its genus. These different variations from the same genus were called χρόαι colours, by Ptolemy. who distinguishes six of them, but the only one used in practice, was that called diatonic-ditonic, whose tetrachord was composed of a weak semitone, and of two major tones. Aristoxenes divides this same genus into only two kinds, viz. the tender or flat diatonic, and the systonic or sharp. This latter answers to the ditonic of Ptolemy. (Vide The Connections of one with the other.)

According to Aristoxenes.
The tetrachord being supposed divided into 60 equal parts.

D I A T O N I C.

Tender or Flat — $12 + 18 + 30 = 60.$
Syntonic or Sharp — $12 + 24 + 24 = 60.$

C H R O M A T I C.

Flat — $8 + 8 + 44 = 60.$
Hemiolian $9 + 9 + 42 = 60.$
Tonic — $12 + 12 + 36 = 60.$

E N H A R M O N I C.

$6 + 6 + 48 = 60.$

According to Ptolemy.
The tetrachord being represented by the reference of its two terms.

D I A T O N I C.

Ditonic $\frac{256}{243} + \frac{9}{8} + \frac{9}{8} = \frac{4}{3}$

C H R O M A T I C.

Flat — $\frac{28}{27} + \frac{15}{14} + \frac{6}{5} = \frac{4}{3}$

Intense, or, Syntonic $\frac{22}{21} + \frac{12}{11} + \frac{7}{6} = \frac{4}{3}$

E N H A R M O N I C.

$\frac{45}{45} + \frac{24}{23} + \frac{5}{4} = \frac{4}{5}$

The

The modern diatonic genus results from the consonant direction of the bass on the chords of a similar mode.

Fundamental and regular Bass of the Scale diatonically ascending by the natural Succession of the *three Cadences*.

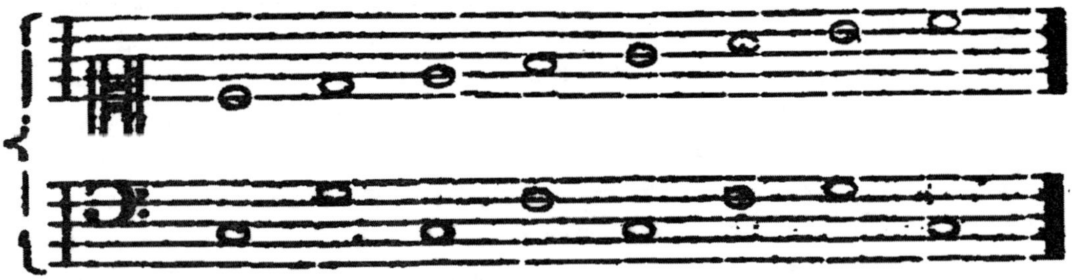

Its references have been fixed by the use of the same chords in different tones, so that, if the harmony has at first lain down the diatonic scale, 'tis the modulation which has modified it, and this scale, such as it is at present, is neither exact in regard to the air, or harmony, but only in regard to the method of employing the same sounds in different uses.

The diatonic genus is, without contradiction, the most natural of the three, since it is the only one which can be used without varying the tone. Its intonation also is incomparably more easy than that of the two others; and there is no doubt but that the first songs were composed in this kind; but we must observe, that, according to the laws of modulation, which permit and prescribes even the passage from one tone to another, we have no pure diatonic in our music. Each particular tone, I will allow, in the diatonic, is good; but we cannot pass from one to the other without some chromatic transition, at least, an omission of the harmony. The pure diatonic, in which no one of the sounds is altered, either by the cleff or accidentally, is called, by Zarlin, diatono diatonic, and he gives the church-music as an example. If the cleff is numbered with a B flat, in that case, according to him, it is a flat diatonic, which must not be confounded with that of Aristoxenes. (Vide Flat.) In regard to the transposition by diesis, this author speaks nothing of it, as it had not been practised in his time. Doubtless he would have given it the name of rough or sharp diatonic, tho' there had even resulted from it a minor mode, as that of E la mi, for in those times, when they had not the harmonic ideas of what we call tones and modes, and where they had already lost the other significations which the ancients fixed to the same words, they paid a greater attention to the particular alterations of the notes than to the general connection which resulted from it. (Vide Transposition.)

DIATONIC SOUNDS or CHORDS. Euclid diſtinguiſhes under this name, amongſt the moveable ſounds, thoſe which do not partake of the greater genus, even in the chromatic and enharmonic. Theſe ſounds in each kind are five in number, i. e. the third of each tetrachord; and they are the ſame which other authors call apycni. (Vide APYCNI, GENUS, TETRACHORD.)

DIAZEUXIS, A Greek word which ſignifies diviſion, ſeparation, disjunction. 'Tis by this term that the tone which ſeparated two tetrachords disjoined, was called in ancient muſic, and which being added to one of the two, formed from it the diapente. It is our major tone, whoſe reference is from 8 to 9, and which in effect is the difference of the fifth and fourth.

The diazeuxis in their muſic was placed between the meſis and parameſis, that is to ſay, between the ſharpeſt tone of the ſecond tetrachord, and the flatteſt of the third, or otherwiſe between the note ſynnemenon, and the parameſis hyperboleon, i. e. between the third and fourth tetrachord, provided that the disjunction was formed in the one or the other, for it could not be practiſed at once in the two

The homologous chords of the two tetrachords, between which there was a diazeuxis, ſounded the fifth, whereas they ſounded in fourth when they were conjoined.

DIESIS, Is, according to old Bacchius, the ſmalleſt interval of the ancient muſic. Zarlin ſays, that Philolaus, the Pythagorean, gave the name of dieſis to the limma; but he adds, a little farther, that the dieſis of Pythagoras is the difference between the limma and apotome. As to Ariſtoxenes, he divided the ton into two equal parts, without many variations, or in three or four. From this laſt diviſion reſulted the dieſis, enharmonic minor, or fourth of a tone; from the ſecond, the minor chromatic dieſis or third of a tone; and from the third, the major dieſis, which made exactly a demi-tone.

DIESIS, Amongſt the moderns, is not properly, as amongſt the ancients, an interval of muſic, but a ſign of that interval which ſpecifies that we muſt raiſe the ſound of the note, before which it is placed, above that which it ought naturally to have, without, however, making its degree or name undergo a change. Moreover, as this elevation may be made, at leaſt, three ways in the eſtabliſhed genera, ſo there are three ſorts of dieſis', viz.

Firſt, The enharmonic minor, or ſimple dieſis, whoſe form is like St. Andrews's Croſs, according to all our muſicians, who follow the practice of Ariſtoxenes, it raiſes the note the fourth of a tone; but properly it was only the exceſs of the ſemi-tone major on the ſemi-tone minor. Wherefore from the natural

natural mi to the fa B flat, there is an enharmonic diesis, whose numerical powers are from 125 to 128.

Secondly, The chromatic diesis, double or ordinary diesis, marked by a double cross, raises the note a semi-tone minor. This interval is equal to that of the B flat, i. e. the difference of the major to the minor semi-tone; wherefore, to ascend from a tone beyond the natural mi, we must pass to the fa diesis. The reference of this diesis is from 24 to 25. (Vide on this article an essential remark at the word semi-tone.)

Thirdly, The enharmonic major, or triple diesis, marked by a triple cross, raises, according to the Aristoxenians, the note about three fourths of a tone. Zarlin says, that it raises it a semi-tone minor, which cannot be understood of, our semi-tone, since in that case, this diesis would be exactly similar to our chromatic diesis.

Of these three diesis', whose intervals were all practised in ancient music, there is only the chromatic which is used in ours; the intonation of the inharmonic diesis' being to us an almost insurmountable difficulty, and the use of them being also abolished by our system.

The diesis, as well as the B flat, is always placed on the left, before the note which ought to bear it; and before or after a cypher, it signifies the same thing as before a note. (Vide CYPHERS.) The diesis' which are intermixt with the cyphers of the thorough bass, are often no more than simple crosses, as the enharmonic diesis: but this cannot cause an equivocation, since it is no longer in use.

There are two methods of making use of the diesis. The one, accidental, when, in the course of the air, we place it on the left of a note. This note, in the major modes, is most generally found the fourth of the tone: In the minor modes, two accidental diesis' are most commonly necessary, particularly in ascending, i. e. one on the sixth note, and another on the seventh. The accidental diesis changes only the note which immediately follows, or, at the most, those which in the same measure are placed on the same degree, and sometimes in the octave, without any contrary sign.

The other method is to make use of the diesis in the cleff, and in that case it is carried thro' the whole continuance of the air, and on all the notes which are placed on the same degree, whereon is the diesis, unless it is opposed by some B flat, or sharp, or that the cleff has no changes.

The position of the diesis' in the cleff is by no means arbitrary, no more than that of the B's flat; otherwise, the two semi-tones of the octave would be subject to be found together out of the prescribed intervals. We must then apply to the diesis' a similar reasoning to that which we have made at the article B flat, and it will be found that the order of the diesis' which is suitable to the cleff, is that of the following notes, beginning by fa, and ascending successively by fifths, or descending by fourths as far as the la, at which we generally stop, because the diesis of mi which would follow, does not differ at all from the fa on our scale.

Order of Diesis' on the Cleff.

Fa, Ut, Sol, Re, La, &c. &c.

We must take notice, that a diesis cannot be used in the cleff without using also those which precede it; wherefore, the diesis of ut is placed only with that of fa; that of sol with the two preceding, &c. &c.

I have given, at the article Transposed cleff, a formula to find immediately if a tone or mode ought to bear diesis' in the cleff, and how many.

Such is the acceptation of the word diesis, and its use, in practice.

The most ancient manuscript, wherein I have seen the sign used, is that of Jean de Muris, which makes me imagine it might have been his invention. But it appears, in his examples, to have only the effect of B sharp; and this author also gives the name of diesis always to the major semi-tone.

In harmonic calculations, we call diesis' certain intervals, greater than a comma, and less than a semi-tone, which make the difference of other intervals engendered by the progressions and references of the consonances. There are three of these diesis'. First, The major diesis, which is the difference between the major and minor semi-tone, and whose numerical powers are from 125 to 128. Secondly, The minor diesis, which is the difference between the semi-tone minor and major diesis, and in reference 3072 to 3125. Thirdly, The diesis maxima, in numerical powers from 243 to 450, which is the difference of the minor tone and greater semi-tone.

It must be confessed, that so many different acceptations of the same word in the same art, are only a cause of frequent equivocations, and produce a continual confusion of errors.

DIEZEUGMENON, A tetrachord diezeugmenon is the name which the Greeks gave their third tetrachord, when it was disjoined from the second. (Vide TETRACHORD.)

DIMINISH'D,

DIMINISH'D, A diminiſh'd interval is every minor interval, from which a ſemitone is taken by a dieſis to the inferior note, or by a B flat to the ſuperior. In regard to the juſt intervals, formed by perfect conſonances, when they are diminiſh'd a ſemitone, they ought not to be called diminiſh'd, but falſe; tho' it is often ſaid, mal-a-propos, a diminiſh'd fourth, inſtead of ſaying falſe fourth; and diminiſh'd octave, inſtead of ſaying falſe octave.

DIMINUTION, An old word, which ſignified the diviſion of a long note, as a minum, or crotchet, into many other ſmaller notes of leſſer powers. It was alſo underſtood, that this word expreſſed thoſe terms which we call by the denomination of trills or quavers. (Vide thoſe words.)

DIOXY, Is, with reference to Nicomachus, a name which the ancients gave ſometimes to the conſonance of the fifth, which they more generally called diapente. (Vide DIAPENTE.)

DIRECT, A direct interval is that which forms any kind of harmony on the fundamental ſound which produces it. Wherefore, the fifth, major third, and the octave, with their redditives, are rigorouſly the only direct intervals; but by extenſion, we call alſo direct intervals all the reſt, as well conſonant as diſſonant, which each part forms with the practiſed fundamental ſound, which ought to be below it. Wherefore, the minor interval is a direct interval on a concord in third minor, and in the ſame manner the ſeventh or ſixth added on the concord which bear their name.

A direct concord is that which has the fundamental ſound in ſharp, and whoſe parts are diſtributed, not according to the moſt natural order, but according to the moſt confined. Wherefore, the perfect direct concord is not octave, fifth, and third, but third, fifth, and octave.

DISCANT, This was, in our muſic, that kind of counterpoint which the ſuperior parts compos'd inſtantly, in ſinging extempore on the tenor or baſs, which forms ſome idea of the ſlowneſs with which the muſic ſhould be directed, to be executed in that manner by muſicians, as little ſkilful as thoſe of that time. "Diſcantant," ſays Jean de Muris, "qui ſimul cum "uno vel pluribus dulciter cantat, ut ex diſtinctis ſonis ſonus "unus fiat, non unitate ſimplicitatis, ſed dulcis concordiſque "mixtionis unione." After having explained what he means by conſonances, and the choice which is neceſſary to make between them, he finds fault ſharply with the ſingers of his time, who practiſed them almoſt indifferently. "With what audacity," ſays he, "if our rules are good, do thoſe dare compoſe "the diſcant, which have not the leaſt comprehenſion of the

" choice of concords, not the least mistrust of those which are " more or less concordant; who neither know from which they " should abstain, nor which they should most frequently use; " neither in what place to employ them, nor any thing which " the practice of an art well understood requires? If they suc- " ceed, it is by chance. Their voices wander without rule on " the tenor, with which they are concordant, if fortune stands " their friend. They throw out their sounds at hazard, as a " stone which an awkward hand aims at a mark, and which in " an hundred times may hit it perhaps once."

The good old Muris touches also these corrupters of pure and simple harmony, in which his age abounded equally with ours. —Heu, proh dolor! His temporibus aliqui suum defectum inepto proverbio colorare moliuntur. Iste est, inquiunt novus discantandi modus, novis scilicet uti consonantiis. Offendunt ii intellectum eorum, qui tales defectus agnoscunt, offendunt sensum, nam inducere cum deberent delectationem, adducunt tristitiam. O incongruum proverbium! O mala coloratio! Irrationabilis excusatio! O magnus abusus, magna ruditas, magna bestialitas, ut asinus sumatur pro homine, capra pro leone, ovis pro pisce, serpens pro salmone! Sic enim concordiæ confunduntur cum discordiis ut nullatenus una distinguatur ab alia. O si antiqui periti musicæ doctores tales audissent discantatores, quid dixissent? Quid fecissent? Sic discantantem in creparent & dicerent. Non hunc discantum, quo uteris, de me sumis. Nom tuum cantum unum & concordantem cum me facis. De quo te intromittis? Mihi non congruis, mihi adversarius, scandalum tu mihi es: O utinam taceres! Non concordas, sed deliras & discordas.

DISCORDANT, By this term is called every instrument which is played on and is not in concord, every voice which sings false, every part which is not concordant with the rest. An intonation which is not just, forms a false tone. A continuance of a whole false, forms a discordant air. This is the difference between these two words.

DISDIAPASON, A name given by the Greeks to the interval which we call double octave.

The disdiapason is nearly of the greatest extent which the human voice can arrive at without forcing itself. There are even very few who can sound it fully. It is for this reason that the Greeks bounded each of their modes by this extent, and gave it the name of a perfect system. (Vide MODE, GENUS, SYSTEM.)

DISJOINT, The Greeks gave the relative name of disjoint to two tetrachords, which immediately followed each other, whilst the deepest chord of the sharp was a tone above the sharpest

ſharpeſt of the flat, inſtead of being ſimilar to it. Wherefore, the two tetrachords, hypaton and diazeugmenon, were disjoint; and the two, ſynnemenon and hyperbolean, were ſo alſo. (Vide TETRACHORD.)

Among us, the name of disjoint is given to the intervals which do not follow each other immediately, but are ſeparated by another interval: wherefore theſe two intervals ut mi and ſol ſi are disjoint. The degrees which are not conjoint, but which are compos'd of two or more conjoint degrees, are alſo called diſjoint degrees. Therefore each of theſe two intervals, of which I have ſpoken, forms a disjoint degree.

DISJUNCTION, Was, in ancient muſic, the ſpace which ſeparated the meſis and parameſis, or in general a tetrachord from one adjoining, when they were not conjoint. This ſpace was a tone, and was called in Greek diazeuxis.

DISSONANCE, Every ſound, which with another forms a concord diſagreeable to the ear, or in a more extenſive ſenſe, every interval which is not conſonant. Moreover, as there are no other conſonances, but which form between themſelves, and with the fundamental, the ſounds of the perfect concord, it follows thence, that every other interval is its true diſſonance. The ancients even counted as ſuch, the thirds and ſixths, which they cut off from the conſonant accords.

The term diſſonance is derived from two words, the one Greek, the other Latin, which ſignify a double ſound. In effect, what renders the diſſonance diſagreeable, is, that the ſounds which form it, far from uniting themſelves to the ear, ſtrike againſt each other, and are heard as two diſtinct ſounds, tho' ſtruck at the ſame time.

The name of interval is given ſometimes to the interval, and ſometimes to each of the two ſounds which form it. But tho' two ſounds are diſſonant between themſelves, the name of diſſonance is given more eſpecially to that of the two which is moſt remote from the concord.

There are an infinity of poſſible diſſonances: but as in muſic all the intervals are excluded, which the received ſyſtem does not furniſh, theſe are reduced to a ſmall number; alſo for practice, we ought to chooſe amongſt thoſe, only thoſe which anſwer to the genus and mode; and laſtly, to exclude from the laſt thoſe which cannot be uſed according to preſcribed rules. What are thoſe rules? Have they any natural foundation, or are they purely arbitrary? This is what I propoſe to examine in this article.

The phyſical principle of harmony is drawn from the production of the perfect concord, by the reſonance of any ſound.

All the consonances arise from thence, and it is nature itself which furnishes them. The dissonance proceeds on a different plan, at least, such as we practice.

We allowedly find its generation in the progressions of consonant intervals, and in their differences, but we cannot discover any physical reason which authorises us to introduce it in the body itself of harmony. P. Mersenne contents himself with shewing the generation by calculation, and the different connections of dissonances, as well of those which are rejected, as of those added; but he mentions nothing of the laws for using them. Mons. Rameau says in formal terms, that the dissonance is not natural to harmony, and that it cannot be used therein without the assistance of art. However, in another work, he endeavours to find its principle by numerical powers, and harmonic and arithmetical proportions, as if there were any identity between the proprieties of the abstracted quantity, and the sensations of hearing.

But after having wasted a quantity of analogies, after a number of metamorphoses of these different proportions, the one within the other, after numerous operations, and useless calculations, he finishes, by establishing, on trifling connections, that dissonance which he gave himself such unwearied pains only to discover. Wherefore, because in the order of harmonic sounds, the arithmetical proportion gives it by the lengths of the chords, a minor third in flat, (take notice that it gives it to the sharp by the calculation of vibrations) he adds to the flat of the subdominant a new minor third. The harmonic proportion gives it a minor third in sharp, (it would give it to the flat by vibrations) and he adds to the sharp of the dominant a fresh minor third. These thirds added, do not, it is true, form any proportion with the preceding references: the references, which themselves ought to have, are often changed; but that signifies little: Mons. Rameau gives powers to every thing for the best. The proportion serves it to introduce the dissonance, and the errors of the proportion to make it felt

The illustrious geometrician, who has deigned to make the world acquainted with Mons. Rameau's system, having suppressed all these vain calculations, I shall follow his example, or will rather transcribe what he says concerning the dissonance; and Mons. Rameau will be indebted to me for having drawn this explanation from the elements of music, rather than from *his* writings.

It being supposed, that the essential chords of the tone, according to Mons. Rameau's system, are known, viz. in the tone of ut, the tonic ut, the dominant sol, and the sub-dominant fa, we muſt alſo be acquainted, that this ſame tone of ut has the two chords ut and ſol common with the tone of ſol; and the two chords ut and fa, common with the tone of fa. Conſequently this direction of the baſs ut ſol may belong to the tone of ut, or to that of ſol; as the direction of the baſs fa ut, or ut fa, may appertain to the tone of ut, or to that of fa.

In that caſe, when we paſs from ut to fa, or to ſol, in a fundamental baſs, we are ſtill ignorant in what tone we are. It would be however ſerviceable to know it, and be able, by ſome method, to diſtingniſh the generator from its fifths.

We may gain this advantage by joining together the ſounds ſol and fa, in the ſame harmony, i. e. by joining to the harmony ſol ſi re of the fifth ſol, the other fifth fa, in this manner, ſol, ſi, re, fa; this fa added, being the ſeventh of ſol, forms a diſſonance; 'tis for that cauſe, that the concord ſol ſi re fa is called diſſonant concord, or concord of the ſeventh. It ſerves to diſtinguiſh the fifth ſol from the generator ut, which always bears, without mixture or alteration, the perfect concord ut mi ſol ut, given by nature herſelf. (Vide CONCORD, CONSONANCE, HARMONY.)

By this means, we ſee that when we paſs from ut to ſol, we paſs at the ſame time from ut to fa, becauſe the fa becomes, by this means, entirely determined, becauſe there is but this tone, to which the ſounds ſol and fa belong at the ſame time.

Let us now ſee continues, Monſ. D'Alembert, what we ſhould add to the harmony fa la ut, from the fifth fa, below the generator, to diſtinguiſh this harmony from that of the ſame generator. It ſeems then, that we ſhould add to it the other fifth ſol, for the purpoſe that the generator ut paſſing to fa, may paſs at the ſame time to ſol, and that the tone may be thereby determined; but this introduction of ſol in the concord of fa la ut would give two ſeconds following each other fa ſol, ſol la, that is to ſay, two diſſonances whoſe union would be too agreeable to the ear; an inconvenience which muſt be avoided; for if, to diſtinguiſh the tone, we alter the harmony of this fifth fa, we muſt alter it as little as poſſible. For this reaſon, inſtead of ſol, we will take its fifth re, which is the ſound neareſt to it, and we ſhall have for the ſub-dominant fa, the concord fa la ut re, which we call concord of greater ſixth, or ſixth added.

We may take notice here of the analogy which is obſerved between the concord of the dominant ſol, and that of the ſub-dominant fa. The dominant ſol, by aſcending above the generator, has a concord entirely compoſed of thirds in aſcending beyond ſol, ſol ſi re fa.

Moreover, the ſub-dominant fa, being below the generator ut, we ſhall find, in deſcending by ut towards fa, by thirds, ut la fa re, which contains the ſame ſounds as the concord fa la ut re gives to the ſub-dominant fa.

We moreover ſee, that the alteration of the harmony of the two fifths, conſiſts only in the minor third re fa, or fa re, added on each ſide to the harmony of theſe two fifths.

This explanation is ſo much the more ingenious, as it ſhews at once the origin, uſe, direction of the diſſonance, its neareſt connection with the tone, and the method of determining reciprocally the one by the other. The fault that I find in it, but an eſſential fault for making the whole glide, is the uſe of a chord unknown to the tone, as the eſſential chord of the tone; and this, by a falſe analogy, ſerving as a baſs to Monſ. Rameau's ſyſtem, deſtroys it, by rendering itſelf erroneous.

I ſpeak of that fifth below the tonic, of that ſub-dominant, between which and the tonic, there cannot be perceived the ſmalleſt union, which can authorize the uſe of this ſub-dominant, not only as an eſſential chord of the tone, but even in any ſenſe. In effect, what is there common between the reſonance, the ſhaking of the uniſon of ut, and the ſound of its fifth below? 'Tis by no means becauſe the entire chord is a fa, that its aliquots reſound at the ſound of ut, but becauſe it is a multiple of the chord ut; and there is no multiple of this ſame ut, which does not render a ſimilar phœnomenon. Take the ſeptuple, it will ſhake and reſound in its parts as well as the triple: Can it be ſaid, that the ſound of this ſeptuple, or its octaves, are the eſſential chords of the tone? Enough is ſaid, ſince it does not even form a commenſurable connection in notes with the tonic.

I know that Monſ. Rameau has pretended, that at the ſound of any chord, another chord in its twelfth below ſhook without reſounding; but, beſides its being a ſtrange phœnomenon in the acouſtic, that a ſonorous chord which ſhakes, does not reſound, it is however known, that this pretended experience is an error, that the ſharp chord ſhakes becauſe it divides itſelf, and that it appears not to reſound, becauſe it forms in its parts only the uniſon of the ſharp, which is not eaſily diſtinguiſhed.

Let Monſ. Rameau then tell us, that he takes the fifth below, becauſe he finds the fifth above; and that this playing with fifths appears to him convenient for the eſtabliſhment of his ſyſtem: We may congratulate him on his invention ſo very ingenious, but let him not authorize it with a chimerical experience; let him not torment himſelf to find, in the variations of harmonic and

and arithmetical proportions, the foundations of harmony, nor take the propriety of numbers for that of ſounds.

Take notice alſo, that if the counter-generation, which he ſuppoſes could have a place therein, the concord of the ſub-dominant fa, ſhould not, by any means, bear a major third, but a minor: becauſe the la Bemol is the true harmonic, which is

1 $\frac{1}{3}$ $\frac{1}{5}$

aſſigned to it by this change ut fa la b. So that according to this computation, the gamut of the major mode ought naturally to have the minor ſixth; but it has the major, as fourth fifth, or as fifth of the ſecond note, wherefore here is a ſecond contradiction.

Laſtly, take notice, that the fourth note given by the ſeries of aliquots, from whence ariſes the true natural diatonic, is by no means the octave of the pretended ſub-dominant, in the reference of 4 to 3, but another fourth note entirely different in the reference of 11 and 8, ſo that every theorician muſt perceive it clearly at firſt ſight.

I, however, appeal to the ear and experience of muſicians.—Let them but liſten to the rough and diſagreeable cadence imperfect of the ſub-dominant to the tonic, when compared with the ſelf-ſame cadence, in its natural place, which is from the tonic to the dominant. In the firſt caſe, can it be ſaid that the ear is ſatisfied after the concord of the tonic? Is it not in expectation of a continuance, or concluſion, at the time it really has it? Moreover, what is a tonic, after the which, the ear ſtill remains unſatisfied? Can it be looked on as a true tonic, and are we not in reality in the tone of fa, while we imagine ourſelves to be in that of ut? Let it be obſerved, how greatly the intonation of the fourth and the ſenſible note, as well aſcending as deſcending, appears ſtrange to the mode, and difficult to the voice. Tho' long cuſtom may have accuſtomed the ear and voice of the muſician to it, the difficulty of beginners to ſound this note ought to ſhew how very unnatural it is. This difficulty is attributed to the three conſecutive tones. Ought it not to be ſeen, that thoſe three conſecutive tones, as well as the note which introduces them, give a barbarous modulation, which has no foundation in nature? She certainly beſtowed a better guidance on the Greeks when ſhe made them finiſh their tetrachord preciſely at the mi of our ſcale, that is to ſay, at the note which precedes this fourth: They choſe rather to take this fourth below, and, by this means, they found by the ear alone. what all our harmonic theory has not rendered perceptible.

If the testimony of the ear, and that of reason unite, at least in the system given, to reject the pretended sub-dominant, not only from the number of essential chords of the tone, but also from the number of sounds which may enter into the scale of the mode, what becomes of all this theory of dissonances? What of the explanation of the minor mode? and of the whole of Monf. Rameau's system?

Not being therefore able to perceive, either in physic or calculation, the real generation of the dissonance, I sought for it, an origin, purely mechanic; and 'tis in the following manner that I endeavoured to explain it in the encyclopœdia, without absenting myself from Monf. Rameau's practical system.

I suppose the necessity of the known dissonance. (Vide HARMONY, CADENCE.)

It now remains to see where that dissonance should be taken, and how used.

If we compare successively all the sounds of the diatonic scale with the fundamental sound in each of the two modes, we shall find for a complete dissonance the second, and the seventh, which is no more than a varied second, and which really forms a second with the octave. That the seventh should be varied from the second, and not the second from the seventh, is evident by the expression of the references, for that of the second 8. 9. being more simple than that of the seventh 9. 16. the interval which it represents, consequently is not the generated, but the generator.

I allow that other altered intervals may become dissonant, but unless it is therein expressed or understood, they are only accidents in the modulation, to which the harmony pays no respect, and these dissonances, in that case, are not treated as such. Wherefore, it is a certain thing, that where there is no second, there is no dissonance; and the second is properly the only dissonance that can be used.

To reduce all these consonances to their smallest space, we need not go out of the octave; they are all therein contained in the perfect concord. Let us then take this concord sol si re sol, and see in what part of that concord, which I as yet suppose in no tone, we may place a dissonance, i. e. a second, to render it as little disgustful to the ear as possible. On the la, between the sol and the si, it would form a second with each, and consequently would be doubly dissonant. It would be the same between the si and re, as between every interval of the third; let the interval of the fourth remain between the re and the sol. Here we may introduce a sound two ways. 1st. We may add the note fa, which will form a second with sol, and a third with re. 2dly. Or the note mi, which will form a second with re, and a third with

with sol. It is evident, that from each of these two ways, will be produced the least rough dissonance that can be, since it will not be discordant with any one sound; and it will produce a new Third, which, as well as the two preceding, will contribute to the sweetness of the whole concord. On one side we shall have the concord of the seventh, and on the other that of the sixth added; the only two dissonant accords admitted in the system of the fundamental bass.

It is not sufficient to cause the dissonance to be heard; it must be pressed; you then disgust the ear only to flatter it afterwards more agreeably. Here are two joint sounds, on one side the fifth and sixth, and the other the seventh and the octave; as long as they will in this manner form the second, they will continue dissonant, but let the parts, which make them to be heard, be distant one degree; let the one ascend, or the other descend diatonically, and the second will on each side become a third; that is, one of the most agreeable consonances. Wherefore, after sol fa will be found sol mi, or fa la; and after re mi, mi ut, or re fa; and this is what is called preventing the dissonance.

It remains to be determined, which of the two joined sounds should ascend or descend, and which should continue as before; but the plan in determination stares us in the face. Let the fifth or the octave remain as principal chords, let the sixth ascend, and the seventh descend, as accessary sounds and dissonances. Moreover, if, of the two joined sounds, that which has the least compass to make, should have the preference, the fa will again descend on the mi after the seventh, and the mi of the concord of sixth added will ascend on the fa, for there is no shorter course to prevent the dissonance.

Let us now see what course the fundamental sound ought to take in relation to the movement assigned to the dissonance. Since one of the two joined sounds remains in its place, it ought to form an union in the following concord. The interval, which the fundamental bass ought to form at quitting the concord, ought then to be determined on these two conditions: 1st. That the octave of the preceding fundamental sound may continue in its place after the concord of the seventh, and the fifth after the concord of sixth added. 2dly. Let the sound, on which the dissonance is resolved, be one of the harmonies of that to which the fundamental bass passes. Moreover, the best movement of the bass being by intervals of the fifth, if it descends from the fifth in the first case, or if it ascends from the fifth in the second, all the conditions will be entirely fulfilled, as it is evident, by the inspection only of the example.

Perfect Concord. Seventh. Sixth added.

From thence is drawn a method of knowing to whatever chord of the tone each of the two concords is most suitable. Which are the two most essential chords in each tone? The tonic and dominant. How can the bass have its direction by descending from the fifth on two essential chords of the tone? It must be by passing from the dominant to the tonic, of which the dominant is the chord to which the concord of the seventh is most suitable. How can the bass by ascending from the fifth have its direction on two essential chords of the tone? 'Tis by passing from the tonic to the dominant, and of which the tonic is the chord to which the concord of sixth added is most apt. The reason for which see in the example, where I have given a diesis to the fa of the concord which follows the latter, for the re being dominant tonic, ought to bear the major third. The bass may have other directions, but those are the most perfect and the two principal cadences. (Vide CADENCE.)

If these two dissonances are compared with the fundamental sound, we find, that that which descends is a minor seventh, and that which rises, a minor sixth; from whence we draw this new rule, that the major dissonances ought to ascend, and the minor descend; for, in general, a major interval has less course to take in ascending, and a minor in descending, and generally also in diatonic directions, the smaller intervals are preferable.

When the concord of the seventh bears a major third, that third forms with the seventh another dissonance, which is the false fifth, or by variation, the triton. This third opposite to the seventh, is also called major dissonance, and it is prescribed to it to ascend, but that is in the quality of a sensible note, and, without the second, that pretended dissonance would by no means exist, or would not be treated as such.

One observation not to be forgotten is, that the two only notes of the scale, which are not found in the harmonics of the two principal chords ut and sol, are precisely those which are therein introduced by the dissonance, and furnish, by this means, the diatonic gamut, which, without this, would be imperfect; and which explains how the fa and la, though strange to the mode, are found in its scale, and why their intonation, always rough, in spite of custom, places at a distance the idea of the principal tone.

We

We muſt alſo take notice, that theſe two diſſonances, viz. the major ſixth and minor ſeventh. differ no more than a ſemi-tone, and would differ ſtill leſs if the intervals were very exact. By the aſſiſtance of this obſervation we may draw from the principle of reaſoning, an origin nearly approaching to both, as I will demonſtrate.

The harmonics which accompany any ſound whatever, are not bounden by thoſe which compoſe the perfect concord. There are an infinity of others leſs ſenſible in proportion as they become ſharper, and their references more compoſed; and theſe references are expreſſed by the natural ſeries of aliquots, $\frac{1}{2}$ $\frac{1}{3}$ $\frac{1}{4}$ $\frac{1}{5}$ $\frac{1}{6}$ $\frac{1}{7}$, &c. The ſix firſt terms of this ſeries give the ſounds which compoſe the perfect concord and its redditives, the ſeventh being excluded; this ſeventh term, however, enters like them in the whole reſonance of the generating ſound, tho' leſs ſenſibly; but it does not enter as a conſonance; it muſt then as a diſſonance; and this diſſonance is given by nature. It remains now to ſee its connection with thoſe of which I have ſpoken.

This connection, moreover, is intermediary between each, and nearly approaching to both; for the reference of the major ſixth is $\frac{3}{5}$; and that of the minor ſeventh $\frac{9}{10}$. Theſe two references being reduced to the ſame terms are $\frac{48}{80}$ and $\frac{45}{80}$:

The reference of the aliquot $\frac{1}{7}$ connected to the ſimple by its octaves, is $\frac{4}{7}$; and this reference reduced to the ſame term with the preceding, is found intermediary between the two, in this manner $\frac{336}{560}$ $\frac{320}{560}$ $\frac{315}{560}$; wherein we ſee, that this connection differs from the major ſixth only a $\frac{1}{35}$, or nearly two commas; and from the minor ſeventh only a $\frac{1}{112}$, which is much leſs than a comma. To make uſe of the ſame ſounds in the diatonic genus, and in different modes, it has been neceſſary to change them; but this change is not great enough to eraſe the traces of their origin.

I have demonſtrated, at the word Cadence, how the introduction of theſe two principal diſſonances, the ſeventh and the ſixth added, gives a method of uniting a continuance of harmony by making it aſcend or deſcend at will, by the interpoſition of diſſonances.

I make no mention here of the preparation of diſſonances, leſs becauſe it has too many exceptions to form from it a general rule, than becauſe this is not its place. (Vide To Prepare.) In regard to the diſſonances by ſuppoſition or ſuſpenſion, vide alſo thoſe two words.

Laſtly, I mention nothing of the diminiſhed ſeventh, a particular concord, which I ſhall have occaſion to ſpeak of at the word Enharmonic.

Tho' this method of conceiving the diſſonance gives a pretty clear idea of it, yet, as this idea is not drawn from the foundation of the harmony, I am very far from endeavouring to give it a greater praiſe than it merits, nor have I ever given it more than its true worth; but they had till now reaſoned ſo ill on the diſſonance, that I do not imagine myſelf to have proceeded worſe than others. Monſ. Tartini is the firſt, and, till now, the only one who has deduced a theory of diſſonances from the true principles of harmony. To avoid uſeleſs repetitions, I convey the reader to the word Syſtem, where I have made the expoſition of his. I will not take upon myſelf to judge if he has found, or not, that of nature; but I ſhould take notice, at leaſt, that the principles of this author appear to have, in their conſequences, that univerſality and connection which is rarely found, unleſs in thoſe which lead to the truth.

One obſervation more on this article. Every commenſurable interval is really conſonant: theſe are truly diſſonant, only thoſe whoſe references are irrational; for theſe are only thoſe to which no common fundamental ſound can be aſſigned. But the point being paſſed, wherein the natural harmonies are ſtill ſenſible, this conſonance of commenſurable intervals is not admitted any more than the induction. In this caſe, the intervals form a great part of the harmonic ſyſtem, ſince they are in the order of its natural generation, and are referred to the common fundamental ſound; but they cannot be admitted as conſonant by the ear, becauſe it does not perceive them in the natural harmony of the corpo ſonoro. Beſides, the more the interval is compoſed, the more it is raiſed to the ſharp of the fundamental ſound, which is proved by the reciprocal generation of the fundamental ſound, and ſuperior intervals. (Vide the Syſtem of Monſ. Tartini.) Moreover, when the diſtance of the fuudamental ſound, at the moſt ſharp of the generator, or generated interval, exceeds the extent of the muſical or perceptible ſyſtem, whatever is beyond that extent, being to be judged void, ſuch an interval has no ſenſible foundation, and ought to be rejected from practice, or only admitted as a diſſonant. This is neither the ſyſtem of Monſ.

Monf. Rameau, or that of Tartini, or mine; but the dictates of nature, the remainder of which I do not pretend to explain.

MAJOR DISSONANCE, Is that which is prevented by afcending. This diffonance is only relative to the minor diffonance, for it forms a third or fixth major on the true fundamental found, and is no other than the fenfible note in a concord dominant, or a fixth added in its own.

MINOR DISSONANCE, Is that which is prevented in defcending. This is always the diffonance properly fo called, i. e. the feventh of the true fundamental found. The major is alfo that which is formed by a fuperfluous interval; and the minor by a diminifhed interval. These different acceptations happen from the word diffonance being equivocal, and fignifying fometimes an interval, and at other times a fimple found.

DITHYRAMB, A kind of Greek fong, which was fung in honour of Bacchus, in the Phrygian mode, and was filled with that fire and gayety that the God infpires to whom it was confecrated. We muft not enquire if our modern men of letters, always wife, have raifed their cries on the diforder and confufion of Dithyrambs. 'Tis very wrong, without doubt, to get drunk, particularly in honour of the Divinity! but I had much rather be intoxicated, than have that filly good-fenfe, which meafures, by cold reafoning, the works and difcourfes of a man in liquor.

DITONE, Was, in the Greek mufic, an interval compofed of two tones, viz. a third major. (Vide INTERVAL, THIRD.)

DIVERTISSEMENT, Is the name given to certain collections of dances and airs, which it is the rule in Paris to infert in each act of an opera, whether comic or tragic. An importunate diverfion, the author of which has taken care to divide the action at fome interefting moment, and which the actors and fpectators, the former feated, the latter ftanding, have the patience to fee and liften to.

DIVISIONS, By this name were called the different methods of applying to the notes, the fyllables of the gamut, according to the different pofitions of the two femitones of the octave, and according to the different routes to come at them. As Aretin invented only fix of thefe fyllables, and as there are feven notes to found in an octave, it muft be neceffary to repeat the name of fome note. This was the reafon that they called always mi fa or fa la, the two notes, between which one of the femitones was placed. Thefe names determined at the fame time thofe of the neareft notes, whether in afcending or defcending. Moreover, as the two femitones are fubject to change their place in the modulation, and as there is in mufic a quantity of different methods to apply the fix fame fyllables to them, thefe methods were called

called divisions, because the same notes therein continually changed their names. (Vide GAMUT.)

In the last age the syllable si was added to the six first of the gamut of Aretin. By this means the seventh note of the scale being found named, the divisions became useless, and were abolished from the French music; but amongst all the other nations, where, according to the genius of the artist, the musicians always take their old track, for the perfection of the art, they have not adopted the si; and there is some appearance, that in Italy, in Spain, in Germany, and in England, the divisions will serve sometimes for the inconvenience of beginners.

DO, A syllable which the Italians substitute in the place of that of ut, the sound of which they find too rough. The same motive has led many persons to undertake, and among others Mons. Sauveur, to change the names of the syllables of our gamut; but the ancient custom has always prevailed amongst us. It is, perhaps, an advantage; it is good to accustom one's self to sol fa by rough syllables, when we have none more sonorous to substitute in their place in singing.

DODECACHORD, This is the title given by Henri Glavean to a large book of his composition, in which, adding four new tones to the eight used in his time, and which still remain in the Roman ecclesiastic canto's, he thinks he has re-established, in their purity, the twelve modes of Aristoxenes, who, however, had thirteen; but this pretence has been refuted by J. B. Doni, on his Treaty on the Genera and Modes.

DOMINANT, A dominant, or sensible concord, is that which is practised on the dominant of the tone, and which announces the perfect cadence. Every major perfect concord becomes dominant as soon as the minor seventh is added to it.

DOMINANT, Is, of the three essential notes of the tone, that which is a fifth above the tonic. The tonic and the dominant determine the tone, they are each the fundamental of a particular concord; whereas the mediant, which constitutes the mode, has no concord with it, and only forms part of that of the tonic.

Mons. Rameau generally gives the name of dominant to every note which bears a concord of the seventh, and distinguishes which bears the sensible concord, by the name of dominant tonic; but on account of the length of the word, this addition has not been adopted by artists, and they continue to call the 5th of the tonic simply dominant, and they do not call them dominants but fundamentals, the other notes bearing the concord of the seventh, which is sufficient for its expression, and prevents confusion.

DOMINANT,

DOMINANT, In church music, is the note which is most struck, in whatever of the tonic we may be. There are in church music a dominant and tonic, but no mediant.

DORIC, The doric mode was one of the most ancient in the Greek music, and it was the flattest and lowest of those which have been since called authentic.

The character of this mode was serious and flat, but of a temperate flatness, which rendered it proper for war, and religious subjects. Platon judges the majesty of the doric mode as very proper to preserve good morals; and 'tis for this reason that he permits the use of it in his republic.

It was called doric because it was in use amongst the people of that name. The invention of this mode was attributed to Thamaris of Thrace, who having been so unlucky as to defy the muses, and be conquered, he was deprived by them of his eyes and lyre.

DOUBLE, Double, or redoubled intervals, are all those which exceed the extent of the octave. In this sense, the tenth is double of the third, and the twelfth double of the fifth. Some give also the name of double intervals to those which are composed of two equal intervals, as the false fifth, which is composed of two minor thirds.

DOUBLE, They call double, the airs of a piece of music simple in itself, which are figured and doubled by the addition of many notes, which vary and adorn the canto, without disfiguring it. This is what the Italians call variazioni. (Vide VARIATIONS.)

There is this difference between the doubles and the flourishes, that the one are at the choice of the musician, which he may make or quit at pleasure to re-take the simple. But the double is never left, for when once it is begun, it must be continued throughout the whole of the air.

DOUBLE, Is also a word made use of in the opera of Paris, to mark out the actors next in order, who supply the place of the principal actors, when they leave them thro' sickness or fantasy, or when an opera is nearly at its end, and another is preparing. We must have seen an opera in doubles to have any conception of such a sight; and how great must be the patience of any one who would visit it in that condition. All the zeal of the good French citizens, well provided with ears to prove it, is hardly sufficient to undergo so detestable a charivari.

TO DOUBLE, To double an air, is to place doubles therein. To double a part, is to substitute one in the place of the principal actor. (Vide DOUBLE.)

DOUBLE CHORD, A kind of play on the violin, which consists in touching two chords at the same time, making two different

different parts. "The double chord has often a great effect." "It is difficult to play justly on the double chord."

DOUBLE DEMI CROTCHET, A note in music equal to the fourth of a minum, or the half of a crotchet. Sixteen double demy crotchets are consequently necessary for a semibreve, or four timed measure. (Vide MEASURE, POWER of the NOTES.)

We here see the figure of the double demi crotchet tied or detached . It is called by that name on account of the double dark at its tail, and which we must distinguish from that properly called so, which makes the subject of the following article.

DOUBLE CROCHET, A note of abbreviation, which shews the division of the notes into double demi crochets, as the simple crochet shews their division into demi crochets. Vide the Figure and effect of the double crochet.

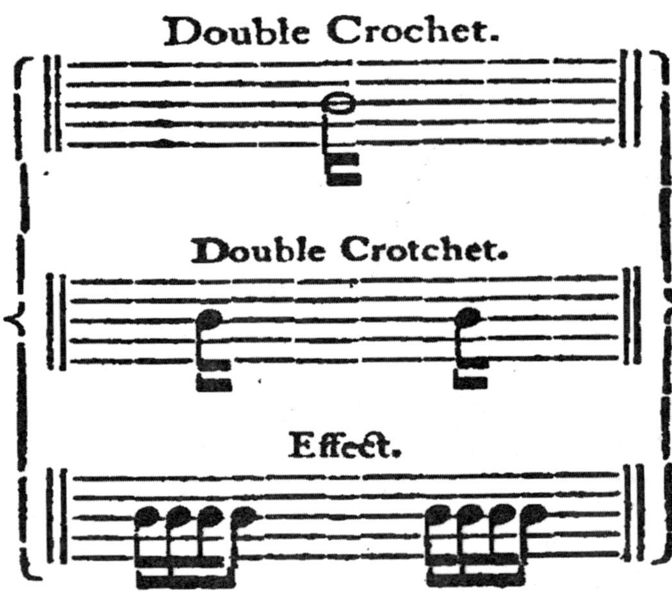

DOUBLE EMPLOI, A name given by Monf. Rameau to the two different methods by which the concord of the sub-dominant may be treated and considered, viz. as fundamental concord of the sixth added, or as concord of the greater sixth, varied from a fundamental concord of the seventh. In effect, these two concords bear exactly the same names, are cyphered in the same manner, and are used on the same chords of the tone, so that often we cannot distinguish which the author intended to use; but by the assistance of the following concord which prevents it, and which in the two cases is different.

To make this distinction, we consider the diatonic progress of the two notes, which form the fifth and sixth, and which making between

between themſelves an interval of the ſecond, are one or the other the diſſonance of the accord.

This progreſs is alſo determined by the movement of the baſs. If then, of theſe two notes, the ſuperior is diſſonant, it will aſcend a degree in the following concord. The inferior will continue in its place, and the concord will be a ſixth added. If it is the inferior which is diſſonant, it will deſcend in the following concord. The ſuperior will remain in its place, and the concord will be that of the greater ſixth. Vide the two caſes in the double emploi.

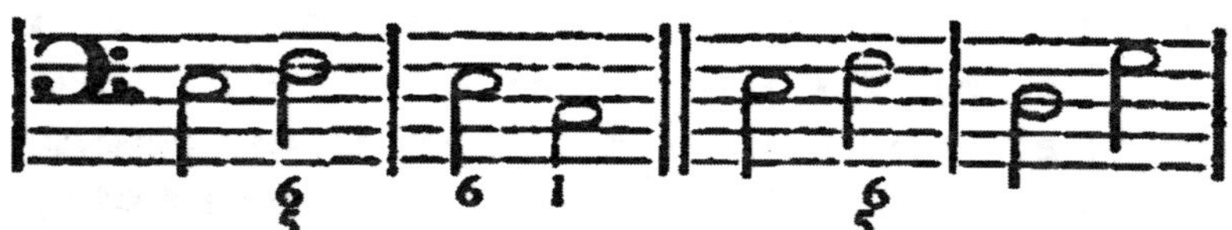

In regard to the compoſer, the uſe he may make of the double emploi, is to conſider the concord, which bears it in one light at going in, and another at going out; ſo that falling in with it, as with a concord of ſixth added, it prevents it as a concord of greater ſixth, and ſo reciprocally.

Monſ. D'Alembert has ſhewn that one of the principal uſes of the double emploi, is to be able to bear the diatonic ſucceſſion of the gamut as far as the octave, without changing the mode, at leaſt in aſcending, for in deſcending it is changed. Vide the example of that gamut and its fundamental baſs.

Gamut intirely in the ſame tone by favour of the Double Emploi.

It is evident, according to Monſ. Rameau's ſyſtem, that all the harmonic ſucceſſion, which reſults from it, is in the ſame tone; for even on a preſſing occaſion, there are uſed only the three concords of the tonic, the dominant, and ſub-dominant; this laſt, giving, by the double emploi, that of the ſeventh of the ſecond note, which is uſed on the ſixth.

In regard to what Monſ. D'Alembert adds in his Elements of Muſic, page 80, and which he repeats in the Encyclopædia, at the article double emploi, viz. that the concord of the ſeventh re fa la ut, even tho' we ſhould look upon it as varied fa la ut re, cannot be followed by the concord ut mi ſol ut; I cannot be of his opinion in that point.

The proof which he gives of it, is, that the diſſonance ut in the firſt concord cannot be prevented in the ſecond, ſince it continues in its place; but in this concord of the ſeventh, re fa la ut, varied from this concord, fa la ut re, in the ſixth added, it is not ut, but re, that is the diſſonance, which conſequently ſhould be prevented by aſcending on mi, as it really does in the following concord, in ſuch a manner, that this courſe is forced within the baſs itſelf, which from re could not, without an error, return to ut, but ought to aſcend to mi, to prevent the diſſonances.

Monſ. D'Alembert then ſhews, that this concord, re fa la ut, preceded and followed by that of the tonic, cannot be authorized by the double emploi; and this is ſtill very true, ſince that concord, tho' cyphered with a 7, is neither treated as a concord of the ſeventh at going in, or coming out, or at leaſt it is not neceſſary to treat it as ſuch, but only as a variation of the ſixth added, whoſe diſſonance is in baſs; in which we ſhould take notice, that this diſſonance is never prepared: Wherefore, tho' in ſuch a paſſage the double emploi is not brought in queſtion, tho' the concord of the ſeventh is only there apparently, and impoſſible to prevent in the rules, this does not hinder the paſſage from being good and regular, as I have proved it to theoricians, and as I am going to prove it to artiſts, by an example of this paſſage, which cannot aſſuredly be condemned by any of them, or juſtified by any other fundamental baſs than mine.

Proof of the ſeventh varied from the ſixth added.

I confeſs that this variation of the ſixth added, which conveys the diſſonances to the baſs, has been blamed by Monſ. Rameau; that author, taking for fundamental the concord of the ſeventh which reſults from it, has choſen rather to make the fundamental baſs deſcend diatonically, and prevent a ſeventh by another ſeventh, than to explain this ſeventh by a variation.

I had

I had removed this error, and and many others in the papers which had continued a long time in Monſ. D'Alembert's hands, when he compoſed his Elements of Muſic, ſo that it is not his ſentiments that I attack, but my own which I defend.

In regard to the concluſion, the double emploi cannot be uſed with too great reſerve, and the greateſt maſters, are thoſe who are moſt wary in employing it.

DOUBLE FUGUE, We make a double fugue, when in the continuance of a fugue already appearing, another fugue is introduced in a quite different method; and this ſecond fugue muſt have its anſwer and entrance juſt as the firſt, which cannot be practiſed, but by four parts. We may, with more parts, make a ſtill greater number of different fugues be heard, but the confuſion is always to be feared, and 'tis then the maſter-piece of the art to treat them nicely. For this purpoſe, ſays Monſ. Rameau, we muſt obſerve, as much as poſſible, to make them enter only one after the other, particularly the firſt time, that their progreſſion be varied; that they be differently characterized; and that, if they cannot be heard together, at leaſt that a portion of the one be heard with a portion of the other. But theſe laborious taſks are made more for the ſcholar than the maſter: Theſe are leaden weights tied to the feet of young runners, to make them more nimble when delivered from them.

DOUBLE OCTAVE, An interval compoſed of two octaves, otherwiſe called fifteenth, and which the Greeks called diſ-diapaſon.

The double octave is in computation doubled from the ſimple octave, and is the only interval which does not change its name, when compoſed with itſelf.

DOUBLE TRIPLE, An ancient name of the triple of minums, or the meaſure of three for two, which is ſtruck as three timed, and contains a minum for each time. This meaſure is no longer in uſe but in France, where it even begins to be aboliſhed.

DOLCE, This word in muſic is oppoſed to forte, and is written above the lines of the French muſic, and below the Italian, where we wiſh to leſſen the noiſe, temperate and ſweeten the vehemence of the ſound, as in echo's and parts of accompaniment. The Italians often write piano in the ſame ſenſe; but their critics in muſic declare them not to be ſynonymous terms, and that it is from abuſe that moſt authors uſe them as ſuch. They ſay, that piano ſignifies only a moderation of the ſound, a diminution of the noiſe; but that dolce denotes, beſides that, a method of playing piu ſoave, ſweeter, more united, and anſwering almoſt to the word louré in French.

The dolce has three divisions, which we must take notice of, viz. the half play, the sweet, and the very sweet. However nearly these divisions may appear to be allied, a well-played band renders them very distinct and sensible.

DRAMATIC, This epithet is given to imitative music, proper to theatrical pieces of singing, as operas. It is also called lyric music. (Vide IMITATION.)

DUET, This name is generally given to all kinds of music in two parts; but at present the sense is restrained to two reciting parts, vocal or instrumental; the simple accompaniments being excluded, which are looked upon as nothing. Wherefore we call duet an air for two voices, tho' there be a third part for the thorough bass, and others for the symphony. In a word, to constitute a duet, two principal parts are necessary, between which the air must be equally distributed.

The rules of the duet, and of two part music in general, are the most rigorous for the harmony; we therein refuse many passages, many movements, which would be permitted to a greater number of parts; for a passage or a concord which would please in a third or fourth sound, becomes disgustful to the ear without them. Moreover, we should be unpardonable to choose ill, having only two sounds to take in each concord. These rules were formerly still more severe, but all that has been now laid aside in these latter times, where all the world set up for composers.

We may view the duet in two lights, viz. simply as a two part air, such as, for instance, the first verse of the stabat of Pergolesis, the most perfect and affecting duet that has come from the pen of any musician; or as a part of imitative and theatrical music, such as the duets in the opera scenes. In each case, the duet is, of all kinds of music, that which requires most taste, choice, and the most difficult to treat on, without going from the unity of melody. I beg to be permitted to make some observations here on the dramatic duet, whose particular difficulties are joined to those which are common to all the duets.

The author of the letter on the opera of Omphale, has sensibly remarked that the duets are out of nature in imitative music; for nothing is less natural than to see two persons speaking to each other for a certain time, either to say the same thing, or to contradict, without ever listening, or answering each other; and tho' this supposition might be admitted in certain cases, it could not still be used in tragedy, where this indecency is neither suitable to the dignity of the persons who speak, or to the education they are supposed to have.

There is nothing then but the transports of passion which can lead two heroic speakers to interrupt each other, to speak both at at once; and, even in ſuch a caſe, it is very ridiculous that theſe pretended diſcourſes ſhould be prolonged ſo as to make a complete piece on both ſides.

The firſt method of preventing this abſurdity is then, to place the duets only in lively and touching ſituations, where the agitation of the ſpeakers throws them into a kind of delirium, capable of making the ſpectators and themſelves forget thoſe theatrical ornaments which ſtrengthen the illuſion in a cold ſcene, and deſtroying it in the heat of their paſſions. The ſecond method is, to uſe the duet as much as poſſible in dialogue. This dialogue ought not to be phraſed and divided into greater periods, as that of the recitative, but formed of interrogations, anſwers, ſhort lively exclamations, which give occaſion to the melody to paſs alternately and nimbly from one part to another, without ceaſing to form a continuance, which may remain on the ear. A third attention is, not to take all the violent paſſions indifferently for ſubjects, but only thoſe which are ſuſceptible of a ſweet melody, and a little contraſt ſuitable to duets, to render its tune accented, and its harmony agreeable. Rage and paſſion are too quick in their courſe. Nothing can be diſtinguiſhed; we hear only a confuſed roar; and the duet has no effect. Moreover, the perpetual return of injuries and inſults would be more ſuitable to herdſmen than heroes; and this is exactly ſimilar to the rhodomontade of thoſe perſons who prefer fear to danger. Much leſs ſhould we make uſe of the ſoft accents, of chains, darts, flames, a flat and cold jargon, which paſſion never knew, and of which good muſic ſtands no more in need than good poetry. The inſtant of a ſeparation, that wherein one of the two lovers goes to death, or into the arms of another, the ſincere reformation of one faithleſs, the touching contention of a mother and her ſon, wiſhing to die for each other: All thoſe moments of affliction, where one cannot fail of ſhedding delicious tears; thoſe are the true ſubjects to be treated in duo, with that ſimplicity of words which is ſuitable to the language of the heart.

All thoſe who have frequented lyric theatres know how much the word addio only excites compaſſion and emotion in the whole audience. But ſo ſoon as a piece of wit, or well-turned phraſe begins to be perceptible, the charm inſtantly vaniſhes, and is ſucceeded by immoderate laughter.

Herein are ſome obſervations which are neceſſary to the poet. In regard to the muſician, it is his duty to find an air ſuitable to his ſubject, and diſtributed in ſuch a manner, that each of the ſpeakers, taking his turn, the whole compaſs may form only one melody; which, without changing the ſubject, or at leaſt without altering the movement, may paſs in its progreſs from one side to the other, without ceasing to be one. The duets which have the greatest effect, are those with equal voices, because their harmony is nearest connected; and amongst equal voices, those which have the greater effect are the treble, because their diapason, being sharper, is more distinct, and the tone more touching. The duets also of this space are the only ones employed by the Italians in their tragedies; and I don't doubt, but the use of castrati, in the parts of men, was due in some measure to this observation. But tho' there should be an equality between the voices, and unity in the melody, it must not be said that the two parts should be exactly similar in their turn of singing; for besides the diversity of styles suitable to them, it is very rare that the situation of two actors should so perfectly be the same, as that they ought to express their sentiments in the same manner; wherefore the musician ought to vary their accent, and give to each of the two the character which best paints the state of his soul, particularly in alternate recitative.

When we join the two parts together (which ought to be done seldom, and continue but little) we must find an air susceptible of a course by thirds or by sixths, in the which the second part may cause its effect, without being divided from the first, (Vide Unity of Melody.) We must preserve the roughness of he dissonances, the piercing and strengthening sounds, the fortissimo of the orchestra for moments of disorder and transport, where the actors, seeming to forget themselves, carry their madness into the soul of every sensible spectator, and make him feel the power of a harmony nicely managed; but such periods should be rare, short, and artfully introduced. One must, by a sweet and affecting music, have already disposed the heart and ear to every emotion, that each of them may unite in their attention to these violent passions; and they must pass with that rapidity which is appropriated to our weakness; for when the agitation is too great, it cannot last, and whatever is beyond nature can make no impression.

As I cannot flatter myself that I am clearly understood throughout the whole of this article, I think it necessary to join an example, on which the reader, comparing my ideas, may have a more easy conception of them. It is drawn from the Olympiad of Metastasio; the curious will do well to look into the music of the same opera, by Pergolesis, how this first musician of his time, and ours, has treated this duet; the subject of which is here presented.

Megacles having engaged to fight for his friend in the games, wherein the reward of the conqueror was the beautiful Aristæa, finds, in this same Aristæa, the mistress whom he adores, delighted with the combat, which he is about to sustain, and which

she

ſhe attributes to his love for him. Ariſtæa ſpeaks on this ſubject the moſt affecting words, to the which he gives a no leſs tender anſwer, but with the ſecret deſpair of neither being able to recall his word, nor diſpenſe, at the expence of his happineſs, with that of a friend to whom he is indebted for his life: Ariſtæa, alarmed at the grief which ſhe ſees painted in his eyes, and which his broken and equivocal diſcourſes confirm, acquaints him with her inquietude; and Megacles being unable to ſupport, at the ſame time, his own deſpair, and the troubles of his miſtreſs, leaves her without an explanation, and relinquiſhes her a prey to the moſt piercing ſorrows. It is in this ſituation that they ſing the following duet:

MEGACLES.

Mia vita . . . . . addio
Ne' giorni tuoi felici
Ricordati di me.

ARISTÆA.

Perchè coſì mi dici,
Anima mia, perchè?

MEGACLES.

Taci, bell' Idol mio.

ARISTÆA.

Parla, mio dolce amor.

TOGETHER.

MEGACLES.—Ah! che parlando, } oh Dio!
ARISTÆA.— Ah! che tacendo, }
Tu mi traffigi il cor!

ARISTÆA, aſide.

Veggio languir chi adoro,
Ne intendo il ſuo languir!

MEGACLES, aſide.

Di geloſia mi moro,
E non lo poſſo dir!

 TOGETHER.

TOGETHER.

Chi mai provò di questo
Affanno più funesto,
Più barbaro dolor ?

As much as this dialogue appears to be only the continuance of the scene, what collects it into one duet only, is the unity of the design, by which the musician re-unites all its parts, according to the poet's intention.

In regard to the burlesque duets, which are used in the intermediaries, and other comic operas, they are not generally for equal voices, but between the bass and the treble. If they have not the pathos of the tragic duets, in lieu of it they are susceptible of a more striking variety, of more different accents, and more expressive characters. All the gentility of coquetry, all the amusement of the laughable characters, all the contrast of the nonsense of one sex, and the cunning of the other; lastly, all the accessary ideas of which the subject is susceptible; all these may occur to throw a prettiness and an interesting harmony in these duets, the rules of which are in other respects the same as the preceding, in what regards the dialogue and unity of melody. To find a comic perfect duo to my liking, in all its parts, I will not omit the immortal author who has furnished me with these two examples, but will cite the first duet of the Serva Padrona: "Lo conosco a quegl' occhietti, &c. &c." and boldly as a model of agreeable singing, unity of melody, simple harmony, pure and brilliant accent, dialogue, and taste, in which nothing can fail, when it is well rendered, if the hearers who understand it, pay it that honour which it merits.

DUPLICATION, A term in church music. The intonation by duplication is made by a kind of perielesis, by doubling the penultimate note of the word, which terminates the intonation, which has no place but when this penultimate is immediately below the last. In that case, the duplication serves to mark it more fully, in the manner of a sensible note.

DURATE, By this term is called every thing which disgusts the ear by its effect. There are voices rough and sliding, instruments sharp and still rough, as well as compositions duraté. The roughness of the B sharp occasioned its formerly receiving the name of B duraté. There are rough intervals in melody, such as the diatonic progress of the three tones, whether in ascending or falling, and such in general are false relations. There are in the harmony rough concords, such as the triton, the superfluous fifth, and, in general, all the major dissonances. The continued roughness is disgusting to the ear, and renders a piece of of music disagreeable; but when managed with art, it answers the purpose of a claro obscure, and makes an addition to the expression.

E.

E SI MI, E LA MI, OR SIMPLY E, Is the third sound of the gamut of Aretin, which is otherwise called mi. (Vide GAMUT.

ECBOLE was, in the most ancient Greek music, an alteration of the enharmonic genus, when a chord was accidentally raised five diesis's above its ordinary concord.

EAR. This word is figuratively used as a musical term. To have an ear, is to have a sensible, clear, and true idea in hearing music; so that, whether for intonation, or for measure, we may be disgusted with the smallest error, and pleased with the beauties of that art, when hearing them. He has a bad ear who is continually singing false, cannot distinguish the true intonation from the false, or who is not sensible of the precision in a measure, and strikes it at an unequal or counter time. Wherefore the word ear is always taken for a nicety in the sensation or judgment of that sensitive faculty. In this acceptation the word ear is never used, but with the singular, and with the partitive article. "To have "an ear," &c. &c. &c.

ECHO. A returned or reflected sound, by a solid body, and which by that means is repeated, and renewed to the ear. This word is derived from the Greek ἦχος, a sound.

We call also by the name of echo, the place where the repetition is heard.

We distinguish the echos taken in this sense into two kinds, viz. 1st, the simple echo, which only repeats the voice once; 2dly, the double, or multiple, which repeats the same sounds twice, or more sounds.

In simple echos, there are some tonics, that is, which only repeat the musical and sustained sound; and others syllabic, which repeat also the words of the voice.

We may draw a part from multiple echos, to form concords and harmony with a single voice, by making between the voice and echo a kind of canon, the measure of which should be directed on the time which passes betwixt the pronounced sounds. This method of making to one's self alone an harmonic concert, must,

must, if the singer be ingenious, and the echo strong, appear astonishing, and almost magical to an unprepossessed hearer.

The name of echo is conveyed in music to those kinds of airs or pieces, in the which, by the imitation of the echo, are repeated now and then, sweet or strong, a certain number of notes. It is on the organ that this method of playing is most commonly used, on account of the facility there is in forming echos on the positive: We may also form echos on the harpsichord, by means of the smaller keys.

The Abbé Brossard says, that the word echo is sometimes used in the place of dolce, or piano, to denote, that the voice, or instrument, should be sweetened as to form an echo. This custom no longer subsists.

ECHOMETRE. A kind of graduated scale, or rule divided into several parts, which is used to measure the duration or length of sounds, to determine their different powers, and even the references of their intervals.

This word is derived from the Greek ἦχος, a sound, and μετρον, a measure. I will not undertake the description of this machine, because no use will ever be made of it; and, as the best echometre is a sensible ear, and long experience in music; those who wish to know more of it, may consult the work of Monsieur Sauveur, inserted in those of the Academy of Sciences, 1701. They will there find two scales of this kind, one of Monsieur Sauveur, and the other of Monsieur Loulie. (Vide Chronometre.)

ECLYSE was, in the most ancient Greek music, an alteration in the enharmonic genus, when a chord was accidentally lowered three diesis's below its ordinary concord; wherefore the eclyse was contrary to the spondeasm.

EIGHTEENTH. An interval which comprehends seventeen conjoint degrees, and consequently eighteen diatonic sounds, counting the two extremes. This is the double octave of the fourth. (Vide fourth.)

EFFECT. An agreeable and strong impression which an excellent music imprints on the ear and mind of an audience; wherefore, the single word effect signifies a pleasing and fine effect in music. We not only say of a work, that it has an effect, but distinguish under the name of circumstances, which are the cause of the effect, all those wherein the produced sensation appears superior the methods employed to raise it.

A continued practice may teach the knowledge of what things produce an effect when laying before the eye, but it is genius only which can discover them. It is the fault of all bad composers and beginners to load parts upon parts, instruments on instruments, to discover the effect which follows from them, and to open, as an ancient said, a wide mouth to blow on a small flute. One would say, to to see their partitions so loaded, so numerous, that they intend to surprise by prodigious effects; and if in hearing the whole you are surprised, 'tis to hear a trifling piece of music, bald, confused, without effect, and more proper to stun the ears than to delight them. On the contrary, the eye wanders over the partitions of great masters to discover those effects, ravishing and sublime, which their music, when executed, produces. It is, that a continued detail is ignorant of true genius, that it affords no amusements by a quantity of silly objects, but that it moves you by great effects, and the strength and simplicity of it united, always form its character.

ELEGY. A kind of composition for the flute, invented, as it is said, by Sacadas, of Argos.

ELEVATION. The elevation of the hand or foot, in striking the time, serves to mark the weaker time, and is properly called raised. Among the ancients it was the contrary. The elevation of the voice in singing, is the movement by which it is carried into sharp.

ELEVENTH. Replique, or octave of the fourth. This interval is called the eleventh, because eleven sub diatonics must be formed to pass from one of these terms to the other.

Monsieur Rameau wished to give the name of eleventh to the concord which is generally called fourth; but as this denomination has not been followed, and as Monsieur Rameau himself has continued to cypher the same concord with a four and not an eleven, we must conform to custom. (Vide concord, fourth supposition.)

ELINE. A name given by the Greeks to a song of the weavers. (Vide SONG.)

ENDEMATIA was the air of a kind of dance peculiar to the inhabitants of Argos.

ENHARMONIC, one of the three genera of the Greek music, often also called harmony by Aristoxenes and his followers.

This genus resulted from a particular division of the tetrachord, according to which, the interval which is placed betwixt the lichanos, or third chord, and the mesis, or fourth being of a triton, or third major, there continues to complete the tetrachord in flat, only a semi tone to divide into two intervals, viz. from the hypaton to the parhypaton, and from the parhypaton to the lichanos. We will explain under the word genus how the division was made.

The enharmonic genus was the sweetest of the three, in the opinion of Aristides Quintilian. It passed as very ancient, and the generality of authors, attributed the invention of it to Olympus, the Phrygian. But his tetrachord, or rather his diatessaron of this genus, contained only three chords, which formed together two uncomposed intervals, the first of a semi tone, and the other a third major; and from these two intervals alone, repeated from tetrachord to tetrachord, resulted at that time all the enharmonic genus. 'Twas not, till after the time of Olympus, that they thought of inserting, in imitation of the other genera, a fourth chord between the two first, to form the division which I have just mentioned. We may see the connections, according to the systems of Ptolomy and Oristoxenes, at the word diatonic.

This genus, so surprising, so admired by the ancients, and according to some, the first discovered of the three, kept not its renown long. Its extreme difficulty rendered it soon forsaken, in proportion as art gained combinations by losing its energy; and when the agility was a substitute for the nicety of the ear. Plutarch also finds great fault with the musicians of his time, for having lost the finest of the three genera, and daring to say, that its intervals were not sensible, as if every thing that escaped their gross senses (adds that great philosopher) must be out of nature.

We have at present a kind of enharmonic genus entirely different from that of the Greeks. It consists, as the two others, in a peculiar progression of harmony, which engenders, in the course of the parts of the enharmonic intervals, by using it successively, or, at the same time, between two notes, which are a tone from each other, the B flat of the inferior, and the diesis of the superior. But though, according to the rigor of the connections, this diesis and B flat ought to form an interval betwixt themselves, (vide scale, and fourth of a tone) This interval is found void, by means of the temperament, which, in the established system, makes the same tone serve two purposes, which does not prevent such a passage from producing, by the force of modulation and harmony, a part of the effect, which we seek in the enharmonic transitions.

As this genus is but little known, and as our authors are contented to give some notions of it too succinct, I think I must explain it here a little more at length.

We must then observe, that the concord of the seventh diminished, is the only one on which we can practice passages truly enharmonic; and that by virtue of that singular propriety which it has of dividing the entire octave into equal intervals. Let us take in the four sounds which compose this concord, that which we wish for fundamental, and we shall always equally find, that the three other sounds form on this a concord of 7th diminished. Moreover, the fundamental sound of the concord of 7th diminished is always a sensible note; so that, without changing any thing in this concord, we may, by a method of double, or quadruple employ, make it serve successively on four different fundamentals, viz. on four different sensible notes.

It

It follows thence, that this same concord, without having any change, either in the accompaniment or the bass, may bear four different names, and consequently be cyphered in four different methods, viz. with a 7 ♮ under the name of diminished seventh; with a 6 + under the name of major fixth and false fifth, with a + 4
5 ♮
under the name of minor third and triton; and lastly, with a + 2 under the name of superfluous second. It must be understood, that the cleff should be numbered differently, according to the tones in which we are supposed to be.

Here then are four methods of going from a concord of diminished seventh, by supposing ourselves successively in four different concords; for the fundamental and natural direction of the sound, which bears a concord of diminished seventh, is to be resolved on the tonic of the minor mode, of which it is a sensible note.

Let us next imagine the concord of the diminish'd seventh on ut diesis, a sensible note. If I take the third mi as fundamental, it will become a sensible note in its turn, and consequently will express the minor mode of fa; moreover, this ut diesis rests certainly in the concord of mi, a sensible note, but it is in quality of re B flat, viz. of the sixth note of the tone, and of the diminish'd seventh of the sensible note; wherefore this ut diesis, which, as a sensible note, was obliged to ascend into the tone of re, becomes re B flat in the tone of fa, and is obliged to descend as diminish'd seventh, which is an enharmonic transition. If instead of the third, we take in the same concord of ut diesis the false fifth sol, as a new sensible note, the ut diesis will again become re B flat, in quality of the fourth note, another enharmonic passage. Lastly, if we take the diminished seventh itself as a sensible note, instead of si B flat, we must necessarily consider it as la diesis, which forms a third enharmonic passage on the same concord.

Through the means of these four different methods of viewing the same concord successively, we pass from one tone to another, which appears very distant from it. We give a different progress to the parts from that, which, in their first place, they ought to have; and these passages when managed a propos, are capable, not only of surprising, but even delighting the audience, when well conducted.

Another source of variety, in the same genus, is drawn from the different methods in which the accord may be resolved which announces it; for though the most natural modulation would be to pass from the concord of diminished seventh, on the sensible note, to that of the tonic in the minor mode, we may, by substituting the major for the minor third, render the mode major, and even

even add to it the ſeventh, to change that tonic in dominant, and by this means to paſs into another tone. By means of theſe different reunited combinations, we may get out of the concord in twelve ways. But, from theſe twelve, there are only nine, which, giving the change of dieſis into B flat, or reciprocally, can be truly enharmonic; moreover, in theſe nine different modulations, there are only three different ſenſible notes, each of which is reſolved by three different paſſages; ſo that, by taking it in its true ſenſe, we find on each ſenſible note no more than three truly enharmonic paſſages, all the reſt not being really enharmonic, or having connection with ſome one of the three firſt. (Vide an example of all theſe paſſages.)

Twelve methods of going out of a concord of diminiſhed ſeventh, wherein are compriſed the three enharmonic tranſitions, and their combinations.

It has been frequently attempted to make entire pieces in the enharmonic genus, in imitation of the modulations in the diatonic genus. To give a kind of rule to the fundamental directions of this genus, it has been divided into diatonic enharmonic, which proceeds by a succession of major semi tones, and in chromatic enharmonic, which proceeds by a succession of semi tones minor.

The air in the first kind is diatonic, because its semi tones are major, and it is enharmonic, because two major semi tones together form a tone of enharmonic interval too strong. To form this kind of air, we must make a bass which descends from fourth, and ascends from major third alternatively. A part of the trio between the parcæ in the opera of Hippolitus, is of this kind, but it could never be executed in the opera house at Paris, though Monsieur Rameau assures us, that it has been performed in other places, by the consent and desire of the musicians, and had a surprising effect.

The air of the second kind is chromatic, because it proceeds by minor semi tones. It is enharmonic, because the two consecutive semi tones minor form too weak a tone of an enharmonic interval.

To form this kind of air, we must make a fundamental bass, which descends from minor third, and ascends from major alternatively. Monsieur Rameau acquaints us, that in the opera of the Gallant Indians, this kind of music met with an applause that shook the very earth; but he was so ill used, as to be obliged to change it into a common music. (Vide the Elements of Music by Monsieur Alembert, page 91, 92, 93, and 166.

In spite of the example cited and authorised by Monsieur Rameau, I think it my duty to acquaint young artists, that the enharmonic diatonic, and enharmonic chromatic, appear to me proper to be rejected as genera, ; and I cannot think that a piece of music, modulated in this manner, even let the execution be the most perfect, can have the smallest merit. My reasons are, that the rough passages of one idea to another, at a great distance, are so frequent therein, that it is not possible for the mind to follow these transitions with the same rapidity as the music presents them; that the ear has not time to perceive the secret and composed connection of the modulations, or to understand the supposed intervals; that there is no longer any shadow of tone, or mode, in such successions; that it is equally impossible to retain that from which we go, or to foresee that to which we are directed; and that amidst all this, we no longer have any idea where we are. The enharmonic is no more than a passage unexpected, the surprising impression of which is formed strongly, and continues a long time; a passage, consequently, which ought not to be repeated too often, or too roughly, for fear the idea of the modulation

lation ſhould be troubled, and become entirely loſt; for as ſoon as we begin to hear ſuch concords as have ſo ſenſible connection, and no common foundation, the harmony has no longer any union, or apparent continuance, and the effect which reſults from it is no more than an empty noiſe, without union or taſte. If Monſieur Rameau, when he ſpent his time in uſeleſs calculations, had paid a greater attention to the metaphyſic of his art, it is to be ſuppoſed, that the natural fire of that artiſt had produced prodigies, the ſeed of which was in his genius, but which his prepoſſeſſions have always ſtifled.

I do not even think, that ſimple enharmonic tranſitions can ever have any ſucceſs, either in choruſſes or airs, becauſe each of theſe pieces forms a whole, wherein ſhould reign unity, and whoſe parts ought to have an union betwixt themſelves more ſenſible than this genus can define it.

What then is the real ſituation for the enharmonic? It is, in my opinion, the forced recitative. It is in a ſublime and pathetic ſcene, when the voice ſhould multiply and vary the muſical inflexions in imitation of the grammatical oratorical accent, an accent often impoſſible to be defined; it is in ſuch a ſcene, I affirm, that the enharmonic tranſitions are well placed, when we know how to manage them for ſublime expreſſions, and ſtrengthen them by ſtrokes of ſymphony, which ſuſpend the words, and give them force to the expreſſion. The Italians, who uſe this method admirably, uſe it only on this plan. We may ſee in the firſt recitative of the Orpheus of Pergoleſis, a ſtriking and ſimple example of the effects which this great muſician knew how to draw from the enharmonic, and how far from producing a rough modulation. Theſe tranſitions, when they become natural and eaſy to ſound, give an energic ſweetneſs to the whole declamation.

I have already ſaid, that our enharmonic genus is entirely different from that of the ancients. I will add, that though we have not, like them, enharmonic intervals to ſound. this does not hinder the modern enharmonic from being of a more difficult execution than theirs. Amongſt the Greeks, the enharmonic intervals, purely melodious, did not require, either in the finger, or audience, any change of ideas, but only a great delicacy in the organs of hearing; whereas, in our muſic, we muſt add to the ſame delicacy an exact knowledge and exquiſite ſentiment of the roughеſt and moſt unnatural harmonic metamorphoſes; for if we do not hear the phraſe, we cannot give the words their neceſſary ſenſe, nor ſing true in an harmonious ſyſtem, if we do not feel the harmony.

TO ENFORCE, is to paſs from the dolce to the forte, or from the forte to fortiſſimo, not on a ſudden, but in a regular gradation, by breathing and augmenting the ſounds, whether on a ſeſſion, or on on a continuance of notes, till we have attained what answers to the term of enforced : We then re-take the ordinary play. The Italians express the word enforced in their music by the term crescendo, or rinforzando indifferently.

ENTRANCE. The air of a symphony, by which a ballet is begun.

The word entrance is used also in an opera, to signify an entire act in those ballet operas, each act of which forms a separate subject. " The entrance of Vertumnus in the elements. The en- " trance of the Inca's in the gallant Indians."

Lastly, Entrance is also said of the instant in which each part which follows another begins to make itself heard.

ÆOLIAN. The æolian tone or mode, was one of the five modes which were the chief in the Greek music, and its fundamental chord was immediately above that of the Phrygian mode. (Vide mode.)

The æolian mode was flat, by the report of Lasus, " I sing, " says he, Ceres, and her sister Melibæa, spouse of Pluto, in the " œolian mode filled with flatness."

The name of æolian, which this mode bore, did not derive itself from the Æolian Islands, but from the Eolia, a country in Asia Minor, where it was first used.

EPIAULIA. A name which the Greeks gave to a song of the millers, called otherwise hymea. (Vide song.)

Quere. Does not the word squawl take its derivation from this word? The squawling of a woman, or child who weeps and is lamenting in the same tone, has some resemblance with the notes of a mill, and, by the metaphor, to that of a miller.

EPILENIA. A song of the grape-gatherers, which was accompanied by the flute. (Vide the fifth book of the Athenæa.

EPINICION. A song of victory, by which was celebrated amongst the Greeks the triumph of a conqueror.

EPISYNAPHIA, is, by the traditions of Bacchus, the conjunction of three consecutive tetrachords, as are the meson, hypaton, and synnemenon. (Vide system tetrachord.)

EPITHALAMIUM. A nuptial air, which was formerly sung at the door of the new-married spouses, to wish them a happy union. Such songs are not in use amongst us ; for we know very well that it is a lost labour. When they are made between friends and acquaintance, we generally substitute, in the place of those simple and chaste thoughts, some ones equivocal and obscene, more conformable to the taste of the age.

EPITRITE. The name of one of the rhimes in the Greek music, with which the times were proportioned in sesqui tierce, or from three to four. This rhime was represented by the foot, which the poets and grammarians call also epitrite, a foot com-

 posed

posed of four syllables, the two first of which are effectually proportioned to the two last; as from three to four. (Vide rhime.)

EPOD. An air of the third couplet, which, in odes, terminated what the Greeks call the period, the which was composed of three couplets, viz. the strophe, the antistrophe, and the epod. The invention of the epod was attributed to Archilochus.

EPTAMERIDES. A name given by Monsieur Sauveur to one of the intervals of his system, lain out in the memoirs of the academy anno 1701. This author then divides the octave into forty-three parts, or merides, then each of those into eptamerides, so that the intire octave comprehends three hundred and one eptamerides, which he again subdivides. (Vide decamerides.) This word is formed from ἑπτα, seven, and μέρις, part.

EPTAPHONIA. The name of a portico in the city of Olympia, in which they had managed an echo, which repeated the voice seven times together. There is a great appearance, that the echo was found there by chance, and that then the Greeks, quacks in their nature, have given the art of it to an architect.

EQUISONANCE. A name by which the ancients distinguished the consonances of the octave and double octave from the rest, the only ones which form a paraphonia. As there has often been a want of the same distinction in modern music, we may make use of it with so much the less scruple, as the sensation of the octave is often confounded to the ear with that of the unison.

EUDROMOS. A name of the air which the hautboys played in the Sthenian games, instituted in Argos in honour of Jupiter. Hierax of Argos was the inventor of this air.

EQUAL. A name given by the Greeks to the system of Aristoxenes, because that author generally divided each of his tetrachords into thirty equal parts, a certain number of which he assigned to each of the three divisions of the tetrachord according to the genus, and the nature of that genus, which he wished to establish. (Vide genus, system.)

EVOVÆ. A barbarous word, formed of six vowels, which denote the syllables of the two words, seculorum amen, and which is only used in church music. It is on the letters of this word that we find marked in the psalters and antiphonaries in the catholic churches, those notes, by which, in each tone, and in the different modifications of the tone, we must terminate the staves of the psalms and cantics.

The evovæ always begins by the dominant of the tone of the antient, which precedes it, and always finishes by the final.

EUTHIA. A term of the Greek music, which signifies a continuance of notes proceeding from the flat to sharp. The euthia was one of the parts of the ancient melopæa.

To

To EXECUTE. To execute a piece of musſic, is to ſing, and play all the parts which it contains, as well vocal as inſtrumental, in the unity which they ought to have; and to render it ſuch as it is pricked in the partition. As muſic is formed to be heard, we cannot judge well of it but by its execution. Such a partition appears admirable to the eye, which cannot be heard in its execution without diſguſt; and another may perhaps appear plain and ſimple to the eye, the execution of which delights by unexpected effects. Under-hand compoſers, attentive to give ſymmetry and play to all their parts, appear generally the moſt ingenious people in the world, whilſt we judge of their works only with the eye. Sometimes alſo they have the cunning to place ſo many different inſtruments, ſo many parts in their muſic, that we cannot, without great difficulty, collect together all the ſubjects neceſſary to execute it.

EXECUTANT. A muſician, who performs his part in a concert. It is the ſame thing as concertant. (Vide concertant.)

EXECUTION. The action of executing a piece of muſic. As muſic is generally compoſed of many parts, whoſe exact connection, whether for the intonation, or the meaſure, is very difficult to obſerve, and the ſtrength of which depends more on taſte than ſigns; nothing is ſo rare as a good execution. It is a trifle to read exactly the muſic by the notes; we muſt enter into all the ideas of the compoſer, feel and render the fire of the expreſſion, and have particularly an ear true, and always attentive to liſten and follow the concinnity. We muſt, in French muſic, particularly be careful, that the principal part underſtands the art of ſoftening or augmenting the movement, according to what the taſte in ſinging, the extent of the voice, and the action of the ſinger require. Conſequently, all the other parts muſt be confined, and attentive to the following of the former. The concinnous in the opera divided into parts, wherein the muſic has no other meaſure than that of the action, would be, in my opinion, the moſt admirable thing in execution.

"If the French (ſays St. Evremond) by their commerce with "the Italians, have attained the art of compoſing with more free-"dom; the Italians alſo have gained, by a commerce with the "French, in what they have learnt from them, the art of ren-"dering their execution more agreeable, more affecting, and "more perfect." The reader will, I imagine, diſpenſe with my commentary on this paſſage. I ſhall only add, that the French imagine the whole world to be employed in their muſic, while, on the contrary, in three parts of Italy, the muſicians do not even know that there exiſts a French muſic different from theirs.

We call alſo *execution* the facility of reading and executing an inſtrumental part; and we ſay, for inſtance, of a ſymphoniſt, that he has great execution when he performs correctly, without hesitation, and at first sight, the most difficult things. Execution, taken in this sense, depends particularly on two things; first, from a perfect knowledge of the touch, and fingering of his instrument; and, secondly, from a long custom in reading music, and phrasing it at sight; for while we see separate notes, we always hesitate in the pronunciation; we acquire a great facility in execution, only by uniting them in the common sense which they ought to form, and in placing the thing itself in the place of the sign. 'Tis in this manner that the memory of the reader is not of less assistance than his eye, and that he would read with difficulty an unknown language, though written in the same characters, and composed of the same words, which he reads without hesitation in his own.

EXPRESSION. A quality, by which the musician has a lively feeling, and renders with energy all the ideas which he should utter, and all the sentiments which he should express. There is one expression in composition, and another in execution; and it is from their concurrence, that the most musical and most agreeable effect results.

To give expression to his works, the composer should seize and compare all the connections which may be found betwixt the strokes of his object and the productions of his art; he ought to know or feel the effect of every character, so that he may convey that which he has chosen to a degree suitable to it: for as a good painter does not give an equal light to all his objects, an ingenious musician should neither give the same energy to all his sentiments, or the same force to all his paintings; and should fix each part in its convenient place, not so much to give powers to it alone, as to afford a greater effect to the whole.

After having carefully sought what he should say, he then seeks the method how; and here begins the application of the precepts in that art, which was a particular language, in the which the musician wishes to make himself understood.

The melody, harmony, movement, and choice of instruments and voices, are the elements of musical language; and the melody, by its immediate connection with the grammatical and oratorical account, is that which gives the character to all the rest. Wherefore, it is always from the air that the principal expression should be drawn, as well in instrumental as vocal music.

That then what we endeavour to render by the melody is the tone, by which we express the sentiments which we wish to represent, and we ought to be very careful to imitate in that the theatrical declamation, which itself is no more than an imitation, but to follow the voice of nature, whose accents are without affectation, and without art. Wherefore the musician must first seek a kind of melody which may furnish musical inflexions, most convenient

venient to the ſenſe of the words, by always ſubordinating the expreſſion of the words to thoſe of the thought, and even thoſe to the ſituation of the ſoul of the ſpeaker; for when we are deeply affected, every diſcourſe which we hold takes a tint of the general ſentiment which reigns in us, and we do not quarrel in regard to what we love, in the ſame tone which agitates us in an indifferent matter.

Our words are differently accented according to the different paſſions that inſpire them; ſometimes ſharp and vehement, ſometimes careleſs and looſe; again varied and impetuous, and then equal and tranquil in its inflexions. From thence the muſician draws the difference of the modes in ſinging which he uſes, and of the different places in the which he maintains his voice; cauſing it to proceed in the lower parts by ſmall intervals, to expreſs the languor of ſorrow and melancholly, drawing from it, in the higher parts, ſharp ſounds from paſſion or grief, and conducting it rapidly through all the intervals of his diapaſon, in the agitation of deſpair, or the oppoſition of contraſted paſſions. We muſt particularly obſerve, that the charm of muſic does not conſiſt only in the imitation, but in an agreeable imitation, and that the declamation itſelf, to cauſe ſo great an effect, muſt be ſobordinate to the melody; ſo that we cannot paint a ſentiment without giving it that charm which is inſeparable from it, nor touch the heart, unleſs we pleaſe the ear. And this alſo is very conformable to nature, which gives the tone of ſenſible perſons an unknown affecting and delightful inflexion, which one without feeling can never inherit. Do not then attempt to take rhodomantade for expreſſion, or roughneſs for energy; neither give a frightful picture of the paſſions you wiſh to expreſs; and, in a word, do not, as in the French Opera, where the tone of paſſion is like to the cries from a cholic, much more than the accents of love.

The phyſical pleaſure which reſults from harmony, augments in its turn the moral pleaſure of the imitation, by uniting the agreeable ſenſations of the expreſſive concords of melody, on the ſame principle as I have juſt mentioned. But harmony does ſtill more: it enforces the expreſſion itſelf, by giving a greater juſtneſs and preciſion to melodious intervals; it animates their character, and ſpecifying exactly their place in the order of modulation, it recalls what preceded, denotes what ought to follow, and thus unites the phraſes in the air, as ideas are united in a diſcourſe. Harmony, examined in this manner, furniſhes the compoſer with variety in expreſſion, which eſcapes him when he ſeeks for expreſſion in one harmony alone; for then, inſtead of animating the accent, he ſtifles it by his concords; and all the intervals, confounded in a continued concourſe, offer nothing more to the ear than a continuance of fundamental ſounds, which have nothing affecting

affecting or agreeable, and whose effect has no impression on our mind. What then must the harmonist do to form a concurrence with the expression of the harmony, and give it a greater effect? He must be careful to avoid to cover the principal sound in the combination of concords; he must subordinate all his accompanyments to the singing part; he must sharpen the energy by the concurrence of the other parts; he must enforce the effect of certain passages by sensible concords; he must introduce others by supposition or suspension, by counting them as nothing on the bass; he must give freedom to the strong expressions by major dissonances, and must retain the minor for softer sentiments. One while he must unite all his parts by continued and flowing sounds; another while he will contrast them in the air by sharp notes. One while he will strike the ear by full concords, and again enforce the accent by the choice of a single interval. On every side he will render the union of modulation present and sensible, and will make the bass and its harmony serve to determine the situation of each passage in the mode, so that we can never hear an interval, or stroke in singing, without feeling at the same time his connections with the whole.

In regard to the rhyme, formerly so powerful in giving force, variety, and taste, to poetic harmony; if our languages, less accented, and less prosodic, have lost the charm which resulted from them, our music substitutes in its place, another more independant of the discourse, in the equality of the measure, and in the different combinations of its times, whether in the whole at a time, or separately in each part. The quantities of language are almost lost under those of the notes, and the music, instead of speaking with the words, borrows, in some respect, a peculiar language from the measure. The force of the expression consists in the part, in re-uniting those two languages as much as possible, and in being careful, that, if the measure and rhyme speak not in the same method, they may at least speak the same things.

The vivacity, which gives a gaiety to all our movements, ought to give the same also to the measure. Sorrow confines the soul, softens the movements, and the same languor is felt in the airs which it inspires; but when the grief is lively, or when the soul is agitated by mighty combats, the words are irregular; its direction is alternate with the slowness of the spondee, and the rapidity of the pyrrhic, and is often retarded instantly as in the forced recitative. It is for this reason, that the most expressive music, or at least the most passionate, is generally that wherein the times, though equal betwixt themselves, are most unequally divided; whereas the image of sleep, repose, peace of the soul, &c. are readily painted with equal notes, whose course is neither quick nor slow.

One

One obſervation, which the compoſer ought not to neglect, is, that the more the harmony is removed, the leſs lively the movement ſhould be; ſo that the mind may have time to catch the courſe of diſſonances, and the quick union in the modulations; it is only the laſt tranſports of paſſion which permit an alliance betwixt the rapidity of the meaſure and the roughneſs of the concords. Then when the ſenſes ſeem to vaniſh, and by dint of agitation the actor appears to have no more knowledge where he is, this energic diſorder may be encreaſed, ſo as to force its entrance into the ſoul of the ſpectator, and even render him inſenſible to every object. But unleſs you are ſublime and great, you muſt be cold and inſipid. Throw your audience into an inſenſibility, or be cautious not to fall into it yourſelf; for he who loſes his reaſon is nothing more than a madman in the eyes of thoſe who preſerve it, and madmen intereſt but little.

Though the greateſt force in expreſſion is drawn from the combination of ſounds, the quality of their tone is not indifferent to cauſe that effect. There are ſtrong and ſonorous voices, whoſe quality is good for a ſtrong impreſſion; others light and flexible, good for things of execution; and ſome ſenſible and delicate, which touch the heart by ſweet and pathetic ſounds. In general, the treble, and all ſharp tones, are proper for expreſſing tenderneſs and ſweetneſs; the baſs and concordant for tranſports of paſſion; but the Italians have baniſhed the baſs from their tragedies, as a part whoſe notes are too rough for the heroic genus; and have ſubſtituted in their places the tenor, whoſe note has the ſame character with a more agreeable effect. They uſe this ſame baſs more ſuitably in the comic for under parts, and generally for all profeſſionary parts.

Inſtruments alſo have very different expreſſions, according to the ſound, whether ſtrong or weak, whether the tone be ſharp or ſweet, the diapaſon ſharp or flat, and whether there can be drawn any ſounds in a greater or ſmaller quantity. The flute is tender, the hautboy gay, the trumpet warlike, the horn ſonorous, majeſtic, and proper for great expreſſion. But there is no inſtrument from which there can be drawn a more varied and univerſal expreſſion, than the violin. This admirable inſtrument forms the foundation of every orcheſtra, and ſuffices, to a great compoſer, to draw from it all the effects which a bad muſician ſeeks in vain in the alliance of different inſtruments. The compoſer ought to be acquainted with the handling the violin, to finger his airs, to diſpoſe his arpeggio's, to know the effect of the chords a vide, and to uſe and chooſe his tones according to the different characters which they have on this inſtrument.

It will be uſeleſs for the compoſer to have a knowledge of animating his work, unleſs the fire which ought to reign therein, is tranſmitted

transmitted to the soul of those who execute it. The singer, who sees the notes of his part only, is not in a condition of catching the expression of the composer, or to give any to what he sings, unless he has a true idea of the sense. We must understand what we read to give a true comprehension of it to others, and it is not sufficient to be sensible in general, unless we are particular also in regard to the energy of the language in which we speak. Begin then by a complete knowledge of the character of the air which you are going to render, of its connection with the sense of the words, the distinction of its phrases, the accent which it has peculiar to itself, that which is supposed in the voice of the executant, the energy which the composer has given to the poet, and those which in your turn you also can give the composer. Then relax your organs to all the fire that their considerations may have inspired you with; do the same as you would, were you at the same time poet, composer, actor, and singer, and you will receive all the expression that you can possibly give the work which you are about to perform. By this method it will naturally follow, that you must place delicacy, and such ornaments in your airs, which can be but elegant and pleasing; fire and sharpness in those which are gay and animated; sighs and plaints in those which are tender and pathetic; and the whole agitation of the forte piano, in the transports of violent passions throughout the whole, where the musical accent is united to the oratorical, throughout the whole where the measure is sensibly felt, and serve as guides to the accents of singing, wheresoever the accomponiment and the voice can accord and unite the effects in such a manner, that nothing dut melody results, and that the deceived audience attribute to the voice the passages with which the orchestra embellishes it; lastly, wheresoever the ornaments, ingeniously managed, can bear witness of the facility of the singer, without covering and disfiguring the air, the expression will be sweet, agreeable, and strong; the ear will be delighted, and the heart moved; the physical and the moral will jointly concur to the pleasure of the audience, and there will reign such a concord betwixt the words and air, that the whole will appear to be only a delightful language, which can express every thing, and always please.

EXTENT. The difference of two given sounds, which have intermediaries, or the sum of all the intervals comprised betwixt the two extremes. Wherefore, the greatest possible extent, or that which comprehends all the rest, is that of all the sensible or perceptible sounds from the flattest to the sharpest, according to the experience of Monsieur Euler; all this extent forms an interval of about eight octaves, between a sound which forms thirty vibrations by second, and another which makes 7552 in the same time.

There

There is no extent in music between two terms, from which we may not insert an infinity of intermediate sounds, which divide it into an infinity of intervals; whence it follows, that the sonorous, or musical extent, is continually divisible ad infinitum, as those of time or place. (Vide interval.)

EXTENT OF THE VOICE. A grace in singing, which is marked by a small note, called, in Italian, appoggiatura, and is practised by ascending diatonically from one note to that which follows it, by an elevation in the throat.

EXTENT OF THE VOICE THROWN OUT, is formed when, ascending diatonically from a note to its third, we fix the third note on the sound of the second; to make the third note only be felt by a redoubled elevation of the throat.

EXTENSION, is, according to Aristoxenes, one of the four parts of the melopæa, which consists in sustaining a long time certain sounds, and even beyond their grammatical quantity. We at present call sounds, thus sustained, tenue, or lene.

F.

F UT FA, F FA UT, or simply F. The fourth sound of the natural and diatonic gamut, which is otherwise called fa. (Vide gamut.)

This is also the name of the lowest of the three cleffs in music. (Vide cleff.)

FALSE. This word is in opposition to just. We sing false when the intervals are not toned in justness, and that the sounds are too high, or too low.

There are false voices, false chords, false instruments. In regard to voices, it is pretended, that the fault lies chiefly in the ear. I have, however, seen many people, who sing very false, and, at the same time, tuned an instrument with very great justness. The fault in their voice had not then any effect in regard to the ear. As for instruments, when their tones are false, it is because the instrument is ill constructed, that its strings are ill proportioned, or the chords false, or out of concord; that he who plays touches falsely, or that he modifies the wind or lips ill.

FALSE CONCORD. Discordant accord, either because it contains dissonances, properly so called, or because its consenances are not just.

FALSE HUMMING. A piece of music in several parts, but simple, and without measure, whose notes are almost all equal,

 and

and whofe harmony is always fyllabic. This is the pfalmody of the Roman Catholics fung in many parts. The air of our pfalme, in four parts, may alfo pafs for a kind of falfe humming, but which proceeds with great gravity and flatnefs.

FALSE FIFTH. A diffonant interval, called by the Greeks hemi diapente, whofe two terms are four diatonic degrees diftant, as well as thofe of the true fifth, but whofe interval is lefs by a femi tone; that of the fifth being of two major femi tones of a minor tone, and a femi tone major; and that of the falfe fifth only of a major tone, a minor, and of two femi tones major. If, on our ordinary keys, we divide the octave into two equal parts, we fhall have on one fide the falfe fifth, as fi fa, and on the other the triton, as fa fi; but thefe two intervals, equal in this fenfe, are not fo, either in the number of the degrees, fince the triton has only three; or in the precifion of the connections, that of the falfe fifth being from forty-five to fixty-four, and that of the triton from thirty-two to forty-five.

The concord of falfe fifth is changed from the dominant accord, by placing the fenfible note in the flat. (Vide at the word concord how this is accompanied.)

FALSE RELATION. A diminifhed or fuperfluous interval. (Vide relation.)

FANTASY. A piece of inftrumental mufic, which is executed when compofed. There is this difference betwixt the caprice and the fantafy; that the caprice is a collection of fingular and droll ideas collected by a warm imagination, and which may even be compofed at leifure; whereas the fantafy may be a very regular piece, which differs from the reft only that it is invented in its execution, and that it has no longer exiftence as foon as it finifhed. Wherefore, the caprice confifts in the nature and affortment of ideas, and the ideas in their quicknefs in prefenting them. It follows thence, that a caprice may be very well written, but never a fantafy; for as foon as it is written or repeated, it is no longer a fantafy, but an ordinary piece.

FEIGNED TREBLE, is that kind of voice, by which a man, leaving the fharp of the diapafon of his natural voice, imitates that of a woman. A man, when he fings the feigned treble, does almoft the fame thing as a pipe of the organ when it plays in octave.

FESTA. A diverfion of finging or dancing, which is introduced in the act of an opera, and which interrupts or always fufpends the action.

Thefe fefta are only amufing, in comparifon with the tirefomenefs of the opera. In an interefting drama, when well conducted, it would be almoft impoffible to endure them.

The

The festa are applied more particularly to tragedies, and divertissements to ballets.

FI. A syllable by which many musicians mark the fa diesis, as they do the ma by mi B flat, which appears, I imagine, sufficiently clear.

FIFTH. The second of the consonances in the order of their generation. The fifth is a perfect consonance. (Vide consonance.) Its sound is connected as from two to three. It is composed of four diatonic degrees, coming to the fifth sound, from whence it has its name of fifth. Its interval is of three tones and a half, viz. two major tones, a minor tone, and a major semi tone.

The fifth may be changed in two ways, viz. by diminishing its interval a semi tone, and then it is called false fifth, and should be stiled diminished fifth; or by increasing the same interval a semi tone, and then it is called superfluous fifth; so that the superfluous fifth has four tones, and the false fifth three only, as the triton, from which, in our system, it only differs by the number of degrees. (Vide false fifth.)

There are two concords which bear the name of fifth, viz. the concord of fifth and sixth, which is also called greater sixth, or sixth added, and the concord of superfluous fifth. The first of these two concords is considered two ways, i. e. as a change from the concord of seventh, the third of the fundamental sound being conveyed to flat; this is the concord of greater sixth. (Vide sixth.) Or as a direct concord, whose fundamental sound is in flat, and it is then the concord of sixth added. (Vide double emploi.)

The second is also considered two ways, the one by the French, the other by the Italians. In the French harmony the superfluous fifth is the dominant concord in the minor mode, below which we make the mediant be heard, which forms a superfluous fifth with the sensible note. In the Italian harmony, the superfluous fifth is used only on the tonic in the major mode, when, by chance, the fa is diesis'd, forming then major third on the mediant, and consequently superfluous fifth on the tonic. The principle of this concord, which appears to go out of the mode, may be found in the exposition of Monsieur Tartini's system. (Vide system.)

It is forbid in composition to make two fifths together, by a similar movement between the two parts; this would disgust the ear, by forming a double modulation.

Monsieur Rameau pretends to give a reason for this rule, by a default of union between the concords. He is deceived. In the first place then, two fifths may be formed, and the harmonic union preserved. Secondly, with this union the two fifths are still ill. Thirdly, we must, on the same principle, extend, as in other places,

places, the rule to the major thirds, which is not, and ought not to be. It does not belong to our hypothesis' to act contrary to the judgment of the ear, but only to give reason for them.

False Fifth, is a fifth counted just in harmony, but which by the force of modulation, is found to be weakened a semi-tone. Such is generally the fifth of the concord of seventh on the second note of the tone in the minor mode.

The False Fifth is a dissonance which must be prevented, but the fifth false may pass as a consonance, and be treated as such, when we compose in four parts.

FIFTH, Is also the name given in France to that instrumental part of the whole, which in Italian is called Viola. The name of this part has passed also to the instrument which plays it, viz. Quinte.

FIFTEENTH. An interval of two octaves. (Vide DOUBLE OCTAVE.)

To FIGURE, Is to pass many notes for one; to form doubles, variations; to add notes to the music in any manner whatsoever; lastly, 'tis to give the harmonious sounds a figure of melody, in uniting them by other intermediate sounds. (Vide DOUBLE, FIGURED HARMONY, &c. &c.)

FIGURED. This adjective is applied either to the notes or harmony; to the notes as in this word, Figur'd-bass, to express a bass, whose notes bearing a concord, are divided into many other notes of less powers. (Vide Figured Bass) To the harmony, when by supposition, and in a diatonic direction, we make use of other notes than those which form the concord. (Vide FIGURED HARMONY and SUPPOSITION.

FINAL. The principal chord of the mode which is also called Tonic, and on which the air or piece ought to finish. (Vide MODE.)

When we compose in many parts, and particularly in chorus, the bass must always fall by finishing exactly on the note of the Final: the other parts may stop on the third or fourth. Formerly it was a rule always given at the end of a piece, the major third must be in final, even in the minor mode. But this custom has been found deficient in taste, and entirely abolished.

FINIS. This word is sometimes placed on the final of the first part of a rondeau, to denote, that having retaken this first part, 'tis on this final we must stop and finish. (Vide RONDEAU.)

This word is no longer used in that sense, the French having substituted in its place, the Final Point, according to the example of the Italians. (Vide FINAL POINT.)

To FINGER, Is to direct the fingers in a convenient and regular manner on any instrument, and chiefly on the Organ or the Harpsichord, to play on it with the most ease and skill possible.

On

On instruments for the breast, such as the violin, and violencello, the principal rule of fingering consists in the different positions of the left hand on the sleeve; it is by this means that the same passages may become easy or difficult, according to the positions and chords, on the which we may take these passages; it is, when a symphonist has attained to the art of passing nimbly with justness and precision through all these different positions, that we say he is expert in the sleeve. (Vide Position.)

On the organ and harpsichord, the fingering is entirely different. There are two methods of playing on these instruments, viz. the accompaniment and pieces. To play the pieces, we pay attention to the facility of the execution, and to a pleasing grace of the hand. As there are an excessive number of possible passages, the greater part of which require a particular way of directing the fingers; and since, besides each country and each master has his rule, there would be required on this part such details as this work would not permit, and in which custom and convenience take place of rules, when once the hand is properly fixed. The general precepts which may be given, are, first, to place both hands on the keys in such a manner, as to have nothing inconvenient in the attitude, which obliges us generally to exclude the thumb of the right hand; because the two thumbs placed on the keys, and principally on the white, would give the arms a situation constrained, and by no means graceful. We must also take notice, that the elbows should be a little raised above the edge of the keys, so that the hand may fall of itself as it were on them, which depends on the height of our seat. Secondly, we must hold the wrist nearly at the height of the keys, i. e. on a level with the elbow: the fingers must be removed from the breadth of the keys which are to be touched, so that they may be in readiness to fall on different ones in their turn. Thirdly, we must not successively convey the same finger on consecutive keys, but make use of all the fingers of each hand: Add to these observations the following rules, which I boldly offer, since I have them from Monsieur Dupli, an excellent master on the harpsichord, and who professes a perfect knowledge of fingering.

This perfection consists in general in a soft, easy, and regular movement. The movement of the fingers is taken from their root, that is, from the joint which fixes them to the hand.

The fingers must be naturally bent, and each finger must have its proper movement, independantly from the rest. The fingers must fall on the keys, and not strike them; and, moreover, must flow one from the other in a succession, that is, we must not leave one key before we have fixed on another. This chiefly regards the French methods of playing.

To continue a shake, we must use ourselves to pass the thumb below any finger whatsoever, and to pass any other finger below the thumb. This method is excellent, particularly when we meet with diesis', or B's flat: then be careful that the thumb be fixed on the key which precedes the diesis, or B flat, or place it immediately after: by this means you will gain as many fingers together as you will have notes to form.

Avoid, as much as possible, to touch a white key with the thumb, or fifth finger, particularly in very quick shakes.

The same shake is often executed with the two hands, the fingers of which, in that case, succeed each other successively. In these shakes the hands pass one on the other, but we must take notice, that the sound of the first key, on which one of these hands passes, must also be united to the precedent sound, as much as if they had been touched by the same hand.

In the harmonious and united kind of music, it is necessary to use ourselves to substitute one finger in the place of another, without raising the key. This method gives facility in the execution, and prolongs the duration of the sounds.

For the accompaniment, the fingering of the left hand is the same as for the pieces, because that hand must always play the bass which is to be accompanied; wherefore the rules of Monsieur Duphli serve equally for that part, except on occasions when we wish to augment the noise by means of the octave, on which we fix the thumb and little finger; for then, instead of fingering, the entire hand is conveyed from one part to another. In regard to the right hand, its fingering consists in the arrangement of the fingers, and in the direction given to them, to make the concords and their succession be heard; so that whosoever hears well the mechanism of the fingers in this part, possesses the art of accompaniment. Monsieur Rameau has very well explained that mechanism in his Dissertation on the Accompaniment, and I think I cannot do better than give here an extract of that part of the dissertation which regards the fingering.

Every concord may be arranged by thirds. The perfect concord, i. e. the concord of a tonic, thus ranged on the keys, is formed from three touches, which ought to be struck with the second, third, and fifth finger. In this situation, it is the lowest finger, that is, the second which touches the tonic; in the two other cases, there is always found a finger less below that same tonic. It must be placed in the fourth. In regard to the third finger, which is fixed above or below the two others, it must be placed in tierce in its turn.

A general rule for the succession of concords is, that there should be an union between them; that is to say, that some one of the sounds of the preceding concord should be prolonged on the following concord, and enter into its harmony. It is from this rule that the whole mechanism of the fingering is drawn. Since to pass regularly from one concord to another, some finger must remain in its place. It is evident, that there are only four methods of regular succession between two perfect concords, viz. the fundamental bass ascending or descending from third or fifth.

When the bass proceeds by thirds, two fingers remain in their place; in ascending, those which formed the third and fifth remain the octave and third; whereas, that which formed the octave, descends on the fifth. In descending, the fingers which formed the octave and third, remain to form the third and fifth; whilst that which formed the fifth ascends on the octave.

When the bass proceeds by fifth, one finger only remains in its place, and the two others take their course; in ascending, it is the fifth which remains to form the octave, whilst the octave and third descend on the third and fifth; in descending, the octave remains to form the fifth, whilst the third and fifth ascend on the octave, and on the third. In all these successions the two hands have always a contrary movement.

By exercising ourselves on different parts of the keys, we are soon familiarized to the play of the fingers on each of these courses, and the continuance of perfect concords can be no longer embarrassing.

In regard to the dissonances, we must first take notice, that every compleat dissonant accord employs the four fingers, all of which may be arranged by thirds, or three by thirds, and the other joined to some one of the first, forming with it an interval of second. In the first case, it is the lowest of all the fingers, i. e. the index which expresses the fundamental sound of the concord; in the second case, it is the highest of the two joined fingers. By this observation, we easily know the finger which forms the dissonance, and which consequently ought to descend to prevent it.

According to the different consonant or dissonant accords, which follow a dissonant accord, we must make one or two fingers descend, or three at the end of a dissonant accord; and the perfect concord which prevents it, is easily found under the fingers. In a course of dissonant accords, when one finger alone descends, as in the interrupted cadence, it is always that which has formed the dissonance; that is to say, the lower of the two joined, or the higher of all, if they are arranged by thirds. Should we make two fingers descend, as in the perfect cadence, add to that which I have mentioned, its neighbour below, and if there is none, the highest of all, those are the two fingers which ought to descend. Should three descend, as in the broken cadence, preserve the fundamental on its key, and make the three others descend.

The course of all these different successions, well studied, shews you the play of the fingers in all possible phrases; and as it is from perfect cadences that the most common succession of harmonic phrases is drawn, it is also in that that we must exercise ourselves most: we shall always find there the fingers directed, and ceasing alternately. If the two higher fingers descend on a concord where the two lower remain in their place, in the following concord the two higher remain, and the lower descend in their turn; or at least, they are the two farthest fingers which form the same play with the two middle.

We may also find an harmonic succession ascending by dissonances, by favour of the sixth added, but this succession, less common than that I have spoken of, is more difficult to manage, less prolonged, and the concords seldom are filled with all their sounds. The course of the fingers should have rules herein always, and, by supposing an union of imperfect cadences, we should always find either the four fingers by thirds, or the two fingers joined. In the first case, it would be to the two lower to ascend, and then to the two higher alternately; in the second, the higher of the two fingers joined, ought to ascend with that that is above it; and if there is none, with the lowest of all, &c. &c. &c.

It cannot be imagined, to what a length the study of fingering, taken in this method, may facilitate the practice of the accompaniment. After a little exercise, the fingers take insensibly the custom of directing themselves as it were voluntarily; they prepossess the mind, and accompany with a facility which has something astonishing. But we must confess, that the advantage of this method is not without its inconveniencies; for, without mentioning the octaves and fifths together, which are met with every moment, there results from all this concourse a rough and disagreeable harmony, with which the ear is strangely disgusted, particularly in concords by supposition.

Masters teach other methods of fingering, founded on the same principles, subject, it is true, to more exceptions, but by which, cutting off the sounds, we hurt the hand less; by a too great extension we avoid the octaves and fifths together, and we produce a harmony not so full, but more pure, and more agreeable.

FIXED. Stable chords or sounds are called fixed. (Vide Sound, Stable.)

FLAT is opposed to sharp. The slower the vibrations of a corpo sonoro are, the more flat the sound is. (Vide Sound, Gravity.)

FLATTE.

FLATTE. A grace in the French finging, difficult to be defined, but whose effect will be sufficiently underftood by an example under the word Accent.

FLEURTIS. A kind of figured counterpoint, which is not fyllabic, or note upon note. It is alfo the collection of different graces, with which a fimple air is adorned. This word is now abolifhed in every fenfe. (Vide Double, Variations, &c.)

FLOURISH. A kind of military air, generally fhort and pleafing, which is performed with trumpets, and imitated on other inftruments. The flourifh is generally with two trebles of trumpets, accompanied by tymbals, and when well executed, has fomething martial and gay, which is very fuitable to its ufe. Of all the European troops, the Germans have the beft military inftruments, and their marches and flourifhes have an admirable effect. It is a remarkable thing, that throughout the whole kingdom of France, there is not one trumpet which founds true; and the moft warlike nation in Europe, has the moft difcordant military inftruments, which is certainly attended with inconveniencies. During the laft wars, the peafants of Bohemia, Auftria, and Bavaria, all muficians born, not being able to think that regular troops had inftruments fo falfe, took thofe old foldiers for new recruits, whom they began to look on with contempt; and it cannot be imagined, how many brave men loft their lives on account of their difcordant mufic. So true it is, that in the preparation of war, nothing fhould be neglected which may ftrike the fenfes.

FLOURISHES. This is faid in mufic of feveral notes which the mufician adds to his part in the execution; to vary an air often repeated, to adorn a too fimple paffage, or to give a brightnefs to the volubility of his throat or fingers. Nothing can better fhew the good or ill tafte of a mufician, than the choice and ufe he makes of thefe ornaments. The vocal French mufic is very cautious in regard to flourifhes; it even becomes more fo every day; and if we except the celebrated Jeliote and Mademoifelle Fel, no French actor will now run the hazard of flourifhing on the ftage; for the French airs having of late years taken a more regular and lamentable tone, will no longer permit it. The Italians go the greateft lengths; amongft them there are contentions who fhall extend it fartheft; an emulation which always leads them to too great a height. However, the accent of their melody being very fenfible, they need not fear that the true air fhould difappear under thefe ornaments which the author himfelf has often fuppofed.

In regard to inftruments, we do as we pleafe in a folo, but a flourifhing fymphonift could not be fuffered in a good band.

FOOT. A meaſure of time, or quantity, diſtributed into two or more equal or unequal powers. There was in ancient muſic this difference between the times and feet, that the times were, as the points or elements, indiviſible, and the feet the firſt compoſed of theſe elements. The feet, in their turn, were the elements of the metre or rhime.

There were ſimple feet, which could only be divided into times, and others compoſed, which might be divided into other feet, as the Choriambic, which might be reſolved into a trochee and a Iambic, the Ionic into a pyrrhic and a ſpondee.

There were rhimic feet, whoſe relative and determined quantities were proper to eſtabliſh agreeable connections, as equal, doubles, ſeſquialters, ſeſqui-thirds, &c. and others not rhimic, between which the references were vague, uncertain, little ſenſible, ſuch, for inſtance, as might be formed from French words, which, from ſhort or long ſyllables, have an infinity of others, without a determined power; or which, long or ſhort in grammar rules only, are not judged as ſuch, either by the ear of the poet, or by the practice of the people.

FORCE. The quality of a ſound, called alſo ſometimes Intenſity, which renders it more ſenſible, and heard at a greater diſtance. The more or leſs frequent vibrations of a ſonorous body, are what render the ſound ſharp or flat; its greateſt or leaſt diſtance from the line of the ſtop, is what renders it ſtrong or weak. When this diſtance is too great, and the inſtrument or voice is forced, (vide To force) the ſound becomes a noiſe, and ceaſes to be agreeable.

TO FORCE THE VOICE, is to exceed its diapaſon, high or low, or its extent by force of the breath; or ſcreaming inſtead of ſinging. Every forced voice loſes its juſtneſs; this even happens to inſtruments where the fiddle-ſtick or the wind is forced, and it is for this reaſon that the French ſeldom ſing true.

FORLANE. The air of a dance of the ſame name, common in Venice, particularly amongſt the Gondoliers. Its meaſure is $\frac{6}{8}$; it is beaten gailey, and the dance alſo is very lively. It is called Forlane, becauſe it takes its origin in Frioul, whoſe inhabitants are called Forlans.

FORTE. This word is written in the parts to denote, that the ſound muſt be forced with vehemence, but without raiſing it, ſung in full voice, and much ſound be drawn from the inſtrument; or ſometimes it is uſed to deſtroy the effect of the word dolce, uſed precedently.

The Italians have ſtill the ſuperlative fortiſſimo, which is not at all wanted in the French muſic, for they generally ſing fortiſſimo without any direction.

FORTE PIANO. An Italian substantive composed, and which the musicians ought to frenchify, as the painters have chiar-scuro, by adopting the idea which it expresses. The forte piano is the art of sweetning and enforcing the sounds in imitative melody, as we do in the words which it ought to imitate. Not only when we speak with passion, we do not always express ourselves in the same tone, but we do not always speak even with the same degree of force. Music, by imitating the variety of the accents and tones, ought also to imitate the intense or remiss degrees of the words, and speak one while dolce, another while forte, sometimes a demi voice, and this is what the word forte piano generally expresses.

FOURTH. The third of the consonances in the order of their generation. The fourth is a perfect consonance; its connection is from three to four: it is composed of three diatonic degrees formed by four sounds, from whence it receives its name of fourth. Its interval is of two tones and a half, viz. a major tone, a minor, and a major semi-tone.

The fourth may be changed two ways, i. e. by diminishing its interval a semi-tone, and then it is called diminished fourth, or false fourth; or by augmenting the same interval a semi-tone, and it is then called superfluous fourth, or triton, because its interval has three full tones: it has only two tones, that is, one tone, and two semi tones in the diminished fourth; but this last interval is banished from the harmony, and only practised in an air.

There is a concord which has the name of fourth, or fourth and fifth. Some call it concord of eleventh. It is that, where, under a concord of seventh, we suppose a fifth sound in the bass, a fifth below the fundamental; for in that case, this fundamental forms a fifth, and its seventh has an eleventh with the supposed sound. (Vide Supposition.)

Another concord is called superfluous fourth, or triton. It is a sensible concord, whose dissonance is conveyed to the bass; for in that case the sensible note forms a triton on that dissonance. (Vide Concord.)

Two true fourths together are permitted in composition, even by a similar movement, provided the sixth be added; but those are passages which must not be used wrong, and which the fundamental bass does not absolutely authorise.

FOURTEENTH. A replique, or octave of the seventh. This interval is called fourteenth, because fourteen sounds must be found to pass diatonically from one of its terms to another.

FRAGMENTS. By this name is called in the opera of Paris, the choice of three or four acts of ballet, which are taken from different operas, and collected together, though they have no connection

nection betwixt themselves, to be represented successively the same day, and with their interludes, equal the duration of an ordinary spectacle. There is no man born with taste who can form any idea of such a mixture, and no theatrical and interesting piece which can permit it.

FREDON. An antient word, which signifies a quick passage, and generally diatonic of many notes on the same syllable. This is nearly what has been since called trill, with this difference, that the trill has a longer duration, and is written, whereas the Fredon is only a short addition in taste, or, as it was formerly called, a diminution, which the singer makes on each note.

FUGUE. A piece of music, wherein we treat, according to certain rules of harmony and modulation, an air called subject, by making it pass successively and alternately from one part to another.

There are the principal rules of the fugue, the one of which are proper to it, and the other common with the imitation.

I. The subject proceeds from the tonic to the dominant, or from the dominant to the tonic, in ascending or falling.

II. Every fugue has its answer in the part, which immediately follows that which has begun.

III. This answer ought to return the subject to the fourth or fifth, and by a similar movement, as exactly as possible proceeding from the dominant to the tonic, when the subject is announced from the tonic to the dominant, and vice versa. One part may also retake the same subject in the octave, or in the unison of the precedent; but in that case it is a repetition rather than a true answer.

IV. As the octave is divided into two unequal parts, the one of which comprehends four degrees in ascending from the tonic to the dominant, and the other only three. This obliges us to have attention to that difference in the expression of the subject, and to make some change in the answer, not to quit the essential chords of the mode. It is another thing when we propose to change the tone; in that case, the exactness of the answer itself, taken on another chord, produces alterations suitable to this change.

V. The fugue must be designed in such a manner, as, that the answer may enter before the end of the first air, that we may hear each of them in part at a time, that by this anticipation the subject may be united, as it were, to itself; and that the art of the composer may be shewn in this collection. It is a joke to give as a fugue, an air, which only passes from one part to another, without any other difficulty than accompanying it immediately. This, at most, deserves only the name of imitation. (Vide Imitation.)

Besides

Besides these rules, which are fundamental, to succeed in this kind of composition, there are others, which, tho' only for taste, are not less essential. The fugues, in general, render the music more noisy than agreeable; for which reason, they are more suitacle in chorusses than any where else. Moreover, as their chief merit is to fix the ear always on the principal air or subject, since, on that account, we make them pass incessantly from part to part, and from modulation to modulation, the composer should be particularly careful to render this air always very distinct, or to hinder its being stifled or confounded amongst the other parts. There are two methods for this; one in the movement, which must be continually contrasted, so that, if the course of the fugue is precipitate, the other parts precede also by long notes; and, in the contrary, if the fugue is directed flatly, the accompaniments labour more: the other method is to separate the harmony, lest the other parts, approaching too near to that which sings the subject, should be confounded with it, and prevent its being heard clearly, so that what would be reckoned a fault every where else, becomes a beauty here.

An Unity of Melody. Here is the grand rule to be practised often by different methods. Me must chuse the concords, the intervals, so that a certain sound, and not an indifferent one, may cause the principal effect, viz. an unity of melody. We must sometimes put into play, instruments or voices of a different kind, so that the part which should predominate may be more easily distinguished, viz. an unity of melody. Another observation, not less necessary, is, in the different unions of modulations, which the force and progress of the fugue bring with them, to take care that all these modulations be correspondent, at the same time, in all their parts; to unite the whole in its progress by an exact conformity of tone, for fear that one part being in one tone, and another in another, the entire harmony should be in neither; and should not present any simple effect to the ear, or simple idea to the mind, viz. an unity of melody. In a word, in every fugue, the confusion of melody and modulation is what, at the same time, is most to be feared, and the most difficult to be avoided; and the pleasure which this kind of music produces, being always middling, we may say, that a good fugue is the unrepaid chef-d'œuvre of a good harmonist.

There are also several other kinds of fugues, as the perpetual fugues, called canons; the double fugues, the counter fugues, each of which may be seen under its title, and, which serve more to extend the art of composers, than to please the ear of an audience.

Fugue is from the Latin fuga, flight; because the parts setting off so successively, seem to fly and pursue each other.

CONFUSED FUGUE, Is that whoſe anſwer is made by a movement contrary to that of the ſubject.

FULL PLAY, Is ſaid of the play of an organ, when all the regiſters are fixed, and the whole harmony is filled ; it is ſaid alſo of bow inſtruments, when we draw from them all the ſound which they can give.

FURCE, A quick and continued ſtroke, which aſcends or falls to join two notes diatonically to a great interval, one from the other, thus :

Unleſs the furce be noted, it is neceſſary, for its execution, that one of the two extreme notes have a duration, on which the furce may be paſſed without changing the meaſure.

G.

G RE SOL, G SOL RE UT, or ſimply G, The fifth ſound of the diatonic gamut, which otherwiſe is called ſol. (Vide Gamut.)

It is alſo the name of the higheſt of the three muſical cleffs. (Vide Cleff.)

GAI, This word written above an air, or a piece of muſic, denotes a middle movement between the quick and moderate : it anſwers to the Italian word, Allegro, uſed in the ſame ſenſe. (Vide Allegro.)

This word may alſo be underſtood of a character of muſic, independantly of the muſic.

GAILLARD, A three-tim'd air, belonging to a lively dance of the ſame air. It was formerly called Romaneſque, becauſe, according to report, it is derived from Rome, or, at leaſt, from Italy.

This dance has been out of uſe ſome time. There is only a ſtep of it that remains, called, " The Gaillard ſtep."

GAMUT, A table or ſcale, invented by Gui Aretin, on the which we learn to name and ſound juſtly the degrees of the octave by the ſix notes of muſic, ut, re, mi, fa, ſol, la, according to all the diſpoſitions that can be given them, which is called in French ſolfier, to ſol fa.

The

The gamut has also been stiled an harmonic hand, because Gui made use of the figure of a hand, on the fingers of which he ranged his notes, to shew the connections of his hexachords with the five tetrachords of the Greeks.

This hand has been in use to teach to name the notes, till the invention of si, which abolishes the divisions amongst us, and, consequently, the harmonic hand which serves to explain them.

Gui Aretin having, according to the general opinion, added to the diagram of the Greeks a tetrachord in sharp, and a chord in flat, or rather, according to Meibornius, having, by these additions, established this diagram in its ancient extent, he called that flat chord hyproposlambanomenos, and marked it by the Γ of the Greeks; and as this letter was found thus at the head of the scale, by placing the flat sounds above, according to the method of the ancients, it caused the name of gamut to be given to this scale.

This gamut then, in the whole of its extent, was composed of twenty chords or notes, viz. of two octaves and a major sixth. These chords were represented by letters and syllables. The letters invariably distinguished each a determined chord of the scale, as they do at present; but as there were then but six letters, that there might be seven, and as it was necessary to re-begin from octave to octave, they distinguished these octaves by the figures of letters. The first octave was marked with capital letters, in this manner, Γ. A. B. &c. The second, in running-hand, g. a. b. And for the supernumerary sixth, they used double letters, gg. aa. bb. &c.

In regard to the syllables, they only represented the names which were to be given to the notes in singing. Moreover, as there were only six names for seven notes, it was through necessity that one name was given to two different notes; which was managed in such a manner, as that these two notes, mi, fa, or la, fa, should fall on semi-tones. Consequently, as soon as a diesis or a B flat presented itself, which brought a new semi-tone, the names were to be again changed, which caused the same name to be given to different notes, and different names to the same note, according to the progress of the air: and these changes of the name were called divisions.

These divisions were then learned by the gamut. At the left of each degree, we saw a letter, which denoted precisely the chord belonging to that degree. On the right, in the cases, we found the different names which that note might bear, in rising or descending by B sharp, or B flat, according to the progress.

The difficulties of this method have caused different changes to be made in the gamut at several times. This plate represents the gamut as it is now used in Italy.

The Italian Gamut.

		B sharp	*natural*	*B flat*
	cc	*la*	*mi*	
	dd	*sol*	*re*	*la*
	cc	*fa*	*ut*	*sol*
	bb	*mi*		
	bb			*fa*
	aa	*re*	*la*	*mi*
	g	*ut*	*sol*	*re*
	f		*fa*	*ut*
	e	*la*	*mi*	
	d	*sol*	*re*	*la*
	c	*fa*	*ut*	*sol*
	b	*mi*		*fa*
	a	*re*	*la*	*mi*
	G	*ut*	*sol*	*re*
	F		*fa*	*ut*
	E	*la*	*mi*	
	D	*sol*	*re*	
	C	*fa*	*ut*	
	B	*mi*		
	A	*re*		
	Γ	*ut*		

It is nearly the ſame thing in Spain and Portugal, unleſs that the column of B ſharp is ſometimes found in the laſt place, which here is the firſt, or ſome other difference of as little ſignification.

To make uſe of this ſcale, if we will ſing in natural, we apply ut to Γ. of the firſt column, the length of which we aſcend as far as la, after which, paſſing to the right in the column of B natural, we name fa; we aſcend to la of the ſame column, and then return in the precedent to mi, and ſo in continuance. Or indeed, we may begin by ut at the C of the ſecond column, and when arrived at la, paſs to mi in the firſt column, and then repaſs in the other column to fa. By this method, one of theſe tranſitions always forms a ſemi-tone, viz. la, fa; and the other, always a tone, viz. la mi. By B flat, we may begin at the ut in c or f, and form the tranſitions in the ſame manner, &c.

In deſcending by B ſharp, we quit the ut of the column in the middle, to paſs to mi from that of the B ſharp, or to fa from that of B flat; then, deſcending as far as ut of that new column, we go out by fa from the left to the right, by mi from right to left, &c.

The

The English do not make use of all the syllables, but only the four first, ut, re, mi, fa, changing thus the column every four notes, or every three, by a method similar to that which I have just explained, unless in the place of la, fa, and la, mi, we must move in fa, ut, and mi, ut.

The Germans have no other gamut than the initial letters, which express the fixed sounds in the other gamuts, and they even sol fa with those letters.

The French gamut, otherwise called gamut of si, prevents the embarrassment of all these transitions. It consists in a simple scale of six degrees on two columns, besides that of the letters.

The French Gamut.

E	*si*	*mi*
D	*la*	*re*
C	*sol*	*ut*
B	*fa*	*si*
A	*mi*	*la*
G	*re*	*sol*
F	*ut*	*fa*

The first column on the left is to be sung by B flat, that is, with a B flat in the cleff. The second is sung in natural. Here lies all the mystery of the French gamut, whose difficulty is as trifling as its use, since every other alteration but a B flat puts it instantly out of use. The other gamuts have only this advantage over it, than having a column for the B sharp also, that is, for a diesis in the cleff; but as soon as we put more than a diesis or a B flat (which formerly was never done) all these gamuts are equally useless.

At present, when the French musicians sing every thing in natural, they have no occasion for a gamut. C sol ut, ut, and C, are, to them, no more than the same thing. But in Gui's system, ut is one thing, and C another, very different; and when he gave each note a syllable and a letter, he did not pretend to make synonymies of them, which would be doubling the names and embarrassments to no purpose.

 GAVOT,

GAVOT, A kind of dance, whose air is two tim'd, and is cut into two repeats, each of which begins with the second time, and finishes on the first. The movement of the gavot is generally pleasing, often lively, sometimes also tender and slow. It marks its phrases and its stops every two measures.

GENIUS. Seek not, young artist, what meaning is expressed by genius. If you are inspired with it, you must fell it in yourself. Are you destitute of it, you will never be acquainted with it. The genius of a musician submits the whole universe to his art. He paints every piece by sounds; he gives a language even to silence itself; he renders ideas by sentiments; sentiments by accents; and the passions which he expresses are drawn from the bottom of the heart. Voluptuousness, by his assistance, receives fresh charms; the grief to which he gives utterance, excites cries; he continually is burning, and never consumes. He expresses with fire even the coldest subjects; even in painting the horrors of death, he conveys to the soul that sentiment of life which never abandons it, and which he communicates to hearts formed to feel it. But alas! his words avail nothing to those wherein his seeds are not implanted; and his prodigies are hardly sensible to those who are incapable of imitating them. Would you then wish to know if any spark of this devouring flame inspires you? Be quick, haste to Naples, listen to the master-pieces of Leo, Durante, Jommilli, Pergolesis. If your eyes are filled with tears, if you feel your heart palpitate, if gaiety agitates you, if sorrow involves you in transports, take Metastasio and labour: His genius will enflame yours; you will form a creation after his example: 'Tis this which forms the genius, and the eyes of others will very soon restore you those tears which your masters have caused you to shed. But if the charms of this grand art leave you contented, if you feel no ravishing transports, if you discover nothing beautiful, but what barely pleases, dare you demand what genius is? Vulgar mortal, dare not profane that heavenly appellation. What would it avail to thee to know it? Thou canst not feel it. Compose in French, and peaceably retire.

GENUS. The division and disposition of the tetrachord considered in the intervals of the four sounds which compose it. We imagine that this definition, which is that of Euclid, is only applicable to the Greek music, which I have spoken of in the first place.

The good regulations of a concord of the tetrachord, viz. the establishment of a regular genus, depended on the three following rules, which I draw from Aristoxenes.

The first was, that the two extreme chords of the tetrachord should always remain unmoveable, that their interval might always

ways be that of a true fourth, or a diateſſaron. In regard to the middle chords, I confeſs, they vary, but the interval of Lichanos in Meſis ought never to paſs two tones, nor diminiſh below a tone; ſo that they had preciſely the ſpace of a tone to vary the concord of the Lichanos, and this is the ſecond rule. The third was, that the interval from the parhypaton, or ſecond chord, ſhould not exceed that of the ſame parhypaton to the Lichanos.

As in general this concord might be diverſified three ways, thi conſtituted three principal genera, viz. the diatonic, chromatic, and enharmonic.

Theſe two laſt genera, or the two firſt intervals, formed always together a ſum leſs than the third interval, and were called, on that account, confined genera.

In the diatonic, the modulation proceeded by a ſemi-tone, a tone, and another tone, ſi, ut, re mi; and as we paſſed through three conſecutive tones, from whence it received the name of diatonic, the chromatic proceeded ſucceſſively by two ſemitones and a hemi-diton, or a minor third, ſi, ut, ut dieſis mi. This modulation was placed in the middle between the diatonic and enharmonic, making, if I may be allowed the expreſſion, different diviſions be felt, juſt as when between two principal colours were introduced ſeveral intermediate properties, and from thence this was called the enharmonic or colour'd genus. In the enharmonic, the modulation proceeded by two fourths of a tone, by dividing, according to Ariſtoxenes, the major ſemitone into two equal parts, or a diton, or major ſixth, as ſi, ſi dieſis enharmonic, ut, and mi, or, according to the Pythagoreans, in dividing the major ſemitone into two unequal intervals, which formed one the minor ſemitone, viz. our ordinary dieſis, and the other the complement of this ſame ſemitone minor to the ſemitone major; and then the diton, as before, ſi, ſi ordinary dieſis, ut, mi. In the firſt caſe, the two equal intervals of ſi to ut were both enharmonic, or the fourth of a tone; in the ſecond caſe, there was no enharmonic but the paſſage of ſi dieſis to ut, viz. the difference between the minor and major ſemitone, which is the dieſis called ſo by Pythagoras, and the true enharmonic interval given by nature.

Therefore, as this modulation, ſays Monſ. Burette, was very much confined, running only through ſmall intervals almoſt imperceptible, it was called enharmonic, as one would ſay, well joined, well collected, probè coagmentata.

Beſides theſe principal genera, there were others which reſulted all from the different parts of the tetrachord, or from methods of turning it differently from thoſe which I have mentioned. Ariſtoxenes ſubdivides the diatonic genus into ſyntonic and diatonic mollare, (vide Diatonic) and the chromatic genus into mollare, mollare hemiolian, and tonic, (vide Chromatic) whoſe differences

 he

he gives as I have ſhewn under their articles. Ariſtides Quintilian mentions many other peculiar genera, and he reckons up ſix as very ancient, viz. the Lydian, Dorian, Phrygian, Ionian, Mixolydian, and Syntonolydian. Theſe ſix genera, which muſt not be confounded with the tones or modes of the ſame names, differ in their degrees, as well as in their concord; the one did not reach the octave, the others reach'd, and others paſs'd it, in ſuch a manner as to partake, at the ſame time, of the genus and the mode. The detail of it may be ſeen in a book, intitled, the Greek Muſician.

In general, the diatonic is divided in as many kinds as can be aſſigned to different intervals between the ſemitone and tone.

The chromatic has as many kinds as may be aſſigned to the intervals between the ſemitone and the enharmonic dieſis.

In regard to the enharmonic, it is not ſubdivided.

Independantly of all theſe ſubdiviſions, there was alſo a common genus, in which were uſed only the ſtable ſounds which belong to all the genera, and a mixt genus, which partook of the character of two or of all the three genera. Moreover, we muſt take notice, that in this collection of genera, which was very rare, there were not more than four chords made uſe of, but they were extended or relaxed differently during the ſame piece, which appears rather difficult to practice. I imagine, that perhaps one tetrachord was tun'd in one genus, and another in another, but authors have not made a clear explanation therein.

We read in Ariſtoxenes, Book I. Part II. that until the time of Alexander, the diatonic and chromatic were neglected by ancient muſicians; and that they practiſed only the enharmonic genus, as the only one worthy of their abilities: but this genus was entirely abandoned in the time of Plutarch, and the chromatic was alſo forgotten before Macrobius.

The ſtudy of the ancient writings, rather than the progreſs of our muſic, has rendered us theſe ideas, loſt amongſt their ſucceſſors. We have, as well as themſelves, the diatonic genus, chromatic and enharmonic, but without any diviſions; and we conſider theſe genera under ideas very different from thoſe which they had. They had as many peculiar manners of conducting the air on certain preſcribed chords. For us, theſe are ſo many manners of conducting the entire body of harmony, which force the parts to follow the intervals preſcribed by theſe genera; ſo that the genus belongs ſtill more to the harmony which engenders it, than to the melody which cauſes its ſenſations.

We muſt obſerve again, that in our muſic, the genera are almoſt always mixt, that is, the diatonic enters very much into the chromatic, and each of them is neceſſarily intermingled with the enharmonic. One entire piece of muſic, in one only genus, would be be very difficult to be conducted, neither would it be supportable; for in the diatonic it would be impossible to change the tone; in the chromatic, we should be forced to change the tone in each note; and in the enharmonic, there would be absolutely no kind of union.

All this is again derived from the rules of harmony, which subject the succession of concords to certain rules, incompatable with a continual succession, enharmonic or chromatic, and also from that of the melody, which cannot extract any kind of pleasing air. It was different with the genera of the ancients, as the tetrachords were equally complete, tho' differently divided in each of the three systems; if, in ordinary melody, one genus had borrowed from another, other sounds than those which were necessarily common between them, the tetrachord would have had more than four chords, and all the rules of their music would have been confounded.

Monf. Serre, of Geneva, has made the distinction of a fourth genus, which I have spoken of in its article. (Vide Diacommatic.)

GIG, The air of a dance which bears the same name, whose measure is a 6=8th, and whose movement lively. The French operas contain many gigs, and the gigs of Correlli have been a long time celebrated; but these airs are entirely out of fashion, and there are no more used in Italy, and very few in France.

GRACES IN SINGING, By this term are called, in the French music, certain turns and shakes in the throat, and other ornaments joined to the notes, which are in such or such a position, according to the rules prescribed by a taste in singing. (Vide Taste in Singing.)

The principal of these graces are "The accent, the flow, the flatte, the martellement, full cadence, broken cadence, and extent of the voice." (Vide those articles.)

GRAVE, An adverb which expresses slowness in a movement, and also, a certain gravity in the execution.

GRAVITY, Is that modification of the sound by which it is considered as grave or bass, in connection with the other sounds, which are called high or sharp. There is no correlative to this word in French, for that of acuity could not express it.

The gravity of the sounds depends on the bigness, length, and extension of the chords, on the length and diameter of the pipes, and, in general, on the extent and mass of sonorous bodies. The more they have of that, the greater is their gravity, but there is no absolute gravity, and no sound is flat or sharp but by comparison.

GROS-FA, Certain ancient pieces of church-music, in square notes. Semibreves, and minums, were formerly called the gros-fa.

GROUP,

GROUP, According to the Abbe Bropart, four equal and diatonic notes, the first and third of which are on the same degree, form a group. When the second descends and the fourth rises, it is an ascendant group; when the second ascends and the fourth falls, it is descendant: and he adds, that this name has been given to these notes on account of the figure which they form together.

I do not remember to have ever heard this word used in speaking, in the sense which the Abbe Bropart gives it, nor to have read it in a similar sense any where but in his dictionary.

GUIDE, Is that part which enters first in a fugue, and announces the subject. (Vide Fugue.) This word is very common in Italy, but seldom used in France in the same sense.

GUIDON, A small sign of music which is placed at the extremity of each stave, on the degree where the note must be placed which begins the following stave. If this first note is accidentally accompanied by a diesis, or B sharp, the guidon should be accompanied also.

In Italy the guidon is no longer used, particularly in partitions, where, each part having its place fixed in the column, we cannot mistake in passing from one to the other. But the guidons are necessary in the French partitions, because, from one line to another, the columns, containing more or less staves, leave you in a continual uncertainty of the stave, correspondent to that which you have left.

GYMNOPOEDIA, An air in strain, to which the young Lacedæmonians danced uncovered.

H.

HARMATIAS, The name of a dactylic air, in the Greek music, invented by the first Phrygian Olympus.

HARMONY, The sense which the Greeks gave to this word in their music, is so much the more difficult to determine, as being originally a proper name it has no root, by which it can be uncomposed to extract its etymology. In the ancient treatises that we have remaining, harmony appears to be the part which has for its object the suitable succession of sounds, insomuch as they are sharp or flat, in opposition to the two other parts, which are called rythmica and metrica; which have connection with the time and measure, which leaves to this convenience a vague and undetermined idea, which cannot be fixed but by an express study of all the rules of the art; and still, after this, the harmony will be very difficult

difficult to be distinguished from the melody, unless they add to the last, the ideas of rhyme and measure, without which, in effect, no melody can have a determined character; whereas the harmony is its own by itself, independant of every other quantity. (Vide Melody.) We see by a passage of Nicomachus, and others, that sometimes the name of harmony was given to the consonance of the octave, and to concerts of the voice, and instruments which were executed by the octave, and which were more commonly called antiphonies.

Harmony, according to the moderns, is a succession of concords according to the laws of modulation. This harmony had, for a long time, no other principles than rules almost arbitrary, or only founded on the approbation of an exercised ear, which judged of the good or ill succession of consonances, and whose decisions were immediately placed in calculation. But, P. Mersenne, and Monf. Sauveur, having found that every sound, tho' simple in appearance, was always accompanied by other sounds less sensible, which formed with it a major perfect concord; Monf. Rameau has left this experience, and has made from it the bass of his harmonic system, with which he has filled many books, and which Monf. D'Alembert has lately taken the trouble of explaining to the public.

Monf. Tartini, leaving another experience more new, more delicate, and not less certain, has attained at conclusions pretty similar, by a quite opposite method. Monf. Rameau engenders the treble by the bass; Monf. Tartini engenders the bass by the treble: The one draws the harmony from the melody, and the former acts quite contrary. To decide from which of the two schools the best works take their origin, we need only know which should be made for the other, the air or the accompaniment. A short exposition of M. Tartini's may be found at the word System. I here continue to speak in that of Monf. Rameau, which I have followed thro' the whole of this work, as the only one admitted in the country where I write.

I ought however to declare, that this system, as ingenious as it may appear, is nothing less than founded on nature, as he incessantly repeats it; that it is established only on analogies and conveniencies, which one, who is tolerable at invention, might overthrow to-morrow, by others much more natural; that lastly, of the experience which he deduces, one is known to be false, and the other does not furnish the consequences which he would draw from it. In effect, when this author wished to decorate, with the title of demonstration, the reasonings on which he establishes his theory, the whole world laugh'd at him. The academy refused, and highly disapproved, this ridiculous qualification; and Monf. Esteve, of the Societé Royale, of Montpelier, clearly shewed him, that to begin

begin by that propofition, viz. that, by the law of nature, the octaves of founds reprefent them, and may be taken for them, was no kind of demonftration, nor even folidly eftablifhed in his pretended demonftration. I now return to his fyftem.

The phyfical principle of the reafonance prefents to us the folitary concords and eftablifhes not the fucceffion. A regular fucceffion is however neceffary. A dictionary of chofen words is not an harangue, nor a collection of good concords a piece of mufic. A fenfe is wanting; an union in the mufic as well as language is neceffary: Something of what precedes muft be tranfmitted to what follows, that the whole may form a concinnity, and may be truly *one*.

Moreover, the compofed fenfation, which refults from a perfect concord, is refolved in the abfolute fenfation of each of the founds which compofe it; and in the compared fenfation of each of thefe intervals which thefe fame founds form between themfelves, there is nothing beyond the fenfible in this concord; from whence it follows, that it is only by the connection of the founds, and the analogy of the intervals, that the union in queftion can be eftablifhed: There lies the true and only principle, whence flow all the laws of harmony and modulation. If then, the whole of harmony was formed only by a fucceffion of perfect major concords, it would be fufficient to proceed to them by intervals fimilar to thofe which compofe fuch a concord; for then, fome found of the preceding concord being neceffarily prolonged on the following, all the concords would be found fufficiently united, and the harmony would be in *one*, at leaft, in this fenfe.

But befides that fuch fucceffions would exclude the whole melody, by excluding the diatonic genus, which forms its bafs, they would not reach the true aim of the art, fince mufic, being a difcourfe, ought, like it, to have its periods, its phrafes, fufpenfions, ftops, and punctūation of every kind; and as the uniformity of the harmonic courfes prefents nothing of thefe properties, the diatonic courfe required the major and minor concords to be intermixt, and we have felt the neceffity of diffonances to mark the ftops and phrafes. Moreover, the united fucceffion of perfect major concords, neither gives the perfect minor concord, the diffonance, or any kind of phrafe, and its punctuation appears entirely erroneous.

Monf. Rameau, infifting abfolutely, in his fyftem, that all our harmony fhould be drawn from nature, has had recourfe, for this purpofe, to another experience of his own invention, which I have fpoken of before, and which is changed from the firft. He has pretended, that any found furnifhed in its multiples a perfect minor concord in flat, whofe dominant or fifth it was, as it furnifhed a major in its aliquots, of which it is the tonic or fundamental.

damental. He has advanced, as a certain thing, that a sonorous made two other flatter chords vibrate in their totality, without, however, making them resound, the one in its major twelfth, and the other in its seventeenth; and from this proposition, joined to the precedent, he has deduced, very ingeniously, not only the introduction of the minor mode, and dissonance in harmony, but the rules of the harmonic phrase, and the whole of modulation, such as we find at the words Concord, Accompaniment, Fundamental Bass, Cadence, Dissonance, Modulation.

But first, the experience is false. It is known, that tuned chords, below the fundamental sound, do not entirely shake with this fundamental sound, but that they are divided to render the unison only, which consequently has no harmonies below. It is also known, that the propriety which the chords have of being divided, is not particular to those which are tuned in the twelfth and seventeenth below the principal sound, but that it is common to all its multiples, from whence it follows, that the intervals of twelfth and seventeenth, not being peculiar in their manner, nothing can be concluded from them in favour of the minor perfect concord which they represent.

Though we should suppose the truth of this experience, this would be very far from removing the difficulties. If, as Mons. Rameau pretends, the whole of harmony is derived from the resonance of a sonorous body, it does not then derive from it the single vibrations of a sonorous body which does not resound. In effect, it is a strange theory to derive from what does not resound, the principles of harmony; and it is strange in physic, to make a sonorous body vibrate and not resound, as if the sound itself was at all different from the air, shaken by these vibrations. Besides, the sonorous body does not only give, besides the principal sound, those sounds which with it compose the perfect concord, but an infinity of other sounds, formed by all the aliquots of the sonorous body. Why are the first sounds consonant, and the other not, since they are all equally given by nature?

Every sound forms a concord truly perfect, since it is formed of all its harmonies, and by them it is that it becomes a sound. These harmonies, however, are not heard, and we distinguish no more than a simple sound, unless it be extremely strong; from whence it follows, that the only good harmony is the unison, and that as we distinguish the consonances, the natural proportion being changed, the harmony has lost its purity.

This alteration is formed two ways: first, by giving a sound to certain harmonies, and not to others, we change the connection of force, which ought to reign amongst them all, to produce the sensation of a sound, and the unity of nature is destroyed. We produce, by doubling these harmonies, an effect similar to that which would be produced by ſtifling all the reſt: for then we muſt not doubt, but that, with the generating ſound, we might hear thoſe of the harmonies which we ſhould have left; whereas, by leaving them all, they deſtroy each other, and concur together to produce and enforce the ſingle ſenſation of the principal ſound. This is the ſame effect which the full play of the organ produces; when removing the regiſters ſucceſſively, we leave with the principal the doublet and the fifth; for then that fifth and that third, which remained confounded, were ſeparately and diſagreeably diſtinguiſhed.

Moreover, the harmonies which were made to ſound, have themſelves other harmonies, which are not from the fundamental ſound: It is by theſe harmonies added, that that which produces them is ſtill more roughly diſtinguiſhed; and theſe ſame harmonies, which make the concord to be thus felt, enter not into their harmony. This is the reaſon why the conſonances which are moſt perfect naturally diſpleaſe the ear, little qualified to underſtand them, and I do not doubt but the octave itſelf would, as well as the reſt, diſpleaſe, if the mixture of the voices of men and women had not given the cuſtom of it from its infant ſtate.

In the diſſonance it is ſtill worſe, ſince not only the harmonies of the ſound which give it, but that ſound itſelf does not enter into the harmonious ſyſtem of the fundamental ſound; which cauſes that the diſſonance is always diſtinguiſhed in a diſagreeable manner amongſt the other ſounds.

Every touch of an organ in full play gives a perfect concord major third, which is not diſtinguiſhed from the fundamental ſound, unleſs we pay an extreme attention, and draw the tones ſucceſſiively; but theſe harmonic ſounds are not confounded with the principal, but by favour of a loud harmony, and an arrangement of regiſters, by which the pipes which make the fundamental ſound reſound, cover with their force thoſe which give their harmonies. Moreover, we do not obſerve, neither can we, that continual proportion in a concert, ſince, in conjunction with the change of the harmony, this greateſt force muſt inſtantly paſs from one part to another, which is not practicable, and would entirely disfigure the melody.

When we play on the organ, each touch of the baſs makes the perfect major concord ſound; but becauſe this baſs is not always fundamental, and as we often modulate in perfect minor concord, this major perfect concord is ſeldom that which the right hand ſtrikes; ſo that we hear the minor third with the major, the fifth with the triton, the ſuperfluous ſeventh with the octave, and a thouſand other cacophonies, with which our ear is little diſguſted, becauſe cuſtom renders them convenient; but it could not be preſumed, that it is the ſame thing with an ear naturally juſt,

just, and which, for the first time, we should put to the proof of this harmony.

Monf. Rameau pretends, that trebles of a certain simplicity naturally suggest their bass, and that a man, who has an ear true, and not exercised, will naturally suggest it. This is a prepossession of a musician, proved erroneous by the whole of experience. Not only he, who shall never have heard bass or harmony, will not find this harmony or bass of himself, but they will displease him as soon as he hears them, and he will prefer greatly the simple unison.

When we reflect, that of all the people of the earth, who all have a music and an air, the Europeans are the only ones who have a harmony and concords, and who find this mixture agreeable; when we reflect, that the world has continued so many years, without, amongst the cultivation of the beaux arts throughout mankind in general, any one's having known this harmony; that no animal, no bird, no being in nature, produces any other concord than the unison, no other music than melody; that the eastern languages, so sonorous, so musical; that the Greek air, so delicate, so sensible, exercised with so much art, have never guided these voluptuous people, fond of our harmony, that without it, their music had such prodigious effects, that with it, ours is so weak; that lastly, it it was reserved for the northern nations, whose rough and brutal organs are more touched with the eclat and noise of the voice, than with the sweetness of the accent, and the melody of the inflections, to make this vast discovery, and to give it as a foundation of all the rules in art: When, I say, we pay attention to the whole of this, it is very difficult not to suspect that all our harmony is but a gothic and barbarous invention, which we should never have followed if we had been more sensible of the true beauties of art, and of music truly natural.

Monf. Rameau, however, pretends that harmony is the source of the greatest beauties in music; but this opinion has been contradicted by facts and reason.—By facts, because all the great effects of music have ceased, and it has lost all its energy and force since the invention of the counter point; to which I add, that beauties purely harmonic, are ingenious beauties, which please only persons versed in the art; whereas the true beauties of music, being those of nature, are, and ought to be, equally sensible to every man, whether learned or ignorant.

By reason, because harmony furnishes no imitation by which the music, forming images, or expressing sentiments, may be raised to the dramatic or imitative genus, which is the most noble part of art, and the only one energetic. Every thing that expresses only the physic of sounds, being greatly bounded in the pleasure which it gives us, and having very little power over the human heart. (Vide Melody.)

HARMONY, A genus of music. The ancients often gave this name to the genus commonly called enharmonic genus. (Vide Enharmonic.)

DIRECT HARMONY, Is that wherein the Baſs is fundamental, and where the ſuperior parts preſerve a direct order between themſelves, and with the baſs. Varied harmony is that where the generating ſound or the fundamental is in ſome one of the ſuperior parts, and where ſome other ſound of the concord is tranſported to the baſs below the reſt. (Vide Direct, &c.)

FIGURED HARMONY, Is that wherein we make ſeveral notes paſs on a concord. We figure the harmony by conjoint or disjoint degrees. When we figure by conjoint degrees, we neceſſarily uſe other notes than thoſe which form the concord; notes which are not on the baſs, and are reckoned as nothing in harmony: Theſe intermediate notes ought not to aſcend to the beginning of the times, and principally the ſtrong times, unleſs it be as flowings, extent of the voice, or when we form the firſt note of the ſhort time to bear up the ſecond. But when we figure by disjoint degrees, we cannot abſolutely make uſe of any notes but thoſe which form the concord, whether conſonant or diſſonant. Harmony alſo figures by ſuſpended or ſuppoſed sounds. (Vide Suſpenſion, Suppoſition.)

HARMONIOUS, Every thing which forms an effect in harmony, and even ſometimes every thing which is ſonorous, and fills the ear, by voices, inſtruments, and ſimple melody.

HARMONIES, Whatever belongs to harmony; as the harmonic diviſions of the monochord, the harmonic proportion, the harmonic canon, &c.

HARMONIC, By this name are called all the concomitant or acceſſary ſounds, which, by the principle of reſonance, accompany any ſound, and render it diviſible. Thus all the aliquots of a ſonorous chord give it harmonies.

HARMONIST, A muſician ingenious in harmony. "Such an one is a good harmoniſt." "Durante is the greateſt harmoniſt in Italy, that is, in the world."

HARMONOMETRE, An inſtrument proper for meaſuring harmonic connections. If we could obſerve and follow with the ear and eye, the bodies, knots, and all the diviſions of a chord ſonorous in its vibration, we ſhould have a natural harmonometre very exact; but our groſs ſenſes not being ſufficient for theſe obſervations, we ſupply them by a monochord, divided at our pleaſure by moveable bridges, and this is the beſt natural harmonometre which has been yet diſcovered. (Vide Monochord.)

HARMONIC

HARMONIC HAND, Is the name which Aretin gave to the gamut which he invented, to shew the connection of his hexachords, of his six letters and six syllables, with the five tetrachords of the Greeks. He represented this gamut by the figure of a left-hand, on the fingers of which were marked all the sounds of the gamut, as well by the correspondent letters as by the syllable which he had joined to them, by passing, by the rule of divisions, from one tetrachord or finger to another, according to the place where the two semitones of the octave were placed by the B sharp or B flat, that is, according as the tetrachords were conjoint or disjoint. (Vide Gamut, Divisions.)

HARPALICE, A kind of song, appropriated to young girls amongst the ancient Greeks. (Vide Song.)

HAUT DESSUS, This is, when the singing treble is divided, the superior part. In instrumental parts we always say, first treble, and second treble; but in vocal, we sometimes say, haut treble, and bass treble.

HAUTE TAILLE or TENOR, Is that part of music which is also simply called tenor. When the tenor is subdivided into two other parts, the lower takes the name of basse Taille, or concordant, and the higher is called haute taille.

HEAD, The head or body of a note is that part which determines its position, and to which the tail is fixed when it has one. (Vide Tail.)

Before the invention of printing, the notes had only black heads, for the greatest part of the notes being square, it would have been too long to make them white in writing them. In the impression, the heads of the notes were made white, that is, vacant in the middle. At present both are in use, and all the rest being equal, a white head always denotes a double power to that of a black. (Vide Notes, Powers of Notes.)

HEMI, A Greek word much used in music, and which signifies half. (Vide Semi.)

HEMIDITON, Was, in the Greek music, the interval of major third diminished a semitone, that is, a minor third. The hemiditon is not, as might be believed, the half of a diton or tone, but it is the diton less than the half of a tone, which is entirely different.

HEMIOLE, A Greek word, signifying the entire and a half, and which has, in some respects, been consecrated to music. It expresses the connection of two quantities, one of which is to the other as 15 to 10, or as 3 to 2. It is otherwise called the sesquialter connection.

It is from this connection that the consonance arises, called diapente or fifth; and the ancient sequialter rhyme arose from it also.

The ancient Italian authors give also the name of hemiole, or hemiolian, to that kind of triple measure, each of whose times is a crotchet. If this crotchet is without a tail, the measure is called hemiolia maggiore, because it is struck more slowly, and that two tailed crotchets are necessary for each time. If each time contains only one tailed crotchet, the measure is struck a double quicker, and is called hemiolia minore.

HEMIOLIAN, This is the name which Aristoxenes gives to one of the three kinds of the chromatic genus, whose divisions he explains. The tetrachord 30 is therein divided into three intervals, the two first of which, equal between themselves, are each the sixth part, and of which the third is two thirds 5+5+20=30.

HEPTACHORD, A lyre or cithara with seven chords, as was that of Mercury, according to the report of many.

The Greeks also gave the name of heptachord to a system of music formed of seven sounds, as our gamut at present. The synemenon heptachord, otherwise called the lyre of Terpander, was composed of sounds expressed by these letters of the gamut, E. F. G. a. b. c. d. The heptachord of Philolaüs substituted B sharp in the place of B flat, and may be expressed thus, E. F. G. a. ♮. c. d. Each chord had a connection with one of the planets. The Hypate to Saturn, the Parhypate to Jupiter, and so on.

HEXACHORD, An instrument of six chords, or system composed of six sounds, as, for instance, the hexachord of Gui d'Arezzo.

HEXARMONIAN, A strain or air, from a loose and effeminate melody, as Aristophanes expresses it, in his reproaches to Philoxenes, its author.

HOMOPHONY, This was, in the Greek music, that kind of symphony which was formed in unison, in opposition to antiphony, which was executed in the octave. This word from ὁμὸς, like, and φωνή, a sound.

HUNTING AIR, This name is given to certain airs and flourishes with horns and other instruments, which, it is said, awaken the idea of the tones, which these same horns give in the chace.

HYMEE, A song of the miller's among the ancient Greeks, otherwise called epiaulia. (Vide that word.)

HYMENÆA, A marriage song amongst the ancient Greeks, otherwise called epithalamium. (Vide Epithalamium.)

HYMN, A song in honour of the gods, or of heroes. There is this difference between the hymn and the cantic, that the latter most commonly relates to actions, and the hymn to persons. The first airs of all nations were either cantics or hymns. Orpheus and Linus passed, amongst the Greeks, for the authors of the first hymns:

hymns: And amongſt Homer's poetry we have ſome remains of a collection of hymns in honour of the gods.

HYPATE, An epithet by which the Greeks diſtinguiſhed the loweſt tetrachord, and the loweſt chord of each of the two loweſt tetrachords; which, to them, was quite the contrary, as they followed, in their denominations, an order retrograde to ours, and placed on high the flat which we place low. This choice is arbitrary, ſince the ideas attached to the word ſharp or flat, have no natural union with the ideas attached to the words high and low.

They called tetrachord hypaton that which was the flatteſt of all, and immediately above the proſlambanomenos, or loweſt chord of the mode; and the firſt chord of the tetrachord which immediately followed that, was called hypate-hypaton; that is to ſay, as the Latins have tranſlated it, "the principal of the tetrachord of the principals." The tetrachord immediately following from flat to ſharp, was called tetrachord meſon, or of the middle, and the flatteſt chord was called hypate meſon, that is, the principal of the middle.

Nicomachus, the Geraſinian, pretends, that this word hypate, principal, elevated or ſupreme, was given to the flatteſt of the chords of the diapaſon, in alluſian to Saturn, which of the ſeven planets is at the greateſt diſtance from us. We have reaſon to imagine from thence that this Nicomachus was a Pythagorean.

HYPATE-HYPATON, This was the loweſt chord of the loweſt tetrachord of the Greeks, and of a higher tone than the proſlambanomenos. (Vide the preceding article.)

HYPATE-MESON, Was the loweſt chord of the ſecond tetrachord, which was alſo the ſharpeſt of the firſt, becauſe theſe two tetrachords were conjoint. (Vide Hypate.)

HYPATOIDES, Flat Sounds. (Vide Lepſis.)

HYPERBOLEAN, A ſtrain or air of the ſame character as the hexarmonian. (Vide that article.)

HYPERBOLEON, The hyperboleon tetrachord was the ſharpeſt of the five tetrachords in the ſyſtem of the Greeks.

This word is the genitive from the plural ſubſtantive ὑπερβόλαι, extremities, the ſharpeſt ſounds being at the extremity of the reſt.

HYPER-DIAZEUXIS, A disjunction of two tetrachords ſeparated by the interval of an octave, as were the tetrachord of the hypate's and hyperbole's.

HYPER-DORIAN, A mode in the Greek muſic, otherwiſe called mixo-lydian, the fundamental or tonic of which was a fourth above that of a Dorian mode. (Vide Mode.)

The invention of the hyperdorian mode is attributed to Pythoclydes.

HYPER-ÆOLIAN, The penultimate in ſharp of the fifteen modes of the Greek muſic, the fundamental or tonic of which was a fourth above that of the æolian. The hyper-æolian mode, no more than the hyper-lydian which follows it, was not ſo ancient as the reſt. Ariſtoxenes does not mention it; and Ptolemy, who admitted no more than ſeven, did not comprehend thoſe two.

HYPERIASTIAN or ſharp MIXO-LYDIAN, Is the name which Euclid, and many of the ancients, give to the mode more commonly called hyper-ionian.

HYPER-IONIAN, A mode in the Greek muſic, called alſo by ſome hyper-iaſtian, or ſharp mixo-lydian, which had its fundamental a fourth above that of the ionian mode. The ionian mode is the twelfth in order from flat to ſharp, according to Alypius's numeration. (Vide Mode.)

HYPER-LYDIAN, The ſharpeſt of the fifteen modes in the Greek muſic, the fundamental of which was a fourth above that of the lydian. This mode, no more than its neighbour the hyper-æolian, was not ſo ancient as the other thirteen; and Ariſtoxenes, who names them all, makes no mention of thoſe two.

HYPER-MIXO-LYDIAN, One of the modes in the Greek muſic, otherwiſe called the hyper-phrygian.

HYPER-PHRYGIAN, Called alſo, by Euclid, hyper-mixco-lydian, is the ſharpeſt of the thirteen modes of Ariſtoxenes, forming the diapaſon, or the octave, with the hypo-dorian, the flatteſt of all. (Vide Mode.)

HYPO-DIAZEUXIS, Is, according to old Bacchius, the interval of fifth, which is found between two tetrachords ſeparated by a disjunction, and moreover, by a third intermediate tetrachord. Wherefore there is a hypodiazeuxis between the tetrachords hypaton and diazeugmenon, and between the tetrachords ſynnemenon and hyperbolean. (Vide Tetrachord.)

HYPO-DORIAN, The flatteſt of all the modes in ancient muſic. Euclid ſays it is the moſt elevated; but the true ſenſe of this expreſſion is explained at the word hypate.

The hypo-dorian mode has its fundamental a fourth below that of the dorian mode. It was invented, as it is ſaid, by Philoxenes: This mode is affecting, but gay, uniting ſweetneſs to majeſty.

HYPO-ÆOLIAN, A mode in ancient muſic, called alſo, by Euclid, flat hypo-lydian. This mode has its fundamental a fourth below that of the æolian mode.

HYPO-IASTIAN. (Vide Hypo-Ionian.)

HYPO-

HYPO-IONIAN, The ſecond of the modes in ancient muſic, beginning by the flat. Euclid calls it alſo hypo-iaſtian, and flat hypo-phrygian. Its fundamental is a fourth below that of the ionian mode.

HYPO-LYDIAN, The fifth mode of ancient muſic, beginning by the flat. Euclid calls it alſo hypo-iaſtian, and flat hypo-phrygian. Its fundamental is a fourth below that of the lydian mode.

Euclid diſtinguiſhes two hypo-lydian modes, viz. the ſharp, which is that of this article, and the flat, which is the ſame as the hypo-æolian.

The hypo-lydian mode was peculiar to funeral ſongs, to ſublime and divine meditations: Some attribute its invention to Polymneſtre, of Colophon; others to Damon, the Athenean.

HYPO MIXO LYDIAN, A mode added by Gui d'Arezzo, to thoſe of the ancient muſic. It is properly the plagal of the mixo lydian mode, and its fundamental is the ſame as that of the dorian.

HYPO-PHRYGIAN, One of the modes in ancient muſic, derived from the phrygian mode, whoſe fundamental was a fourth above that of the other. Euclid ſpeaks of another hypo-phrygian mode in the flat of this: It is what is more correctly called hypo-ionian. (Vide that word.)

The character of the hypo-phrygian mode was calm, peaceable, and proper to temperate the vehemence of the phrygian. It was invented, they ſay, by Damon, the friend of Pythias, and pupil of Socrates.

HYPO-PROSLAMBANOMENOS, The name of a chord added, as it is pretended, by Gui d'Arezzo, a tone lower than the proſlambanomenos of the Greeks, that is, below the whole ſyſtem. The author of this new chord expreſſed it by the letter Γ of the Greek alphabet, and from thence we receive the name of gamut.

HYPORCHEMA, A ſort of cantic, by which the feaſts of the gods were danced.

HYPO-SYNAPHE, Is, in the Greek muſic, the disjunction of two tetrachords ſeparated by the interpoſition of a third, conjoint with thoſe two, ſo that the homologous chords of the two tetrachords, disjoined by hypo-ſynaphe, have five tones, or a minor ſeventh of interval between them. Such are the tetrachords hypaton and ſynnemenon.

I.

IALEME, A kind of air peculiar to funerals, formerly in use among the Greeks, as the Linos amongst the same people, and the Muneros amongst the Egyptians. (Vide Song.)

IAMBIC. There were in the ancient music two kinds of iambic verses, one of which were only recited by the sound of instruments, whereas the rest were sung. We do not comprehend what effect the accompaniment of instruments on a simple recital could produce, and all that can be reasonably concluded from it, is, that the most simple method of pronouncing the Greek poetry, or at least the iambic, was made by appreciable sounds, and even then received much from the intonation of the air.

IASTIAN, A name given by Aristoxenes and Alypius to the mode which other authors more generally call ionian. (Vide Mode.)

IMITATION. Dramatic and theatrical music concurs to imitation, as well as poetry or painting; 'tis to this principle that all the fine arts are connected, as Mons. le Batteux has demonstrated. But this imitation has not the same extent for all. All that the imagination can represent to itself has its origin from poetry. Painting, which does not offer its picture to the imagination, but to the sense, and that one sense alone, paints only objects peculiar to the sight. Music would appear to have the same bounds in regard to the hearing: however it paints all, even the objects which are only visible, by a transformation almost inconceivable, it seems to place the eye in the ear, and the greatest surprise of an art, which agitates only in the movement, is to be able to form from it even the image of a repose. Night, sleep, solitude, and silence, enter into the number of the extensive paintings of music. We know that noise can produce the effect of silence, and silence the effect of noise; as when we slumber at an equal and monstrous lecture, and awaken at the instant that it ceases. But music agitates nearer on us, in exciting, by a sense, affections similar to those which may be excited by another, and as the connection cannot be sensible unless the impression is strong, so painting, stript of that force, cannot render to music the imitations which that draws from it. Let all nature be in a slumber, he that contemplates it, sleeps not; and the art of the musician consists in substituting, in the place of the insensible image of the object, that of the movements which his presence excites in the heart of the contemplator. He will not only agitate the sea, animate the flame of a conflagration, make rivulets flow, the rain fall,

fall, and torrents swell, but he will paint the horrors of a boundless desart, calm the tempest, render the air tranquil and serene, and spread over the orchestra, a new and pleasing freshness. He will not directly represent things, but excite in the soul the same movement which we feel in seeing them.

I have said, under the word Harmony, that no principle is drawn from it which leads to musical imitation, since there is no connection between the concords, and the objects we wish to paint, or the passions we would express. I will shew, at the word Melody, what this principle is, which harmony does not furnish, and what strokes, given by nature, are used by music to represent these objects and these passions.

IMITATION, In its technical sense, is the use of the same air, or one similar, in many parts, which make it heard one after the other in the unison, the fifth, the fourth, the third, or in any interval whatsoever. The imitation is always well taken, even in changing several notes, provided that this same air be always known in itself, and that we do not remove far from the laws of a good modulation. Often, to render the imitation more sensible, we make precede a silence or long notes, which seem to stifle the air at the moment that the imitation re-animates it. We treat the imitation as we please, we leave it, we re-take it, and begin another at pleasure: In a word, its rules are as relaxed as those of the fugue are severe, for which reason great masters disdain it, and every imitation too affected, almost always cools a young scholar in composition.

IMPERFECT. This word has several significations in music: An imperfect concord is in opposition to a perfect concord, that which bears a sixth or dissonance, and in opposition to the full concord, it is that which has not all the sounds suitable to it, and which ought to render it complete. (Vide Concord.)

The imperfect mode or time was, in our ancient music, that of the double division. (Vide Mode.)

An imperfect cadence is that which is otherwise called irregular cadence.

An imperfect cadence is that which may be major or minor, as the third and sixth. (Vide Consonance.)

In church-music, they call imperfect modes those which are defectuous high or low, and rest below one of the two terms which they ought to reach.

IMPROVISARE, Is to compose and sing a song extempore, with airs or words, accompanied commonly by a guittar, or any other such instrument. There is nothing more common in Italy than to see two marks meet, challenge, attack, and form alternate couplets on the same air, with a vivacity of dialogue, air, and accompaniment, which cannot be believed but by on eye witness.

INHARMONIC. An inharmonic relation is, according to Monf. Saverien, a term of mufic; and he fends us, for an explanation, to the word Renvoi, where he does not mention it. In regard to fuch a term as this, I am entirely ignorant.

INSTRUMENT, A term of genus, under which we comprehend all artificial bodies which may render and vary the founds, after the example of the voice. All bodies capable of agitating the air by any fhock, and then to excite, by their vibrations, in that agitated air, ondulations pretty frequent, may afford a found; and all bodies capable of accelerating or retarding thefe ondulations, may vary the founds. (Vide Sound.) There are three methods of rendering founds on inftruments, viz. by the vibrations of the chords, by thofe of certain elaftic bodies, and by the collection of the air fhut up within the pipes. I have fpoken, at the word Mufic, of the invention of thefe inftruments.

They are generally divided into chord inftruments, wind, and percuffion inftruments. The chord inftruments, amongft the ancients, were very numerous. The moft known are the following: Lyra, Pfalterium, Trigonium, Sambuca, Cithara, Pectis Magas, Barbiton, Teftudo, Epigonium, Simmicium, Epandoron, &c. All thefe inftruments were touched with the fingers, or with the plectrum, a kind of bow.

For their principal wind inftruments, they had thofe call'd tibia, fiftula, tuba, cornu, lituus, &c.

The inftruments of percuffion were thofe which they named Tympanum, Cymbalum, Crepitaculum, Tintennabulum, Crotalum, &c. But many of thofe did not vary their founds.

We cannot here find articles for thofe inftruments, or for thofe of the modern mufic, whofe number is exceffive. The inftrumental part, not being entered within the plan of my work, for the encyclopœdia, has hindered me, by the extent of the knowledge which it requires, from placing it in this.

INSTRUMENTAL, What belongs to the play of inftruments. "An inftrumental turn in finging." "Inftrumental mufic."

INTENSE. Intenfe founds are thofe which have the greateft force, which are heard at the greateft diftance. They are alfo thofe, which, being rendered by well extended chords, vibrate by their means even more ftrongly. This word is Latin, as well as that of Remifs oppos'd to it, but, in theoric writings, both the one and the other is frenchified and anglicifed.

INTERCIDENCE. A term in church-mufic. (Vide Diaptofis.)

INTER-ACT, A fpace of time which paffes between the end of the act of an opera, and the beginning of the following act; and, during which, the reprefentation is fufpended, whilft the action is fuppofed to continue elfewhere. The orcheftra fills

fills this ſpace, in France, by the execution of a ſymphony, which has alſo the name of interlude.

It does not appear, that the Greeks ever divided their drama's by acts, and, conſequently, had no interludes.

The repreſentation was not ſuſpended on their theatres from the beginning of the piece to the end. It was the Romans, who, little ſmitten with the ſpectacle, began firſt to divide it into many parts, whoſe intervals offered a relaxation to the attention of the ſpectators, and this cuſtom has been continued amongſt us.

Since the interlude is formed to ſuſpend the attention and quiet the mind of the ſpectator, the theatre ſhould remain empty, and the intermedes with which it was formerly filled, formed an interruption of very bad taſte, which could not fail of injuring, by rendering the thread of the action forgotten. However, Moliere himſelf did not ſee this ſimple truth, and the inter-acts of his laſt piece were filled with intermedes. The French, whoſe ſpectacles have more reaſon than fire, and who do not love to be kept long in ſilence, have, of late, reduced the inter-acts to the ſimplicity which they ought to have; and it is to be deſired, for the perfection of the theatre, that their example ſhould be every where followed.

The Italians, whom an exquiſite ſentiment often guides more than reaſon, have proſcribed the dance of the dramatic action. (Vide Opera.) But by a conſequence which ariſes from the too great duration that they would give the ſpectacle, they fill their inter-acts with ballets, which they baniſh from the piece; and tho' they may avoid the abſurdity of a double imitation, they fall into that of the tranſpoſition of the ſcene; and leading the ſpectator thus from object to object, make him forget the principal action, loſe the intereſting parts, and, to give him the pleaſure of the eye, take from him that of the heart. They, however, begin to feel the error of this monſtrous aſſemblage, and, after having almoſt already baniſhed the intermedes of inter-acts, doubtleſs they will not heſitate to aboliſh the dances, and to preſerve it, as is becoming, to make a ſeparate and brilliant ſpectacle at the end of the piece.

But tho' the theatre remains empty in the inter-act, I do not ſay that the muſic ſhould be interrupted, for, in the opera, where it makes a part of the exiſtence of things, the ſenſe of hearing ought to have ſuch an union with that of the ſight, that whilſt we ſee the ſituation of the ſcene, we may hear the harmony, which we muſt ſuppoſe inſeparable; ſo that its concurrence may not at length appear ſtrange or new under the air of authors.

The difficulty which is preſented on this ſubject, is to know what the muſician ought to dictate to the orcheſtra, when there paſſes nothing more on the ſtage. For, if the ſymphony, as well as as dramatic mufic, is no more than a continual imitation, what fhould it fay when no one fpeaks? What fhould it do when there is no longer any kind of action? I anfwer to that, that though the theatre be empty, the foul of the audience is not fo: there muft have remained on them a ftrong impreffion of what they have juft feen and heard. 'Tis for the orcheftra to nourifh and fuftain this impreffion during the inter-act, fo that the fpectator may not reach the conclufion of the following act with the fame coldnefs as he began the piece; and that intereft may be united in his foul as are the events in the reprefented action. By this means, the mufician never ceafes to have an object of imitation, either in the fituation of the characters, or that of the fpectators. The one never hearing but the expreffion of thofe fentiments which they feel go out from the orcheftra, are, as it were, identified with what they hear, and their condition is fo much the more pleafant, as there reigns in it a more perfect concord between what ftrikes their fenfes, and touches their heart.

The ingenious mufician draws alfo from his orcheftra another advantage, to give the reprefentation all the effect that it can have, by leading gradually the fpectator, attentive to the moft favourable fituation of the foul, to the effect of the fcenes which he is about to fee in the approaching act.

The duration of the inter-act has no fixed meafure, but it is fuppofed more or lefs great in proportion to the time which that part of the action requires which paffes behind the theatre. However, that duration ought to have the bounds of fuppofition, relatively to the hypothetic duration of the whole action, and thofe of reallity, relative to the duration of the reprefentation.

This is not the place for examining if the rule of the 24 hours has a foundation fufficient, and if it is never permitted to break through it.

But if we would give to the fuppofed duration of an inter-act, the bounds drawn from the nature of things, I cannot fee that any others can be found than thofe of the time during which no fenfible and regular change was made in nature, as there is none made apparently in the fcene during the inter-act. Moreover, this time is, in its greateft extent, nearly twelve hours, which form the middle duration of a day and night. This fpace being paffed, there is no more poffibility, nor illufion in the duration of an inter-act.

In regard to the real duration, it ought to be, as I have faid, proportioned, both to the duration of the reprefentation, and to the partial and relative duration of what paffes behind the fcenes. But there are other bounds drawn from the general end, which we propofe, viz. the meafure of attention; for we ought to be

very

very cautious not to make the inter-act continue ſo far as to let the ſpectator fall into a delirium and draw near to ſlumbering. This meaſure has not ſuch a preciſion in itſelf, but that the muſician, who has fire and genius of ſoul, may, with the aid of his orcheſtra, extend it much farther than any other. I do not even doubt but there are methods of deceiving the ſpectator by the effective duration of the inter-act, by making him eſteem it more or leſs great, by the methods of inter-fixing the characters of the ſymphony. But it is time to finiſh this article, which is already too long.

INTERLUDE, A piece of muſic or dancing, inſerted at the Opera-Houſe, and ſometimes the Play-Houſe, between the acts of a long piece, to enliven and eaſe the minds of the ſpectators, ſorrowful thro' the tragic, and intereſted in its grand concern.

There are interludes, which are real comic or burleſque drama's, the which dividing thus an intereſting part by one intereſting alſo, toſs and turn the attention of the ſpectator in contrary ſenſes, and in a method quite oppoſite to taſte and reaſon. As dancing, in Italy, does not, and ought not, to enter into the conſtitution of the lyric drama, we are obliged to admit it on the theatre, to uſe out in a detached manner from the piece. It is not that which I find fault with; on the contrary, I think it neceſſary to efface, by an agreeable ballet, the ſad impreſſions left by the repreſentation of a tragic opera; and I highly approve, that this ballet forms a ſubject which has no connection with the piece; but what I diſapprove, is, that they divide the acts by ſimilar ballets, which, dividing thus the action, and deſtroying the intereſting parts, make, as it were, a freſh piece of every act.

INTERVAL, The difference of one ſound and another between the flat and ſharp: This is the whole ſpace which one of the two would have to paſs thro' to reach the uniſon of the other. The difference between interval and extent, is, that the interval is conſidered as undivided, and the extent as divided. In the interval we conſider the two terms only: in the extent, we ſuppoſe their intermediaries: The extent forms a ſyſtem, but the interval may be uncompoſed.

To take this word in its moſt general ſenſe, it is evident that there are an infinity of intervals; but as, in muſic, we bound the number of ſounds to thoſe which compoſe a certain ſyſtem, we bound alſo, by that means, the number of intervals to thoſe which theſe ſounds may form between themſelves. So, that by combining two by two, all the ſounds of any ſyſtem ſoever, we ſhall have all poſſible intervals in the ſame ſyſtem; on which it will remain to reduce under the ſame kind, all thoſe which ſhall be found equal.

The

The ancients divided the intervals of their music in simple or uncomposed intervals, which they called diastems, and in composed intervals, called systems.

The intervals, says Aristoxenes, are different five ways. First, In extent. A great interval differs thus from a smaller. Secondly, In resonance or concord. By this a consonant interval differs from a dissonant. Thirdly, In quantity, as a simple interval differs from one composed. Fourthly, In genus. Thus the diatonic, chromatic, and enharmonic genera, differ in themselves. Fifthly, In the nature of their connection, as the interval, whose rates may be expressed by numbers, differs from an irrational interval. Let us speak a few words on all these differences.

I. The smallest of all the intervals, according to Bacchius, is the enharmonic diesis. The greatest, to take it, at the flat extremity of the hypo-dorian mode, to the sharp extremity of the hypo-mixo-lydian, would be of three compleat octaves; but as there is a fifth to be removed, or even a sixth, according to a passage of Adrastes, cited by Meibonius, the fourth remains above the dis diapason; that is, the eighteenth, as the greatest interval of the Greek diagram.

II. The Greeks divided, as we do the intervals, into consonant and dissonant, but their divisions were not the same as ours, (Vide Consonance.) They again sub-divided the consonant intervals into two kinds, without reckoning the unison, which they called homophony, or a similarity of sounds, and whose interval is void. The first kind was the antiphony, or opposition of sounds, which was made in the octave, and was properly no more than a replique of the same sound, but however an opposition from flat to sharp. The second kind was a paraphony, or distinction of sounds, under which was comprehended every consonance except the octave and its repliques: All the intervals, says Theon, of Smyrna, which are neither dissonant, nor in unison.

III. When the Greeks speak of their diastems, or simple intervals, we must not take this term in its full rigour, for the diesis itself was not, according to them, exempt from composition; but we must always connect it with the genus, to which the interval is applied. For instance, the semitone is an interval simple in the chromatic genus, and in the diatonic, composed in the enharmonic. The tone is composed in the chromatic, and simple in the diatonic; and the diton itself, or major third, which is an interval composed in the diatonic, is uncomposed in the enharmonic. Wherefore, what is a system in one genus, may be a diastem in another, and so reciprocally.

IV. On the genera: Divide successively the same tetrachords, according to the diatonic genus, the chromatic, and enharmonic, you

you will have three different concords, which, compared together, instead of three intervals, will produce nine, bedsides the combinations and compositions which can be made of them, and the difference of all these intervals, which will produce a multitude of others. If you compare, for instance, the first interval of each tetrachord in the enharmonic, and flat chromatic of Aristoxenes, you will have, on one side, a fourth, or $\frac{3}{12}$ of a tone, on the other, a third, or $\frac{4}{12}$, and the two sharp chords will make together an interval; which will be the difference of the two preceding, or the twelfth part of a tone.

V. Passing next to the connections, this article leads me to a small digression.

The Aristoxenians pretended that their music was very well simplified by their equal divisions of intervals, and laughed exceedingly at the whole of Pythagoras's calculation. It seems, however, to me, that this pretended simplicity consisted only in the words, and that if the Pythagoreans had understood their master, and their music, a little better, they would very soon have ceased railing at their adversaries.

Pythagoras did not form those sounds, and their connection, which he first calculated. Guided by experience, he only took an abridgement of his observations. Aristoxenes, incommoded with all his calculations, formed in his brain a system quite different, and, as if he could have changed nature at his pleasure, to have simplified the words, was, he thought, simplifying things, whereas in reality it was entirely contrary.

As the connections of the consonances were simple and easy to be expressed, these two philosophers were in agreement thereon: they were so even on the first dissonances; for they equally agreed that the tone was the difference of the fourth and fifth. But how could they determine this difference otherwise than by calculation? Aristoxenes seems to desire none, and on this tone, whose connection he boasted to be ignorant of, he built his whole musical doctrine. What could there be more easy than to shew him the falseness of his operations, and the justness of those of Pythagoras? But, should he have said, I always take doubles, or halves, or thirds. This is more simple, and more easily made than your commas, your limma and apotomes.—I confess it, Pythagoras had answered: but tell me, I beg, how you take these doubles, halves, and thirds? The other had replied, that he toned them naturally, or that he took them on his monochord.—Well, had answered Pythagoras, tone me the fourth of tone justly. If the other had been quack sufficient to have done it, Pythagoras had added. But is your monochord well divided? Shew me, I beg, what method you have used to take therein the third or fourth of a tone? I cannot see, in such a case, what Aristoxenes could have answered. For, to say that the instrument had been tuned by the voice, besides that it would have been falling into the circle, this was not agreed to by the Aristoxeneans, since they all avowed by their cleff, that the voice should be a long time exercised on an instrument of the greatest justness, to be able to tone the intervals of the flat chromatic, and enharmonic genus.

Moreover, since calculations not less composed are necessary, and even geometrical operations more difficult, to measure the thirds and fourths of the tone of Aristoxenes, than to assign the connections of Pythagoras, it is with reason that Nicomachus, Boetius, and many other theoricians preferred the just and harmonic connections of their master to the divisions of the Aristoxenian system, which were not more simple, and which gave no interval in the justness of its origin.

We must take notice, that those reasonings which were proper to the music of the Greeks, cannot be equally suitable to ours, because all the sounds of our system concur in consonances, which could not be done in theirs, but for the diatonic genus only.

It follows hence, that Aristoxenes distinguished with reason the intervals into rational or irrational; since, though they were all rational in the system of Pythagoras, the greatest part of the dissonances was irrational in his.

In modern music, we consider the intervals also many ways, viz. either generally, as the space or distance of some one of these given sounds; or, as that only of the distances which may be marked; or lastly, as those which are marked on different degrees. According to the first sense, every numerical power, as is the comma, or silent, as the diesis of Aristoxenes, may express an interval. The second sense is applied to the intervals only received in the system of our music, the least of which is the minor semi-tone, expressed on the same degree by a diesis, or B flat. (Vide Semi-tone.) The third acceptation supposes some difference in position: that is, one or more degrees between the two sounds which form the interval. 'Tis in this last acceptation that the word is fixed in practice; so that two equal intervals, such as are the false fifth and triton, bear however different names, if the one has more degrees than the other. We divide, as the ancients did the intervals, into consonants and dissonants. The consonants are perfect or imperfect. (Vide Consonance.) The dissonances are so by nature, are become so accidentally. There are only two intervals dissonant by their nature, viz. the second and seventh, by understanding their octaves and repliques. These

These two alſo may be reduced into one only, but all conſonances may become diſſonant by accident. (Vide Diſſonance.)

Moreover, every interval is ſimple or redoubled. The ſimple interval is that which is contained within the bounds of the octave. Every interval which exceeds this extent is redoubled; that is compoſed of one or more octaves, and of the ſimple interval whoſe replique it is.

The intervals which are ſimple are again divided into direct and varied. Take as a direct any ſimple interval ſoever, its complement in the octave is always varied from that, and reciprocally.

There are only ſix kinds of ſimple intervals, three of which make complements of three others in the octave, and conſequently their variations only. If you then take the ſmalleſt intervals, you will have for direct, the ſecond, third, and fourth; for varied, the ſeventh, ſixth, and fifth. Let the one be direct, the others will be varied, and ſo reciprocally.

To find the name of any interval ſoever, we muſt only add the unity to the number of the degrees which it contains. Wherefore the interval of one degree will give the ſecond; of two, the third; of three, the fourth; of ſeven, the octave; of nine, the tenth, &c. &c. But this is not ſufficient to determine an interval; for under the ſame name it may be major or minor, juſt or falſe, diminiſhed or ſuperfluous.

The imperfect conſonances, and the two natural diſſonances, may be major or minor, which, without changing the degree, makes, in the interval, the difference of a ſemi-tone. If from a minor interval, we take again a ſemi-tone, this interval becomes diminiſhed. If we augment a major interval a ſemitone, it becomes ſuperfluous.

The perfect conſonances are invariable by their nature. When their interval is what it ought to be, they are called juſt. If we change this interval a ſemi-tone, the conſonance is called falſe, and becomes a diſſonance; ſuperfluous, if the ſemi-tone is added; diminiſhed, if it is cut off. The name of falſe fifth is given improperly to the diminiſhed fifth: it is taking the kind for the genus. The ſuperfluous fifth is quite as falſe as the diminiſhed, and even in many reſpects more ſo.

T A B L E

OF ALL THE

SIMPLE INTERVALS

Practicable in Muſic.

Intervals expreſſed by Notes.	Name of the Interval.	Degrees which it contains	Power in Tones and Semi-tones.	Reference in Numbers.
Ut ✱ — re ♭	Second diminiſhed	— 1 —	—— 0 ——	375 —— 384
Si —— ut	Second minor	— 1 —	1 Semi-Tone	15 —— 16
Ut —— re	Second major	— 1 —	1 Tone	8 —— 9
Ut —— re ✱	Second ſuperfluous	— 1 —	1 ½ Tone	64 —— 75
Si —— re ♭	Tierce diminiſhed	— 2 —	1 Tone	125 —— 144
Mi —— ſol	Tierce minor	— 2 —	1 ½ Tone	5 —— 6
Ut —— mi	Tierce major	— 2 —	2 Tones	4 —— 5
Fa —— la ✱	Tierce ſuperfluous	— 2 —	2 ½ Tones	96 —— 125
Ut ✱ — fa	Fourth diminiſhed	— 3 —	2 Tones	75 —— 96
Ut —— fa	Fourth juſt	— 3 —	2 ½ Tones	3 —— 4
Ut —— fa ✱	Fourth ſuperfluous called Triton	— 3 —	3 Tones	32 —— 45
Fa ✱ — ut	Fifth diminiſhed called falſe Fifth.	— 4 —	3 Tones	45 —— 64
Ut —— ſol	Fifth juſt	— 4 —	3 ½ Tones	2 —— 3
Ut —— ſol ✱	Fifth ſuperfluous	— 4 —	4 Tones	16 —— 25
La ✱ — fa	Sixth diminiſhed	— 5 —	3 ½ Tones	125 —— 192
Mi —— ut	Sixth minor	— 5 —	4 Tones	5 —— 8
Sol —— mi	Sixth major	— 5 —	4 ½ Tones	3 —— 5
Re ♭ — ſi	Sixth ſuperfluous	— 5 —	5 Tones	72 —— 125
Re ✱ — ut	Seventh diminiſhed	— 6 —	4 ½ Tones	75 —— 128
Mi —— re	Seventh minor	— 6 —	5 Tones	5 —— 9
Ut —— ſi	Seventh major	— 6 —	5 ½ Tones	8 —— 15
Sol ♭ — fa ✱	Seventh ſuperfluous	— 6 —	6 Tones	81 —— 160
Ut —— ut	Octave	— 7 —	6 Tones	1 —— 2

We

We here find a table of all the ſimple intervals practicable in muſic, with their names, their degrees, their powers, and references.

We muſt take notice in this table, that the interval, called by the harmoniſts, ſuperfluous ſeventh, is only a major ſeventh, with a peculiar accompaniment ; the true ſuperfluous ſeventh, as it is marked in the table, not having a place in harmony, or only ſucceſſively, as an enharmonic tranſition, never rigorouſly in the ſame concord.

We ſhould obſerve alſo, that the greateſt part of theſe references may be determined ſeveral ways: I have preferred the moſt ſimple, and that which gives the feweſt numbers.

To compoſe or redouble one of theſe intervals that are ſimple, it is ſufficient to add to it the octave as many times as we chuſe, and to have the name of this new interval, we muſt add to the ſimple name of interval as many times ſeven as it contains octaves. Reciprocally, to know the ſimple of a redoubled interval, whoſe name it has, we muſt only reject ſeven as often as we can. The reſt will give the name of the ſimple interval which produced it. Chuſe you a redoubled fifth ? that is, the octave of the fifth, or the fifth of the octave ? To five add ſeven, you will have twelve. The redoubled fifth is then a twelfth. To find the ſimple of a twelfth, reject ſeven from the number twelve as many times as you can, the remaining five ſhews you its fifth. In regard to the connection, we muſt only double the conſequence, or take the half of the antecedent of the ſimple powers as many times as we add octaves, and we ſhall have the powers of the redoubled ratio. Wherefore, two three, being the ratio of the fifth ; one three, or, two ſix, will be that of the twelfth, &c. Wherein we muſt obſerve, that in muſical terms, to compoſe or rodouble an interval, is not to add it to itſelf, but to add to it an octave : to triple it, is to add two of them, &c.

I ought to mention here, that all the intervals expreſſed in this dictionary by the names of notes, ought always to be reckoned from flat to ſharp, ſo that this interval, ut ſi, is not a ſecond, but a ſeventh ; and ſi ut, is not a ſeventh, but a ſecond.

INTONATION, The action of tuning. (Vide To Tune.) The intonation may be juſt or falſe, too high or too low, too ſtrong or too weak, and then the word intonation, accompanied with an epithet, is underſtood of the method of tuning.

IONIAN or IONIC, The ionian mode was, counting from flat to ſharp, the ſecond of the five middle modes of the Greek muſic. This was alſo called iaſtian, and Euclid calls it the Phrygian flat. (Vide mode.)

IRREGULAR. Irregular modes in church-muſic, are thoſe whoſe extent is too great, or who have ſome other irregularity.

Formerly,

Formerly, that cadence which did not fall on one of the essential chords of the tone was called irregular; but Monf. Rameau has given this name to a particular cadence, in which the fundamental bafs afcends from fifth, or defcends from fourth, after a concord of fixth added. (Vide Cadence.)

J.

TO JAR, Is to lofe the intonation; that is, to change improperly the juftnefs of the intervals, and, confequently, to fing falfe. There are fome muficians, whofe ear is fo juft, that they form no jar, but fuch as are rather uncommon. Many others do not jar for another reafon, fince, to lofe the tone it muft firft have been found. To fing without a key, to bawl, force the voice too high or too low, and to have more regard to the extent than to the juftnefs, are methods almoft fure to fpoil the ear, and at the fame time to jar.

JARGON, Is, in general, every emotion of the air which renders itfelf fenfible to the audible organs. But in mufic, the word jargon is oppofed to found, and is underftood of every fenfation of the hearing, which is not fonorous and appreciable. We may fuppofe, to explain the difference in regard to this, between the jargon and found, that the laft is appreciable only by the concourfe of its harmonies, and the jargon is not fo, becaufe it is deprived of it. But befides that this method of appreciation is difficult to conceive, if the emotion of the found, caufed by the found, makes the aliquots of that chord vibrate with another, we cannot fee why the emotion of the air, caufed by the jargon, fhaking that fame chord, fhould not, at the fame time, fhake its aliquots. I do not know that any propriety of the air has been made which can make it fufpected, that the agitation which produces the found, and that which produces the prolonged jargon, fhould not be of the fame nature; and that the action and re-action of the air and the fonorous body, or of the air and the jarring body, fhould be caufed by different laws in the effect of each.

Might it not be conjectured, that the jargon is not of a different nature from the found, that itfelf is only the fum of a confufed multitude of different founds, which are heard at a time, and render, in fome fort, their ondulations mutually contrary. All elaftic bodies feem to be more fonorous in proportion as their matter

matter is more homogenous, as the degree of cohesion is more equal throughout, and as the body is not, as it were, divided into a multitude of small masses, which, having different solidities, resound consequently in different tones. Why should not the jargon be from the sound, since it excites it? For every jargon makes the chords of a harpsichord resound, not some ones as does a sound, but all together, because there is not one which finds its unison, or its harmonies. Why should not the jargon be from the sound, since by sounds the jargon is made? Touch, at the same time, all the keys of an instrument, and you will produce a total sensation, which will be a jargon only, and whose effect will be prolonged by the resonance of the chords, only as every other noise which would make the same chords resound. Why should not the jargon be from the sound, since a too strong sound is veritably a jargon, as a voice which screams to its utmost height, or particularly as the sound of a large bell, which we hear even in the clapper itself. For it is impossible to appreciate it, unless, when issuing from the clapper, the sound be sweetened by a convenient distance.

But it may be said, how happens this change of an excessive sound into a jargon? It is because the violence of the vibrations renders the resonance of so great a number of aliquots sensible; because the mixture of so many different sounds forms then its ordinary effect, and is no longer any thing more than noise. Wherefore the aliquots which resound are not only the half, third, fourth, and all the consonances, but the seventh part, the ninth, the one hundredth, and still farther. All this forms an effect similar to that of all the keys of a harpsichord struck at the same time, and by this means the sound becomes a jargon.

The name of jargon is given, in contempt, also to a confused and noisy piece of music, wherein more *Fracas* is heard than harmony, and more clamour than air. "This is only jargon." "This opera makes a great jargon, and little effect."

JULE, The name of a kind of hymn or song amongst the Greeks, in honour of Ceres and Proserpine. (Vide Song.)

JUST. This epithet is generally given to the intervals whose sounds are exactly in the connection which they ought to have, and to voices which strike these intervals always in justness; but it is especially applied to perfect consonances. The imperfect may be major or minor; the perfect are only just: as soon as they are altered a semi-tone, they become false, and consequently dissonances. (Vide Interval.)

JUST, Is sometimes an adverb also. "To sing just." "To play just."

K.

KEYS, A general ſtave or ſum of the ſounds of all the ſyſtem, which reſults from the relative poſitions of the three cleffs. This poſition gives an extent of twelve lines, and, conſequently, of twenty-four degrees, or three octaves and a fourth. All that exceeds this ſpace, above or below, cannot be marked but by the aſſiſtance of one or more accidental lines, added to the fifth which compoſe the ſtave of a cleff.

The notes or diatonic touches of the keys, which are always conſtant, are expreſſed by the letters of the alphabet, with the difference of the notes of the gamut, which, being moveable and relative to the modulation, bear names which expreſs theſe connections. (Vide Gamut.)

Each octave of the keys comprehend thirteen ſounds, ſeven diatonic and five chromatic, repreſented on the inſtrumental cleff by ſo many touches. Formerly theſe thirteen touches anſwered to fifteen chords, viz. one more between the re dieſis and the natural mi, the other between the ſol dieſis and the la; and theſe two chords which formed enharmonic intervals, and which were made to ſound at will by means of two broken touches, were looked upon then as the perfection of the ſyſtem; by virtue of our rules of modulation, theſe two have been cut off, becauſe it would have been neceſſary for them to be placed every where. (Vide Cleff.)

KNOTS, Thoſe fixed points were called knots in the which a ſonorous chord, put into vibration, was divided into vibrating aliquots, which render another ſound than that of the entire chord. For inſtance, if of two chords, one of which will be the triple of the other, we make the ſmalleſt ſound, the greater will anſwer, not by the ſound which it has as an entire chord, but by the uniſon of the ſmalleſt; becauſe, in that caſe, the greater chord, inſtead of vibrating in its totality, is divided, and vibrates only by each of its thirds.

The immoveable points, which are the diviſions, and which, in ſome reſpect, take the place of bridges, are what Monſ. Sauveur has called knots; and he has called ventres the middle points of each aliquot, where the vibration is greateſt, and where the chord is fartheſt removed from the line of the ſtop.

If, inſtead of making another ſmaller chord ſound, we divide the greater to the point of one of its aliquots, by a trifling obſtacle which retards it without ſubjecting it, the ſame caſe will again be met with by making one of the two parts reſound, for

for then the two will reſound in the uniſon of the ſmall, and we ſhall ſee the ſame knots, and the ſame venties as before.

If the ſmaller part is not the immediate aliquot of the greater, but that they have only one common aliquot, they will then be divided both according to their common aliquot, and we ſhall ſee knots and venties, even in the ſmaller parts.

If the two parts are incommenſurable, that is, that they have no common aliquot, then there will be no reſonance, or there will be only that of the ſmaller part, unleſs we ſtrike ſtrong enough to force the obſtacle and make the entire chord reſound.

Monſ. Sauveur found a method to ſhew theſe knots, &c. to the academy, in a very ſenſible manner, by placing on the chord papers of two colours, one in the diviſions of the knots, and the other in the middle of the ventres; for then at the ſound of the aliquot we always ſaw the papers of the ventres fall, and thoſe of the knots remain in their place.

Sonorous Chord in Vibration by its Aliquots at the Sound of one between them.

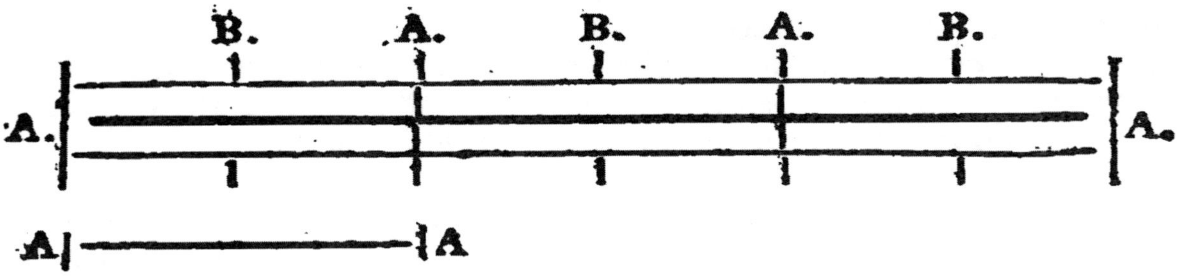

A. Knots, where were the papers of one Colour.
B. Ventue, where were the papers of another Colour.

L.

LA, The name of the ſixth note of our gamut, invented by Guy Aretin.

LARGE, The name of a kind of note in our old muſic, whoſe powers were augmented by drawing ſeveral ſtrokes, not only on the ſides, but thro' the middle of the note, which Muris forcibly blames, as an unnatural innovation.

LARGO. This word written at the head of an air, ſpecifies a ſlower movement than the adagio, and the laſt of all in ſlowness. It shews that we must extend the long sounds, time and measure, &c.

The diminutive larghetto denotes a movement rather quicker than largo, more slow than andante, and approaching nearly to andantino.

LEAP. Every passage from one sound to another by disjoint degrees is a leap. There is a regular leap, which is always made on a consonant interval, and an irregular on a dissonant. This distinction happens from all the dissonances, except the second, which is not a leap, being more difficult to tune than the consonances. A necessary observation in melody to compose easy and agreeable airs.

LEMME, A silence or pause of a short time, in the catalectic rhyme. (Vide Rhyme.)

LENE, A sound sustained by a part during two or more measures, whilst the other parts are changing. (Vide Measure.) It happens sometimes, but seldom, that all the parts are lene's at the same time, and in that case the lene must not be so long, that the sentiment of the measure be forgotten.

LEPSIS, The Greek name of one of the three parts of the ancient melopœa, called also sometimes Euthia, by which the composer discerns, if he ought to place his air in the system of bass sounds called hypatoïdes, in that of sharp sounds called netoides, or that of middling sounds called mesoïdes. (Vide Melopœa.)

LICENCE, A liberty which the composer takes, and which seems contrary to rules, tho' it be in their principle; for herein the licences are distinguished from faults. For instance, it is a rule in composition not to ascend from the minor third, or minor sixth, to the octave. This rule is derived from the law of harmonic union, and from that of the preparation. When then we ascend from the minor third, or minor sixth, to the octave, so that there be however an union between the two concords, or that the dissonance is prepared, we use a Licence: but if there be neither union nor preparation, we make a fault. It is a rule also not to make two just fifths together between the same parts, particularly by a similar movement: the principle of this rule is in the law of the unity of the mode. Every time then that these two fifths may be made without making two modes be felt, it is a licence, but there is no fault. This explanation was necessary, because the musicians have no clear idea of this word licence.

As the greatest part of the rules of harmony are founded on arbitrary principles, and change by custom and the taste of the composers, it happens thence that these rules vary, are subject to the mode, and that what is a licence at one time, is not so at another. Two or three ages back, it was not permitted to make

two

two thirds together, particularly of the same kind; however, entire pieces are now made by thirds. Our ancients did not permit three consecutive tones to be tuned diatonically: at present, we tune, without hesitation, as many as the modulations will permit. It is the same thing with false relations, syncopated harmony, and a thousand other accidents of composition, which were first faults, then licences, and, at present, have not any irregularity at all.

LICHANOS, Is the name, which, among the Greeks, the third chord of their two first tetrachords bore, because that third chord was touched by the index, which they called Lichanos.

The third chord, in the sharp of the lowest tetrachord, which was that of the hypate's, was formerly called lichanos hypaton, sometimes hypaton diatonos, enharmonios, or chromatiké, according to the Greeks. That of the second tetrachord, or tetrachord of the middle, was called lichanos meson, or meson diatonos, &c.

LIGATURE, Was, in our ancient music, the union by a stroke of two or more passed notes, or diatonically, or by disjoint degrees on the same syllable. The figure of these notes, which was square, gave a great facility in uniting them so, which cannot be done at present but by means of the chapeau, on account of the roundness of our notes.

The power of notes which composed the ligature, varied much, according as they ascended or descended; according as they were differently united with a tail, or without; according as these tails were placed on the right or left, ascending or descending; lastly, according to a number of rules so entirely forgotten at present, that perhaps there is not a musician in Europe who is able to decypher the music of some distant antiquity.

LIMMA, An interval of the Greek music, which is less by a comma than a major semi-tone, and, being cut off from a major tone, leaves the apotome for a remainder.

The connection of the limma is from 243 to 256, and its generation is found, beginning by ut, at the fifth fifth si, for then the quantity by which this si is surpassed by the adjoining ut, is precisely in the connection which I have laid down.

LINE. The lines in music are those horizontal and parallel strokes which compose the stave, and on which, or in the spaces which separate them, we place the notes according to their degrees. The stave in church-music has only four lines, that of music in general has five firm and complete, besides the additional lines often added above or below the stave for the notes which pass its extent.

The lines, whether in church-music, or in any other kind, are reckoned, beginning at the most bass. This most bass is the first, the

the higheſt is the fourth, in church-muſic, the fifth in others. (Vide Stave.)

LINOS, A kind of ruſtic air amongſt the ancient Greeks; they had alſo a funeral air of the ſame name, which anſwers to what the Latins called nænia. The one ſay that the linos was invented in Ægypt; others attribute its invention to the Eubeian Linus.

LIVELY, In Italian vivace: This word denotes a gay, quick, animated movement, a bold execution, full of fire.

LONGUE, Is, in our ancient muſic, a ſquare note with a tail on the right, thus 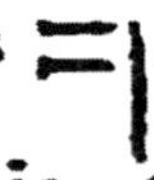. It is ordinarily equal to four two-timed meaſures, that is, two breves; ſometimes it is equal to three according to the mode. (Vide Mode.)

Muris, and his contemporaries, had longues of three kinds, viz. the perfect, the imperfect, and the double. The perfect longue has, on the right ſide, a tail deſcending  or . It is equal to three perfect times, and is itſelf called perfect, on account, ſays Muris, of its numerical reference to the Trinity. The imperfect longue is figured as the perfect, and is not diſtinguiſhed but by the mode: It is called imperfect, becauſe its courſe is not alone, and as it ought always to be preceded or followed by a breve. The double longue contains two equal times imperfect; it is figured as the ſimple longue but with twice the bigneſs . Muris cites Ariſtotle to prove that this note is not belonging to church-muſic.

At preſent, the word longue is the correlative of breve, (vide Breve) wherefore every note which precedes a breve, is a longue.

TO LOOSEN, Is, on ſleeve inſtruments, ſuch as the violin, the violincello, &c. to remove the left hand from its natural poſition, to advance it on a poſition higher, or more in ſharp. (Vide Poſition.) The compoſer ought to know the extent which the inſtrument has, without looſening, ſo that when it paſſes this extent, and looſens, that may be done in a practicable manner.

LOURE, A kind of dance, whoſe air is rather ſlow, and is ordinarily marked by the meaſure $\frac{6}{4}$. When each time bears three notes, the firſt is pointed, and that of the middle is render'd a breve. Loure is the name of an ancient inſtrument, on which the air of the dance in queſtion was played.

LOW, In muſic, ſignifies the ſame thing as grave, and this term is oppoſed to high and ſharp. We ſay alſo, that the tone is too low, that one ſings too low, that the ſound muſt be en-

forced

forced lower. Low ſignifies ſometimes alſo ſlowly, and in this ſenſe it is oppoſed to ſtrong. We ſay, to ſpeak low, to ſing in low or baſs voice. "He ſung or ſpoke ſo low, that it was with difficulty he was heard."

Low again is uſed in the ſub-diviſion of the ſinging trebles, in ſpeaking of that of the two which is below the other; or to ſpeak in other words, low treble is a treble, whoſe diapaſon is below the ordinary medium. (Vide Treble.)

LUTHIARY, A workman who makes violins, violincellos, and other ſimilar inſtruments. This word, which ſignifies a maker of lutes, has been tranſmitted by Synecdoche to this kind of workmen, becauſe, formerly, the lute was the inſtrument moſt uſed in former times, and which were moſt made.

LYDIAN, The name of one of the modes of the Greek muſic, which was placed in the middle between the æolian and hyperdorian. It was called alſo ſometimes the barbarous mode, becauſe it bore the name of an Aſiatic people.

Euclid diſtinguiſhes two lydian modes. The above, properly called ſo, and another which he calls flat lydian, and which is the ſame with the æolian mode, at leaſt in regard to its fundamental. (Vide Mode.)

The character of the lydian mode was animated, ſtriking, ſorrowful however, pathetic, and proper for ſoftneſs, for which reaſon, Plato baniſhed it from his Republic. It is on this mode that Orpheus, it is ſaid, attracted the very beaſts, and with which Amphion built the walls of Thebes. It was invented, the one ſay, by Amphion, the ſon of Jupiter and Antiope; others, by Olympus, a Myſian, a deſciple of Marſias; others alſo, by Melampides; and Pindar ſays, that it was uſed, for the firſt time, at the marriage of Niobe.

LYRIC, What belongs to the lyre: This epithet was formerly given to the poetry made to be ſung and accompanied by the lyre, or cithara, by the ſinger, as odes and other ſongs, with the difference of the dramatic and theatrical poetry, which was accompanied with flutes by others, but at preſent it is applied contrariwiſe to the ſilly poetry of our opera's, and by extenſion, to the dramatic and imitative muſic of the theatre. (Vide Imitation.

LYTIERSE, A ſong of the reapers amongſt the ancient Greeks.

M.

MA, A syllable with which some musicians sol fa the mi B flat, as they sol fa by si the fa diesis.

MACHICOTAGE. By this term is called, in church-music, certain additions and compositions of notes, which fill, by another diatonic course, the intervals of tierces and others. The name of this kind of air comes from that of the Ecclesiastics, called machicots, which formerly executed it after the children of the band.

MADRIGAL, A piece of music well studied and ingenious, which was very much in fashion in Italy in the sixteenth age, and even at the beginning of the precedent. The madrigals were generally composed for the voice in five or six parts, all forced, on account of the fugues and designs with which these pieces were filled; but the organists composed and executed also the madrigals on the organ; and it is even pretended, that it was on this instrument that the madrigal was invented. This kind of counter-point, which was subjected to very rigorous laws, bore the name of magridalesque stile. Many authors, for having excelled in it, have immortalized their names in the annals of art. Such were amongst others, Luca Marentio, Luigi Prenestino, Pomponio Nenna, Tommaso Pecci, and particularly the famous Prince of Venosa, whose madrigals, full of knowledge and taste, were admired by all the masters, and sung by all the ladies.

MAGADIZARE, Was, in the Greek music, to sing in the octave, as the voices of men and women did naturally when united together; wherefore the magadized airs were always antiphonies. This word comes from magas, the bridge of an instrument, and by extension, an instrument with double chords, each ascending to the octave by means of a bridge, as, at present, our harpsichords.

MAGASIN, The Hôtel de la Dependance of the opera at Paris, where the directors and other persons employed in the opera house lodged, and in which is a little theatre, called also theatre, or theatre du magasin, on which the first repetitions were made. This is the odeum of the French music. (Vide Odeum.)

MAJOR. The intervals susceptible of variation are called major, when they are so large as to be so without becoming false.

The intervals called perfect, such as the octave, the fifth, and fourth, have no variation, and are only just, as soon as they are altered, they become false. The other intervals may, without changing their names, and without ceasing to be just, vary a

certain

certain difference: when this difference may be removed, they are major; minors, when it may be added.

These variable intervals are five in number, viz. the semi-tone, the tone, the third, the sixth, and seventh. In regard to the tone and semi-tone, their difference from major to minor cannot be expressed in notes, but in numbers only. The major semi-tone is the interval of a minor second, as from si to ut, or from mi to fa, and its connection is from fifteen to sixteen. The major tone is the difference of the fourth and fifth, and its connection is from eight to nine.

The three other intervals, viz. the third, the sixth, and the seventh, always differ a semi-tone from major to minor, and these differences may be noted. Wherefore the minor third has one tone and a half, and the major third two tones.

There are some other smaller intervals, as the diesis and the comma, which may be distinguished in less, minor, middle, major, and maxima; but as these intervals cannot be expressed but in numbers, these distinctions are useless in practice.

Major is also said of a mode when the tierce of the tonic is major, and then the word mode often is only understood "To pass from major to minor." (Vide Mode.)

MARCH, A military air, which is played by instruments of war, and denotes the metre and cadence of the drums, which is properly the march.

Chardin says, that in Persia, when they are desirous of building houses, flattening a piece of ground, or making some other expeditious work, which requires a quantity of hands, they assemble together the inhabitants of one quarter, that they may labour with the sound of the instruments; and that, by this means, the work may be transacted with much greater zeal and quickness, than if the instruments were not used.

The Marechal de Saxe has shewn, in his reveries, that the effect of the drums was not bounded by a vain noise without utility, but that, according as the movement was more lively or slower, they naturally transported the soldier to press or slacken his pace; we may also say, that the airs of the marches should have different characters, according to the occasion wherein they were used; and this is what they ought to have reflected on to a certain point, when they were distinguished and diversified, one for the assembling together, another for the march, another for the charge, &c. &c. But it would have answered very well if they had profited by this principle as much as they might have done. They have, till now, confined themselves to the composing of tunes which might make the metre be felt, and the beating of the drum be clearly heard. The airs of marches also very often are deficient in that particular.

The

The French troops having few military inſtruments for the infantry, except the fifes and drums, have alſo very few marches, and the greateſt part very badly compoſed; but there are ſome admirable in the German armies.

As an example of the concord and tune of the march, I have given the firſt part of that of the French muſqueteers.

March of the Muſqueteers of the King of France.

There are only the infantry and light cavalry which have marches amongſt the troops. The tymbals of the cavalry have no fixed march; the trumpets have only one tone almoſt uniform, and ſome flouriſhes.

MARTELLEMENT. A kind of grace in the French ſinging. When diatonically deſcending from one note on another by a trill, we enforce the ſound of the firſt note on the ſecond, falling immediately on that ſecond note, by a ſingle turn of the voice, that is called forming a martellement.

MAXIMUM. We call the interval miximum, that which is greater than the major of the ſame kind, and which cannot be marked; for if it could be marked, it would not be called maximum, but ſuperfluous.

The ſemi-tone maximum forms the difference of the minor ſemi-tone and the major tone, and its connection is from twenty-five to twenty-ſeven. There would be between the ut dieſis, and the re, a ſemi-tone of that kind, if all the ſemi-tones were not rendered equal, or ſuppoſed ſuch by the government.

The

The dieſis maximum is the difference between the minor tone and ſemi-tone maximum, in reference from 243 to 250.

Laſtly, The comma maximum, or comma of Pythagoras, is the quantity by which is made the difference between the two terms neareſt to each other, by the progreſſion of fifth, and by a progreſſion by octaves; that is, the exceſs of the twelfth fifth ſi dieſis, on the ſeventh octave ut, and this exceſs, in the reference of 524288 and 531441, is the difference which the government cauſes to be null.

MAXIM, Is a note made in a long horizontal ſquare, with a tail on the right ſide in this manner 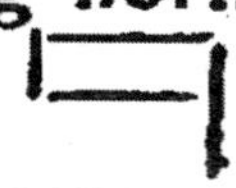, which is equal to eight two-timed meaſures, viz. two longues, and ſometimes three, according to the mode. (Vide Mode.) This kind of note is no longer uſed, ſince the meaſures are ſeparated by bars, and the length or continuities of ſounds are marked with ties. (Vide Meaſure.)

MEASURE, The diviſion of the duration or time into ſeveral equal parts, long enough for the ear to catch and ſubdivide their quantity, and ſhort enough for the idea of the one not to be effaced before the return of the other, and for its equality to be felt.

Each of theſe equal parts is alſo called meaſure; they are ſubdivided into other aliquots, called times, and which are marked by equal motions of the hand or foot. (Vide To beat Time.) The equal duration of each time or meaſure is filled by ſeveral notes, which paſs quicker or ſlower in proportion to their number, and to which different figures are given to make their different durations. (Vide Power of the Notes.)

Many, conſidering the progreſs of our muſic, imagine the meaſure to be a new invention, becauſe it was once neglected. But on the contrary, the ancients not only practiſed the meaſure, but even gave it rules very ſevere, and founded on principles which ours know nothing of. In effect, to ſing without meaſure, is not to ſing; and the ſentiment of the meaſure, not being leſs natural than that of the intonation, the invention of theſe two things could not be made ſeparately.

The meaſure of the Greeks was confined to their language. It was poetry which gave it to muſic: the meaſures of the one anſwered to the feet of the other. Proſe could not have been meaſured in muſic. Amongſt us, it is quite contrary; the little proſody of our languages cauſes the power of the notes in our airs to determine the quantity of the ſyllables: it is on the melody that we are obliged to ſcan our diſcourſe. We do not even perceive whether what we ſing is proſe or verſe: our poetry having no feet, our vocal muſic has no meaſure. The air guides, and the language obeys. The measure fell into oblivion, tho' the intonation was always cultivated, when, after the victories of the Barbarians the language changed their character, and lost their harmony. It is not surprising, that the metre, which served to express the measure of the poetry, should be neglected in those times, when it was no longer felt, and when verse was sung less than prose.——The people, at that time, knew hardly any other amusement than the ceremonies of the church, no other music than that of their devotions; and, as this music did not require a regularity of rhyme, that part was at length entirely forgotten. Gui marked his music with points, which did not express different quantities; and the invention of notes was certainly since the time of that author.

This invention of different powers of notes is generally attributed to Jean de Muris, about the year 1330. But P. Mersenne denies it with reason; and one must have never read the writings of that canon, to sustain an opinion which they so clearly refute. He not only compares the powers which the notes had before him to those which were given them in his time, and which he does not pretend to be the author of, but he even speaks of the measure, and says that the moderns, that is, his contemporaries, nunc morosâ multum utuntur mensurâ, which evidently supposes that the measure, and, consequently, the power of the notes, were known and used before him. Those who would wish to enter a more extensive search where that part of music was in the time of that author, should consult his manuscript treatise, intitled, Speculum Musicæ, which is in the king of France's library, numero 7207, page 280.

The first who gave the notes any rules of quantity, were more attentive to the powers, or relative durations of these notes, than to the measure itself, or to the character of the movement; so that before the distinction of the different measures, there were notes of, at least, five different powers, viz. The maximum, the longue, the breve, the semi-breve, and minime, which may be seen at their articles. What there is of certainty, is, that all these different powers are found, and even more, in the manuscripts of Machault, without finding therein any sign of measure.

In the end, the connection in power of one of these notes to the other, depended on the time, the prolation, and mode. By the mode was determined the connection of the maximum with the longue, or of the longue with the breve; that of the longue with the breve, or of the breve with the semi-breve; and by prolation, that of the breve with the semi-breve, or of the semi-breve with the minor. (Vide Mode, Prolation, Time.) In general, all these different modifications may be connected with the

the double or triple measure, that is, with the division of each power into two or three equal times.

This method of expressing the time or measure of the notes changed entirely during the course of the last age. As soon as it was the custom to enclose each measure within two bars, it was absolutely necessary to proscribe all the kinds of notes which enclosed more measures. Its measure became clearer, the partitions better ordered, and the execution easier, which was very necessary to compensate for the difficulties which music acquired in becoming every day more composed. I have seen excellent musicians very much embarrassed to execute in measure the trios of Orlando and Claudin, composers in the time of Henry III. of France.

Till that time the triple had passed as the most perfect; but at length the double took the ascendant, and the six or four-timed measure was taken as the base of all the rest. Moreover, the four-timed measure is always resolved into one of two times, wherefore, it is properly to the double measure that all the rest are connected, at least in regard to the powers of the notes, and signs of the measures.

Instead then of maximums, longues, breves, semi-breves, &c. were substituted minums, crotchets, demi-crotchets, double and triple demi-crotchets, &c. which were all taken in a sub-double division, so that every kind of note was precisely equal to the half of the precedent. A division clearly insufficient, since the triple measure being preserved, as well as the double or quadruple, and every time being divisible, as every measure into a sub-double or sub-triple power, at the will of the composer, it was necessary to assign, or, rather, preserve to the notes, divisions that answered to these two calculations.

The musicians soon found out the error; but, instead of establishing a new division, they endeavoured to supply that by some new invented sign; wherefore, not being able to divide a minum into three equal parts, they were contented with writing three crotchets, adding the cypher three on that of the middle. This cypher itself, at last, appeared too troublesome for them, and to lay a surer net for those who read their music, they have taken the resolution to suppress the three, or even the six; so that to know if the division is double, or triple, we have no other step to take than to count the notes, or guess.

Tho' there are in our music only two kinds of measures, there are so many divisions made, that at least sixteen kinds may be reckoned, whose signs are these.

2 or ₵ $\frac{2}{4}$ · $\frac{6}{4}$ · $\frac{6}{8}$ · $\frac{6}{16}$, 3, $\frac{3}{2}$ · $\frac{3}{4}$ · $\frac{9}{4}$ · $\frac{3}{8}$ · $\frac{9}{8}$ · $\frac{3}{16}$ · C. $\frac{12}{4}$ · $\frac{12}{8}$ · $\frac{12}{16}$.

(Vide the Examples.)

Two-Times.
1
Of two Times.
2
Two-four.
Of two Times.
3
Six-four.
Of two Times.
4
Three-eight.
Of one Time or of three.
5
Six-eaght
Of two Times
6
Six-fixteen.
Of two Times.
7
Three-Times.
Of three Times.
8
Three-two.
Of three Times.
9
Nine-four.
Of three Times.
10
Nine-eight.
Of three Times.
11
Three-four.
Of three Time.
12
Three-fixteen.
Of one Time.
13
Four-Times.
Of four Time.
14
Twelve-four.
Of four Time.
15
Twelve-eight.
Of four Times.
16
Twelve-fixteen.
Of four Times.

Of all these measures there are three which are called simple, because they have only a single cypher or sign, viz. the 2 or ⊄, the 3, and the C, or four Times. All the rest, which are called double, take their denomination and signs from this last, or from the round note which fills it. This is the rule.

The inferior cypher denotes a number of notes of equal powers, forming together, the duration of a semi-breve, or a four-timed measure. The superior cypher shews how many of those same notes are necessary to fill each measure of the air we are to write.

By this rule, we see that three minums are necessary to fill a measure with the sign $\frac{3}{2}$, two crotchets for that with the sign $\frac{2}{4}$, three demi-crotchets for that with the sign $\frac{3}{8}$, &c. All this confusion of cyphers is ill understood; for why is this connection of so many different measures to that of four times, which is so little like them? or why this connection of so many different notes to a crotchet, whose duration is so little determined? If all these signs are intitled to mark so many different kinds of measures, there are a great deal too many: and if they are to express the different degrees of movements, there are not enough; since, independant of the nature of the measure and division of the times, we are almost always constrained to add a word at the beginning of an air to determine its time.

There are really no more than two kinds of measures in our music, viz. of two and of three equal times; but as each time, as well as each measure, may be divided into two or three equal parts, this makes a sub-division, which gives four kinds of measure in all: We have no more.

We might, however, add a fifth, by combining the two first in a measure of two unequal times; the one composed of two notes, and the other of three. We may find, in this measure, airs very well cadenced, which it would be impossible to mark by an usual measure. I here give an example.

Example

Example of a Measure Sesqui-alter, of two unequal Times.

The Sieur Adolphats made, at Genes, in 1750, an Essay of this Measure, in the grand orchestra, in the air se la sorte mi condanna, of his opera d'Ariane. This piece succeeded, and was applauded. In spite of that, I do not find that his example has been followed.

MEDIANT, Is the chord or note which divides into two thirds the intervals of fifth, which is found between the tonic and dominant. The one of these thirds is major, the other minor;

minor; and it is their relative position which determines the mode. When the major third is in flat, that is, between the mediant and tonic, the mode is major; when the major third is in sharp, and the minor in flat, the mode is minor. (Vide Mode, Tonic, Dominant.)

MEDIATION, A parting of each verse in a psalm into two divisions: the one sung by one side of the band, and the other by the other, in catholic churches.

MEDIUM, That situation of the voice which is equally distant from from flat and sharp. The higher is more striking, but it is always forced; the bass is grave and majestic, but it is more rough. A pleasing medium, in which we suppose a certain latitude, gives the best formed sounds the most melodious, and strikes the ear much more agreeably. (Vide Sound.)

MEDLEY, One of the parts of the ancient melopoea, called agoge by the Greeks, which consisted in interplacing, and properly mixing, the modes and genera. (Vide Melopoea.)

MELODY, A succession of sounds, so ordered, according to the laws of rhyme and modulation, that it forms a sensation agreeable to the ear. The vocal melody is called air, the instrumental, symphony.

The idea of rhyme enters necessarily into that of melody, an air is an air no longer than it is measured; the same succession of sounds may receive as many characters, as many different melodies, as it can be differently scann'd; and the smallest change of the power of the notes can disfigure this same succession, so far, as to render it dubious. Wherefore the melody is nothing by itself: it is the measure which determines it, and there is no air without its time. We ought not then to compare melody with harmony, an abstraction made from the measure in each; for it is essential to the one, and not to the other.

Melody has reference to two different principles, according to the manner in which we consider it. Taken in the connection of sounds, and by the rules of the mode, it has its principle in harmony; since it is an harmonic analysis which gives the degrees of the gamut, the chords of the mode, and the laws of the modulation, the only elements of singing. According to this principle, the whole force of melody is bounded to the flattering the ear by agreeable sounds, as one flatters the eye by agreeable concords of colours; but when taken as an art of imitation, by which the mind may be affected with different images, the heart moved by different sentiments, the passions excited or calmed, in a word, moral effect be operated, which surpass the immediate empire of the sense, another principle must be sought for it, for we see no one taken, by which the harmony alone, and whatever comes from it, can affect us thus.

What

What is this second principle? It is in nature as well as the first, but to discover it therein, a more nice observation is necessary, tho' more simple, and a greater sensibility in the observer. This principle is the same which makes the tone of the voice vary when we speak, according to the things we say, and the movements we use in speaking. It is the accent of the language which determines the melody in each nation; it is the accent which makes us speak while singing, and speak with more or less energy, according as the language has more or less accent. That, whose accent is most expressed, should produce a melody more lively and more passionate. That which has little or no accent, can have only a cold and languishing melody, without character or expression. Herein are the true principles: As long as we leave them, and attempt to speak of the power of music on the human heart, we shall speak unintelligibly,—we shall know nothing of what we say.

If music paints only by melody, and receives from thence its whole force, it follows, that every music, which does not sing, however harmonious it may be, is not an imitative music; and not being able either to touch or paint with its beautiful concords, soon fatigues the ear, and always leaves the heart in a state of coldness. It follows also, that in spite of the diversity of parts, which harmony has introduced, and which at present are so much abused, that as soon as two melodies are heard at the same time, they efface each other, and are of no effect, however beautiful each of them may be separately; from whence we may judge with what taste the French composers have introduced in their operas, the use of making an air of accompaniment serve in the place of a chorus; or another air, which is as if they had taken into their heads to make two discourses at the same time, to give a greater force to their eloquence. (Vide Unity of Melody.)

MELODIOUS, Whatever produces a melody. Melodious, in general, is said of agreeable sounds, sonorous voices, sweet and pleasing airs, &c.

MELOPOEA. This was, in ancient music, the regular use of all the harmonic parts: that is, the art or rules of the composition of an air, the practice and effect of which was call[ed] melody.

The ancients had different rules for the method of conducting their airs by conjoint degrees, disjoint, or mixed, in ascending or falling. We find many in Aristoxenes, which all depend on this principle, that in every harmonic system, the third or fourth sound after the fundamental, ought always to strike its fourth or fifth, according as the tetrachords are conjoint; or disjoint, a difference

difference which renders a mode authentic or plagal, at the pleasure of the composer. This collection of all the rules is called melopœa.

The melopœa is composed of three parts, viz. the prise, lepsis, which teaches the musician in what extent of the voice he ought to establish his diapason; the medley, mixis, according to which he unites or mixes properly the genera, or the modes; and the use, chreses, which is sub-divided into three other parts. The first, called euthia, directs the course of the air, the which is, either direct from flat to sharp, or changed from sharp to flat; or mixt, that is, composed of each. The second, called agogé, moves alternatively by disjoint degrees in ascending, and conjoint in descending, or the contrary. The third, called petteïa, by which he discerns and picks out the sounds to be rejected, those to be admitted, and those to be used most frequently.

Aristides Quintilian divides the whole melopœa into three kinds, which are connected with as many modes, taking this last name in a new sense. The first kind was the hypatoïdes, called so from the chord hypate, the principal or most bass, because the air, directing only the flat sounds, was not at a distance from that chord, and this air was proper to the tragic mode. The second kind was the mesoïdes, from mese, the chord of the middle, because the air reigned on the middling sounds, and this answered to the nomic mode, consecrated to Apollo. The third was called netoïdes, from nete, the last or highest chord: its air was extended only on the sharp sounds, and constituted the dithyrambic or bacchic mode. These modes had others, which were subordinate to them, and varied the melopœa; such as the erotic or amorous, the comic, and encomiac destined to praises.

All these modes, being proper to excite or calm certain passions, had great influence on the manners, and by a reference to this influence, the melopœa was again divided into three genera, viz. the systaltic, or that which inspired tender and affecting passions, the sorrowful, and those capable of engaging the heart, according to the sense of the Greek word. Secondly, the diastaltic, or that which was proper to express noble sentiments, in exciting joy, courage, magnanimity. Thirdly, the euchastic, which was between the other two, and which restored the soul to a state of tranquility. The first kind of melopœa was convenient for amorous poetry, sorrows, bewailings, and other similar expressions. The second was suitable for tragedies, warlike airs, and heroic subjects. The third to hymns, praises, or instructions.

MELOS, Sweetness of singing. It is difficult to distinguish, in the Greek authors, the sense of the word melos from that of melody. Plato, in his Protagoras, places the melos in simple discourse, and seems to understand by it the tune of the word.

The melos appears to be that by which the melody was rendered agreeable. This word is derived from μέλι, Honey.

MESIS, The name of the ſharpeſt chord of the ſecond tetrachord among the Greeks. (Vide Meſon.)

Meſe ſignifies middle, and this name was given to that chord, not, as the Abbé Bropard ſays, becauſe it is common between the two octaves of the ancient ſyſtem, for it bore that name before this ſyſtem had acquired that extent; but becauſe it formed preciſely the middle between the two firſt tetrachords, of which this ſyſtem was then compoſed.

MESOIDES, A kind of melopœa, whoſe airs always were directed on the middle chords, which were alſo called the meſoides of the meſis, or tetrachord meſon.

MESOIDES, Middle ſounds, or ſounds taken in the medium of the ſyſtem. (Vide Melopœa.)

MESON, A name given by the Greeks to their ſecond tetrachord, beginning to reckon by flat; and this is alſo the name by which each of theſe four chords is diſtinguiſhed from thoſe which correſpond to them in the other tetrachords. So, in that I am ſpeaking of, the firſt chord was called hypate-meſon; the ſecond, parhypate-meſon; the third, lichanos-meſon, or meſon-diatonos; and the fourth, meſis. (Vide Syſtem.)

Meſon is the genitive plural of meſis, middle, becauſe the tetrachord meſon is placed in the middle between the firſt and third; or rather, becauſe the chord meſis gives its name to the tetrachord, whoſe ſharp extremity is formed.

A general Diagram of the Greek Syſtem for the diatonic Genus.

	Modern Names.	Ancient Names.	
	La	Neté hyperboleon	Tetrachord hyperboleon.
	Sol	Hyperboleon diatonos	
	Fa	Trite hyperboleon	
	Mi	Neté diezeugmenon —	Synaphe ou conjunction.
Tetrachord Synnemenon.	Re	Diezeugmenon diatonos / Neté ſynnemenon	Tetrachord diazeugmenon.
	Ut	Synnemenon diatonos / Trite ſynnemenon	
	Si	Paramefis — —	Diazeuxis ou disjunction.
	Si bemol	Trite ſynnemenon	
	La	Meſis — — —	
	Sol	Meſon diatonos — —	Tetrachord meſon.
	Fa	Parhypate meſon — —	
	Mi	Hypate meſon — —	Synaphe ou conjunction.
	Re	Hypaton diatonos — —	Tetrachord hypaton.
	Ut	Parhypate hypaton —	
	Si	Hypate hypaton — —	
	La	Proſlambanomenos	

MESOPYCNI,

MESOPYCNI, By this name the ancients called, in the confined genera, the second sound of each tetrachord. The sounds mesopycni were five in number. (Vide Sound, System, Tetrachord.)

METRIC, The metric measure, according to Aristides Quintilian, is the part of music, in general, which has, as its object, the letters, syllables, feet, verses, and the poem. And there is this difference between the metric and rhymic, that the first is only used in the form of the verses, and the second in that of the feet which compose them, which can be applied even to the prose. From whence it follows, that the modern languages may even have a metric music, since they have a poesy, but not a rhymic music, because their poesy has no direction by feet. (Vide Rhyme.)

MI, The third of the six syllables invented by Gui Aretin, to name the notes when the words are not joined to the music. (Vide E si mi, Gamut.)

MINIME, We call interval minime, or lesser, that which is less than the minor of the same kind, and which cannot be marked, for if it could be, it would not be stiled minime, but diminished.

The minime semi-tone is the difference between the semi-tone maximum, and the middle, in reference from 125 to 128. (Vide Semi-tone.)

MINIME, In connection with the duration or time, is, in ancient music, the note which at present we call minum. (Vide Power of the Notes.)

MINIME REST, A silence equivalent to a crotchet, and which is marked by a bent stroke approaching to the figure of 7, a cypher, but turned in a contrary sense, in this sort, 1. (Vide Silence, Notes.)

MINOR, A name borne by certain intervals, when they are small enough to be so without becoming false. (Vide Major, Interval.)

Minor is also said of the mode, when the third of the tonic is minor. (Vide Mode.)

MINUM, Is the name of a note, which is equal to two crotchets, or the half of a semi-breve. (Vide Notes.)

MIXIS, MEDLEY, One of the parts of the ancient melopœa, by which the composer learns to combine properly the intervals, and to distribute the genera and modes according to the character of the air which he has proposed to form. (Vide Melopœa.)

MIXO-LYDIAN, The name of one of the modes of ancient music, called otherwise hyper-dorian. (Vide this word.) The mixo-lydian mode was the sharpest of the seven, to which Ptolomy had reduced all those of the Greek music.

This mode is affecting, passionate, suitable to the greater movements, and, by that means, to tragedy itself. Aristoxenes assures us, that Sappho was the inventress of it; but Plutarch says, that some ancient tables attribute it to Pytoclides. He also says, that the Argians punished the first that used it, and who had introduced in music the use of seven chords, that is, a tonic on the seventh chord.

MIXT, We call mixt, or connexed modes, in church music, the airs whose extent exceeds their octave, and enters from one mode into another, partaking, by this means, from the authentic and the plagal. This medley is composed of equal modes, as of the first tone with the second; of the third with the fourth; in a word, of the plagal with its authentic, and reciprocally.

MOBILE, The two middle chords of each tetrachord were called mobile chords in the Greek music, because they accorded differently according to the genera, with the difference of the two extreme chords, which, never varying, were called stable chords. (Vide Tetrachord, Genus, Sound.)

MODE, The regular disposition of an air and its accompaniment, in relation to certain principal sounds, on the which a piece of music is constituted, and which are called the essential chords of the mode.

The mode differs from the tone, in that the former denotes only the chord, or place of the system which ought to serve as a base to the air, and the mode determines the third, and modefies the whole scale on this fundamental sound.

Our modes are not founded on any characteristic sentiment, like those of the ancients, but only on our harmonic system. The chords essential to the mode are three in number, and form together a perfect concord. First, the tonic, which is the fundamental chord of the tone and mode. (Vide Tone and Tonic.) Secondly, the dominant in the fifth of the tonic. (Vide Dominant.) Thirdly, the mediant, which constitutes the mode properly, and which is in the third of the same tonic.

As this third may be of two kinds, there are two different modes. When the mediant forms a major third with the tonic, the mode is major; it is minor when the third is minor.

The major mode is immediately engendered by the resonance of the sonorous body, which renders the major third of the fundamental sound; but the minor mode is not given by nature: it is found only by analogy and variations. This is true in the system of Mons. Tartini, as well as in that of Mons. Rameau.

This last author, in his different successive works, has explained that origin of the minor mode in different methods, no one of which has contented his interpreter M. D'Alembert. For which reason, D'Alembert founds that same origin on another principle, which

which I cannot display better than by transcribing the very terms of that great geometrician. " In the air ut mi sol, which
" constitutes the major mode, the sounds mi and sol are such,
" that the principal sound ut makes them both sound, but the
" second sound mi does not make sol sound, which is only its
" minor third.

" Moreover, let us suppose, that in the place of this sound mi,
" we place between ut and sol another sound, which has, as well
" as the sound ut, the property of making sol resound, and which,
" however, is different from ut; this sound, which we seek for,
" ought to be such, as to have for major seventeenth the sound
" sol, or one of the octaves of sol; consequently, the sought
" sound should be in the major seventeenth below sol, or, which
" is the same thing, in the major third below the same sound
" sol. Moreover, the sound mi being in minor third below sol,
" and the major third being a semi-tone greater than the minor,
" it follows, that the sound we seek will be a semi-tone lower
" than the mi, and will consequently be mi B flat. This new
" arrangement, ut, mi B flat, sol, in which the sounds ut and
" mi B flat, each make sol resound, without ut making mi B flat
" resound, is not, in reality, as perfect as the first arrangement
" ut, mi, sol; because, in the one, the two sounds mi and sol
" are each engendered by the principal sound ut, whereas, in the
" other, the sound mi B flat is not engendered by the sound ut;
" but this arrangement ut mi B flat sol, is so dictated by na-
" ture, tho' less immediately than the first, and, in effect, ex-
" perience proves that the ear is but little accommodated to
" it.

" In the course ut, mi B flat, sol, ut, it is evident, that the
" third of ut to mi B flat is minor, and such is the origin of the
" genus or mode called minor."

Elements of Music, Page 22.

The mode being once determined, all the sounds of the gamut take a relative or fundamental name, and proper to the place which they hold in that mode. Here are all the names of the notes in relation to their mode, taking the octave of ut as an example of the major mode, and that of la of the minor.

Major	Ut	re	mi	fa	ſol	la	ſi	ut
Minor	La	ſi	ut	re	mi	fa	ſol	la
	Tonic.	Second Note.	Mediant.	Fourth Note, or Sub-dominant.	Dominant.	Sixth Note, or Sub-dominant.	Seventh Note.	Octave.

We muſt take notice, that when the ſeventh note is only in a ſemi-tone of the octave, that is, when it forms the major third of the dominant, as the ſi natural in major, or the ſol dieſis in minor, then that ſeventh note is called a ſenſible note, becauſe it expreſſes the tonic, and makes the tone felt.

Not only each degree takes the name ſuitable to it, but each interval is determined in relation to the mode. Theſe are the rules eſtabliſhed for the purpoſe: Firſt, The ſecond note ought to form a major ſecond on the tonic, the fourth, and dominant, a juſt fourth and fifth, and this equally in the two modes.

Secondly, In the major mode, the mediant or third, the ſixth and ſeventh of the tonic ought always to be major: this is the character of the mode. For this ſame reaſon, theſe three intervals ought to be minor in the minor mode; however, as we muſt perceive therein the ſenſible note, which cannot be done without a falſe relation, whilſt the ſixth note remains minor; this cauſes exceptions, to which we muſt pay attention in the courſe of harmony and ſinging; but the cleff with its tranſpoſitions muſt always give all the determined intervals by connection with the tonic, according to the nature of the mode: We may find at the word cleff a general rule for it.

As all the natural chords of the octave of ut give, in relation to that tonic, all the intervals preſcribed for the major mode, and as it is the ſame thing with the octave of la for the minor mode, the precedent example, which I have propoſed only for the names of the notes, ought to ſerve alſo as formula for the rule of intervals in each mode.

This rule is not, as might be believed, eſtabliſhed on principles purely arbitrary; it has its foundation in the harmonic generation, at leaſt to a certain point.

If you give the perfect concord major to the tonic, the dominant, and ſub-dominant, you will have all the ſounds of the diatonic ſcale for the major mode. To have that of the minor mode, leaving always the major third to the dominant, give the minor

minor third to the two other concords. Such is the analogy of the mode.

As this medley of major and minor concords introduces, into the minor mode, a false relation between the sixth note and the sensible, we sometimes give, to avoid this false relation, a major third to the fourth note in ascending, or the minor third to the dominant in descending, particularly by variation; but in that case there are exceptions.

There are properly only two modes, as we have just seen; but as there are twelve fundamental sounds, which give as many tones in the system, and as each of these tones is susceptible of the major and minor modes, we may compose in twenty-four modes or methods. There are even thirty-four possible in the method of marking the notes, but in practice we exclude ten, which, in reality, are only the repetition of ten others, under relations much more difficult, where all the chords would change their names, and wherein we should, with difficulty, know our situation. Such are the major modes on the diesis'd notes, and the minor modes on the B's flat. So, instead of composing in sol diesis major third, you will compose in la B flat, which gives the same touches; and instead of composing in re B flat minor, you will take ut diesis by the same calculation, viz. to avoid on one side an F double diesis, which would become a G natural, and on the other a B double, which would become a natural A. We do not always remain in the tone, or the mode, by which we begin an air, but, whether for expression, or for variety, we change the tone and mode, according to harmonic analogy, returning, however, always to that, which he has made to be first heard, which is called to modulate.

From thence arises a new distinction of the mode in principal and relative: the principal is that by which the piece begins and finishes; the relatives are those which are intermixt with the principal in the course of the modulation. (Vide Modulation.)

The Sieur Blainville, an eminent musician of Paris, proposed, in 1751, the attempt of a third mode, which he calls mixt mode, because it partakes in the modulation of the two others, or is rather composed of them; a medley which the Author does not look upon as inconvenient, but rather as an advantage, and a source of variety, and of liberty in the airs and harmony.

This new mode not being given by the analysis of three concords, as the two others, is not determined, like them, by harmonies essential to the mode, but by an entire gamut, which is suitable to it, as well in ascending as falling; so that in our two modes the gamut is given by the concords, and in the mixt mode, the concords are given by the gamut.

The

The formula of this gamut is in the aſcendant and deſcendant ſucceſſion of the following notes:

Mi, fa, ſol, la, ſi, ut, re, mi,

whoſe eſſential difference, in regard to the melody, is in the poſition of the two ſemi-tones; the firſt of which is found between the tonic, and the ſecond note; and the other between the fifth and ſixth; and, in regard to harmony, in that which it bears on the tonic minor third in beginning, and major in finiſhing, as may be ſeen.

Gamut and Accompaniment of the mixt Mode of Mr. Blainville.

In

In the accompaniment of this gamut, as well in ascending or falling, as it was given by that author, and executed in the spiritual concert the 30th of May, 1751.

It is objected to the Sieur de Blainville, that his mode has neither concord, essential chord, or cadence suitable to it, and which distinguishes sufficiently major or minor. He answers to this, that the difference of his mode is less in harmony than melody, and less in the mode than even in the modulation; that it is distinguished in its beginning from the major mode by its minor third, and in its end from the minor mode by its plagal cadence. To which we answer, that a modulation which is not exclusive is not sufficient to establish a mode, that its own is inevitable in the two other modes, particularly in the minor; and, in regard to its plagal cadence, that it has necessarily a place in the same minor mode every time that we pass from the concord of the tonic to that of the dominant, as that was formerly practised even on the finals in the plagal modes, and in the tone of the fourth. From whence it is concluded, that his mixt mode is less a peculiar kind, than a new denomination with methods for intermixing and combining the major and minor modes, as ancient as harmony, practised in every age: and that appears so true, that even in beginning his gamut, the author neither dares to give the fifth or sixth to his tonic, for fear of determining a tonic in minor mode by the first, or a mediant in major mode by the second. He leaves an equivocation in not filling his concord.

But whatever objection may be made against the mixt mode, whose name is more rejected than its practice, this will not hinder the master, with which the author establishes and treats it, from making itself known to a man of sense, and a musician well versed in the principles of his art.

The ancients differed greatly on the definitions, divisions, and names of their tones or modes. Obscure in every part of their music, they are almost unintelligible in regard to this. All agree, its true, that a mode is a certain system, or a constitution of sounds; and, it appears, that this constitution is nothing else in itself than a certain octave filled with all the intermediate sounds, according to the genus. Euclid and Ptolomy seem to make it consist in the different positions of the two semi-tones of the octave, in relation to the principal chord of the mode, as we may see still in the eight tones of church-music; but the greatest number appear to place this difference only in the place which the diapason of the mode employs in the general system, that is, inasmuch as the base or principal chord of the mode is sharper or flatter, being taken in different parts of the system; all the chords of the series always preserving a similar connection with the

the fundamental, and, consequently, changing the concord at each mode to preserve the analogy of this connection: such is the difference of the tones in our music.

According to the first sense, there would be only seven possible modes in the diatonic system, and, in effect, Ptolomy admits no more; for there are only seven methods to vary the position of two semi-tones in relation to the fundamental sound, preserving between these two semi-tones the prescribed interval. According to the second sense, there would be as many possible modes as sounds, i. e. an infinity; but if we confine ourselves, even in the diatonic system, there will be no more than seven found, unless we chuse to take, as new modes, those which would be established in the octave of the first.

By combining together these two methods, we now want only seven modes; for if these modes are taken in different places of the system, we find, at the same time, the fundamental sounds distinguished from flat to sharp, and the two semi-tones differently situated in relation to the principal sound.

But besides these modes, we may form many others, by taking in the same series, and on the same fundamental sound, different sounds, as the essential chords of the mode: for instance, when we take for dominant the fifth of the principal sound, the mode is authentic; it is plagal if we choose the fourth; and there are properly two different modes on the same fundamental. Moreover, as to constitute an agreeable mode, we must, say the Greeks, render the fourth and fifth just, or, at least, one of the two; it is evident that we have, in the extent of the octave, only five fundamental sounds, on each of which may be established an authentic mode and a plagal. Besides these ten modes, we find other two; the one authentic, which cannot furnish a plagal, because its fourth forms the triton; the other plagal, which cannot furnish an authentic, because its fifth is false. It is, perhaps, in this manner that we must understand a passage of Plutarch, where the music complains that Phrynis has corrupted it by desiring to draw from five, or, rather seven chords, twelve different harmonies. Here then are twelve possible modes in the extent of an octave, or two disjoint tetrachords: if we come to join these two tetrachords together, that is, to give a B flat to the seventh in cutting off the octave; or if we divide the entire tones by chromatic intervals, to introduce therein new intermediate modes, or if, having an attention to the differences only, from flat to sharp, we place other modes to the octave of the preceding; all this will furnish different methods of multiplying the number of the modes far beyond twelve. And those are the only methods of explaining the different numbers of the modes admitted or rejected by the ancients at different times.

The

The ancient music being then confined within the narrow bounds of the tetachord, the pentachord, the hexachord, the eptachord, and the octachord, there were at first only three modes admitted, whose fundamentals were at a tone distance from each other. The flattest of the three was called the dorian, the phrygian was in the middle, and the sharpest was the lydian. In dividing each of these tones into two intervals, place was made to the two other modes, the ionian and æolian, the first of which was inserted between the doric and phrygian, the second between the phrygian and lydian.

In the end, the system being extended to sharp and flat, the musicians established on each side, new modes which took their denomination from the five first, by joining the preposition hyper, upon, for those above, and the propofition hypo, under, for those below. Wherefore the lydian mode was followed by the hyper-dorian, the hyper-ionian, the hyper-phrygian, the hyper-æolian, and the hyper-lydian in ascending; and after the dorian mode came the hypo-lydian, the hypo-æolian, the hypo-phrygian, the hypo-ionian, and the hypo-dorian in descending. We find the numbering of these fifteen modes in Alypius, a Greek author,

A GENERAL TABLE

Of all the Modes in the Ancient Music.

N. B. As authors have given different names to a great number of these modes, the names least used are placed in smaller characters.

	No.	Note	Mode	Other names
Sharp.	15	Si —	Hyper Lydian.	
	14	Si B flat	Hyper-Æolian.	
	13	La —	Hyper-Phrygian.	Hyper-mixo-Lydian.*
	12	La B flat	Hyper-Ionian.	Hyper-Iastian. Mixo-Lydian aigu.
	11	Sol -	Hyper-Dorian. Mixo-Lydian.	
Middle.	10	Fa Diesis	Lydian.	
	9	Fa —	Æolian.	Lydian flat.
	8	Mi —	Phrygian.	
	7	Mi B flat	Ionian.	Iastian. Phrygian flat.
	6	Re —	Dorian.	Hypo-mixo-Lydian.
Flat.	5	Ut Diesis	Hypo-Lydian.	
	4	Ut —	Hypo-Æolian.	Hypo-Lydian flat.
	3	Si —	Hypo-Phrygian.	
	2	Si B flat	Hypo-Ionian.	Hypo-Iastian. Hypo-Phrygian flat.
	1	La —	Hypo-Dorian.	Common. Locrian.

* I have here placed the hyper-mixo-lydian mode, finding it so marked in my manuscripts under the citation of Euclid. But the true place of this mode ought to be, I think, a semi-tone above the hyper-lydian; for which reason Euclid has been deceived, or, that I have erroneously transcribed it.

Their order and their intervals expressed by the names of the notes in our music. But we must take notice, that the hypo-dorian

dorian was the only mode executed in its whole extent; during the time that the reſt aſcended, the ſounds in ſharp were cut off, not to exceed the extent of the voice. This obſervation ſerves to the intelligence of ſome paſſages of the ancients, by which they ſeem to ſay, that the flatteſt modes had a ſharper air, which was true, in that theſe airs were raiſed more above the tonic. Thro' an ignorance of this, Le Doni has been greatly embarraſſed in theſe apparent contradictions.

Of all theſe modes, Plato rejected many, as capable of changing the manners. Ariſtoxenes, in conjunction with Euclid, admitted only thirteen, ſuppreſſing the two moſt raiſed, viz. the hyper-æolian and hyper-lydian. But in the work which remains to us from Ariſtoxenes, he named only ſix, on which he connects the different ſentiments, which were permanent in his time. Laſtly, Ptolomy reduced the number of theſe modes to ſeven, ſaying, that the modes were not introduced in the deſign of varying the airs according to flat and ſharp, for it is evident that they might have been multiplied much beyond fifteen, but rather for the ſake of facilitating the paſſage of one mode to another, by conſonant intervals eaſy to ſound.

He confined all the modes in the ſpace of an octave, of which the doric mode ſerved as a centre, ſo that the mixo-lydian was a fourth above, and the hypo-dorian was a fourth below; the phrygian a fifth above the hypo-dorian; the hypo-phrygian a fourth below the phrygian; and the lydian a fifth above the hypo-phrygian; from whence it appears, that by reckoning from the hypo-dorian, which is the loweſt mode, there was, to the hypo-phrygian, the interval of a tone; from the hypo-phrygian to the hypo-lydian, another tone; from the hypo-lydian to the dorian, a ſemi-tone; from that to the phrygian, a tone; from the phrygian to the lydian, another tone; and from the lydian to the mixo-lydian, a ſemi-tone; which forms the extent of a ſeventh in this order.

1—Fa—Mixo-Lydian.
2—Mi—Lydian.
3—Re—Phrygian.
4—Ut—Dorian.
5—Si—Hypo-Lydian.
6—La—Hypo-Phrygian.
7—Sol—Hypo-Dorian.

Ptolomy aboliſhed all the other modes, pretending that a greater number could not be placed in the diatonic ſyſtem of an octave, all the chords which compoſed it being found employed. Thoſe are the ſeven modes of Ptolomy, which, by joining the hypo-mixo-lydian, added, they ſay, by Aretin, form at preſent the eight tones of church-muſic. (Vide Tones of the Church.)

This is the cleareſt notion that can be drawn from the tones or modes of ancient muſic, whilſt they were looked upon as differing only from ſharp to flat, but they had ſtill other differences which characterized them more particularly in regard to the expreſſion. They were drawn from the genus of poetry which was ſet to muſic, from the nature of the inſtrument which ſhould accompany it, from the rhyme and cadence therein obſerved, from the form in which certain airs were placed amongſt certain people, and from whence are derived originally the names of the principal modes, the doric, the phrygian, lydian, ionian, and æolian.

There were alſo other ſorts of modes, which might have been better called ſtyles or genera of compoſition. Such were the tragic mode deſtined for the theatre; the Nomiach mode conſecrated to Apollo; the Dithyrambic to Bacchus, &c. (Vide Style and Melopœa.)

In our ancient muſic, they called alſo modes, in reference to the meaſure or the time, certain methods of fixing the relative powers of all the notes by a general ſign: the mode was then nearly what is now called meaſure; it was marked in the ſame manner after the cleff, by circles and demi-circles, punctuated or without points, followed by the cyphers 2 or 3 differently combined, to which were added or ſubſtituted in the courſe, different perpendicular lines, according to the mode, in number and in length; and it is from this ancient cuſtom, that the uſe of the C and C barr'd has remained to us. (Vide Prolation.)

There were, in this ſenſe, two kinds of modes, the major, which was connected to the maximum; and the minor, which was for the longue. Each was divided into perfect and imperfect.

The major perfect mode was marked with three lines, each of which filled three ſpaces of the ſtave; and three others, which filled only two. Under this mode the maximum was equal to three longues.

Major Perfect Mode.

The major imperfect mode was marked by two lines, each of which croſſed three ſpaces, and two others which croſſed only two, and in that caſe the maximum to two longues only.

Major Imperfect Mode.

The minor perfect mode was marked by one ſingle line which croſſed three ſpaces, and the longue was equal to three breves.

Minor Perfect Mode.

The minor imperfect mode was marked by a line which croſſed two ſpaces only, and its longue was equal only to two breves.

Minor Imperfect Mode.

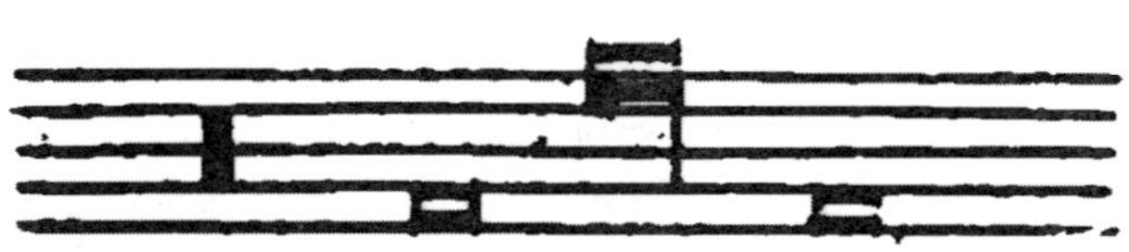

The Abbe Broſſard has improperly mixed the circles and demi-circles with the figures of thoſe modes. Thoſe reunited ſigns had no place in the ſimple modes, but only when the meaſures were double or conjoint.

All this has been long ſince out of uſe: but we muſt neceſſarily underſtand theſe ſigns to be ſkilled in decyphering the ancient muſic, in which the moſt ingenious muſicians are often greatly embarraſſed.

MODERATE. This word expreſſes a middle movement between the ſlow and lively: It anſwers to the Italian andante. (Vide Andante.)

MODIFICATION. An operation by which, thro' means of a trifling alteration in the intervals, making the difference of two neighbouring sounds vanish, they are confounded in one, which, without disgusting the ear, forms the respective intervals of each. By this operation, we simplify the scale in diminishing the number or necessary sounds. Without the modification, instead of twelve sounds only, which the octave contains, there would be more than sixty wanting to modulate in all the tones.

On the organ, the harpsichord, and every other instrument with keys, there neither is, nor can be, an interval perfectly in concord, except the octave only. Its numerical powers are only three major thirds, or four minor thirds, before the making a just octave; the one pass it, and the others do not reach it.

$$\text{For } \frac{5}{4}+\frac{5}{4}+\frac{5}{4}=\frac{125}{64}<\frac{128}{64}=\frac{2}{1}\ \&\ \frac{6}{5}+\frac{6}{5}+\frac{6}{5}=\frac{1295}{623}>\frac{12}{6\text{-}8}=\frac{2}{1}.$$

Wherefore we are constrained to enforce the major thirds, and to weaken the minor, so that the octaves, and all the other intervals, may correspond exactly, and that the same touches may be used under their different connections. In one moment I will explain the method of managing this.

This necessity was not felt immediately, or discovered before the meliorating of the musical system. Pythagoras, who first found the connection of the harmonic intervals, pretended that these connections were observed in all the mathematical rigour, without allowing any thing to the tolerance of the ear. This severity might be very suitable in its time, when the whole extent of the system was still bounded by so small a number of chords. But as the greatest part of the ancient instruments were composed of chords which were touched a vide, and as, in consequence a chord was necessary for each sound, in proportion as the system extended, they perceived that the rule of Pythagoras, multiplying the chords too much, hindered them from drawing from them their proper uses.

Aristoxenes, the disciple of Aristotle, seeing how much the exactness of calculations hurt the progress of music, and the facility of the execution, took all of a sudden the other extremity, abandoning the calculation almost entirely; he pleaded to the judgment of the ear only, and rejected, as useless, the whole that Pythagoras had established.

This formed in music two sects, which have for some time divided the Greeks, the one of the Aristoxenians, which were the musicians

musicians of practice; the other, of the Pythagoreans, which were the philosophers. (Vide Aristoxenians and Pythagoreans.)

In the end, Ptolomy and Didymus, finding, with reason, that Pythagoras and Aristoxenes had fallen into two excesses equally faulty, and consulting at the same time sense and reason, laboured each, on their own part, towards a reformation of the ancient diatonic system. But as they were not greatly removed from the principles established for the division of the tetrachord, and, at last, distinguishing the difference between the major and minor tones, they did not dare touch upon the one to divide it, as the other, by a chromatic chord, into two equal parts: the system continued a long time in a state of imperfection, which did not permit us to perceive the true principle of the modification.

Lastly came Gui d'Arezzo, who, in some respects, re-founded the music, and, as they say, invented the harpsichord. Moreover, it is certain, that that instrument could not exist any more than the organ, had not the modification been found out at the same time; without which, it is impossible to accord them, and impossible, at least, that the first invention can have much preceded the second. This is nearly all that we know of it.

But though the necessity of the modification has been long since known, it is different, in regard to the best rule, to be followed for its determination.

The last age, which was the age of discoveries in every kind, is the first which has given us any clear insight on this head. Le P. Mersenne, and Mons. Loulié, have made calculations; Mons. Sauveur has found divisions which furnish all possible modificatio . Lastly, Mons. Rameau, after all the rest has imagined to have found the true theory of modification first, and has even pretended, on this theory, to establish, as new, a very ancient practice, which I shall speak of instantly.

I have said that it was necessary, for temperating the sounds of the keys, to enforce the major thirds to weaken the minor, and to distribute these alterations so as to render them as little sensible as possible. For this purpose, we must return on the concord of the instrument, and this concord is generally made by fifths: it is therefore by its effect on the fifths, that we should consider the modification.

If we tune very justly four fifths together, as ut sol re la mi, we shall find that this fourth fifth mi, with the ut, from whence we set off, will form a major discordant third, and much too strong; and, in effect, this mi, produced as the fifth of la, is not the same sound which ought to form the major third of ut. Herein lies the proof.

The

The connection of the fifth is $\frac{2}{3}$ or $\frac{1}{3}$ on account of the octaves 1 and 2 taken indifferently for each other. Wherefore the succession of fifths, forming a triple progression, will give ut 1, sol 3, re 9, la 27, and mi 81.

Let us now consider this mi as major third of ut: its connection is $\frac{4}{5}$ or $\frac{1}{5}$, four being only the double octave of one. If from octave to octave, we draw near to the mi of the precedent, we shall find mi 5, mi 10, mi 20, mi 40, and mi 80. Wherefore the fifth of la being mi 81, and the major third of ut being mi 80, these two mi's are not the same, and their references are $\frac{80}{81}$, which form precisely the major comma.

If we pursue the progression of fifths as far as the twelfth power, which happens at si diesis, we shall find, that this si exceeds the ut, whose unison it ought to make in the connection of 531441 and 524288, a connection which gives the comma of Pythagoras. So that by this calculation, the si diesis ought to exceed the ut of three major comma's; and by the other, it exceeds it only by the comma of Pythagoras.

But the same sound mi which forms the fifth of la, must also serve to form the major third of ut; the same si diesis which forms the twelfth fifth of the same ut, must form the octave also; and lastly, these different concords must concur to constitute the general system without multiplying the chords. This is what is executed by means of the modification.

For this purpose, first, we begin by ut in the middle of the keys, and weaken the four first fifths in ascending, until that the fourth mi forms a major third, absolutely just with the first sound ut, which we call the first proof.

Secondly, In continuing to tune by fifths, as soon as we are arrived on the diesis's, we enforce the fifths a little, though the thirds may suffer, and when we are arrived to the sol diesis, we stop. This sol diesis ought to make, with the mi, a just major third, or at least tolerably so; this is the second proof.

Thirdly, We take the ut again, and tune the fifths in flat, viz. fa, si B flat, &c. weak of consequence; then enforcing them by degrees, that is, weakening the sounds till we come to the re B flat, which, taken as ut diesis, ought to be found in concord, and form a fifth with the sol diesis, at which we had before stopt. This is the third proof.

The

The last fifths will be found rather strong, as well as the major thirds, which renders the major thirds of si B flat, and mi B flat, heavy, and rather rough. But this roughness will be supportable if the partition is well formed; and besides, these thirds, by their situation, are less used than the first, and ought to exist only by choice.

The organists and factors look upon this modification as the most perfect that can be used. In effect, the natural tones enjoy, by this means, all the purity of harmony; and the transposed tones, which form less frequent modulations, offer great assistance to the musician when he is in want of marked expressions; for it is good to observe, says Monf. Rameau, that we receive different impressions from the intervals in proportion to their different alterations. For instance, the major third, which naturally excites a joy in us, impresses on us even the ideas of fury, when too strong; and the minor third, which inspires us with tenderness and sweetness, changes our sensations into those of sorrow, when too weak.

Ingenious musicians, continues the same author, know how to make a good use of these different effects of the intervals, and, by the expression which they draw from them, make the alteration flourish, which might be condemned.

But in his harmonic generation, this same Monf. Rameau speaks quite another thing. He reproaches himself for his condescension for actual custom, and destroying all that he had before established; he gives a formula of eleven methods proportionate between the two terms of the octave, on which formula he insists on the whole succession of the chromatic system being established, so that this system resulting from the twelve semi-tones perfectly equal, it is of necessity that all the intervals which are formed from it, should be perfectly equal between themselves.

For practice, says he, take whatever key you please; tune then its fifth just, diminish it a very little; proceed in this manner from one fifth to another, always ascending, that is, from sharp to flat, until the last whose sharp sound must have been the flat of the first, you may then be certain that the harpsichord will be quite in tune.

This method which Monf. Rameau proposes, had already been proposed, and abolished by the famous Couperin. We may find it also at full length in P. Mersenne, who names one Gallee as its author, and who has even taken the trouble to calculate the eleven proportionate methods, of which Monf. Rameau gives us the Algebraic formula.

In

In ſpite of the ſcientific appearance of this formula, we do not find that the practice which reſults from it has been yet approved, either by muſicians or factors. The firſt cannot reſolve to deprive themſelves of the energic variety which they find in the different affections of the tones which the eſtabliſhed modification occaſions. Monſ. Rameau tells them in vain, that they are deceived, that the variety is found in the uniſon of the modes, or in the different degrees of the tonics, and not at all in the alteration of the intervals; the muſician anſwers, that the one does not exclude the other; that he does not think himſelf convinced by an aſſertion, and that the different affections of the tones are not in any reſpect proportionate to the different degrees of their finals. For, ſay they, tho' there is only a ſemitone diſtance between the final of re and that of mi B flat, as between the final of la and that of ſi B flat; however, the ſame muſic will affect us very differently in A la mi re, than in B fa; and in D ſol re, than in E la fa; and the attentive ear of the muſician can never be deceived, though even the general tone ſhould be raiſed or lowered a ſemi-tone and more: an evident proof that this variety comes elſewhere than ſimply from the different elevation of the tonic.

In regard to inſtrument makers, they find, that a harpſichord tuned in this manner, is not really ſo concordant as Monſ. Rameau pretends. The major thirds appear to them rough and diſguſting; and when we tell them that they have only to act in the alteration of thirds, as they did before in that of fifths, they anſwer, that they can't conceive how the organ can be managed to ſuppreſs the beatings which are heard therein by this method of tuning, or how the ear can fail to be diſguſted.

Since, by the nature of conſonances, the fifths may be more changed than the third without diſguſting the ear, or cauſing beatings, is it not neceſſary to throw the alteration on that ſide where it is leaſt diſguſting, and to leave the intervals, in preference, more juſt where they cannot be changed without being rendered diſcordant.

P. Merſenne aſſures us, that, in his time, they ſaid that the firſt who practiſed ſemi-tones on the keys, tuned all the fifths nearly according to the equal concord propoſed by Monſ. Rameau, but that their ear not being able to endure the diſcordance of the major thirds, neceſſarily too ſtrong, they modified the concord by weakening the firſt fifths to lower the major thirds. It appears, therefore, that to uſe ones ſelf to this method of concord, is a habit difficult to be followed by an exerciſed and ſenſible ear.

As

As to what remains, I cannot be prevented to remind my readers of what I have said at the word consonance, on the cause of that pleasure which the ear receives from consonances, drawn from the simplicity of the connections. The connection of a modified fifth, according to Monf. Rameau's method, is this, $\underline{\overset{4 \text{———} 3}{V\,80 + } \; \overset{4\text{———}}{V\,81}}$. This connection, however, pleases the ear. I would know whether its simplicity is the cause of it.

MODULATION. This is properly the method of establishing and treating the mode; but this word, at present, is more generally taken for the art of conducting the harmony, and the air successively in several modes, by a method agreeable to the ear, and conformable to rules.

If the mode is produced by harmony, from thence also arise the laws of modulation. These laws may be simply conceived, but are difficult to be observed. Herein lies their consistent rules.

To modulate well in a same tone, we must first go through all its sounds with a fine music, by striking the essential chords oftener, and resting on them longer: that is to say, that the sensible concord, and the concord of the tonic, ought to be shewn therein frequently, but under different appearances, and by different courses, to prevent the monotony. Secondly, To establish Cadences and stops only on these two concords, or, at most, on that of the sub-dominant. Thirdly and lastly, never to alter any of the sounds of the mode; for we cannot, without quitting it, make a diesis or a B flat be heard, which does not belong to it, or remove any one that does belong to it.

But to pass from one tone to another, we must consult the analogy, and pay attention to the connection of the tonics, and to the quantity of chords common to the two tones.

Let us now depart from the major mode: whether we consider the fifth of the tonic, as having with it the simplest of all the connections after that of the octave, or whether we consider it as the first of the sounds which enter in the resonnance of this same tonic, we shall always find that this fifth, which is the dominant of the tone, is the chord on which we may establish the most analogous modulation to that of the principal tone. This dominant, which formed part of the perfect concord of the first tonic, forms also a part of its own, of which it is the fundamental sound. There is then an union between these two concords. Moreover, this same dominant, bearing, as well as the concord, a perfect major concord by the principle of resonance, these two concords differ between themselves only by the dissonance, which, passing from the tonic to the dominant, is the sixth added; and from the dominant, repassing to the tonic, is the se-

 venth

venth. Moreover, theſe two concords, thus diſtinguiſhed by the diſſonance which ſuits each, form, by the ſounds which compoſe them, rang'd in order, preciſely the octave or diatonic ſcale, which we call gamut, which determines the tone.

This ſame gamut of the tonic forms, only changed by a dieſis, the gamut of the tone of the dominant, which ſhews the great analogy of theſe two tones, and gives the facility of paſſing from one to the other by means of a ſingle alteration. The tone of the dominant is then the firſt which is preſented after that of the tonic in the order of modulations. The ſame ſimplicity of connection which we find between a tonic and its dominant, is alſo found between the ſame tonic and its ſub-dominant; for the fifth, which the dominant forms in ſharp with this tonic, the ſub-dominant forms in flat; but this ſub-dominant is the fifth of the tonic only by a variation; it is directly fourth by placing this tonic in flat, as it ought to be, which eſtabliſhes the gradation of the connections: for in this ſenſe, the fourth, whoſe connection is from three to four, follows the fifth immediately, whoſe connection is from two to three. If this ſub-dominant does not enter, in the ſame manner, in the concord of the tonic, in return, the tonic enters into its concord. For ſhould ut mi ſol be the concord of the tonic, that of the ſub-dominant will be fa la ut; wherefore, it is the ut which forms here the union, and the two other ſounds of this new concord are preciſely the two other ſounds of the precedent. Moreover, we muſt not change more ſounds for this tone than for that of the dominant: there are in each all the ſame chords of the principal tone, very nearly. Give a B flat to the ſenſible note ſi, and all the notes of the tone of ut will ſerve to that of fa. The tone of the ſub-dominant is not then leſs analogous to the principal tone than that of the dominant.

We ought alſo to take notice, that after having uſed this firſt modulation to paſs from a principal tone ut to that of its dominant ſol, we are obliged to uſe the ſecond to return to the principal ſound; for if ſol is dominant of the tone of ut, ut is ſub-dominant to the tone of ſol; wherefore, one of theſe modulations is not leſs neceſſary than the other.

The third ſound, which enters in the concord of the tonic, is that of its third or mediant, and is alſo the ſimpleſt of the connections after the two precedent $\frac{2}{3}\ \frac{3}{4}\ \frac{4}{5}$.

Here then is a new modulation, which is preſented, and as much more analogous, as two of the ſounds of the principal tonic enter alſo into the minor concord of its mediant; for the firſt concord

concord being ut mi sol, this will be mi sol si, where we see that mi and sol are common.

But what removes this modulation to a little distance, is the quantity of sounds which must be changed, even for the minor mode, which is most suitable to this mi. I have given before the formula for these two modes; therefore, applying this formula to the minor mode mi, we find, in reality, only the fourth sound fa changed by a diesis in descending; but in rising, we find two others also, viz. the principal tonic ut, and its second note re, which becomes here a sensible note: it is certain, that the alteration of so many sounds, and particularly of the tonic, distances the mode, and weakens the analogy.

If we vary the third as we have the fifth, and take that third below the tonic on the sixth note la, which we ought also to call sub-mediant, or mediant below, we shall form on this la a modulation more analogous to the principal tone than was that of mi; for the perfect concord of this sub-mediant being la ut mi, we find therein, as in that of the mediant, two of the sounds which enter into the concord of the tonic, viz. ut and mi; and moreover, the scale of this new tone being composed, at least in descending, of the same sounds as that of the principal tone, and having only two sounds changed in ascending, i. e. one less than the scale of the mediant; it follows thence, that the modulation of the sixth note is preferable to that of this mediant, inasmuch, as the principal tonic forms therein one of the essential chords of the mode, which is more suitable for connecting the idea of the modulation. The mi may follow afterwards.

Here then are four chords, mi fa sol la, on each of which we may modulate, going out of the major tone of ut. Let the re and si remain the two harmonies of the dominant. This last, as a sensible note, cannot become tonic by any good modulation, at least immediately. This would be applying roughly to the same sound, ideas too much opposed, and giving it an harmony too distant from the principal. For the second note re, we may also, by favour of the consonant direction of the fundamental bass, modulate therein in minor third, provided that we do not remain therein more than an instant, so that we may not have time to forget the modulation of the ut, which itself is changed; otherwise it would be necessary, instead of returning immediately in ut, to pass by other intermediate tones, where it would be dangerous to be led into an error.

By following the same analogies, we shall modulate in the following order to go out of a minor tone: the mediant first, then the dominant, the sub-dominant, and the sub-mediant, or sixth note. The mode of each of these accessary tones is determined by its mediant, taken in the ſcale of the principal tone. For inſtance, going out of a major tone ut to modulate on its mediant, we render the mode of this mediant minor, becauſe the dominant ſol of the principal tone forms a minor third on this mediant mi. On the contrary, going out of a minor tone la, we modulate on its mediant ut in major mode, becauſe the dominant mi of the tone, from whence we go out, forms a major third on the tonic of that wherein we enter, &c.

Theſe rules, confined in a general formula, are, that the modes of the dominant, and the ſub-dominant, are ſimilar to that of the tonic, and that the mediant and ſixth note bear the oppoſed mode. We muſt take notice, however, that in virtue of the right we have to paſs from major to minor, and reciprocally, in a ſame tone, we may alſo change the order of the mode from one tone to the other: but in thus removing from the natural modulation, we muſt be attentive to the return, for this is a general rule, which every piece of muſic ought to finiſh in the tone by which it began.

I have collected, in two ſhort examples, all the tones in which we may immediately paſs: the firſt, by going from the major mode; and the other by going from the minor mode. Every note expreſſes a modulation; and the power of the notes in each example, ſpecifies alſo the relative duration ſuitable to each of theſe modes, according to its connection with the principal tone.

Table of all the immediate Modulations.

Going out of the major mode. Going out of the minor.

Theſe immediate modulations furniſh the methods of paſſing by the ſame rules, in the moſt diſtant rules; and of immediately returning to the principal tone, which we muſt never loſe ſight of. But it is not ſufficient to know the courſes which we ought to follow; we muſt alſo know the method of entering on them. Here is the ſummary of the precepts which may be given in regard to this. In melody, we muſt, to expreſs the modulation we have choſen, only make the alterations be heard, which it produces in the ſounds of the tone from whence we go out, to render them proper to the tone wherein we enter.

Are we in ut major? We have only to ſound a fa dieſis to expreſs the tone of the dominant, or a ſi B flat to ſpecify the tone of the ſub-dominant. Then paſs through the eſſential chords of the tone wherein you enter: If it is well choſen, your modulation will

will always be good and regular. In the harmony, there is a little more difficulty; for as the change of the tone muſt be made at the ſame time in all the parts, we ought to be careful, in the harmony and air, to avoid following two different modulations at the ſame time. Huyghens has very well remarked, that the proſcription of the two conſecutive fifths has this rule as its principle: in effect, we cannot form, in any manner, ſeveral juſt fifths together, between two parts, without modulating in two different tones.

To announce a tone, many perſons pretend that it is ſufficient to form the perfect concord of the tonic, and that this is indiſpenſable for the giving of the mode; but it is certain, that the tone cannot be determined but by the concord ſenſible or dominant: we muſt then make this concord be heard in beginning the new modulation. The beſt rule would be, that the ſeventh or minor diſſonance ſhould be always prepared therein, at leaſt, the firſt time that we make it audible; but this rule is not practicable in all the permitted modulations; and provided that the fundamental baſs is directed by conſonant intervals, that we obſerve the harmonic union, the analogy of the mode, and avoid the falſe relations, the modulation is always good. Compoſers give as another rule, to change the tone only after a perfect cadence, but this rule is uſeleſs, and nobody ſubmits to it.

All the poſſible methods of paſſing from one tone into another, are reduced to five for the major mode, and four for the minor, which we have announced by a fundamental baſs for each modulation.

	Major.	
Tone of the	Dominant —	A
	Sixth Note —	B
	Mediant —	C
	Sub-Dominant	D
	Second Note	E

	Minor.	
Tone of the	Mediant —	F
	Dominant —	G
	Sub-Dominant	H
	Sixth Note —	I
	Idem — —	K

If there is any other modulation which does not come within any of theſe nine, unleſs it be enharmonic, that modulation is infallibly bad. (Vide Enharmonic.)

TO MODULATE, Is to compoſe or prelude, whether in writing, or on an inſtrument, or with the voice, in following the rules of modulation. (Vide Modulation.)

MOLLARE, An epithet, given by Ariſtoxenes and Ptolomy, to a kind of the diatonic genus, and of the chromatic alſo, which I have ſpoken of at the word Genus.

In modern muſic, the word Mollare is only uſed in the compoſition of the word B mollare or B flat, in oppoſition to B ſharp, formerly called B rough.

Zarlin, however, calls diatonic mollare, a kind of the diatonic genus, which I have ſpoken of before. (Vide Diatonic.)

MONOCHORD, An inſtrument having only one chord, which is divided ad libitum by moveable bridges, the which ſerves to find the connections of the intervals, and all the diviſions of the harmonic canon. As the part of inſtruments does not appertain to my plan, I ſhall not extend any farther on this article.

MONODY, A ſong for a ſingle voice, in oppoſition to what the ancients called chorodies, or muſic executed by a band.

MONOLOGUE, The ſcene of an opera, wherein the actor is alone, and ſpeaks only to himſelf. It is in the monologues that all the force of muſic is diſcovered, the muſician being able to give ſcope to the whole fire of his genius, without being confined in the length of his pieces by the preſence of a ſecond ſpeaker.—Theſe kinds of recitative, which have a place, and cauſe ſuch an effect in the Italian opera, are only uſed in monologues.

MONOTONY, Is properly a pſalmody, or piece of muſic, which always moves on the ſame tone; but this word is at preſent uſed only in figured muſic.

MORES. A conſiderable part of the Greek muſic, called by them hermoſmenon, which conſiſted in underſtanding and chooſing the beautiful of every kind, and did not permit them to give to each ſentiment, to each object, to each character, all the forms of which it was ſuſceptible: but obliged them to confine themſelves to what was ſuitable to the ſubject, the occaſion, perſons, and circumſtances. The Mores conſiſted alſo in tuning and proportionating in ſuch a manner in a piece, all the parts of the muſic, the mode, the time, the rhyme, melody, and even the changes, that a certain conformity might be felt throughout the whole, which ſhould leave no diſagreement, but render it perfectly one. This ſingle part, the idea of which is not even known in our muſic, ſhews to what point of perfection an art might be carried, in which the pleaſing, ſuitable, and agreeable, was reduc'd to rules.

MOTET. This word, in ancient times, ſignified a very laboured compoſition, enriched with all the beauties of art, and this within a very ſhort period; from whence, according to ſome, it takes its name of motet, as if it was one ſingle word.

At preſent, the name of motet is given to every piece of muſic made in Latin words, as was cuſtomary in the Roman-church, as pſalms, hymns, antiennes, &c. and this, in its general ſenſe, is called Latin muſic.

The French ſucceeded better in this kind of muſic than in their own, the language being more favourable; but they make uſe of too great labour, and, as the Abbé du Bos has accuſed them, they

they play too much on the words. In general the Latin music has not sufficient gravity for the use to which it is allotted. We ought not to aim therein at imitation, as in theatrical music. Sacred airs ought not to represent the tumult of the human passions, but only the majesty of him to whom they are addressed, and the resignation of soul in those who pronounce them. Whatever may be expressed in the words, every other language in the air is a contrary sense. We should have, I do not say no piety, but no taste, if we preferred the general music to that of the church, for the church itself.

The musicians of the thirteenth and fourteenth age, gave the name of mottelus to that part which is now called counter-tenor. This name, and others as strange, often cause a great embarrassment to those who study the decyphering of ancient manuscripts of music, which was not written in partition as at present.

MOTIVE. This word is seldom used but in a technical sense by the composers. It signifies the primitive and principal idea, on which the composer determines his subject and arranges his design. 'Tis the motive which bids him put pen to paper to write such a thing, and not another. In this sense, the principal motive ought to be always present in the mind of the composer, and he ought to manage that it should be so also in that of his audience.

Besides this motive, which is only the principal idea of the piece, there are particular motives, which are the determining ideas of the modulation, the union, the harmonic textures; and on these ideas, which we hasten in the execution, we judge if the author has properly followed his motives, or if he has taken the changes, as it often happens to those who proceed note by note, and who are deficient in knowledge and invention. It is in this acceptation that we say, motive of the fugue, motive of the cadence, motive of the changes in the mode, &c.

TO MOVE. This term is used figuratively in music, and is said of the succession of sounds, or concords, which follow each other in a certain order. "The bass and treble move by contrary movements." "To move in counter-time," &c.

MOVEMENT, A degree of quickness or slowness, which the character of the piece we execute gives to the measure. Every kind of measure has a movement peculiar to itself, and which is designed in Italian by these words, Tempo giusto. But besides this, there are five principal modifications of movement, which, in the order from slow to quick, are expressed by the words, Largo, adagio, andante, allegro, presto; and these words in English are rendered, by slow, moderate, pleasing, gay, quick. We must, however, take notice, that, the movement always having much lefs precifion in the French mufic, the words that exprefs it have a fenfe much more vague than in the Italian.

Each of thefe degrees is fub-divided and modified into others alfo, in which we muft diftinguifh thofe which exprefs the degree only of quicknefs or flownefs, as larghelto, andantino, allegretto, preftiffimo, and thofe, moreover, which mark the character and expreffion of the air, as agitato, vivace, guftofo, combrio, &c. The firft may be rendered by all the muficians, but there are only thofe which have fentiment and tafte, who feel and render the others.

Tho', in general, flow movements are fuitable to forrowful paffions, and animated movements to the gay, there are, however, often modifications by which a paffion fpeaks on the tone of another. It is true, that gayety cannot be expreffed with flownefs, but often the moft lively griefs have the moft unbounded language.

MOVEMENT, Is alfo the courfe or progrefs of founds from flat to fharp, or from fharp to flat: wherefore, when we fay that we muft, as much as poffible, make the bafs and treble move by contrary movements, this fignifies that one of the parts ought to afcend, whilft the other defcends. Some call oblique movement, that wherein one of the parts remains in its place, whilft the other afcends or defcends.

The ingenious Jerome Mei, in imitation of Ariftoxenes, diftinguifhes in general, in the human voice, two kinds of movements, viz. that of the fpeaking voice, which he calls continued movement, and which is not fixed till the moment we are filent; and that of the finging voice, which moves by determined intervals, and which he calls diaftematic, or intervallative movement.

MUSETTE, A kind of air fuitable to the inftrument of this name, whofe meafure is two or three timed, the character fweet and original, the movement a little flow, bearing generally a bafs in the line or point of the organ, fuch as may make it a mufette, and which is fo called on account of this bafs. On thefe airs we form the dances of a fuitable character, and which alfo have the name of mufettes.

MUSICIAN. This name is given equally to him who compofes mufic, and him who executes it. The firft is alfo called compofer. (Vide that word.)

The ancient muficians were poets, philofophers, and orators of the higheft order. Such were Orpheus, Terpander, Sterichorus, &c. Boetius alfo will not honour with the name of mufician, him, who only practices the mufic by the fervile ufe of fingers and voice, but him who poffeffes that knowledge by reafon and fpeculation. And it moreover feems, that to raife one's felf to the lofty expreffions of oratorical and imitative mufic, we muft have

have made the human paſſions, and the language of nature, our particular ſtudy. The muſicians, however, of our time, confined in general to the practice of notes, and ſome turns in the air, cannot be highly offended, I imagine, if they are not eſteemed as great philoſophers.

MUSIC, The art of combining the ſounds in a manner pleaſing to the ear. This art becomes a ſcience, and even very profound, when we attempt to find the principles of theſe combinations, and the cauſes of the pleaſure which they inſpire us with. Ariſtides Quintilian defines muſic as the art of the beautiful, and pleaſing in the voices and movement. It is not ſtrange, that with definitions ſo vague and general, the ancients have given a prodigious extent to the art which they thus defined.

We generally ſuppoſe, that the word muſic is derived from muſa, becauſe we believe that the muſes have invented this art; but Kircher, after Diodorus, derives this word from an Ægyptian name, pretending, that it was in Ægypt that the muſic began firſt to eſtabliſh itſelf after the deluge, and that the firſt idea of the ſound was received by the reeds which grew on the banks of the Nile, when the wind blew in the hollow of their pipes. Whatever may be the etymology of this word, the origin of the art is certainly more applicable to mankind; and if the words did not begin with the air, it is at leaſt certain, that wherever we ſpeak, we ſing.

Muſic is naturally divided into theoretic or ſpeculative, and practical.

Speculative muſic is, if I may be allowed the expreſſion, the knowledge of muſical matter, that is, the different connections from flat to ſharp, quick to ſlow, ſour to ſweet, ſtrong to weak, of which the ſounds are ſuſceptible; connections, which comprehending all poſſible combinations of the muſic and ſounds, ſeem to comprehend alſo all the cauſes of the impreſſions which their ſucceſſion may form on the ear and the ſoul.

Practical muſic is the art of applying and making uſe of the principles of the ſpeculative; that is, to conduct and diſpoſe the ſounds in connection with the conſonance, in duration, ſucceſſion, in ſuch a manner, as that the whole may produce on the ear the propoſed effect. It is this art which is called compoſition. (Vide this word.) In regard to the actual production of the ſounds by voices or inſtruments, which is called execution, it is the part purely mechanic and operative, which, only ſuppoſing the faculty of ſounding the intervals juſt, of marking the durations true, to give to the ſounds the degree preſcribed in the tone, and the powers preſcribed in the time, requires rigorouſly no other knowledge than that of the characters of muſic, and cuſtom in expreſſing them.

Speculative music is divided into two parts, viz. the knowledge of the connection of the sounds, or their intervals, and that of their relative durations, that is, of the measure and time.

The first, is properly that which the ancients called harmonic music; it teaches in what consists the nature of the air, and marks what is consonant, dissonant, agreeable, or displeasing to the ear. In a word, it gives a knowledge of the different methods with which the sounds affect the ear by their tone, their force, their intervals, which is equally applied to their concord, and their succession.

The second has been called rhymic, because it treats the sounds in regard to the time and quantity. It contains the explanation of the rhyme and metre, long measures and short, lively and slow, the times and different parts into which they are divided, to apply to them the succession of the sounds.

The practical music is divided also into two parts, which answer to the two preceding.

That which answers to the harmonic music, and which the ancients called melopoea, contains the rules for combining and varying the consonant and dissonant intervals, in an agreeable and harmonious manner. (Vide Melopoea.)

The second, which answers to the rhymic music, and which they call rythmopoea, contains the rules for the application of the times, feet, measures, in a word, for the practice of rhyme. (Vide Rhyme.)

Porphyrius gives another division of music, whilst it has for its object the mute and sonorous movement; and, without distinguishing it into speculative and practical, there are found in it the six following parts: the rhymic, for the movements of dancing; the metric, for the cadence and number of verses; the organic, for the practice of instruments; the poetic, for the tones and accent of poesy; the hypocritic, for the attitudes of pantomimes; and the harmonic, for the air.

The music is divided, at present, more simply into melody and harmony; for the rhymic is no longer regarded amongst us, and the metric is very trifling, since our verses, in airs, take nearly their measure from music, and lose the little which they receive from it by themselves.

By melody, we direct the succession of the sounds, so as to produce an agreeable air. (Vide Melody, Air, Modulation.)

Harmony consists in uniting to each of the sounds, in a regular succession, two or more other sounds, which, striking the ear at the same time, flatter it by their concurrence. (Vide Harmony.)

We might, and, perhaps, ought to divide the music into natural and imitative. The first, confined to the physic of the sounds only, and acting on the sense only, cannot carry its impressions to the heart, and gives sensations only more or less agreeable. Such is the music of the songs, hymns, cantics, and of all the airs, which are only combinations of melodious sounds, and all music in general which is not harmonious.

The second, by inflexions lively and accented, and, as it were, speaking, expresses all the passions, paints every picture, renders every object, submits the whole of nature to its ingenious imitations, and, by this means, conveys to the soul of the man those sentiments proper for moving it. This truly lyric and theatrical music was that of ancient poems, and it is that which at present we apply to the drama's, executed in music on our theatres. It is only in this music, and not in the harmonic or natural, that we must seek the cause of the prodigious effects which it formerly produced. How much soever we may seek for moral effects in the physic of sounds only, we shall never find them, and our reasoning will be without understanding.

The ancient writers differ greatly on the nature, the object, extent, and the parts of music. In general, they gave this word much more extensive than that which remains to it at present. They not only comprehended, under the name of music, as we have seen, the dance, gesture, and poetry, but even the collection of all the sciences. Hermes defines music as the knowledge of the order in every thing. This was also the doctrine in the school of Pythagoras, and that of Plato, who taught, that every thing in the universe was music. According to Hesychius, the Athenians gave the name of music to all the arts; and all this is no longer astonishing, since, that a modern musician has found in music the principal of all references, and the foundation of every science. From thence are all those sublime pieces of music, which the philosophers have handed down to us, divine music, music of mankind, celestial music, terrestrial, active, contemplative, enunciative, intellective, oratorical, &c.

It is under these vast ideas that we must understand several passages of the ancients on music, which would be unintelligible in the sense which we at present give to this word.

It appears that music has been one of the first arts; we find it mixt among the most ancient monuments of human kind. It is also very probable, that the vocal music was found before the instrumental, if among the ancients there ever was a music truly instrumental; i. e. formed for instruments entirely. Not only mankind, before discovering any instrument, must have made observations on the different tones of their voice, but they must have learned very early, by the natural concert of birds, to modify their voice and throat in an agreeable and melodious manner. After this, the wind instruments must have been the first invented. Diodorus, and other authors, attribute the invention

to

to an obſervation of the blowing of the wind in reeds or other hollow plants. This is alſo a ſentiment of Lucretius.

At liquidas avium voces imitarier ore
Antè fuit multò, quam levia Carmina cantu
Concelebrare homines poſſint, aureiſque juvari ;
Et Zephyri cava per calamorum ſibila primùm
Agreſteis docuêre cavas inflare cicutas.

In regard to other kinds of inſtruments, the ſonorous chords are ſo common, that mankind muſt have early obſerved the different tones which have given birth to the different chord inſtruments. (Vide Chord.)

Thoſe inſtruments which are ſtruck to draw a ſound from them, as drums and tymbals, owe their origin to the deafening noiſe which hollow bodies emit when ſtruck.

It is difficult to leave theſe generalities to fix on ſome certainty on the invention of muſic reduced into an art. Without aſcending to times before the flood, ſeveral of the ancients attribute this invention to Mercury, as well as that of the lyre. Others fix on Cadmus as the introductor of it among the Greeks, who, flying from the court of the king of Phænicia, carried with him into Greece, the muſician, Hermione, or Harmony ; from whence it would follow, that this art was known in Phænicia before Cadmus. In a part of Plutarch's Dialogue on Muſic, Lyſias names Amphion as the inventor ; in another, Soterichus ſays it was Apollo ; and in a third, he ſeems to give the honour to Olympus : there is no agreement on this matter, and, it muſt be confeſſed, it is of little conſequence. To theſe firſt inventors ſucceeded Chiron, Demodocus, Hermes, Orpheus, who, in the opinion of ſome, invented the lyre.

After thoſe, came Phæmius, then Terpander, contemporary of Lycurgus, and who laid down the rules of muſic. Some attribute to him the invention of the firſt modes. Laſtly, we add Thales and Thamiris, who is ſaid to have been the inventor of muſical inſtruments. Theſe great muſicians lived moſt of them before Homer. Others, more modern, are Laſus of Hermione, Melnippipes, Philoxenes, Timotheus, Phrynnis, Epigonius, Lyſander, Simmicus, and Diodorus, who all have conſiderably improved the muſic.

Laſus is, as it is reported, the firſt who has written on this art, in the time of Darius Hyſtaſpes. Epigonius invented the inſtrument of forty chords, which bore his name. Simmicus invented alſo an inſtrument of thirty-five chords, called Simicium.

Diodorus improved the flute, and added new holes to it ; and Timotheus the lyre, by adding a new chord to it, which was the occaſion of his ſuffering a fine by the Lacædemonians.

As

As the ancient authors express themselves very obscurely on the inventors of musical instruments, they are also very unintelligible on the instruments themselves. Hardly do we know any thing more of them than their names. (Vide Instrument.)

Music was in its greatest esteem among the different people of antiquity, and particularly among the Greeks; and this esteem was proportionate to the power and surprising effects which they attributed to this art. Their authors do not think they have given us a too great idea of it, when they told us it was used in heaven; and that it formed the chief amusement of the gods and souls of the blessed. Plato does not hesitate to say, that there can be no change in music, but there must be one also in the constitution of the state; and he pretends, that sounds may be assigned capable of raising the ideas of a base soul, insolence, &c. with all their contrary virtues. Aristotle, who seems to have written his political works only to oppose his sentiments to those of Plato, is, however, in concord with him in regard to the power of music over the manners. The judicious Polybius tells us, that music was necessary to sweeten the manners of the Arcadians, who dwelt in a country where the air was cold and wintry; that those of Cynetes who neglected music, surpassed all the Greeks in cruelty, and that there was no country which was equal to it in crimes. Athenæus assures us, that in former times, all laws, human and divine, exhortations to virtue, the knowledge of what concerned the gods and heroes, the lives and actions of illustrious men, were written in verse, and sung publicly in choirs by the sound of instruments; and we see, by sacred writings, that such were the customs of the Israelites from the earliest times. There had been no method found more efficacious to engrave, on the minds of men, the principles of morality and love of virtue; or, rather, all this was not the effect of a premeditated design, but of the grandeur in its sentiments, and the elevation of the ideas which sought, by proportioned accents, to form to themselves a language worthy of them.

Music formed a part of the study of the ancient Pythagoreans. They used it to excite the soul to laudable actions, and to inflame each other with the love of virtue. According to the philosophers, our souls were formed of nothing but harmony; and they expected to re-establish, by the means of sensual harmony, the intellectual and primitive one of the faculties of the soul; that is to say, that which, according to them, existed in it before it animated our bodies, and whilst it dwelt in heaven.

Music is at present sunk from that degree of power and majesty, so far as to make us doubt of the truth of those wonders which it formerly performed, tho' attested by the most judicious

 historians,

historians, and graveſt philoſophers of antiquity. However, in modern hiſtory, we may find ſome ſimilar facts. If Timotheus excited the fury of Alexander by the phrygian mode, and calmed it by the lydian, a muſic, ſtill more moderate, has ſurpaſſed it, by exciting, they ſay, in Erric, king of Denmark, ſuch a fury, that he kill'd his moſt faithful ſervants. Doubtleſs theſe wretches were leſs ſenſible of muſic than their prince, otherwiſe he might have run half the danger. D'Aubigny recounts another hiſtory quite ſimilar to that of Timotheus. He tells us, that in the reign of Henry III. the muſician Claudin, playing at the marriage of the Duc de Joyeuſe, in the phrygian mode, animated, not the king, but a courtier, who ſo far forgot himſelf as to draw his ſword in the preſence of his ſovereign; but the muſician quickly calmed him by taking the hypo-phrygian mode. This is ſaid with as much aſſurance, as if the muſician Claudin knew in what conſiſted the phrygian and hypo-prhygian modes.

If our muſic has little power over the affections of the ſoul, in return, it is capable of acting phyſically on the body, as in the hiſtory of the Tarantula, too well known to want mentioning here: as a proof of which, I bring the Chevalier Gaſcon which Boyle mentions, who, at the ſound of a cornemuſe, or bag-pipe, could not contain his urine; to which ſhould be added, what the ſame author recounts of ſome women, who burſt into tears at the hearing of a certain tone, with which the reſt of the audience were not at all affected; and I know a woman of faſhion at Paris, who cannot liſten to any kind of muſic whatſoever, without being ſeized with an involuntary and convulſive laughter. We read alſo in the hiſtory of the Academy of Sciences, at Paris, that a muſician was cured of a violent fever, by a concert performed in his chamber.

Sounds act even on inanimated bodies, as we may ſee by the ſhaking and reſonance of a ſonorous body at the ſound of another, with which it is connected in ſome reſpect. Morhoff mentions a certain Peter, a Dutchman, who broke a glaſs by the ſound of a voice. Kirtcher ſpeaks of a large ſtone, which trembled at the ſound of a certain pipe in an organ. P. Merſenne ſpeaks alſo of a kind of waggon, which the playing of the organ ſhook as though it had been an earthquake.

Boyle adds, that the *Stalls* often ſhake at the ſound of the organ, and that he has himſelf felt them tremble under his hand at the ſound of the organ or the voice, and that he has been aſſured, that thoſe which were well formed, trembled all at ſome determined tone. The whole world have heard mention of the famous pillar at the church in Rheims, which ſenſibly ſhakes at the ſound of a certain bell, whilſt the other pillars continue immoveable;

moveable;

moveable: but that which transmits the honour of the marvellous to the sound, is, that this same pillar equally shakes when the clapper of the bell is removed.

All these examples, the greatest part of which belong rather to the sound than to the music, and of which physic may give some explanation, neither makes them more credible or intelligible to us, tho' the ancients held them in music as marvellous and almost divine. Many authors have puzzled their brains to endeavour to give a cause for them. Wallis attributes them partly to the novelty of art, and partly rejects them on the exaggeration of authors.

Others imagine that the Greeks, more sensible than ourselves, by the constitution of their climate, or by their method of living, might be mov'd by things which could make no impression on us. Monf. Burette, even in adopting all these facts, pretends, that they do not prove the perfection of the music which produced them: he sees nothing in it, but what the sad scrapers of a country village might have done, in his opinion, quite as well as the first musicians of the world.

The generality of these sentiments are founded on the persuasion we are in of the excellence of our music, and the contempt we have for that of the ancients. But is this contempt as justly founded as we pretend? This has been several times examined; and when we consider the obscurity of the matter, and the insufficiency of judges, has great need of undergoing a better search. Of all those who have yet employed themselves in this examination, Vossius, in his Treatise de Viribus Cantûs & Rhythmi, appears to have best discussed the question, and draws the nearest to truth. I have thrown some ideas thereon in a writing not yet made public, where my thoughts will be more suitably placed than in this work, which is not intended to stop the reader for the discussion of my opinion.

It has been much wished to see some fragments of ancient music. P. Kircher and Monf. Burette have laboured thereon to satisfy the curiosity of the public. To give them a greater chance of profiting by their labours, I have transcribed here two pieces of Greek music, turn'd into modern notes by those authors.

An Ode of Pindar. A Piece of ancient Music.

The Chorus which follows is sung with sound of the Harp.

An Hymn to Nemesis 2d. a Piece of ancient Music.

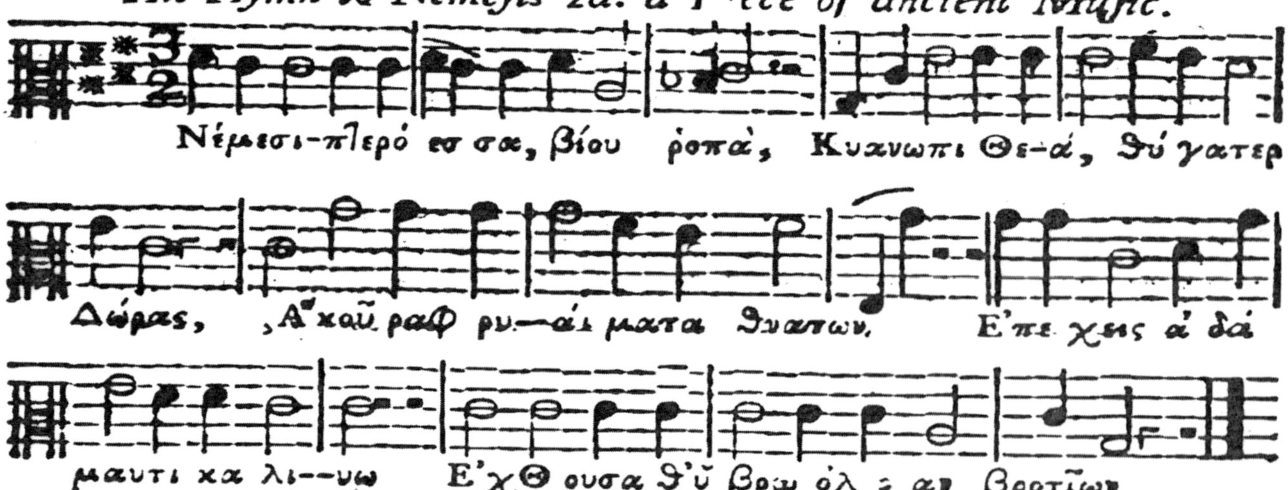

But who can dare to judge of ancient music by such examples? I imagine them to be faithful. I even wish that those who would judge of it, could sufficiently know the genius and accent of the Greek,

Greek, that they would reflect, that an Italian is judged incapable of a French air; that a Frenchman knows nothing of the Italian melody: when he has compared time and place, then let him speak if he dare.

To put the reader in a way to judge of the different musical accents of different people, I have transcribed also a Chinese air, drawn from P. du Halde.

A Chinese Air.

A Persian Air, taken from the Chevalier Chardin.

Translation of the Persian Words.

Your countenance is vermilion, like the flowers of Granada;
Your words a perfume, from which I am inseparable.
The world has nothing fix'd: Every thing changes.
Bring odorous flowers to animate the heart of my monarch.

Song of the Savages in Canada, drawn from P. Merſonne.

We ſhall find in theſe pieces a conformity of modulation with our muſic, which muſt make one admire the excellence and univerſality of our rules, and may render the underſtanding or fidelity of thoſe who have tranſmitted to us thoſe airs, ſomewhat ſuſpicious to others.

The Ranz des Vaches.

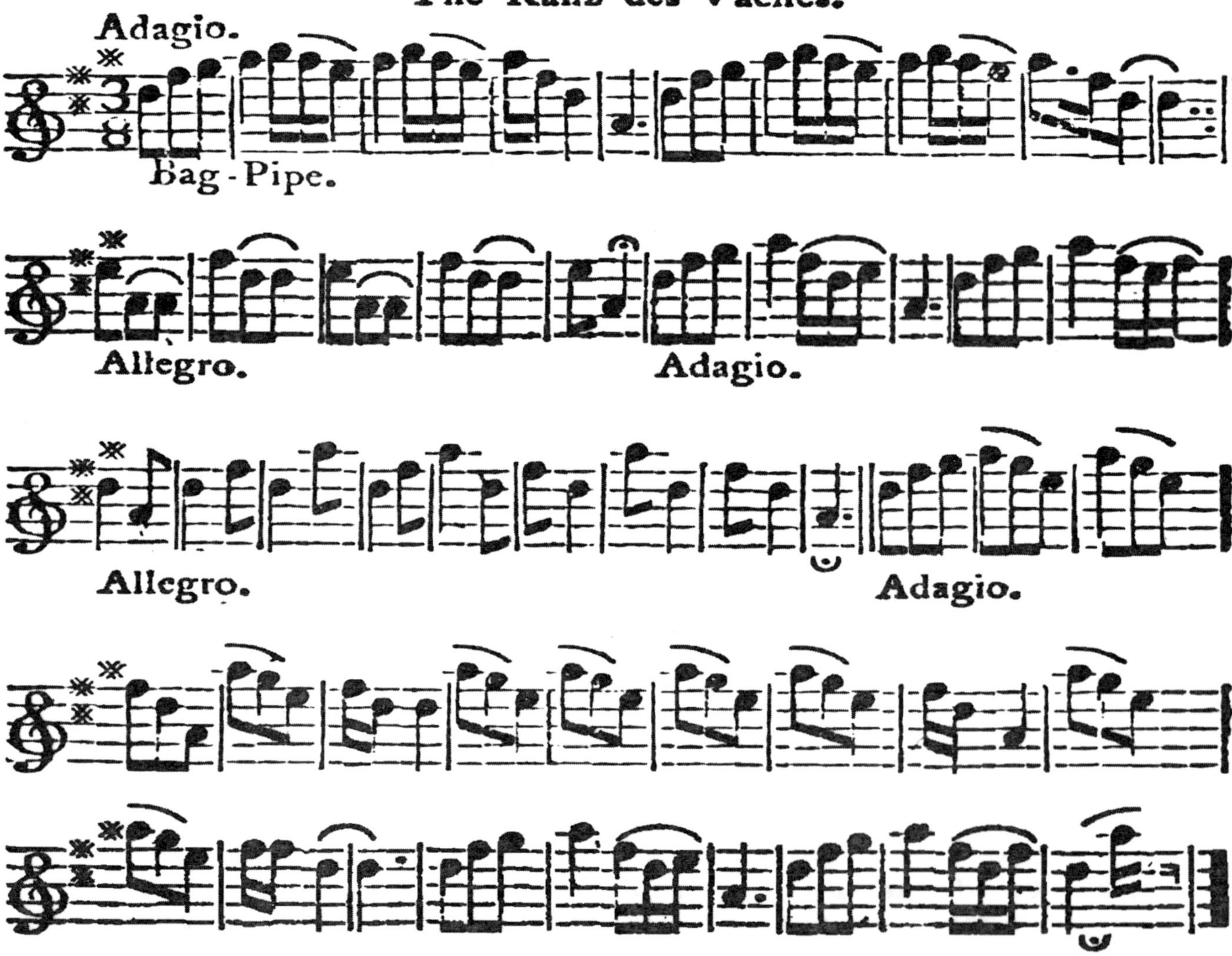

The above celebrated Air, called Ranz des Vaches, was ſo generally beloved among the Swiſs, that it was forbidden to be play'd in their troops under pain of death, becauſe it made them burſt

burst into tears, desert, or die, whoever heard it; so great a desire did it excite in them of returning to their country. We shall seek in vain to find in this air any energic accents capable of producing such astonishing effects. These effects, which are void in regard to strangers, come alone from custom, reflections, and a thousand circumstances, which, retrac'd by those who hear them, and recalling the idea of their country, their former pleasures, their youth, and all their joys of life, excite in them a bitter sorrow for the loss of them. The music does not in this case act precisely as music, but as a memorative sign. This air, tho' it continues the same, does not produce, at present, the same effects which it produc'd before amongst the Swiss; because, having lost the taste for their ancient simplicity, they no longer regret it, but when reminded. So true it is, that it is not in their physical action, we should seek for the greatest effects of sounds on the human heart.

The method, by which the ancients prick'd their notes, was established on a very simple foundation, which was the connection of cyphers; i. e. by the letters of their alphabet; but instead of confining themselves on this idea to a small number of characters easy to retain, they were lost in multitudes of different signs, with which they confused their music in return, so that they had as many methods of marking as genera and modes. Boetius took from the Latin alphabet characters corresponding to those of the Greek. Pope Gregory perfected this method. In 1024, Gui d'Arezzo, benedictine, introduced the use of stave, (vide Stave) on lines, on which he marked the notes in form of points, (vide Notes) expressing, by their position, the elevation or the lowering of the voice. Kircher, however, pretends, that this invention was prior to Gui, and, in effect, I have not seen in the writings of this monk, that he claims it to himself; but he invented the gamut, and applied to the notes of his hexachord, names drawn from the hymn of St. John Baptist, which they preserve at present. This man, lastly, born for music, invented different instruments, called polyplectra, such as the harpsichord, spinnet, viol, &c. &c.

The characters of music, have, according to the general opinion, received their last considerable augmentation in 1330, at the time, they say, when Jean de Muris, call'd improperly by some Jean de Mæurs, or de Muria, doctor of Paris, tho' Gesner makes him an Englishman, invented the different figures of the notes which express the duration or the quantity, and which we now call semi-breves, minums, crotchets, &c. But this sentiment, tho' very common, appears to me rather dubious, to judge of it by his Treatise of Music, intitled Speculum Musicæ, which I

 have

have had the boldneſs to read almoſt all through, to conſtitute therein the invention attributed to this author. As to the remainder, this great muſician has had, like the king of poets, the honour to be claimed by different people; for the Italians alſo pretend he is of their nation, perhaps deceived by a fraud or error of Bontempi, who calls him Penigino inſtead of Panigino.

Laſus is, or ſeems to be, as I have ſaid before, the firſt who has written on muſic; but his works are loſt, as well as ſeveral other books of the Greeks and Romans on the ſame ſubject. Ariſtoxenes, the diſciple of Ariſtotle, and chief of the muſical ſect, is the moſt ancient author who remains to us in that ſcience. After him comes Euclid of Alexandria. Ariſtides Quintilian wrote after Cicero. Alypius comes next; then Gaudentius, Nicomachus, and Bacchius.

Marc Meibomius has given us a beautiful edition of theſe ſeven Greek authors, with a Latin tranſlation and notes.

Plutarch has written a Dialogue on Muſic. Ptolomy, a celebrated mathematician, wrote, in Greek, the Principles of Harmony, about the time of the emperor Antoninus. This author preſerves a medium between the Pythagoreans and Ariſtoxeneans. A long time after, Manuel Bryennius wrote alſo on the ſame ſubject. Amongſt the Latins, Boetius has written in the time of Theodoric; and not far from the ſame time, Martianus, Caſſiodorus, and Saint Auguſtine.

The moderns are many in number. The moſt known are Zarlin, Salerias, Valgulio, Galilée, Mei, Doni, Kircher, Merſenne, Parran, Perrault, Wallis, Deſcartes, Holder, Mengoli, Malcolm, Burette, Valloti: laſtly, Monſ. Tartini, whoſe book is full of profundity, genius, tautology, and obſcurity; and Monſ. Rameau, whoſe writings have this ſingularity, that they have gain'd him a great fortune without having ever been read by any one. This lecture is beſides become abſolutely ſuperfluous, ſince, that M. d'Alembert has taken the trouble of explaining to the public the ſyſtem of the fundamental baſs, the only thing uſeful and intelligible which can be met with in the writings of this muſician.

MUSIC MASTER. A muſician hir'd to compoſe and execute muſic. It is the muſic-maſter who beats time, and directs the muſicians. He ſhould be ſkill'd in compoſition, tho' he does not always compoſe the muſic which he makes others execute. In the opera-houſe of Paris, for inſtance, the employment of beating time is a particular office; whereas, the muſic of the opera is compoſed by whomſoever has talent and will. In Italy, he who has compoſed an opera directs always its execution, not in beating time, but with the harpſichord. Wherefore, the office of

muſic-maſter

music-master has no foundation but in churches: for which reason, we do not say in Italy *Music-Master*, but *Master of the Chapel*, a denomination which begins to be used at present in France.

MUTATIONS. By this term were call'd, in ancient music, generally, all the passages of an order, or subject of one air to another.

Aristoxenes defines the mutation as a kind of passion in the order of melody; Bacchius, as a change in the subject, or the transposition of a like into an unlike place; Aristides Quintilian, as a variation in the proposed system, and the character of the voice; Martianus Capella, as a transition of the voice in another order of sounds.

All these definitions, obscure and too general, have need of being cleared by divisions, but authors do not agree better on these divisions than on the definition itself. However, we just gather, that all these mutations may be reduced to five principal kinds.

First, A mutation in the genus, when the air pass'd, for instance, from diatonic to chromatic, or to the enharmonic, and reciprocally.

Secondly, In the system, when the modulation united two disjoint tetrachords, or separated from them two conjoint, which answers to the passage of the B sharp to B flat, and reciprocally.

Thirdly, In the mode, when, for instance, we pass from the doric to the phrygian or lydian, and reciprocally, &c.

Fourthly, In the rhyme, when we pass'd from quick to slow, or from one measure to another.

Fifthly and lastly, in the melopœa, when we interrupted a heavy, serious, magnificent air, by a lively, gay, and quick change, &c.

N.

NATURAL. This word has several senses in music. First, Natural music is that which the human voice forms by opposition, to the artificial music which is executed with instruments. Secondly, We say that an air is natural when it is easy, sweet, pleasing; that a harmony is natural, when it has few variations or dissonances, that it is produced by chords essential and natural to the mode. Thirdly, Natural is also said of every piece of music which is neither forced or obscure, which neither goes too high or too low, neither too quick or too slow. Fourthly and lastly, The most common signification, and the only one which the Abbe Bropard has not mentioned, is applied to the tones or modes, from whence the sounds are drawn in the ordinary gamut without any alteration, so that a natural mode is that in which neither diesis or B flat is used. In the exact sense, there could be only one natural tone, which would be that of ut, or C major third; but we extend the naturals to all the tones, whose essential chords, bearing neither diesis's or B's flat, permit that we should number the cleff neither with one or the other: such are the major modes of G and F, the minor modes of A and D, &c. (Vide Transposed Cleffs, Modes, &c.)

The Italians always mark their recitative to the natural, the changes of tone being so frequent therein, and the modulations so confined, that, whatever way we number the cleff for a mode, we could not spare either diesis's or B's flat for the rest, and we should throw ourselves, in the end of the modulation, in very embarassing confusions of signs, when the notes changed in the cleff, by a sign, are found changed by the contrary sign accidentally.

To sol fa in natural, is to sol fa by the natural. (Vide Recitative) Names of the sounds in the ordinary gamut, without regard to the tone which we are in.

NETE. This was, in the Greek music, the fourth chord, or sharpest of each of the three tetrachords, which followed the two first from flat to sharp.

When the third tetrachord was conjoint with the second, this was the tetrachord synnemenon, and its nete was called nete synnemenon.

This third tetrachord bore the name of diezeugmenon when it was disjoint, or separated from the second by the interval of a tone, and its nete was called nete diezeugmenon.

Lastly, The fourth tetrachord, always bearing the name of hyperboleon, its nete was always called also nete hyperboleon.

In regard to the two first tetrachords, as they were always conjoint, they had no nete, either of them; the fourth chord of the first, being always the first of the second, was called hypate meson; and the fourth chord of the second, forming the middle of the system, was called mesis. *Nete*, says Boetius, *quasi neate, id est, inferior*, for the ancients, in their diagrams, placed the flat sounds above, and the sharp below.

NETOIDES. Sharp sounds. (Vide Lepsis.)

NEUME. A term in church-music. The neume is a kind of short recapitulation of the air in a mode, which is made at the end of an ancient, by a simple variety of sounds, and without joining

joining to them any words. The Catholics authorize this fingular cuftom on a paffage of St. Auguftine, who fays, that no words being poffible to be worthy of pleafing God, it is laudable to addrefs him in a confufed mufic of jubilation. "For to whom is "fuch a jubilation fuitable, unlefs to an ineffable Being? and "how can we celebrate this ineffable Being, fince we cannot be "filent, or find any thing in our tranfports which can exprefs "them, unlefs unarticulated founds?"

NIGLARIAN. The name of a nome, or air of an effeminate and foft melody, as Ariftophanes reproaches Philoxenes its author.

NIMBLY. This word expreffes a movement ftill quicker than gay, a movement which is a medium between gay and quick. It anfwers nearly to the Italian term vivace.

NINETEENTH. An interval which comprehends eighteen conjoint degrees, and, confequently, nineteen founds of the diatonic, reckoning the two extremes. This is the double octave of the fifth. (Vide Fifth)

NINTH. The octave of the fecond. This interval has the name of ninth, becaufe we muft form nine confecutive founds to arrive diatonically from one of its terms to the other. The ninth is major or minor, as the fecond, of which it is the replique. (Vide Second)

There is a concord by fuppofition, which is called concord of the ninth, to diftinguifh it from the concord of the fecond, which is prepared, accompanied and prevented differently. The concord of the ninth is formed, by a found placed in the bafs, a third below the concord of feventh, which is the occafion of the feventh itfelf making a ninth on this new found. The ninth is accompanied, confequently, by the third, the fifth, and fometimes the feventh. The fourth note of the tone is generally that on which this concord is moft fuitable, but it may be placed every where in harmonic unions. The bafs ought always to arrive by afcending to the note which bears the ninth. The part which forms the ninth ought to fyncopate, and prevents this ninth as a feventh, defcending diatonically from one degree on the octave, if the bafs continues in its place, or on the third, if the bafs defcends from the third. (Vide Concord, Suppofition, Syncope)

In the minor mode, the fenfible concord on the mediant lofes the name of concord, and takes that of fuperfluous fifth. (Vide Superfluous Fifth)

NOELS, or CHRISTMAS CAROLS. Kinds of airs allotted to certain cantics, fung by the people in the celebration of Chriftmas. The airs of thefe carols fhould have a rural and paftoral character, fuitable to the fimplicity of the words, and to that of the ſhepherds, who, we ſuppoſe, ſung them at going to pay homage to the infant Jeſus in the manger.

NOME. Every air determined by rules which it was not permitted to break, bore amongſt the Greeks the name of nome.

The nomes received their denominations, firſt, either from certain people, æolian nome, lydian nome; ſecondly, or from the nature of the rhyme, orthian nome, dactylic nome, trochaïc nome; or thirdly, from their inventors, Hieracian nome, Polymneſtant nome; fourthly, or from their ſubjects, pythian nome, comic nome; fifthly or laſtly, from their mode, hypatoïd or flat nome, netoïd or ſharp nome, &c.

There were two-part nomes which were ſung on two modes. There was alſo a nome called three parts, which was ſung on three modes, viz. the doric, the phrygian, and the lydian. (Vide Song, Mode)

NOMIC. The nomic nome, or the genus of the muſical ſtyle which bore this name, was conſecrated, among the Greeks, to Apollo, god of ſongs and verſes, and wherein they endeavoured to render the airs brilliant, and worthy of the god to whom they were conſecrated. (Vide Mode, Melopœa, Style.)

NOMION. A kind of love ſong amongſt the Greeks. (Vide Song)

NOTES. Signs or characters uſed to mark, that is, to write the muſic.

The Greeks made uſe of the letters of their alphabet to mark their muſic. Moreover, as they had twenty-four letters, and as their greateſt ſyſtem, which was only of two octaves in a ſame mode, did not exceed the number of ſixteen ſounds, it would ſeem that the alphabet muſt have been more than ſufficient to expreſs them, ſince their muſic, being only their poetry marked, the rhyme was ſufficiently determined by the metre, without there being wanting for that abſolute powers, and ſigns peculiar to muſic; for tho' by ſuperabundance they had characters alſo to mark the different feet, it is certain, that vocal muſic was not in want of it; and inſtrumental muſic, being only the vocal play'd by inſtruments, had neither need of it, ſince the words were written, or the ſymphoniſt knew them by heart.

But we muſt take notice, in the firſt place, that two ſame ſounds, one while at the extremity, and another while in the middle of the third tetrachord, according to the place wherein the disjunction is made, (Vide that word) they gave to each of thoſe ſounds, names and ſigns which expreſſed theſe different ſituations. Secondly, that theſe ſixteen ſounds were not all the ſame in the three genera; that there were ſome common to the three, and others peculiar to each; and that notes were conſequently

quently neceſſary to expreſs theſe differences. Thirdly, that muſic was differently noted for inſtruments than for the voice, as we have at preſent, for certain chord inſtruments, a table which has no reſemblance to that of ordinary muſic in the leaſt. Laſtly, that the ancients having as many as fifteen different modes, according to the numbering of Alypius, (Vide Mode) it was neceſſary to appropriate characters to each mode, as we ſee in the tables of the ſame author. All theſe modifications required a multitude of ſigns, for which the four and twenty letters were very far from ſufficing. From thence ariſes the neceſſity of uſing the ſame letters for ſeveral ſorts of notes, which obliged them to give to thoſe letters different ſituations to couple them, maim them, and lengthen them in different ſenſes. For inſtance, the letter Pi written in all theſe forms Π, Ш, ⊏⊐ , Г, Π, expreſſed five different notes.

By combining all the modifications which theſe different circumſtances required, we find nearly 1620 different notes, a prodigious number, which muſt have rendered the ſtudy of muſic a thing of the greateſt difficulty. It was certainly ſo in the time of Plato, who adviſes young men to ſpend two or three years in ſtudying its rudiments only. The Greeks, however, had not ſo great a number of characters, but the ſame note had ſometimes different ſignifications, according to occaſion; wherefore, the ſame character which marks the proſlambanomenos of the lydian mode, marks the parhypate meſon of the hypo-iaſtian mode, the hypate meſon of the hypo-phrygian, the lichanos hypaton of the hypo-lydian, the parhypate hypaton of the iaſtian, and the hypate hypaton of the phrygian. The note changes alſo ſometimes, tho' the ſound continues the ſame; as, for inſtance, the proſlambanomenos of the hypo-phrygian, which has the ſame ſign in the hyper-phrygian, hyper-dorian, phrygian, dorian, hypo-phrygian, and hypo-dorian modes, and another ſame ſign, in the lydian and hypo-lydian modes.

Notes

Notes of the Ancient Greek Music,

Diatonic Genus, Lydian Mode.

N. B. The first Note is for Vocal Music, the Second, for the Instrumental.

Modern Names.	Ancient Names.	Notes.		Explanation.
La	Proslambanomenos	Ζ	⊥	Zeta imperfect, and Tau couchant
Si	Hypaté hypaton	Ι	Γ	Gamma backwards, and Gamma just.
Ut	Parhypaté Hypaton	R	L	Beta imperfect, and Gamma varied.
Re	Hypaton Diatonos	Φ	F	Phi, and Digamma.
Mi	Hypaté meson	C	C	Sigma, and Sigma.
Fa	Parhypaté meson	Ρ	Ɔ	Rho, and Sigma couchant.
Sol	Meson Diatonos	M	ℸ	Mu, and Pi prolong'd.
La	Mesis	I	<	Iota, and Lambda couchant.
Si b	Trité Synnemenon	Θ	V	Theta, and Lambda varied.
Si ♮	Paramesis	Z	⊏	Zeta, and Pi couchant.
※ Ut	Synnemenon Diatonos	Γ	N	Gamma, and Nu.
+ Re	Neté Synnemenon	Ʊ	Z	Omega varied, and Zeta.
※ Ut	Trité Diezeugmenon	E	Ш	Eta and Pi varied, and prolong'd.
+ Re	Diezeugmenon Diatonos	comme	la	Neté Synnemenon, which is the same chord.
Mi	Neté Diezeugmenon	Φ	Ш	Phi couchant, and Eta courant prolong'd.
Fa	Trité hyperboleon	⅄	⊀	Upsilon varied, and Alpha with the right stroke cut off.
Sol	Hyperboleon Diatonos	M	ℸ	Mu, and Pi prolong'd, top'd with an accent.
La	Neté hyperboleon	I	≮	Iota, and Lambda couchant, top'd with an accent.

REMARKS.

REMARKS.

Tho' the chord diatonos of the tetrachord synnemenon, and the trité of the tetrachord diezeugmenon, have different notes, they are only the same chord, or two chords in unison. It is the same thing with the two chords, neté synnemenon and diezeugmenon diatonos; these two also have the same chords. We must also take notice, that the mesis and nete hyperboleon bear the same note for the vocal, tho' they are in the octave of each other: It is apparent, that in practice there was some other method of distinguishing them in music.

The curious, who would wish to know the notes of all the genera and modes, may consult, in Meibomius, the tables of Alypius and Bacchius.

We here find the table of notes in the diatonic genus in the lydian mode, which was the most used; these notes having been preferred to those of the other modes by Bacchius, are sufficient to understand all the examples which he gives in his work; and the music of the Greeks being no longer in use, this table suffices also to put an end to the errors of the public, who think their manner of marking notes so entirely lost, that this music would be impossible for us to decypher. We might decypher it as exactly as the Greeks themselves could have done, but to phrase it, to accent it, to understand it, to judge of it, is possible to no one, and never can become so. In every kind of music, as well as in every language, to decypher, and to read, are two things very different. The Latins, who, in imitation of the Greeks, marked also their music with the letters of their alphabet, removed also a great quantity of their notes, the enharmonic genus having ceased its practice entirely, and several modes being no longer in use. It appears that Boetius established the use of fifteen letters only; and Gregory, bishop of Rome, considering that the connections of the sounds are the same in each octave, reduced these fifteen notes also to the seven first letters of the alphabet, which were repeated in different forms from one octave to another.

Lastly, In the eleventh age, a benedictine of Arezzo, named Gui, substituted, in the place of these letters, points placed on different parallel lines, to each of which a letter served as cleff. In the end, these points were enlarged; it was also thought convenient to place some in the spaces comprised between these lines, and these lines and spaces were multiplied as occasion required. (Vide Stave)

The

The notes had for some time no other use than to mark the degrees and differences of intonation. They were all, in regard to duration, of equal powers; and received, in regard to this, no other difference than those of long and short syllables, on which they were sung: It is nearly in this condition that the church-music the Catholics has continued to this day; and the music of the psalms, amongst the protestants, is still more imperfect; since, in their use, the lengths of the breves, or the rounds of the minums, were not even distinguished, tho' they preserved two different figures.

This indistinction of figures continued in the general opinion, as far as 1338, when Jean de Muris, a doctor and canon of Paris, gave, it is pretended, different figures to the notes, to mark the connections of duration which they had between each other: he also invented certain signs of measure, called modes or prolations, to determine, in the course of an air, if the reference of long to short should be double or triple, &c. Many of the figures no longer subsist. There have been others substituted in their place at different times. (Vide Measure, Time, Power of Notes.) Vide also, at the word Music, what I have said of this opinion.

To read music written by notes, and to render it exactly, there are eight things to be considered. First, the cleff and its position. Secondly, the diesis's or B's flat which may accompany it. Thirdly, the place or position of each note. Fourthly, its interval, that is, its connection with that which precedes, or with the tonic, or some fixed note whose tone we have. Fifthly, its figure, which determines its powers. Sixthly, the time wherein it is found, and the place it occupies. Seventhly, the diesis B flat, or accidental B sharp, which may precede it. Eighthly, the kind of the measure, and character of the movement. And all this, without reckoning either the words or syllables to which each note belongs, the accent, or the expression suitable to the sentiment, whereon we reflect. One of these eight observations only omitted, may make it jar, or play out of time.

The music has had the lot of those arts which improve but slowly.

The inventors of notes have been attentive to the state only, wherein it was in their time, without reflecting on that to which it might be raised; and in the end, their marks have been found so much the more defective, as the art has been since improved. In proportion as they advaneed, they established new rules to remedy the present inconveniencies; by multiplying the signs, they have multiplied the difficulties; and by dint of additions and cyphers, they have drawn, from a simple principle, a system very confused, and very badly regulated.

We

We may reduce its faults to three principals: The firſt is the multitude of ſigns and their combinations, which load the mind and memory of beginners in ſuch a manner, that the ear is form'd, and the organs have acquired habit, and a neceſſary facility, a long time before they are able to ſing *à livre ouvert*; from whence it follows, that the difficulty is intirely in an attention to the rules, and not at all in the execution of the air. The ſecond, is the little evidence in the nature of major, minor, diminiſhed, and ſuperfluous intervals, all indiſtinctly confounded in the ſame poſitions; a fault of ſuch influence, that it is not only the principal cauſe of the ſlowneſs in the progreſs of ſcholars, but, moreover, there is no muſician form'd, who can fail of being incommoded in the execution. The third, is the extreme diffuſion of the characters, and the too great extent which they take up, which, join'd to thoſe lines, to thoſe ſtaves ſo inconvenient to trace, becomes a ſource of embarraſſment of more than one kind. If the firſt advantage of inſtituting ſigns, was, that they ſhould be clear, the ſecond is, that they ſhould become conciſe; what judgment then we form of an order of ſigns in which both the one and the other are wanting?

Muſicians, it is true, cannot ſee any thing of this. Cuſtom has habituated them to this. Muſic to them is not the knowledge of ſounds; it is that of crotchets, minums, demi-crotchets, &c. &c. As ſoon as theſe figures ceaſe to be preſent, they cannot ſatisfy themſelves that they ſee muſic. Moreover, what they have learnt with difficulty, how can they render it eaſy to others? It is not then the muſician who ſhould be conſulted herein, but the man who *underſtands* muſic, and who has reflected on the art.

There are not, in this laſt claſs, two that agree in the errors of our notes; but ſtill theſe faults are eaſier to know than to correct. Many have endeavoured at this correction without ſucceſs for ſome time. The public, without any great diſcuſſion on the advantage of the ſigns propoſed to it, always embrace thoſe which are already eſtabliſhed, and muſt always prefer a bad method of knowing, to a better of learning. Wherefore, becauſe a new ſyſtem is rejected, is no ſolid proof of any thing more, than that the author came too late; and we may always diſcuſs and compare the two ſyſtems, with any regard on this point, to the judgment of the public.

All the methods of marking notes, which have not had for their grand law the evidence of intervals, do not ſeem to me worthy of the trouble of being removed. I will not then make any ſtop at that of Monſ. Sauveur, which may be ſeen in the Memoirs of the Academy of Sciences, anno 1721, nor at that of

Monſ.

Monſ. Demaux, given ſome years after. In theſe two ſyſtems, the intervals being expreſſed by ſigns intirely arbitrary, and without any true connection with the thing repreſented, eſcape the moſt attentive eyes, and can be fixed on the memory alone; for of what ſervice are heads differently figured, and tails differently directed, to the intervals which they ought to expreſs? Such ſigns as thoſe have nothing in them which ſhould make them preferable to others; the neatneſs of the figure, and the little place which it takes up, are advantages which might be found in a ſyſtem entirely different: chance may have given the firſt ſigns, but we muſt have a choice more peculiar to the thing in thoſe which ſhould be ſubſtituted in their place. Thoſe which have been propoſed in 1743, in a little work, intitled, "Diſſertation on the Modern Muſic," having this advantage, their ſimplicity perſuades me to lay down their abridged ſyſtem in this article.

The characters of muſic have a double object, viz. to repreſent the ſounds, firſt, according to their different intervals from flat to ſharp, which conſtitutes the air and harmony. Secondly, according to their different relative durations from quick to ſlow, which determines the time and meaſure.

In the firſt caſe, in whatever method we turn and combine written and regular muſic, we can never find any combinations therein but of the ſeven notes of the gamut, carried in different octaves, or tranſpoſed on different degrees, according to the time and mode which we have choſen. The author expreſſes theſe ſeven ſounds by the ſeven firſt cyphers; ſo that the cypher 1 forms the note ut, 2 the note re, 3 the note mi, &c. and he traverſes them with a horizontal line, as in the example.

The Octave in aſcending.

—1—2—3—4—5—6—7—$\overline{1}$—

ut, re, mi, fa, ſol, la, ſi, ut.

He writes above the line the notes which continuing to aſcend, would be found in the ſuperior octave; wherefore ut, which immediately follows ſi, aſcending a ſemi-tone, ſhould be above the line in this manner $\overline{}{+}^{1}$; and in the ſame manner the notes which belong to the ſharp octave, of which this ut is the beginning, ought to be all above the ſame line. If we entered into a third octave in ſharp, we have only to traverſe the notes by a ſecond accidental line above the firſt.

If, on the contrary, we would deſcend into the octave inferior to that of the principal line, we muſt write immediately below that line, the notes of the octave which follow it deſcending: if

then

then you descend an octave, add a line below, as you have placed one above, to ascend, &c. By means of three lines only, you may go through the whole extent of five octaves, which cannot be done in our ordinary music in less than eighteen.

We may even manage without drawing any line. We place all the notes horizontally in the same rank: if we find a note which passes the si of the octave wherein we are in ascending, i. e. which enters into a higher octave, we place a point on this note. This point suffices for all the following notes which remain without interruption in the octave wherein we are entered. If we re-descend from one octave to the other, it will require another point under the note by which we enter therein, &c. We see in the following example the progress of two octaves, as well ascending as descending, marked in this manner.

1 2 3 4 5 6 7   1 2 3 4 5 6 7   1 7 6 5 4 3 2   1 7 6 5 4 3 2 1

The first method of marking with lines is suitable to music greatly laboured, and very difficult for large partitions, &c. The second with points is proper for simple music, and trifling airs, but nothing hinders us from using it at our pleasure in the place of the other; and the author has made use of it in transcribing the famous Arietta, "*L'Objet qui regne dans mon Ame*," which we find pricked in partition by the cyphers of that author, at the end of his work.

By this method, all the intervals become so evident, that nothing can equal it: the octaves always bear the same cypher; the simple intervals are always known in their doubles or composition.

We instantly discover in the tenth $\overset{3}{\overline{\;1\;}}$ or 13, that it is the octave of the major third; the major intervals can never be confounded with the minor: 24 will be continually a minor third; 46 a major third. The position has nothing to do with that.

After having thus reduced the whole extent of the keys, under a much smaller compass, with much clearer signs, we now pass to the transpositions.

There are only two modes in our music. What is singing or playing in re major? It is transporting the scale or the gamut of ut a tone higher, and placing it on re as tonic or fundamental.

All the references which belonged to ut pass to re by this transposition. It is to express this system of connections, raised or lowered so much, that so many alterations of diesis and B's flat have been thought necessary on the cleff. The author of the New System suppresses all this embarrassment at a stroke. The single word re, plac'd at top, and in the margin, gives us

 notice,

notice, that the piece is in major re; and as then the re takes all the connections which ut had, it takes alſo its ſign and name. It is marked with the cypher 1, and all its octave follows by the cyphers 2, 3, 4, &c. as before. The re of the margin ſerves as its cleff, it is the touch re or D of the natural key; but this ſame re becomes a tonic under the name of ut, and becomes alſo the fundamental of the mode.

But this fundamental, which is tonic in the major tones, is only mediant in the minor; the tonic which takes the name of la, being then found a minor third below this fundamental. This diſtinction is made by a ſmall horizontal line drawn under the cleff. Re, without this line, expreſſes the major mode of re; but re, with the line under it, deſigns the minor mode of ſi, of which this re is the mediant. This diſtinction, which ſerves only to determine clearly the tone by the cleff, is not more neceſſary in the new ſyſtem than in the ordinary note, wherein it is not placed. Wherefore, though no attention ſhould be paid to it, we could not ſol fa leſs exactly. Inſtead of the ſame names of the notes, we might make uſe, for cleffs, of the letters of the gamut, which anſwers to them, C for ut, D for re, &c. (Vide Gamut)

The muſicians affect a great deal of contempt for the method of tranſpoſitions, doubtleſs, becauſe it renders the art too eaſy. The author ſhows that this contempt is ill founded: that it is their method we ſhould deſpiſe, ſince it is laborious to no end; and the tranſpoſitions, whoſe advantage he ſhows, are, even without reflecting on them, the true rule which all the great muſicians and good compoſers follow. (Vide Tranſpoſition)

The tone, the mode, and all their connections well determined, it is not ſufficient to make all the notes of each octave be known, nor the paſſage from one octave to another by clear and preciſe ſigns; we muſt, beſides, expreſs the part of the keys, which theſe octaves employ. If I have a ſol to tune, it muſt be known which, for there are five in the keys, the one high, the other middle, the other low, according to the different octaves; theſe octaves have each their letters; and one of theſe letters placed on the line, which ſerves as a ſtave, denotes to what octave that line belongs, and, conſequently, the octaves which are above and below. We muſt ſee the figure at the end of his book, and the explanation the author gives to it, to be able to judge of this part of his ſyſtem, which is amongſt the moſt ſimple.

It remains, for the expreſſion of all the poſſible ſounds in our muſical ſyſtem, to render the accidental alterations introduced by the modulation, which may be eaſily done. The dieſis is form'd by traverſing the note with a ſtroke aſcending from the left to the

the right, in this manner: fa dieſis 4; ut dieſis 1. We mark the B flat by a ſimilar mark deſcending, ſi B flat 7; mi B flat 3. In regard to B ſharp, the author ſuppreſſes it as an uſeleſs ſign in his ſyſtem.

This part being thus filled, we muſt now come to the time and meaſure. The author lays all waſte before him on this crowd of different meaſures, with which the muſic has been ſo improperly loaded. He knows only two like the ancients, viz. two-tim'd and three-tim'd meaſures. The times of each of theſe meaſures may, in their turn, be divided into two or three equal parts. From theſe two combined rules, he draws exact expreſſions for all the poſſible movements.

We connect in ordinary muſic the different powers of the notes to that of a particular note, which is the ſemi-breve, which cauſes that the powers of this note continually varying, the notes compared with it have no fixed powers. The author handles it differently. He determines the power of the notes only on the kind of meaſure in which they are uſed, and on the time which they employ therein, which diſpenſes him from having, for theſe powers, any particular ſign beſides the place which it fills.

One ſingle note between two bars fills a whole meaſure. In the meaſure of two times, two notes filling up the meaſure, form each of them a time. Three notes do the ſame thing in a three-tim'd meaſure. If there are four notes in a two-tim'd meaſure, or ſix in a meaſure of three, it is, that each time is divided into two equal parts; we paſs then two notes for a time; we paſs three when there are ſix notes in one, and nine in the other. In a word, when there is no ſign of inequality, the notes are equal, their number is diſtributed in a meaſure according to the number of the times, and the nature of the meaſure: To render this diſtribution more eaſy, we ſeparate, if we chuſe it, the times by comma's; ſo that in reading muſic, we ſee clearly the power of the notes, without its being neceſſary to give them, on that account, any particular figures.

Example of equal Powers.

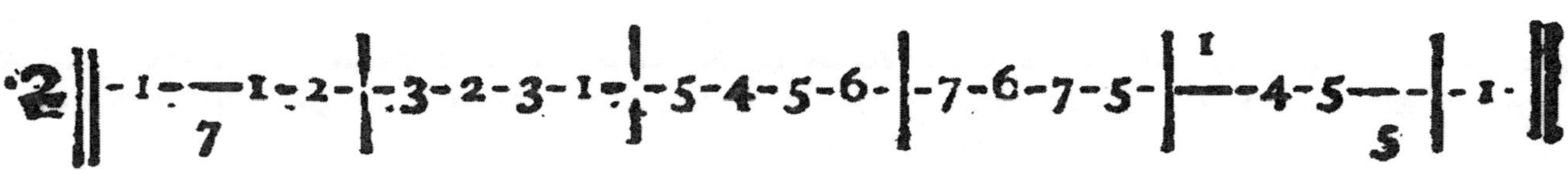

Idem,

Idem, ſeparating the Times by Comma's, &c.

2‖—1———1—2———3—2,—3—1———5—4,—‖
7,

The unequal diviſions are marked with the ſame facility. Theſe inequalities are never more than ſub-diviſions, which are brought into an equality by a ſtroke, with which two or more notes are covered. For inſtance, if a time contains a demi-crotchet and two double demi-crotchets, a ſtroke in a right line above or below the two double demi-crotchets, will ſhew that they form together only a quantity equal to the preceding, and conſequently, one demi-crotchet; wherefore, the entire time is found divided into two equal parts, viz. The ſingle note, and the ſtroke which comprehends two. There are alſo ſub-diviſions of inequality, which may require two ſtrokes, as, if a demi-crotchet pointed was followed by two triple demi-crotchets, in that caſe, a ſtroke on the two notes would be firſt neceſſary, to repreſent the triple demi-crotchets, which would render them together equal to the point; then a ſecond ſtroke, which covering the precedent ſtroke and the point, might render all that it cover'd equal to the demi-crotchet. But whatever quickneſs the notes may have, theſe ſtrokes are never neceſſary but when the powers are unequal, and whatever inequality there may be therein, we ſhall never want more than two ſtrokes, particularly in ſeparating the times by ſtops, as we may ſee in the example following.

The author of the new ſyſtem uſes the point alſo, but otherwiſe than in ordinary muſic: In this, the point is equal to half of the note which precedes it; in his, the point, which alſo marks the prolongation of the preceding note, has no other power than that of the place which it fills: If the point fills a time, it is equal to a time; if it fills a meaſure, it is equal to a meaſure; if it is in a time with another note, it is equal to the half of this time. In a word, the point is reckoned as a note, is meaſured as the notes, and to mark line's or ſyncope's, we may make uſe of ſeveral points together, of equal or unequal powers, according to thoſe of the times or meaſures which theſe points are to fill.

All the ſilences are in want of one character only, which is the O. This is uſed as the notes, and as the point. The point is marked after it to prolong a ſilence, as after a note to prolong a ſound. (Vide the example of this):

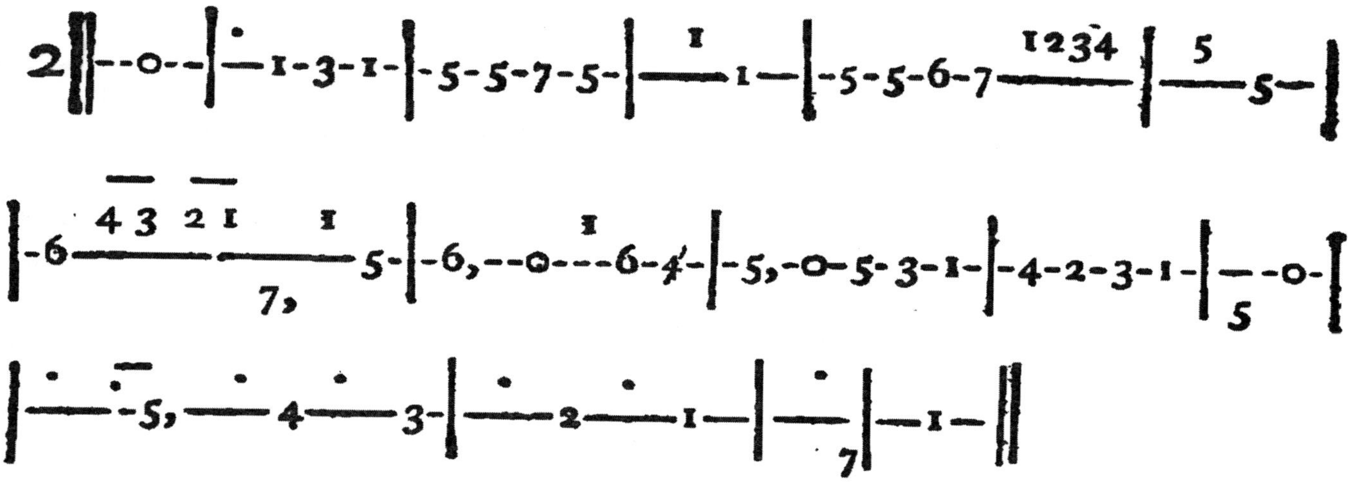

Such is the abridgement of this new system. We will not follow the author in the account of his rules, or in the comparison which he makes with the characters used, and his own; we must certainly expect he will place all the advantage on his own side; but this prepossession should not lead the reader, who is impartial, from examining the reasons which the author gives in his book. As the author is the composer of this Dictionary, he cannot mention any thing more under this article, without removing from the duty which he ought to attend to herein. —— Vide an air written in new characters, but it will be very difficult to decypher the whole of it properly, without recourse to the book itself, because an article of this Dictionary ought not to be a book, and in the explanation of so complicated an art, it is impossible to say all in a few words.

Air to sing with a Base.

Continued.

Continued.

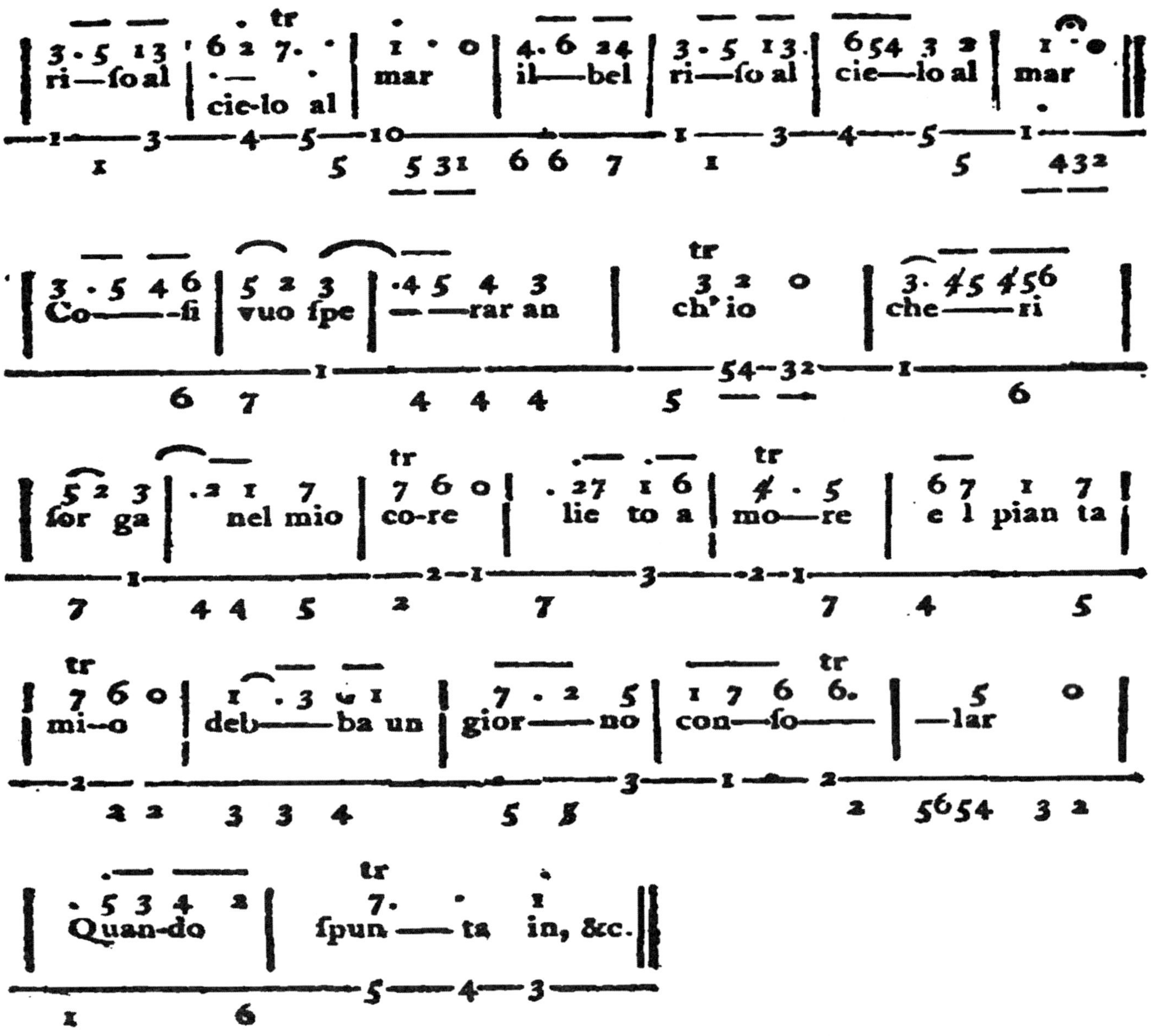

SENSIBLE NOTE, Is that which is a major third above the dominant, or a ſemi-tone below the tonic. The ſi is a ſenſible note in the tone of ut, the ſol dieſis in the tone of la.

It is called ſenſible note becauſe it makes the tone and tonic be felt, on which, after the concord dominant, the ſenſible note taking the ſhorteſt way, is obliged to aſcend; which occaſions that ſome treat this ſenſible note as a major diſſonance, thro' fault of ſeeing that the diſſonance, being a connection, cannot be conſtituted but by two notes.

I do not ſay that the ſenſible note is the ſeventh of the tone, becauſe, in the minor mode, this ſeventh note is ſenſible only in aſcending; for, in deſcending, it is a tone of the tonic, and in the minor third of the dominant. (Vide Mode, Tonic, Dominant.)

NOTES OF TASTE. There are two kinds of them. The one which belongs to the melody, but not to harmony; ſo that tho' they enter into the meaſure, they do not in the concord: theſe are marked in full. The other notes of taſte, entering neither into harmony or melody, are marked only with ſmall notes, which are not reckoned in the meaſure, and whoſe very rapid duration is taken on the note which precedes, or that which follows. Vide an example of the notes of taſte in their two kinds.

Notes of Taſte of the firſt Kind.

Notes of Taſte of the ſecond Kind.

NOTHUS. This is the epithet given by ſome to the hypophrygian mode, which has its final in ſi, and conſequently its fifth falſe, which cuts it off from the authentic modes; and to the æolian, whoſe final is in fa, and the fourth ſuperfluous, which removes it from the number of plagal modes.

TO NUMBER THE CLEFF. Is to place in it the number of dieſis's, or B's flat, ſuitable to the tone and mode in which we chuſe to write our muſic. (Vide B Flat, Cleff, Dieſis.)

NUNNIA. Was, amongſt the Greeks, a ſong peculiar to nurſes. (Vide Song.)

O.

O. This capital letter, form'd in a circle, or double C Ɔ, is, in our ancient music, the sign which is called perfect time; that is, of triple measure, or three-tim'd, with the difference of the imperfect time, or double measure, which was marked by a simple C, or an O divided on the right or left C or Ɔ.

The imperfect time was sometimes marked by a simple O; sometimes by an O pointed within, in this manner, ʘ; or by an O barr'd, ⦶. (Vide Time.)

OBLIG'D. We call an oblig'd part, that which sometimes recites, that which we cannot remove without spoiling the harmony or the air, which distinguishes it from the parts of fulness, which are added only as a greater perfection of harmony, but by the removal of which, the piece is by no means mutilated. Those who are in the parts of fulness may stop when they choose; the music proceeds the same: But he who is buried in the oblig'd parts, cannot quit them an instant without failing in the execution.

OCTACHORD. An instrument or system of music, composed of eight sounds or seven degrees. The octachord or lyre of Pythagoras comprehended the eight sounds expressed by these letters, E, F, G, a, ♮, c, d, e, that is, two disjoint tetrachords.

OCTAVE. The first of the consonances in the order of their generation. The octave is the most perfect of the consonances; it is, after the unison, that of all the concords whose connection is the most simple; the unison is in the computation of equality, that is, as 1 to 1. The octave is in double computation, that is, as 1 to 2. The harmonies of the two sounds agree in each without exception, which has no place in any other interval.

Lastly, these two concords have so much conformity, that they are often confounded in melody, and in harmony itself we take them indifferently one from the other.

This interval is called octave, because, to move diatonically from one of these terms to the other, we must pass by seven degrees, and make eight different sounds be heard.

Here are the properties which distinguish the octave so singularly from all the other intervals.

I. The octave confines within its bounds all the primitive and original sounds; so after having established a system, or a collection of sounds, in the extent of an octave, if we wish to prolong that collection, we must necessarily retake the same order in a second octave, by a similar series, and the same thing for a third

third and fourth octave, where we ſhall not find any ſound which is not the replique of the firſt. Such a ſeries is called ſcale of muſic in its firſt octave, and replique in all the reſt. It is in virtue of this propriety of the octave, that it has been called diapaſon by the Greeks. (Vide Diapaſon.)

II. The octave takes in alſo all the conſonances, and all their differences; that is, all the ſimple intervals, as well conſonant as diſſonant, and, conſequently, the whole of harmony. Let us eſtabliſh all the conſonances on a ſame fundamental ſound, we ſhall have the following table:

$$\frac{120}{120}.\quad \frac{100}{120}.\quad \frac{96}{120}.\quad \frac{90}{120}.\quad \frac{80}{120}.\quad \frac{75}{120}.\quad \frac{72}{120}.\quad \frac{60}{120}.$$

which anſwers to this:

$$1.\quad \frac{5}{6}.\quad \frac{4}{5}.\quad \frac{3}{4}.\quad \frac{2}{3}.\quad \frac{5}{8}.\quad \frac{3}{5}.\quad \frac{1}{2}.$$

Where we find all the conſonances in this order: the minor third, the major third, the fourth, the fifth, the ſixth minor, the ſixth major, and, laſtly, the octave. By this table, we ſee that the ſimple conſonances are all contained between the octave and uniſon. They may even be heard at a time in the extent of an octave without any mixture of diſſonances. Strike, at the ſame time, theſe four ſounds, ut, mi, ſol, ut, aſcending from the firſt ut to its octave, they will form together all the conſonances, except the major ſixth, which is compoſed, and will form no other interval. Take any two of theſe ſounds, the interval will be always conſonant: 'tis from this uniſon of all the conſonances that the concord which produces them is called perfect concord.

The octave, giving all the conſonances, gives, conſequently, all their differences, and by them all the ſimple intervals of our muſical ſyſtem, which are only the differences themſelves. The difference of the major and minor third gives the minor ſemi-tone; the difference of the major third and fourth gives the major ſemi-tone; the difference of the fourth and fifth gives the major tone; and the difference of the fifth and ſixth major gives the minor tone. Moreover, the minor ſemi-tone, the major ſemi-tone, the minor and major tones, are the only elements of all the intervals in our muſic.

III. Every ſound conſonant with one of the terms of the octave, is conſonant alſo with the other. Conſequently, every ſound diſſonant with one, is diſſonant with the other.

IV. Lastly, the octave has this propriety also, the most singular of all, that it can be added to itself, tripled, and multiplied at pleasure, without changing its nature, and without its product ceasing to be a consonance.

This multiplication of the octave, as well as its division, is however bounded in regard to us, by the capacity of the auditive organ; and an interval of eight octaves already exceeds that capacity. (Vide Extent.) The octaves themselves lose something of their harmony in being multiplied; and, beyond a certain measure, all the intervals are less easy for the ear to catch; a double actave begins already to be less agreeable than a simple; a triple than a double; lastly, in the fifth octave, the extreme distance of its sounds deprives the consonance nearly of the whole of its beauty.

It is from the octave that we draw the ordained generation of all the intervals by harmonic divisions and sub-divisions. Divide harmonically the octave 3. 6. by the number 4. you will have on one side the fourth, 3. 4. and on the other side the fifth, 4. 6.

Divide, in the same manner, the fifth, 10. 15. harmonically by the number 12. you will have the minor third, 10. 12. and the major third 12. 15. Lastly, divide the major third 72. 90. again, harmonically by the number 80. you will have the minor tone 72. 80. or 9. 10. and the major tone 80. 90. or 8. 9, &c.

We must take notice, that these harmonic divisions give always two unequal intervals, the least of which is in flat, and the greater in sharp. If we make the same divisions in arithmetical proportion, we shall have the smallest interval in sharp, and the greater in flat. Wherefore the octave 2. 4. arithmetically divided, will immediately give the fifth 2. 3. in flat, then the fourth 3. 4. in sharp. The fifth 4. 6. will first give the major third 4. 5. then the minor third 5. 6. and so with the rest. We should have the same connections in contrary senses, if, instead of taking them, as I do here, by vibrations, we took them by the lengths of the chord. This knowledge is besides of little utility in itself, but it is necessary to understand the ancient authors.

The complete and rigorous system of the octave is composed of three major tones, two minor, and two major semi-tones. The temperated system is of five equal tones, and 2 semi-tones, forming together as many diatonic degrees on the seven sounds of the gamut, as far as the octave of the first. But as every tone may be divided into two semi-tones, the same octave is divided also chromatically into twelve intervals, each of a semi-tone, the seven precedent of which retain their name, and the five others take

take each the name of the diatonic ſound neareſt to it, below by dieſis, and above by B flat (Vide Scale.)

I do not ſpeak here of diminiſhed or ſuperfluous octaves, becauſe this interval is ſeldom changed in melody, and never in harmony.

It is forbidden, in compoſition, to make two octaves together, between different parts, particularly in a ſimilar movement; but this is permitted, and even elegant, formed on purpoſe, and à propos, through the whole of an air or a period: It is in this manner, that in ſeveral concerto's, all the parts take by intervals the rippieno, in octave or uniſon.

On the rule of the octave. (Vide Rule.)

TO OCTAVE. When we force the air in a wind inſtrument, the ſound immediately aſcends to the octave: this is what we call to octave. In ſtrengthening the inſpiration thus, the air being incloſed in the pipe, and conſtrained by the exterior air, is obliged, in yielding to the quickneſs of the oſcillations, to be divided into two equal columns, having each the half of the length of the pipe: It is in this manner that each of theſe halves ſounds the octave of the whole. A chord of the violincello octaves by a ſimilar principle, when the ſtroke of the bow is too rough, or too near the bridge. It is a fault in the organ when a pipe octaves. This happens from its receiving too much air.

ODE. A Greek word which ſignifies an air, or ſong.

ODEUM. This was, amongſt the ancients, a place deſtined for the repetition of the muſic which was to be ſung on the ſtage, as in the opera of Paris, is the little theatre du Magaſin.

The name of odeum was given ſometimes to buildings which had no connection with the theatre. We read in Vitruvius, that Pericles ordered an odeum to be built at Athens, where they diſputed for the rewards of muſic; and in Pauſanias, that Herod, the Athenian, conſtructed a magnificent odeum, as the ſepulchre of his wife.

The Eccleſiaſtic writers deſign alſo ſome times the choir of a church, by the word odeum.

OPERA. A dramatic and lyric ſpectacle, where we uſe our endeavours to reunite all the charms of the fine arts, in the repreſentation of a paſſionate action, to excite, by the aſſiſtance of agreeable ſenſations, the intereſt and illuſion.

The conſtitutive parts of an opera, are the poem, the muſic, and the decorations. By poetry we ſpeak to the mind; by muſic to the ear; and by painting to the eyes; and the whole ought to be reunited to move the heart, and convey to it, at the ſame time, the ſame impreſſion through different organs. Of theſe three parts, my ſubject does not permit me to conſider the firſt and

and laſt, but by the connection which they may have with the ſecond. Wherefore I paſs immediately to *that*.

The art of combining the ſounds agreeably, may be viewed under two different aſpects. Conſidered as an inſtitution of nature, muſic bounds its effect by the ſenſation and phyſical pleaſure which reſults from it, by the melody, harmony, and rhyme. Such is ordinarily the church-muſic; ſuch are the tunes for dancing, and thoſe of ſongs. But as an eſſential part of the lyric ſcene, whoſe principal object is the imitation, muſic becomes one of the fine arts, capable of painting every picture, of exciting every ſentiment, of harmonizing with poetry, giving it a new ſtrength, embelliſhing it with new charms, and triumphing by its means at the time that it crowns it.

The ſounds of the ſpeaking voice, neither ſuſtained, nor harmonious, are not appreciable, and, conſequently, cannot be agreeably allied with thoſe of the ſinging voice and inſtruments, at leaſt, in our languages, too much removed from a muſical character; for we cannot underſtand the paſſages of the Greeks in their method of reciting, but by ſuppoſing their language to be accented in ſuch a manner, that the inflections of the diſcourſe in a ſuſtained declamation, form between themſelves muſical and appreciable intervals; ſo we may ſee that their theatrical pieces were a kind of opera, and 'tis for this ſame reaſon, that there could be no opera properly called ſo amongſt them.

By the difficulty of uniting the air to the diſcourſe in our languages, it is eaſy to perceive, that the intervention of the muſic, as an eſſential part, muſt give the lyric poem a character different from that of tragedy and comedy, and make a third from it in the nature of a drama, which has its particular rules; but theſe differences cannot be determined without a perfect knowledge of the part added, of the methods to unite it with the words, and of its natural relation with the human heart: ſtudies which belong leſs to the artiſt than to the philoſopher, and which muſt be left for a pen formed to brighten every art, to ſhew to thoſe who profeſs them, the principles of their rules, and to men of taſte, the ſources of their pleaſures.

Confining myſelf, then, to ſome obſervations on this ſubject, more hiſtorical than reaſoned, I ſhall firſt take notice, that the Greeks had not, in their theatre, a lyric genus as ourſelves; and what they called by that name, was not at all ſimilar to it. As they had much accent in their lauguage, and but little *noiſe* in their concerts, all their poetry was muſical, and all their muſic declamatory; ſo that their airs were little more than a ſuſtained diſcourſe, and they really ſung their verſes as they expreſs at the head of their poems, which has given the Latins firſt, then ourſelves,

ourſelves, by imitation, the ridiculous cuſtom of ſaying, "I ſing," when we do not ſing. "Arma virumque *Cano*." In regard to what they called lyric genus in particular, it was an heroic poeſy, whoſe ſtyle was pompous and ſigured, which was accompanied by the lyre or cithara, in preference to every other inſtrument. It is certain, that the Greek tragedies were recited in a manner very ſimilar to the air, that they were accompanied with inſtruments, and that choruſſes compoſed a part of them.

But if, on this account, it is thought that they were opera's like to ours, we muſt then imagine opera's without airs, for it ſeems to me ſufficiently proved, that the Greek muſic, without even excepting the inſtrumental, was nothing more than a real recitative. It is true, that this recitative, which reunited the charm of the muſical ſounds to the whole harmony of poetry, and to all the force of declamation, muſt have much more energy than the modern, which cannot enjoy one of theſe advantages but at the expence of the reſt. In our living languages, which in general carry with them the ſcent of the rudeneſs of that climate wherein they are original, the application of the muſic to the words is much leſs natural. A doubtful proſody is a bad agreement with the regularity of meaſure. Syllables mute without ſound, articulations which are rough, ſounds little harmonious and leſs varied, are with difficulty connected to melody; and a poetry cadenc'd by the number of ſyllables only, receives a harmony little felt in muſical rhyme, and is inceſſantly oppoſed to the diverſity of powers and their movements. Here are difficulties which ſhould be conquered or eluded in the invention of the lyric poem. It was then endeavoured, by a choice of words, turns and verſes, to make a proper language; and this language, which was called lyric, was rich or poor, in proportion to the ſweetneſs or roughneſs of that from whence it was derived.

Having, in ſome reſpects, prepared the words for the muſic, it was then neceſſary to apply the muſic to the words, and to render it proper in ſuch a manner on the lyric ſcene, that the whole might be taken for a ſingle and the ſame idiom, which produced the neceſſity of continually ſinging, to appear always ſpeaking; a neceſſity which reaſonably ariſes from a language being little muſical: for the leſs ſweetneſs and accent a language has, the more the alternative paſſage of the words to the air, and the air to the words, becomes rough and diſguſting to the ear. From thence ariſes the want of ſubſtituting, in the place of the diſcourſe in recital, a diſcourſe in muſic, which might ſo nearly imitate it, that there ſhould be only the juſtneſs of the concords which could diſtinguiſh it from the words. (Vide Recitation.)

This

This method of uniting on the theatre the music to the poetry, which amongst the Greeks was sufficient for the interest and illusion, because it was natural, by the contrary reason could not suffice amongst us by the same ending. In listening to a constrained and hypothetic language, we have some trouble to conceive what is said: with much noise they afford little emotion. From thence arises the necessity of introducing a physical pleasure to the assistance of the moral, and to supply, by the attraction of harmony, what is wanting in the energy of expression. Wherefore, the less we know how to touch the heart, the more we must endeavour to flatter the ear. We are obliged to seek in sensation, that pleasure which sentiment denies us. Hence is the origin of airs, choirs, symphony, and of that enchanting melody with which modern music is often embellished, at the expence of the poetry, but which the man of taste banishes from the theatre, when he is flattered without emotion.

At the first rise of the opera, its inventor, wishing to elude what had very little nature, viz. the union of music to the discourse, in the imitation of human life, resolved to transport the scene to the heavens and hell, and, thro' an ignorance of making mankind speak, they chose rather to make gods and devils sing, than heroes and shepherds. Very soon the marvellous became the foundation of the lyric theatre, and, contented with enriching themselves with a new genus, they did not even pay attention to find whether they had chosen one that was suitable. To sustain so strong an illusion, it was necessary to drain all that human art could imagine most seducing amongst a people whose most ardent passions were the love of pleasure, and that of the fine arts. That celebrated nation, in which there remains nothing of its ancient grandeur, but that of the ideas in the fine arts, lavished all its taste and ingenuity to give this new spectacle all the eclat it stood in need of. Through the whole of Italy were seen theatres equal to the palaces of their kings, and, in elegance, like the monuments of antiquity, with which it was filled. They invented, to adorn them, the art of perspective and decoration. Artists of every kind displayed their talents to the utmost. The most ingenious machines, the boldest flights, tempests, thunder, lightning, and all the inventions of art, were used to fascinate the eye, whilst multitudes of instruments and voices astonished the ear.

With all this the action continued cold, and every situation was uninteresting. As there was no plot but what was easily discovered by the assistance of some god, the spectator, who knew the whole power of the poet, left him quietly the function of preserving his heroes from the greatest dangers. Wherefore, the preparations

preparations were immenſe, and produced little effect, becauſe the imitation was always flat and imperfect; the action taken unnaturally was unintereſting to us; and the ſenſes pay little regard to the illuſion when the heart is unconcerned; ſo that on a computation of the whole, it would have been difficult to have tir'd an audience with greater expence.

This ſpectacle, imperfect as it was, became a long time the admiration of contemporaries, who knew no better. They even congratulated it on the diſcovery of ſo fine a genus. "Here, "ſaid they, is a new principle joined to thoſe of Ariſtotle: here "is admiration joined with terror and pity." They did not perceive that this apparent richneſs was at bottom no more than a ſign of ſterility, as the flowers which cover the field before harveſt. It was a want of knowing how to touch the paſſions that they wiſhed to ſurpriſe; and this pretended admiration, was, in effect, no more than a childiſh aſtoniſhment, which they ought to have bluſh'd at. A falſe appearance of magnificence and enchantment, impoſed on them to ſuch a degree, that they ſpoke with enthuſiaſm of a theatre, which deſerved only hiſſings: They had, with the moſt profound belief, as much veneration for the ſtage itſelf, as for the chimerical objects which they endeavoured to repreſent on it: as if there was a greater merit in making the king of gods ſpeak flatly, than the loweſt mortal; and that Moliere's valets were not preferable to Pradon's heroes.

Tho' the authors of theſe firſt operas had hardly any other aim than to dazzle the eye and ſtun the ear, it was difficult for the muſician not to be tempted to ſeek to draw from his art the expreſſions of the ſentiments ſcattered in the poem.

The ſongs of nymphs, the hymns of prieſts, the cries of warriors, the infernal howls, did not ſo much fill theſe vulgar drama's, but that there was ſome moment found of intereſt and ſituation, where the ſpectator requires only to take breath. Very ſoon they began to perceive, that, independantly of the muſical declamation, which the language often ill ſuited the choice of the movement, the harmony and airs was not indifferent to the things which they had to ſay, and that, conſequently, the effect of the muſic alone, bounded thus far to the ſenſes, might even reach the heart. The melody, which was ſeparated from poetry only thro' neceſſity, took a part of this independance, to give itſelf beauties, abſolute, and purely muſical: The harmony diſcovered or improved, opened new paths for it to pleaſe and move the ſoul; and the meaſure, freed from the hindrance of poetic rhyme, acquired alſo a kind of ſeparate cadence, which it held of itſelf alone.

Muſic, being by this means become a third art of imitation, had very ſoon its language, expreſſion, and paintings, independant

 of

of poetry. The symphony itself, taught to speak without the assistance of words, and very often, as lively sentiments came from the orchestra as from the lips of the actors. It was then, that, beginning to be disgusted with all this chinking emptiness, childish parade of machinery, and fantastic images of things that were never seen, they sought in the imitation of nature, paintings more interesting and more credible. Till that time, the opera had been constituted as it could be; for what better use could be made on the stage, of a music which could paint nothing, than to use it in the representation of things that could not exist, and on which no one was in a condition of comparing the image with the object? It is impossible to know if we are affected by the painting of the marvellous, as we should be, were it present; whereas every man may judge by himself, if the artist has given the passions their true language, and if the objects of nature are truely imitated. As soon as music had learnt to paint and speak, the charms of sentiment soon made those of fable give way: The theatre was purged of its jargon of mythology; interest was substituted in the place of the marvellous; the machines of poets and carpenters were destroyed; and the lyric drama took a more noble and gigantic form. All that could touch the heart was used therein with success; they were no longer in want of imposing by beings of invention, or rather of folly; and the gods were turned off the stage, when they were able to represent mankind. This form, more sensible and more regular, is also more suitable to the illusion; they saw, that the master-piece of music was to make itself forgotten; that by throwing disorder and trouble into the soul of the spectator, it hindered him from distinguishing the tender and pathetic accents of a groaning heroine, from the real ones of grief; and that Achilles in a rage might chill us with horror, in the very same language that would have disgusted us from his lips at another time.

These observations gave cause to a second reformation, not less important than the first. They perceived, that nothing cold and reasoned was necessary to the opera; nothing that the spectator could listen to quietly enough to reflect on the absurdity of what he heard, and 'tis in that particularly, that the essential difference of the lyric drama and simple tragedy consists. All politic deliberations, all projects of conspiration, expositions, recitals, sententious maxims, in a word, every thing that speaks to reason only was banished from the language of the heart, with the turns of the mind, madrigals, and every thing which proceeds from the thoughts only. The tone itself of simple gallantry, which agrees ill with the greater passions, was hardly admitted in tragic situations, whose effect it almost always spoils;

for we never perceive better that the actor sings, than when he speaks a song.

The energy of all the sentiments, the violence of all the passions, are then the principal object of the lyric drama; and the illusion which forms its charm, is always destroyed as soon as the author and actor leave the spectator a moment to himself.

Such are the principles on which the modern opera is established. Aportolo Zeno, the Corneille of Italy, his tender pupil, who is its Racine, have opened and improved this new career. They have dared to place the heroes of history on a theatre, which seemed to agree only to the phantoms of fable. Cyrus, Cæsar, Cato himself, have appeared on the stage with success; and those spectators who were most averse to hearing such men sing, very soon forgot that they sung; subjugated and ravished by the eclat of a music, as full of noble dignity as of enthusiasm and fire. We easily suppose, that sentiments so different from ours, ought to be also expressed in another tone.

These new poems which genius had created, and which itself only could sustain, were out of the depth of those musicians who had only the mechanism of their art; and who, deprived of the fire of invention, and the gift of imitation, made opera's as they would have made wooden shoes. Hardly were the cries of the bacchanals, the conjurations of sorcerers, all the airs which were no more than a real noise, banished from the theatre; hardly had they endeavoured to substitute in the place of this barbarous *fracas*, the accents of passion, grief, threats, tenderness, tears, and groans, and all the motions of a troubled soul, when, obliged to give sentiments to their heroes, and a language to the human heart, the Vinci's, Leo's, Pergolesis's, disdaining a servile imitation of their predecessors, and opening to themselves a new path, protected it under the wings of genius, and found themselves successful even in their first attempts. But we cannot long continue in the route of the *bon Goût*, without ascending or falling; and perfection is a point wherein it is difficult to maintain our ground. After having endeavoured and felt its force, music, in a condition of moving by itself, begins to disdain the poetry which it ought to accompany; and thinks to succeed better by her own separate beauties, than by those which she drew from her companion. It is true, she proposes to render the ideas and sentiments of the poet, but takes, in some respects, a different language; and tho' the object is the same, the poet and the musician too, separated in their labours, offer at the same time two resembling images, but distinct, which are of mutual injury to each other. The mind, obliged to divide itself, chooses and fixes on one image rather than another. The musician then, if if he has more art than the poet, eclipses him and effaces his glory: The actor, seeing that the spectator sacrifices the words to the music, sacrifices in his turn the gesture and theatrical action to the air and beauties of the voice, which makes the piece quite forgot, and changes the spectacle into a real concert. If, on the contrary, the advantage is found on the side of the poet, the music, in its turn, will become almost indifferent; and the spectator deceived by the noise, may take the change so far as to attribute, to a bad musician, the merit of an excellent poet; and think he admires master-pieces of harmony, whilst his admiration is directed only to a well composed poem.

Such are the errors which the absolute perfection of music, and its want of application to language, may introduce into opera's in proportion to the concourse of these two causes. Whereon we should remark, that the languages most proper to bend under the laws of measure and melody, are those where the duplicity which I have spoken of is least apparent; because, the music being connected only with the ideas of poetry, this in its turn is connected with the inflections of melody; and when the music ceases to observe the rhyme, the accent, and harmony of the verse, the verse gives way, and is used in the cadence of the measure and musical accent. But when the language has neither sweetness or flexibility, the confinement of poetry hinders it from being connected with the air; the sweetness of the melody itself hinders it from being united with the true recitation of verses; and we perceive, in the forced union of these two arts, a perpetual constraint which disgusts the ear, and destroys, at the same time, the attraction of melody, and the effect of declamation. This error is without remedy; and to attempt to apply forcibly the music to a language which is not musical, is to give it a greater roughness than it would have had without it.

By what I have said thus far, it must be seen, that there is a greater connection between the eye and the decoration, and the ear and music, than there appears between two senses which appear to have nothing common in them; and that, in certain respects, the opera constituted as it is, is not so completely monstrous as it seems to be. We have seen, that by desiring to offer to the eye the interest and movements, which were wanting in the music; they had imagined the low inventions of flying-machines; and that until they knew how to move us, they were contented with surprising us. It is therefore very natural, that music, become passionate and pathetic, should banish to strolling players, those silly supplements which it stood in no need of it itself. The opera then, purged of all the marvellous which debased it,

became

became an entertainment equally touching and majestic, worthy of pleasing persons of taste, and interesting a sensible heart.

It is certain, that as much of the pomp might have been removed from the spectacle as was added to the interest of the action; for the more persons there are who act, less we are employed in the objects which surround them; but still the situation of the scene must be suitable to the actors who speak therein: and the imitation of nature, often more difficult, and always more agreeable, than that of imaginary beings, became more interesting as it became more natural. A beautiful palace, pleasing gardens, well executed ruins, please the eye much more than the fantastic image of Tartarus, Olympus, or the chariot of the sun; an image as much inferior to that which we trace in ourselves, as in chimerical objects: it costs nothing to the mind to go beyond possibility, and to make to itself models of every imitation. From thence it happens, that the marvellous, tho' misplaced in tragedy, is not so in the epic poems, where the imagination, always industrious and magnificent, is charged with the execution, and draws from it quite a different part than that which the best machinist can form on our theatre, or the splendor of the most potent monarch.

Tho' music, taken as an art of imitation, has still more connection with poetry than painting, that, in the *manner* it is used on the stage, is not so subject as poetry to form with the music a double representation of the same object; because the one renders the sentiments of mankind, and the other the image only of the place wherein they are fixed; an image which strengthens the illusion, and transports the spectator to every part wherein the actor is supposed to be placed. But this removal from one place to another, ought to have rules and boundaries: It is not permitted, in regard to this, to call forth the agility of the imagination, but by consulting the law of nature; and tho' the spectator seeks only an attention to those fictions from whence he draws his whole pleasure, we must not abuse his credulity so far as to make him ashamed of it. In a word, we must remember, that we speak to sensible hearts, without forgetting that we address ourselves to reasonable people. Not that I would transmit to the opera, that rigorous unity of place which is required in tragedy, and which cannot be attended to but at the expence of the action, so that we are exact in one particular to be abused in a thousand others. It would be besides to deprive ourselves of the advantage in the change of scenes, which make each other mutually prosper; it would be exposing ourselves by a vicious uniformity, to oppositions badly conceived, between the scene which remains continually, and the situations which change;

it would be spoiling, by each other, the effect of music and that of decoration, as if we introduced voluptuous symphonies amongst rocks, or lively airs in the palaces of kings.

It is then with reason that the changes of the scene are left to subsist from act to act; and for their being regular and admissible, it is sufficient that they can naturally go from the place whence they go out, to the place whereto they pass, in the interval of time which passes, or which the action supposes between the two acts; so that, as the unity of time ought to be confined nearly within the duration of twenty-four hours, the unity of place should be confined nearly within the space of a day's journey. In regard to the changes of the scene, practised sometimes in the same act, they appear to me equally contrary to illusion and reason, and ought to be entirely abolished from the theatre.

Here then is the method by which the concurrence of the acoustic and perspective may improve the illusion; flatter the senses by different, but analogous impressions; and convey to the soul the same interest with a double pleasure. Wherefore it would be a great error to imagine, that the regulation of the theatre has nothing in common with that of music, if it was only from the general agreement which they draw from the poem. 'Tis for the imagination of the two artists to determine together, what that of the poet has left to their disposal; and to agree so well in that, that the spectator may always feel the perfect concord of what he sees and what he hears. But it must be confessed, that the task of the musician is the greatest. The imitation of painting is always cold, because it wants that succession of ideas and impressions which inflames the soul by degrees, and every thing is said at the first view. The imitative powers of that art, with several apparent objects, are confined in effect to very weak representation. It is one of the great advantages of the musician, to be able to paint things which cannot be heard; whilst it is impossible for the painter to paint those which cannot be seen; and the greatest prodigy of an art which has activity by its movements only, is to be able to form them as far as the representation of repose. Sleep, the calm of night, solitude and silence themselves, enter into the number of musical paintings. The noise sometimes produces the effect of silence; the silence that of noise: as when a man sleeps at an equal and monotonous lecture, and wakes at the same instant it ceases; and it is the same thing with other effects. But art has substitutions more fertile, and much nicer than those: it knows how to excite, by one sense, motions similar to those which may be excited by another; and as the connection cannot be sensible but when the impression is strong, the painting, stripp'd of that force, gives, with difficulty, those imitations

imitations to music which it draws from it. Though all nature should slumber, he who contemplates it sleeps not; and the art of the musician consists in substituting, in lieu of the insensible image of the object, that of the movements which its presence excites in the mind of the spectator: It does not directly represent the thing, but it awakens in our soul the same sentiment which we feel at the sight of it.

So, how little soever the painter has to draw from the partition of the musician, the skilful musician will not leave the works of the painter without some profit. He will not only agitate the sea at pleasure, excite the flames of a conflagration, make rivers flow, the rain fall, and the torrents enlarge, but he will increase the horror of a frightful desert; will strengthen the walls of a subterraneous prison, will calm the storm, render the air peaceful, the sky serene, and will extend, throughout the orchestra, a new and lively freshness.

We have now seen how the union of the three arts, which constitute the lyric scene, forms between themselves a whole, aptly united. We have endeavoured to introduce a fourth, which remains to be spoken of.

All the motions of the body, ordered according to certain laws to effect the eye, take in general the name of gestures. The gesture is divided into two kinds: One is used as an accompaniment to the words; and the other as a supplement. The first, natural to every man who speaks, is differently modified, according to men, languages and characters. The second, is the art of speaking to the eyes without the assistance of writing; by motions of the body, become signs of convention. As this gesture is most laborious, less natural to us than the use of words, and that it renders it useless, it excludes it, and even supposes its privation: this is what was called the art of pantomimes. To this art add a choice of agreeable attitudes, and cadenc'd movements, you will then have what we call the dance, which by no means deserves the name of art, when it speaks nothing to the mind.

This finished, it is our next concern to know if dancing, being a language, and, consequently, an art capable of imitation, may enter with the three others in the course of the lyric action; or if it can interrupt and suspend this action, without spoiling the effect and unity of the piece.

Moreover, I do not see that this last case may even demand a question. For every one perceives, that all the interest of a followed action depends on the continued and redoubled impression, which its representation makes on us; that all the objects which suspend or divide the attention, are as many counter-charms which

which deſtroy that of intereſt; that by dividing the ſpectacle by other ſpectacles which are unconcerned with it, we divide the principal ſubject into independant parts, which have nothing common between them but the general connection of the matter which compoſes them; and that laſtly, the more agreeable the inſerted ſpectacles are, more the mutilation would be deformed. So that, ſuppoſing an opera divided by ſome *divertiſements* which may be imagined, if they ſuffered the principal to be forgotten, the ſpectator, at the end of each *fête*, would be as little moved as at the beginning; and to animate him afreſh, and inſpire him with a new movement, we ſhould be obliged to begin again for ever. This is the reaſon why the Italians have baniſhed from the interludes of their opera's, the comic intermedes that had been inſerted; a kind of agreeable ſpectacle, ſtriking and taken from nature, but ſo miſplaced in the middle of a tragic action, that the two pieces would mutually injure each other, and that one of the two could never intereſt but at the expence of the other.

It remains then to ſee, if, ſince the dance cannot enter into the compoſition of the lyric genus, as a different ornament, we could not make it enter as a conſtitutive part; and make an art, which ought not to ſuſpend the action, form a concurrence with it. But how can we admit, at the ſame time, two languages which mutually exclude each other, and join the pantomimic art to words which render it ſuperfluous? The language of the geſture being the reſource of dumb Perſons, or thoſe who cannot underſtand each other, becomes ridiculous between thoſe who ſpeak. We do not anſwer words by antic tricks, or geſtures by diſcourſe; otherwiſe, I do not ſee why he who underſtands the language of another, ſhould not anſwer him in the ſame tone. Suppreſs then the words if you wiſh to make uſe of dancing. As ſoon as you introduce the pantomime into an opera, you muſt inſtantly baniſh poetry, becauſe of all the unities, that of language is moſt neceſſary; and it is abſurd and ridiculous to ſay, at the ſame time, the ſame thing to the ſame perſon, both by writing, and by word of mouth.

The two reaſons that I have alledged are united in their whole force to baniſh *fêtes* and *divertiſſimens* from the lyric drama, which not only ſuſpend its action, but either ſpeak nothing, or roughly ſubſtitute another oppoſite language, whoſe contraſt deſtroys nature, weakens the intereſting parts, and, whether continued in the ſame action, or in an inſerted epiſode, equally gives a wound to reaſon. It would be much worſe, if theſe *fêtes* preſented the ſpectator with nothing but a leap without union, and a dance without an object; a gothic and barbarous tiſſue, in a kind of work, wherein every thing ſhould be painting and imitation.

We

We must however confess, that the dance is so advantageously placed on the stage, that it would be depriving it of one of its greatest beauties, to remove it entirely. So, though we ought not to debase a tragic action by leaps, and inter-leaps, we may still terminate a spectacle very agreeably, by giving a ballet after the opera. as a little entertainment after the tragedy. In this new spectacle, which has no reference to the precedont, we may also make choice of another language: It is another nation which appears on the stage. The pantomimic art or dance becoming then the language of convention, the words should be banished from it in their turn; and the music, continuing the method of union, is applied to dancing in a small piece, as it was applied to the words in a greater. But before using this new language, we must create it. To begin then by giving ballets in action, without having first established the convention of gestures, is to speak a language to persons who have not its dictionary, and who, consequently, will not understand it in the least.

OPERA. Is also a word consecrated to distinguish the different works of the same author, according to the order in which they have been printed or engraved, and which he marks himself in general by cyphers. These two words are principally used for compositions of symphony.

ORATORIO. A kind of drama in Latin, or a vulgar language, divided by scenes, in imitation of theatrical pieces, but which is always on some sacred subject; and set to music, to be executed in some church during Lent, and at other times. This custom, so common in Italy, is not admitted in France. The French music is so little suitable to the dramatic genus, that it is sufficient, for its insufficiency, to be shewn on the theatre, without displaying it in the church.

ORCHESTRA. This was, amongst the Greeks, the lower part of the theatre; it was formed in a half circle, and adorned with seats on all sides. It was called orchestra because it was there that the dances were performed.

Amongst them the orchestra formed a part of the theatre: at Rome it was separated from it, and filled with seats appropriated to the senators, magistrates, vestals, and other persons of distinction. At Paris, the orchestra of the French and Italian play-houses, and what is besides called the *Parquet*, is put to a similar use.

At present, this word is more particularly applied to music, and means sometimes the place where those sit who play on the instruments, as the orchestra of the opera-house; and sometimes the place where the whole band in general are fixed, as the orchestra of the spiritual concert at the Chateaû de Tuilleries; and again the collection of all the symphonists. It is in this last sense, that we say of the execution of music, that the orchestra was good or bad, to express that the instruments were well or ill played.

In the numerous pieces of music in symphonists, such as that of an opera, the true distribution of an orchestra is a care not to be neglected. We owe in great part to this care, the astonishing effect of the symphony in the operas of Italy. The first attention is paid towards the fabric of the orchestra, that is, of the materials which it contains. They give it propositions proper for the symphonists to be most assembled and distributed in the properest manner. They take care to make the case of it of a light thin wood, to establish it on a *vide*, with arches for supporters, to remove the spectators from it by a partition placed in the pit, at a foot or two distance; so that the body of the orchestra, being in a manner borne in the air, and touching hardly any thing, vibrates and resounds without any obstacle, and acts as a large instrument, which answers to all the rest, and increases their effect.

In regard to the interior distribution, we must be careful, first, That the number of each kind of instruments be proportioned to the effect which they should all produce together; that, for instance, the bass should not be stifled by the treble, or stifle it; that the hautboys should not predominate over the violins; neither the seconds on the firsts. Secondly, Thar the instruments of each kind, except the basses, should be collected together, for them to agree and move together with more exactness. Thirdly, That the basses be dispersed around the two harpsichords, and throughout the orchestra, because it is the bass which should direct and sustain all the other parts, and all the musicians should equally hear it. Fourthly, That all the symphonists have their eyes on the master of his harpsichord, and the master on each of them, that in the same manner each violin be seen by the first, and the first see the rest; for which reason, this instrument, being the most numerous, as it ought to be, should be distributed into two lines which regard each other, viz. the one sitting in front of the theatre, with their back to the spectators, and the others seated opposite to them, with their backs to the theatre, &c.

The first orchestra in Europe, for the number and intelligence of symphonists, is that of Naples; but the best distributed, and which form together in the most perfect manner, is the orchestra at the opera-house of the king of Poland, at Dresden, directed by the illustrious Hasse. Following is the representation of this orchestra, where, without attention to the measures, which have not been taken in their places, we can judge better by the eye of the whole distribution, than we could have done on a longer description.

Diftribution of the Orcheftra at the Opera-Houfe of Drefden.

Directed by le Sr. Haffe.

Explanation of the Cyphers.

1. Harpfichord of the Mafter de Chapelle.
2. Ditto of Accompaniment.
3. Violoncellos.
4. Counterbaffes.
5. Firft Violins.
6. Second Violins, with the Back towards the Theatre.

7. Hautboys, the fame.
8. Flutes, the fame.

a. Tenors, the fame.
b. Baffoons.
c. Hunting Horns.
d. A Tribune on each Side for the Timballs and Trumpets.

It

It has been remarked, that of all the orchestras of Europe, that of Paris, tho' one of the most numerous, caused the least effect: The reasons may be easily discovered; First, the bad construction of the orchestra, sunk within the earth, and formed of materials of rough wood, massy, and loaded with iron, stifles every resonance. Secondly, the bad choice of symphonists, the greatest number of which, received thro' favour, hardly understand music, and have no idea of concinnity. Thirdly, their continual custom of scraping, agreeing and preluding with the greatest noise, without ever being in concord. Fourthly, the French genius, which generally neglects and disdains every thing that becomes a daily duty. Fifthly, the shocking instruments for symphony, which, continuing fixed on the place, are intended to bellow during the time of representation, and grow rotten in the interim. Sixthly, the bad placing of the master, who, at the forepart of the theatre, and quite busied with the actors, cannot be sufficiently attentive to his orchestra, and has it behind him, instead of before his eyes. Seventhly, the insupportable noise of his time-stick, which covers and stifles all the effect of the symphony. Eighthly, the bad harmony of their compositions, which, being never pure and chosen, gives the sound of a deafening and confused collection of instruments, instead of things which may produce an effect. Ninthly, not sufficient counter-basses and violoncellos, the sounds of which, trained after their method, stifle the melody and deafen the spectator. Tenthly and lastly, the errors of the measure, and the undetermined character of the French music, where it is the actor always who directs the orchestra, instead of the orchestra directing the actor; and where the treble introduces the bass, instead of the bass conducting the treble.

ORGANIC. This was, amongst the Greeks, that part of music which was executed on instruments; and this part had its characters, its peculiar notes, as may be seen in the Tables of Bacchius and Alypius. (Vide Music, Notes.)

TO ORGANIZE. This was, in the beginning of the invention of the counter-point, the insertion of some thirds in a collection of church-music, in unison; so that, for instance, that a part of the choir singing these four notes, ut, re, si, ut; the other part sung, at the same time, these other four, ut, re, re, ut. It appears, by the examples cited by l'Abbe de Bœuf and others, that the organization was seldom practised but on the sensible note, at the approach of the final; from whence it follows, that they hardly ever organized but by a minor third. For a concord so easy and so little varied, the choristers who organized did not fail being paid at a dearer rate than the rest.

In

In regard to the organum triplum, or quadruplum, which was alſo called triplum or quadruplum ſimply, it was the ſame thing as the identical air of the organizing parts, toned by counter-tenors at the octave of the baſſes, and by trebles at the octave of the tenor.

ORTHIAN. The orthian nome, in the Greek muſic, was a dactylic, invented, according to ſome, by the ancient Phrygian Olympus; and according to others, by the Myſian. It is on this orthian nome, ſay Herodotus and Aulugelles, that Arion ſung when he threw himſelf into the ſea.

OVERTURE. A piece of ſymphony, which we endeavour to render ſplendid, flattering, harmonious, and which ſerves as an introduction to operas, and other lyric dramas of a certain extent.

The overtures of the French opera are almoſt all calculated on thoſe of Lully. They are compoſed of a continuing piece, called *Grave*, which is generally played twice, and of a dancing *Repriſe*, called gay, which is commonly fugued. Several of theſe *Repriſes* are admitted alſo into the *Grave* at its concluſion.

There was a time when the French overtures ſerved as a model for all Europe. Not ſixty years ago, they ſent from France overtures, to place at the head of their operas in Italy. I have even ſeen many ancient Italian operas marked with an overture of Lully at their head. This is what the Italians at preſent contradict, ſince the whole has had ſuch a change; but, nevertheleſs, the fact is very certain.

The inſtrumental muſic having had an aſtoniſhing progreſs within about forty years, the ancient overtures, made for the ſymphoniſts, who were little ſkilled in managing their inſtruments, were very ſoon left for the French; and they have been contented with nearly preſerving their diſpoſition. The Italians themſelves have not been ſlow in ſecuring themſelves from this hindrance; and they at preſent diſtribute their overtures in another manner. They began by a lively and pleaſing piece of two or four times; then they give an andante *á Demi jeu*, in which they aim at diſplaying all the graces of a fine muſic; and they finiſh by a brilliant allegro, generally of three times.

The reaſon they give for this diſtribution, is, that in a numerous ſpectacle, where the ſpectators make great noiſe, they ſhould perſuade them to ſilence at the firſt ſtroke, and fix their attention by ſome bold beginning which may ſtrike them. They ſay, that the grave of our overtures is neither heard, or liſtened to, by any one; and that our firſt ſtroke of the fiddle-ſtick, which we boaſt of with ſo great emphaſis, leſs noiſy than the concord of inſtruments which precedes it, and with which it is confounded, is

 more

more suitable for persuading the audience to slumber than attention.

They add, that after having rendered the spectator attentive, it is necessary that he should be interested with less noise by an agreeable and flattering air, which may dispose him to the tenderness with which he is to be inspired; and lastly, to put an end to the overture in another character, which, being connected with the beginning of the drama, denotes, by finishing with *eclat*, the silence which the actor, at his entrance on the stage, requires of the spectators.

Our old course of overtures has caused a pleasant idea to be circulated in France: Many have imagined, that there was such an agreement between the form of Lully's overtures, and every opera, that it could not be changed without spoiling the effect of the whole; so that, of the beginning of a symphony, which should be in a different taste, such, for instance, as an Italian overture, they would say with contempt, that it was a sonata, and not an overture, as if every overture was not a sonata.

I know very well, that it would be a desirable thing for a proper and sensible connection to be between the character of an overture, and that of the work which it introduces; but instead of saying that all overtures should be cast in the same mould, this says precisely the contrary. Besides, if our musicians fail so often in catching the true connection of the music to the words in each piece, how can they catch the finer and more remote connections between the ordonnance of an overture, and that of the entire body of the work? Some musicians have flattered themselves to have caught these connections by collecting, before-hand in the overture, all the characters expressed in the piece, as if they would express the same action twice, and that what is to come should be already passed. It is not this. The best understood overture, is that which disposes the heart of the spectator in such a manner, as that it opens naturally to the interest which they endeavour to give it from the very beginning of the piece. This is the real effect that a good overture must produce. This is the plan on which it must be directed.

OXIPYCNI. Is the name which the ancients gave, in the crowded genus, to the third sound in ascending from each tetrachord. Wherefore, the oxipycni sounds were five in number. (Vide Apycni, Crowded, System, Tetrachord.)

P.

P.

P. By abbreviation, ſignifies piano, that is, *ſweet*. (Vide Sweet.)

The double PP. ſignifies pianiſſimo, that is, very ſweet.

PANTOMIME. An air on which two or more dancers execute an action, which bears alſo the name of pantomime. The airs of pantomimes are generally a principal couplet, which returns often in the courſe of the piece, and which ſhould be ſimple, for the reaſon given at the word *Country Dance*; but this couplet is intermixed with others more lively, which ſpeak, as it were, and form an image in the ſituation where the dancer ſhould place a determined expreſſion.

PAPER RUL'D. By this name is called the paper prepared with the ſtaves entirely drawn, to mark the muſic thereon. (Vide Stave.)

There is rul'd paper of two kinds, viz. that whoſe length exceeds its breadth, ſuch as is commonly uſed in France; and that whoſe breadth is greater than its length. This laſt is the only one uſed in Italy. However, by a whim, the reaſon of which I know not, the paper-makers of Paris call *Paper rul'd a la Françoiſe*, that which is uſed in Italy; and *Paper rul'd a l'Italienne*, that which is preferred in France.

The form whoſe breadth exceeds its length, appears moſt commodious in my opinion, either becauſe a book of this form is better laid open on a deſk, or becauſe the ſtaves, being longer, they are leſs frequently changed: Moreover, it is in the changes that muſicians are ſubject to take one ſtave for another, particularly in partitions. (Vide Partition.)

The rul'd paper uſed in Italy, has always ten ſtaves, neither more or leſs; and that makes exactly two lines or columns in the ordinary partitions, where we have always five parts, viz. two trebles of violins, the viola, the ſinging part, and the baſs. The diviſion being always the ſame, and each one finding, in the partitions, his part placed in like manner, paſſes always from one column to another without embarraſſment, or fear of miſtaking. But in the French partitions, where the number of ſtaves is not fixed and determined, either in the pages or columns, we are always obliged to heſitate at the end of each ſtave, to find, in the column that follows, the ſtave correſpondent to that wherein we are, which renders the muſician more doubtful, and the execution more ſubject to a failure.

PARADIAZEUXIS. Was, in the Greek musſic, by the tradition of old Bacchius, the interval of one tone only between the chords of two tetrachords; and ſuch is the nature of the disjunction which acts between the tetrachord ſynnemenon, and the tetrachord diazeugmenon. (Vide thoſe words.)

PARAMESIS. This was, in the Greek muſic, the name of the firſt chord of the tetrachord diazeugmenon. We muſt remember, that the third tetrachord may be conjoined with the ſecond; then its firſt chord was the meſis, or the fourth chord of the ſecond; that is, this meſis was common to the two.

But when this third tetrachord was disjoint, it began by the chord called parameſis, which, inſtead of being confounded with the meſis, was placed a tone higher; and this tone formed the disjunction or diſtance between the fourth chord, or the ſharpeſt of the tetrachord meſon; and the firſt, or ſharpeſt of the tetrachord diazeugmenon.

Parameſis ſignifies near to meſis; becauſe, in effect, the parameſis was only a tone diſtant, tho' there was ſometimes a chord between two. (Vide Trite.)

PARANETE. Was, in ancient muſic, the name given, by ſeveral authors, to the third chord of each of the three tetrachords ſynnemenon, diazeugmenon, and hyperboleon; a chord which ſome diſtinguiſhed only by the name of the genus, wherein theſe tetrachords were uſed. So the third chord of the tetrachord hyperboleon, which is called hyperboleon diatonos, by Ariſtoxenes and Alypius, is called paranete hyperboleon, by Euclid.

PARAPHONY. Is, in ancient muſic, that kind of conſonance which does not reſult from the ſame ſounds, as the uniſon, which is called homophony; nor from the replique of the ſame ſounds as the octave, which is called antiphony; but ſounds really different, as the fifth and fourth, the only paraphonies admitted in this muſic: for, as to the ſixth and third, the Greeks did not place them in the rank of paraphonies, not even admitting them as conſonances.

PARENTHESIS. A ſign of abbreviation in the note. It is a ſmall ſtroke acroſs at the tail of a minum or crotchet, to expreſs its diviſion into demi-crotchets, to preſerve place, and prevent confuſion. The parentheſis denotes, conſequently, four demi-crotchets inſtead of a minum; or two inſtead of a crotchet. The *round* having no tail, cannot bear a parentheſis; but we may alſo make eight demi-crotchets from it, by abbreviations, by dividing it into two minums or four crotchets, to which we add the parentheſis. The copier ſhould be careful to diſtinguiſh the figure of the parentheſis, which is only an abbreviation of that of the demi-crotchet, which ſhews a real power.

PARHYPATE.

PARHYPATE. The name of the chord which immediately follows the hypate from sharp to flat. There were two parhypates in the diagram of the Greeks, viz. the parhypate hypaton, and the parhypate meson. This word parhypate signifies subprincipal, or bordering on the principal. (Vide Hypate.)

PARODY. An air of symphony, of which a singing air is formed by adjusting the words. In music, well-composed, the air is made on the words; and in the parody, the words are made on the air: All the couplets of a song, except the first, are kinds of parodies; and this is, in general, what is felt too much by the method of murdering the prosody. (Vide Song.)

PART. This is the name of every voice or separated melody, whose re-union forms the concert. To constitute a concord, two sounds must be heard at a time, at least, which a single voice cannot do. To form, in singing, a harmony, or a collection of concords, many voices are necessary. The air which belongs to each of these voices is called part; and the collection of all the parts of a same work, written below each other, is called partition. (Vide Partition.)

As a complete concord is composed of four sounds, there are also, in music, four principal parts, the sharpest of which is called treble, and is sung by the voices of women, children, or musici: The other three are the counter tenor, the tenor, and bass; which all belong to the voices of men.

Extent of the four Vocal Parts.

We may here see the extent of the voice in each of these parts, and the cleff which belongs to it. The white notes show the full sounds, where each part may reach to an equal height and an equal descent; and the demi-crotchets which follow, show the sounds, where the voice begins to be forced, and which it ought to form in passing only. The Italian voices almost always exceed this extent in ascending, particularly the trebles; but the voice becomes then a kind of *faucet*, and, whatever art it may use to disguise it, it is certainly so.

Some one, or each of theſe parts, is ſub-divided, when we compoſe with more than four parts. (Vide Treble, Tenor, Baſs.)

In the firſt invention of the counter-point, there were at firſt only two parts; one of which was called tenor, and the other diſcant. Laſtly, a third was added, which had the name of triplum; and a fourth, ſometimes called quadruplum, but more commonly mottetos. Theſe parts were confounded very frequently one with the other: 'Tis but by little and little, that, extending themſelves to ſharp and flat, they have taken, with the moſt ſeparated and moſt fixed diapaſons, thoſe names which they have at preſent.

There are alſo inſtrumental parts. There are even inſtruments, as the organ, the harpſichord, the viol, which may form ſeveral parts at a time. We divide alſo the inſtrumental muſic in four parts, which anſwer to thoſe of the vocal muſic, and are called treble, fifth, tenor, and baſs; but the treble is generally ſeparated into two, and the fifth is united with the tenor, under the common name of viol.

Extent of the four Inſtrumental Parts.

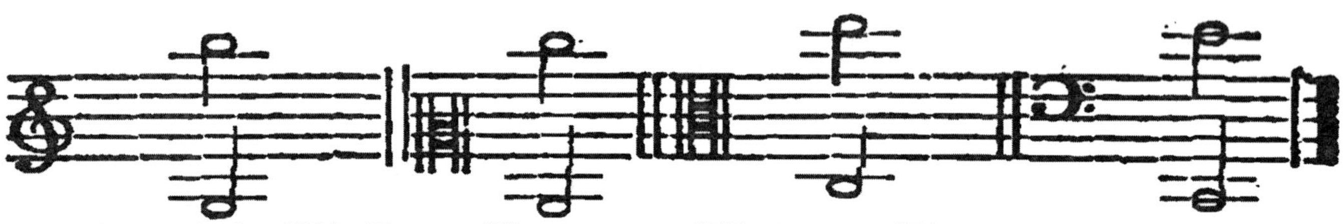

Treble of the Violin. Tenor. Viola, or Fifth. Baſs.

We here find the cleffs and extent of the four inſtrumental parts; but we muſt take notice, that the generality of inſtruments have not preciſe bounds above, and that they may be extended as far as poſſible, at the expence of the ears of the audience; whereas, in the lower parts, they have a fixed term which they cannot paſs. This term is on the note which I have marked; but I have marked above only that which we may reach without looſening.

There are parts which ought to be ſung by one voice alone, or played by a ſingle inſtrument; and thoſe are called reciting parts. Other parts are executed by ſeveral perſons ſinging, or playing in uniſon; and are called concertant parts, or parts of chorus.

We call alſo part, the paper of muſic on which is written the ſeparated part of each muſician. Sometimes ſeveral ſing or play on the ſame paper; but when each has his own, as is the general practice

practice in great pieces of music, then, tho' in this ſenſe each concertant has his part, it cannot be ſaid, in the other ſenſe, that there are ſo many parts of concertants, whilſt the ſame part is often doubled, trebled, and multiplied in proportion to the total number of executants.

PARTITION. A collection of all the parts in a piece of muſic, where we ſee, by the re-union of the correſponding ſtaves, the harmony which they form together. We write, for this purpoſe, all the parts from ſtave to ſtave, the one below the other, with the cleff ſuitable to each, beginning by the ſharpeſt, and placing the baſs below all We arrange them, as I have ſaid at the word Copier, ſo that each meaſure of a ſtave be perpendicularly placed above or below the correſpondent meaſure of other parts, and encloſed within the ſame bars prolonged from one to another, ſo that we may ſee, at firſt ſight, all that ſhould be underſtood at a time.

As in this diſpoſition, one ſingle line of muſic comprehends as many ſtaves as there are parts, we confine all theſe ſtaves by a ſtroke of the pen, which is called column, and which is drawn on the margin at the beginning of the line thus compoſed; then we re-begin, by a new line, to trace a new column, which is filled with the remainder of the ſame ſtaves, written in the ſame order.

So, when we wiſh to follow a part, after having gone thro' the ſtave to the end, we do not paſs to that which is immediately below, but we examine what rank the ſtave that we quit holds in the column; we ſeek in the column which follows the correſpondent part, and we find therein the continuance of the ſame part.

The uſe of partitions is indiſpenſable for compoſition. He alſo who conducts a concert, muſt have the partition under his eye, to ſee if each one follows his part, and to replace thoſe who are in error. It is even uſeful to the accompaniſt to follow the harmony truly; but in regard to other muſicians, we give generally his ſeparate part to each, it being uſeleſs for him to ſee that which he does not execute.

There are, however, ſome caſes where we join, in a ſeparate part, other parts in ſimilar partitions, for the convenience of the executants. Firſt, in vocal parts we generally note the thorough baſs in partition with each reciting part, either to prevent the ſinger from the trouble of reckoning his pauſes in following the baſs, or that he may himſelf accompany in repeating or reciting his part. Secondly, the two parts of a ſinging duet are marked in partition in each ſeparate part, ſo that every ſinger, having before the dialogue under his eye, may better enter into the spirit of it, and accord more easily with its counter-part. Thirdly, in the instrumental parts, we are cautious, in confined recitatives, to mark always the singing part in partition with that of the instrument; so that, in those alternatives of unmeasured airs and measured symphony, the symphonist may take the time of the rittornels true without hesitating or erring.

PARTITION. Is also, amongst organ and harpsichord makers, a rule for according the instrument, beginning by a chord or pipe of each touch, in the extent of an octave or rather more, taken near the middle of the keys; and on this octave or partition we accord all the rest afterwards. This is the method we follow for the formation of a partition.

On a sound given by an instrument, which I shall speak of at the word Tone, we accord in the unison or octave the C sol ut, which belongs to the cleff of that name, and which is found at the middle of the keys, or nearly. We then concord the sol, fifth sharp of that ut; then the re, sharp fifth of this sol; after which, we re-descend to the octave of this re, on the side of the first ut. We ascend to the fifth la, then again to the fifth mi. We re-descend to the octave of this mi, and continue in the same manner, ascending from fifth to fifth, and re-descending to the octave when we advance too much in sharp: When we have reached sol diesis, we stop.

We then retake the first ut, and accord its sharp octave; then the fifth flat of that octave fa, the sharp of this fa; next the si B flat, fifth of this octave; lastly, the mi B flat, fifth flat of this si B flat, the sharp octave from which mi B flat ought to form a true fifth, or nearly so with the la B flat or sol diesis, precedently accorded. When this happens, the partition is just, otherwise it is false; and this happens from not having exactly followed the rules explained at the word Modification.

Partition for the Concord of the Organ and Harpsichord.

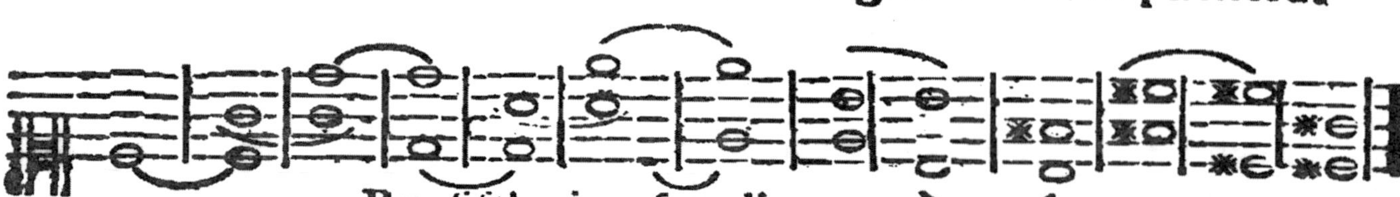

Vide the above succession of concords which form the partition.

The partition being well formed, the remaining concord is very easy, since there is no longer any thing more than unisons and octaves to finish the concordance of the whole keys.

PASSACAILLE. A kind of chacon, whose air is more tender and the movement slower than in the ordinary ones. (Vide Chacon.)

The passacaille's of Armeda and Isa are celebrated in the French opera.

PASSAGE. An ornament by which a stroke of music is ornamented, in general rather short, which is composed of several notes or diminutions, which are sung or played very lightly. This is what the Italians call also passo. But every singer in Italy is obliged to understand the composition of the passi, whereas the generality of French singers never remove from the notes, and form only those passages which are written for them.

PASSE PIED. The air of a dance of the same name, very common, whose measure is triple, is marked $\frac{3}{8}$, and beaten with one time. Its movement is more lively than that of the minuet; the character of the air somewhat similar, except that the passe pied admits the syncope, and the minuet does not. The measure of each reprise ought to enter in this manner, in an equal number. But the air of the passe pied, instead of beginning on the stroke of the measure, should, in every reprise, begin on the demi-crotchet which precedes it.

PASTORAL. A rural opera, whose personages are shepherds, and whose music should be assorted to the simplicity of the taste and manners supposed to them.

A pastoral is also a piece of music formed on words relative to a pastoral condition; or an air which imitates that of the shepherds, which has its sweetness, tenderness, and nature: The air of a dance composed in the same character, is also called pastoral.

PASTORELLA. An Italian air in the pastoral genus. The French airs called pastorals, are generally of two times, and in the character of the musette. The Italian pastorals have more accent, more grace, as much sweetness, and less flatness. Their measure is always the 6—8th.

PATHETIC. A kind of dramatic and theatrical music, which tends towards the painting and touching the nobler passions, and more particularly grief and sorrow. All the expression in the French music, in the pathetic genus, consists in trained and

and enforced ſounds, and in ſuch a ſlowneſs of movement, that all ſentiments of the meaſure are effaced. From thence it happens, that the French think every thing pathetic that is ſlow, and that all ſhould be ſlow that is *pathetic*. They even have airs which become gay and trifling, or tender and pathetic, according as they are ſung quick or ſlow. Such is an air ſo celebrated in Paris, to which the firſt character is given on theſe words, "Il "y a trente ans que mon cotillon trâine," &c. and the ſecond on theſe, "Quoi vous partez ſans que rien vous arrête," &c. This is the advantage of French melody, it ſerves for whatever we chuſe.—Fiet avis, & cum volet, arbor.

But the Italian muſic has not the ſame advantage: Each air, each melody has its character ſo appropriated, that it cannot be deprived of it. Its pathetic of accent and melody is felt in every kind of meaſure, and even in the moſt lively movements.

The French airs change their characters as the movement is preſſed or ſlackened. Each Italian air has its movement ſo determined, that it cannot be changed without overthrowing the melody. The air, thus disfigured, does not change its character, it loſes it: It is no longer an air; it is nothing in the character of the movement, neither can it be in the genus, in the mode, or in the harmony; ſince there are pieces equally pathetic in the three genera, in the two modes, and all imaginable harmony. The true pathetic is in the paſſionate accent, which is not determined by rules; but which the genus finds, and the heart feels, without the art being able to give its laws in any reſpects.

PAVANE. The air of an ancient dance of the ſame name, which has not been in uſe for ſome time. This name of pavane was given it becauſe the figurants formed, in looking at each other, a kind of tail after the manner of the peacock's. The man made uſe of his cape and ſword, which he uſed in this dance, and 'tis in alluſion to the vanity of this attitude that they have formed the reciprocal verb *ſe pavanor*.

PAUSE. An interval of time, which, in the execution, ought to paſs in ſilence by the part where the pauſe is marked. (Vide Silence.)

The name of pauſe may be applied to ſilences of different durations, but it is underſtood of a full meaſure. This pauſe is marked by a demi-bâton, which, leaving one of the interior lines of the ſtave, deſcends as far as the half of the ſpace compriſed between this line, and the line immediately below. When we have ſeveral pauſes to mark, we ſhould then make uſe of figures, which I have ſpoken of at the word *Reſt*.

In

In regard to the demi-pause, which is equal to a minum, or the half of a four-timed measure, it is marked as the entire pause, and with this difference, that the pause belongs to a line above, and that the demi-pause is below.

We must take notice, that the pause is always equal to a just measure, in whatever kind of measure it may be, whereas the demi-pause has a fixed and invariable power; so that, in every measure, which is superior or inferior to a semi-breve, or two minums, we ought not to use the demi-pause to mark a demi-measure, but other silences which express its just powers.

In regard to the other kind of pauses known in our ancient music, under the name of *useless pauses*, because they were placed after the cleff, and which served not to express silences, but to determine the modes; this name of pauses was given them only thro' error; for which reason I transmit the reader to the words Rest and Mode, on that article.

TO PAUSE. To press on a syllable in singing: We ought not to pause but on long syllables, and never on the e mute.

PEAN. An air of victory amongst the Greeks, in honour of the gods, and particularly of Apollo.

PENTACHORD. Was, amongst the Greeks, sometimes an instrument of five chords, and sometimes an order or system formed of five sounds. It is in this last sense, that the fifth, or diapente, was sometimes called pentachord.

PENTATONON. Was, in ancient music, the name of an interval which we, at present, call superfluous sixth. (Vide Sixth.) It is composed of four tones, of a major semi-tone, and a minor; from whence it receives the name of pentatonon, which signifies five tones.

PERFECT. This word, in music, has several senses. When joined to the word concord, it signifies a concord which comprehends all the consonances without any dissonance. When joined to *cadence*, it expresses that which bears the sensible note, and the dominant falls on the final. When joined to the word consonance, it expresses a just and determined interval, which can neither be major or minor; so the octave, the fifth, and fourth, are perfect consonances; and these are the only ones. When joined to mode, it is applied to the measure, by an acceptation which is no longer known, and must be explained for the understanding of the ancient authors. They divided the time or mode, in reference to the measure, into perfect and imperfect; and, pretending that the ternary number was more perfect than the binary, which they proved by the trinity, they called perfect time or mode, that whose measure was of three times; and they marked it by an an O or circle, sometimes single, and sometimes barred ⦶. The imperfect time, or mode, formed a measure of two times, and was marked by a divided O or C, sometimes single, and sometimes barred. (Vide Measure, Mode, Prolation, Time.)

PERFIDIA. A term of the Italian music, which signifies a certain affectation of always doing the same thing, and always following the same design, preserving the same movement, the same character of the air, the same passages, the same figures of the notes. (Vide Design, Air, Movement.) Such are the constrained basses, as those of the ancient chacons, and an infinity of methods in constrained accompaniment, or perfidiato, which depend on the caprice of the composers.

This term is not used in France; and I don't know if it has ever been written in this sense, otherwise than in Bropard's Dictionary.

PERIELESIS. A term of church-music. It is the interposition of one or more notes in the intonation of certain pieces of music, to assure their final, and specify to the choir that it belongs to them to take and pursue what follows.

The perielesis is otherwise called cadence, or small neuma, and is formed three ways: viz. First, by circumvolution; Secondly, by intercidence, or diatopse; or Thirdly, by simple duplication. (Vide those words.)

PERIPHERES. A term of the Greek music, which signifies a collection of notes, as well ascending as falling, and which return, as it were, on themselves. The peripheres was formed of the anacamptos and euthia.

PETTEIA. A Greek word which has nothing correspondent to it in our language, and which is the name of the last of the three parts into which the melopœa is sub-divided. (Vide Melopœa.)

The petteïa is, according to Aristides Quintilian, the art of discerning the sounds which ought, or ought not, to be used, those which should be more or less frequent, and those by which we ought to begin or finish.

It is the petteïa which constitutes the modes of music; it determines the composer in the choice of the genus of melody, relative to the movement which he would paint or excite in the soul, according to persons or occasions. In a word, the petteïa, a part of the hermosmenon which regards the melody, is, in this respect, what the *mores* are in poetry.

We cannot see what moved the ancients to give it this name, unless they took it from πεττεία, their games at dice: the petteïa in music being a rule to combine and arrange the sounds, as the game of dice is to arrange the pieces called πέττοι, *calculi*.

PHILÆLIA.

PHILÆLIA. Was a kind of hymn amongſt the Greeks, or ſong in honour of Apollo. (Vide Song.)

PHONIC. The art of treating and combining the ſounds on the principles of the acouſtic. (Vide Acouſtic.)

PHRASE. A continuance of an air or harmony, which forms, without interruption, a ſenſe more or leſs finiſhed, and which is terminated on a ſtop, by a cadence more or leſs perfect.

There are two kinds of muſical phraſes. In melody the phraſe is conſtituted by the air; that is, by a collection of ſounds ſo diſpoſed, whether in connection to the tone or movement, that they form the whole well united, which is reſolved on an eſſential chord of the mode in which we are.

In harmony, the phraſe is a regular continuance of concords all united together by diſſonances, expreſſed or underſtood, which is reſolved on an abſolute cadence: according as the ſenſe is more or leſs finiſhed, the ſtop alſo is more or leſs perfect.

It is in the invention of muſical phraſes, in their proportions, in their inter-mixture, that the real beauties of muſic conſiſt.

A compoſer, who punctuates and phraſes well, is a clever fellow; a ſinger, who feels, marks well his phraſes and their accent, is a man of taſte: but he who can only ſee, and render the notes, the tones, times, and intervals, without entering into the ſenſe of the phraſes, however ſure, however exact he may be, in every other reſpect, he is no more than a ſapſcull.

PHRYGIAN. The phrygian-mode is one of the four principal and moſt ancient modes of the Greek muſic. Its character was bold, lofty, impetuous, vehement, terrible: According to Athenæus alſo, the trumpets, and other military inſtruments, were founded on the phrygian mode.

This mode, invented, they ſay, by the Phrygian Marſyas, is placed in the middle, between the lydian and doric, and its final is at a tone diſtance from that of each.

PIECE. A work in muſic of a certain extent, ſometimes of a ſingle diviſion, ſometimes of ſeveral, forming a concinnity and a totality, formed to be executed together. So, an overture is a piece, tho' compoſed of three diviſions; and an opera itſelf is ſo, tho' divided by acts. But, beſides this general acceptation, the word piece was alſo a more peculiar one in inſtrumental muſic, and only for certain inſtruments, ſuch as the viol and harpſichord. For inſtance, we do not ſay, "A piece for the violin," but "*A ſonata*;" and we never ſay a ſonata for the harpſichord, but a piece.

PINCH. A kind of grace proper for certain inſtruments, and particularly the harpſichord; it is formed by ſtriking alternatively the ſound of the written note, with the ſound of the inferior note, and obſerving to begin and finiſh by the note which bears the pinch. There is this difference between the pinch and trill, that the latter is ſtruck with the ſuperior note, and the pinch with the inferior. So the trill on ut is ſtruck on the ut and re; and the pinch on the ſame ut is ſtruck on the ut and ſi. The pinch is marked, in the pieces of Couperin, with a ſmall croſs, very ſimilar to that with which the trill is marked in ordinary muſic. Vide the ſigns of the one and the other, at the head of that author's pieces.

TO PINCH. Is to uſe the fingers, inſtead of the bow, to make the chords of an inſtrument ſound. There are chord inſtruments which have no bow, and which are played only by pinching, ſuch as the lute, guittar, &c. but we alſo ſometimes pinch thoſe where we generally uſe the bow, as the violin and violincello; and this method of playing, almoſt unknown in the French muſic, is marked in the Italian by the word pizzicato.

PIZZICATO. This word, written in the Italian muſic, denotes that we muſt pinch. (Vide To Pinch.)

PLAGAL. A plagal tone or mode. When the octave is found arithmetically divided, according to the ordinary language, that is, when the fourth is in flat, and the fifth in ſharp, we ſay that the tone is plagal, to diſtinguiſh it from the authentic, where the fifth is in flat, and the fourth in ſharp.

Let us ſuppoſe the octave A a divided into two parts by the dominant E. If you modulate between theſe two la's, in the ſpace of an octave, and make your final on one of them, your mode is authentic. But if, modulating between theſe two la's, you make your final on the dominant mi, which is intermediary, or modulating from the dominant to its octave, you make the final on the intermediary tonic, in theſe two caſes the mode is plagal.

Here then is all the difference by which we ſee that all the tones are really authentic, and that the diſtinction is only in the diapaſon of the air, and in the choice of the note on which we ſtop, which is always the tonic in the authentic, and ofteneſt the dominant in the plagal.

The extent of the laws, and the diviſion of the parts, has made theſe diſtinctions diſappear in muſic, and they are no longer known but in that of the church. We count therein four plagal or collateral terms, viz. the ſecond, fourth, ſixth, and eighth, all thoſe whoſe number is equal. (Vide Tones of the Church.)

PLAY. The action of playing on an inſtrument. We ſay full play, demi play, according to the ſtronger or ſweeter manner of drawing the ſounds from an inſtrument.

TO PLAY. On inſtruments, is to execute airs of muſic on thoſe inſtruments, particularly thoſe proper to them, or airs noted for them. We ſay, To play on the violin, the baſs, the hautboy, the flute; To touch the harpſichord, the organ; To ſound the trumpet; To finger the guittar, &c. But an affectation of theſe peculiar terms, borders on pedantry. The term *to play* becomes general, and ſuits inſenſibly every kind of inſtrument.

PLICA. A kind of ligature in our ancient muſic. The plica was a ſign of heſitation, or ſlowneſs, (Signum moroſitatis, as Muris ſays). It was made by paſſing from one ſound to another, from the ſemi-tone to the fifth, whether in aſcending or falling, and there were four ſorts: Firſt, The plica long, and aſcending, is a quadrangular with a ſingle aſcendant ſtroke to the right, or with two ſtrokes, one of which on the right is the greateſt . Secondly, The long deſcending plica has two deſcendant ſtrokes, one of which on the right is the greater . Thirdly, The ſhort aſcendant plica has its ſtroke aſcending from the left, longer than that on the right . Fourthly, The deſcendant has the ſtroke deſcending from the left greater than that on the right 

POINT. This word, in muſic, ſignifies ſeveral different things. There are, in our ancient muſic, ſix ſorts of points, viz. Point of perfection, point of imperfection, point of increaſing, point of diviſion, point of tranſlation, and point of alteration.

I. The point of perfection belongs to the ternary diviſion. It renders every note perfect, that is followed by another note, leſs by the half of its figure; then, by force of the intermediary point, the precedent note is equal to the triple inſtead of the double of that which follows.

II. The point of imperfection, placed on the left of the longue, diminiſhes its powers, ſometimes of a round, or ſemi-breve, ſometimes of two. In the firſt caſe, we place a ſemi-breve between the longue and the point; in the ſecond, we place two ſemi-breves at the right of two longues.

III. The point of increaſing belongs to the binary diviſion, and, between two equal notes, makes that ſuperior which precedes the double of that which follows.

IV. The point of diviſion is placed before a ſemi-breve, followed by a breve in the perfect time. It takes away a time from this breve, and makes it equal only to two ſemi-breves, inſtead of three.

V. If a ſemi-breve, between two points, ſhould be followed by two or more breves in imperfect time, the ſecond point tranſfers its ſignification to the laſt of theſe breves, renders it perfect, and makes its powers three times. This is the point of tranſlation.

VI. A point between two ſemi-breves, placed themſelves between two breves or ſquares in perfect time, takes a time from each of theſe breves, ſo that each breve is only equal to two ſemi-breves inſtead of three. This is the point of alteration.

This ſame point before a ſemi-breve, followed by two other ſemi-breves, between two breves or ſquares, doubles the powers of the laſt of theſe ſemi-breves.

As theſe ancient diviſions of time into perfect and imperfect, are no longer uſed in muſic, all theſe ſignifications of the point, which in reality are very confuſed, have been long aboliſhed.

At preſent, the point, taken as a power of the note, is always equal to the half of that which precedes it. So, after the ſemi-breve, the point is equal to a minum; after the minum, to a crotchet; after the crotchet, to a demi-crotchet, &c. But this method of fixing the powers of a point is not certainly the beſt that might be imagined, and often cauſes uſeleſs embarraſſments.

ORGAN or STOP POINT. Is a kind of point which I have ſpoken of at the word couronne. It is in relation to that kind of point that we generally call organ-points, thoſe kinds of muſic, meaſured or not meaſured, written or not, and all thoſe harmonic ſucceſſions which paſs on a ſingle note of the baſs always prolonged. (Vide Cadenza.)

When this ſame point, ſurmounted by a couronne, is written on the laſt note of an air, or a piece of muſic, it is then called final point.

Laſtly, there is another kind of point alſo, called detached points, which are placed immediately above or below the head of the notes: Several are generally placed together, and this ſhows that the notes thus pointed ſhould be marked by equal tones of the tongue, or bow, bold and detached.

TO POINT. Is, by means of the point, to render alternatively long and ſhort, the collection of notes naturally equal; ſuch, for inſtance, as a continuance of demi crotchets. To point them on the note, we add a point after the firſt; a double demi-crotchet on the ſecond; a point after the third; then a double crotchet; and ſo on. In this manner they keep, two by two, the ſame powers which they had before; but this power is unequally diſtributed between the two demi-crotchets, ſo that the firſt, or longue, has three quarters, and the ſecond or breve, the other quarter. To point them in the execution, we paſs them unequal,

equal, according to these same proportions, tho' they should even be marked as equal.

In the Italian music, all the demi-crotchets are always equal, unless they are marked as pointed. But in the French music we do not make the demi-crotchets exactly equal but in the four timed measure. In all the rest they are always pointed a little, unless it be written "Equal demi-crotchets."

POLYCEPHALE. A sort of nome for the flutes, in honour of Apollo.

The polycephale nome was invented, according to some, by the second Phrygian Olympus, and, according to others, by Crates, a disciple of the same Olympus.

POLYMNASTIC. A name for flutes, invented, according to some, by a woman named Polymneste; and, according to others, by Polymnestus, son of Colophonian Meles.

POSITION. A part of the stave, where a note is placed to fix the degree of elevation of the sound which it represents.

The notes, in connection with the lines, have only two different positions, viz. on a line, or in a space; and these positions are always alternative when we move, or diatonically so. It is next the place which the line or space fills, and in connection with the cleff, which determines the real position of the note in a general key.

We call also position in the measure, that time which is marked in beating, in lowering, or fixing the hand, and which is generally called the stroke. (Vide Thesis.)

Lastly, we call position, in the playing of sleeve-instruments, the place where the hand is placed on the sleeve, according to the tone on which we play. When we have the hand at the height of the sleeve against the finger board, so that the index is placed at a tone of the chord à jour, it is the natural position. When we loosen, we reckon the positions by diatonic degrees, which the hand is distant from on the finger board.

POWER OF THE NOTES. Besides the position of the notes which marks its tone, they all have some determined figure, which marks its duration on time, that is, which determines the powers of the notes.

The invention of this is attributed to Jean de Muris, about the year 1330, for the Greeks had no other power of notes than the quantity of syllables, which alone must prove that they had no music purely instrumental. However, P. Mersenne, who had read the works of Muris, assures us that he saw nothing to confirm that opinion; and myself, after having read the greatest part, have not been more lucky than himself. Moreover, the examination of manuscripts, in the fourteenth age, which are in the

the French king's library, does not perſuade us to judge that the different figures of notes, which are found therein, were of ſo new an inſtitution. Laſtly, it is difficult to be believed, that, during three hundred years and more, which have paſſed between Gui Aretin and Jean de Muris, the muſic ſhould have been entirely deprived of the rhyme and meaſure, which are its fire and principal beauty,

However it may be, it is certain, that the different powers of the notes are of very ancient invention. I find, in the earlieſt times, five ſorts of figures for them, without reckoning the ligature and point. Theſe five are the maximum, the longue, the breve, the ſemi-breve, and minime. See Plate A. Fig. I.

All theſe different notes are black in the manuſcript of Guillaume de Machault. It is only ſince the invention of painting, that they have thought of making them white, and adding new notes to diſtinguiſh the powers by the colour as well as the figure.

The notes, tho' figured the ſame, had not always the ſame equality. Sometimes the maximum was equal to two longues, or the longue to two breves; ſometimes it was equal to three: this depended on the mode. (Vide Mode.) It was the ſame thing with the breve, in connection with the ſemi-breve, and this depended on the time. (Vide Time.) Laſtly, it was ſimilar with the ſemi-breve, in connection with the minime, and this depended on the prolation. (Vide Prolation.)

There were then double longue, perfect longue, imperfect longue, perfect breve, changed breve, major ſemi-breve, and minor ſemi-breve: ſeven different powers, to which four figures only anſwer, without reckoning the maximum or minime, a note of more modern invention. (Vide theſe different words.) There were alſo ſeveral other methods of modifying the different powers of theſe notes, by the point, the ligature, and poſition of the tail. (Vide Ligature, Plica, Point.)

The figures which were added in the continuance of theſe five or ſix firſt, were the crotchet, the demi-crotchet, the triple, and even quadruple demi-crotchet, which would make eleven figures in all; but as ſoon as it was the cuſtom to ſeparate the meaſures by bars, all the figures of notes were abandoned, which were equal to ſeveral meaſures, as the maximum, which equalled eight; the longue equal to four; and the breve to two.

The ſemi-breve, which equals an entire meaſure, is the longeſt power of notes remaining in uſe, and on which all the powers of the other notes have been determined; and as the binary meaſure, which had paſſed a long time for leſs perfect than the ternary, took laſtly the treble, and ſerved as the baſs of all the other

other measures; so the sub-double division carried it on the sub-triple, which had also passed as the most perfect: sometimes the semi-breve was not equal to three minums, but two only; the minum two crotchets; the crotchets two demi-crotchets; and so on to the quadruple demi-crotchet; unless in the cases of exception, where the sub-division has been preserved, and expressed by the cypher 3 placed above or below the notes.

The ligatures were also abolished at the same time, at least in regard to the changes which they produced in the power of the notes. The tails, in whatever manner they are placed, had no more than a fixed sense, and always the same; and lastly, the signification of the point was also bounded by the half of the note, which is immediately before it. Such is the condition in which the figures of the notes have been placed, in regard to their powers, and where they actually are.

The equivalent silences are explained at the article *Silence*.

The author of the dissertation on modern music, finds all this to be ill imagined. I have said, at the word *Note*, some one of the reasons which he alledges.

PRELUDE. A piece of symphony, which serves as an introduction and preparation to a piece of music. In which sense, the overtures of the opera are preludes; as also the ritournels, which are very often at the beginning of scenes or monologues.

Prelude is also a stroke in singing, which passes thro' the principal chords of the tone, to announce it, to verify if the instrument is in tune, &c.

TO PRELUDE. Is, in general, to sing or play some stroke of irregular fantasy, rather short, but passing by the essential chords of the tone, either to establish or to dispose the voice, or to place the hand well on an instrument before the beginning of a piece of music.

But on the organ and the harpsichord, the art of preluding is more considerable. It is to compose and play extempore pieces, filled with all that composition has most ingenious, in design, in fugue, in imitation, modulation, and harmony. It is chiefly in preluding, that great musicians, exempted from that extreme slavery to rules, which the eye of the critic imposes on them on paper, makes those transitions shine which ravish the ear of the audience. It is here that it is not sufficient to be a good composer, or to possess one's key well, or even to have a good and well exercised hand: We must, moreover, abound in that fire of genius, and that inventive ingenuity, which find and execute instantly the subjects most favourable to harmony, and most flattering to the ear. It is by this grand art of preluding that excellent organists shine in France; such as the Sieurs Claviere

and

and Daquin, who were ſtill ſurpaſſed by Monſ. le Prince d'Ardore, ambaſſador of Naples, who, for vivacity of invention, and force of execution, eclipſes the moſt illuſtrious artiſts, and cauſes the admiration of connoiſſeurs at Paris.

PREPARATION. The act of preparing the diſſonance. (Vide To Prepare.)

TO PREPARE. To prepare a diſſonance, is to treat it in harmony, ſo that, by favour of that which precedes, it may be leſs rough to the ear than it would be without this precaution: According to this definition, every diſſonance muſt be prepared. But when, to prepare a diſſonance, we require that the ſound which forms it ſhould have made a conſonance before, in that caſe, there is fundamentally only one diſſonance which is prepared, viz. the ſeventh. This preparation, moreover, is not at all neceſſary in the ſenſible concord, becauſe then the diſſonance, being characteriſtic, and in concord and mode, is ſufficiently announced; the ear attends to it, admits it, and is neither deceived on the concord, or its natural progreſs. But when the ſeventh is heard on the fundamental ſound, which is not eſſential to the mode, we ought to prepare it to ſuit every equivocation, to hinder the ear of the audience from inattention; and as this concord of ſeventh is overthrown and combined in ſeveral methods, from thence alſo ariſe different methods, apparently of preparation, which at bottom, however, always return to the ſame.

We muſt conſider three things in the practice of diſſonances, viz. the concord which precedes the diſſonance, that wherein it is found, and that which follows it. The preparation regards only the two others. For the third, vide To Save.

When we would prepare a diſſonance regularly, we muſt chuſe to arrive at the concord, ſuch a continuance of the fundamental baſs, that the ſound, which forms the diſſonance, may be a prolongation in the ſtrong time of a conſonance, ſtruck on a weak time in the precedent concord, which we call to ſyncopate.

From this preparation reſult two advantages; viz. I. That there is neceſſarily an harmonic connection between the two concords, ſince the diſſonance itſelf forms that connection; and ſecondly, That this diſſonance, being only the prolongation of a conſonant ſound, becomes much leſs rough to the ear than it would be on a ſound freſh ſtruck. Herein, moreover, is all that is ſought in the preparation. (Vide Cadence, Diſſonance, Harmony.)

We ſee, by what I have juſt ſaid, that there is no part particularly deſtined in the preparation of the diſſonance, than that itſelf which makes it heard; ſo that if the treble ſounds the diſſonance,

dissonance, it is dependant on it to syncopate; but if the dissonance is in the bass, the bass must syncopate. Tho' there is nothing that can be more simple, the masters of composition have terribly confused it. There are dissonances never prepared, such as the sixth added: others which are prepared but seldom, such as the diminished seventh.

PRESTO, This word, written at the head of a piece of music, denotes the quickest and most animated of the five principal movements established in the Italian music. Presto signifies quick. Sometimes we express a movement still quicker by the superlative prestissimo.

TO PRICK NOTES. Is to write music with characters destined for that purpose, and which are called notes. (Vide Notes.)

There is, in the method of marking music, an elegance of copy, which consists less in the beauty of the note, than in a certain exactness to place all the signs suitably, and which renders music, thus *marked*, much easier to execute; which has been explained at the word Copist.

PRIMA INTENZIONE. A technical Italian word, which has no correspondent in French, and which wants none, since the idea which this word expresses is not known in the French music. An air, a piece *di prima intenzione*, is that which is formed on a sudden, quite entire, and with all its parts in the mind of the composer, as Pallas came completely armed from the brain of Jupiter. The pieces, *di prima intenzione*, are such uncommon strokes of genius, all whose ideas are so narrowly united, that they form, as it were, only one alone, and cannot be presented to the mind without the other. They are similar to those long periods of Cicero, tho' eloquent, the sense of which suspended during all their duration, is determined only at the last word, and which, consequently, have formed only one single thought in the mind of the author. There are, in arts, inventions produced by such efforts of genius, and all the reasonings of which, intimately united one with the other, cannot be formed successively, but are necessarily offered to the mind, all at the same time, since the first, without the last, would form no sense. Such is, for instance, the invention of that prodigious machine of the *Mætier a bas*, which may be looked on, says the philosopher who has described it in the Encyclopœdia, as a single and only reasoning, the fabrication of whose work is the conclusion. These kinds of operations of the understanding, which are difficultly explained, even by the analysis, are prodigies for reason, and are only conceived by a genius capable of producing them: Its effect is always proportioned to the labours of the brain which they

 have

have cost; and, in music, the pieces di prima intenzione, are the only ones which can cause extasies, delights, those transports of the soul which convey the hearer from himself; we feel them, we enter into them at a moment; connoisseurs can never be deceived in them. At the end of one of these sublime pieces, run through one of these extempore airs. All whose phrases have been composed one after the other, or are only one phrase changed into different tones, and whose accompaniment is only a collection made without labour, and with whatever taste this last piece may be composed, if the remembrance of the other leaves you any attention to bestow on it, it will be only to be frozen, as it were, and impatient for it. After an air di prima intenzione, every other music loses its effect.

PROGRESSION. A continued proportion, prolonged beyond three times. (Vide Proportion.) The continuances of equal intervals are all in progression, and it is in identifying the neighbouring terms of different progressions, that we are able to complete the diatonic and chromatic scale, by means of the modification. (Vide Modification.)

PROLATION. Is, in our ancient music, a method of determining the power of semi-breve notes on that of the breve, or of the minime's on that of the semi-breve. This prolation was marked after the cleff, and sometimes after the sign of the mode, by a circle or demi-circle, punctuated or not punctuated, according to the following rules.

Considering the sub-triple division always as the most perfect, the prolation was divided into perfect and imperfect, and each into major or minor, in the same manner as for the mode.

The perfect prolation was for the ternary measure, and was marked by a point in the circle when it was major, that is, when it denoted the connection of the breve to the semi-breve; or by a point in a demi-circle when it was minor, that is, when it expressed the connection of the semi-breve with the minime. See Fig. II. and Fig. III. Plate I.

The imperfect prolation was for the binary measure, and was marked as the time by a single circle when major, or by a demi-circle when minor. See Fig. IV. and Fig. V. Plate I,

Some other signs have been since added to the perfect prolation. Besides the circle and demi-circle, they made use of the cypher $\frac{3}{1}$ to express the power of three semi-breves, for that of the breve, and of the cypher $\frac{3}{2}$, to express the powers of three minums for the semi-breve.

A

At present, all prolations are abolished. The sub-double division has gained the point over the sub-ternary; and we must have recourse to exceptions and particular signs, to express the division of any note into three others that are equal. (Vide Power of the Notes.)

We find, in the Academical Dictionary, that prolation signifies trill. I have never heard, or read, any where else, that this word had such a sense.

PROLOGUE. A kind of smaller opera, which precedes the greater, announces it, and serves as its introduction. As the subject of prologues is generally elevated, marvellous, magnificent, and full of praises, its music should be brilliant, harmonious, and more tender than pathetic. We ought not to drain, in the prologue, the grand movements we would excite in the piece; and the musician must, without being flat and tiresome in the delivery, still know how to manage so as to shew himself interesting and fresh in the body of the work. This gradation is neither felt, or rendered by the generality of composers, but it is still necessary, tho' difficult. The best way would be, not to be in want of it, and to suppress entirely the prologues, which only tire and hurry the spectator, or injure the interest of the piece, by employing the methods of interesting before-hand. The French opera's are the only ones, which have preserved prologues: They, moreover, suffer them only because they dare not murmur against the flatness which they contain.

TO PROLONG A SOUND. Is, in singing, to manage the voice, so that we may continue it a long time without taking breath. There are two methods of prolonging a sound: the first, in sustaining it always equally, which is generally done on lene's, and laboured accompaniment; the second, in strengthening it, which is more used in passages and trills. The first method requires more justness, and the Italians prefer it: the second has more eclat, and pleases the French more.

PROPERLY. To sing or play properly, is to execute the melody with the ornaments suitable to it. This melody being nothing by the force only of the sounds, and having no character by itself, takes one only by the affected turnings given to it in its execution. These turnings, taught by the masters of the taste in singing, are what are called the graces of the French music. (Vide Graces.)

PROPORTION. An equality between two connections. There are four kinds of connection, viz. the arithmetical, geometrical, harmonic, and counter-harmonic. We must have the idea of these different proportions to understand the calculations, with which authors have loaded the theory of music.

Let there be four times or quantities, a, b, c, d; if the difference of the firſt term a to the ſecond b, is equal to the difference of the third c to the fourth d, theſe four terms are in arithmetical proportion: ſuch are, for inſtance, the following numbers, 2, 4, 8, 10.

If, inſtead of having regard to the difference, we compare theſe terms by the method of containing, or being contained; if, for inſtance, the firſt a is to the ſecond b, as the third c is to the fourth d, the proportion is geometrical: ſuch is that which theſe four numbers form, 2, 4, 8, 16.

In the firſt example, the exceſs by which the firſt term 2 is ſurpaſſed by the ſecond 4, is 2; and the exceſs by which the third 8 is ſurpaſſed by the fourth 10, is alſo 2: theſe four terms are then in arithmetical proportion.

In the ſecond example, the firſt term 2 is the half of the ſecond 4; and the third term 8 is alſo the half of the fourth 16: theſe four terms are then in geometrica lproportion.

A proportion, whether arithmetical or geometrical, is called inverſe or reciprocal; when after having compared the firſt term with the ſecond, we do not compare the third with the fourth, as in direct proportion, but the fourth with the third, and the connection being thus taken, are found equal. Theſe four numbers, 2, 4, 8, 6, are in reciprocal arithmetical proportion; and theſe four, 2, 4, 6, 3, are in reciprocal geometrical proportion.

When, in a direct proportion, the ſecond term, or conſequence of the firſt connection, is equal to the firſt term, or antecedent of the ſecond counection, theſe two terms being equal, are taken for the ſame, and written only once inſtead of twice. So in this arithmetical proportion, 2, 4, 4, 6, inſtead of writing the number 4 twice, we write it but once, and the proportion is placed thus, ÷ 2, 4, 6.

In the ſame manner, in this geometrical proportion, 2, 4 :: 4, 8, inſtead of writing 4 twice, we write only one, in this manner, ∺ 2, 4, 8.

When the conſequence of the firſt connection ſerves as antecedent to the ſecond, and the proportion is placed in three times, this proportion is called thorough, becauſe, between the ſecond references which form it, there is no interruption found therein, when it is placed in four times.

Theſe three terms ÷ 2, 4, 6, are in thorough arithmetical proportion, and theſe other three ∺ 2, 4, 8, are in thorough geometrical proportion. When a thorough proportion is prolonged, that is, when it has more than three times, or two equal references, it is called progreſſion.

So theſe four terms, 2, 4, 6, 8, form an arithmetical progreſſion, which may be prolonged as much as we pleaſe, in adding the

the difference to the laſt term; and theſe four terms, 2, 4, 8, 16, form a geometrical progreſſion, which may be prolonged in the ſame manner, as much as we pleaſe, in doubling the laſt term, or in general, by multiplying it by the quotient of the ſecond term, divided by the firſt, which quotient is called the expoſition of the connection or progreſſion.

When three terms are ſuch as the firſt to the third, as the difference of the firſt to the ſecond is to the difference of the ſecond to the third, theſe three terms form a kind of proportion, called harmonic. Such are, for inſtance, theſe three numbers, 3, 4, 6; for as the firſt 3 is the half of the third 6; in the ſame manner the exceſs 1 of the ſecond on the firſt, is the half of the exceſs 2 of the third on the ſecond.

Laſtly, when three terms are ſuch, that the difference of the firſt to the ſecond is in the difference of the ſecond to the third, not as the firſt is to the third, as in harmonic proportion, but, on the contrary, as the third is to the firſt, then theſe three terms form together a kind of proportion, called counter harmonic proportion. So theſe three numbers, 3, 5, 6, are in counter harmonic proportion.

Experience has ſhewn, that the connections of three chords, ſounding the perfect major concord third together, formed between themſelves, the ſort of proportion which, on that account, was called harmonic; but this is a pure propriety of numbers, which has no affinity with the ſounds, or with their effect, on the auditive organ; ſo the harmonic and counter harmonic proportion belong no more to the art than arithmetical proportion, or the geometrical, which are even of much greater utility. We muſt always think, that the proprieties of abſtracted quantities are not proprieties of ſounds; and not ſeek, in imitation of Pythagoreans, ſome ſilly chimerical analogies between things of different natures, which have only connections of convention between them.

PROPRIETY. The execution of the air with the ornaments ſuitable to it, and which are called graces in ſinging. (Vide Graces.)

PROSLAMBANOMENOS. Was, in ancient muſic, the flatteſt ſound of all the ſyſtem, a tone below the hypate hypaton.

This name ſignifies ſuper-numerary, acquired or added, becauſe the chord which renders that ſound was added below all the tetrachords to continue the diapaſon, or the octave with the meſis; and the diapaſon or double octave, with the nete-hyperboleon, which was the ſharpeſt chord of all the ſyſtem. (Vide Syſtem.)

PROSODIAC. The proſodiac nome was ſung in honour of Mars, and was, they ſay, invented by Olympus.

PROSODY. A kind of nome for flutes, and peculiar to the cantics which were sung, amongst the Greeks, at the entrance of sacrifices. Plutarch attributes the invention of prosodies to Clonas, of Tegæa, according to the Arcadians, and Thebes, according to Boetius.

PROTESIS. The pause of a long time in ancient music, with the difference of the limma, which was the pause of a short time.

PYTHAGOREANS. The name of one of the two sects into which the Theoricians were divided in the Greek music: it took its name from Pythagoras, its chief, as the other sect took its name from Aristoxenes.

The Pythagoreans fixed all the intervals, as well consonant as dissonant, by the calculation of connections. The Aristoxenians, on the contrary, said that they appealed to the judgment of the ear. But, at bottom, their dispute was only a dispute of words; and under more simple denominations, the halves or fourths of the tone, amongst the Aristoxenians, either signified nothing, or required no calculations less composed than those of the limma, comma's, and apotomes, fixed by the Pythagoreans. In proposing, for instance, to take the half of a tone, what did an Aristoxenian propose? Nothing on which the ear could place a fixt judgment. Either he knew not what he would say, or proposed to find a medium proportionate between 8 and 9. This proportionate medium if the square root of 72, and this square root is an irrational number, there was no other possible method of assigning this half of the tone but by geometry; and this geometrical method was not more simple than the references, from number to number, calculated by the Pythagoreans. The simplicity of the Aristoxenians was only apparent; it was a simplicity similar to that of the system ef Mons. Boisgelou, of which I shall speak hereafter. (Vide Interval, System.)

Q.

QUADRUPLE DEMI CROTCHET. A note of music, equal to the fourth of a demi-crotchet, or the half of a double demi-crotchet. Sixty-four quadruple demi-crotchets are necessary for a four timed measure; but a measure is seldom filled, or even a time, with that kind of note. (Vide Power of the Notes.)

The quadruple demi-crotchet is almost always united with other notes of equal or different powers, and is thus figured:

 or . It takes its name from four strokes, or parenthesis's, which it bears.

QUANTITY. This word, in music as well as in prosody, does not signify the number of notes or syllables, but the relative duration which they ought to have. The quantity produces the rhyme, as the accent produces the intonation. From the rhyme and intonation results the melody. (Vide Melody.)

QUARREE or BREVE. A kind of note formed thus, ⊟. and which takes its name from its figure. In our ancient music, it was sometimes equal to three semi-breves, and sometimes two, accordingly as the prolation was perfect and imperfect. (Vide Prolation.)

The quarree, however, is always equal to two semi-breves, but it is very seldom used.

QUARTER OF A MINIME REST. A power of silence, which, in the Italian music, is figured thus, γ, in the French ⊣; and which denotes, as its name expresses, the fourth part of a minime rest, that is, the equivalent of a double demi-crotchet. (Vide Minime Rest, Power of the Notes.)

QUARTER OF A TONE. An interval introduced into the enharmonic genus, by Aristoxenes, and whose computation is sordato. (Vide Enharmonic, Scale, &c.)

We have neither in the ear, or in harmonic calculations, any principle which can furnish us the exact interval of the quarter of a tone; and when we consider what geometrical operations are necessary to determine it on the monochord, we are nearly tempted to suspect that we have, perhaps, never toned, and never shall tone the quarter of a tone just, either by the voice, or any instrument.

The musicians call also the quarter of a tone, the interval which from two notes at a tone from each other, is found between the B flat of the superior, and the diesis of the inferior.

an interval which the modification causes to vanish, but which the calculation may determine.

This fourth of a tone is of two kinds, viz. the major enharmonic, in the connection of 576 to 625, which is the complement of two semi-tones to the major tone; and the enharmonic minor, in the computation of 125 to 128, which is the complement of the two same semi-tones minor with the minor tone.

QUATUOR. This is the name given to pieces of vocal and instrumental music, which are of four reciting parts. (Vide Parts.) There are no true quatuors, or they are to no purpose. In a good quatuor, the parts must be almost always alternative, because, in every concord, there are only two parts, at the most, which form an air, and which the ear can distinguish at the same time: the two others are only as a filling up; and we ought never to place any filling up in a quatuor.

QUINQUE. A name given to pieces of vocal and instrumental music, which are of five reciting parts. Since there is no true quatuor, for a much better reason, there is no veritable quinque. Each of these words, tho' passed from the Latin to the French, are pronounced as in Latin.

QUICK. In Italian Presto. This word, at the head of an air, denotes the quickest of all the movements; and it has after it only its superlative prestissimo, or presto assai, or very fast.

R.

RANZ DES VACHES. A celebrated air among the Swiss, and which their young herdsman play on the bag-pipe, while they keep their herds on the mountains. (Vide Music.)

RAVALEMENT. The keys, or system a ravalement, is that which, instead of being bounded by four octaves, as the ordinary key, is extended to five, adding a fifth below the ut, a fourth above it, and by this means comprehending five octaves between the two fa's. The word ravalement comes from the organ and harpsichord makers, and those are the only instruments on which we can comprehend five octaves. The sharp instruments pass even the ut seldom above, without playing false; and the concord of the basses does not permit them to pass the ut below.

RE. A syllable by which we sol fa the second note of the gamut. This note, in natural, is expressed by the letter D. (Vide D and Gamut.)

RECHERCHE.

RECHERCHE. A kind of prelude, or fantasy on the organ or harpsichord, in which the musician affects to search for, and gather, the principal strokes of harmony and music, which have been executed, or which are going so to be in a concert. This is ordinarily made immediately without preparation, and, consequently, requires a great deal of skill.

The Italians call recherches, or cadences, those arbitrii, or organ points, which the singer takes the liberty of making on certain notes of his part, suspending his part, passing thro' the different chords of the mode, and even in going out sometimes, according to the different ideas of his genius, and the turns of his throat, whilst all the accompaniment ceases, till he thinks it proper to finish.

RECITAL. The general name of all that is sung with a single voice. We say, a recital of the bass, a recital of counter-tenor. This word is applied, in this sense, to instruments: We say, a recital of the violin, the flute, the hautboy. In a word, *to recite*, is to sing or play alone on any part, in opposition to the choir, or symphony in general, wherein several sing or play the same part in unison.

We may also call recital, the part wherein the principal subject reigns, and of which all the rest are only the accompaniment. They have placed, in the Dictionary of the French Academy, "The recitals are not at all subject to the measure as the airs." A recital is often an air, and, consequently, measured.—Quere, Can the Academy, perhaps, have confounded the recital with the recitative?

RECITING. A reciting part is that which is sung by a single voice, or played by a single instrument, in opposition to the parts of symphony and chorus, which are executed in unison by several concertants. (Vide Recital.)

RECITATION. The action of reciting music. (Vide To Recite.)

TO RECITE. Is to sing or play alone in music. To execute a recital. (Vide Recital.)

RECITATIVE. A discourse recited in a musical and harmonious tone. It is a method of singing which approaches nearly to speech, a declamation in music, in which the musician should imitate, as much as possible, the inflexions of the declaiming voice. This air is called recitative, because it is applied to narration, recital, and is used in the dramatic dialogue. They have placed in the Dictionary of the Academy, that the recitative should be uttered distinctly: There are recitatives which should be so, and others which should be sustained.

The perfection of the recitative depends much on the character of the language; the more the language is accented and melodious,

dious, the more the recitative is natural, and draws near to real discourse: it is only the accents marked in a language truly musical; but in a heavy, flat, and unaccented language, the recitative is only notes, cries, psalmody. The words are no longer discovered. Here, I think, is the only true principle, drawn from the nature of the thing, on which we ought to fix, to judge of the recitative, and compare that of one language to another, viz. that the best recitative is that wherein we sing the least.

Amongst the Greeks, all their poetry was in recitative, because, the language being melodious, it was sufficient to add to it the cadence of the metre, and the sustained recitation, to render this recitation entirely musical; from whence it comes, that those who verify call it singing. This custom, having ridiculously passed into other languages, causes the poet to say, I sing, when there is no singing in the case. The Greeks could sing in speaking; but amongst us we must either sing or speak: we cannot do both at the same time. 'Tis this very distinction which has rendered the recitative necessary for us. The music predominates too much in our airs; the poetry is almost forgotten; our lyric dramas are too much sung to be so always. An opera, which should be only a collection of airs, would tire almost as much as a whole single air of the same length. We must divide and separate the airs by conversation; but this conversation should be modified by music. The ideas should change, but the language must continue the same. This language being once given, to change it in the course of a piece, would be to speak half French, half German. The passage from discourse to the air, and reciprocally, is too unequal. It disgusts nature and the ear at the same time; true interlocution should speak or sing; they cannot do alternatively one and the other. The recitative, moreover, is the method of union between the air and the words; it is that which separates and distinguishes the airs; which quiets the ear, astonished at what preceded; and disposes it to taste what follows. Lastly, 'tis by assistance of the recitative, that what is only dialogue, recital, narration in the drama, may be rendered without going out of the given language, and without displacing the eloquence of the airs.

The recitative is not measured in singing. This measure, which characterises the airs, would spoil the reciting declamation. It is the accent, whether grammatical or oratorical, which ought alone to direct the slowness or rapidity of the sounds; in the same manner also their elevation or lowering. The composer, in making the recitative on some determined measure, has nothing in view but to fix the correspondence of the thorough bass and music, and to denote, nearly, how the quantity of the syllables should be mark'd, cadenc'd, and the verses scann'd. The

Italians never make uſe, for their recitative, of any but the four-tim'd meaſure; but the French intermix their's of all ſorts of meaſures.

Theſe laſt number the cleff alſo with all kinds of tranſpoſitions, as well as for the recitative as for the airs, which the Italians do not; but they always mark the recitative in natural: The quantity of modulations with which they are loaded, and the promptitude of the tranſitions, cauſing that the tranſpoſition ſuitable to one tone is not ſo to thoſe in which it paſſes, would multiply the accidents on the ſame notes too much, and would render the recitative almoſt impoſſible to follow, and very difficult to be marked.

In effect, it is in the recitative that we ought to make uſe of the moſt laboured harmonic tranſitions, and the moſt ingenious modulations. The airs, offering only a ſentiment, and an image, encloſed, laſtly, within ſome unity of expreſſion, do not permit the compoſer to be diſtant from the principal tone; and if he wiſhed to modulate much in ſo ſhort a ſpace, he would offer only murdered phraſes, without union, taſte, or melody: A fault very common in the French and German muſic.

But in the recitative, where the expreſſions, the ſentiments, the ideas, vary every inſtant, we ought to make uſe of modulations equally varied, which may repreſent, by their contextures, the ſucceſſions expreſſed by the diſcourſe of the recitant. The inflexions of the ſpeaking voice are not bounded by muſical intervals. They are uncontrouled, and impoſſible to be determined. Not being able then to fix them with a certain preciſion, the muſician, to follow the words, ſhould, at leaſt, imitate them as much as poſſible; and for the purpoſe of conveying to the mind of the audience the idea of intervals and accents, which cannot be expreſſed in notes, he has recourſe to tranſitions which ſuppoſe them: If, for inſtance, the interval of the major or minor ſemi-tone is neceſſary, he will not mark them; he cannot: but he will give you the idea of them by the aſſiſtance of an enharmonic paſſage. A motion of the baſs is often ſufficient to change all the ideas, and to give the recitative that accent and inflexion, which the actor is unable to execute.

In regard to what remains, as it is neceſſary for the audience to be attentive to the recitative, and not the baſs, which ought to form its effect without being liſtened to, it thence follows, that the baſs ſhould continue in the ſame note as long as poſſible; for it is in the moment that its note changes, and it ſtrikes another chord, that it is attended to. Theſe moments being uncommon and well choſen, do not uſe any great effect; they remove the ſpectator leſs frequently, and leave him more eaſily in the perſuaſion, that he hears ſpeaking only, tho' the harmony ſhould continually act on his ear. Nothing denotes a worſe recitative than theſe baſſes perpetually leaping, which run from demi-crotchet to demi-crotchet after this harmonic ſucceſſion, and form, under the melody of the voice, another kind of melody more flat and tireſome. The compoſer ſhould know the art of prolonging and varying his concords on the ſame note of the baſs, and change them only in the moment when the inflexion of the recitative, becoming more lively, receives greater effect by this change of baſs, and prevents the audience from taking notice of it.

The recitative ſhould ſerve only to unite the contexture of the drama, to ſeparate and give weight to the airs, to prevent the wearineſs which the continuance of a great noiſe would cauſe; but however eloquent the dialogue may be, however energic and ingenious the recitative may be, it ought to continue no longer than is neceſſary to its object, becauſe it is not in the recitative that the charm of muſic acts, and that the opera was inſtituted only to diſplay this charm. Moreover, it is in this that the error of the Italians lies, who, by the extreme length of their ſcenes, make an ill uſe of this recitative. However beautiful it may be in itſelf, it tires, becauſe it continues too long; and that it is only to hear the recitative that we go to the opera.

Demoſthenes ſpeaking the whole day, would tire in the end; but it would not thence follow, that Demoſthenes was a tireſome orator. Thoſe who ſay that the Italians find their recitative bad, ſay it very frankly; ſince, on the contrary, there is no part in muſic of which the connoiſſeurs make ſuch great account, and on which they are ſo difficult. It is even ſufficient to excel in this ſingle part, were we but middling in every other, to be raiſed in that country to the rank of the moſt illuſtrious artiſt, and the celebrated Porpora, was only immortaliſed by that method.

I add, that tho' we do not ſeek in general in the recitative for the ſame energy of expreſſion as in the airs, it is ſtill found ſometimes; and when it is found, it forms a greater effect than in the airs themſelves. There are good opera's, where ſome principal piece of recitative excites the admiration of connoiſſeurs, and an intereſt in the whole ſpectacle: The effect of theſe pieces ſhows ſufficiently that the fault imputed to the genus, lies only in the method of treating it.

Monſ. Tartini relates having heard, in 1714, at the operahouſe in Ancona, a piece of recitative of one ſingle line, and without any accompaniment but the baſs, form a prodigious effect, not only on the profeſſors of the art, but on all the ſpectators. "It was, ſays he, at the beginning of the third act. At

"each

"each representation, a profound silence amongst the whole audience announced the approach of this terrible piece. The faces grew pale; they felt themselves shiver; and they beheld each other with a kind of terror: It was neither tears nor groans; it was a certain sensation of rough and disdainful rigour, which troubled the soul, confined the heart, and froze the blood." We should transcribe the original passage: these effects are so little known on our theatre, that our language is almost incapable of expressing them.

L'Anno quatordecimo del Secolo presente nel dramma che si representava in Ancona, v'era su'l principio dell' Attoterzo una riga di recitativo non accompagnato da altri stromenti che dal basso: per cui, tanto in noi professori, quanto negli ascoltanti, si destava una tal e tanta commozione di animo, che tutti si guardavano in faccia l'un l'altro, per la evidente mutazione di colore che si faceva in ciascheduno di noi. L'Effetto non era di pianto (mi recordo benissimo che le parole erano di sdegno); ma di un certo rigore e freddo nel sangue, che di fatto turbava l'animo. Tredeci volte si recito il dramma, e sempre segui l'effeto stesso universalmente: di che era segno palpabile il sommo previo sdenzio, con cui l'uditorio tutto si apparecchiava a goderne l'effetto.

RECITATIVE ACCOMPANIED. Is that to which, besides the thorough bass, is added an accompaniment of violins. This accompaniment, which cannot by any means be syllabic, together with the rapidity of the utterance, is generally formed of long notes sustained on entire measures; and we write, for this purpose, on all the parts of the symphony, the word sostenuto, chiefly in the bass, which, without that, would strike only flat and detached strokes at each change of the note, as in the ordinary recitative; whereas we must, in that case, prolong and sustain the sounds, the whole power of the notes. When the accompaniment is measured, this obliges us to measure the recitative, which then follows and accompanies in some kind of accompaniment.

RECITATIVE MEASUR'D. These two words are contradictory. Every recitative, wherein we find any other measure than that of the verses, is no longer recitative. But an ordinary recitative is often changed on a sudden in music, and takes from measure and melody, whatever is marked in writing on the parts a tempo, or a battula. This contrast, this well managed change, produces surprising effects. In the course of a recitative, a tender and plaintive reflexion takes the musical accent, and is displayed instantly by the sweetest inflexions of the music; then, being cut in the same manner by some other lively and impetuous reflexion, it is roughly interrupted to take, at a moment, the whole utterance

ance of the words. These short and measured pieces, accompanied, in general, with flutes and horns, are not uncommon in grand Italian recitatives.

The recitative is also measured when the accompaniment with which it is charged, being tuneful and measured itself, obliges the recitant to conform his voice to it. It is less than a measured recitative, than, as I have said above, a recitative accompanying the accompaniment.

RECITATIVE CONFIN'D. Is that which, being intermixt with rittornels and strokes of symphony, confines, as it were, the recitant and orchestra, one towards the other, so that they ought to be attentive in a mutual degree. These alternative passages of recitative and melody, clothed with all the eclat of the orchestra, are the most touching, most ravishing, and most energic parts of the modern measure. The actor agitated, transported with a passion which does not suffer him to go through his speech, is interrupted, breaks off, makes a stop, during which time the orchestra speaks for him; and these silences, thus filled, affect the audience infinitely more than if the actor himself spoke all that the music makes them understand. Thus far, the French music has not been able to make any use of the confined recitative. They have endeavoured to give some idea of it in a scene, *Du Devin du Village*; and it appears, that the public has found, that a situation, when lively and thus managed, became much more interesting. What would not the confined recitative do in grand and pathetic scenes, if so great an acquisition can be drawn from it in a rustic and jocular genus.

RECLAME or CATCH WORD. Is, in church-music, that part of the answer which is re-begun after the verse. (Vide Answer.)

REDOUBLED. We call a redoubled interval, every simple interval carried in its octave. So the thirteenth, composed of a sixth and octave, is a redoubled sixth; and the fifteenth, which is an octave added to the octave, is a redoubled octave. When, instead of an octave, we add two, the interval is triple; and quadruple when three are added.

Every interval, whose name passes seven in number, is always at least redoubled. To find the simple of any redoubled interval, throw out seven as often as you can from the name of this interval, and the remainder will be the name of the simple interval. From thirteen throw out seven, six remains; so the thirteenth is a redoubled sixth. From fifteen take away twice seven, or fourteen, one remains; so the fifteenth is a tripled unison or doubled octave.

Reciprocally,

Reciprocally, to redouble any simple interval, add to it seven, and you will have the name of the same redoubled interval. To triple a simple interval, add to it fourteen. (Vide Interval.)

REDUCTION. A collection of notes diatonically descending. The term, as well as its contrary deduction, is no longer used but in church-music.

RELATION. A connection which the two sounds that form an interval have with one another, considered by the genus of that interval. The relation is just when the interval is just, major or minor: it is false, whether superfluous or diminished. (Vide Interval.)

Amongst false relations, we consider as such in harmony, those only whose two sounds cannot enter into the same mode. So the triton, which in melody is a false relation, is not so in harmony but when one of the sounds which form it is a chord unknown to the mode. The diminished fourth, tho' banished from harmony, is not always a false relation. The diminished and superfluous octaves, being not only intervals banished from harmony, but also impracticable in the mode, are always false relations. It is the same thing with the diminished and superfluous thirds and sixths, tho' the last be admitted at present.

In former times false relations were forbidden; at present, they are almost all permitted in melody, but not in harmony. We may, however, make them understood, provided that one of the two sounds, which form a false relation, be not admitted as a note of taste, and not as the constitutive part of the concord.

We call also enharmonic relation, between two chords which are at a tone of interval, the connection which is found between the diesis of the inferior, and that of the superior. It is by the modification, the same touch on the organ and harpsichord; but in rigour, it is not the same sound, and there is between them an enharmonic interval. (Vide Enharmonic.)

REMISS. Remiss sounds are those which have little strength, those which, being very flat, cannot be rendered but by very loose chords, or heard very near. Remiss is opposed to intense; and there is this difference between remiss and weak, in the same manner as between intense and strong, that low and high are said of the sensation which the sound conveys to the ear, whereas intense and remiss are rather connected with the cause that produces it.

RENVOI. A sign figured at will, placed commonly above the stave, which corresponding with another similar sign, marks that we must, whence is the second, return where the first is, and from thence follow until we find the final point. (Vide Point.)

REPERCUSSION.

REPERCUSSION. A frequent repetition of the ſame ſounds. This is what happens in every modulation well determined; where the eſſential chords of the mode, thoſe which compoſe the harmonic triad, ſhould be reſtruck oftener than any of the reſt. Amongſt the three chords of this triad, the two extremes, that is, the final and dominant, which are properly the repercuſſion of the tone, ſhould be oftener ſtruck than that of the middle, which is only the repercuſſion of the mode.

REPETITION. An eſſay particularly made of a piece of muſic, which is to be executed in public. Repetitions are neceſſary to certify that the copies are exact, that the actors may foreſee their parts, that they may concert together and accord, that they may expreſs the ſpirit of the work, and render faithfully what they have to ſpecify. Repetitions ſerve the compoſer alſo to judge of the effect of his piece, and make the changes it may want.

REPLIQUE. This term in muſic ſignifies the ſame thing as the octave. (Vide Octave.) Sometimes, in compoſition, the uniſon of the ſame note is alſo called replique, in two different parts.

There are neceſſarily repliques in each concord, throughout the whole of muſic of more than four parts. (Vide Uniſon.)

REPEAT. Every part of an air which is repeated twice is called by this term. It is in this ſenſe that we ſay the firſt repeat of an overture is flat, and the ſecond gay. Sometimes alſo, by repeat, we underſtand only the ſecond part of an air. We ſay alſo, that the repeat of Dardanus's beautiful minuet is worth nothing. Laſtly, repeat is alſo each of the parts of a rondeau, which has often three, and ſometimes more, the firſt of which only is repeated.

In notes we call repeat a ſign, which marks that the part of the air which precedes it ſhould be repeated, which prevents the trouble of writing it twice. In this ſenſe, we diſtinguiſh two repeats, the greater and ſmaller. The greater repeat is figured in the Italian manner, by a double perpendicular bar, with two points beyond each ſide; or in the French, by two perpendicular bars, a little more diſtant, which traverſe the whole ſtave, and between which a point is placed in each ſpace; but this ſecond method is gradually aboliſhed: for, not being able to imitate the Italian muſic entirely, we, at leaſt, take the words and ſigns; as thoſe youths who think they follow Voltaire's ſtyſe by imitating his orthography.

This repeat, thus punctuated on the right and left, generally denotes, that we muſt begin again twice, as well the part which precedes

precedes as that which follows, for which reaſon, it is generally found near the middle of paſſe pieds, minuets, gavots, &c.

When the repeat has points on the left only, it is for the repetition of that which precedes; and when on the right, it is for the repetition of what follows. It would be at leaſt to be wiſhed, that this convention, adopted by ſome, was entirely eſtabliſhed; for it appears to me very convenient. Vide the form of theſe different repeats.

REPEATS.

In the Italian Form. In the French Form.

The ſmaller repeat is, when after a greater repeat we begin ſome others of the laſt meaſures before we finiſh. There are no peculiar ſigns to the ſmaller repeat, but we commonly uſe ſome ſign of the Renvoi figured above the ſtave. (Vide Renvoi.)

We muſt take notice, that thoſe who mark correctly always take care that the laſt note of a repeat be exactly connected for the meaſure, both to that which begins the ſame repeat, and to that which begins the following, when there is one. If the reference of theſe notes does not exactly fill the meaſure, after the note which terminates a repeat, we add two or three notes of that which ought to be re-begun, until we have ſufficiently ſpecified how the meaſure is to be filled. Moreover, as at the end of a firſt part, we have firſt the firſt part to repeat, then the ſecond part to begin; and as that is not always done in times, or ſimilar parts of times, we are often obliged to mark the final of the firſt repeat twice; one before the ſign of repeat, with the firſt notes of the firſt part; the other, after the ſame ſign, to begin the ſecond part. We then draw a chapeau or half-circle after that firſt final until its repetition, to denote that the ſecond time we muſt paſs, as null, all that is compriſed under the demi-circle. I cannot render this explanation more clear, ſhorter, or more exact, but the following method will ſhow it more perfectly.

Method of Repeating.

RESONNANCE. A prolongation or reflection of the sounds, whether by the continued vibrations of the chords of an instrument, or by the tinkling of a sonorous body, or the collision of the air enclosed in a wind instrument. (Vide Sound, Music, Instrument.)

Elliptic and parabolic vaults resound; that is, reflect the sound. (Vide Eccho.)

According to Monf. Dodart, the nose, mouth, and its parts, as the palate, the tongue, the teeth, the lips, have no connection with the tone of the voice; but their effect is very great in resonnance. (Vide Voice.)

A very sensible example is drawn from a maple instrument, called guimbard, which, if we hold it with the fingers, and strike on the languette or tongue, will give no sound; but, if holding it between the teeth, we do the same, it will render a sound, which is varied by confining it more or less, and is heard very far, particularly in the bass.

In chord instruments, such as the harpsichord, the violin, the violincello, the sound comes from the chord only; but the resonnance depends on the case of the instrument.

RESPONSE. A kind of redoubled ancient, which is sung in the Roman Church after the morning lesson, and which finishes in the method of a rondeau by a repeat, called reclame.

The air of the response ought to be more ornamented than that of an ordinary ancient, without, however, going out of the flat melody, or of that of the mode which we have chosen. It is not, however, necessary for the verse of a response to be terminated by the final note of the mode: It is sufficient that this final terminates the response itself.

RESPONSE. Is also, in a fugue, the entrance of the subject by another part, after the first has made it to be heard; but it is particularly in a counter fugue, the entrance of the subject varied from that which has been just heard. (Vide Fugue, Counter Fugue.)

REST. A kind of thick bar which perpendicularly traverses one or more lines of the stave, and which, according to the number of lines which it comprehends, expresses a greater or smaller quantity of measures, which ought to be passed in silence.

Anciently there were as many kinds of rests as different powers of the notes, from the semi-breve, which is equal to a measure, to the maximum, which equals eight, and whose duration, in silence, was empowered by a rest, which, going of from one line, traversed three spaces, and joined the fourth line.

At present, the greatest rest is of four measures. This rest, going off from one line, traverses the following, and is joined to the third.

It

Rests of four Measures. Rest of two Measures.

It is repeated once, twice, or as many times as are necessary to express eight measures, or twelve, or every other multiple of four; and we generally add a cypher, which dispenses with calculating the powers of all these rests. So the signs covered by the cypher 16, in the above plate, denote a silence of sixteen measures. I do not see very clearly the great utility of a double sign to the same thing. So the Italians, to whom a greater practice of music always suggests the first methods of abridging its signs, begin to suppress rests; in the place of which they substitute the cypher which expresses the number of measures to be counted. But an attention, which we must have in that case, is not to confound these cyphers in the stave with other similar cyphers, which may mark the space of the measure we make use of.

31 Measures to be counted.

So, in the above figure, we must take care to distinguish the sign of three times from that with the number of pauses to be counted, for fear, that instead of 31 measures or pauses, we should reckon 331.

The smallest rest is of two measures, and traversing a single space is only extended to the line nearest to it,

The other less silences, as a measure, half measure, time, demi-time, &c. are expressed by the words pause, demi-pause, &c. (Vide those words.)

It is easy to understand, that in combining all these signs, we may express, at pleasure, silences of any duration.

We must not confound, with rests of silences, other rests precisely of the same figure, which, under the name of initial pauses, served in our ancient music to announce the mode, that is, the measure, which I have have spoken of at the word Mode.

RHYME. Is, in its most general definition, the proportion that the parts of a whole have between each other. It is, in music, the difference which results from quickness or slowness, length or brevity of the times.

Aristides Quintilian divides the rhyme into three kinds, viz. the rhyme of immoveable bodies, which results from the just proportion of their parts, as in a well made ſtatue; the rhyme of local movement, as in dancing, the walk well compoſed, and the attitudes of pantomimes; and the rhyme in movements of the voice, or relative duration of ſounds, in ſuch a proportion, that, whether we always ſtrike the ſame chord, or vary the ſounds from ſharp to flat, we always make agreeable effects reſult from their ſucceſſion in their duration and quantity. This laſt kind of rhyme is the only one which I ſhall here ſpeak of.

The rhyme applied to the voice may be underſtood either of words or muſic. In the firſt ſenſe, it is from the rhyme, that the number and harmony of eloquence ariſe; the meaſure and cadence of poetry: in the ſecond, the rhyme is properly applied to the power of notes, and is now called meaſure. (Vide Meaſure.)

It is alſo to this ſecond acceptation that I ſhould confine what I have to ſay here on the rhyme of the ancients.

As the ſyllables of the Greek language had quantity and more ſenſible powers, as well as more determined than thoſe of our language; and as the verſes which were ſung were compoſed of a certain number of feet, which theſe ſyllables formed long or ſhort, differently combined, the rhyme of the muſic regularly followed the movement of thoſe feet, and was properly its expreſſion. It was divided as well as thoſe into two times, the one ſtruck, the other raiſed. They counted three genera, ſometimes four, and more, according to the different connections of the time. Theſe genera were *the equal*, which was alſo called dactylic, wherein the rhyme was divided into two equal times: The double, trochaïe or Iambic, in which the duration of one of the two times was double to that of the other. The ſeſquialter, which was alſo called peonic, whoſe duration, in one of the two times, was to that of the other in numerical powers as 3 to 2; and laſtly, the epitrite, leſs uſed, where the connection of the two times was as 3 to 4.

The times of theſe rhymes were ſuſceptible of more or leſs ſlowneſs, by a greater or leſs number of ſyllables, or long and ſhort notes, according to the movement; and in this ſenſe, a time might receive as far as eight different degrees of movement by the number of ſyllables which compoſed it; but the two times always preſerved together the connection determined by the genus of the rhyme.

Beſides that, the movement and motion of the ſyllables, and, conſequently, of the times and rhyme which reſulted from them, were ſuſceptible of acceleration and ſlackening, at the pleaſure of the poet, according to the expreſſion of the words and character of the paſſions which were to be expreſſed. So from theſe two meaſures combined together, aroſe a quantity of poſſible modifications

difications in the movement of a ſame rhyme, which had no other bounds than thoſe above or below, which the ear was not of an extent to perceive their proportions.

The rhyme, in reference to the feet which entered into poetry, was divided into three other genera. The ſimple, which admitted only one kind of feet; the compoſed, which reſulted from two or more kinds of feet; and the mixt, which might be reſolved into two or more rhymes, equal or unequal, according to the different combinations of which it is ſuſceptible.

Another ſource of variety in the rhyme was the difference of the movements or ſucceſſions of this ſame rhyme, according to the inter-mixture of the different verſes. The rhyme might be always uniform; that is, be ſtruck by two times always equal, as in the hexameter, pentameter, adonian, and anapeſtic verſes, &c. or always unequal, as in the pure iambic verſes; or diverſified, that is mixed with equal and unequal feet, as in the ſcazons, choriambics, &c. But in all theſe caſes, the rhymes, even ſimilar or equal, might, as I have ſaid, be very different in quickneſs, according to the nature of the feet. So of two rhymes of the ſame genus, reſulting one from two ſpondees, the other from two pyrrhics, the firſt would be double to the other in duration.

Silences were alſo found in the ancient rhyme, not in truth, as ours to make only ſome one of the parts be ſilent, or to give certain characters to the muſic, but only to fill the meaſure of theſe verſes called catalectics, which wanted a ſyllable; ſo the ſilence never could be found but at the end of the verſe to ſupply that ſyllable.

In regard to Lene's, they knew them without doubt, ſince they had a word to expreſs them. Its practice, however, muſt have been very uncommon amongſt them; at leaſt this may be inferred by the nature of their rhyme, which was only the expreſſion of the harmony, and of the harmony of the verſes. Neither does it appear that they practiſed trills and ſyncopes, or the points, unleſs the inſtruments formed ſomething ſimilar in accompanying the voice, of which we have no *Indice*.

Voſſius, in his book De Poematum Cantis & Veribus, raiſes the ancient rhyme greatly, and attributes to it all the force of the ancient muſic. He ſays, that a rhyme detached as ours, which repreſents no image of things, can have no effect, and that the ancient poetic numbers had been invented only for the very end that we neglect. He adds, that language and modern poetry are little ſuitable to muſic; and that we ſhall never have good vocal muſic till we make verſes favourable to the air; that is, till we confine our language, and give it, after the example of the ancients, the quantity and meaſured feet, by proſcribing for ever the barbarous invention of the rhyme.

Our verses, says he, are precisely as if they had only one single foot; so that we have no veritable rhyme in our poetry: and, in fabricating our verses. we only take care to introduce a certain number of syllables, without scarcely taking notice of what nature they are. Surely this is not a fit composition for music.

The rhyme is an essential part of music, and particularly in the imitative. The melody is nothing without it; and by itself it is something, as we find by the effect of drums. But whence comes the impression which the measure and cadence occasion on us? What is the principle by which these returns, sometimes equal, and sometimes varied, affect our souls, and may convey to them the sentiment of the passions? Enquire of the metaphysician. All that we can say hereon is, that as the melody takes its character from the accents of the language, the rhyme draws its own from that of the prosody, and in that case it acts as an image of the words; to which we will add, that certain passions have naturally a rhymic character, as well as a melodious one, absolute, and independant of the language, as sorrow, which moves by slow and equal paces, as well as by low and slackened tones; joy, by lively and quick tones, as well as by sharp and intense tones; from whence, I presume, that we might observe in all the other passions, a peculiar character, but more difficult to catch, because the generality of these other passions being composed, partake more or less of precedents, as well as from each other.

RHYMIC. A part of the art of music, which taught the practice of rules of movement and rhyme, according to the laws of the rhymopæa.

The rhymic, to speak a little more in detail, consists in knowing how to chuse, between the three modes established by the rhymopæa, the most suitable to the character in question; to know and possess all kinds of rhymes in their foundation; to discern and make use of the most suitable on each occasion; to intermix them at the same time in the most expressive and agreeable method; and lastly, to distinguish the arsis and thesis, by the most sensible and best cadenced movement.

RHYMOPÆA. A part of the musical science, which prescribed to the rhymic art, the laws of rhyme, and of all that belongs to it. (Vide Rhyme.) The rhymopæa was to the rhymic what the melopæa was to melody.

The rhymopæa had for its object the movement, or the time whose measure it denoted, divisions, order, and mixture, whether to move the passions, to change them, or to calm them. It comprehends also the science of mute movements, called orchesis, and in general of all the regular movements. But it was principally connected with poetry, because then poetry alone regulated the movements

movements of music, and as there was no music purely instrumental which had an independant rhyme.

We know that the rhymopæa was divided into three principal modes or tropes, the one low and confined, another raised and great, and the middle tranquil and peaceable; but, besides, the ancients have left us nothing but very general precepts on this part of their music; and what they have said of it has its connection always to the verses and words destined for the music.

RIGADOON. A kind of dance, the air of which is struck in two times, of a lively movement; and is generally divided into two repeats, phrased from four to four measures, and beginning by the last note of the second time.

I have heard say, by a dancing-master, that the name of this dance was derived from that of the inventor, who was called Rigaud.

RIPPIENO. An Italian word, which is frequently found in church-music, and is similar to the word Chorus.

RITTORNEL. A stroke of symphony which is used after the manner of prelude to a head of the air, by which the air is ordinarily announced; or, at the end, to imitate and certify the end of the same air; or, in the middle, to repose the voice, to strengthen the expression, or simply to embellish the piece.

In recueils or partitions of ancient Italian music, the rittornels are often designed by the words si suona, which signifies that the instrument which accompanies should repeat what the voice has sung.

Rittornel comes from the Italian Rittornello, and signifies a small return. At present, that symphony has taken a more brilliant character, and almost independant of the vocal, we pay no more attention to simple repetitions. Wherefore the word rittornel has grown obsolete.

ROLL. The separated paper which contains the music that a concertant ought to execute, and is called part in a concert, but roll in an opera. Wherefore, we ought to distribute a part to each musician, and a roll to every actor.

ROMANCE. An air on which we sing a small poem of the same name, divided by couplets, whose subject is generally some amorous, and often tragic history. As the romance should be written in a simple touching style, and a rather antique taste, the air ought to answer to the character of the words: No ornaments; a sweet, natural, rural melody, which may produce its effect by itself, independantly of the method of singing it. It is not necessary that the air should be striking; it is sufficient that it is lively, that it does not over-shadow the words, that it makes them very clearly be heard, and requires not too great an extent of voice. A well composed romance which has nothing soaring, does not immediately affect; but each couplet adds something to the effect of the preceding; the interest augments insensibly, and we find ourselves sometimes melted into tears, without being able to discover the charm which has produced that effect. It is a certain experience, that every accompaniment of instruments weakens this impression. For the air of a romance, we require only a just, clear voice, which pronounces well and sings with simplicity.

ROMANESQUE. An air for dancing.

RONDEAU. A kind of air with two or more repeats, and whose form is such, that after having finished the second repeat, we retake the first, and so on, returning always and finishing by the same repeat with which we began. For this purpose, we should so conduct the modulation, that the end of each repeat might be suitable to the beginning of all the rest; and that the end of all the rest may suit the beginning of that first.

The grand Italian airs, and all our arietta's, are in rondeau, as well as the greatest part of French pieces for the harpsichord.

The *Routines* are magazines of a contrary sense, for those who follow them without reflexion. Such is for musicians that of rondeau's. A great discernment is necessary to make a choice of words which are proper to them. It is ridiculous to place a complete thought in rondeau, divided into two branches. It is ridiculous to put in rondeau a comparison, whose application is made only in the second branch, in re-taking the first, and finishing by it. Lastly, it is ridiculous to place in rondeau a general thought limited by an exception, relative to the condition of him who speaks; so that, forgetting the exception which has reference to himself, he may finish in re-taking the general thought.

But every time that a sentiment expressed in the first branch, brings with it a reflexion which enforces it, and places it in the second; every time that a description of the condition of him who speaks, filling the first branch, clears a comparison in the second; every time that an affirmation in the first branch contains its proof, and its confirmation in the second; lastly, every time that the first branch contains the proposition of doing a thing, and the second the reason of the proposition; in these different cases, and in others similar, the rondeau is always well placed.

RULE OF THE OCTAVE. An harmonic formula, published the first time in 1700, which determines, on the diatonic motion of the bass, the concord suitable to each degree of the tone, as well in major mode as minor, and as well ascending as the contrary.

We find this formula cyphered here on the octave of the major mode, and again on the octave in minor.

Rule

Rule of the Octave.

In mode major.

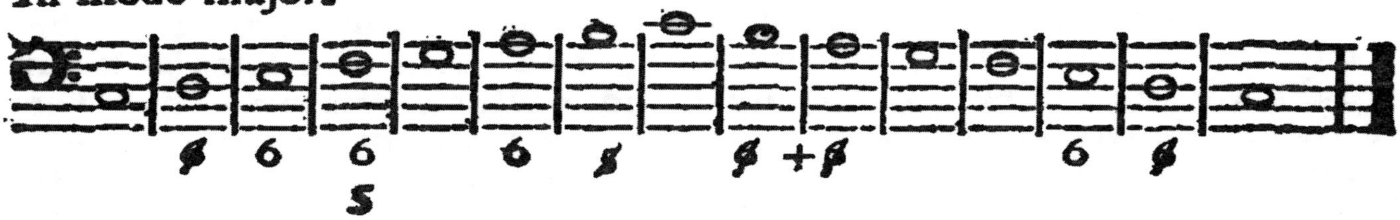

In mode minor.

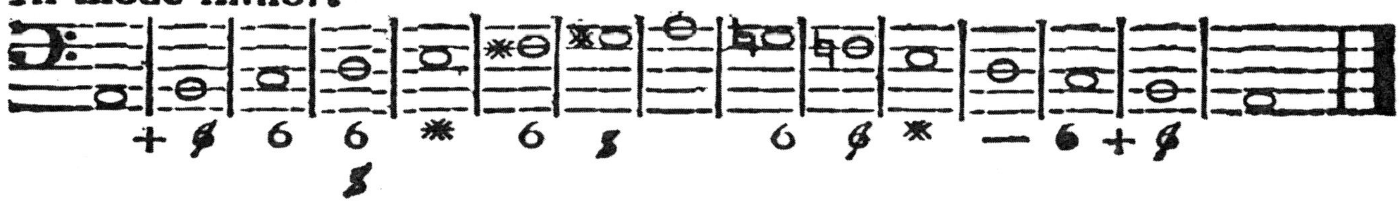

Provided that the tone be well determined, we ſhall not miſtake in accompanying on this rule, as long as the author continues in the ſimple and natural harmony which the mode bears. If he leaves that ſimplicity by ſuppoſed concords, or other licences, it is his buſineſs to expreſs it by ſuitable cyphers, which he alſo ought to do at each change of the tone; but all that is not cyphered ſhould be accompanied according to the rule of the octave; and this rule ſhould be ſtudied on the fundamental baſs, to have a right comprehenſion of its ſenſe.

It is however unlucky, that a formula, deſtined to the practice of elementary rules in harmony, ſhould contain a fault againſt thoſe ſame rules. It is to give early inſtructions to beginners to tranſgreſs the laws that are given them. This fault is in the accompaniment of the ſixth note, with which the concord cyphered by a 6, offends againſt the rules; for we can find no union; and the fundamental baſs deſcends diatonically from a perfect concord on another perfect concord. A liberty to be formed into a rule.

We might manage that there could be an union, by adding a ſeventh to the perfect concord of the dominant; but then this ſeventh, becoming an octave on the following note, would not be preſerved; and the fundamental baſs, deſcending on a perfect concord diatonically, after a concord of ſeventh, would make a movement quite intolerable.

We might alſo give to this ſixth note, the concord of ſmaller ſixth, the fourth of which would form an union; but this would be fundamentally a concord of ſeventh with minor third, where the diſſonance ſhould not be prepared, which is alſo againſt the rules. (Vide To Prepare.)

We might cypher ſixth fourth on this ſixth note, and it would be then the perfect concord of the ſecond; but I am in doubt if the muſicians would approve a variation ſo ill underſtood as that;

a variation which the ear does not adopt, and on a concord which removes too much the idea of the principal modulation.

We might change the concord of the dominant, giving it the ſixth fourth inſtead of the ſeventh, and then the ſimple ſixth would ſuit very well on the ſixth note which follows; but the ſixth fourth would ſuit very ill on the dominant, unleſs it was followed by the perfect concord, or the ſeventh, which would bring back the difficulty. A rule, which ſerves not only in practice, but as a model for practice, ſhould never be drawn from thoſe theoretic combinations rejected by the ear; and each note, particularly the dominant, ſhould convey to it its proper concord whenever it has one.

I look on it then as a certain thing that our rules are bad, or that the concord of ſixth, with which we accompany the ſixth note in aſcending, is a fault that ſhould be corrected; and that to accompany this note regularly, as is neceſſary in a formula, there is only one concord to give it, viz. that of the ſeventh; not a fundamental ſeventh, which, in this movement, not being able to be preſerved but by another ſeventh, would be a fault; but a ſeventh varied by a concord of ſixth added on the tonic: It is clear, that the concord of the tonic is the only one which can be regularly inſerted between the perfect concord, or of ſeventh on the dominant, and the ſame concord on the ſenſible note which immediately follows. I wiſh ſome ingenious perſons may find this correction good: I am ſure, at leaſt, that they will find it regular.

TO RULE THE PAPER. Is to mark on fair paper, the ſtaves to mark the muſic on. (Vide Ruled Paper.)

RULER. A workman whoſe profeſſion conſiſts in ruling the papers for muſic. (Vide Copiſt.)

RULING. The method by which the paper is ruled. "This ruling is too black." "There is pleaſure in writing notes on a neat ruling." (Vide Ruled Paper.)

S.

S. This letter written alone in the reciting part of a concert, ſignifies ſolo, and is then alternative with T, which ſignifies tutti.

SARABAND. The air of a dance, which bears the ſame name, which ſeems to have been tranſmitted from Spain, and was formerly danced with caſtagnetto's. This dance is no longer uſed

used, unless in some old French operas. The air of the saraband is at three slow times.

TO SAVE. To save, or preserve a dissonance, is to resolve it, according to rules of the consonance of a following concord. There is a movement prescribed to this, both in the fundamental bass of the dissonant accord, and in the part which forms the dissonance. There is no method of saving, which is not derived from an act of cadence; it is then by the nature of the cadence we would make, that the movement of the fundamental bass is determined. (Vide Cadence.)

In regard to the part which forms the dissonance, it ought neither to continue in its place, nor to move by disjoint degrees; but it ought to ascend or descend diatonically, according to the nature of the dissonance. Masters say, that the major dissonance ought to ascend, and the minor to descend; which is not without exception, since in certain chords of harmony, a seventh as well major, ought not to ascend, but fall; unless in the concord, termed very incorrectly, concord of superfluous seventh: It is better then to say, that the seventh and every dissonance deriving from it, ought to descend, and that the sixth added, and every dissonance deriving from it, should rise. This is a rule really general and without any exception. It is the same thing with the law of saving the dissonance: there are dissonances which we may prepare; but there is no one, that we should not save.

In regard to the sensible note, improperly called major dissonance, if it ought to ascend, it is less by the rule of saving the dissonance, than by that of the diatonic movement, and to prefer the shortest way; and effectually there are cases, as, that of the intererrupted cadence, where this sensible note does not ascend.

In concords by supposition, a same concord furnishes two dissonances, as the seventh and ninth, the ninth and fourth, &c. These dissonances should then have been prepared, and ought both to be saved; that is, we must pay attention to all that has a dissonance, not only on the fundamental bass, but also on the thorough.

SCALE. This name is given to the diatonic succession of the seven notes, ut re mi fa sol la si, of the gamut, because these notes are found ranged in the manner of scales on the staves of our music. This enumeration of all the diatonic sounds of our system, ranged in order, which we call scale, was called by the Greeks, tetrachord, because in effect their scale was composed of only four sounds, which they repeated from tetrachord to tetrachord, as we do from octave to octave. (Vide Tetrachord.)

Saint Gregory was, they say, the first who changed the tetrachords of the ancients, into a heptachord, or system of seven notes: at the end of which, beginning another octave, we find similar sounds repeated in the same order. This discovery is very ingeni ous, and it muſt appear ſingular, that the Greeks, who ſaw very clearly the properties of the octave, ſhould, in ſpite of that, have thought, they ſhould continue attached to their tetrachords. Gregory expreſſed theſe ſeven notes, by the firſt ſeven letters of the Latin alphabet. Gui Aretin gave names to the ſix firſt, but he neglected to give one to the ſeventh; which in France, has ſince been called ſi, and which has no other name yet than B mi, amongſt the other european nations.

We muſt not think, that the connections of the tones, and ſemitones; of which the ſcale is compoſed, are things purely arbitrary; and that by other diviſions as good, an order, and different connections could have been given to the ſound of this ſcale. Our diatonic ſyſtem is better in certain reſpects, becauſe it is engendered by the conſonances, and the difference there are between them. "Let a perſon hear, ſays Monſ. Sauveur, ſeveral times the concord of the fifth, and that of the fourth, he is naturally led to imagine the difference which is betwixt them. It is united, and conjoined with thoſe in our mind, and partakes of their graces; this is the major tone. It is the ſame thing with the minor tone, which is the difference of the minor third and the fourth, and the major ſemitone, which is that of the ſame fourth in major third". Morevover, the major tone, the minor tone, and the major ſemi-tone, are the diatonic degrees of which our ſcale is compoſed, according to the following references,

Major Tone	Minor Tone	Semi Tone Major	Major Tone	Minor Tone	Major Tane	Major Semi Tone	
Ut	Re	Mi	Fa	Sol	La	Si	Ut
$\frac{3}{9}$	$\frac{3}{10}$	$\frac{15}{16}$	$\frac{8}{9}$	$\frac{9}{10}$	$\frac{8}{9}$	$\frac{15}{16}$.	

To make a proof of this calculation, we muſt compoſe all the connections compriſed between two conſonant terms, and we ſhall find, that their product gives exactly the reference of the conſonance; and if we re-unite all the terms of the ſcale, we ſhall find the total connection in ſub-double numerical powers; that is, as 1 to 2, which is in effect the exact connection of two extreme terms, viz. of the ut to its octave.

The

The ſcale we have now ſeen, is that which is called natural or diatonic; but the moderns, dividing its degrees into other ſmaller intervals, have derived from it another ſcale, which they have called ſemi-tonic or chromatic ſcale, becauſe it proceeds by ſemi-tones.

To form this ſcale, we have only divided into two equal intervals, or ſuppoſed ſo, each of the five entire tones of the octave, without diſtinguiſhing the major tone from the minor; which, with the two major ſemi-tones which were already found, forms a ſucceſſion of twelve ſemi-tones on thirteen conſecutive ſounds, from one octave to the other.

The uſe of this ſcale is to give the methods of modulating on whatever note we chooſe, as fundamental; and of being able, not only to form any interval on this note, but to eſtabliſh a diatonic ſcale on it, ſimilar to the diatonic ſcale of ut. Whilſt we are contented to have, as tonic, a note of the gamut taken at pleaſure, without troubling ourſelves if the ſounds by which the modulation ought to paſs, were with that note, and between themſelves, in ſuitable references, the ſemi-tonic ſcale was little neceſſary; whatever fa dieſis, whatever ſi B flat, compoſed what was called the ſharps of muſic, there were only two touches to add to the diatonic keys. But ſince we have thought to have felt the neceſſity of eſtabliſhing a perfect ſimilitude between the different tones, it has been neceſſary to find methods of tranſporting the ſame airs and the ſame intervals, higher or lower, according to the tone which we may have choſen. The chromatic ſcale is then become of indiſpenſable neceſſity; and 'tis by its means that we convey an air on ſuch degree of the keys as we would chooſe, and that we render it exactly on this new poſition, ſuch as it may have been imagined for another.

Theſe five added ſounds form no new degrees in muſic; but they are all marked on the neareſt degree, by a B flat if the degree is higher, by a dieſis if it is lower; and the note always takes the name of the degree on which it is placed. (Vide B Flat and Dieſis.)

To aſſign, however, the connections of theſe new intervals, we muſt know, that the two parts or ſemi-tones which compoſe the major tone, are in the references of 15 to 16, and 128 to 135; and that the two which compoſe the minor tone alſo, are in the references of 15 to 16, and 24 to 25; ſo that in dividing the whole octave according to the ſcale of ſemi-tonic, we have all its terms in the references placed on the following figure.

Chromatic Scale drawn from Monſ. Malcolm.

Major.	Middle.	Major.	Minor.	Major.	Middle.	Major.	Major.	Minor.	Major.	Middle.	Major.
Ut, ut ✱,	re,	mi b,	mi,	fa,	fa ✱,	ſol,	ſol ✱,	la,	ſi b,	ſi,	ut
$\frac{15}{16}$	$\frac{128}{135}$	$\frac{15}{16}$	$\frac{24}{25}$	$\frac{15}{16}$	$\frac{128}{135}$	$\frac{15}{16}$	$\frac{15}{16}$	$\frac{24}{25}$	$\frac{15}{16}$	$\frac{128}{135}$	$\frac{15}{16}$

But we muſt take notice that this diviſion, drawn from Monſ. Malcolm, ſeems to want juſtneſs in many reſpects. Firſt, the ſemi-tones which ought therein to be minor, are major; and that of ſol dieſis in la, which ought to be major, is minor. In the ſecond place, ſeveral major thirds, as that of la in ut dieſis, and of mi in ſol dieſis, are too ſtrong by a comma, which muſt render them inſupportable. Laſtly, the middle ſemi-tone, being there ſubſtituted in the place of the ſemi-tone maximum, gives falſe intervals wherever it is uſed. On which we ought not to forget, that this middle ſemi-tone is greater than the major itſelf, i. e. middle between the maximum and major.

A better and more natural diviſion would then be, to divide the major tone, into two ſemi-tones; the one minor from 24 to 25, the other maximum from 25 to 27, leaving the minor-tone divided into 2 ſemi-tones, the one major, and the other minor, as in the table above. There are ſtill two other ſemi-tonic ſcales, which are derived from two other different methods of dividing the octave by ſemi-tones.

The firſt is made by taking an harmonic, or arithmetical middle, between the two terms of the major tone, and another betwixt thoſe of the minor tone, which divides the one and the other tone into two ſemi-tones almoſt equal; ſo the major tone $\frac{8}{9}$ is divided into $\frac{16}{17}$ and $\frac{17}{18}$ arithmetically, the numbers repreſenting the length of the chords; but when they repreſented the vibrations, the lengths of the chords are reciprocal, and in harmonic proportion, as one $\frac{16}{17}$ $\frac{8}{9}$ which places the greater ſemi-tone in flat.

In the ſame manner the minor tone $\frac{9}{10}$ is arithmetically divided

into

into two ſemi-tones $\frac{18}{19}$ $\frac{19}{20}$ or reciprocally one $\frac{18}{19}$ $\frac{9}{10}$ but this laſt diviſion is not harmonic.

The whole octave thus calculated, gives the references expreſſed in the following ſcale.

Chromatic Scale by Monſ. Malcolm.

$\frac{16}{17}$	$\frac{17}{18}$	$\frac{18}{19}$	$\frac{19}{20}$	$\frac{15}{16}$	$\frac{16}{17}$	$\frac{17}{18}$	$\frac{18}{19}$	$\frac{19}{20}$	$\frac{16}{17}$	$\frac{17}{18}$	$\frac{15}{16}$	
Ut,	ut ✱,	re,	mi♭,	mi,	fa,	fa ✱,	ſol,	ſol ✱,	la,	ſi ♭,	ſi,	ut.

Monſ. Salmon relates, in his Philoſophical Tranſactions, that he made, before the Royal Society, a tryal of this ſcale, on chords exactly divided according to theſe proportions, and that they were perfectly in concord with the other inſtruments touched by the beſt hands.

Monſ. Malcolm adds, that having calculated and compared theſe connections, he found a greater number of faults in this ſcale than in the precedent; but that the errors were conſiderably leſs, which makes ſome compenſation.

Laſtly, the other ſemi-tonic ſcale is that of the Ariſtoxenians, which P. Merſenne has very largely treated, and which M. Rameau has endeavoured to renew in theſe laſt times. It conſiſts in geometrically dividing the octave by eleven methods proportioned in twelve ſemi-tones perfectly equal. As their connections are not rational, I will not give here thoſe references which cannot be expreſſed but by the formula itſelf, or by logarithms of the terms of progreſſion between the extremes 1 and 2. (Vide Modification.)

As in the diatonic and chromatic genus the harmoniſts add a third, viz. the enharmonic, this third genus ſhould have its ſcale alſo, at leaſt by ſuppoſition; for tho' the truly enharmonic intervals do not exiſt in our keys, it is yet certain, that every enharmonic paſſage ſuppoſes them; and that the mind, correcting the ſenſation of the ear on this point, paſſes then from one idea to another, only through favour of this interval underſtood. If every tone was exactly compoſed of two minor ſemi-tones, every enharmonic interval would be null, and this genus could no longer exiſt. But as a minor tone itſelf contains more than two minor ſemi-tones, the complement of the ſum of theſe two ſemi-tones to the tone, that is, the ſpace which remains between the dieſis of the inferior note, and the B flat of the ſuperior, is preciſely the enharmonic interval, called commonly the fourth of the

the tone. This fourth of the tone is of two kinds, viz. the major and the minor enharmonic, whoſe connections may be found at the word *Quarter of a Tone*.

This explanation ought to ſuffice to every reader, for the eaſy conception of the enharmonic ſcale, which I have calculated, and here inſerted.

Enharmonic Scale.

Ut, ut ✱, re b, re, re ✱, mi b, mi, mi ✱, fa, fa ✱, ſol b,

$\frac{24}{25}$	$\frac{576}{625}$	$\frac{24}{25}$	$\frac{24}{25}$	$\frac{125}{128}$	$\frac{24}{25}$	$\frac{24}{25}$	$\frac{125}{128}$	$\frac{24}{25}$	$\frac{576}{625}$	$\frac{24}{25}$

ſol, ſol ✱, la b, la, la ✱, ſi b, ſi, ſi ✱, ut.

$\frac{24}{25}$	$\frac{125}{128}$	$\frac{24}{25}$	$\frac{24}{25}$	$\frac{576}{625}$	$\frac{24}{25}$	$\frac{24}{25}$	$\frac{125}{128}$

Thoſe who would chuſe a clearer account of this point, muſt turn to the word Enharmonic.

SCENE. We diſtinguiſh in lyric muſic, the ſcene from the monologue, in that, there is only one actor in the monologue, and at leaſt two ſpeakers in the ſcene. Conſequently in the monologue, the character of the muſic ſhould be one, at leaſt in regard to the perſon: but in the ſcenes, the muſic ſhould have as many different characters as there are ſpeakers. In effect, as in ſpeaking, each one always continues the ſame voice, the ſame accent, and generally the ſame ſtyle in all that he ſays; ſo every actor, in the different paſſions he expreſſes, ſhould always preſerve a character peculiar to him, and which may diſtinguiſh him from another actor. The grief of an aged man, has not the ſame tone as that of a young one; the paſſion of a Billingſgate fiſh-woman, has different accents from that of a warrior: A Barbarian can never ſay "I adore you," as a profeſſed amoroſo.

We muſt then in ſcenes, render not only the character we would paint, but that of the perſon whom we make to ſpeak. This character is partly denoted by the kind of voice appropriated to each part; the turn in ſinging of a counter-tenor is different from that of the baſs tenor. We place more gravity in the airs of baſs trebles, and more vivacity in thoſe of ſharper voices. But beſides theſe differences, the ingenious compoſer muſt find individual ones to characterize his perſonages, ſo that one ſhall know in a moment, by the peculiar accent of the recitative or air, if it is Mandane or Emira, if its Olintes or Alceſtes, whom

we

we hear. I agree that there are only men of genius, who feel, and mark these differences; but I say however, that it is only in the observation of them, and others similar, that we are able to produce the illusion.

SCHISMA. A small interval, which is equal to the half of a comma, and whose numerical powers are consequently mute, since, to express it in numbers, it would be necessary to find a proportional medium between 80 and 81.

SCHOENION. A kind of nome for flutes in the ancient Greek music.

SCHOLIA. A kind of song amongst the ancient Greeks, whose characters were extremely diversified according to subjects and persons. (Vide Song)

SECOND. An interval of a conjoint degree, wherefore the diatonic movements are all made on the intervals of the second.

There are 4 kinds of seconds. The first called diminished second, is made on a major tone, whose inferior note is connected by a diesis, and the superior by a B flat; such, for instance is the interval of the re B flat, to the ut diesis. The connection of this second is from 375 to 384; but it is of no use, unless in the enharmonic genus: the interval also is found null in virtue of the modification. In regard to the interval of one note to its diesis, which Brossart calls diminished second, it is not a second, it is a changed unison.

The second, which is called minor second, is constituted by the major semi-tone, as of si to ut, or of mi to fa; its connection is from 15 to 16. The third is the major second, which forms the interval of a tone; as this tone may be major or minor, the reference of this second, is from 8 to 9 in the first case, from 9 to 10 in the second. But this difference is null in our music.

Lastly, the fourth is the superfluous second, composed of a major tone, and a minor semi-tone, as from fa to sol diesis: Its connection is from 64 to 75.

There are in harmony two concords, which bear the name of second, the first is simply called concord of second. It is a concord of varied seventh, whose dissonance is in the bass; from whence it follows very clearly, that the bass should syncopate to prepare it. (Vide to Prepare.)

When the concord of seventh is dominant, i. e. when the third is major, the concord of the second is called concord of triton, and the syncope is not necessary, because the preparation is not so.

The other is called concord of superfluous second. It is a concord varied from that of diminished seventh, the seventh of which itself is conveyed to the bass. This concord is equally good with or without a syncope. (Vide Syncope.)

SEMI. A word borrowed from the Latin, which signifies half, We use it in music, instead of the hemi of the Greeks, to compose ſeveral technical words very barbarouſly, the half Greek and the half Latin. This word, before the Greek name in any interval whatever, always ſignifies a diminution, not the half of this interval, but only a minor ſemi-tone; wherefore ſemi-diton is the minor third; ſemi-diapente, the falſe fifth; ſemi-diateſſaron, the diminiſhed fourth.

SEMI BREVE. Is, in our ancient muſic, a power of notes or meaſure of a time, which comprehends the ſpace of two minime's, that is, the half of a breve. The ſemi-breve is however called round, becauſe it has that figure; but formerly it was in a lozenge.

Anciently the ſemi-breve was divided into major and minor, the major is equal to two thirds of the perfect breve, and the minor to the other third of the ſame breve; wherefore the major ſemi-breve contains two minors

The ſemi-breve, before the minime was invented, being the note of leſs power, was not ſub-divided. This indiviſibility, they ſay, is expreſſed in ſome meaſure, by its figure of a lozenge terminated above, below, and at the two ſides, by points. Moreover Muris proves, by the authority of Ariſtotle and Euclid, that the point is indiviſible; from whence he concludes, that the ſemi-breve encloſed between four points is indiviſible as themſelves.

SEMI TONE. Is the ſmalleſt of all the intervals admitted in modern muſic; it is nearly equal to the half of a tone.

There are ſeveral kinds of ſemi-tones, two are diſtinguiſhed in practice, the major, and the minor; three others are known in harmonic calculations, viz. The ſemi-tone maxime, the minime, and the middle; the ſemi-tone major is the difference of the major third to the fourth, as mi fa. Its connection is from 15 to 16, and it forms the ſmalleſt of all the diatonic intervals.

The minor ſemi-tone is the difference of the major third to the minor. It is marked on the ſame degree by a dieſis or a B flat: It forms only one chromatic interval, and its reference is from 24 to 25.

Though we place a difference between theſe two ſemi-tones by the method of noting them, there is none, however, on the organ and harpſichord; and the ſame ſemi-tone is ſometimes major and ſometimes minor, ſometimes diatonic and ſometimes chromatic, according to the mode in which we are however in practice. We call ſemi-tones minor, thoſe, which being marked by a B flat or dieſis, do not change their degree; and ſemi-tones major, thoſe, which form an interval of the ſecond.

In regard to the three other ſemi-tones admitted only in theory, the ſemi-tone maxime is the difference of the tone major to the ſemi-tone minor, and its connection is from 25 to 27. The middle ſemi-tone is the difference major to the tone major, and its connection is from 128 to 135. Laſtly, the ſemi-tone minime,

is

is the difference of the ſemi-tone maxime to the middle ſemi-tone, and its connection is from 125 to 128, of all theſe intervals, there is only the major ſemi-tone, which, in quality of ſecond, may be ſometimes admitted into harmony.

SEMI TONIC. A ſemi-tonic or chromatic ſcale. (Vide Scale.)

SENSIBILITY. A diſpoſition of the ſoul which inſpires the compoſer with the lively ideas which he wants; the executant, with the lively idea of theſe ſame expreſſions; and the auditor, with the lively impreſſion of the beauties and errors of muſic which he is made to hear. (Vide Taſte.)

SENSIBLE. A ſenſible concord is that which is otherwiſe called dominant concord. (Vide Concord.)

It is practiced only on the dominant of the tone; from whence it receives the name of dominant concord, and it always bears the ſenſible note for third of that dominant, from whence it receives the name of ſenſible concord. (Vide Concord.)

In regard to the ſenſible note. (Vide Note.)

SEVENTH. A diſſonant interval varied from the ſecond, which is called by the Greeks, heptachordon, becauſe it is formed of ſeven ſounds, or ſix diatonic degrees. There are four ſorts of them. The firſt is the minor ſeventh compoſed of four tones, three major and a minor, and of two major ſemi-tones, as from mi to re: and chromatically of 10 ſemi-tones, ſix major and four minor. Its connection is from 5 to 9.

The ſecond is the major ſeventh, compoſed diatonically of five tones, three major and two minor, and of a major ſemi-tone; ſo that no more than one major ſemi-tone is neceſſary to compoſe an octave, as from ut to ſi, and chromatically of 11 ſemi-tones, ſix major, and five minor. Its connection is from 8 to 15.

The third is the diminiſhed ſeventh, it is compoſed of three tones, two minor and one major, and of three major ſemi-tones, as from ut dieſis, to ſi B flat. Its connection is from 75 to 128.

The fourth is the ſuperfluous ſeventh, it is compoſed of five tones, three minor and two major, a ſemi-tone major, and a ſemi-tone minor as from ſi B flat, to la dieſis, ſo that there is only a comma wanting to it to form an octave. Its connection is from 81 to 160, but this laſt kind is not uſed in muſic, unleſs in ſome enharmonic tranſitions.

There are three concords of the ſeventh.

The firſt is fundamental, and bears ſimply the name of ſeventh, but when the third is major, and the ſeventh minor, it is called ſenſible or dominant concord. It is compoſed of the third, the fifth, and the ſeventh.

The ſecond alſo is fundamental, and is called concord of diminiſhed ſeventh; it is compoſed of the minor third, the falſe fifth,

 and

and the diminiſhed ſeventh, whoſe name it takes, that is, of three minor conſecutive tones, and is the only concord, which is thus formed of equal intervals: It is made on the ſenſible note only. (Vide Enharmonic.)

The third is called concord of ſuperfluous ſeventh; it is a concord by ſuppoſition formed by the dominant accord, below which the baſs makes the tonic be heard.

There is alſo a concord of ſeventh and ſixth, which is only a variation of the concord of the ninth. It is only practiſed in the organ points on account of its duration. (Vide Concord.)

SERENADE. A concert given in the night under the windows of ſome one.

It is generally compoſed of inſtrumental muſic; ſometimes however the voice is added to it. We call ſerenades alſo the pieces compoſed or executed on theſe occaſions. The mode of ſerenades has been long obſolete; they continue no longer but amongſt the lower people, and that is a pity. The ſilence of the night, which baniſhes all confuſion, makes the muſic ſuperior, and renders it more delicious.

This word, Italian in its origin, comes without doubt from ſereno, or from the Latin ſerum, in the evening. When the concert is performed in the morning, or at break of day, it is called aubade.

SESQUI. A particle often uſed by our ancient muſicians in the compoſition of words, ſerving to expreſs the different ſorts of meaſures.

They called Seſqui Alter's, the meaſures whoſe principal note was equal to the half more than its ordinary powers, that is, three of the notes, of which otherwiſe it would have only equalled two, which had place in all the triple meaſures, whether in major, where the breve itſelf without points was equal to three ſemi-breves, or in the minor, where the ſemi-breve equalled three minime's, &c.

They called the triple alſo ſeſqui alter, marked by this ſign C $\frac{9}{8}$, double ſeſqui fourth, the triple marked C $\frac{9}{4}$, and ſo on with the reſt. Seſqui diton, or hemi diton, in the Greek muſic, is the interval of a minor third.

SEXTUPLE. A name given rather improperly to meaſures of two times compoſed of ſix equal notes, three for each time. Theſe kinds of meaſures have been alſo called by ſome improperly, "ſix timed meaſures."

We may reckon five kinds of theſe ſextuple meaſures, that is, as many as there are different powers of the notes, from that which is compoſed of ſix rounds or ſemi-breves, called in France triple of

ſix

six for one, and which is expressed by this cypher $\frac{6}{1}$ to that called triple of six for sixteen, composed only of six double demi-crotchets only, and which is marked also $\frac{6}{16}$. The greatest part of these distinctions are abolished, and in effect they are rather useless, since all these different figures of notes, are less different measures than modifications of the movement in the same kind of measure; which is still better marked by a single word written at the head of the air, than with all the confusion of cyphers and notes, which only serve to increase the difficulty of an art which is puzzling enough in itself. (Vide Double, Triple, Time, Measure, &c.)

SHARP. The alteration of a note or an interval by a diesis or B flat. This is properly the common and general name of the accidental diesis's and B's flat. The word is no longer in use, but there is no other substituted in its place. The fear of using superannuated terms daily enervates our language; the fear of using old terms decreases it daily; Its greatest enemies will ever be those who purify it.

They called sharp also the chromatic touches of the keys, which we now call, white touches, and which were formerly made black, because our rude ancestors had not the ingenuity of making the keys black, to give a greater eclat to the Ladies fingers. We call at present cut sharps, those of the touches which are broken to supply the *Ravalement*.

TO SKIP. We skip a tone, when giving a Flute too much wind, or in the pipe of a wind instrument, we force the air to be divided, and make instead of the full tone of the flute, or pipe, only some one of its harmonies. When the skip is of an entire octave, it is called to octave. It is clear that to vary the sounds of the trumpet and french-horn, we must necessarily skip, and it is only in skipping that we make octaves on the flute.

SI. One of the seven syllables which they make use of in France to sol-fa their notes. Guy Aretin in composing his gamut, invented only six of these syllables, because he only changed in hexachords, the Greek tetrachords, tho' in the end, his gamut, as well as ours, was composed of seven notes. It happened from thence, that to name the seventh, it was necessary every movement to change the names of the rest, and to name them in different manners: an embarrassment which continues no longer, since the invention of si, on the gamut, from which a musician, named de Nevers, made, in the beginning of this century, an express work.

Bropard, and those who have followed him, attribute the invention of si to another musicain, named Le Maire, betwixt the middle and end of the last century; others give the honour of it to a certain Vander

Vander Pullen: others aſcend as far as Jean de Muris, about the year 1330, and the Cardinal Bona, ſays, that about the eleventh age, which was that of Aretin, Ericius Dupuis added a note to the ſixth of Guy, to avoid the difficulties of the diviſions, and facilitate the ſtudy of muſic.

But, without attending to the inventions of Ericius Dupuis, which without doubt died with him, or on which Bona, later by five centuries, may have been deceived; it is even eaſy to prove, that the invention of ſi is much later than Jean de Muris, in whoſe writings we ſee nothing ſimilar to it.

In regard to Vander Pullen, I cannot ſay any thing as I am not acquainted with him Le Maire now remains, in whoſe favour the voices of all ſeem to unite; If the invention conſiſts in having brought into practice the uſe of this ſyllable ſi, I do not ſee many reaſons for diſputing the honour with him. But if the true inventor is he, who has firſt found the neceſſity of a ſeventh ſyllable, and who has added one in conſequence, we need not ſearch far to find, that Le Maire has no claim to this title; for we find in ſeveral parts of P. Merſenne's writings, the neceſſity of the ſeventh ſyllable to avoid the diviſions; and he witneſſes that ſeveral had invented or practiſed this ſeventh ſyllable nearly in the ſame time; and amongſt others, Gilles Grand Jean, writing maſter of Sens; but that ſome named that ſyllable ci, others di, others ni, others ſi, others za, &c. Even before P. Merſenne, we find, in a work of Banchieri, monk of Olivet, printed in 1614, and entituled Caſtella di Muſici, the addition of the ſame ſeventh ſyllable; he calls it Bi by B ſharp, Ba by B flat, and he aſſures us, that this addition has been very much approved at Rome. So that all the pretended invention of Le Maire conſiſts, at the moſt, in having written or pronounced ſi, inſtead of having written or pronounced Bi or Ba, Ni or Di, and this is what has immortalized Le Maire. As to what remains, the uſe of the ſi is known only in France, and in ſpite of what the monk Banchieri ſays of it, it is not even preſerved in Italy.

SICILIAN. A kind of air for dancing, in the 6—4 or 6—8 meaſures of a movement much ſlower, but yet more ſpecified than the jig.

SIGNS. Are, in general, all the different characters made uſe of to mark the muſic. But this word is more particularly underſtood of the dieſis's B's flat, B's ſharp, points, repeats, pauſes, guidons, and other ſmall detached characters, which without being real notes, are modifications of notes and of the method of executing them.

SILENCES. Signs anſwering to the different powers of the notes, which, put in the place of thoſe notes, mark, that the whole of their time ſhould be paſſed in ſilence.

Tho' there are 10 powers of different notes, from the maximum to the quadruple demi-crotchet, there are however only 9 different characters for the filences; for that which ought to correfpond to the maximum, has always failed, and to exprefs its duration, we double the reft four meafures, being of an equality with the longue.

Thefe different filences are then, firft, the reft of four meafures, which is equal to a longue; Secondly, the reft of two meafures, equal to a breve; Thirdly the paufe, equal to a femi-breve; Fourthly the demi-paufe, equal to a minime; Fifthly the minime reft, equal to a crotchet; Sixthly, the demi-minime reft, equal to a demi-crotchet; Seventhly, the quarter-minime reft equal to a double demi-crotchet; Eighthly, the demi-quarter minime reft, equal to a triple demi-crotchet; and Ninthly the fixteenth of a minime reft, equal to a quadruple demi-crotchet.

We muft take notice, that the point has no place among filences as among notes; for tho' a crotchet and minime reft may be of equal powers, it is not cuftomary to point the latter to exprefs the powers of a pointed crotchet, but we ought, after the minime reft, to write alfo a demi-minime reft. However, as fome point the filences alfo, the executant muft be ready to all.

SIMPLE. In doubles and variations, the firft couplet, or original air, fuch as it is now marked, is called the fimple. (Vide Double, Variations.)

TO SING. Is, in its moft general acceptation, to form ftrong and varied founds by the voice. But it is moft generally the formation of different inflexions in the voice, fonorous, agreeable to the ear, by intervals admitted in mufic and within the rules of modulation.

We fing more or lefs agreeably, in proportion as the voice is more or lefs agreeable and fonorous; the ear more or lefs juft; the organs more or lefs flexible; the tafte more or lefs formed; and more or lefs practifed in the art of finging. To which we fhould add, in imitative and theatrical mufic, the degree of fenfibility which affects us, more or lefs, with the fentiments we are to render. We have alfo more or lefs difpofition towards finging, according to the climate in which we are born, and according to the more or lefs accent in our natural language. For the more accented the language is, and, confequently, the more melodious, more thofe who fpeak it have the facility of finging it.

There has been compofed an art of finging, that is, obfervations on thofe voices which fung the beft; there have been compofed, rules for facilitating and improving the ufe of this natural endowment. But there remain many difcoveries to be made, on the eafieft, fhorteft, and fureft method of acquiring that art.

SINGER.

SINGER. A musician who sings in a concert.

SINGING MASTER. A musician who teaches the reading of vocal music, and singing on the notes.

The functions of the singing-master relate to two principal objects. The first, which regards the culture of the voice, is to draw from it all that can be given in regard to singing, whether by the extent, by the justness, by the sound, by the nimbleness, or by the art of enforcing and sweetening the sounds, and learning to manage and modify them with all the ingenuity possible.

The second object regards the study of the signs, that is, the art of reading the notes on the paper, and the custom of decyphering it with so much facility, that, at the opening of the book, we may be able to sing every kind of music. (Vide Notes.)

A third part of the functions of the singing-master regards the knowledge of the language, particularly of the accents, of the quantity and best method of pronouncing them; because the errors of pronunciation are much more sensible in a song, than in conversation; and a well composed vocal, should be only a more energic and more agreeable method of marking the prosody and accents. (Vide Accent.)

SIXTH. The second of two imperfect consonances, called hexachord by the Greeks, because its interval is formed of six sounds, or five diatonic degrees. The sixth is a natural consonance, but only by combination; for there is not in the order of consonances, any simple or direct sixth.

To consider the sixth only by their intervals, we find four kinds, two consonant and the dissonant.

The consonants are, first, the minor sixth composed of three tones and two semi-tones major, as mi ut. Its relation is from five to eight. Secondly, the major sixth, composed of four tones and a major semi-tone, as sol mi. Its connection is from three to five. The dissonant sixths are, first, the diminished sixth, composed of two tones and three major semi-tones, as ut diesis la B flat; and whose relation is from 125 to 192. Secondly, the superfluous sixth, composed of four tones, a major semi-tone, and a minor semi-tone, as si B flat, and sol diesis. The relation of this sixth is from 72 to 125.

These two last intervals are never used in melody; and the diminished sixth is omitted in harmony.

There are seven concords which have the name of sixth. The first is simply called concord of sixth; it is the perfect concord, whose third is conveyed to the bass. Its place is on the mediant of the tone, or on the sensible note, or on the sixth.

The second is called concord of sixth-fourth. This is also the perfect concord, whose fifth is conveyed to the bass. It is never made but on the dominant or on the tonic.

The

The third is called concord of ſmaller ſixth. It is a concord of ſeventh, whoſe fifth is conveyed to the baſs. The ſmaller ſixth is conveyed ordinarily on the ſecond note of the tone, or on the ſixth.

The fourth is the concord of ſixth and fifth, or greater ſixth. It is alſo a concord of ſeventh, but whoſe third is conveyed to the baſs. If the fundamental concord is dominant, then the concord of greater ſixth loſes this name, and is called concord of falſe fifth. (Vide Falſe Fifth.) The greater ſixth is commonly placed only on the fourth note of the tone.

The fifth is the concord of ſixth added. A fundamental concord, compoſed, as that of the greater ſixth, of a third, a fifth, a major ſixth; and which is placed in the ſame manner on the tonic or fourth note. We can then diſtinguiſh theſe two concords only by the method of ſaving them; for if the fifth deſcends, and the ſixth remains, it is the concord of greater ſixth, and the baſs forms a perfect cadence; but if the fifth remains, and the ſixth aſcends, it is the concord of ſixth added, and the fundamental baſs forms an irregular cadence. Moreover, as, after having ſtruck this concord, we are maſters of one of theſe two methods, this keeps the audience in ſuſpence on the true foundation of the concord, until the end has determined it: and 'tis this liberty of chooſing, that Monſ. Rameau calls double-employ. (Vide that word.)

The ſixth concord is that of major ſixth and falſe fifth, which is no more than a concord of ſmaller ſixth in minor mode, in which the falſe fifth is ſubſtituted in place of the fourth; or, to expreſs myſelf differently, it is a concord of diminiſhed ſeventh, in which the third is conveyed to the baſs. It is placed only on the ſecond note of the tone.

Laſtly, The ſeventh concord of ſixth, is that of the ſuperfluous ſixth. It is a kind of ſmaller ſixth, which is never practiſed but on the ſixth note of a minor tone deſcending on the dominant; as then the ſixth of this ſixth note is naturally major; it is ſometimes rendered ſuperfluous by adding to it a dieſis. That ſuperfluous ſixth then becomes an original concord, which is not overthrown or varied. (Vide concord.)

SLOWLY. This word anſwers to the Italian largo, and denotes a ſlow movement. The ſuperlative ſound, very ſlowly, marks the ſloweſt of all the movements.

SOL. The fifth of the ſix ſyllables invented by Aretin, to pronounce the notes of the gamut. The natural ſol anſwers to the letter G. (Vide Gamut.)

TO SOL FA. Is, in tuning the ſounds, to pronounce at the ſame time the ſyllables of the gamut which correſpond to them. This exerciſe is that by which thoſe begin who learn muſic, that the idea of these different syllables uniting in their mind to that of the intervals which have relation to it, these syllables assist them to recall these intervals.

Aristides Quintilian teaches us, that the Greeks had four syllables or denominations of notes to sol fa, which they repeated at each tetrachord, as we repeat seven in each octave. These four syllables were the following, te, ta, thè, tho. The first answered to the first sound, or the hypate of the first tetrachord, and the following; the second to the parhypate; the third to the lichanos; the fourth to the nete; and so on in re-beginning: a method of sol-faing, which, shewing us clearly that their modulation was confined within the extent of the tetrachord, and that the homologous sounds, preserving both the same connections, and the same names, from one tetrachord to another, were repeated from fourth to fourth, as amongst us from octave to octave, proves, at the same time, that their harmonic generation, had no relation with ours, and was established on principles entirely different.

Guy d'Arezzo, having substituted his hexachord in the place of the ancient tetrachord, substituted also, to sol-fa it, six other syllables to the fourth which the Greeks used differently. These six syllables are the following, ut, re, mi, fa, sol, la; drawn, as every one knows, from the Hymn of St. John Baptist. But every one does not know, that the air of this hymn, as it is now sung in the Roman-church, is not exactly that from which Aretin took his syllables; since the sounds which bear them in this hymn, are not those which bear them in his gamut. We find, in an ancient manuscript, in the library of the Chapter of Sens, this hymn; such, probably, as it was sung in the time of Aretin; and in which each of the six syllables is exactly applied to the correspondent sound of the gamut, as may be seen in Fig. VI. Plate I.

It seems that the use of the six syllables of Guy was not very soon extended out of Italy, since Muris witnesses having heard in Paris, the syllables, pro, to, do, no, a, instead of those. But in time, those of Guy gained the day, and were received in France as in the rest of Europe. There is now Germany alone where they sol-fa by the letters of the gamut only, and not by syllables; so that the note which in sol-faing we call la, they call A; that which we call ut, they call C. For the diesis'd notes, they add an s to the letter, and pronounce that s is; so that, for instance, to sol-fa re diesis, they pronounce dis. They have also added the letter h, to remove the equivocation of si, which is b only by being b flat; when it is b sharp, it is h.

They know in sol-faing no other b flat than that alone; instead of the b flat of every other note, they take the diesis of that

that which is below; so for la b flat, they sol fa G s; for mi b flat, D s; and this method of sol-faing is so rough and confused, that one must be a German to make use of it, and to become by that means a great musician.

Since the establishment of the gamut of Aretin, they have endeavoured, at different times, to substitute other syllables in the room of his. As the voice of the three first is rather dull, Mons. Sauveur, in changing the method of pricking the notes, changed also that of sol-faing; and named the eight notes of the octave by the eight following syllables, pa, ra, ga, da, so, bo, lo, do. These names had no better success than the notes; but as to the syllable do, it was prior to M. Sauveur. The Italians have always used it, instead of ut, to sol-fa, though they name it *ut*, and not *do*, in the gamut. In regard to the addition of si, vide Si.

In regard to the notes changed by diesis or b flat, they convey the name of the note to the natural, and that causes, in the method of sol-faing, many difficulties, which M. de Boisgelou has proposed to remedy, by adding five notes to complete the chromatic system, and giving a particular name to each note. These names, with the ancients, are in all about twelve in number, as many as there are chords in this system, viz. ut, de, re, ma, mi, fa, fi, sol, be, la, sa, si. By means of these five notes added, and of the names which they bear, all the b's flat and diesis's are annihilated; as may be seen at the word System, in the exposition of that of Mons. de Boisgelou.

There are different methods of sol-faing, viz. by divisions, by transposition, and in the natural. The first method is the most ancient; the second, the best; and the third, the most general in France. Several nations have preserved, in the divisions, the ancient nomenclator of the six syllables of Aretin.

Others have retrenched them, as the English, who sol-fa on these four syllables only, mi, fa, sol, la. The French, on the contrary, have added a syllable to confine, under different names, all the seven diatonic sounds of the octave.

The inconveniencies of Aretin's method are considerable, for thro' the not rendering the gamut complete, the syllables of that gamut signify neither the fixed touches of the keys, nor the degrees of the tone, nor even the determined intervals. By the divisions, la fa, you may form an interval of major third in descending, or minor third in ascending, as may be easily seen by the gamut, &c. (Vide Gamut.)

It is still worse in the English method. We find every moment different intervals which cannot be expressed but by the same syllables; and the same names of the notes return in every fourth, as among the Greeks, instead of returning only at every octave, as in the modern system.

The method of sol-faing established in France, by the addition of si, is certainly much superior to all this; for the gamut being found complete, the divisions become useless, and the analogy of the octaves is perfectly observed. But the musicians have again spoilt this method, by the strange imagination of rendering the names of the notes always fixed and determined on the touches of the keys; so that these touches have all a double name, whilst the degrees of a transposed tone have none: an error which loads, universally, the memory with all the diesis's or B's flat of the cleff; which removes from the names of the notes the expression of the intervals proper to them; and which effaces, lastly, as much possible, all the traces of modulation.

Ut or re are not, or ought not to be such, or such a touch of the keys, but such a chord of the tone. In regard to the fixed touches, it is by the letters of the alphabet that they are expressed. The touch which you call ut, I call C; that which you call re, I call D. They are not signs that I invent; they are signs entirely established, by which I very clearly determine the fundamental of a tone. But this tone being once determined, tell me, I beg, in your turn, how you name the tonic which I name ut, and the second note, which I name re, and the mediant, which I name mi?

For these names, relative to the tone and the mode, are essential for the determination of ideas, and the justness of the intonations. If we give it a due reflexion, we shall find, that what the French musicians call *to sol-fa in natural*, is entirely out of nature. This method is unknown in every other nation, and cannot certainly gain success in any; every one must feel the contrary, that nothing is more natural than to sol-fa by transposition when the mode is transposed.

We have, in Italy, a recueil of lessons to sol-fa, called Solfeggi. This recueil, composed by the celebrated Leo, for the use of beginners, is very highly esteemed.

SOLO. This Italian word is anglicised in music, and applied to a piece which is sung with a single voice, or which is played on one instrument, with a simple accompaniment of bass, or harpsichord; and this is what distinguishes the solo from the recital, which may be accompanied by the whole orchestra. In the pieces called concerto's, we write always the word solo on the principal part when it recites.

SONATA. A piece of instrumental music, composed of three or four consecutive pieces of different characters. The sonata is nearly for instruments, what the cantata is for the voice.

The ſonata is ordinarily made for a ſingle inſtrument which recites, accompanied by a thorough baſs; and in ſuch a compoſition, we are attached to whatever is moſt favourable to make the inſtrument ſplendid, for which we labour; whether by the turn of ſinging, or by the choice of the ſounds which are moſt ſuitable to that kind of inſtrument, or by the boldneſs of the execution. There are alſo ſonata's in trio, which the Italians generally call ſinfonie; but when they paſs three parts, or there is ſome one reciting, they take the name of concerto. (Vide Concerto.)

There are ſeveral kinds of ſonata's. The Italians reduce them to two principal ſorts: the one which they call Sonate di Camera, ſonata's for a private room, which are compoſed of ſeveral familiar or dancing tunes; ſuch nearly as thoſe recueils which, in France, they call ſuites. The other kind is called Sonate da Chieſa, church ſonata's, in the compoſition of which, there ought to enter more labour, pains, harmony, and airs more ſuitable to the dignity of the place. Of whatever kind the ſonata's may be, they generally begin by an adagio; and after having paſſed by two or three different movements, finiſh by an allegro, or a preſto.

Now, that inſtruments form the moſt important part of muſic, the ſonata's are extremely a-la-mode, as well as every kind of ſymphony; the vocal is only acceſſary, and the air accompanies the accompaniment. We receive this ill taſte from thoſe who, wiſhing to introduce the turn of Italian muſic in a language not ſuſceptible of it, have obliged us to endeavour to make with inſtruments, what was impoſſible for us to form with the voice. I. dare to foretell, that ſo unnatural a taſte cannot continue. Muſic, purely harmonic, is trifling: to pleaſe conſtantly, and prevent languor, it ought to be raiſed to the rank of imitative arts; but its imitation is not always immediate, as thoſe of poetry and painting; the words is the method by which the muſic determines ofteneſt the object whoſe image it offers us; and it is by the touching ſounds of the human voice, that this image awakens in our ſouls the ſentiment which it ought to produce. Who does not feel how far the pure ſymphony, in which we ſeek only to render the inſtrument brilliant, is from that energy? Can all the trifles of Monſ. Mondonville's violin ſtrike me as two ſounds of Mad. Le Maure's voice? Symphony animates the muſic, and adds to its expreſſion, tho' it does not ſupply the place of it. To know what all this fracas of ſonata's would mean, with which we are loaded, we muſt do as the ignorant painter, who was obliged to write under his figures, "This is a tree." "This is a man." "And this is a horſe."

SONG. A kind of very ſhort lyric poem, which generally acts in agreeable ſubjects, to which a tune is added, to be ſung on familiar

familiar occasions; as at table, with one's friends, with one's mistress, and even alone, to remove, for some moments, wearisomeness, if we are rich; and to support poverty and labour with more resolution, if poor.

The use of songs seems to be a natural consequence from that of words, and, in effect, is not less general; for wherever they speak, they sing. It is only necessary, for the conception of them, to extend the organs, give an agreeable turn to the ideas we are delighted with, and fortify by the expression, of which the voice is capable, the sentiments we would chuse to render, or the image we would paint. The ancients had not the art of writing at the time they had of singing. Their laws and their histories, the praises of their gods and heroes, were sung before they were written. And from thence it happens, according to Aristotle, that the same Greek name was given to the laws and songs.

All the lyric poetry was properly consisting of songs only; but I ought to confine myself here to speaking of that which bore this name particularly, and which had its character in the most complete manner, according to our ideas.

Let us begin by songs for the table. In the most distant times, says Mons. de la Nauze, all the guests, according to Dicearchus, Plutarch, and Artemon, sung together, and in the same strain, the praises of the Divinity. Wherefore, these songs were veritable pæans, or sacred cantics. The gods were not disturbers of their feasts, and thus disdained not to admit them to their pleasures.

In the end the guests sung successively, each in his turn, holding a branch of myrtle, which passed from the hand of him who had sung, to him who sung next. Lastly, when music was improved in Greece, and the lyre was used in feasts, there were, say the authors already cited, only the ingenious who were qualified to sing at table, at least, when accompanied by the lyre. The others, obliged to confine themselves to the branch of myrtle, gave rise to a Greek proverb, by which they said, that a man sung with the myrtle, when they would tax him with ignorance.

These songs accompanied with the lyre, and of which Terpander was the inventor, were called scoliæ, a word which signifies oblique, to denote, according to Plutarch, the difficulty of *the song*, or, as Artemon will have it, the irregular situation of those who sung; for, as they were obliged to be ingenious for this method of singing, each one did not sit in his rank, but only those who understood music, which were dispersed here and there, and placed obliquely with relation to each other.

The subjects of the scholiæ were drawn not only from love and wine, or pleasure in general, as at present, but from history also, war, and even morality. Such is the song of Aristotle on the death

death of Hermias, his friend and ally, which occasioned the author the accusation of impiety.

"O virtue, who, spite of the difficulties which thou presentest "to impotent mortals, art the charming object of their searches! "Virtue pure and lovely! Amongst the Greeks, a death for "thee was reckoned enviable; the suffering with constancy a "dread calamity more than praise-worthy. Such are the seeds "of immortality which thou expandest over the heart. They "fruits are more to be valued than gold, than the love of pa-"rents, or the most tranquil slumbers. For thee the god-like "Hercules, and the son of Leda, endured ten thousand toils, "and the success of their exploits proclaimed thy power. It is "through love for thee that Ajax and Achilles descended to Plu-"tonian mansions; and 'twas in view of thy celestial beauty "that the Prince of Atarnes deprived himself of Sol's bright "beam: a prince immortalised for ever. The daughters of me-"mory shall ever sing his glory, when tuning their soft lyres to "hospitable Jove, and the value of a sincere and lasting friend-"ship."

All their moral songs were not so grave as that: here is one of a different taste, taken from Athenæus.

"The chief of all blessings is health; the second, beauty; the "third, riches honestly collected; and the fourth, the juvenile "days we pass with our friends."

In regard to the scholiæ, which consist of love and wine, we may judge of them by the seventy odes of Anacreon, which remain to us. But even in these kind of songs, we may see that love of their country and liberty most clearly shine, with which the Greeks were ever animated.

"Wine and health, says one of these songs, for my Clitagora "and myself, with assistance from the Thessalians." That is, besides that Clitagora was a Thessalian, the Athenians had formerly received succour from the Thessalians, against the tyranny of Pysistratides.

They had also songs for the different professions. Such were the songs of the shepherds; one kind of which, called bucoliasm, was absolutely the song of those who drove the herds; and the other, which is properly the pastoral, was an agreeable imitation of it. The song of the reapers, called the Lytierse, so called from the son of Midas, who took a pleasure in that employment. The song of the millers, called Hymee, or Epiaulia, as this taken from Plutarch, "Grind, Mule, grind, for Pittacus, who reigns "in splendid Mitylene, delights in eating," because Pittacus was a great Glutton. The song of the weavers, which was called Eline; the yule song of the wool-carders; that of the nurses, which was called Catabaucalesis, or Nunnia; the song of lovers,

lovers, called Nomion; that of the ladies, called Calyce; and Harpalyce, that of young girls. These two songs, by changing the sex, became also songs of love.

For particular occasions, they had the marriage song, called Hymenæa, Epithalamium; the song of Datis on merry occasions; for lamentations, the Jaleme; and Linos for funerals, and other mournful occasions. This Linos was sung also by the Ægyptians, and called by them Maneros, from the name of one of their princes, at whose burial it had been sung. By a passage of Euripides, cited by Athenæus, we may see that the Linos also might express joy.

Lastly, there were also hymns or songs in honour of the gods and heroes. Such were the Jule's of Ceres and Proserpine; the Philælia of Apollo; the upinges of Diana, &c.

This genus passed from the Greeks to the Latins, and several odes of Horace are gallant or bacchic songs. But this nation, more warlike than sensual, made, for a long time, but a trifling use of music and songs, and never approached on this point to the graces of the Greek.

It seems that music always remained rough and discordant amongst the Romans. What they sung at marriages, was rather a clamour than songs; and it cannot be presumed, that the satyrical songs of the soldiers, at the triumph of their generals, had a very agreeable melody.

The moderns have their songs also of different kinds, according to the genius and taste of each nation. But the French bore off the palm from the rest of Europe, in the art of composing them; if not for the turn and melody of the airs, at least for their wit, the grace and ingenuity of the words, tho' in general the wit and satyr, shew much better than the sentiment in such a composition. They pay more attention to this amusement, and have ever excelled in it. This happy people are always gay, turning every thing into merriment: their ladies are very gallant; the gentlemen very dissipated; and the country produces excellent wine. How can they then refrain from continually singing? We have still some ancient songs of Thibàult, Comte de Champagne, the most gallant man of his time, set to music by Guillaume de Machault; Marot has made several which remain; and thro' favour of the airs of Orlando and Claudin, we have also several of the Pleyade of Charles IX. I shall make no mention of more modern songs, by which the musicians, Lambert, du Bousset, la Garde, and others, have gained a name; and amongst whom we find as many poets as there are *Gens de Plaisir*, in a nation which is given most to it, though not all so celebrated as le Comte de Coulanges, & l'Abbe de Lattaignant. Neither have Provence and Languedoc

guedoc degenerated from their first talents. We see in these provinces an air of gaiety reign throughout, which incessantly invites the people to singing and dancing. One of Provence, they say, menaces his enemy with a song, as an Italian would attack his with a rapier. Other Countries have also their provinces for singing. In Great-Britain, it is Scotland; in Italy, it is Venice.

Our songs are of several sorts, but in general on Love or Wine, or sometimes on Satyr. The love songs are, the tender airs which are also called serious; the romances, whose character is to move the soul insensibly by the tender and lively recital of some amorous and tragic history; the pastoral and rustic songs, many of which are made for dancing, as the Musettes, the Gavots, &c.

The drinking songs are generally airs of bass, or semi-breves for the table. It is with great reason that few are made for the treble, for there is not a viler and more disgusting idea of debauchery than a drunken woman.

In regard to satyric songs, they are comprized under the name of Vaudevilles, and dart their rays indifferently on vice and virtue, by rendering them equally ridiculous; which ought to proscribe the vaudeville from the lips of persons of morality.

We have also a kind of song which is called parody. These are words adjusted as we can, on airs of the violin, or other instruments, and which are rhymed either well or ill, without paying attention to the measure of the verses, or to the character of the air, or to the sense of the words, or even often to common delicacy. (Vide Parody.)

SONOROUS. Which renders a sound, "A sonorous metal" From thence, "A sonorous body". (Vide corpo sonoro.)

Sonorous is said particularly, and with excellence of all that renders mellow, strong, clear, just sounds, and well tuned. "A sonorous bell" &c.

SOTTO VOCE. This Italian word specifies, in the places in which it is written, that we must only sing a demi-voix, or play only a *demi jeu*. Mezzo forte, and mezza voce, signify the same thing.

SOUND. When the agitation communicated to the air by the collision of a body struck by another, reaches as far as the auditive organ, it produces a sensation called noise. But there is a resounding noise called sound. Searches on the absolute sound belong to the physician. The musician examines only the relative sound. He only examines by sensible modification, and it is according to this last idea, that we enquire into it in this article.

There are three principal objects to be considered in the sound; the tone, the force, and the modification. Under each of these relations the sound is conceived as modifiable. First from flat to ſharp ; ſecondly from ſtrong to weak ; thirdly from ſharp to ſweet, or from the dull to the lively, and ſo reciprocally.

I firſt ſuppoſe, that whatever may be the nature of the ſound, that its vehicle is the air itſelf ; in the firſt place, becauſe the air is the only intermediary body of the exiſtence, which we are perfectly aſſured of, between the ſonorous body, and the auditive organ : ſince we muſt not multiply the beings without a neceſſity ; as the air is ſufficient to explain the formation of the ſound ; and, moreover, becauſe experience teaches us, that a ſonorous body renders no ſound in a place quite deprived of air.

If we would imagine another fluid, we may eaſily apply to it all that I have ſaid on the air in this article.

The reſonance of the ſound, or to ſpeak more clearly, its permanence and prolongation, can ariſe only from the duration of the agitation of the air. As long as this agitation continues, the ſhaken air inceſſantly ſtrikes the auditive organ, and by this means prolongs the ſenſation of the ſound.

But there is not a more ſimple method of conceiving this duration, than by ſuppoſing in the air vibrations which ſucceed each other, and thus renew the impreſſion every inſtant. Moreover, this agitation of the air, of whatever kind it may be, cannot be produced but by a ſimilar agitation in the parts of the ſonorous body. Moreover, it is a certain fact, that the parts of the ſonorous body undergo ſuch vibrations. If we touch the body of a violincello at the time we draw the ſound, we feel it ſhake under our hand, and we ſee very ſenſibly, the vibrations of the chord continue till the ſound is extinguiſhed.

It is the ſame thing with a bell, which we make ſound by ſtriking it with the clapper ; we feel it, we ſee it even ſhake, and we perceive the grains of ſand leap up, which are thrown on the ſurface.

If the chord looſens, or the bell burſts, there is more ſhaking and more ſound. If then, neither this bell nor this chord can communicate to the air any movements, but what themſelves have, we cannot doubt, but that the ſound produced by the vibrations of the ſonorous body, extends itſelf by ſimilar vibrations which this body communicates to the air.

All this being ſuppoſed, let us firſt examine what conſtitutes the relation of ſounds from flat to ſharp.

I. Theon, of Smyrna, ſays that Laſus of Hermione, as well as the Pythagorean Hyppaſes of Metapont, to calculate the relation of conſonances, made uſe of two ſimilar veſſels, which reſounded in uniſon. That leaving one of theſe empty, and filling a quarter of the other, the percuſſion of each produced the conſonance of a fourth ; that, then filling the ſecond a third, then again the half, the

the percussion of the second had produced the consonance of the fifth, then of the octave.

Pythagoras, according to Nichomachus and Censorinus, managed in another manner, the calculation of the same connections. He suspended, they say, different weights to the same sonorous chords, and determined the references of the different sounds, on those which he found between the hanging weights; but the calculations of Pythagoras are too just to have been made in this manner; since every one knows at present on the experience of Vincent Galilæus, that the sounds are together, not as hanging weights, but in the sub-double computation of these same weights.

Lastly, was invented the monochord, called by the ancients Canon Harmonicus, because it gave the rule of harmonic divisions. We must explain its principles.

Two chords of the same composition equal, and equally extended, form a perfect unison in every sense. If the lengths are unequal, the shortest will give a sharper sound, and make more vibrations in a given time; from whence we may conclude that the difference of sounds from sharp to flat, proceeds only by that of vibrations formed in the same space of time, by the chords or sonorous bodies which make them heard: wherefore we express the connections of sounds by the numbers of vibrations which give them.

We also know, by as certain experience, that the vibrations of the chord, equal in every other respect, are always reciprocal in the lengths. So the double chord of another, will make, at the same time only the half of the number of vibrations of the latter, and the relation of the sounds, which they will cause to be heard is called octave. If the chords are as 3 to 2, the vibrations will be as 2 to 3, and the connection of the sounds will be called fifth, &c. (Vide Interval.)

We see by this means, that with moveable bridges it is easy to form on a single chord, the divisions which produce sounds in all possible connections, whether together, or with the entire chord. This is the monochord which I have just mentioned. (Vide Monochord.)

We may render sharp or flat sounds by other means; two chords of equal length do not always form the unison, for if the one is greater or less extended than the other, it will form less vibrations in equal times, and consequently, will give a sharper sound. (Vide chord.)

It is easy to explain on these principles the construction of chord instruments, such as the Harpsichord, and the playing of Violins or Basses, which by the different impression of the fingers or moveable bridges on the chords, produces the diversity of sounds drawn from

from thoſe inſtruments. We muſt reaſon in the ſame manner for the wind inſtruments. The holes, as in the flute and haut-boy, ſerve to ſhorten them, to render the ſound more ſharp. In giving more wind, they are made to octave, and the ſound becomes ſtill ſharper. The column of air forms the ſonorous body, and the different tones of the trumpet and french-horn, have the ſame principles as the harmonious ſounds of the violincello and violin, &c. (Vide harmonic ſound.)

If we make one of the grand chords of a violin or violincello reſound with ſome force, in paſſing the fiddle-ſtick rather nearer to the bridge than ordinary, we ſhall hear diſtinctly, however little our ear may be exerciſed or attentive, beſides the ſound of the entire chord, at leaſt that of its octave, that of the octave of its 5th, and that of the double octave of its third; we ſhall even ſee ſhake and reſound all the chords, aſcending to the uniſon of thoſe. Theſe acceſſary ſounds always accompany any ſound whatſoever, but when this principal ſound is ſharp, the other are leſs ſenſible.

We call theſe the harmonies of the principal ſound; it is by them, according to Monſ. Rameau, that every ſound is appreciable, and 'tis in them that himſelf and Monſ. Tartini, have ſought the principle of all harmony, but by routs directly oppoſite. (Vide harmonic ſyſtem.)

One difficulty which remains to be explained in the theory of the ſound, is to know how two or more ſounds may be heard at the ſame time. When we hear, for inſtance, the two ſounds of the fifth, one of which forms two vibrations, whilſt the other makes three, we cannot well conceive how the ſame maſs of air may furniſh at the ſame time theſe different numbers of vibrations diſtinct from each other; and ſtill leſs, when it makes more than two ſounds together, and that they are all diſſonant with each other.

Mengoli and others manage the buſineſs by compariſons. It is the ſame thing, ſay they, as with two ſtones thrown in the water at the ſame time, and whoſe different circles lie croſs ways without confounding each other. Monſ. de Mairan, gives a more philoſophical explanation. The air, according to him, is divided into particles of different ſizes, each of which is capable of a peculiar tone, and ſuſceptible of no other; ſo that in every ſound which is formed, the particles of air analogous to it only, are ſhaken, thoſe and their harmonies, whilſt all the reſt remain tranquil, till moved in their turn by ſounds correſpondent to them. So that we hear at the ſame time two ſounds, as we ſee two colours; becauſe, being produced by different parts, they affect the organ in different points.

This ſyſtem is ingenious, but the imagination is with difficulty united to the infinity of the particles in the air, differing in ſize, and

mobility,

mobility, which ought to be expanded in each point of the ſpace, to be always ready on neceſſity, to render an infinity of all the poſſible ſounds in every place. When they are once arrived at the drum of the ear, we have ſtill leſs conception, how, in ſtriking ſeveral together, they can produce a ſhake capable of conveying the ſenſation of each in particular to the brain. It appears, that this difficulty has been rather removed than reſolved. They alledge in vain the example of light, whoſe rays meet in a point without confounding the objects; for, beſides that one difficulty is not reſolved by another, the ſimile is not exact, ſince the object is ſeen without exciting in the air a movement ſimilar to that which a ſonorous body muſt occaſion to be heard. Mengoli ſeems deſirous of preventing this objection, by ſaying that the maſſes of the air, charged, as it were, with different ſounds, ſtrike the drum only ſucceſſively, alternatively, and each in its turn, without paying too great attention, how he ſhould employ thoſe, which are obliged to wait till the firſt have diſcharged their office; or without explaining how the ear, ſtruck with ſo many ſucceſſive impreſſions, can diſtinguiſh thoſe which belong to each ſound. In regard to the harmonies which accompany any ſound ſoever, they offer rather a new caſe of the precedent difficulty, than a ſeparate embarraſſment; for as ſoon as it is explained how many ſounds may be heard at a time, we may eaſily explain the phœnomena of harmonies. For inſtance, let us ſuppoſe that a ſound puts in motion the particles of air ſuſceptible of that ſame ſound, and the particles ſuſceptible of ſharper ſounds, ad infinitum, from theſe different particles, there will then be ſounds, whoſe vibration beginning and finiſhing exactly with the ſonorous body, will be continually aided and renewed by thoſe of the other; theſe particles will be thoſe which give the uniſon. Next comes the octave, whoſe two vibrations concording with one of the principal ſounds, are aſſiſted and enforced by it from two to two: conſequently, the octave will be ſenſible, but leſs than the uniſon. Then comes the twelfth, or octave of the fifth, which forms three preciſe vibrations, whilſt the fundamental ſound makes one; wherefore, receiving a freſh ſtroke only at each third vibration, the twelfth will be leſs ſenſible than the octave, which receives this freſh ſtroke at the ſecond. By following the ſame gradation, we find the concourſe of vibrations more ſlow, the ſtrokes leſs renewed, and conſequently the harmonies always leſs ſenſible, until the references are compoſed to that point; that the idea of the concurrence not ſufficiently frequent, be effaced, and the vibrations having the time to be extinguiſhed before they are renewed, the harmonic is no longer heard at all.

Laſtly, when the reference ceaſes to be rational, the vibrations no longer concur. Thoſe of the ſharper ſound, always contrary, are

are very soon stifled by those of the chord, and this sharp sound is absolutely dissonant and null.

Such is the reason why the first harmonies are heard, and all the rest are not so. But I have written already too much on the first quality of the sound. Let us now pass on to the rest.

II. The force of the sound depends on that of the vibrations of the sonorous body, the more these vibrations are strong, the more vigorous the sound is, and is heard at the greater distance. When the chord is sufficiently extended, and the voice or instrument not too much forced, the vibrations always remain isochronous, and consequently the tone continues the same, whether we strengthen or weaken the sound; but in striking too forcibly with the bow, in slackening the chord too much, in singing too high, we may make the vibrations lose the necessary isochronism for the identity of the tone; and this is one of the reasons, why, in the French music, wherein the grand merit is to scream, we are more subject to sing false than in the Italian, where the voice is moderated with more sweetness.

The quickness of the sound, which would seem to depend on its force, does not so. This quickness is always equal, and constant, unless accelerated or retarded by the wind; that is to say, that the sound, strong or weak, will be always uniformly extended; and in two seconds will always go twice the distance it would do in one. According to Halley and Flampstead, the sound in England goes 1070 French feet in a second, and at Peru, 174 fathoms, according to Monf. de la Condamine. P. Mersenne, and Gassendi have assured us that a favourable or contrary wind neither accelerates or retards the sound; but since the experience that Derham and the Academy of Sciences have made on this subject, this passes as an error.

Without slackening the motion the sound is weakened in extending itself, and this weakening, if the propagation is free, if it is not prevented by any obstacle, or slackened by the wind, ordinarily follows the reason of the square of distances.

III. In regard to the difference, which is found also between the sounds by the quality of the modification, it is evident, that it holds neither to the degree of elevation, nor even to that of the force. It will be in vain for a hautboy to place itself in unison with a flute, it will be in vain to sweeten the sound to the same degree. The sound of the flute will always have, a *je ne sais quoi* of mellow and sweet, that of the hautboy something rude and sharp, which will prevent the ear from confounding them; without mentioning the diversity of the modification of the voice. (Vide Voice.)

There is not an instrument which has not its peculiar tone, which has no connection with that of another, and the organ alone has

twenty

twenty methods of playing all of a different modification. No one, however, that I know of has examined the ſound in this particular; which as well as the reſt will perhaps be found to have ſome difficulties; for the quality of the modification cannot depend, either from the number of vibrations, which forms the degree from flat to ſharp, or from the greatneſs or force of theſe ſame vibrations, which forms the degree from ſtrong to weak. We muſt then find in the ſonorous body a third different cauſe from theſe two, to explain this third quality of the ſound, and its differences; which perhaps, is not too eaſy.

The three principal qualities which I have mentioned enter all, though in different proportions, into the object of muſic, which is ſound in general.

In effect, the compoſer does not only conſider if the ſound which he uſes ought to be high or low, flat, or ſharp, but if they ought to be ſtrong or weak, diſguſting or ſweet, dull or pleaſing: and he diſtributes them to different inſtruments and different voices, in recitatives or choruſſes, at the extremities or in the medium of the inſtruments or voices, with the dolce and forte, according as theſe are ſuitable.

But it is true, that it is only in the compariſon of ſounds from flat to ſharp, that the whole harmonic ſcience conſiſts; ſo that, as the number of ſounds is infinite, we may ſay in the ſame ſenſe, that this ſcience is infinite in its objects. We conceive no preciſe ſounds to the extent of ſounds from flat to ſharp, and however ſmall the interval may be, which is between two ſounds, we ſhall always conceive it diviſible by a third ſound; but nature and art have limited this infinity in the practice of muſic. We very ſoon find in inſtruments, the bounds of practicable ſounds, as well in flat as in ſharp. Lengthen or ſhorten a ſonorous chord to a certain point, it will have no more a ſound. We can neither augment or diminiſh, at will, the capacity of a flute, or the pipe of an organ, neither its length. There are bounds paſſed which neither can any longer reſound. The breathing has alſo its meaſure and its laws. When too weak, it renders no ſound, when too ſtrong, it produces only a piercing cry, which it is impoſſible to appreciate. Laſtly, it is agreed, by a thouſand experiences, that all ſenſible ſounds are confined within a certain latitude, paſſed which, either too flat or too ſharp, they are no longer perceived, or become inappreciable to the ear. Monſ. Euler has, in ſome reſpects, fixed its limits; and according to his obſervations, ſhewn by Monſ. Diderot, in his principles of the acouſtic, all ſenſible ſounds are comprized between the numbers 30 and 7552; that is to ſay, that, according to this great geometrician, the flatteſt ſound perceptible to the ear forms 30 vibrations a ſecond, and the sharpest 7552 vibrations at the same time; an interval, which nearly comprehends eight octaves.

On the other hand, we see by the harmonic generation of sounds, that amidst their infinity, there are very few which can be admitted into the harmonious system. For all those which do not form consonances with the fundamental sounds, or which do not arise mediately or immediately, from the differences of these consonances, ought to be proscribed from the system. This is the reason, that however perfect ours may be supposed at present, it is however bounded to twelve sounds only in the extent of an octave; from which twelve, all the other octaves contain no more than repliques. If we chuse to reckon all these repliques for so many different sounds, in multiplying them by the number of octaves, to which the extent of appreciable sounds is confined, we shall find ninety-six in all, as the greatest number of practicable sounds in our music on the same fundamental sound.

We could not reckon, with the same precision, the number of sounds practicable in ancient music. The Greeks formed, as it were, as many systems of music as they had different methods of tuning their tetrachords. It appears, by reading their treatises of music, that the number of these methods was great, and perhaps undetermined. Moreover, each particular concord changed the sounds of half the system, that is, of two moveable chords in each tetrachord. So that we plainly see, that they had sounds in a single method of concord; but we cannot justly calculate how much this number was multiplied in all the changes of genus and mode which introduced new sounds.

In regard to their tetrachords, they distinguished the sounds into two general classes, viz. the stable and fixed sounds, whose concord never changed; and the moveable sounds, whose concord changed with the nature of the genus. The first were eight in all, viz. the two extremes of each tetrachord, and the chord proslambanomenos; the second were also at least eight in number, sometimes nine or ten, because two adjoining sounds were sometimes confounded in one, and sometimes separated.

In the pycni genera, they divided the stable sounds into two kinds; one of which contained three sounds, called apycni, because they formed neither semi-tones, or smaller intervals in flat; these three sounds apycni, were the proslambanomenos, the nete synnemenon, and the nete hyperboleon. The other kind took the name of sounds barypycni, because they formed the flat of the smaller intervals: The sounds barypycni were five in number, viz. the hypate hypaton, the hypate meson, the mesis, the paramesis, and the nete diezeugmenon.

The

the moveable tones were ſubdivided in the ſame manner into meſophycni ſounds, which were alſo five in number, viz. The ſecond in aſcending of each tetrachord; and in five other ſounds called oxiphycni, which were the third in aſcending of each tetrachord. (Vide Tetrachord.)

In regard to the twelve ſounds of the modern ſyſtem, their concord never change, and they continue immoveable. Broſſard pretends, that they are all moveable, founding it on their being to be changed by dieſis or B flat; but it is one thing to change the chord, and another to change the concord of the chord.

FIXED SOUND. To have what we call a fixed ſound, we muſt be aſſured, that this ſound would always be the ſame, in all times and in all places. Moreover, we muſt not think it ſufficient for this purpoſe, to have a pipe, for inſtance, of a determined length; for firſt, the pipe always continuing the ſame, the weight of the air will nevertheleſs change; the ſound will alter and become flatter or ſharper according as the air is lighter or heavier. For the ſame reaſon, the ſound of the ſame pipe will again change with the column of the atmoſphere, according as this ſame pipe is raiſed or lowered, in mountains or in vallies.

In the ſecond place, this pipe, whatever may be its compoſition, will be ſubject to the variations that heat and cold cauſes in the dimenſions of every body. The pipe ſhortening or lengthening itſelf, will become proportionally ſharper or flatter; and from theſe two combined cauſes, comes the difficulty of having a fixed ſound, and the almoſt impoſſibility of being aſſured of the ſame ſound, in two places at the ſame time, or twice in the ſame place.

If we could reckon exactly the vibrations which a ſound makes in a given time, we might, by the ſame number of vibrations, be aſſured of the identity of the ſound; but this calculation being impoſſible, we can only certify the identity of the ſound by that of the inſtruments which give it, viz. The pipe, in regard to its dimenſion; and the air, as to its weight. Monſ. Sauveur propoſed, for this purpoſe, a method, which by experience did not ſucceed. Monſ. Diderot has ſince propoſed ſome more practicable, and which conſiſts in graduating a pipe of a ſufficient length, that its diviſions may be juſt and ſenſible, in compoſing it by two moveable parts, by which it may be lengthened or ſhortened, according to the dimenſions proportional to the alterations of the air, expreſſed by the thermometer, in regard to their temperature, and by the barometer as to their weight.

Vide the principles of acouſtic by that author to form a judgment of it.

FUNDAMENTAL SOUND. A fundamental ſound is that which ſerves as a foundation to the concord. (Vide Concord,) or to the tone. (Vide Tone.)

Fundamental bass, is that which serves as a foundation to harmony. (Vide Fundamental Bass.)

A fundamental concord is that whose bass is fundamental, and whose sounds are arranged according to the order of their generation; but as this order removes the parts extremely, we connect them by combinations or variations; and provided that the bass continues the same, the concord does not on that account fail to bear the name of fundamental.

Such is, for instance, this concord ut mi sol, confined in an interval of 5th, whereas in the order of its generation ut sol mi, it comprehends a 10th, and even a 17th, since the fundamental ut is not the 5th of sol, but the octave of that 5th.

HARMONIC SOUNDS. A singular kind of sounds, which are drawn from certain instruments, such as the violin and the violincello, by a particular motion of the fiddle-stick, which is drawn nearer to the bridge, and the finger lightly placed on certain divisions of the chord. Their sounds are very different for their modifications and for the tone, from what they would be, if the finger was constantly fixed. In regard to the tone, for instance, they will give the 5th, when they would have given the 3d, the 3d, when they would give the 6th, &c. As to the modifications, they are much sweeter than those which are drawn full from the same division, by carrying the chord towards the sleeve, and on account of this sweetness, they are called fluted sounds. One must, to have a a clear judgment of them, have heard Monf. Mondonville draw on his violin, or Monf. Bertaud on his violincello, the consequences of these beautiful sounds. By sliding the finger slightly from sharp to flat, from the middle of a chord which we touch at the same time with the bow in the aforesaid manner, we hear distinctly a succession of harmonic sounds from flat to sharp; which very much astonishes those unskilled in the theory of them.

The principle on which this theory is founded, is, that a chord being divided into two commensurable parts together, and consequently with the entire chord, if the obstacle which is placed at the point of division hinders only imperfectly the communication of vibrations from one part to another, every time that the chord is sounded in this state, it will not render the sound of the entire chord, nor that of its greater part, but that of the smaller part, if it measures exactly the other; or, if it does not measure it, the sound of the greatest aliquot common to these two parts.

Let a chord 6 be divided into two parts 4 and 2, the harmonic sound will resound by the length of the small part 2, which is aliquot of the greater part 4; but if the chord 5 is divided by 2 and 3, then as the small part does not measure the greater, the harmonic sound will only resound, according to the half 1 of this same

ſame ſmaller part, which half is the greateſt common meaſure of the two parts 3 and 2, and of the whole chord 5.

By means of this law drawn from obſervation, and conformable to the tryals made by Monſ. Sauveur, at the Academy of Sciences, all the marvellous diſappears. With a very ſimple calculation, we aſſign to each degree the harmonic ſound which anſwers to it. In regard to the finger ſliding the length of the chord, it gives only a continuance of harmonic ſounds, which ſucceed each other rapidly in the order they ought to have according to that of the diviſions on which we paſs the finger ſucceſſively, and the points which form no exact diviſions, or which form thoſe that are too compoſed, give no ſenſible or appreciable ſound.

A Table of Harmonic Sounds ſenſible and appreciable on the Violincello.

The chord á vidi	gives	The uniſon.
The minor third		The 19th or double octave of the fifth.
The major third		The 17th or double octave of the ſame major third.
The fourth		The double octave.
The fifth		The 12th or octave of the ſame fifth.
The minor ſixth		The triple octave.
The major ſixth		The 17th major or double octave of the third.
The octave		The octave.

We here find a table of harmonic ſounds, which may facilitate the ſearch of them, to thoſe who deſire to practice them. The firſt column denotes the ſounds which the diviſions of the inſtruments would render when touch'd in full; and the ſecond, the fluted ſounds correſponding when the chord is harmonically touch'd.

After the firſt octave, that is, after the middle of the chord, advancing towards the bridge, we again find the ſame harmonic ſounds in the ſame order, on the ſame diviſions of the ſharpeſt octave, that is, the nineteenth on the minor tenth, the ſeventeenth on the major tenth, &c.

I have made, in this table, no mention of the harmonic ſounds relative to the ſecond and ſeventh; firſt, becauſe the diviſions which form them, having only very ſmall aliquots together, would render their ſounds too ſharp to be agreeable, and too difficult to be drawn by the ſtroke of the fiddle ſtick; and moreover, becauſe one muſt enter into the ſub-diviſions too much extended, which cannot be admitted but in practice; for the harmonic ſound of the major tone would be the twenty-third, or the triple octave of the ſecond; and the harmonic of the minor tone would be the twenty-fourth, or triple octave of the minor third: But what ear is fine enough, and what hand ſufficiently juſt, to diſtinguiſh and touch, at will, a minor or a major tone?

The whole play of the marine-trumpet is in harmonic ſounds, which is the reaſon that we cannot draw every kind of ſound from it with eaſe.

TO SOUND. We ſay, in compoſition, that a note ſounds on the baſs, when it enters into the concord and forms a harmony, allowing the difference of the notes, which are thoſe of taſte, and ſerve only to figure, but have no ſound. We alſo ſay, to ſound a note, or a concord, to expreſs the ſtriking or cauſing a ſound to be heard, the harmony of that note or that concord.

SOURDINE. A ſmall inſtrument of copper or ſilver, which is applied to the bridge of a violin or violincello, to render the ſounds weaker, by intercepting and preventing the vibrations of the entire body of the inſtrument. The ſourdine, by weakening the ſounds, changes their modification, and gives them an exceeding moving and mournful character. The French muſicians, who think that a ſweet play produces the ſame effect as the ſourdine, and who do not admire the trouble of placing and diſplacing, make no uſe of it; but they make uſe of it with great effect in all the orcheſtras of Italy; and it is becauſe the word ſordini is found very often in their ſymphonies, that I have made an article of it. There are ſordini alſo for the French-horn, for the harpſichord, &c.

SPACE. A fair interval, or diſtance, which is found in the ſtave between a line, and that which follows it immediately above or below. There are four ſpaces in the five lines, and two beſides, the one above, the other below the entire ſtave: We find, when neceſſary, theſe two indefinite ſpaces, by additional lines added above or below, the which augment the extent of the ſtave, or furniſh new ſpaces. Each of theſe ſpaces divides the interval of two lines which terminate it, into two diatonic degrees, viz. one from the inferior line to the ſpace, and the other from the ſpace to the ſuperior line. (Vide Stave.)

SPICCATO. An Italian word, which, written on muſic, denotes ſtrong and well detached ſounds.

SPONDAULA. Was, amongſt the ancients, a player on the flute, or ſome other ſimilar inſtrument, who, while the ſacrifice was offered, played in the ear of the prieſt ſome ſuitable air, to prevent his liſtening to any thing which might interrupt him.

This word is formed from the Greek σπουδὶς, a libation, and ἀυλὸς, a Flute.

SPONDIASM. Was, in the moſt ancient Greek muſic, an alteration in the harmonic genus, when a chord was accidentally elevated

elevated three diesis's above its ordinary concord, so that the spondiasm was precisely the contrary to the Eclysis.

STABLE. The stable chords or sounds were, besides the chord proslambanomenos, the two extremes of each tetrachord, which extremes sounding the diatepason or fourth together, the concord never changed, as did that of the chords in the middle, which were extended or slackened, according to the genera, and on that account were called moveable chords or sounds.

STAVE. The stave or line of music is composed of five parallel lines, on or between which the different positions of the notes mark their intervals or degrees. The stave of church-music has only four lines: It formerly had eight, according to Kircher, each marked with a letter of the gamut; so that there was only one conjoint degree from one line to another: When the degrees were doubled, by placing notes in this manner in the intervals, the stave of eight lines being reduced to four, was found of the same extent as before.

To this number of five lines in music, and four in that of the church, are added, additional or accidental lines, when necessary, and the notes pass the extent of the stave above or below. This extent, in a stave of music, is in the whole of eleven notes forming ten diatonic degrees, in church-music of nine notes forming eight degrees. (Vide Cleff, Notes, Lines.)

STOP. Is the termination of the phrase, on which termination the air reposes, more or less perfectly. The stop cannot be established but by a full cadence; if the cadence is avoided, there can be no true stop: for it is impossible for the ear to repose on a dissonance. We see by this means, that there are precisely as many kinds of stops, as sorts of full cadences (Vide Cadence,) and these different stops produce in music, the effect of the punctuation in discourse.

Some confound, very improperly, the stops with the silences, tho' these two things are very different.

STRUCK. This is the time when the hand or foot is lowered, and when we beat to mark the measure. (Vide Thesis.) We strike with the foot in general only the first time of each measure, but those who cut in two, the measure of four, strike also the third. In striking the measure with the hand, the French never beat but in the first time, and mark the rest by different movements of the hand; but the Italians strike the two first of the measure of three, and raise the third. They strike in the same manner the two first in the measure of four, and raise the two others. These movements are more simple, and appear more convenient,

STYLE. The distinctive character of composition or execution. This character varies greatly, according to the countries, the taste ot the people, the genius of authors, &c. according to matter, place, ſubject, expreſſion, &c.

We ſay, in France, the ſtyle of Lully, of Rameau, of Mondonville, &c. In Germany, the ſtyle of Haſſe, of Gluck, of Graun. In Italy, the ſtyle of Leo, of Pergoleſis, of Jomelli, of Buranello. The ſtyle of church-muſic is not the ſame as that for the theatre or a private room. The ſtyle of German compoſitions is lively, divided, but harmonious. That of the French compoſition is flat, rough, ill cadenced, monotonous. That of the Italian compoſitions, flouriſhing, pleaſing, energetic.

The dramatic or imitative ſtyle is proper for exciting or painting the paſſions. The ſtyle of the church is ſerious, majoſtic, grave. The ſtyle of the Motet, where the artiſt affects to ſhew himſelf as ſuch, is more claſſic and ingenious, than energetic and affecting. The hyporchematic ſtyle is peculiar to joy, pleaſure, dancing, filled with lively movements, gay and well expreſſed. The ſymphonic or inſtrumental ſtyle. As every inſtrument has its touch, its fingering, its character peculiar to it, it alſo has its ſtyle. The meliſmatic or natural ſtyle, which is firſt preſented to perſons who have not yet ſtudied. The ſtyle of fantaſy, little united, filled with ideas, free from every conſtraint. The choraic or dancing ſtyle, which is divided into as many different branches as there are characters in dancing.

The ancients had alſo their different ſtyles. (Vide Mode and Melœpea.)

SUB-DOMINANT. A name given, by Monſ. Rameau, to the fourth note of the tone, which is, conſequently, in the ſame interval of the tonic in deſcending, as is the dominant in aſcending. This denomination happens from the affinity which this author finds by variation, between the minor mode of the ſub-dominant, and the major mode of the tonic. (Vide Harmony.)

SUB-MEDIANT. Is alſo, in Monſ. Rameau's Vocabulary, the name of the ſixth note of the tone. But this ſub-mediant, as it ought to be in the ſame interval of the tonic below, as is the mediant above, ſhould form a major third under this tonic, and conſequently minor third on the ſub-dominant, and it is on this analogy that the ſame Monſ. Rameau eſtabliſhes the principal of the minor mode; but it would follow from thence, that the major mode of a tonic, and the minor mode of its ſub-dominant, muſt have a great affinity; which is no ſuch thing: ſince, on the contrary, it is very ſeldom that we paſs from one of theſe two modes to another, and that the almoſt entire ſcale is altered by ſuch a modulation.

I may be deceived in the acceptation of theſe two precedent words, not having Monſ. Rameau's writings before me whilſt I write this article. He, perhaps, underſtands ſimply by ſub-dominant,

nant, the note, which is a degree below the dominant; and by sub-mediant, the note which is a degree below the mediant. What keeps me in suspense between these two senses, is, that in each the sub-dominant is the same note fa for the tone of ut, but it would not be the same thing with the sub-mediant: It would be la in the first sense, and re in the second. The reader may verify which of the two is Mons. Rameau's: what may be depended on, is, that what I have given is preferable for the use of composition.

SUBJECT. A term of composition. This is the principal part of the design, the idea which serves as a foundation to all the rest. (Vide Design.)

All the other parts require only art and labuor: this depends only on the genius, and, tis in this, that invention entirely consists. The principal subjects in music, produce Rondeau's, Imitations, Fugues, &c. (Vide those Words.)

A barren and cold composer, after having discovered with difficulty some scattered subject, only turns it and changes it from modulation to modulation; but the artist who has fire, and a clear imagination, without suffering his subject to be forgotten, gives it a new air every time it is represented.

SUPERFICIES. A combination, either of the sounds of a concord, beginning by one of those sounds, and taking the rest according to their natural connection, or, from the touches of the keys which form the same concord. From whence it follows, that a concord may have as many superficies as there are sounds which compose it, for each may be the first in its turn.

The perfect concord ut mi sol, has 3 superficies. By the first all the fingers are ranged by thirds, and the tonic is under the index; by the second mi sol ut, there is a fourth between the two last fingers, and the tonic is under the last; by the third sol ut mi, the fourth is between the index and fourth finger, and the tonic is under the latter. (Vide Variation.)

As the dissonant accords have generally four sounds, they have also four superficies, which may be found with the same facility.

SUPERSUS. A name formerly given to trebles when they were very sharp.

SUPERNUMERARY. Was the name of the lowest chord in the Greek system; they called it also in their language proslambanomenos. (Vide that Word.)

SUPPOSITION. This word has two senses in music. First, when several notes ascend or fall diatonically in a part on the same note of another part; these diatonic notes cannot then all form a harmony, or enter at the same time into the same concord. There are some then counted for nothing, and those are the notes foreign to harmony which are called notes by supposition.

The general rule is, when the notes are equal, that all thofe which ftrike on the ftrong time bear the harmony, thofe which pafs on the weak time are notes of fuppofition, which are placed for the air only, and to form conjoint degrees. Take notice that by ftrong and weak time, I underftand lefs the principal times of the meafure than the parts themfelves of each time. So, if there are two equal notes in a fame time, it is the firft which bears the harmony: the fecond is of fuppofition. If the time is compofed of four equal notes, the 1ft and 3d bear the harmony, and the 2d and 4th are the notes of fuppofition, &c.

Sometimes this order is perverted: we pafs the firft note by fuppofition, and we make the fecond borne, but then the powers of this fecond note are generally augmented by a point at the expence of the firft.

All this always fuppofes a diatonic movement by conjoint degrees; for when the degrees are disjoint, there is no fuppofition, and all the notes ought to enter in the concord.

Secondly, we call concords by fuppofition, thofe where the thorough bafs adds or fuppofes a new found below the fundamental bafs: which occafions that fuch concords always exceed the extent of the octave. The diffonance of concords by fuppofition fhould be always prepared by fyncope's, and faved in defcending diatonically on the founds of a concord, under which the fame fuppofed bafs may act as fundamental bafs, or, at leaft as thorough bafs. Which occafions the concords by fuppofition, well examined, may all pafs as pure fufpenfions. (Vide Sufpenfion.)

There are three forts of concords by fuppofition. All are concords of the 7th: The firft, when the added found is a third below the fundamental, fuch is the concord of the 9th, if the concord of the 9th is formed by the mediant added below the fenfible concord in the minor mode, the concord then takes the name of fuperfluous 5th.

The fecond kind is when the fuppofed found is a 5th below the fundamental, as in the concord of 4th, or 11th, if the concord is fenfible and the tonic fuppofed, the concord takes the name of fuperfluous 7th.

The third kind is that where the fuppofed found is below a concord of diminifhed 7th, if it is a third below, that is, that the fuppofed found be the dominant, the concord is called concord of fecond minor and third major. It is very little in ufe, if the found added is a fifth below, or that this found be the mediant, the concord is called concord of 4th, or fuperfluous 5th, and if it is a 7th below, that is, the tonic itfelf, the concord takes the name of minor 6th and fuperfluous 7th.

In regard to the variations of these different concords, where the supposed sound is transported in the superior parts, being admitted only by licence, they ought only to be practised with choice and circumspection. We may find at the word concord all those which may be tolerated.

SUSPENSION. There is suspension in every concord on the bass, from which we sustain one or more sounds of the precedent concord, before we pass to those which belong to it; as if, when the bass passes from the tonic to the dominant, I prolong some moments on that dominant, the concord of the tonic which precedes it before, resolving it on its own, it is a suspension.

There are suspensions which are cyphered and enter into harmony.

When they are dissonant, they are always concords by supposition, other suspensions are only of taste; but whatever may be their nature, we ought always to subject them to the three following rules.

I. The suspension ought always to be made on the stroke of the measure, or at least on a strong time.

II. It ought always to be diatonically resolved, whether in ascending or falling, that is, that each part, which has suspended, ought not immediately to ascend or fall, but a degree to arrive at the natural concord of the note of the bass, which has borne the suspension.

III. Every suspension cyphered ought to be saved in descending, except the single sensible note, which is saved in rising.

By the method of these precautions there is no suspension but what may be practised with success, because in that case the ear, presenting on the bass the movement of the parts, supposes beforehand the concord which follows. But it belongs to the taste alone to choose and distribute, a propos, the suspensions in singing and harmony.

TO SUSTAIN, Is to make the sounds continue exactly their whole powers, without suffering them to be extinguished before the end, as musicians very often do, and particularly symphonists.

SYLLABLE. This name has been given by some of the Ancients, and Nichomachus amongst the rest, to the consonance of the fourth, which they commonly called diatessaron. Which also proves by etymology, that they looked upon the tetrachord as we do on the octave, as comprehending all the radical or composed sound.

SYMPHONIST. A composer of Church music. This term is become technical since it has been used by Monf. L'Abbe le Beuf.

SYMPHONY, This word, formed from the Greek σὺν with, and φωνὴ sound, signifies, in ancient music, that union of the sounds which

which form a concert. It is a ſentiment received, and, I believe demonſtrated, that the Greeks underſtood not the harmony in the ſenſe which we at preſent give to this word.

Their ſymphony formed no concords, but reſulted from the concurrence of ſeveral voices or inſtruments, or of inſtruments joined with the voice, ſinging or playing the ſame part. This was done two ways, where the whole concerted in uniſon, and the ſymphony was then more particularly called homophony, where the half of the concertants was in the octave, or even in the double octave of the other, and this was called antiphony. We find the proof of theſe diſtinctions in the problems of Ariſtotle, Section 19.

At preſent, the word ſymphony is applied to all inſtrumental muſic, as well for pieces which are deſtined only for inſtruments, as Sonata's and Concerto's, as for thoſe, where the inſtruments are found mixed with the voice, as in our Opera's, and in ſeveral ſorts of muſic. We diſtinguiſh vocal muſic into muſic without ſymphony, which has at leaſt a treble of inſtruments, violins, flutes, or hautboys. We ſay of a piece, that it is in grand ſymphony, when, beſides the baſs and treble it has alſo two other inſtrumental parts, viz. tenor, and 5th of the violin.

The muſic of the King's Chapel, that of ſeveral Churches, and of the Opera-Houſe, are almoſt always in grand ſymphony.

SYNAPHE. The conjunction of two tetrachards, or more preciſely the reſonance of 4th or diateſſaron, which is made between the homologous chords of two conjoint tetrachords. Wherefore, there are three ſynaphes on the ſyſtem of the Greeks. The one between the tetrachord of the hypates, and that of the meſis: the other, betwixt the tetrachord of the meſis and that of the conjoint, and the third between the tetrachord of the diſjoint and that of the hyperboles. (Vide Syſtem, Tetrachord.)

SYNAULIA. A concert of ſeveral muſicians, who, in Ancient muſic, played and anſwered each other alternatively on flutes, without any union of the voice.

Monſ. Malcolm, who doubts whether the Ancients had a muſic compoſed only for inſtruments, does not fail to cite this ſynaulia from Athenæus, and he is in the right; for theſe ſynaulias were no more than a vocal muſic played by inſtruments.

SYNCOPE. A prolongation on the ſtrong time of a ſound begun on the weak time; wherefore, every ſyncopated note is in counter time, and every collection of ſyncopated notes is a movement in counter time.

We muſt take notice that the ſyncope does not exiſt leſs in harmony, tho' the ſound which forms it, inſtead of being continued ſhould be ſtruck by two or more notes, provided that the diſpoſition of theſe notes which repeat the ſame ſound, be conformable to the definition.

The

The syncope has its uses in melody, for the expression and taste of singing, but its principal utility is in the harmony for the practice of dissonances. The first part of the syncope serves for the preparation. The dissonance is struck on the second, and in a succession of dissonances, the first part of the following syncope serves at the same time to save the dissonance which precedes, and and to prepare that which follows.

Syncope is from σὺν with and κόπτω I cut, because the syncope cuts off from each time, opposing, as it were with the other. Mons. Rameau derives this word from the noise of the sounds which knock against each other in some kind of dissonance; but the syncopes are anterior to our harmony, and there are often syncopes without a dissonance.

SYNNEMENON. Is the name which the Greeks gave to their third tetrachord, when it was conjoint with the second, and divided from the fourth; when on the contrary, it was conjoint to the fourth and divided from the second, this same tetrachord took the name of diezeugmenon. (Vide that Word.)

SYNNEMENON DIATONOS. Was, in Ancient music, the third chord of the tetrachord synnemenon in the diatonic genus, and as that third chord was the same as the second of the tetrachord of disjoints, it bore also in this tetrachord the name of trite diezeugmenon. (Vide Trite, System, Tetrachord.)

This same chord, in the two other genera, bore also the name of the genus in which it was used, but then it was not confounded with the trite diezeugmenon. (Vide Genus.)

SYNTONIC. Is the epithet by which Aristoxenes distinguishes that of the two spaces of the ordinary diatonic genus, whose tetrachord is divided into a semi-tone and two equal tones; whereas in the flat diatonic, after the semi-tone, the first interval is three quarters of a tone, and the other five. (Vide Genus, Tetrachord.)

Besides the syntonic genus of Aristoxenes, called also diatono diatonic, Ptolomy establishes another, by which he divides the tetrachord into three intervals. The first of a semi-tone major; the second of a tone major; and the third of a tone minor. This syntonic diotonic of Ptolomy remains, and it is also the only diatonic of Didymus, allowing this difference, that Didymus having placed this minor tone in flat, and the major tone in sharp, Ptolomy varied that order.

We may see, with a cast of the eye the difference of these two syntonic genera, by the connections of the intervals which compose the tetrachord in each.

The Syntonic of Ariſtoxenes $\frac{3}{20}+\frac{6}{20}+\frac{6}{20}=\frac{3}{4}$

The Syntonic of Ptolomy $\frac{15}{16}+\frac{8}{9}+\frac{9}{10}=\frac{3}{4}$

There were alſo other ſyntonics, and they reckoned 4 principal kinds, viz. The ancient, the reformed, the temperated, and the equal. But it is loſing time, and abuſing that of the reader, to examine every one of theſe diviſions

SYNTONO LYDIAN. The name of one of the modes in ancient muſic. Plato ſays, that the mixo-lydian modes and ſyntono-lydian are peculiar to tears.

We ſee in the firſt book of Ariſtides Quintilian a liſt of the different modes which we muſt not confound with the tones which bear the ſame name, and which I have ſpoken of at the word mode, to be conformable to the modern cuſtom introduced very improperly by Glarean. The modes were different methods of varying the order of intervals. The tones differed as at preſent by their fundamental chords. It is in the firſt ſenſe that we muſt underſtand the ſyntono lydian mode of which Plato ſpeaks, and of which, beſides, we have no other explanation.

SYSTEM. This word having ſeveral acceptations, will oblige me to render it a very long article.

To begin by the proper and technical ſenſe, I ſhall firſt ſay that the name of ſyſtem was given to every compoſed interval, or conceived as compoſed of other ſmaller intervals, which conſidered as the elements of the ſyſtem, are called diaſteme.

There are an infinity of different intervals, and conſequently an infinity alſo of poſſible ſyſtems. To confine myſelf here to ſomething real, I ſhall only ſpeak of the harmonic ſyſtems, that is of thoſe, whoſe elements are either conſonances, or differences of conſonances, or differences of thoſe differences. (Vide Interval.)

The ancients divided the ſyſtems into general and particular. They called *particular ſyſtem*, all that was compoſed at leaſt of two intervals; ſuch as are or may be conceived, the octave, the 5th, the 4th, the 6th, and even the third. I have ſpoken of the particular ſyſtems at the word interval.

The general ſyſtems, which were more commonly called diagrams, were formed by the ſum of all the particular ſyſtems, and conſequently comprehended all the ſounds uſed in muſic. I confine myſelf here to the examination of their ſyſtem in the diatonic genus; the difference of the chromatic and enharmonic being ſufficiently explained in their articles.

We

We ought to judge of the condition and progress of the ancient system, by those of the instruments destined for their execution.

For these instruments accompanying the voice in unison, and playing all which they sung, must form as many different sounds as there entered into the system.

The chords of these first instruments were always touched, a vide, where were then as many chords necessary as the system contained sounds, and 'tis by this means that, since the origin of music, we may determine on the number of the chords of the instrument, the number of the sounds in the system.

The whole system of the Greeks was at first composed only of four sounds at the most, which formed the concord of their lyre or cithara. These four sounds according to some, were by conjoint degrees, according to others they were not diatonic; but the two extremes sounded the octave, and the two middle divided it into a fourth on each side, and a tone in the middle, in the following manner;

Ut ——— Trite Diezeugmenon
Sol ——— Lichanos Meson
Fa ——— Parhypate Meson
Ut ——— Parhypate Hypaton

This is what Boetius calls the tetrachord of Mercury, tho' Diodorus advances that Mercury's lyre had only three chords. This system did not long continue confined to so few sounds. Chorebe, Son of Athis, King of Lydia, added a 5th chord; Hyagnis a 6th; Terpander a 7th to equal the number of the planets; and lastly, Lychaon of Samos, an 8th.

This is what Boetius says: but Pliny says that Terpander having added three chords to the four ancient, played first on the cithara with 7 chords; that Simonides joined to it an 8th, and Timotheus a 9th. Nicomachus the Gerasinian attributes this 8th chord to Pythagoras, the 9th to Theophrastus of Pieria, then a 10th to Hystæus of Colophon, and an 11th to Timotheus of Milet. Pherecrates in Plutarch makes a more rapid progress to the system; he gives 12 chords to the system of Menalippedes, and as many to that of Timotheus. And as Pherecrates was contemporary with this great musician, supposing him effectually to have said what Plutarch makes him say, his witnessing is of great weight on a fact which he had before his eyes.

But how can we be assured of the truth amid so many contradictions, either in the doctrine of authors, or in the order of facts as they are reported? For instance, the tetrachord of Mercury evidently gives the octave on the diapason. How then could it be, that after the addition of three chords, the whole diagram should be found diminished a degree, and reduced to an interval of 7th?

This

This is however what the generality of authors would ſeem to underſtand, and amongſt the reſt Nicomachus, who ſays that Pythagoras finding the whole ſyſtem compoſed only of two conjoint tetrachords, which between their extremities formed a diſſonant interval, rendered it conſonant, in dividing theſe two tetrachords by the interval of a tone, which produced the octave.

However it be, it is a certain thing at leaſt, that the ſyſtem of the Greeks was inſenſibly extended as well above or below, and that it attained and even paſſed the extent of the dis-diapaſon or double octave, an extent which they called ſyſtema perfectum, maximum, immeſtatum, the grand ſyſtem, the perfect ſyſtem; ſo that betwixt its extremities, which formed together a perfect conſonance were contained all the ſimple conſonances, double, direct, and varied, all the particular ſyſtems, and according to them, the greateſt intervals which can have place in melody.

This entire ſyſtem was compoſed of four tetrachords, 3 conjoint, and 1 disjoint, and a tone beſides, which was added below all to compleat the double octave, from whence the chord which formed it, took the name of Proſlambanomenos or added. This could not, it ſeems have produced more than 15 ſounds in the diatonic genus; It has however formed 6. This is that the disjunction making itſelf perceived, ſometimes between the ſecond and third tetrachord, ſometimes between the third and fourth; it happened in the firſt caſe, that after the ſound la, the ſharpeſt of the ſecond tetrachord, followed in aſcending the ſi natural which began the third tetrachord; or, in the ſecond caſe, that this ſame ſound la beginning itſelf the third tetrachord, was immediately followed by ſi b flat; for the firſt degree of each tetrachord in the diatonic genus, was always of a ſemi-tone. This difference produced then a 16th ſound on account of the ſi, which was natural on one ſide, and b flat on the other.

The 16 ſounds were repreſented by 18 names; that is to ſay, that the ut and re being either ſharp ſounds, or the middle of the third tetrachord, according to theſe two caſes of disjunction, a name was given to each of theſe two ſounds which determined its poſition.

But as the fundamental ſound varied according to the mode, there followed from thence for the place which each mode occupied in the whole ſyſtem, a difference from flat to ſharp, which multiplied ſeveral ſounds; for if the different modes had ſeveral common ſounds, they had alſo ſome peculiar to each, or to a few only. So, in the ſingle diatonic genus, the extent of all the ſounds, admitted in the 15 modes, numbered by Alipius, is of three octaves; and, as the difference of the fundamental ſound of each mode, to that of its neighbour was only of a ſemi-tone, it is evident

dent that all this ſpace graduated from ſemi-tone to ſemi-tone, produced, in the general diagram, the quantity of 34 ſounds practiſed in the ancient muſic. If, deducing all the repliques of the ſame ſounds, we confine ourſelves within the bounds of an octave, we ſhall find it divided chromatically into 12 different ſounds, as in the modern muſic; which is manifeſted by the inſpection of the tables placed by Meibomius at the head of the work of Alipius.

Theſe remarks are neceſſary for eradicating the error of thoſe, who believe in the faith of ſome moderns, that ancient muſic was compoſed in the whole of 16 ſounds.

In regard to the enharmonic genera and chromatic, the tetrachords were therein found very well divided according to other proportions, but as they always contained equally 4 ſounds, and 3 conſecutive intervals, in the ſame manner as the diatonic genus, each of theſe ſounds bore the ſame name in their genus, which correſponded to them in the other; for which reaſon I have given no particular tables for each of theſe genera.

The curious may conſult thoſe which Meibomius has placed at the head of the work of Ariſtoxenes. We ſhall find 6, one for the enharmonic genus, 3 for the chromatic, and 2 for the diatonic, according to the diſpoſitions of each of theſe genera, in the Ariſtoxenian Syſtem.

Such was, in its perfection, the general ſyſtem of the Greeks, which remained nearly in this condition to the 11th century; the time, when Gui d' Arezzo made a conſiderable change. He added below a new chord which he called Hypoproſlambanomenos, or ſub-added, and above, a 5th tetrachord, which he called the tetrachord of the ſur-ſharp.

Beſides that, he invented, they ſay, the b flat neceſſary for diſtinguiſhing the ſecond chord of a tetrachord conjoint with the firſt chord of the ſame disjoint tetrachord; that is to ſay, that he fixed that double ſignification of the letter B, which St. Gregory, before him, had already aſſigned to the note ſi. For ſince it is certain that the Greeks had, for a long time theſe ſame conjunctions and disjunctions of tetrachords, and conſequently, ſigns to expreſs each degree in theſe two different caſes, it follows thence that it was not a new ſound introduced in the ſyſtem of Guy, but only a new name, which he gave to this ſound, reducing by this means to one ſame degree, what amongſt the Greeks formed two.

We muſt alſo ſay of theſe hexachords ſubſtituted in the place of their tetrachords, that it was leſs a change to the ſyſtem, than to the method, and that all which reſulted from it, was another method of ſol-faing the ſame ſounds. (Vide Gamut, To Sol-fa.)

We eaſily conceive that the invention of the counter-point, to whatever author it is due, muſt very ſoon draw back the bounds of this

this ſyſtem. Four parts ought to have more extent than one alone. The ſyſtem was fixed to four octaves, and this is the extent of the keys in all the ancient organs. But at laſt they found them ſelves incommoded by limits, whatever ſpace they might contain, they went beyond them ; they extended above and below ; they formed keys a ravalement ; they forced the voice ; and at laſt gave ſo much extent to this ſyſtem, that it has no greater bounds than thoſe of the violin.

As we cannot even looſen to deſcend, the loweſt chord of the ordinary baſſes does not paſs the C ſol ut, but we ſhall equally find the method of obtaining on that ſide the tone of the general ſyſtem ; that is even what they have begun to do, and I look on it as a certain thing, that in France the tone of the opera is lower at preſent than at the time of Lully. On the contrary, that of the inſtrumental muſic is aſcended as in Italy, and theſe differences become ſufficiently ſenſible to be perceived in practice.

In Plate II. Fig. I. Is given a table, of the entire ſet of keys a ravallement, and of all the ſounds contained therein in the extent of five octaves.

SYSTEM. Is alſo, either a method of calculation to determine the relations of ſounds admitted in muſic, or an order of ſigns eſtabliſhed to expreſs them. It is in the firſt ſenſe that the ancients diſtinguiſhed the Pythagorean ſyſtem, and the Ariſtoxenian. (Vide thoſe Words.)

It is in the ſecond that we at preſent diſtinguiſh the ſyſtem of Gui, that of Sauveur, of Demos, and Souhaiti, &c. of which I have ſpoken at the word note.

We muſt take notice that ſome one of theſe ſyſtems bear this name in either acceptation, as that of M. Sauveur, which gives at the ſame time, rules for determining the relations of ſounds and notes to expreſs them ; as may be ſeen in the Memoirs of that author, expanded in thoſe of the Academy of Sciences. (Vide Merides, Eptamerides, Decamerides.)

Such is alſo another ſyſtem ſtill newer, which being in manuſcript, and perhaps never intended to be ſeen entirely by the Public, is deſerving to have an extract here, which has been communicated to us by the author Monſ. Roualle de Boiſgelou, counſellor to the grand counſel, already mentioned in ſome articles of this Dictionary.

The firſt thing neceſſary, is to determine the exact relation of the ſounds in the diatonic and chromatic genera, which being done in an uniform manner for the tones, conſequently diſperſes the modification.

The whole ſyſtem of Monſ. de Boiſgelou is ſummarily confined in the four formilæ which I am going to tranſcribe, after having put the reader in mind of the rules eſtabliſhed in different parts of this

this Dictionary on the method of comparing and composing the intervals, or relations which express them. We must then remember, I. That to add one interval to another, we must compose its references si, for instance, adding the 5th $\frac{2}{3}$ to the 4th $\frac{3}{4}$, we have $\frac{6}{12}$ or $\frac{1}{2}$: that is, the octave

II. To add an interval to itself, we must only double its connection, so to add a 5th to another 5th, we must only raise the reference of the 5th to its second power $\frac{2^2}{3^2} = \frac{4}{9}$.

III. To connect or simplify a redoubled interval, such as this $\frac{4}{9}$, it is sufficient to add the small number to itself, one time or more: that is, to lower the octaves until the two terms, being as nearly connected as possible, give a simple interval. So from $\frac{4}{9}$, we have as a product of the redoubled 5th, the reference of the major tone, I will add, that in this dictionary, I have always expressed the connections of the intervals by those of the vibrations, whereas Monf. de Boisgelou expresses them by the lengths of the chords, which renders its expressions inverse to mine. So, the reference of the 5th by the vibrations, being $\frac{2}{3}$, is $\frac{3}{2}$ by the lengths of the chords. But we shall now see that this connection is approached only in the system of Monf. de Boisgelou.

There are however the four formulæ of this author with their explanation.

Formulæ

$$\begin{cases} \text{A.} & 12\,f - 7\,\underline{r + t} = 0 \\ \text{B.} & 12\,x - 5\,\underline{t + r} = 0. \end{cases}$$

$$\begin{cases} \text{C.} & 7\,f - 4\,\underline{r + x} = 0. \\ \text{D.} & 7\,x - 4\,\underline{t + f} = 0. \end{cases}$$

The Explanation.

Connection of ehe octave ——— 2 — 1.
Connection of the 5th ——— n — 1.
Connection of the 4th ——— 2 — n.

Connection of the interval which comes from the 5th — n^{r}. 2^{s}.
Connection of the interval which comes from the 4th 2^{s} — n^{r}.

r. The number of 5ths or 4ths of the interval.
ſ. The number of the combined octaves of the interval.
t. The number of ſemi-tones in the interval.
x. The diatonic gradation of the interval. That is the number of major and minor diatonic ſeconds of the interval.
$\underline{x + 1}$. Gradations of the terms from whence the interval takes its name.

The firſt caſe of each formulæ is placed when the interval comes from 5ths. The ſecond caſe of each formulæ is placed, when the interval is derived from 4ths.

To render this clearer by examples, let us begin by giving names to each of the 12 touches of the keys.

Theſe names, in the arrangement of the keys propoſed by Monſ. de Boiſgelou, are the following:

	de	ma	fa	ſol	la	ſi	
Ut	re	mi	ſi	be	ſa	ut	

Every interval is formed by the progreſſion of 5ths or 4ths, conveyed to the octave. For inſtance, the interval ſi ut is formed by this progreſſion of 5 fourths, ſi mi la re ſol ut, or by this progreſſion of 7 fifths, ſi fi de be ma ſa fa ut.

In the ſame manner the interval fa la is formed by this progreſſion of 4 fifths, fa ut ſol re la, or by this progreſſion of 8 fourths, fa ſa ma be de fi ſi ma la.

Since that the connection of every interval which is derived from 5ths, is $n^{r} : 2^{s}$. and that which comes from 4ths, is $2^{s} : n^{r}$. it follows

follows from thence that we have for the connection of the interval si ut, when it comes from 4ths, this proportion $2^s - n^r - 2^3 - n^s$. This is the method of proving the analogy.

The number of 4ths from whence this interval si ut is derived, being 5, the connection of that interval is of $2^5 - n^5$, since the connection of the 4th is $2 : n$.

But this connection $2^5 - n^5$, would design an interval of 2^5 semi-tones, since each 4th has five semi-tones, and that interval has 5 fourths. So, the octave having only 12 semi-tones, the interval si ut would pass two octaves.

Then that the interval si ut may be less than the octave, we must diminish this reference $2^5 : n^5$. of two octaves; that is, of the connection of $2^2 : 1$. Which is done by a connection composed of the direct reference $2^5 - n^5$, and of the reference $1 - 2^2$ inverse of that $2^2 - 1$, in this manner: $2^5 + 1 . n^5 + 2^2 :: 2^5 . 2^2 n^5 :: 2^3 : n^5$. The interval si ut, moreover coming from fourths, its connection, as I have said before, is $2^s : n^r$. Then $2^s : n^r :: 2^3 : n^5$. and again $s = 3$ and $r = 5$.

So, reducing the letters of the second case of each formulæ to the correspondent formulæ, we have for C $7s - 4r - x = 21 - 20 - 1 = 0$, and for D $7x - 4t - s = 7 - 4 - 3 = 0$.

When the same interval si ut, comes from 5ths, it gives this proportion $n^r : 2^s :: n^7 : 2^4$. So, we have $r = 7$, $s = 4$, and consequently, for the A of the first formulæ $12 - 7r - t = 48 - 49 + 1 = 0$. And for B. $12x - 56 + r = 12 - 5 - 7 = 0$.

In the same manner the interval fa la coming from 5th, gives this proportion $n^r : 2^s :: n^4 : 2^2$, and consequently we have $r = 4$ and $s = 2$. The same interval coming from 4ths, gives this proportion, $2^s : n^r :: 2^5 : n^8$.

It would be too tedious to explain here the method of finding the connections, and the whole which concerns the intervals by the method of formulæ. It will be placing an attentive reader on the ramble, to give him the computation of n and of its powers.

Computation of the Powers of n.

$n^4 = 5$ is an experienced truth.

Wherefore, $n^8 = 25$ $n^{12} = 125$, &c.

The precise Computations of the three first Powers of n.

$n = \sqrt[4]{5}$, $n^2 = \sqrt{5}$, $n^3 = \sqrt[4]{127}$.

The nearer Computations of the three first Powers of n.

$$m = \frac{3}{2},\ m^2 = \frac{3^2}{2^2},\ m^3 = \frac{3^3}{2^3}.$$

The connection $\frac{3}{2}$ then, which till now has been thought to have been that of the true 5th, is only a relation of approximation, and gives too strong a 5th ; and from thence the real principle of the modification; which is called so only through abuse, since the 5th must be weak to be true.

Remarks on the Intervals.

An interval of a given number of semi-tones, has always two different connections : the one as coming from 5ths, and the other as coming from 4ths. The sum of these two powers of r in these two connections equal 12, and that of the two powers of s equals 7.

That of the two connections of 5ths or 4ths, in which r is smaller, is the diatonic interval ; the other is the chromatic. So the interval si ut, which has these two connections $2^3 : n^5$ and $n^7 : 2^4$. is a diatonic interval, as coming from 4ths, and its connection is $2^3 : n^5$; but this same interval si ut, is chromatic as coming from 5ths, and its connection is $n^7 : 2^4$, because in the first case r + 5 is less than r = 7 of the second.

On the contrary, the interval fa la, which has its two connections $n^4 : 2^2$: and $2^5 : n^8$: is diatonic in the first case, where it comes from 5ths, and chromatic in the second, where it comes from 4ths.

The interval si ut diatonic, is a second minor : The interval si ut, chromatic, or rather the interval si si diesis (for then ut is taken as si diesis) is a superfluous unison.

The interval fa la diatonic, is a major third : The interval fa la chromatic, or rather the interval mi diesis la (for then fa is taken as mi diesis) is a dimished fourth : So with the rest.

It is evident, I. That to each diatonic interval there corresponds a chromatic of the same number of semi-tones, and vice versa. These

These two intervals of the ſame number of ſemi-tones, the one diatonic and the other chromatic, are called correſpondent intervals.

Secondly. When the power of r is equal to one of theſe numbers 0, 1, 2, 3, 4, 5, 6, the interval is diatonic, whether that this interval comes from 5ths or 4ths; but if the R is equal to one of theſe numbers 7, 8, 9, 10, 11, 12, the interval is chromatic.

Thirdly. When r = 6 the interval is in the ſame time diatonic and chromatic, whether it comes from 5ths or 4ths, ſuch are the two intervals fa ſi, called triton, and ſi fa, called falſe fifths.

The triton fa ſi is in the reference $n^{6} : 2^{3}$, and comes from 6 fifths: the falſe 5th ſi fa is in the connection $2^{4} : n^{6}$, and comes from 6 fourths: where we ſee, that in the two caſes we have r = 6. So the triton, as a diatonic interval, is a major 4th and as a chromatic interval, as ſuperfluous 4th. The falſe 5th ſi fa, as a diatonic interval, is a minor 5th; as a chromatic interval, a diminiſhed 5th. There are but theſe two intervals and their repliques which are able to be at the ſame time diatonic and chromatic.

The diatonic intervals of the ſame name, and conſequently of the ſame gradation, are divided into major and minor. The chromatic intervals are divided into diminiſhed and ſuperfluous. To each diatonic interval minor, there correſponds a chromatic ſuperfluous interval; and to each diatonic major interval, there correſponds a chromatic diminiſhed interval.

Every interval in aſcending which comes from 5ths is major or diminiſhed, according as that interval is diatonic or chromatic; and reciprocally every major or diminiſhed interval comes from fifths.

Every interval in aſcending which comes from 4ths, is minor or ſuperfluous, according as that interval is diatonic or chromatic, and vice verſa, every minor or ſuperfluous interval comes from fourths.

It would be the contrary if the interval was taken in deſcending.

Of two intervals, correſpondant, that is, the one diatonic and the other chromatic, and which conſequently come, the one from 5ths, and the other from 4ths, the greater is that which comes from 4ths; and it ſurpaſſes that which comes from 5ths in regard to the gradation, by an unity, and, in regard to the intonation, by an interval, whoſe connection is $2^{7} : n^{12}$: that is, 128. 125. This interval is the diminiſhed ſecond called commonly grand comma, or quarter of the tone; and here is a door opened to the enharmonic genus.

To proceed in placing the reader in a right view for the formulæ, peculiar to the improvement of the theory of muſic, I have here given

given the two tables of progreſſion performed by Monſ. de Boiſgelou, by which we ſee with a caſt of the eye the connections of each interval, and the powers of the terms of thoſe connections, according to the number of 4ths or 5ths which compoſe it.

Progreſſion by 5ths beginning by fa.

ut	de	re	ma	mi	fa	ſi	ſol	be	la	ſa	ſi	ut
2	2^5	2^2	2^6	2^3	1	2^4	2	2^5	2^2	2^6	2^3	1
n	n^8	n^3	n^{10}	n^5		n^7	n^2	n^9	n^4	n^{11}	n^6	12

Progreſſion by 4ths beginning by ſi.

ut	de	re	ma	mi	fa	ſi	ſol	be	la	ſa	ſi	ut
n^5	n^{10}	n^3	n^8	n	n^6	n^{11}	n^4	n^9	n^2	7	1	n^5
2^2	2^5	2	2^4		2^3	2^6	2^2	2^5	2	2^4		2^3

We ſee, in theſe formulæ, that the ſemi-tones are really the primitive and elementary intervals which compoſe all the reſt; which has engaged the author to make for this ſame ſyſtem, a conſiderable change in the characters, by chromatically dividing the ſtave, by intervals, or equal degrees, and all of a ſemi-tone; whereas in the ordinary muſic, each of theſe degrees is ſometimes a comma, ſometimes a ſemi-tone, ſometimes a tone, and ſometimes a tone and a half; which leaves to the eye the equivocation, and to the mind, the doubt of the interval, ſince the degrees being the ſame, the intervals are ſometimes the ſame, and ſometimes different.

For this reformation it is ſufficient to make the ſtave of 10 lines inſtead of 5, and to aſſign to each poſition one of the 12 notes of the chromatic keys before mentioned, according to the order of theſe notes, which always remaining the ſame, determine their intervals with the niceſt preciſion, and render all the dieſis's B's flat, or B's ſharp abſolutely uſeleſs, in whatever tone we may be, and as well in the cleff as accidentally. I have here given the chromatic ſcale without either dieſis or b flat.

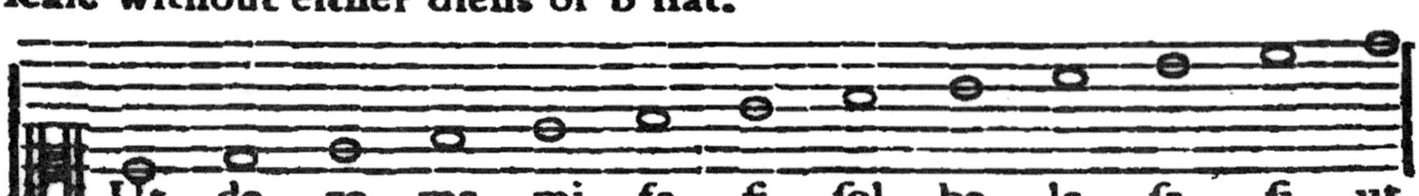

and

and alſo the diatonic ſcale.

However little we practice on this new method of pricking and reading the muſic, we ſhall be ſurprized at the neatneſs, and ſimplicity which it gives the notes, and the ſimplicity it conveys in the execution; without its being poſſible to ſee any other inconvenience in it, than that it fills a little more ſpace on the paper, and perhaps may dazzle the eye, in the quicker parts, by the multitude of its lines, and particularly in the ſymphony.

But as this ſyſtem of notes is abſolutely chromatic, it ſeems to me to be inconvenient to ſuffer the denominations of the diatonic degrees to be ſubſtituted in the place of it, and that according to Monſ. Boiſgelou, ut re ought not to be a ſecond, but a third; neither ut mi a third but a fifth; nor ut ut an octave, but a twelfth; ſince each ſemi-tone really forming a degree on the note, ſhould alſo take its denomination; then x + 1 being always equal to t in the formulæ of that author, theſe formulæ would be found extremely ſimplified. This ſyſtem beſides, appears to me equally profound and advantageous. It would be a deſirable thing for it to be explained, and publiſhed by the author, or ſome ingenious theorician.

SYSTEM. Laſtly is the collection of rules in harmony, drawn from ſome common principles which gather them together, which form their union, from which they flow, and by which we form a computation of them.

Until our age, the harmony, born ſucceſſively, and, as it were by chance, had only ſcattered rules, eſtabliſhed by the ear, confirmed by cuſtom, and which appeared abſolutely arbitrary. Monſ. Rameau is the firſt, who, by the ſyſtem of the fundamental baſs, has given the principles of theſe rules. The ſyſtem on which this dictionary has been compoſed, being ſufficiently explained in the principal articles, ſhall not be treated of in this, which is already too long, and which theſe ſuperfluous repetitions would extend to an exceſs. Beſides, the plan of this work does not oblige me to expoſe all the ſyſtems, but only to give a true explanation what a ſyſtem is, and to ſtrengthen, when neceſſary, that explanation by examples. Thoſe who would wiſh to ſee the diffuſed obſcure ſyſtem of Monſ. Rameau by his writings, lain out with a clearneſs of which it could not have been thought ſuſceptible, may have recourſe to the elements of muſic by Monſ. D' Alembert.

Mon.

Monſ. Serre, of Geneva, having found Monſ. Rameau's Principles inſufficient in many reſpects, planned another ſyſtem on his, in which he pretends to ſhew, that the whole of harmony is borne on a double fundamental baſs: and as this author, having travelled in Italy, was not ignorant of Monſ. Tartini's experiments, he compoſed from them, joining them with thoſe of Rameau, a mixed ſyſtem which was printed at Paris in 1753, under this Title "Eſſay on the Principles of Harmony." The facility that each one has of conſulting this work, and the advantage to be found by reading the whole of it, diſpenſe with my giving any account of it to the public. It is different with that of the illuſtrious Monſ. Tartini, which remains to be ſpoken of; the which as it is written in a foreign language often profound, and always diffuſed, cannot be conſulted but by few people, the greateſt part of which are diſcouraged by the obſcurity of the book, before they have entered upon its beauties. I ſhall, as briefly as poſſible, make an extract of this new ſyſtem, which, if it is not that of nature, is at leaſt, amongſt all that have been yet publiſhed, that, whoſe principle is the moſt ſimple, and from which the whole laws of harmony ſeem to ariſe leaſt arbitrarily.

System of Monſ. Tartini.

There are three methods of calculating the connections of ſounds.

I. In cutting on the monochord, the entire chord into its parts by moveable bridges, the vibrations or ſounds will be in the inverſe proportion of the lengths of the chord and its parts.

II. In extending equal chords, by unequal weights, the ſound will be as the ſquare roots of the weights.

III. In extending by equal weights, chords, equal in thickneſs and unequal in length, or equal in length and unequal in thickneſs, the ſound will be in the inverſe proportion of the ſquare roots of the dimenſion, wherein the difference is found.

In general, the ſounds are always together in the inverſe proportion of the cubic roots of ſonorous bodies. The ſounds of the chords are moreover changed three ways, viz. in altering either the thickneſs, that is the diameter of the thickneſs, or the length, or tenſion. If all this is equal, the chords are in uniſon. If only one of theſe is changed, the ſounds follow, in inverſe proportion, the connections of the alterations. If two or all the three are changed, the ſounds are, in inverſe proportion, as the roots of the compoſed connections of the alterations. Such are the principles of all the phænomena, which we obſerve in comparing the connections of the ſounds, and thoſe of the dimenſions of the ſonorous bodies.

This

This being understood, having placed every thing necessary, touch on the organ the key which renders the lowest note as follows:

All the other notes marked above, will resound at the same time, and still you will hear only the flattest sound.

The sounds of this series being confounded in the flat sound, will form in their connections, the natural consequence of the fractions $\frac{1}{1}\ \frac{1}{2}\ \frac{1}{3}\ \frac{1}{4}\ \frac{1}{5}\ \frac{1}{6}$, which consequence is an harmonic progression.

This same series will be that of equal chords, hung by weight, which would be as the squares $\frac{1}{1}\ \frac{1}{4}\ \frac{1}{9}\ \frac{1}{16}\ \frac{1}{25}\ \frac{1}{36}$, &c. of the abovesaid fractions.

And the sounds which these chords would render, are the same, expressed in notes in the example.

By this means, all the sounds which are in harmonic progression after the unity, are reunited to form one only sensible to the ear, and the whole harmonic system is found in the unity.

There is no sound, which makes any resonance but from its aliquots, because in every other fraction, as this would be $\frac{3}{5}$, it is found after the division of the chord in equal parts; a remainder, whose vibrations strike against each other, stops the vibrations of the equal parts, and are equally prevented by them; so that of the two sounds which would result from it, the weakest is destroyed by the shock of the rest.

Moreover, its aliquots being all comprised in the series of the fractions $\frac{1}{1}\ \frac{1}{2}\ \frac{1}{3}\ \frac{1}{4}$, &c. before given, each of these aliquots is what Mons. Tartini calls unity or harmonic monad, from the concurrence, whence a sound results. So, the whole of harmony being necessarily comprised betwixt the monad or composing unity, and the full sound or composed unity, it follow that harmony has, on both sides, the unity for its term, and consists in that unity essentially.

The following experiment, which serves as the principle of all artificial harmony, places this truth even in a clearer light.

Every time that two strong times, true and sustained, are heard at the same moment, there results from their shock a third sound, more or less sensible, in proportion to the simplicity in the connection of the two first, and the nicety of the ear in the audience.

To render this experiment as sensible as possible, we should put two hautboys of a good concord, at some paces of interval, and place ourselves between them, at an equal distance from each. If we should be in want of hautboys, we may take two violins, which, tho' the sound should be weaker, may, by being touched with force and justness, be sufficient to make a third sound be distinguished.

The production of this third sound, by each of our consonances is as follows:

And we may continue it below the consonances, by all the intervals represented by the aliquots of unity.

The octave gives none, and that is the only interval excepted.

The 5th gives the unison of the flat sound, an unison, which, with attention we cannot fail to distinguish.

The third sounds produced by the other intervals, are all in flat.

The 4th gives the octave of the sharp sound.

The major third gives the octave of the flat sound, and the minor sixth, which is varied from it, gives the double octave of the sharp sound.

The minor third gives the major tenth of the flat sound; but the sixth major, which is varied from it, gives only the major tenth of the sharp sound.

The major tone gives the 15th, or double octave of the flat sound.

The minor tone gives the 17th, or double octave in the major third of the sharp sound.

The semi tone major gives the 22d, or triple octave of the sharp sound.

Lastly, the semi-tone minor, gives the 26th of the flat sound.

We

We see, by comparing the four last intervals, that a change hardly perceptible in the interval, changes very sensibly the produced or fundamental sound. So, in the major-tone, confine the interval by lowering the superior sound, or elevating the inferior only $\frac{80}{81}$, immediately the produced sound will ascend a tone.

Form the same operation on the major semi-tone, and the produced sound will descend a 5th.

Tho' the production of the third sound is not confined to these intervals, our notes not being able to express any more composed, it is useless for the present to go below those.

We see in the regular movement of the consonances which compose this table, that they are all connected with one common bass, and all produce exactly the same third sound.

Here then, by this new phænomenon, is a physical demonstration of the unity in the principle of harmony.

In the Physico Mathematic Sciences, such as music, the demonstrations should be very geometrical, but physically deduced from the thing demonstrated. 'Tis then alone that the union of calculation to physic, furnishes, in established truths, both on experience and geometrically demonstrated, the true principles of this art. Otherwise geometry alone will give certain theorems, but without use in practice: Physic will give particular facts, but without union together, and any general law.

The physical principle of harmony is one, as we have seen, and is resolved in an harmonic proportion. Moreover, these two proprieties are suitable to the circle; for we shall soon perceive, that the two extreme unities of the monad and sounds are found therein; and in regard to the harmonic proportion, it is found also, since in whatever point C, we unequally cut the diameter A B, for which see Fig. II. Plate II.

The square of the ordinated C D, will be a proportionate harmonic means between the two rectangles of the parts A C, and C B, of the diameter by the ray; a propriety which is sufficient to establish the harmonic nature of the circle. For, tho' the ordinated parts are geometrical means between the parts of the diameter, the square of these ordinated parts being harmonic means between the rectangles, their connections representing so much the more exactly those of the sonorous bodies, than the connections of these chords, where the hanging weights are also as the squares, whilst the sounds remain as the roots.

From the diameter A B, divided according to the series of the fractions $\frac{1}{2}\ \frac{1}{3}\ \frac{1}{4}\ \frac{1}{5}\ \frac{1}{6}$, which are in harmonic progression, let there be drawn the ordinated C, C C; G, G G; c, c c; e, e e; and g, g g; See Fig. III. Plate II.

The diameter repreſents a ſonorous chord, which divided into the ſame computations gives the following ſounds.

To avoid the fractions, let us give 60 parts to the diameter, the ſections will contain theſe entire numbers, $BC = \frac{1}{2} = 30$; $BG, = \frac{1}{3} = 20$; $Bc = \frac{1}{4} = 15$; $Be = \frac{1}{5} = 12$; $Bg = \frac{1}{6} = 10$.

From the points where the ordinated parts cut the circle, let us draw on each ſide chords to the two extremities of the diameter; the ſum of the ſquare of each chord, and of the ſquare of the correſpondant chord, which I call its complement, will always be equal to the ſquare of the diameter. The ſquares of the chords will be always together as the correſpondent abſciſſes, conſequently alſo in harmonic proportion, and in the ſame manner will repreſent the above example, allowing the exception of the firſt ſound.

The ſquares of the complements of theſe ſame chords will be together as the complements of the abſciſſes in the diameter, conſequently in the following proportions.

$$\overline{AC}^2 = \frac{1}{2} = 30.$$

$$\overline{AG}^2 = \frac{2}{3} = 40.$$

$$\overline{Ac}^2 \ \frac{3}{4} = 45$$

$$\overline{Ae}^2 = \frac{4}{5} = 48$$

$$\overline{Ag}^2 = \frac{5}{6} = 50.$$

and

and will reprefent the founds of the following example,

P 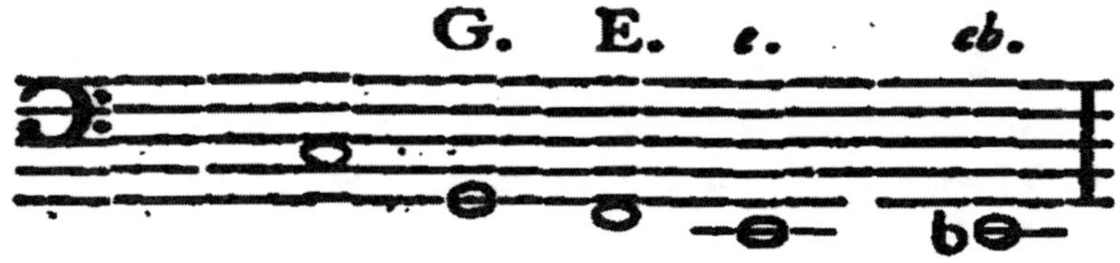

on which we ought to take notice, in paffing, that this example, compared to the following,

Q 

and to the firft, gives the natural foundation of the rule of contrary movements.

The fquares of the ordinated parts will be in the following proportions to the fquare 3600 of the diameter:

$$\overline{AB}^2 = 1 = 3600$$

$$C,\ \overline{CC}^2 = \frac{1}{4} = 900$$

$$G,\ \overline{GG}^2 = \frac{2}{9} = 800$$

$$c,\ \overline{cc}^2 = \frac{3}{16} = 675$$

$$e,\ \overline{ee}^2 = \frac{4}{25} = 576$$

$$g,\ \overline{gg}^2 = \frac{5}{36} = 500$$

and will reprefent the founds in the above example.

Moreover, this laft feries which has nothing homologous in the divifions of the diameter, and without which, we cannot however compleat the harmonic fyftem, fhews the neceffity of feeking in the proprieties of the circle, for the true foundations of the fyftem, which cannot be found either in the ftraight line, or in the abftracted numbers.

I designedly pass all the other propositions of Monf. Tartini, on the nature of Arithmetic, of the harmony and geometry of the circle, as well as on the bounds of the harmonic series given by the sextuple computation; because its proofs, expressed only in cyphers, establish no general demonstration; and, what is more, by often comparing heterogeneous magnitudes, he finds proportions where we cannot even see connections. So, he would prove that the square of a line is a proportional means of such a computation, he makes no other proof, but that such a number is a proportional means between two such other numbers. For the surfaces and abstracted numbers not being of the same nature, cannot be compared.

Monf. Tartini perceives this difficulty, and endeavors to prevent it; we may see his reasonings in his book.

This theory being established, we must now deduce its given proofs and the rules of the harmonic art.

The octave, which engenders no fundamental sound, not being essential to harmony, may be removed from the constitutive parts of the concord. So, the concord, reduced to its greatest simplicity, should be considered without it. It is then composed of these three terms, $1\ \frac{1}{3}\ \frac{1}{5}$, which are in harmonic proportion, and where the two monades $\frac{1}{3}\ \frac{1}{5}$ are the only true elements of sonorous unity; for the fraction $\frac{1}{4}$ is the element $\frac{1}{2}$, and the fraction $\frac{1}{6}$ is octave of the monade $\frac{1}{3}$.

This perfect concord $\frac{1}{3}\ \frac{1}{5}$ produced by a single chord, and whose terms are in harmonic proportion, is the general law of nature, which serves as a bass to all the sciences of sounds; a law, which physic may endeavour to explain, but whose explanation is useless to the rules of harmony.

The calculations of the chords, and pendant weights, serve to give in numbers the connections of the sounds which cannot be considered as quantities but by favor of these calculations.

The third sound, engendered by the concurrence of two others, is as the product of their quantities; and when in a common cathegory this third sound is always found the same, tho' engendered by different intervals, it is, that the products of the generations are equal together.

This

This is manifeſtly deduced from the precedent propoſitions.

What, for inſtance is the third ſound which reſults from C B and G B? It is the uniſon of C B. Why ſo? Becauſe in the two harmonic proportions, whoſe ſquares of the two ordinated parts C, C C, and G, G G, are proportional means, the ſums of the extremes are equal together, and conſequently produce the ſame common ſound C B or C, C C.

In effect, the ſum of the two rectangles B C, by C, C C, and of A C, by C, C C is equal to the ſum of the two rectangles of B G by C, C C, and of G A by C, C C: for each of theſe two ſums is equal to twice the ſquare of the ray. From whence it follows, that the ſound C, C C, or C B, ſhould be common to the two chords; moreover, this ſound is preciſely the note of the laſt plate.

Whatever ordinated parts you may take in the circle, to compare them 2 by 2, or even 3 by 3, they will always engender the ſame third ſound repreſented in the plate; becauſe the rectangles of the two parts of the diameter by the ray, will always give equal ſums.

But the octave X Q engender harmonics only in ſharp, and by no means the fundamental ſound, becauſe we cannot elevate the ordinated part on the extremity of the diameter, and conſequently the diameter and the ray, in their harmonic proportions, have any common product.

Inſtead of harmonically dividing the diameter by the fractions $\frac{1}{2}$ $\frac{1}{3}$ $\frac{1}{4}$ $\frac{1}{5}$ $\frac{1}{6}$, which give the natural ſyſtem of the major concord, if we divide it arithmetically into 6 equal parts, we ſhall have the ſyſtem of the major concord varied, and this variation gives exactly the minor concord. See Fig. IV. Plate II.

One of theſe parts will have the 19th, that is, the double octave of the 5th, two will give the 12th, or the octave of the 5th, three will give the octave, four the 5th, and five the minor 3d.

But, as ſoon as uniting two of theſe ſounds, we ſeek the third ſound, which they engender, theſe two ſounds, inſtead of the ſound C,

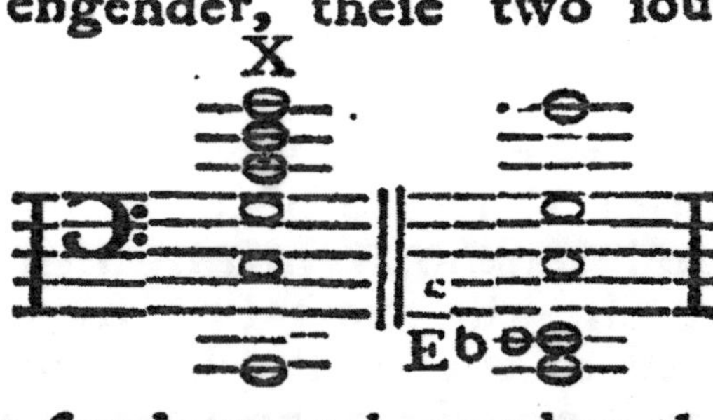

will never produce as fundamental, any but the ſound E b; which proves, that neither the minor concord, or its mode, are given by nature. If we make two or more intervals of the minor concord ſound together, the fundamental ſounds will be multiplied, and in relation

relation to theſe ſounds; we ſhall hear ſeveral major concords, at the ſame time, without any minor concords.

So, by an experiment formed in preſence of eight celebrated profeſſors of muſic, two hautboys and a violin ſounding the white notes together marked as follows:

A 

the ſounds marked in blank in the ſame figure, are diſtinctly heard, viz. Thoſe which are marked aſide as follows, for the intervals which are above,

B 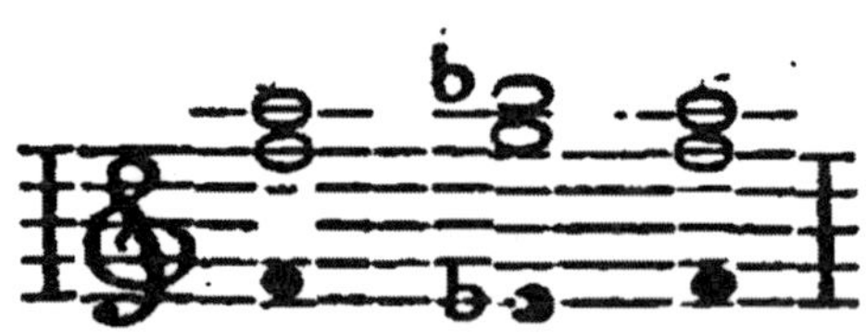

and thoſe marked next, for the intervals below.

C 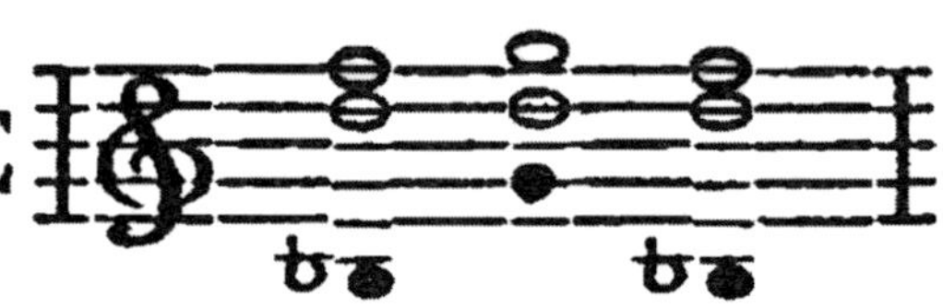

In judging of the horrible cacophony, which ſhould reſult from this concinity, we ſhould conclude that all muſic in the minor mode would be inſupportable to the ear, if the intervals were true enough and the inſtruments ſufficiently ſtrong to render the engendered ſounds as ſenſible as the generators.

I beg leave to remark, *en paſſant*, that the inverſe of two modes marked in a precedent plate, is never bounded to the fundamental concord which conſtitutes them, but that it may be heard throughout the whole air, and harmony; which, noted in a direct ſenſe within the major mode, when we reverſe the paper, and place cleffs at the end of thoſe lines that are become the beginning, preſents another *ſuite* of air and harmony in minor mode, exactly the inverſe of the firſt, wherein the baſs becomes the treble, and vice verſa. This is the cleff of the method of compoſing then double canons which I have ſpoken of at the word canon. Monſ. Serre, before mentioned, who has very clearly explained in his book this harmonic curioſity, introduces a ſymphony of this kind, compoſed by Monſ. de Merambeſt, who ſhould have had it engraved.

That

That would have been certainly better than having it executed.

A composition of this nature must be better to present to the eye than the ear.

We have seen that from the harmonic division of the diameter, results the major mode, and from the arithmetical division, the minor mode. It is besides a known thing of all the theoricians, that the connections of the minor concord are found in the arithmetical division of the 5th. To find the first foundation of the minor mode in the harmonic system, it is sufficient to shew in this system the arithmetical division of the 5th.

The whole harmonic system is founded on a double computation, the connection of the entire chord to its octave, or of the diameter to the ray; and on the sesqui alter computation, which gives the first harmonic or fundamental sound, to which all the rest are connected.

Moreover, if in the double computation, we compare successively the second note G, and the third F of the series P to the fundamental sound Q, and to its flat octave which is the entire chord, we shall find that the first is an harmonic means, and the second an arithmetical means between those two terms.

In the same manner, if in the sesqui alter computation we compare successively the 4th note e, and the 5th eb of the same series, to the entire chord, and its 5th G, we shall find that the 4th e is an harmonic means, and the 5th eb an arithmetical means betwixt the two terms of this 5th. The minor mode then being founded on the arithmetical division of the 5th, and the note eb, taken in the series of the complements in the harmonic system, giving this division, the minor mode is founded on that note in the harmonic system.

After having found all the consonances in the harmonic division of the diameter, the major mode in the direct order of these consonances, the minor in their retrograde order, and in their complements, there remains to examine the third example, which expresses in notes the connections of the squares in the ordinated parts, and which gives the system of dissonances.

If we join, by consonances, the successive intervals of the above example, we shall find that to square the ordinated parts, is to double the interval which they represent. So, adding a third sound, which represents the square, this added sound will always double the interval of the consonance, as we see in the following plate.

Thus the first note K of the above example doubles the octave, the first interval of the other example; the second note L doubles the fifth, the second interval; the third note M doubles the fourth the third interval, &c. and tis this doubling of intervals which is expressed as follows

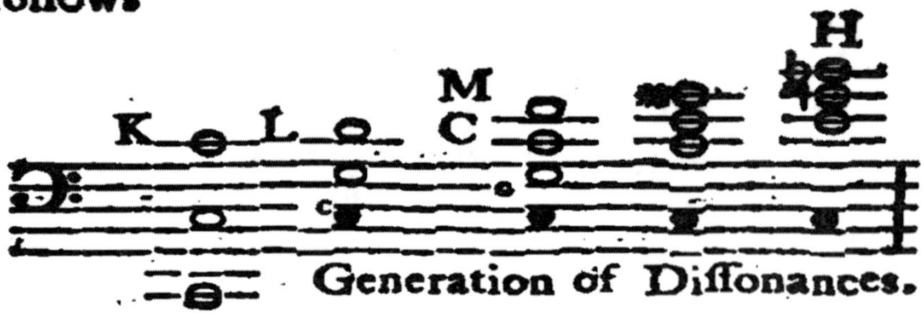

Generation of Dissonances.

Leaving aside the octave of the first interval, which engendering no fundamental sound, ought not to pass as harmonic, the added note L forms, with the two which are below it, a thorough geometrical proportion in sesquialter computation, and the following, always doubling the intervals, form also always geometrical proportions.

But the proportions and progressions harmonic and arithmetical, which constitute the consonant major and minor system, are opposed, by their nature, to the geometrical progression; since this results essentially from the same, connections, and the others from connections always different. Then, if the two proportions harmonic and arithmetical are consonant, the geometrical proportion will be necessarily dissonant; and, consequently, the system which results from the former example, will be the system of dissonances.

But this system drawn from the squares of the ordinated parts is united to the two precedent, drawn from the squares of chords. The dissonant system is then united in the same manner to the universal harmonic system.

It follows from thence, first, That every concord will be dissonant, when it contains two similar intervals, others than the octave; whether these two intervals be found conjoint with, or separated from the concord. Secondly, that of these two intervals, that which belongs to the harmonic or arithmetical system shall be consonant, and the other dissonant. So in the two examples S T of dissonant concords in the following plate, the intervals G C and c e are consonant, and the interval's C F and e g dissonant,

S. T.

In connecting however each term of the dissonant series to the fundamental sound or engendered C of the harmonic series, we shall find that the dissonances which result from this connection will be the

the following, and the only direct ones which can be established on the harmonic system.

I. The first is the 9th, or double 5th L.

II. The second is the 11th, which must not be confounded with the simple 4th, provided that the first 4th, or simple 4th G C, being in the particular harmonic system, is consonant; which is not the second fourth, or 11th C M, foreign to this same.

III. The third is the 12th or superfluous fifth, which Monf. Tartini calls the concord of a new invention, either because he first discovered its principles, or because the sensible concord in minor mode on the mediant, which we call superfluous 5th, has never been admitted on account of its horrid roughness. Vide the practice of this concord a la Francoise,

and the practice of the same a l' Italienne.

Before we conclude the enumeration we have begun, I should take notice, that the same distinction of the two fourths, consonant and dissonant, which I have made before, should be understood in the same manner of the two major thirds of this concord, and the two minor thirds of the following.

IV. The 4th and last dissonance given by the series, the 14th H that is, the octave of the 7th, a 14th which is reduced to the simple only by licence, and according to the right which we attribut

 but

bute to ourſelves in the cuſtom of indifferently confounding the octaves.

If the diſſonant ſyſtem is deduced from the harmonic ſyſtem the rules of preparing and ſaving the diſſonances are not leſs deduced, and we ſee, in the conſonant and harmonic series, the preperations of all the ſounds in the arithmetical ſeries. In effect, comparing the three ſeries O P Q, we always find in the ſucceſſive progreſſion of the ſounds of the ſeries O, not only, as we have ſeen, the ſimple computations, which, when doubled, give the ſounds of the ſeries Q but alſo the ſame intervals, which the ſounds of the two P and Q form together. So that the ſeries O always prepares beforehand, what the two ſeries P and Q immediately produce.

So, the firſt interval of the ſeries O, is that of the chord, a vide, to its octave, and the octave is alſo the interval or concord, which the firſt ſound of the ſeries Q produces, compared to the firſt ſound of the ſeries B.

In the ſame manner, the ſecond interval of the ſeries O (always reckoning from the entire chord) is a 12th; the interval or concord of the ſecond ſound of the ſeries Q compared to the ſecond ſound of the ſeries P, is alſo a 12th.

The third on each ſide, is a double octave, and ſo on.

Moreover, if we compare the ſeries P to the entire chord,

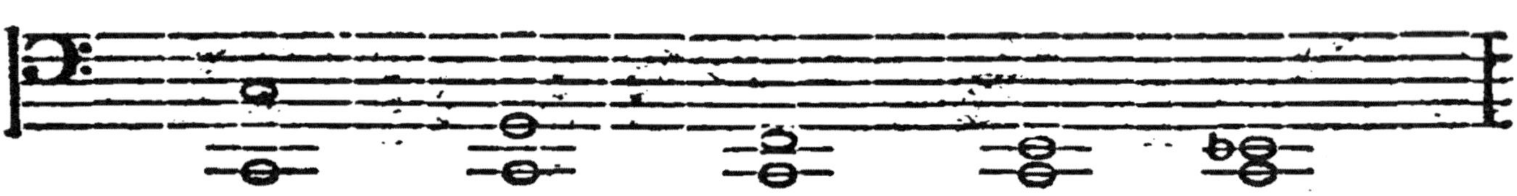

We ſhall find exactly the ſame intervals which the ſeries O gives beforehand, viz. the octave, 5th, 4th, major 3d, and minor 3d.

From whence it follows, that the particular harmonic ſeries gives preciſely, not only the exemplar and model of the two ſeries arithmetical and geometrical, which it engenders, and which with it compleat the univerſal harmonic ſyſtem; but alſo preſcribes to one, the order of the ſounds, and prepares for the other the uſe of the diſſonances.

This preparation, given by the harmonic ſeries, is exactly the ſame which is eſtabliſhed in practice; for the 9th doubled from the 5th, is alſo prepared by a movement of the 5th. The 11th doubled from the 4th, is prepared by a movement of the 4th. The 12th, or ſuperfluous 5th, doubled from the major third, is prepared by a movement of major third; laſtly the 14th, or falſe 5th, doubled from the minor third, is alſo prepared by a movement of the minor third.

It is true that we muſt not ſeek theſe preparations in the movements called fundamental in Monſ. Rameau's ſyſtem; but which are

are not so in that of Monf. Tartini; and it is true also that the same dissonances are prepared in several different ways, either by the variations of harmony, or by a substituted bass; but the whole depends on the same principle, and this is not the place to enter into a detail of rules.

That of resolving and saving the dissonances arises from the same principle as their preparation: for as each dissonance is prepared by the antecedent connection of the harmonic system, so it is saved by the consequent connection of the same system.

So, in the harmonic series the connection $\frac{2}{3}$, where the progress of 5th being that whose 9th is prepared and doubled, the following connection $\frac{3}{4}$ or progress of 4th is that whose same 9th ought to be saved. The 9th ought then to descend a degree, to seek in the harmonic series the unison of the second progress, and consequently the octave of the fundamental sound.

General System of Dissonances.

By following the same method, we shall find that the 11th F should in the same manner descend a degree on the unison E of the harmonic series, according to the correspondant reference $\frac{4}{5}$, that the 12th or superfluous 5th G diesis, ought to redescend on the same G natural, according to the reference $\frac{5}{6}$; and we see the reason, till now unknown, why the bass ought to ascend to prepare the dissonances, and the treble descend to save them. We may also take notice that the 7th, which, in Monf. Rameau's system is the first and almost the only dissonance, is placed the last in that of of Monſ. Tartini; ſo much it was decreed theſe authors ſhould be contradictory in every circumſtance.

If we have clearly underſtood the generations and analogies of the three orders or ſyſtems, all founded on the firſt, given by nature, and all repreſented by the parts of the circle or their powers, we ſhall find firſt, That the particular harmonic ſyſtem, which gives the major mode, is produced by the ſextuple diviſion in harmonic progreſſion of the diameter, or the entire chord, conſidered as the unity. Secondly, that the arithmetical ſyſtem, from whence the minor mode reſults, is produced by the arithmetical ſeries of the complements; taking the ſmaller term for the unity, and raiſing it from term to term as far as the ſextuple computation, which at laſt gives the diameter, or the entire chord. Thirdly, that the geometrical ſyſtem, or the diſſonant is alſo drawn from the harmonic ſyſtem, by doubling the powers of each interval; from whence it follows, that the harmonic ſyſtem of the major mode, the only one immediately given by nature, ſerves as a principle and foundation to the reſt.

By what has been yet ſaid, we ſee that the harmonic ſyſtem is not compoſed of parts which reunite to form the whole, but on the contrary, it is from the diviſion of the whole, or the integral unity, that the parts are drawn; that the concord forms to itſelf no ſounds, but that it gives them; and that laſtly, whereſoever the harmonic ſyſtem has a place, the harmony does not derive from the melody, but the melody from the harmony.

The elements of the diatonic melody are contained in the ſucceſſive degrees of the ſcale or octave of the major mode, beginning by C, from which is derived alſo the ſcale of the minor mode, beginning by A.

This ſcale not being exactly in the order of the aliquots is no more than that which the natural diviſions of horns, trumpets, and other ſimilar inſtruments produce, as may be ſeen in the plate by the compariſon of theſe two ſcales, a compariſon, which ſhews at the ſame time the cauſe of the falſe tones given by theſe inſtruments.

Diatonic Scale.

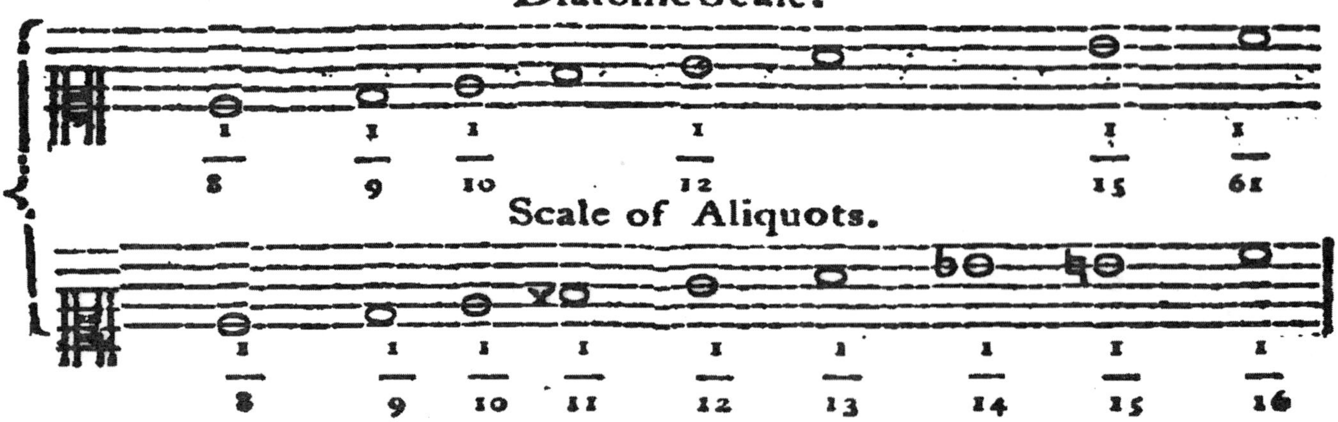

However, the common scale, tho' not in concord with the series of the aliquots, has not a less physical and natural origin to be explained.

The portion of the first series O, which determines the harmonic system, is the sesquialter or 5th C G; that is, the octave harmonically divided.

Besides, the two terms, which correspond to those in the series P of the complements, are the notes G F. These two chords are the middle; the one harmonic the other artificial, betwixt the entire chord and its half, or between the diameter and the ray; and these two middle G and F being connected both to the same fundamental, determine the tone and even the mode, since the harmonic proportion predominates over it; and they appear before the generation of the minor mode, having no other law than that which is determined by the harmonic series, from whence they are derived; they ought each to bear the character, viz. The perfect major concord, composed of major 3d and 5th.

If then we connect and range successively, according to the nearest order, the notes which constitute these three concords, we shall have very exactly, as well in musical notes, as in numerical connections, the octave or ordinary diatonic scale rigorously established.

In notes, the thing is evident by a single operation.

In numerical connections, this is almost as easily proved, for supposing 360 for the length of the entire chord, these three notes C, G, F, will be as 180, 240, 270; their concords will be as follows:

and the entire scale seduced from it, will be in the connections marked as follows:

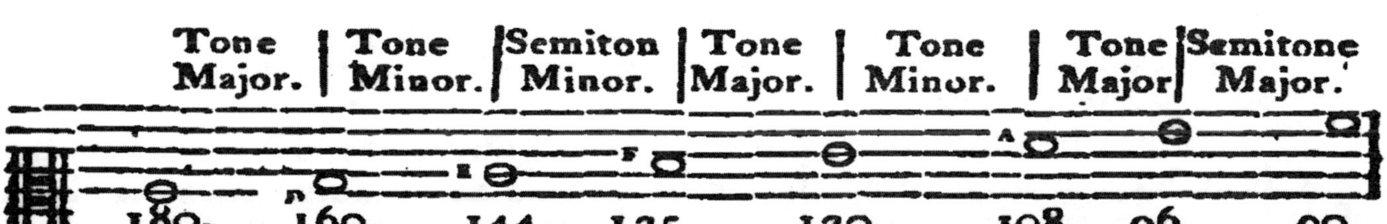

Where we see that all the intervals are just, except the perfect concord, D F A, in which the 5th D A is weak by a comma, as well as the minor third D F, on account of the minor tone D E; but in every system this error, or an equivalent one is inevitable.

In

In regard to the other alterations, which the neceſſity of uſing the ſame touches in different tones, introduces into our ſcale), Vide Modification.) The ſcale being once eſtabliſhed, the principal uſe of the notes C G F, from whence it is derived, is the formation of the three cadences, which giving a progreſs of fundamental notes from one to the other, are the baſs of all modulation. G being an harmonic means, and F, an arithmetical means betwixt the two terms of the octave, the paſſage from the middle to the extreme forms a cadance which takes its name from the middle which produces it, G C is then an harmonic cadence; F C an arithmetical; and we call mixt cadence, that which, paſſing from the arithmetical means to the harmonic means, is compoſed of the two before reſolving on the extreme.

Harmonic Cadence. Arithmetical Cadence. Mixt Cadence.

Of theſe three cadences, the harmonic is the principal and the firſt in order: Its effect is of a flat harmony, ſtrong, and terminating in an abſolute ſenſe.

The arithmetical is weak, ſweet, and leaves a ſomething ſtill to be deſired. The mixt cadence ſuſpends the ſenſe, and produces nearly the effect of the interrogative and admirative point.

From the natural ſucceſſion of theſe three cadences, ſuch as we ſee it in a former plate. There reſults exactly the fundamental baſs of the ſcale; and from their different intermixtures is derived the method of treating any tone, and modulating on it a ſeries of airs, for each note of the cadence is ſuppoſed to bear the perfect concord as has been ſaid before.

In regard to what is called "The Rule of the Octave", it is evident, that tho' we ſhould not even admit the harmony which it ſpecifies as pure and regular, as it is found only through dint of art and deductions, it can never be propoſed, in quality of principle and a general law.

The compoſers of the 15th age, the generality of whom were excellent harmoniſts, uſed the whole ſcale as a fundamental baſs of as many perfect concords as it had notes, except the 7th on account of the falſe 5th; and this harmony well conducted, would have formed a very great effect, if the perfect concord on the mediant had not been rendered too harſh by theſe two falſe relations with the concord which precedes it, and that which follows.

To

To render this series of perfect concords as pure and sweet as possible, we must reduce it to this other fundamental bass, which furnishes with the precedent, a new source of varieties.

As we find in this formula, two perfect concords in minor third, viz. D A, it will be necessary to seek the analogy which the major and minor tones should have together in a regular modulation.

Let us consider the note eb of the example P, united to the two correspondent notes of the examples O and Q, taken as fundamental: it is found by this means as the Base, or foundation of a concord in major third; but taken as an arithmetical means between the entire chord and its fifth, as in the example X of the other plate: it is then found mediant or second base of the minor mode: So this same note, considered under two different references, and both deducted from the system, gives two harmonies; from whence it follows, that the scale of the major mode is a minor third above the analogous scale of the minor mode.

Wherefore the minor mode analogous to the scale of ut, is that of la, and the minor mode analogous to that of fa, is that of re.

Moreover, la and re, give exactly, in the fundamental bass of the diatonic scale, the two minor concords analogous to the two tones of ut and fa, determined by the two harmonic cadences of ut to fa and of sol to ut. The fundamental bass, wherein we make these two concords enter, is then as regular, and more varied than the precedent, which only contains the harmony of the minor mode.

In regard to the two last dissonances n and r of the example q, as they come from the diatonic genus, we will not yet speak of them.

The origin of the measure, the periods, phrases, and all the musical rhyme, is found also in the generation of the cadences, in their natural series, and their different combinations. First, the means being homogenous to its extreme, the two members of a cadence ought in their first simplicity, to be of the same nature and equal powers. Consequently the eight notes which form the four cadences, the fundamental bass of the scale, are equal together; and forming also four equal measures, one for each cadence, the whole gives a compleat sense, and an harmonic period.

Moreover, as the whole harmonic system is founded on the double and sesqui alter computation, which on account of the octave is confounded with the triple powers, in the same manner every good and sensible measure is resolved on that of two times, or that of three, all which is below, often attempted, and always unsuccessful, not being able to produce any good effect.

From the different foundations of harmony given by the three sorts of cadence, and from the different methods of intermixing them, arises the variety of the senses, of phrases, and the whole melody,

lody; of which the ingenious musician expresses all that of the phrases for discourse, and punctuates the sounds as correctly as the Grammarian does the words.

From the measure given by the cadences, there results also the exact expression of the prosody and rhyme; for as the short syllable rests on the long, in the same manner the note which prepares the cadence, in rising, sustains itself and pauses on the note which resolves it in striking; which divides the times into strong and weak, as the syllables into long and short.

This shews how we can, even in observing the quantities, reverse the prosody and measure the whole *à contre tems*, when we strike the short syllables and raise the long; tho' we should think we observed their relative durations and musical powers.

The use of dissonant notes by conjoint degrees in the weak times of the measure, is also deduced from principles established thereon; for let us suppose the diatonic and measured scale as follows,

X

Z

it is evident, that the note sustained or struck in the bass x, instead of the notes in the bass z, is only thus tolerated, because always returning on the strong times, it easily escapes our attention in the weaker; and the cadences, whose place it has, are not less supposed, which could not be, if the dissonant notes changed place, and were struck on the strong times.

Let us next see what sounds may be added or substituted to those of the diatonic scale, for the formation of the chromatic and enharmonic genera.

By inserting in their natural order the sounds given by the series of dissonances, we shall first have the note sol diesis n, which gives the chromatic genus, and the regular passage of the major tone of ut to its minor corresponding la.

Chromatic

Chromatic Tetrachord.

We have next the note r or ſi b flat, which with that I have ſpoken of, gives the enharmonic genus.

Tho' in regard to the diatonic, the whole harmonic ſyſtem is, as has been ſeen, contained in the ſextuple computation, yet the diviſions are not ſo bounded to this extent, but betwixt the 19th or triple fifth $\frac{1}{6}$, and the 22d or quadruple octave $\frac{1}{8}$, we may inſert an hormonic means $\frac{1}{7}$ taken in the order of aliquots, and given alſo by nature in the french-horns and trumpets, and of an intonation very eaſy on the violin.

This term $\frac{1}{7}$, which harmonically divides the interval of the 4th ſol ut or $\frac{6}{8}$, does not form with the ſol a juſt minor third, whoſe reference would be $\frac{5}{6}$, but an interval a little leſs, whoſe whoſe reference is $\frac{6}{7}$, ſo that we cannot exactly expreſs it in notes; for the la dieſis is already too ſtrong: We ſhall repreſent it by the note ſi, preceded by the ſign |ↄ, a little different from the ordinary b flat.

The ſcale augmented, or as the Greeks ſay, the Epaiſſi Genus of theſe three new ſounds placed in their rank, will be then as the example.

Genus épaiſſi.

The

The whole for the same tone, or at least for the tones naturally analogous.

Of these three added sounds, the first of which, as Tartini shews, constitutes the chromatic genus, and the third the enharmonic; the sol diesis and the si b flat are in the order of dissonances; but the si ↄ does not fail to be consonant, tho' it does not belong to the diatonic genus; being out of the sextuple progression which contains and determines this genus; for since it is immediately given by the harmonic series of the aliquots, since it is the harmonic medium between the 5th and octave of the fundamental sound, it follows from thence that it is consonant as themselves, and neither wants to be prepared or saved: This is also what the ear confirms perfectly in the regular use of this kind of 7th.

By the assistance of this new tone, the bass of the diatonic scale returns exactly on itself, in descending, according to the nature of the circle which represents it; and the 14th or 7th redoubled, is then found regularly saved by this note on the tonic or fundamental bass, as all the other dissonances.

Would you wish to deduce from the principles before placed, the rules of modulation, take the three major relative tones, ut, sol, fa, and the three minor analogous tones la, mi, re, you will have 6 tonics; and these are the only ones on which we can modulate, in going from the principal tone: Modulations which we intermix by choice, according to the character of the air, and the expression of the words; not, however that amongst these modulations there are some preferable to others: These preferences even immediately discovered by the sentiment, have also their principles and numerical powers, and their exceptions, whether in the different impressions which the composer would make, or in the greater or lesser union he gives his phrases. For instance, the most natural and most agreeable modulation in major mode, is that which passes from the tonic ut, to its dominant sol, because the mode major, being founded on harmonic divisions, and the dominant harmonically dividing the octave, the passage from the first term to the middle is the most natural. On the contrary, in the minor mode la, founded on the arithmetical proportion, the passage from the tone to the 4th note re, which arithmetically divides the octave, is much more natural than the passage from the dominant to the tone mi, which harmonically divides the same octave, and if we examine attentively, we shall find, that the modulations more or less agreeable, all depend on the greater or smaller references established in this system.

Let us next examine the concords or particular intervals in the minor mode, which are deduced from the sounds added to the scale.

The

The analogy between the two modes gives the three following concords,

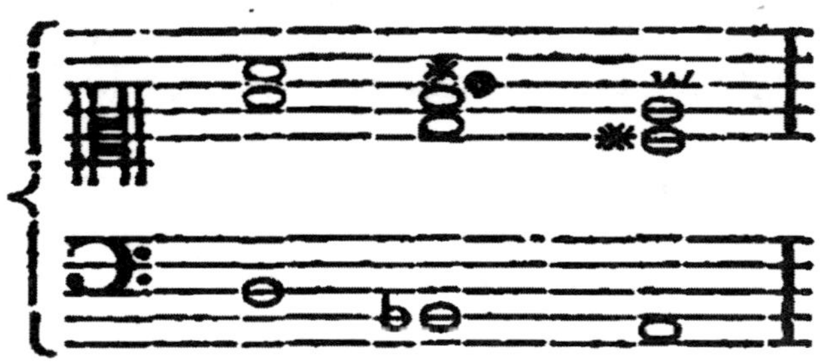

all whose sounds have been found consonant in the establishment of the major mode. There is only the added sound g ✕ whose consonance can be disputed.

We must next take notice, that this concord is not resolved in the dissonant concord of diminished 7th, which would have sol diesis for bass, because besides the diminished 7th sol diesis and fa natural, there is also found a diminished third sol diesis, and si b flat, which breaks all proportion, which experience confirms by the unsurmountable roughness of this concord. On the contrary, besides that this arrangement of superfluous 6th pleases the ear, and is very harmoniously resolved, Monf. Tartini pretends that the interval is really good, regular, and even consonant, First, because this 6th is very nearly an harmonic 4th, to the three notes B b, d, f, represented by the fractions $\frac{1}{4}$ $\frac{1}{5}$ $\frac{1}{6}$, of which $\frac{1}{7}$ is the proportional exact harmonic 4th. Secondly, because that same 6th, is very nearly the harmonic means of the 4th fa, si b flat, formed by the 5th of the fundamental sound and its octave. If, on this occasion, we make use of the note marked sol diesis, rather than the note marked la b flat, which seems to be the true harmonic means, it is not only that this division would remove us very far from the mode, but even that this same note la b flat, is only an harmonic means in appearance, provided that, the 4th fa si b flat, is changed and too weak by a comma; so that sol diesis, which has a less connection to fa, draws nearer to the true harmonic means than la b flat, which has a greater connection to the same fa.

We ought besides to observe that all the sounds of this concord, which re-unite in a regular harmony, are exactly the four same sounds furnished beforehand, in the dissonant series Q by the complements of the divisions of the harmonic sextuple: which, in some respect, closes the harmonic circle, and confirms the union of all the parts in the system.

By the assistance of this 6th, and all the other sounds, which harmonic and analogous proportion furnish in the minor mode, we we have a very eaſy method of prolonging and varying the harmony, without going out of the mode, or even of making uſe of any real diſſonance, as may be ſeen in the example of the counter-point given by Monſ. Tartini, and in which he pretends not to have uſed any diſſonance unleſs the 4th, and final 5th.

This ſame ſuperfluous 6th, has alſo more important and nicer uſes in modulations, turned by enharmonic paſſages, in that it may be indifferently taken in practice for the 7th bemolized by the ſign | ↄ ↄ, from which this dieſis'd 6th differs very little in calculation, and not at all on the keys. In that caſe, this 7th, or that 6th always conſonant, but marked ſometimes by dieſis, and ſometimes by b flat, according to the tone from whence we go out, and that which we enter, produces in harmony apparent and ſudden metamorphoſes, of which, though regular in this ſyſtem, the compoſer would be very much embarraſſed to give a reaſon in any other, as may be ſeen in the following examples,

I.

II.

Corrected

III.

Corrected

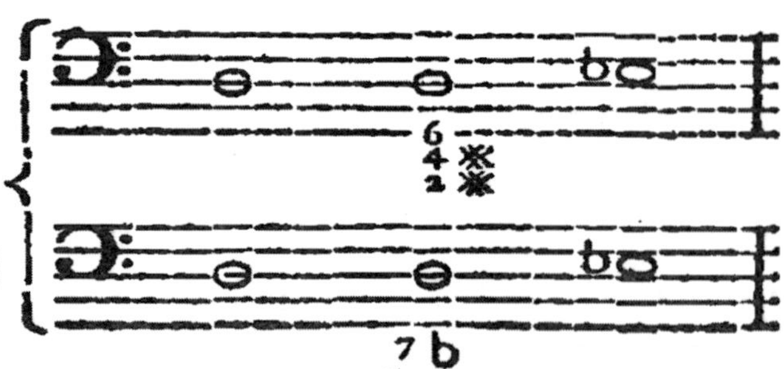

8 particularly

particularly in that marked +, when the fa taken as natural, and forming an apparent 7th which cannot be ſaved, is at bottom, no more than a ſuperfluous 6th formed by a mi dieſis, on the ſol of the baſs; which enters into the rigor of the rules. But it is ſuperfluous to extend on the fineſſes of the art, which does not eſcape ingenious harmoniſts, and which others would only abuſe, in uſing them *mal a propos*. It is ſufficient to have ſhewn that the whole is held on ſomething, and that the true ſyſtem of nature leads to the moſt intricate and hidden turnings of the art.

T.

T. This letter is ſometimes written in partitions to deſign the part of the tenor, when this tenor takes the place of the baſs, and is written on the ſame ſtave, the baſs preſerving the pauſe.

Sometimes in the parts of ſymphony, the T ſignifies tutti, and is oppoſed to the letter S, or the word ſolo, which in that caſe muſt have neceſſarily been written before in the ſame part.

TA. One of the four ſyllables with which the Greeks ſol-fa their muſic. (Vide to Sol-fa.)

TABLATURE. This word formerly ſignified the totality of the ſigns in muſic; ſo that, whoever underſtood the notes, and could ſing *á livre ouvert*, was ſaid to be ſkilled in the tablature.

At preſent the word tablature is reſtrained to a certain method of marking by letters, which we uſe for the chord inſtruments touched by the fingers, ſuch as the Lute, the Guittar, and formerly the Theorb, and the Viol.

To mark in tablature, we draw as many parallel lines as the inſtrument has chords. We then write on thoſe lines ſome letters of the alphabet, which expreſſes the different poſitions of the fingers on the chords, from ſemi-tone to ſemi-tone. The letter A denotes the chord a vide, b, expreſſes the firſt poſition, c the ſecond, d the third, &c.

In regard to the powers of the notes, they are marked by ordinary notes of ſimilar powers, all placed on the ſame line, becauſe theſe notes ſerve only to mark the power, and not the degree.

When the powers are always ſimilar, that is, that the method of ſcanning the notes is the ſame in all meaſures, we are ſatisfied with marking it on the firſt, and we proceed.

Herein lies all the myſtery of the tablature which we will aſſiſt towards an explanation by the inſpection of Fig. V. Plate II.

Wherein I have pricked down the firſt couplet of the *Folies d Eſpagne* in tablature for the guittar.

As

As the generality of instruments, for which the tablature measured, are out of use, and as we have found the ordinary notes more convenient for those which are still played, the tablature is almost entirely laid aside or only serves for a scholar's first lessons.

TACET. A Latin word used in music to denote the silence of a part. When, in the course of a piece of music, we would mark a silence of a certain time, we write it with rests or pauses. But when some part ought to preserve a silence throughout an entire piece, we express it by the word tacet, written in the part below the name, or first notes of the air.

TAIL. We distinguish in notes the head and the tail. The head is the body of the note itself. The tail is that perpendicular stroke which is fixed to the head, and which ascends or falls indifferently across the stave. In church music, the greatest part of the notes have no tail, but in our music there is only the semi-breve without it. Formerly the breve had none also; but the different positions of the tail served to distinguish the powers of the other notes and particularly the plica.

At present the tail added to the notes of church music prolongs their duration; it abridges it, on the contrary, in ours, since a minum is equal to only half a semi-breve.

TAMBOURIN. A kind of dance very much in fashion at present on the French stage. Its air is very lively, and is struck in two quick times. It ought to be well cadenced and bold, in imitation of the flute amongst those of Provence, and the bass ought to re-strike the same note, in imitation of the Galoubé, with which the player on the flute is generally accompanied.

TASTE. Of all natural gifts, taste is that which is most felt and least explained: It would not be what it is, if it could be defined; for it judges of objects, in which the judgment is not concerned, and serves, as it were, as spectacles to reason.

There are in melody, some airs more agreeable than others, tho' equally well modulated. There are, in harmony things striking, and others not so, all equally regular. There is in the union of pieces, an exquisite art of making the one receive a power from the other, which depends on something more nice than the law of contrasts. There are in the execution of the same piece, different methods of rendering it, without ever removing it from its character: Of these methods, the one pleases more than the others, and far from being able to submit them to rules, we cannot even determine them. Reader, give me a cause for their differences, and I will explain you what is taste.

Each man has his peculiar taste, by the which he gives to things, which he calls beautiful and excellent, an order which belongs to himself alone. One is more touch'd with pathetic pieces; the other prefers a gay air. A sweet and flexible voice will

will fill its tunes with agreeable ornaments, a sensible and strong voice will animate them with the accents of passion. The one will seek simplicity in melody, the other will aim at laboured strokes, and each will cal that an elegance of taste, which he has preferred.

This diversity comes sometimes from the different dispositions of the organs, from which taste is extracted; Sometimes from the particular character of each man, which renders him more sensible to one pleasure or failing, than to another; sometimes from the divinity of age or sex, which turns the desires towards the different objects. In all these cases, each having only his own taste to oppose to that of another, it is evident, that there is no dispute to be made.

But there is also a general taste, on which all organised persons agree, and it is this only, to which we can absolutely give the name of taste. Let a concert be heard by ear sufficiently exercised, and men sufficiently instructed; the greatest number will generally agree on the judgment of the pieces, and on the order of preference convenient to them. Ask each one the reason of his judgment; there are things on which they will give an almost unanimous opinion. These are the things which may be submitted to rules, and this common judgment is that of the artist and the connoisseur. But amongst these things, which they agree to find good or ill, there are some on which they cannot authorize their judgment by any reason, solid and common, to the rest; and this last judgment belongs to a man of taste. If there is not found a perfect unanimity, it is, that all have not equally good organs; that all are not persons of taste; and that the prejudices of custom or education, often change, by arbitrary conventions, the order of natural beauties. In regard to this taste, we may dispute on it, by another method of determining the variance, than that of counting the notes, when we do not even agree to that of nature. Here then is what ought to decide, in respect to the preference of French and Italian music.

Genius creates, but taste makes the choice; and a too abundant genius is often in want of a severe censor, to prevent it from abusing its valuable riches. We can do great things without taste, but it is that alone which renders them interesting. It is taste, which makes the composer catch the ideas of the poet: It is taste, which makes the executant catch the ideas of the composer.

It is taste, which furnishes to each whatever may adorn and augment their subject; and it is taste which gives the audience the sentiment of their agreements.

Taste however is by no means sensibility. We may have much taste, with a frigid soul; and a man transported with things really passionate, is little touched with the pleasing. It seems that taste is more particularly connected with the smaller expressions, and sensibility to the greater.

TASTE in SINGING. By this term is called in France, the art of singing or playing the notes with the graces suitable to them, to cover a little the flatness of the French airs. We find at Paris several instructors of this taste, whose principles may be found at the word *graces*.

The taste in singing consists also much in artificially giving to a singer, the tone, whether good or ill, of some actor or actress in vogue. Sometimes it consists in squeaking thro' the nose, sometimes in imitating a duck, a goat, &c. &c, but all these, are temporary graces, which change incessantly with their authors.

TASTO SOLO. These two Italian words written in a thorough bass, and generally under some organ point, mark that the accompanist ought to make no concord with the right hand, but only to strike with the left the marked note, and at most, its octave, without adding any thing; provided that it would be almost impossible for him to follow the turning of the harmony or notes of taste, which the composer makes to pass on the bass during that time.

TE. One of the four syllables by which the Greeks sol fa the music.

TENDERLY. This adverb written at the head of an air, expresses a slow and sweet movement, sounds drawn pleasingly and animated both tender and touching. The Italians make use of the word amoroso, to express nearly the same thing; but the character of the amoroso has more accent, and breathes a *je ne sais quoi* of less flat and more passionate.

TENEDIUS. A kind of nome for flutes in the ancient Greek music.

TENOR. The second of the four parts of music, counting from flat to sharp. It is the part which is most convenient to the common voice of a man; which is the cause of its often being called thro' preference "The human Voice".

The tenor is sometimes divided into two other parts; the one more elevated which we call first of counter tenor, the other lower, called second or bass tenor. This last is in some respects a midling or common part, between the tenor and bass, and is also called on that account *Concordant*. (Vide Parts.)

We hardly make use of any tenor in the French operas: On the contrary, the Italians prefer in theirs the tenor to the bass, as a voice more flexible, as sonorous, and much less rough.

TENOUR. A term of church music which marks in psalmody the part which reigns from the end of the intonation as far as the mediation, and from the mediation, as far as the termination.

This

This tenour, which we may call the dominant of the pfalmody, is almoft always on the fame tone.

TENTH. An interval, which comprehends nine conjoint degrees, and confequently 10 diatonic founds, in reckoning the two which form it. This is the octave of the third, or the third of the octave, and the 10th is major or minor, as the fimple interval, whofe replique it is. (Vide Third.)

TETRACHORD. Was, in ancient mufic, an order or particular fyftem of founds, whofe extreme chords founded the 4th.

This fyftem was called tetrachord, becaufe the founds which compofed it, were generally four in number; which however was not always true.

Nichomachus, according to Boetius, fays, that mufic in its firft fimplicity had only four founds or chords, whofe two extremes founded the diapafon together; whereas the two mean diftances of a tone one from the other, founded each the fourth with the extreme, to which it was neareft, and the fifth with that from which it was moft diftant. He calls that the tetrachord of Mercury, from the name of him who was faid to be its inventor.

Boetius alfo fays, that after the addition of three chords made by different authors, Lychaon of Pamos, added an 8th, which he placed betwixt the trite and paramefis, which were formerly the fame chord; which rendered the octachord complete, and compofed of two disjoint tetrachords from the conjoint, which they were formerly in the heptachord.

I have confulted the work of Nicomachus, and it appears to me that there is nothing faid to that purpofe. He fays on the contrary, that Pythagoras having remarked, that, tho' the mean found of the two tetrachords founded the confonance of the 4th with each of the extremes, thefe extremes compared together were entirely diffonant; he inferted between the two tetrachords an 8th found, which, dividing them by a tone of interval, fubftituted the diapafon or the octave in the place of the 7th between their extremes, and produced alfo a new confonance between each of the two mean chords and the extreme oppofed to it.

On the method, by which this addition was made, Nicomachus and Boetius are equally in an error; and not contented with contradicting each other, each of them even contradicts himfelf. (Vide Syftem, Trite, Paramefis.)

If we paid attention to what Boetius and other more ancient writers fay, we could give no fixed bounds to the extent of the tetrachord; but whether we divide or flatten the voice, we fhall find, that the moft exact definition is that of old Bacchius, and that alfo which I have preferred.

In effect, this interval of 4th is effential to the tetrachord; for which reafon the extreme founds, which form this interval are called

called immoveable or fixed, by the ancients; whereas they call moveable or changing the middle ſounds, becauſe they may be concordant in ſeveral methods.

On the contrary, the number of four chords, from whence the tetrachord has taken his name, is ſo little eſſential to it, that we ſee, in ancient muſic, ſome tetrachords which had only three. Such were, at one time, the enharmonic tetrachords. Such was according to Meibomius, the ſecond tetrachord of the ancient ſyſtem, before a new chord was inſerted. In regard to the firſt tetrachord, it was certainly complete before Pythagoras, as we ſee in the Pythagorean Nicomachus; which does not hinder Monſ. Rameau from affirming, that, according to the unanimous report Pythagoras found the tone, the diton, the ſemi-tone; and that, on the whole, he formed the diatonic tetrachord, (Take notice that that would make a tetrachord), inſtead of ſaying that Pythagoras found only the computations of thoſe intervals, which, according to a more unanimous report, were known a long time before him.

The tetrachords did not long continue bounded to the number of two: there was very ſoon a third formed, then a fourth; a number, to which the ſyſtem of the Greeks continued fixed.

All theſe tetrachords were conjoint; that is, the laſt chord of the firſt, always ſerved as the firſt chord of the ſecond, and ſoon, except a ſingle place in flat, or in ſharp of the third tetrachord, where there was a disjunction, which placed a tone of interval betwixt the higher chord of the inferior tetrachord, and the loweſt of the ſuperior. (Vide Synaphe, Diazeuxis.) Moreover, as this disjunction of the third tetrachord, was ſometimes made with the ſecond, ſometimes with the fourth; this made a particular name peculiar to this third tetrachord, in each of the two caſes.

So that, though there were properly only four tetrachords, there were however five denominations.

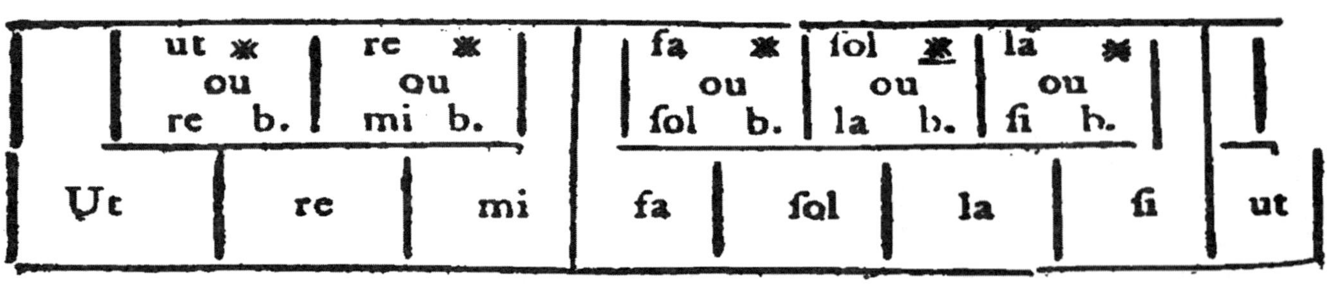

Here are the names of theſe tetrachords. The flatteſt of all the four, and which was placed a tone above the chord proſlambanomenos, is called the tetrachord hypaton; The ſecond in aſcending, which was always conjoint with the firſt, was called the tetrachord meſon;

meson; The third, when it was conjoint to the second, and separated from the fourth, then this third tetrachord took the name of diezeugmenon. Lastly, the fourth was called the tetrachord hyperbolean. Aretin added to this system a 5th tetrachord, which Meibomius pretends that he only re-established. However it may be, the particular systems of the tetrachords gave at last place to that of the octave, which furnished them all,

The two extreme chords of each of these tetrachords were called immoveable, because their concord never changed; but each contained also two middling chords, which, tho' in true concord in all the tetrachords, were however subject, as I have said, to be raised or lowered, according to the genus, and even the kind of the genus; which was equally done in all the tetrachords. For this reason the chords were called moveable.

There were six principal kinds of concord, according to the Aristoxenians, viz. Two for the diatonic genus, three for the chromatic, and one only for the enharmonic. Ptolomy reduces these six kinds to five.

These different kinds, reduced to the most common practice, formed only three, one for each genus.

I. The diatonic ordinary concord of the tetrachord formed three intervals, the first of which was always of a semi-tone, and the two others each of a tone, in this manner: mi, fa, sol, la.

For the chromatic genus, it was necessary to lower the third chord a semi-tone, and they had two consecutive semi-tones, then a minor third, mi, fa, fa diesis, la.

Lastly, for the enharmonic genus, it was necessary to lower the two chords from the middle, till we had two fourths of consecutive tones, then a major third, mi, mi demi diesis, fa, la, which formed between the mi diesis and the fa, a real enharmonic interval.

The similar chords, though they are sol-fa'd by the same syllables, did not bear the same names in all the tetrachords, but in the flat tetrachords they had denominations different from those which they had in the sharp tetrachords.

The homologous chords, considered as such, bore general names which expressed the connection of their position in their respective tetrachords; wherefore, the name of Barypycni was given to the first sounds of the confined interval, that is, to the flattest sound of each tetrachord; from the mesopycni to the seconds or means, from the oxypycni to the third or sharp, and from the apycni to those, which did not touch the confined intervals on any side. (Vide System.)

This division of the system of the Greeks by similar tetrachords, as we divide ours by octaves similarly divided, proves, I think that this system had been produced by no sentiment of harmony, but that they endeavoured to render, by more confined intervals, the

the inflexions of the voice, which their ſonorous and harmonious language gave to their ſuſtained recitation, and particularly to that of their poetry, which was then a veritable muſic; ſo that the muſic was then no more than the accent of the words, and did not become a ſeparated art till after a long track of time. However it may be, it is certain that they confined their primitive diviſions to four chords, all the reſt of which were only repliques, and that they looked on all the other tetrachords, only as ſo many repetitions of the firſt. From whence I conclude, that there is no more analogy between their ſyſtem and ours, than between a tetrachord and an octave, and that the fundamental movement in our mode, which we give as a baſs to their ſyſtem, has no connection with it in any reſpect.

I. Becauſe a tetrachord formed for them as complete a whole, as an octave forms for us.

II. Becauſe they had only four ſyllables to ſol fa, whereas we have ſeven.

III. Becauſe their tetrachords were conjoint, or disjoint at will, which expreſſed their entire reſpective independance.

IV. And laſtly, becauſe the diviſions were exactly ſimilar in each genus, and were practiſed in the ſame mode, which could not be done in our ideas by any truly harmonic modulation.

TETRADIAPASON. Is the Greek name of the quadruple octave, which we alſo called 29th. The Greeks knew no more than the name of this interval, for their ſyſtem of muſic did not reach it. (Vide Syſtem.)

TETRATONON. Is the Greek name of an interval of four tones, called at preſent ſuperfluous 5th. (Vide Fifth.)

TEXT. Is the poem, where the words are, which are ſet to muſic. But this word is abſolete in this ſenſe, and *text* is no longer uſed amongſt muſicians, but the *words*.

THE. One of the four ſyllables which the Greeks uſed to ſol fa.

THESIS. Lowering, or poſition. By this name was formerly called the ſtrong, or ſtruck time of the meaſure.

THO. One of the four ſyllables which the Greeks uſed to ſol fa.

THIRTEENTH. An interval, which forms the octave of the 6th or the 6th of the octave. This interval is called 13th, becauſe it is formed of 12 diatonic degrees, that is, of 13 ſounds.

TIE. There is a tie in harmony, and a tie in muſic.

The tie has a place in harmony, when this harmony proceeds by ſuch a progreſs of fundamental ſounds, as that ſome one of the ſounds which accompany that we leave, continues and accompanies that which we paſs. There is a tie in the concords of the tonic, and dominant, ſince the ſame ſound forms the 5th of the firſt and the octave of the ſecond; there is a tie in the concords of the tonic

and

and sub-dominant, provided that the same sound serves as 5th to one, and octave to the other. Lastly, there is a tie in the dissonant concord every time that the dissonance is prepared, since the preparation itself is nothing else than the tie.

The tie in the air has place every time that we pass two or more notes, under a single stroke of the bow, or the throat, and is marked by a bent stroke, with which the notes are covered, which ought to be united together.

In church music we call a tie, a continuance of several notes passed on the same syllable, because on the paper they are generally tied or united together.

Some name a tie also what is properly called syncope.

TIED. We call tied notes, two or more notes, which we pass with a single stroke of the bow on the violin, and the violincello; or with a single stroke of the tongue on the flute, and the hautboy: In a word, all the notes which are under the same tie.

TIERCE. The last of the simple and direct consonances in the order of their generation, and the first of the two imperfect consonances.

As the Greeks did not admit it as consonant, it had no general name amongst them; but it took only the name of less or greater interval, from which it was formed. We call it tierce, because its interval is always composed of two degrees, and three diatonic sounds. To consider the tierces only in the last sense, that is, by their degrees, we find of four sorts, two consonant, and two dissonant. The consonants are first. The major tierce, which the Greeks called diton, composed of two tones, as from ut to mi. Its connection is from 4 to 5. Secondly, the minor third called by the Greeks hemiditon, and composed of a tone and a half, as mi sol. Its connection is from 5 to 6.

The dissonant tierces are first. The diminished tierce, composed of two major semi-tones, as si ré b flat, whose reference is from 125 to 144. Secondly, the superfluous tierce, composed of two tones and a half, as fa la diesis. Its reference is from 96 to 125.

This last interval not having place in a same mode, is never used either in harmony, or in melody. The Italians practice sometimes the diminished third in the air, but it has no place in any harmony; and this is the reason that the concord of superfluous 6th has no variation.

The consonant tierces are the spirit of harmony, particularly the major third, which is sonorous and brilliant; the minor third is more tender and sorrowful. It has great sweetness when its interval is redoubled, that is, when it forms the 10th. In general the tierces must be carried above; below they are flat and little harmonious,

harmonious, for which reaſon a duet of baſſes has never a good effect.

Our ancient muſicians had almoſt as ſevere laws on the tierces as on the 5ths. It was forbidden to make two together, even of different kinds, particularly by ſimilar movements. At preſent that we have generalized by the good laws of the mode, the peculiar rules of the concord, we form without any error, by ſimilar or contrary movements, by conjoint and disjoint degrees, as many conſecutive major or minor tierces as the modulation can ſuffer, and we have very agreeable duets which from beginning to end, proceed only by tierces.

Tho' the tierce enters into the generality of concords, it does not give its name to any, unleſs to that which ſome call concord of tierce 4th, and which is moſt commonly known by the name of ſmaller 6th. (Vide Concord Sixth.)

TIERCE of PICARDY. The muſicians call by this term, thro' pleaſantry, the major tierce given, inſtead of the minor, to the final of a piece, compoſed in minor mode. As the major perfect concord is more harmonious than the minor, it was formerly a law to finiſh on the firſt; but this final, tho' harmonious, had ſomething grating which cauſed it to be forſaken. We always finiſh now by the concord which is ſuitable to the mode of the piece, unleſs when we would paſs from minor to major, for then the final of the firſt mode bears the major third elegantly to announce the ſecond.

It was called tierce of Picardy, becauſe the uſe of this final continued longeſt in the church muſic, and conſequently, in Picardy, where they have muſic in a great number of Cathedrals and other Churches.

TIME. The meaſure of a ſound, in regard to its duration.

A ſucceſſion of ſounds, however well it may be directed in its movement, in its degrees from flat to ſharp, or ſharp to flat, produces no more, as it were, than indeterminate effects. It is the relative and proportional durations of theſe ſame ſounds, which fix the true character of muſic, and give it its greateſt energy. The time is the ſpirit of the air: Thoſe airs, whoſe meaſure is ſlow, lead us naturally to ſorrow; but a gay, lively and well cadenced air excites a joy in us, and the feet can hardly be retained from dancing. Remove the meaſure, deſtroy the proportion of the times, the ſame airs which theſe proportions would render agreeable, being left without charms and without force, will become incapable of pleaſing or intereſting. The time on the contrary has its force in itſelf, it depends on that alone, and may ſubſiſt without the diverſity of ſounds. The drum gives us an inſtance of it, always rough and very imperfect, becauſe the ſound of it cannot be ſuſtained.

We

We conſider time in muſic, either with regard to the general movement of an air, and in this ſenſe we ſay that it is ſlow or quick. (Vide Meaſure, Movement,) or, according to the aliquot parts of each meaſure, parts, which are expreſſed by movement of the hand or foot, which are particularly called times; or laſtly, according to the peculiar power of each note. (Vide Power of the Note.)

I have ſufficiently ſpoken, at the word rhyme, of the times in Greek muſic, it remains now to ſpeak of thoſe in modern muſic.

Our ancient muſicians were acquainted with no more than two kinds of meaſure or of time: the one of three times, which thy called perfect meaſure; the other of two, treated as an imperfect; and they called time, modes or prolations, the ſigns which they added to the cleff to determine one or the other of theſe meaſures.

Theſe ſigns did not ſerve that ſingle purpoſe as at preſent, but they fixed alſo the relative power of the notes, as we may have already ſeen at the words mode and prolation, in regard to the maximum, the longue and ſemi-breve. In regard to the breve, the method of dividing it, was, what they preciſely called time, and this time was perfect or imperfect.

When the time was perfect, the breve was equal to three ſemibreves, and they expreſſed that by an entire circle, barred or not barred, and ſometimes alſo by this compoſed cypher $\frac{3}{1}$.

When the time was imperfect, the breve was equal to only two ſemi-breves, and they expreſſed that by a demi-circle or C. Sometimes they turned the C backwards, and this marked a diminution of the half on the powers of each note. We denote the ſame thing at preſent in barring the C. Some have alſo called minor times, that meaſure of the barred C, where the notes continue only the half of their ordinary power; and major time, that of the full C, or of the ordinary meaſure in four times.

We have well retained the triple meaſure of the ancients as well as the double, but by their ſtrange methods of dividing the notes in two methods, we have retained only the ſub-double, tho' we are not leſs in want of the other; ſo that to divide a meaſure or a time into three equal parts, ſigns are wanting to us; and it is with difficulty we know the art of managing them. We muſt have recourſe to the cypher 3, and other expedients, which may ſhew the inſufficiencyof the ſigns.

We have added to ancient muſic, a combination of times, which is the four timed meaſure; but as it may be always reſolved into two 2 timed meaſures, we may ſay that we have abſolutely no more than two times or three times for the aliquot parts of all our different meaſures.

There are as many different powers of times as there are kinds of meaſures and modifications of the movement. But when once the meaſure and movement are determined, all the meaſures ought to be perfectly equal, and all the times of each meaſure perfectly equal together. Moreover, to render this ſenſibility equal, we ſtrike each meaſure, and mark each time by a movement of the hand or foot, and on theſe different movements, we rule exactly the different powers of the notes, according to the character of the meaſure.

It is an aſtoniſhing thing to ſee with what preciſion, we learn the art, by the aſſiſtance of a little cuſtom, of making and following all the times with ſo perfect an equality, that there is no pendulum, which ſurpaſſes the hand or foot of a good muſician in juſtneſs; and that laſtly the ſentiment of this equality alone is ſufficient to guide him, and ſupplies the place of every ſenſible movement; ſo that in each concert the ſame meaſure follows with the greateſt preciſſion, without another taking notice of it, or even himſelf remarking it.

In the different time of a meaſure, there are ſome more ſenſible, more marked than the reſt, tho' of equal powers. The time which marks moſt, is called ſtrong time; that which is marked leſs, is called weak. This is what Monſ. Rameau, in his treatiſe on harmony, called good and ill time. The ſtrong times are, the firſt in the meaſure of two times; the firſt and third in the meaſures of three and four. In regard to the ſecond time it is always weak in all the meaſures, and it is the ſame thing with the fourth in the four timed meaſure.

If we ſub-divide each time, into two other equal parts, which we may call alſo times, or half times, we ſhall have beſides a ſtrong time, for the firſt half, a weak time for the ſecond, and there is no part of a time, which may not be ſub-divided in the ſame manner.

Every note which begins on the weak time, and finiſhes on the ſtrong is a note *à contre tems*, and becauſe it diſguſts and roughens the meaſure in ſome reſpects, it is called ſyncope. (Vide Syncope)

Theſe obſervations are neceſſary to learn a good method of treating the diſſonances. For every diſſonance well prepared ſhould be on the weak time, and ſtruck on the ſtrong; except however in the courſe of avoided cadences, where this rule, tho' applicable to the firſt diſſonance, is not equally ſo to the reſt. (Vide Diſſonance, &c.

TONE. This word has ſeveral ſenſes in muſic.

Firſt. It is taken for an interval, which characteriſes the ſyſtem and the diatonic genus. In this acceptation, there are two ſorts of tones, viz. The major tone, whoſe reference is from 8 to 9, and which reſults from the difference of the 4th to the 5th; and the minor tone, whoſe reference is from 9 to 10, and which reſults from the difference of the minor third to the fourth.

The

The generation of the major tone, and that of the minor are equally found in the second fifth re beginning by ut; for the quantity by which this re surpasses the octave of the first ut, is in the connection from 8 to 9, and that, in which this re is surpassed by mi, major third of this octave, is in the connection from 9 to 10.

Secondly. We call tone the degree of elevation which the voice takes, or on which the instruments ascend, to execute the music.

It is in this sense that we say, in a concert, that the tone is too high or too low. In the churches, there is a tone of chorus peculiar to their music. There is a chapel tone, and an opera tone for the music. This last has nothing fixed, but in France it is generally lower than the other.

Thirdly. We give also the same name to an instrument which serves to give the tone of the concord to the whole orchestra.

This instrument which some call also chorist, is a whistle, which by means of a kind of graduated sucker, by which we lengthen or shorten the pipe at will, gives always nearly the same sound under the same division. But that which depends on the variations of the air, nearly prevents us from being assured of a fixed sound, that it should be exactly the same. Perhaps, since it exists from music, we have never concerted it twice on the same tone. Monf. Diderot, has given, in his principles of accoustic, the methods of fixing the tone with much more precision, by remedying the variations of the air.

Fourthly, and lastly. Tone is taken for a rule of modulation relative to a note or principal chord, which is called tonic. (Vide Tonic.)

On the tones of the ancients. (Vide Mode.)

As our modern system is composed of 12 chords or different sounds, each of these sounds may serve as a foundation to a tone, that is, be its tonic. There are already 12 tones, and as the major and minor modes are applicable to each tone, there are 24 modulations, of which our music is succeptible on these 12 tones. (Vide Modulation.)

These tones differ together by the different degrees of elevation, betwixt the flat and sharp which the tonics maintain. They differ also by the divers alterations of the sounds and intervals, produced in each tone by the modification, so that, on a well tuned harpsichord, a skilful ear recollects without trouble whatsoever sound he hears by the modulation; and these tones are equally known on tuned harpsichords higher or lower the one than the other; which shews that this knowledge comes at least as much from the different modifications as from the degree of elevation which the tonic maintains on the keys.

From thence arises a source of varieties and beauties in the modulation, a diversity and admirable energy in the expression. From thence arises lastly the faculty of exercising different sentiments with similar concords struck in different tones. Are we in want of the majestic, the flat? L F ut fa, and the major tones by b flat will express it nobly. Is the gay, the brilliant wanting? Take A mi la, Da la re, the major tones by diesis. Do we require the affecting, the tender? Take the minor tones by b flat. C sol ut minor conveys tenderness in the soul; F ut fa minor reaches the mournful, and expresses sorrow. In a word, each tone, each mode, has its peculiar expression, which we must study, and herein is one of the methods which render an ingenious composer master, in some respects, of the affections of those who listen to him: It is a kind of equivalent to the ancient modes, tho' very much removed from their variety and their energy.

It is, however, of this agreeable and rich diversity, that Monsf. Rameau would deprive the music, by introducing an entire equality and monotony in the harmony of each mode, by its rule of the modification; a rule already so often proposed and abandoned before him. According to this author, it would render the harmony more perfect. It is certain, however, that nothing can be gained in this on one side, which is not lost on the other; and tho' we should suppose (which is not) that harmony, in general, would be rendered more pure, would that make any amends for what is lost on the side of the expression? (Vide Modification.)

TONE OF THE FOURTH. By this term the organists and musicians of the church have called the plagal of the minor mode, which stops and finishes on the dominant instead of falling on the tonic. This name of the tone of fourth is derived from such; being the modulation of the fourth tone in church music.

TONES OF THE CHURCH. These are the methods of modulating the church-music on such or such a final, taken in the prescribed number, by following certain rules admitted in all the churches where the Gregorian chant is practised.

We reckon eight regular tones, four of which are authentic or principal, and four plagal or collateral. We call authentic tones those where the tonic occupies nearly the lowest degree of the music; but if the air descends three degrees lower than the tonic, in that case the tone is plagal.

The four authentic tones have their finals a degree one from the other, according to the order of these four notes, re, mi, fa, sol. So the first of these tones answering to the doric mode of the Greeks, the second answers to the phrygian; the third to the æolian, (and not to the lydian, as the symphonists say); and the last to the mixo-lydian. It is Saint Miroclet, bishop of Milan,

lan, or, according to others, Saint Ambrose, who, about the year 370, chose these four tones to compose the chant of the church of Milan; and it was, they say, the choice and approbation of these two bishops which occasioned the name of authentics to be given to these four tones.

As the sounds used in these four tones, did not take up all the disdiapason, or the 15 chords of the ancient system, Saint Gregory formed the project of using them all by the addition of four new tones called plagal, which having the same diapasons as the precedent, but their final being raised a fourth, answers properly to the hyper-dorian, the hyper-phrygian, the hyper-æolian, and the hyper mixo lydian. Others attribute the invention of this last to Gui d' Arezzo.

It is from thence that the four authentic tones have each a plagal, as collateral, or supplement; so that after the first tone, which is authentic, comes the second tone, which is its plagal; the third authentic, the fourth plagal, and so on. Which causes that the modes or authentic tones are also called unequal, and the plagal, equal, in regard to their place in the order of sounds.

The discernment of the authentic or the plagal tones is indispensable in him who gives the tone of the chorus; for if the air is in a plagal tone, he must take the final nearly in the medium of the voice; and if the tone is authentic, he should take it in the bass.

Thro' a failure of this observation, the voice is often obliged to be forced or not distinctly heard.

There are also tones called mixed, that is, partaking of the authentic and plagal, or which are in principal and collateral parts; they are also called common modes or tones. In this case, the numerical name of the denomination of the tone is taken from that of the two which predominates, or which is most felt, particularly at the end of a piece.

Sometimes we make transpositions in a tone to the fifth. So, instead of re in the first tone, we shall have la as final, si for mi, ut for fa, and so on. But if the order and modulation do not change, neither does the tone, tho' for the convenience of the voice the final may be transposed. These are observations to be made by the singer or organist who gives the intonation. To appropriate, as much as possible, the extent of all these tones, to that of a single voice, the organists have sought for the tones of music most correspondant to those. Here are those which are established.

1st Tone — — — Re minor
2d Tone — — — Sol minor
3d Tone — — — La minor or Sol
4th Tone — — — La minor, finishing on the dominant

5th

5th Tone———————————Ut major or re
6th Tone———————————Fa major
7th Tone——————— ———Re major
8th Tone——————————— { Sol major, causing the tone to be felt in the tone of ut

We might reduce these eight tones even to a smaller extent by placing in unison the highest note of each tone; or, if we chuse, that which is most struck, and which is called, in the terms of church music, *dominant*; but as it has not been found that the extent of all these tones thus managed exceeds that of the human voice, they have not thought proper to diminish this extent by transpositions more difficult and less harmonious than those in use.

The tones of the church have shewn no submission to the laws of the tones in music. They have no interest in a mediant, or a sensible note, their mode is little determined, and they leave the semi-tones, where they are found in the natural of the scale; provided only that they neither produce a triton or false fifth on the tonic.

TONIC. The name of the principal chord on which the tone is established. All airs finish generally by this note, particularly in the bass. It is that kind of tierce, which the tonic supports, that determines the mode. Wherefore we can compose in the two modes on the same tonic. Lastly, the musicians find this property in the tonic, that the perfect concord rigourously belongs to it alone. When we strike this concord on another note, either some dissonance is understood, or that note becomes tonic for the moment.

By the method of transpositions, the tonic bears the name of ut in major mode, and of la in minor. (Vide Tone, Mode, Gamut, to sol fa, &c.)

Tonic is also the name given by Aristoxenes, to one of the three kinds of the chromatic genus, whose divisions he explains, and which is the ordinary chromatic of the Greeks, preceeding by two consecutive semi-tones, then a minor third. (Vide Genus.)

Tonic is sometimes an adjective. We say the tonic chord, tonic note, tonic concord, &c.

TRAIN. When two notes are separated by a disjoint interval, and this interval is filled with all its diatonic notes, this is called a train. The train differs from the fusee, in that the intermediary sounds which unite the two extremities are very quick, and not sensible in the measure, whereas those of the train having a sensible power, may be slow and even unequal.

The ancients called in Greek ἀγωγὶς, and in Latin Ductus, what we at present call train, and they distinguished three kinds of them

them. First. If the following sounds followed each other in descending, they called that εὐθεῖα, ductus rectus. Secondly. If they followed each other in descending, it was ἀνακάμπτουσα, ductus revertens. Thirdly. If after having ascended by b flat, they redescended by b sharp, or reciprocally, that was called περιφερὴς, ductus circumcurrens. (Vide Cuthia, Anacamptos.)

We should have enough to do at present, that the music is so laboured, if we were to give names to all these different passages.

TRANSITION. Is, in music, a method of sweetening the mount of a disjoint interval, by inserting diatonic sounds between those which form this interval.

The transition is properly a train not marked: Sometimes also it is only an extent of the voice, when the question is only to render the passage of a diatonic degree more sweet.

So, to pass from ut to re, with more sweetness, the transition is taken on ut.

Transition, in harmony, is a fundamental movement proper to change the genus or the tone in a sensible regular manner, and sometimes by intermediaries. So, in the diatonic genus, when the bass moves so as to require, in the parts, the passage of a minor semi-tone, it is a chromatic transition. (Vide Chromatic.)

If we pass from one tone to another by favour of a concord of diminished 7th, it is an enharmonic transition. (Vide Enharmonic.)

TRANSLATION. Is, in our ancient music, the removal of the signification of a point, to a note separated by other notes of this same point. (Vide Point.)

TO TRANSPOSE. This word has several senses in music.

We transpose in executing, when we transpose a piece of music in another tone, than that wherein it is written. (Vide Transposition.)

We transpose in writing, when we mark a piece of music in another tone of music than that in which it has been composed. Which obliges us not only to change the positions of all the notes in the same connection, but also to number the cleff differently, according to the rules prescribed at the article cleff transposed.

We lastly transpose in sol-faing, when without paying attention to the natural name of the notes, we give them those that are relative to the tone, and to the mode in which we sing.

TRANSPOSITION. A change, by which we transport an air or a piece of music from one tone to another.

As there only two modes in our music, to compose in such or such a tone, is nothing else than to fix on such or such a tonic

tonic, that of the two modes which we have chosen. But as the order of sounds is not found naturally disposed on all the tonics, as it ought to be for the establishment of a same mode, we correct these differences by means of the diesis's or b's flat, with which the cleff is numbered, and which transports the two semi-tones from the place where they were, to that where they ought to be for the mode and tone in question. (Vide Transposed Cleff.)

When then we would transpose in a tone a composed air into another, it is first necessary to raise or lower its tonic and all the notes one or more degrees, according to the tone which we have chosen; then to number the cleff as the analogy of this new tone requires. All this is equal for the voice, for in calling ut always the tonic of the major mode, and la, that of the minor, they follow all the affections of the mode, without even paying attention to it. (Vide to Sol-fa.) But it is not a trifling attention for a symphonist to play in one tone what is marked in another; for, tho' he is guided by the notes which he has before him, his fingers must sound very different ones, and he should alter them quite differently according to the varied method with which the cleff should be numbered for the marked tone, and for the transposed, so that often he ought to form diesis's where he sees b's flat, and vice versa, &c.

It is, I think, a great advantage of the system of the author of this Dictionary, to render the pricked music equally proper to all the tones, by changing one single letter. This occasions, that in whatsoever tone we transpose, the instruments which execute have no other difficulty than that of playing the notes, without ever having the embarrassment of the transposition. (Vide Notes.)

TREBLE. The sharpest of the parts in music, that which reigns above all the rest. It is in this sense that we say of the instrumental music, a treble of the violin, a treble of the flute and hautboy, and in general a treble of symphony.

In vocal music, the treble is executed by the voices of women, children, and also by castrats, whose voices, by reports difficult to conceive, gains an octave above, and loses one below, by means of this mutilation.

The treble is generally divided into first and second, and even sometimes into third.

The vocal part, which executes the second treble, is called bass treble, and there are also made recitatives for the voice only for this part. A beautiful bass treble full and sonorous, is not less esteemed in Italy, than the clear and sharp voices; but they pay no regard to them in France. However, by a caprice of the fashion, I have seen a Mad. Gondre, at the Parisian Opera very much applauded, who had in effect a very beautiful bass treble.

TREMBLING

TREMBLING. A grace of singing which the Italians call trillo, and which is oftener designed in french by the word cadence.

They also in former times made use of the term of trembling, in Italian tremelo, to advise those who played bow instruments to strike several times the note, with the same stroke of the bow as for the imitation of the trembling on the organ. Neither the name or the thing are used at present,

HARMONIC TRIAD. This term in music has two different senses. In calculation, it is the harmonic proportion; in practice, it is the perfect major concord which results from this same proportion, and which is composed of a fundamental sound, of its major third and its fifth.

It is called triad, because composed of three times.

And harmonic, because it is in harmonic proportion, and is the source of all harmony.

TRIHEMITON. Is the name which the Greeks gave to the interval which we call minor third; they called it also sometimes hemiditon. (Vide Hemi, or Semi.)

TRILL. A passage in the air of several notes on the same syllable.

The trill is only an imitation of the instrumental melody, in the occasions where, whether for the gaiety of the air, or for the truth of the image, or for the force of the expression, it is necessary to suspend the discourse and prolong the melody; but we must besides manage that the syllable be long, its tone lively, and proper for leaving the throat, the facility of sounding clearly and lightly the notes of the trill, without tiring the organs of the singer, and consequently, neither those of the audience.

The most favourable vowels to extend the voice, are A's, then the full O's and E's; the I and U are little sonorous, much less the diphthongs. In regard to the nazal vowels, they ought never to form a trill. The Italian language abounding in O and A, is much properer for the inflections of the voice than the French, neither are the Italian musicians sparing of them. On the contrary, the French, obliged to compose almost all their syllabic music on account of the few fabourable vowels, are constrained to give the notes a slow and plac'd movement, or to make the consonants disgustful, in making the syllables concur, which necessarily renders the air languishing or hard. I do not see how the French music can ever surmount this inconvenience.

It is a popular prejudice to think that a trill is always out of place in a sad and pathetic air; on the contrary, when the heart is moved in the most lively manner, the voice finds the accents more easily in words, than the mind can, and from thence comes the use of the interjections in all languages. (Vide Neuma.)

It is not a leſs error to think that a trill is always well placed on a ſyllable, or in a word which bears it, without conſidering of the ſituation of the ſinger, if the ſentiment which he ſhould enter into, be at all ſuitable. The trill is an invention of modern muſic. It does not appear that the ancients made any uſe of it, or even ſtruck more than two notes on the ſame ſyllable. This difference is an effect of that of two pieces of muſic, one of which was ſubmiſſive to the language, whilſt the other gave it the law.

TRIMELES. A kind of nome for the flutes in the ancient muſic of the Greeks.

TRIMERES. A name which was executed in three conſecutive modes, viz. the phrygian, the doric, the lydian. Some attribute the invention of this compoſed nome to Sacadas of Argos, others to Clonos Thegeates.

TRIO. In Italian Perzetto. A muſic with three principal or reciting parts. This kind of compoſition is looked upon as the moſt excellent, and ought alſo to be the moſt regular of all. Beſides the general rules of the counter point, there are more rigorous ones for the trio, whoſe perfect obſervation tends to produce the moſt agreeable to all the harmonies. Theſe rules all flow from this principle, that, the perfect concord being compoſed of three different ſounds, we muſt in each concord, to fill the harmony, diſtribute theſe three ſounds, as much as poſſible, to the three parts of the trio. In regard to the diſſonances, as we ought never to double them, and as their concord is compoſed of more than three ſounds, there is alſo a great neceſſity for diverſifying them, and to make a good choice beſides of the diſſonance of the ſounds alſo, which ought in preference to accompany it. From thence ariſe theſe different rules, of never paſſing a concord without cauſing the third or ſixth to be heard; conſequently of avoiding to ſtrike at the ſame time the 5th and octave, or the 4th and 5th; of not practiſing the octave but with great precaution; and never to ſound two together, even between different parts; to avoid the fourth as much as poſſible, for all the parts of a trio, taken 2 by 2 ought to form perfect duets. From thence, in a word, are all thoſe ſmaller rules of detail, which we practice without even ſtudying them, when we are well acquainted with their principle.

As all theſe rules are incompatable with the unity of melody, and as we never hear a regular and harmonious trio have a determined and ſenſible air in the execution, it follows, that the rigorous trio, is an erroneous genus in muſic. Theſe ſo ſevere rules have been long ſince aboliſhed in Italy, where they never looked on a piece of muſic that does not ſing as good, however harmonious it may be in other reſpects, and whatever trouble its compoſition may have coſt.

We

We should here recollect what I have said at the word duet.

These terms, duet and trio, are only understood of the principal and forced parts; and we omit the comprehension of accompaniments, &c. so that a piece with 4 or 5 parts, cannot still be more than a trio.

The French, who are very fond of the multiplication of parts, provided they find concords more easily than airs, not satisfied with the difficulties of the ordinary trio, have imagined what they also call double trio, whose parts are doubled, and all forced. They have a double trio of the Sieur Duché, which passes for a master piece in harmony.

TRIPLE. A kind of measure, in which the measures, the times, or the aliquots of those times, are divided into three equal parts.

We may reduce to two general classes, this infinite number of triple measures, with which Bononcini, Lorenzo, and Brossard after them, have loaded, the one his Musico Practico, the other his Alberi Musicali, and the third his Dictionary. These two classes are the measure ternary, or of three times, and the binary, whose times are divided into sub-triple powers.

Our ancient musicians looked upon the three timed measure as much superior to the binary, and gave it, on that account the name of perfect mode. We have explained at the words mode, time, prolation, the different signs which they made use of to express these measures according to the different powers of the notes, which filled them; but whatever these notes were, as soon as the measure was triple or perfect, there was always a kind of note, which even without point, filled exactly a measure, and was sub-divided into three other equal notes, one for each time. So in the triple perfect, the breve was equal, not to two, but three semi-breves, and in the same manner with the other kinds of triple measures. There was however, a case excepted; it was when this breve was immediately preceded or followed by a semi-breve, for then the two together forming only a just measure, whose semi-breve was equal to a time, there was a necessity for the breve to be equal to two only, and so with the other measures.

By this means were formed the times of the triple measure, but in regard to the sub-divisions of these same measures; they were always formed according to the sub-double computation, and I know no ancient music, where the times are divided into sub-triple powers. The moderns also have several three timed measures of different powers, the simplest of which was marked by a 3, and filled with a pointed minum, forming a note for each time. All the rest are measures, called doubles, on account of their sign being composed of two cyphers. (Vide Measure.)

The second kind of triple is that which is connected, not to the number of the times in the measure, but to the division of each time

time in sub-triple computation. This measure is, as I have just said, of modern invention, and is subdivided into two kinds, two imed and three timed measures, the one of which may be consider-ed as doubly triple measures, viz. 1st. By the three times of the measure, and 2dly, by the three equal parts of each time. The triples of that last kind are all expressed in double measures. The triples of this last kind are all expressed in double measures.

Here is a recapitulation of all the triple measures used at present. Those marked with an asterisk, are no longer used.

I. Triples of the first kind, that is, whose measure is three timed, and each time divided into sub-double computation.

*3	3	3	3	3	*3
*3.	1	2	4	8	16.

II. Triples of the second kind, that is, whose measure is two timed, and each time, sub-divided into sub-triple computation.

6	6	6	12	*12
2	4	8	8	16

These two measures are struck at four times.

III. Composed triples, that is, whose measure is three timed, and each time again divided into three equal parts.

*9	9	*9
4	8	16

All these triple measures are also more simply divided into three kinds, reckoning as such only those which are struck at three times viz. The triple of minum's, which contains a minum by time, and is thus marked $\frac{3}{2}$.

The triple of notes, which contains a crotchet by time, and is thus marked $\frac{3}{4}$.

[And

And the triple of demi crotchets, which contained a demi crotchet by time, or a pointed crotchet by measure, and is thus marked $\frac{3}{8}$.

TRIPLED. A tripled interval is that which is conveyed to the triple octave.

TRIPLUM. Is the name given to the sharpest part in the beginnings of the counter point.

TRITE. Was reckoning from sharp to flat, as the ancients did the third chord of the tetrachord, that is, the second in reckoning from flat to sharp. As there were five different tetrachords, there ought to have been as many trites; but this name was not in use, but in the three sharp tetrachords. For the two flat, Vide Parhypate.

Wherefore there were the hyperbolean trite,, the diezeugmenon and synnemenon. (Vide System, Tetrachord.)

Boetius says, that the system not being yet composed of more than two conjoint tetrachords, the name of trite was given to the fifth chord which was also called paramesis; that is, to the second chord on ascending from the tetrachord: But that Lycaon the Samian, having inserted a new chord between the 6th or paranete and trite, this preserved the single name of trite, and lost that of paramesis, which was given to this new chord. This is not entirely what Boetius says; but in this manner it must be explained to understand it.

TRITON. A dissonant interval composed of three tones, two major and a minor, and which may be called superfluous fourth.

This interval is equal on the keys, to that of the false fifth; however its numerical powers are not equal, that of the triton being only from 32 to 45; which comes from the triton, being no more than a major tone in the equal intervals on each side, instead of the two major semi-tones in the false 5th.

But the most considerable difference of the false 5th, and the triton is that the one is a major dissonance, which the parts save, in being removed; and the other a minor dissonance, which the parts save by drawing near to them.

The concord of the triton is only the over throwing of the sensible concord, whose dissonance is conveyed to the bass. From whence it follows, that this concord ought to be placed only on the fourth note of the tone, which should be accompanied by the second and saved by the sixth.

TO TUNE an Instrument.

Is to extend, or to loosen the chords, to lengthen or shorten the pipes, to increase or diminish the mass of the sonorous body, until all

all the parts of the inſtrument are in the tone which they ought to have.

To tune an inſtrument, we muſt firſt fix a ſound, which ſerves others as a term of compariſon. This is what we call to take or give the tone. (Vide Tone.) This ſound is generally the ut for the organ and harpſichord; the la for the violin and baſs; which have this la on a chord, a vide, and in a medium proper for being eaſily caught by the ear.

In regard to flutes, hautboys, baſſoons, and other wind inſtruments, they have their tone nearly fixed, which cannot by any means be changed but in changing ſome piece of the inſtrument. We may alſo lengthen them a little at the junction of the pieces, which rather lowers the tone; but there muſt neceſſarily reſult falſe tones from theſe variations, becauſe the juſt proportion is broken between the total length of the inſtrument, and the diſtances from one tone to another.

When the tone is determined, we connect with it all the other ſounds of the inſtrument, which ought to be fixed by the concord according to the intervals ſuitable to them. The organ and the harpſichord accord by 5ths until the partition be made, and by octaves for the remainder of the keys; the baſs and the violin by 5ths. The viol and guittar by 4ths and 3rds, &c. In general we chooſe conſonant and harmonious intervals, that the ear may more eaſily catch their juſtneſs.

This juſtneſs of intervals, cannot be obſerved in practice, in all its rigor, and for them all to accord together, each one in particular muſt undergo ſome alteration. Each kind of inſtrument has particular rules, and a method of according for this purpoſe. We take notice that the inſtruments, from whence we draw the ſounds by breathing, as the flute and hautboy, riſe inſenſibly when we have played ſome time, which happens,according to ſome from the humidity, which proceeding from the mouth with the air, breathes into and ſhortens them; or rather, according to the doctrine of Monſ. Euler, is, that the heat and refraction which the air receives during the inſpiration, renders its vibrations more frequent, diminiſh the weight, and by this means augmenting the relative weight of the atmoſphere, render the ſound rather ſharper.

Whatever the cauſe may be, we muſt in tuning, pay attention to the neareſt effect, and force the word a little when we give or receive the tone on theſe inſtruments; for to remain in tune during the concert, they ſhould be a little too low in beginning.

TUNIST. We call tuniſts of the organ or harpſichord, thoſe who go in churches or houſes, to accommodate and tune the inſtruments, and which in general, are the makers of them.

TUNE. A kind of modification of the human voice, by which we form varied and appreciable ſounds. Let us take notice, that to give

give all the univerſality to this definition which it ought to have, we muſt not only underſtand by appreciable ſounds, thoſe which may be aſſigned by the notes of our muſic, and rendered by the touches of our keys; but all thoſe, by which we may prove or feel the uniſon, and calculate the intervals in any manner ſoever. It is very difficult to determine in what the voice which forms the words, differs from that which forms the tune.

This difference is ſenſible, but we cannot very clearly perceive in what it conſiſts, and when we ſeek to find it, we find it not. Monſ. Dodart has made anatomic obſervations, by favor of which he thinks really to diſcover, in the different ſituations of the larynx, the cauſe of two kinds of voice. But I do not know if theſe obſervations or the conſequences drawn from them, are to be depended on. There ſeems to be wanting to the ſounds which form the diſcourſe, no more than permanence, to form a real tune: It appears alſo, that the different inflexions which we give to the voice in ſpeaking, form intervals which are not at all harmonic, which form no parts of the ſyſtem in our muſic, and which conſequently not being expreſſed in notes, are not properly a tune for us.

The tune does not ſeem natural to mankind. Tho' the ſavages of America ſing, becauſe they ſpeak, yet a true ſavage never ſung.

The dumb dont ſing, they form only accents without permanence, a diſguſtful bellowing which their wants draw from them.

I ſhould doubt, if the Sieur Pereyre, with all his ingenuity, could ever draw from them any muſical air. Children ſcream, cry, but they dont ſing. The firſt expreſſions of nature have nothing in them melodious or ſonorous, and they teach to ſing, as to ſpeak. The melodious and appreciable tune, is only an artificial imitation of the accents in the ſpeaking or paſſionate voice. We cry, we complain, without ſinging; and as, of all imitations, the moſt intereſting is that of the human paſſions, ſo of all the methods of imitating, the moſt agreeable is the tune.

Tune, applied more particularly to our muſic, in its melodious part, is that which reſults from the duration and ſucceſſion of ſounds, that, from whence the whole of the expreſſion depends, and to which all the reſt are ſubordinate. (Vide Muſic, Melody.) Agreeable tunes ſtrike immediately, they are eaſily engraved in the memory; but they are often the rock of compoſers, becauſe knowledge is only neceſſary for the heaping together of concords, but talents are wanting for a pleaſing air. There are in every nation turns of muſic trivial and worn out, into which muſicians are inceſſantly falling. There are others rough, which are never uſed, becauſe the public always oppoſe them. To invent new tunes, belongs to the man of genius; to find thoſe that are beautiful, belongs to the man of taſte.

Laſtly

Lastly, in its most confined sense, tune is said only of vocal music and in that which is mingled with symphony; we call the parts in tune those which are destined for the voice.

TUTTI. This word is often written in the parts of symphony in a concerto, after this other word solo, which marks a recitative.

The word tutti expresses the place where a recitative finishes, and where the whole orchestra begins afresh.

TWELFTH. An interval composed of 11 conjoint degrees, that is, of 12 diatonic sounds, reckoning the two extremes. It is the octave of the 5th.

Every sonorous chord renders, with the principal sound, that of the 12th, rather than that of the 5th, because this 12th is produced by an aliquot of the entire chord, which is the third; whereas the two thirds which would give the 5th, are not an aliquot of this same chord.

U.

UNCOMPOSED. An uncomposed interval is that which cannot be resolved into smaller intervals, and has no other element than itself, such for instance, as the enharmonic diesis, the comma, and even the semi-tone.

Amongst the Greeks, the uncomposed intervals were different in the three genera, according to the method of tuning the tetrachords. In the diatonic, the semi-tone, and each of the two tones which follow it, were uncomposed intervals. The minor third, which is found between the 3rd and 4th chord in the chromatic genus, and the major third between the same chords in the enharmonic, were also uncomposed intervals. In this sense, there is only a single uncomposed interval in the modern system, viz. The semi-tone. (Vide Semi-tone.)

UNISON. An unison of two sounds, which are in the same degree, one of which is neither flatter or sharper than the other, and whose interval being null, gives only a reference of equality.

If two chords are of the same matter, equal in length, in thickness, and equally extended; they will be always in unison.

But it is false to say that two sounds in unison are so perfectly confounded, and have such an identity that the ear cannot distinguish them; for they may differ much in regard to the modification and the degree of force. A bell perhaps may be in unison with the chord of a guittar, a viella with the unison of a flute, and yet the sounds are not confounded.

The zero is not of the number, nor is the unison an interval, but the unison is in the series of intervals, what the zero is, in that of numbers; it is the term from whence they go out; it is the point of their beginning.

What constitutes the unison, is the equality of a number of vibrations made in equal times by two sounds. As soon as there is an inequality betwixt the numbers of these vibrations, there is an interval between the sounds that give them. (Vide Chord, Vibration.)

They tormented themselves greatly to know if the unison was a consonance: Aristotle denies it, Muris affirms it, and P. Mersenne, ranges himself in the lists of the latter. As that depends on the definition of the word consonance, I do not see what dispute could be occasioned on it. If we do not understand this word consonance, but as an union of two sounds agreeable to the ear, the unison will be assuredly a consonance; but if we add to it a difference from flat to sharp, it is clear that it will not be so. A more important question, is to know which is most agreeable to the ear of the unison or a consonant interval, such, for instance, as the octave or 5th. All those who have an ear exercised in harmony, prefer the concord of the consonances to the identity of the unison; but all those, who, without the custom of harmony, have no prejudice in regard to the ear, have quite a contrary judgment. The unison alone pleases them, or at most the octave. Every other interval appears to them discordant; from whence it would follow, I think, that the most natural harmony, and consequently the best, is in unison. (Vide Harmony.)

It is a known observation of all musicians, that that of the shaking and resonance of the chord, to the sound of another chord, ascends to the unison of the first, or even to its octave, or the octave of its 5th, &c.

The phænomenon may be explained in this manner.

The sound of a chord A puts the air in motion. If another chord B is found in the sphere of the movement of that air, it will act on it. Each chord, in a given time is only susceptible of a certain number of vibrations. If the vibrations, of which the chord B is susceptible, are equal in number to those of the chord A, the airs shaken by the one, acting on the other, and finding it disposed to a movement similar to that it has received, communicates it to it.

The two chords moving thus in equal pace, all the impulsions which the air receives from the chord A, and which it communicates to B, are co-incident with the vibrations of that chord, and consequently will augment its movement, instead of acting contrary to it. This movement, thus successively augmented, will very soon approach to a sensible shake. The chord B will then render a

 sound

ſound for every ſonorous chord which ſhakes, ſounds, and this ſound will neceſſarily be in uniſon with that of the chord of A.

By the ſame reaſon, the ſharp octave will ſhake and reſound alſo, but with leſs ſtrength than in the uniſon; becauſe the co-incidence of the vibrations, and conſequently the impulſion of the air, is leſs frequent by the half. It is even ſtill leſs in the 12th, or re-doubled 5th, and leſs in the 17th of major triple tierce, the laſt of the conſonances which ſhakes and reſounds ſenſibly and directly; for in regard to the minor third and ſixths, they reſound only by combination.

Every time that the numbers of the vibrations of which two chords are ſuſceptible in equal time, are commenſurable, we cannot doubt but that the ſound of the one will communicate to the other ſome ſhake by their common aliquot; but this ſhake being no longer ſenſible below the four preceding concords, it is reckoned as nothing in the remainder. (Vide Conſonance.)

It appears by this explanation, that a ſound never makes another re-ſound but by virtue of ſome uniſon; for any ſound ſoever always gives the uniſon of its aliquots; but as it cannot give the ſound of its multiples, it follows, that a chord ſonorous in its movement, can never make one reſound flatter than itſelf. Whereon we may judge of the truth of the experiment from whence Monſ. Rameau takes the origin of the minor mode.

UNISSONI. This Italian word written at length, or abridged in a partition on the ſtave vide of the ſecond violin, denotes, that it ſhould play in uniſon on the part of the firſt; and this ſame word, written on the ſtave vide of the firſt violin, ſhews, that it ſhould play in uniſon on the part of the air.

UNITY of MELODY. All the fine arts have ſome unity of object, a ſource of the pleaſure which they give to the mind; for the attention divided is by no means at eaſe, and when two objects employ us, it is a proof that neither of them ſatisfies us. There is, in muſic, a ſucceſſive unity which is connected to the ſubject, and by which, all the parts, well united, compoſe a ſingle *totum*, whoſe concinnity and connections we may eaſily perceive.

But there is another unity of object more clear and more preſerved, and from whence there ariſes, without any attention being paid, the energy of muſic, and the force of its expreſſions.

When I hear our Pſalms ſung in four parts, I always begin to be ſeized, raviſhed, with this full and nervous harmony; and the firſt concords, when they are truly toned, incite me even to a ſhivering. But hardly have I heard the continuance of it for ſome minutes, than my attention is relaxed, the noiſe ſtuns me by degrees, ſoon it fatigues me, and in the end I am tired of hearing nothing but concords.

This effect does not happen when I hear good modern music, though the harmony is less vigorous; and I remember, that at the Opera House of Venice, far from a fine air fatiguing me, when well executed, I gave it, however great the length might be, continually a fresh attention, and listened to it with more pleasure at the end than the beginning.

This difference is derived from that of the character of the two modes, one of which is only a continuance of concords, and the other a *suite* of the air. The pleasure, besides of the harmony is only a pleasure of a pure sensation, and the enjoyment of the senses is always short: Satiety and fatigue are its close attendants. But, the pleasure of melody and music, is a pleasure of interest and sentiment, which speaks to the heart, and which the artist can always sustain and renew by dint of genius.

The music ought then necessarily to sing for the touching, the pleasing, and sustaining the interest and attention. But how in our systems of concords and harmony, can the music manage towards the singing parts? If each part has its peculiar air, all these airs, heard at the same time, will be mutually destroyed, and will no longer form an air. If all the parts form the same air, we shall have no more harmony, and the concert will be entirely in unison.

The method by which a musical instinct, a certain and dull sentiment of genius, has removed this difficulty without seeing it, and has even drawn an advantage from it, is very remarkable.

The harmony, which ought to stifle the melody, animates it, enforces it, determines it. The different parts without being confounded, answer the same effect; and tho' each of them appears to have its proper air, yet of all these re-united parts, we hear only one and the same air proceed. This is what I call unity of melody.

Here is the method of the harmony's itself concurring to this unity, instead of injuring them. They are our modes which characterise our music, and our modes are founded on our harmony.

Every time then that the harmony strengthens or determines the sentiment of the mode and modulation, it adds to the expression of the air, provided that it does not cover it.

The art of the composer, is then in relation to the unity of melody, 1st. When the mode is not sufficiently determined by the music, to determine it better by harmony. 2dly. To choose and turn its concords, so that the most lively sound may be that which sings, and that which makes it proceed best, may be in bass. 3dly. To add to the energy of each passage by rough concords if the expression is rough, and sweet if the expression is sweet. 4thly. To pay attention in the turning of the accompaniment to the forte piano of melody. 5thly, and Lastly, to manage so that the air of of the other parts, far from being contrary to that of the principal part, may ſuſtain it, ſecond it, and give it a livelier accent.

Monſ. Rameau, to prove that the energy of the muſic is all taken from harmony, gives the inſtance of a ſame harmony, which he calls a ſame air, which takes entirely different characters, according to the different methods of accompanying it. Monſ. Rameau has not ſeen that he proved quite the contrary, from what he would prove, for in all the examples he gives, the accompaniments of the baſs ſerves only to determine the air. A ſimple interval is not an air, it becomes air only when it has its place aſſigned in the mode; and the baſs, in determining the mode and the place of the mode, which this interval occupies, determines in that caſe that interval to be of ſuch or ſuch an air; ſo that if by what precedes the interval in the ſame part, we determine the place, which it has in its modulation, I declare, that it will have its effect without any baſs; wherefore harmony acts, in this occaſion, only in determining the melody to be ſuch or ſuch; and it is purely as melody that the interval has different expreſſions according to the place of the mode wherein it is uſed.

The unity of melody requires that we never hear two melodies at a time, but not that the melody ſhould never paſs from one part to another: On the contrary, there is often elegance and taſte to manage á propo's, this paſſage, even from the air to the accompaniment, provided that the words be all underſtood. There is even harmony ingenious, and well managed, wherein the melody, without being in any part, reſults only from the effect of the whole.

We here find an example, which, tho' rough, is ſufficient to make what I have ſaid, clearly underſtood.

A

A treatiſe would be neceſſary to ſhew in detail the application of this principle in duets, trios, quatuors, in choruſſes, and pieces of ſymphony. Men of genius will ſufficiently diſcover the extent and uſe of it, and their works will inſtruct others. I conclude then, and I ſay, that from the principle which I have juſt eſtabliſhed, it follows, 1ſt. That all muſic which does not ſing, is tireſome, whatever harmony it may have. 2dly. That all muſic, wherein we diſtinguiſh ſeveral airs together, is ill, and that there reſults from it the ſame effect as from two or more diſcourſes pronounced at the ſame time, on the ſame tone. By this judgment, which admits of no exception, we ſee what we ought to think of theſe marvellous pieces of muſic, where one air ſerves as an accompaniment to another. It is in the principle of unity of melody, that the Italians have felt and followed, without knowing it, but which the French have neither known or followed; it is, I ſay, in this grand principle, that the eſſential difference of two pieces of muſic conſiſts; and it is, I believe, what every impartial judge muſt ſay, who would give to each the ſame attention, if the thing might in all reſpects be poſſible.

When I had diſcovered this principle, I wiſhed before I propoſed it, to try at the application of it by myſelf: This eſſay produced *Le Devin de Village*, after the ſucceſs of it, I ſpoke of it in my *Letter on the French Muſic*. It belongs to maſters of the art to judge if the principle is good, and if I have truly followed the rules which iſſue from them.

UNIVOCAL. The univerſal conſonances are the octave and its repliques, becauſe all bear the ſame name. Ptolomy was the firſt which gave them this name.

UPHOLDING or BURDEN. The termination of all the couplets in a ſong, by the ſame words, and by the ſame air, which is ordinarily ſaid twice.

UPINGE. A kind of ſong conſecrated to Diana amongſt the Greeks. (Vide Song.)

UT. The firſt of the ſix ſyllables of the gamut of Aretin, which anſwers to the letter C.

By the method of tranſpoſitions, we always call ut the tonic of the major modes, and the mediant of the minor modes. (Vide Gamut, Tranſpoſition.)

The Italians finding this ſyllable ut too dull, ſubſtitute in its place, in ſol-faing, the ſyllable do.

V

V. This capital letter serves to express the parts of the violin, and when it is a double V, it marks that the first and second are in unison.

VARIATION. A change of order in the sounds which compose the concords, and in the parts which compose the harmony, which is formed in substituting in the place of the bass, by octaves, the sounds which ought to be above; or in that of the extremeties, those which ought to occupy the middle, and reciprocally.

It is certain, that in every concord there is a fundamental and natural order, which is that of the generation of the concord itself; but the circumstances of a succession, the taste, the expression, the beauties of the air, the variety, the attraction of harmony, often oblige the composer to change this order in varying the concords, and consequently the disposition of the parts.

As three things may be ordered in 6 methods, and 4 things in 24 ways, it seems at first that a perfect concord should be susceptible of 6 variations, and a dissonant concord of 24; since the one is composed of 4 sounds, and the other of 3, and that the variation consists only in the transpositions of octaves. But we must take notice, that in harmony we do not reckon as variations, all the different dispositions of the superior sounds, whilst the same sound continues in flat. Wherefore these two orders of the perfect concord ut mi sol, and ut sol mi, are taken only for the same name; which reduces all the vibrations of the perfect concord to three; and to four, all those of the dissonant concord; that is, to as many variations as enter into the different sounds of the concord: for the repliques of the same sounds are here looked upon as nothing.

Every time then that the fundamental bass is heard in the flattest part, or, if the fundamental bass is removed every time that the natural order is preserved in the concord, the harmony is direct.

As soon as this order is changed, or the fundamental sound without being in flat, are heard in some other part, the harmony is varied. It is a variation of the concord, when the fundamental sound is transposed. It is the variation of harmony, when the treble, or some other part moves, as the bass ought to do.

Wheresoever a direct concord is well placed, its variation will be also well placed, in regard to harmony, for it is always the same fundamental succession. So in each note of the fundamental, we are masters of disposing the concord at will, and consequently of making every moment a different variation; provided that we make

make no change in a regular and fundamental succession; that the dissonances are always prepared and saved by the parts which make them heard; that the sensible note always ascend; and that we avoid the false relations too rough in a same part. Herein lies the cleff of these mysterious differences which the composers place between the concords or treble syncope, and those wherein the bass ought to syncopate; as, for instance, between the 9th and the 2nd. This is, that in the first the concord is direct and the dissonance in the treble; in the others the concord is varied and the dissonance is in bass.

In regard to concords by supposition, we want more precautions to vary them. As the sound, which we add to the bass, is entirely strange to the harmony, it is often suffered only on account of its great distance from the other sound, which renders the dissonance less rough. If this added sound comes to be transposed in superior parts, as it is sometimes, unless this transposition is done with much art, it can produce therein a very bad effect; and this can never be practised happily, without cutting off any other sound of the concord. Vide at the word *concord*, the cases and choice of these cuttings off.

The perfect understanding of the variation depends only in study and art. The choice is another thing. We want an ear and taste. Experience is necessary in different effects; and tho' the choice of the variation is indifferent for the foundation of the harmony, it is not so for the effect and expression. It is certain that the fundamental bass is made to sustain the harmony, and reign below it.

Every time then that we change the order, and vary the harmony, we ought to have good reasons for it, without which we shall fall into the error of our modern music, where the treble sing sometimes as basses, and the basses always as trebles; where the whole is confused, varied, ill ordered, without any other reason than to pervert the order established, and to spoil the harmony.

On the organ and harpsichord the different variations of a concord, as long as they may be done with a single hand, are called superficies.

VARIATIONS. We understand under this name, all the methods of ornamenting and doubling an air, whether by diminutions, or by passages, or other graces, which adorn and figure this air. To whatever degree we multiply and charge the variations, it is always necessary, that across these flourishes we should have a view to the foundation of the air, which we call simple; and the character of each variation must at the same time be marked by differences which sustain the attention and prevent fatigue.

The

The ſymphoniſts often form variations extempore, or ſuppoſed ſo; but they are more often marked. The different couplets of the Folies d'Eſpagne, are ſo many marked variations. We often alſo find ſome in the French chacons, and in the ſmall Italian airs for the violin and violincello. All Paris have gone to admire, at the ſpiritual concert, the variations of the Sieurs Guignon and Mondonville; and more recently of the Sieurs Guignon and Gaviniés, on the airs of the Pont-neuf, which had no other merit than to be thus varied by the moſt ingenious violin players in France.

VAUDEVILLE. A kind of ſong with couplets, which generally moves on laughable or ſatyrical ſubjects. We make the origin of this little lyric poem aſcend to the reign of Charlemagne; but, according to the moſt common opinion, it was invented by a certain Baſſelin, of Vire in Normandy; and as to dance on theſe airs, they aſſembled in the Val de Vire, they were called they ſay, vaux de vire, and by corruption, vaudevilles.

The air of the vaudevilles is generally little muſical. As we pay attention therein to the words only, the air ſerves only to render the recitative a little more forcible. We perceive beſides in general, neither taſte, or air, or even meaſure. The vaudeville belongs excluſively to the French, and they have ſome very ſtriking and agreeable.

VIBRATION. The ſonorous body in action removes from its ſtate of quick, by gentle ſhakes, but ſenſible, frequent, and ſucceſſive, each of which is called a vibration. Theſe vibrations communicated to the air, bears the ſenſation of the ſound to the ear, by this vehicle; and this ſound is flat or ſharp, according as the vibrations are more or leſs frequent at the ſame time. (Vide Sound.)

VICARIER. A familiar word by which Church Muſicians expreſs what thoſe do, who run from town to town, and from Cathedral to Cathedral, to gather up ſome retributions, and live at the expence of the muſic maſters, who are on their route.

VIDO. Chord a vido, is, on ſleeve inſtruments, ſuch as the viol or violin, the ſound which we draw from the chord in the whole of its length, from the ſounding board as far as the bridge, without placing any finger on it.

The ſound of the chords a vido, is not only flatter, but more reſonant and full than when we place thereon a finger; which is cauſed by the ſoftneſs of the finger, which hurts and intercepts the play of the vibrations. This difference occaſions that good players on the violin avoid touching the chords a vido, to remove that inequality

inequality of the tone which has a bad effect, when it is not managed á propos. This method of executing requires laboured positions, which increase the difficulties of the play. But still, when we have once acquired a habit, we are really masters of our instrument; and in the most difficult tones, the execution then moves as in the easiest.

VILLANELLE. A kind of rustic dance, the air of which should be very gay, and of a very sensible measure. The foundation of this air is generally a couplet rather simple, on which we form doubles and variations.

VIOL. By this name, in the Italian music, is called that part which the French stile tenor; for the French often double this part, that is, make two for one: a thing which the Italians never do. The viol serves to unite the treble to the bass, and to fill, in an harmonious manner, the too great vido which must remain between them. For which reason, the viol is always necessary for the concordance of the whole, even when it only makes the bass play on the octave, as it often happens in Italian music.

VIOLIN. The thing for the person. A symphonist who plays on the violin in an orchestra. The violins are generally divided into first, which play thefirst treble; and second, which play the second.. Each of these two parts has its chief, or guide, which is also called the first; viz. The first of the first; the first of the seconds. The first of the first violins is also called in brief, first violin; it is the chief of the whole orchestra; it is that which gives the tone, guides all the symphonies, which rectifies them when in an error, and on which they must all depend.

VIRGULUM. By this term the musicians called that part of the note which has been since called tail.

VOCAL. What belongs to the tone of voices. "A vocal turn in singing." "Vocal music."

THE VOCAL. We sometimes take this adjective substantively, to express that part of the music which is executed by voices. "The symphonies of such an opera are tolerably good; but the vocal is shocking."

VOICE. The sum of all the sounds which a man can, in speaking or singing, crying, &c. draw from his organs, forms what is called the voice; and the qualities of this voice depend also from those of the sounds which form them. So we may apply to the voice, all that I have already said of sound in general. (Vide Sound.)

I. The physicians distinguish the voice as a simple sound, such as the cry of children.

II. As an articulated sound, such as in discourse.

III. In music, which adds to the modulation and variety of the tones.

IV. In declamation, which ſeems to depend on a new modification in the voice, and even on the ſubſtance itſelf: a modification different from that of the muſic, and that of the words, ſince it may be united to each, or be cut off from it.

We may ſee, in the Encyclopædia, at the article "Declamation des *Anciens*," from whence theſe diviſions are drawn, the explanation which Monſ. Duclos gives of theſe different kinds of voices. I ſhall content myſelf with tranſcribing here what he ſays of the ſinging or muſical voice, the only one which is connected with my ſubject. "The ancient muſicians eſtabliſhed, "after Ariſtoxenes, 1ſt. That the voice of muſic ſhould paſs from "one degree of elevation or lowering, to another; that is, from "one tone to another, by a leap, without paſſing through the "interval which ſeparates them; whereas that of the diſcourſe "is raiſed and lowered by a continued movement. Secondly, "That the ſinging voice ſhould be ſuſtained on the ſame tone, "conſidered as an indiviſible point, which does not happen in "ſimple pronunciation.

"This movement by leaps and ſtops, is, in effect, that of the "voice in ſinging: but is there nothing more in muſic?

"There has been a tragic declamation which admitted the "paſſage from one tone to another by a leap, and the ſtop on a "tone. We take notice of the ſame thing in certain orators. This "declamation, however, is different from the voice in ſinging.

"Monſ. Dodart, who joined to the ſpirit of labour and diſcuſ"ſion, the greateſt knowledge of phyſic, of anatomy, and the "play of the parts in the human body, has particularly given "an attention to the organs of the voice. He obſerves, firſt, "that ſuch a man, whoſe voice in diſcourſe is diſpleaſing, may "ſing very agreeably. And ſo, on the contrary, ſecondly, That "if we have not heard a perſon ſing, whatſoever knowledge we "may have of his ſpeaking voice, we can form no true idea of "his voice in ſinging.

"Monſ. Dodart, continuing his reſearches, diſcovered, that in "the ſinging voice, there is, beſides that of the words, a move"ment of the whole larynx; that is, from the part of the tra"chean artery, which forms as a new canal, terminated in the "glotta, which ſuſtains and ſurrounds its muſcles. The differ"ence between the two voices comes then from that which is "between the larynx, ſeated and in peace on thoſe which are "attached to it in words; and this ſame larynx ſuſpended on "its attached parts in action, and moved by a balance from high "to low, and from low to high. This balance may be com"pared to the movement of the birds which hover in the air, "or of the fiſh which are continued in the ſame place againſt "the courſe of the tide; though the wings of the one, and the

"fins

"fins of the other, appear immoveable to the eye, they form "continual vibrations; but so short and quick, that they are "imperceptible.

"The balance of the larynx produces, in the singing voice, a "kind of ondulation, which is not in simple discourse. The "sustained and modulated ondulation, in fine voices, is too much "felt in the weak and decayed. This ondulation ought not to "be confounded with the cadences and trills which are formed "by the very quick and very delicate movements of the opening of "the throat, and which are composed of the interval of a tone, "or demi-tone.

"The voice, whether for music or discourse, comes entirely "from the throat, in regard to the sound and the tone; but the "ondulation comes entirely from the balance of the whole la-"rynx: It does not form a part of the voice, but it affects its "totality. It results from what I have lain down, that the "voice in music consists in the movement, by a leap from one "tone to another, in the continuance of the tones, and in that "ondulation of the larynx which affects the totality, and even "substance of the sound."

For, first we may, at will, give or remove from the voice that ondulation when we sing; and we do not less sing when we clip an united sound without any kind of ondulation. Secondly, the sounds of the instruments do not differ in any kind from those of the singing voice, in regard to their nature of musical sounds, and have nothing by themselves by this ondulation. Thirdly, This ondulation is formed in the tone, and not in the modification: The proof of it is, that on the violin and other instruments, we imitate this ondulation, not by any balance similar to the supposed movement of the larynx, but by a balance of the finger on the chord, which, thus shortened and lengthened alternatively, and almost imperceptibly, renders two alternative sounds, in proportion as the finger draws back, or advances. So the ondulation, whatever Monf. Dodart says, does not consist in a very light balance of the same sound; but in the more or less frequent alteration of two very neighbouring sounds; and when the sounds are too distant, and the alternative succours are too rough, in that case the ondulation roughens.

I should think, that the true distinctive character of the voice in music, is to form appreciable sounds, by which the unison may be taken or felt, and passed from one to the other by harmonic and commensurable intervals; whereas, in the speaking voice, either the sounds are not sufficiently sustained, and, as it were, not in proper union to be appreciated, or the intervals which separate them are not sufficiently harmonic, or their connections sufficiently simple.

The obſervations which Monſ. Dodart makes on the difference of the ſpeaking voice, and that of ſinging, in the ſame man, far from being contrary to this explanation, confirm it; for as there are languages more or leſs harmonious, whoſe accents are more or leſs muſical, we take notice alſo, in theſe languages, that the ſpeaking and ſinging voices are connected or removed in the ſame proportion. So, as the Italian language is more muſical than the French, the words are leſs diſtant from it in the muſic; and it is more eaſy to have the knowledge of a man we have heard ſpeak, by his ſinging in that language. In a language which would be completely harmonious, as was the Greek at the beginning, the difference of the ſpeaking and ſinging voices is null: We ſhould have the ſame voice for ſpeaking and ſinging. Perhaps that may be at preſent the caſe of the Chineſe.

Here may perhaps be too much on the different genera of the voice: I now return to the ſinging voice, and ſhall confine myſelf to it during the remainder of this article.

Each individual has his particular voice, which diſtinguiſhes him from every other voice by ſome peculiar difference, as one face is diſtinguiſhed from another; but there are alſo ſome of theſe differences, which are common to ſeveral, and which forming ſo many kinds of voices, require a particular denomination of each.

The moſt general character which diſtinguiſhes the voices, is not that which is drawn from their tone or volume; but from the degrees which this volume occupies in the general ſyſtem of ſounds.

We diſtinguiſh in general, the voices into two claſſes, viz. the ſharp and flat voice. The known difference between each, is nearly an octave; which cauſes that the ſharp voice really ſings in the octave of the flat, when they ſeem to ſing in uniſon.

The flat voices are the moſt general for men, the ſharp for women; Eunuchs and children have nearly the ſame diapaſon of voice as women. All men however may even approach it in ſinging the faucet. But of all the ſharp voices, we muſt agree, in ſpite of the prevention of the Italians for caſtrati, that there is no kind of voice comparable to that of women, either for the extent, or the beauty of the tone. The voice of children has little conſiſtence, and no baſs. That of eunuchs on the contrary, excells in alto; and as to the faucet, it is the moſt diſagreeable of all the tones in the human voice. It is ſufficient to be of that ſentiment, to be attentive to the choruſſes of the ſpiritual concert at Paris, and to compare their trebles with thoſe at the opera.

All theſe different diapaſons, reunited and put in order, form a general extent nearly of three octaves, which have been divided into four parts, three of which, called counter tenor, tenor and baſs, belong to the flat voice; and the fourth only called treble, is aſſigned

aſſigned to ſharp voices. On which ſubject, here are ſome remarks which I preſent to the reader.

I. According to the ſtave of the ordinary voices, which may be fixed nearly to a major 10th, by placing two degrees of interval between each kind of voice, and that which follows it, which is all the difference that can be given them, the general ſyſtem of the human voice in the two ſexes, which we make to paſs three octaves, ought to contain only two octaves and two tones. It was in effect to this extent, that the four parts of muſic were bounded, long after the invention of the counter point, as we ſee in the compoſitions of the 14th age; where the ſame cleff, on four ſucceſſive poſitions from line to line ſerves as the baſs, which they called tenor; for the tenor, which they called contratenor; for the counter, tenor, which they called mottetu; and for the treble, which they called triplum. This diſtribution muſt really render the compoſition more difficult, but at the ſame time the harmony more confined and more agreeable.

II. To advance the vocal ſyſtem to the extent of three octaves with the gradation I have mentioned, we ſhould want ſix parts inſtead of four; and nothing would be more natural than this diviſion: not on account of its connection with the harmony, which does not carry ſo many different ſounds, but in regard to the voices, which are actually rather ill diſtributed. In effect, why ſhould there be three parts in a man's voice, and one only in that of a woman; of the totality of the latter contains as great an extent as the totality of the reſt? Let an interval of the ſharpeſt ſounds of the ſharpeſt female voices be meaſured, with the flatteſt ſounds of the flatteſt female voices. Let the ſame thing in a man's voice, and we ſhall not only find a ſufficient difference to eſtabliſh three parts on one ſide, and one only on the other; but this difference itſelf, if there is one, will be reduced almoſt to nothing. To judge clearly of this, we muſt not be confined to the mere examination of things ſuch as they are, but ſhould ſee what they might be, and conſider that cuſtom contributes much to the formation of voices on the character which we would give them. In France, where they are in want of baſſes, or counter tenors, and pay no attention to the baſs trebles, the voices of their men take different characters, and the female voices keep one only; but in Italy, where they look on a beautiful baſs treble as equal to the ſharpeſt voice, there may be found amongſt their women, very beautiful flat voices, which they call Contr' Alti, and very beautiful ſharp voices, which are called Soprani. On the contrary, in the voice of the recitative, they have only tenors; ſo that, if there is only one character of voice for women in our operas, in theirs there is only one character for that of men.

In regard to the chorusses, the parts are generally so distributed in Italy, as in France, it is an universal custom, but arbitrary, which has no natural foundation. Besides, do we not admire in several places, and particularly in Venice, very beautiful music in grand chorus, executed by young girls only ?

III. The too great distance of the voices between each other, which makes them all exceed their staves, obliges several to be subdivided. By this means we divide the basses, into counter basses, and bass tenors ; the tenors into counter-tenors and concordants ; the trebles into first and seconds ; but in all this we perceive nothing fixed, nothing regulated on this principle. The general scheme of the French composers, is always to force the voice to make it screem rather than sing. 'Tis for this reason, that they appear at present to confine themselves to the basses, and counter tenors, which are in the two extremes. In regard to the tenor, a part so natural to man, that it is called for excellence, the human voice, it is already banished from our operas, where they forsake every thing natural ; and by the same reason it will not be long before it is entirely extirpated from the French music.

We distinguish the voices by many other differences than those from flat to sharp. There are strong voices, whose sounds are bold and noisy ; sweet voices, whose sounds are soft and fluted ; lengthened voices, which have a great extent ; fine voices, full, just, and harmonious. Amongst the many voices that I remarked in my short excursion to the metropolis of England, I observed several of the kind abovementioned. In what I have stiled the fine voice, the Scotch were particularly excellent. I should not omit, tho' partiality might urge me, to pay that difference to a Foreigner which his merit demands, on which account, I must beg leave to make this short digression, to pay that respect to Mr. Keard's excellence, which the fullness, justness, and harmony of his voice may claim, without the smallest deviation from his modesty, tho' that extends so far as to require a foreign pen to tell his merits to the world. There are also the contraries to all this ; there are rough and heavy voices ; there are voices flexible and easy ; there are some, whose sounds are unequally distributed to the one above, to others in the medium, to others below. There are equal voices also, which make the same tone be felt in their whole extent. It is the part of the composer to abstract from each voice, whatever may be advantageous to his character. In Italy, where every time that an opera is introduced on the stage, it is always a new music, the composers are always careful to appropriate all the parts to the voices which ought to sing them. But in France, where the same music continues for ages, each part must always serve to every voice of the same kind ; and this is perhaps one of the reasons, why the

the French airs, far from acquiring any perfection, become day by day, more disgusting and tedious.

The most extended, the most flexible, the sweetest, the most harmonious voice that ever existed, appears to have been that of the Chevalier Balthasar Ferri, a Perusian of the last age; a singer uncommonly excellent, whom every sovereign in Europe retained in his court by turns, who was loaded with honours during his life, and whose glory and talents were celebrated after death by all the muses of Italy. All the writings composed to the praise of this celebrated musician, breathe delight and enthusiasm; and the agreement of all his contemporaries, shews, that so perfect and so uncommon talents were beyond envy. Nothing, say they, can express the graces of his voice, or the eclat of his music. He had, in the highest degree, all the characters of perfection in every kind: He was gay, bold, lively, grave, tender, at will, and every heart gave way to his pathos. Among the infinity of strong turns which he executed by his voice, I will cite one only. He ascended and re-descended, in one breath, two full octaves in a continual trill, marked on all the chromatic degrees with so much justness, though without accompaniment, that if any one had struck this accompaniment under the note where he was found, whether B flat or diesis, they instantly perceived so just a concord, as surprised all the audience. We call voice also, the vocal and reciting parts for which a piece of music is composed: So we say a molet for a single voice, instead of saying a molet in recitative; a cantata for two voices, instead of a cantata in duet, or with two parts. (Vide Duo, Trio.)

VOLTE. A kind of three timed air peculiar to a dance of the same name, which is composed of several turns and returns, whence it receives the name of volte. This dance is a kind of gaillard, and has not been used for some time.

VOLUME. The volume of a voice, is the extent or interval which is between the sharpest and flattest sounds which it can render. The volume of ordinary voices is about eight or nine tones: The most remarkable voices hardly ever pass the two octaves in just and full sounds.

W.

WORDS. Is the name given to the poem which the composer sets to music, whether this poem be small or great, whether it be a drama or a song. The fashion is to say of a new opera,

opera, that the music is tolerably good, but the words detestable. We might say the contrary of the ancient operas of Lully.

WORK. We say the third work of Corelli, the fifth of Vivaldi, &c. &c. But these titles are no longer in use. In proportion as music improves, it loses these pompous names, by which our ancients thought they increased its merit.

Z.

ZA. The syllable by which is distinguished in church-music, the si B flat from the si natural, to which is left the name of si.

FINIS.

Plate I.

Fig-1. Adant Silences

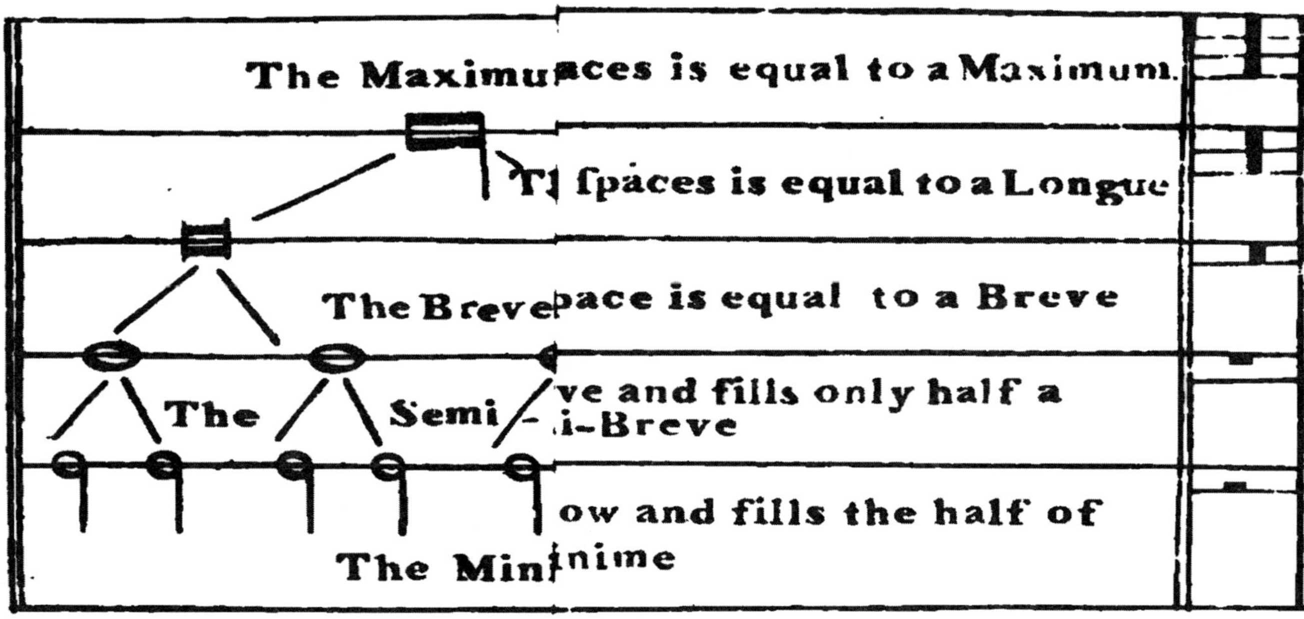

Fig.2.

Fig.3.

Fig.4.

Fig.5.

Fig. 1.

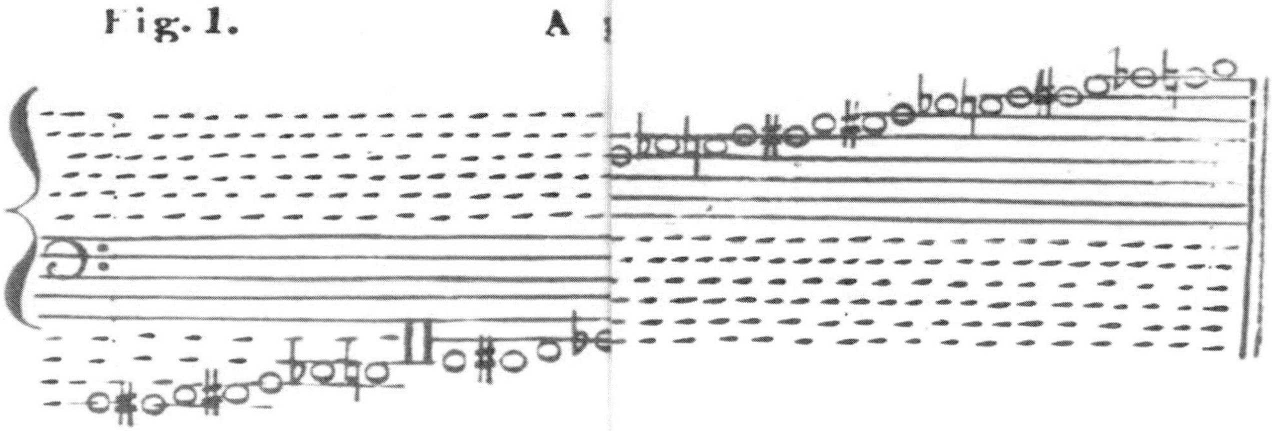

Fig. 2.

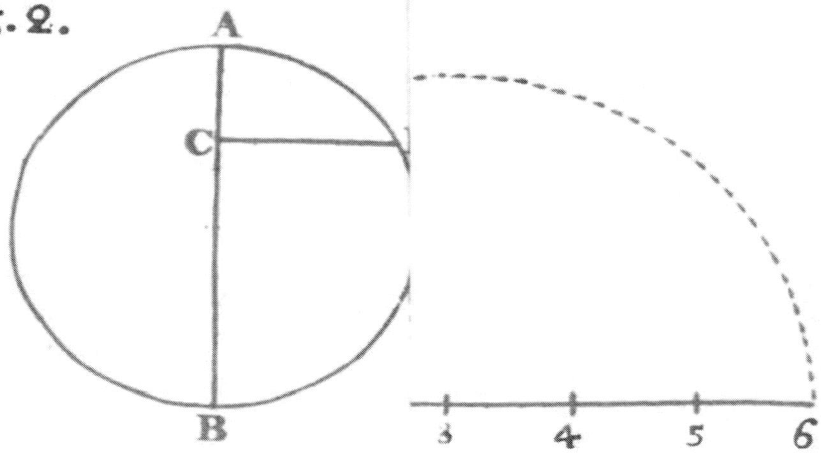

Fig. 5.

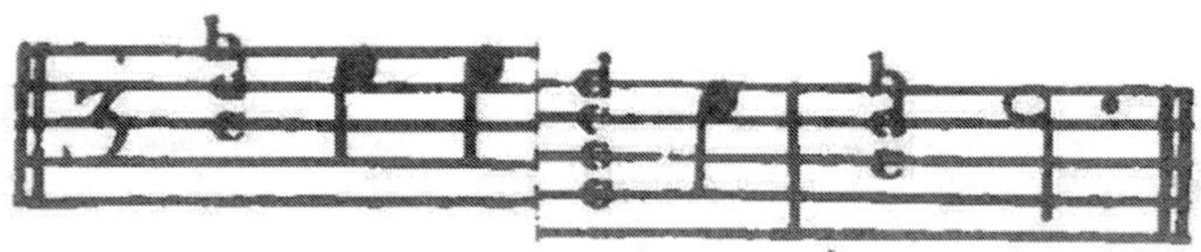